VIRGINIA TAX PAYERS

1782-87

*Other Than Those
Published by the United
States Census
Bureau*

By

AUGUSTA B. FOTHERGILL

and

JOHN MARK NAUGLE

Originally published: Richmond, Virginia, 1940
Reprinted: Genealogical Publishing Co., Inc.
1001 N. Calvert St., Baltimore, Md. 21202
1966, 1971, 1974, 1978, 1986, 1999
Library of Congress Catalogue Card Number 66-30321
International Standard Book Number 0-8063-0147-3
Made in the United States of America

The Act for the first census to be taken was passed at the second session of the First Congress and was signed by President Washington on March 1,1790.

This census was to include free white males over sixteen years of age,free white males under sixteen years of age,free white females,all other free persons and slaves.

These lists for Virginia,as well as several other states,were destroyed when the British burnt Washington during the War of 1812 so an effort was made to locate duplicates but there seemed to be only some copies of State enumerations extant.

My effort has been to make use of the first personal property tax lists for those counties then extant in order to supply this deficiency. The lists are not absolutely conclusive since some men did not pay taxes if they were indigent,exempt for physical disabilities or if they held certain political or military offices.However,in some instances we find that some of the latter paid on some of their personalty.

Ordinarily it would have seemed wiser to have published the tax payers as they occurred in the original lists but in all but ten of the counties they have already been letter grouped by the enumerators so that any value as to neighbors has been destroyed.

Fayette and Lincoln Counties of the present Kentucky have been included,then being in Virginia, but the lists for Jefferson County having been removed to Kentucky could not be included as I am only using those lists in our State Archives.

The first tax assesments were ordered to be made in the year 1782 but some of them are not to be found so they were used for the extant counties,not included in the first census,at the first date to be found: Accomac for the year 1787; Augusta for the year 1782; Bedford for the year 1782; Berkeley for the year 1782;Botetourt for 1784; Brunswick for 1782; Buckingham for the year 1782; Campbell County for 1785; Caroline for 1783;Charles City for 1783; Culpeper County for 1783; Dinwiddie County for the year 1782; Elizabeth City for the year 1782; Fauquier County for the year 1782; Fayette,for the year 1787; Goochland County for 1782; Hardy County for the year 1786;Henrico County for the year 1782; Henry County for 1782; James City County for the year 1782; King George County for the year 1782; King & QueenCounty 1782; King William County 1782; Lincoln,1787; Louisa County year 1782; Loudon County 1782; Lunenburg County 1782; Montgomery County 1782; Northampton County 1782; Prince George County 1782; Prince William County 1782; Rockbridge County 1782;Southampton County 1782; Spotsylvania,1782; Washington County 1782; Westmoreland County 1783; York County 1784.

I have used the following abbreviations for the county names:

Aug.	for	Augusta County.	Ja.Cy	for	James City County
Acco.	"	Accomac	"	K.Wm.	"	King William
Bot.	"	Botetourt	"	K.&Q	"	King & Queen
Buck.	"	Buckingham"		K.Geo.	"	King George
Berk.	"	Berkley		Lun.	"	Lunenburg
Brun.	"	Brunswick	"	Lou.	"	Loudon
Bed.	"	Bedford	"	Loui.	"	Louisa
Cul.	"	Culpeper	"	Mont.	"	Montgomery
Cha.Cy"	Charles City		Nor.	"	Northampton
Caro.	"	Caroline		Pr.Wm.	"	Prince William
Camp.	"	Campbell		Pr.Geo.	"	Prince George
Din.	"	Dinwiddie		Rock.	"	Rockbridge
Eli.Cy"	Elizabeth City		Spots.	"	Spotsylvania
Fau.	"	Fauquier		So'n	"	Southampton
Gooch."	Goochland		Wash.	"	Washington
Hen.	"	Henrico		West.	"	Westmoreland
Henry	"	Henry		York	"	York
Har.	"	Hardy				

Augusta B. Fothergill

VIRGINIA TAX PAYERS

TAX PAYER	Poll	Slave	County	TAX PAYER	Poll	Slave	County	TAX PAYER	Poll	Slave	County
Abbet,Ishmael	1		Mont.	Adams,Elizabeth,	1		Lou.	Adams,Wilson,	1		Loui.
Abbett,James,	1	1	Spots.	Adams,Evan,			Cul.	Aday,Walter,	1		Bed.
Abbett,Thomas,	1		Rock.	Adams,Francis,	1	10	Lou.	Adcock,Anderson,	1	6	Buck.
Abbott,Daniel,	3		Cul.	Adams,Feathergill,	2	4	Fau.	Adcock,Carter,			Buck.
Abbot,Elizabeth,		5	Cul.	Adams,Gawen,	1		Pr.Wm.	Adcock,Edmund,	1	2	Buck.
Abbott,George,	1		Buck.	Adams,George,	1		Loui.	Adcock,Elizabeth,		5	Buck.
Abbott,Jacob,	1	1	K.& Q.	Adams,George,	1	5	Din.	Adcock,George,	1	1	Buck.
Abbott,Joseph,	1		Lou.	Adams,George,	1	2	K.Wm.	Adcock,John,	2	6	Buck.
Abbott,Roger,	1	10	Cul.	Adams,George,	1	1	Fau.	Adcock,John,Jr.,	1		Buck.
Abbott,Thomas,	1		Bot.	Adams,Henry,	1		So'n	Adcock,Joseph,		1	Buck.
Abdale,Abel,	1	1	Nor.	Adams,Henry,		2	So'n	Adcock,William,	1		Buck.
Abdale,Amos,	1		Nor.	Adams,Isaac,	1		Brun.	Adderson,Jonathan,	2	2	Acco.
Abdal,Elisha,	1	1	Acco.	Adams,James,	1		Mont.	Adderson,John,			Acco.
Abdal,Ezekiel,	1		Acco.	Adams,James,	1		Lou.	Adderson,John,	1		Acco.
Abdale,Henry,	1	1	Nor.	Adams,Jacob,	1		Henry,	Adderson,Littleton,	1	2	Nor.
Abdale,Jacob,	1	1	Nor.	Adams,Jacob,	1		Henry,	Adderson,Margaret,		2	Nor.
Abdale,William,		3	Nor.	Adams,John,	1	1	So'n	Adderson,Nathan,	2	6	Acco.
Abbernatha,David,	1	2	Lun.	Adams,John,	1		Loui.	Adderson,Thomas,Sr.,	1	6	Nor.
Abernathy,Charles,	1	4	Brun.	Adams,John,	1	4	Mont.	Adderson,Thomas,Jr.,	1	3	Nor.
Abernathy,Frederick,	1	1	Brun.	Adams,John,			Cul.	Addison,John,			Buck.
Abernathy,James,		1	Brun.	Adams,John,	1		Bed.	Adkins,Alexander,	2		Spots.
Abernathy,John,Sr.,	1	1	Brun.	Adams,John,Sr.,			Bed.	Adkins,Bartlet,	1		Lin.
Abernathy,John,Jr.,	1	2	Brun.	Adams,John,Jr.,	1		Bed.	Adkins,David,	1		Henry
Abernathy,Liles,	1	4	Din.	Adams,John,			K.& Q.	Adkins,David,	1		Hen.
Abernathy,Mary,		1	Din.	Adams,John,			Lou.	Adkins,James,	3		Brun.
Abernathy,Robert,	1	3	Brun.	Adams,John,	1		Lou.	Adkins,James,Jr.,			Brun.
Abernathy,Signal,	1	2	Din.	Adams,John,	1		Camp.	Adkins,James,	1		West'd
Abernathy,William,	2	9	Brun.	Adams,John,	1		Camp.	Adkins,James,			Cul.
Abington,John,	1	1	Henry	Adams,Littleton	1	5	Fau.	Adkins,Jesse,	1		Lin.
Able,James,	1		Pr.Wm.	Adams,Mary,		4	So'n	Adkins,Pleasant,	1		Goock.
Able,Jeremiah,	1		Wash.	Adams,Moses,			Bed.	Adkins,Rowland,	1		Bed.
Able,Lewis,	1		Mont.	Adams,Nathaniel,	1	1	Lou.	Adkins,William,	1		Mont.
Abney,John,	1	3	Aug.	Adams,Patrick,	1		Mont.	Adkins,William,			Brun.
Abrahams,Joseph,	1	5	K.Wm.	Adams,Reuben,	1	1	Brun.	Addleman,Daniel,	1		Lou.
Abrahams,Levy,	1		Aug.	Adams,Col.Richard,	1	14	Gooch.	Adney,Thomas,	1		Bed.
Abrahams,Mordecai,	1	23	K.Wm.	Adams,Col.Richard,		11	Hen.	Adson,Charles,			Din.
Abrahams,Solomon,	1	5	K.Wm.	Adams,Richard,	2	22	Hen.	Aeemster,Thomas,	1	6	Aug.
Abrel,James,	1		Berk.	Adams,Richard,Jr.,			Hen.	Aelord,Amos,	1		Wash.
Abrell,Jacob,	1		Berk.	Adams,Richard,			K.Wm.	Aeres,James,	1		K.& Q.
Abshear,Abraham,	1		Bed.	Adams,Richard,	1	1	Henry	Aerey,Seaton,			K & Q.
Abshear,Christian,	1		Bed.	Adams,Samuel,	1		Lou.	Agee,Isaac,	1		Buck.
Abshear,Lodowick,	1		Bed.	Adams,Samuel,	1	4	Lou.	Agee,James,	2	14	Buck.
Abston,Jesse,	1	2	Bed.	Adams,Samuel,	1		Bed.	Agee,James,Jr.,	1	1	Buck.
Ackman,John,John,	1		Berk.	Adams,Samuel,	1		Bot.	Agee,Jacob,	1		Buck.
Acors,J.,	1		Pr.Wm.	Adams,Sarah,		12	Fau.	Agee,John,			Buck.
Acres,Alexander,	1		K.Geo.	Adams,Thomas,	1		So'n	Agee,Noah,			Buck.
Acre,William,	1		K.Wm.	Adams,Thomas,	1	1	Pr.Geo.	Agnew,William,	1		Lou.
Acre,William,	1		Cul.	Adams,Thomas,	2	40	Aug.	Ahern,William,	1		Loui.
Acton,Francis,	1	4	Lou.	Adams,Thomas,	1		Henry	Akers,Blackburn,	1		Mont.
Acton,James,	1		Henry,	Adams,Thomas,	1	2	Henry	Akers,John,	1		Buck.
Acton,Richard,	1		Har.	Adams,Thomas,	1		Berk.	Akers,John,			Buck.
Acuff,Cain,	1		Spots.	Adams,Thomas,	3		Lou.	Akers,Peter,	1		Camp.
Acuff,John,	2		Henry	Adams,Thomas,	1	6	Loui.	Akers,Peter,	1		Lou.
Acuff,William,	1		Henry	Adams,Thomas,			K.Wm.	Akers,Ralph,	1		Lou.
Acuff,William,	1		Henry,	Adams,Thomas,	1	3	Fau.	Akers,Robert,	1		Lou.
Acworth,Patience,		6	Acco.	Adams,W.	1		Pr.Wm.	Akers,Solomon,	1		Mont.
Adair,James,	1		Mont.	Adams,William,	1		So'n	Akers,William,	1	2	Camp.
Adair,James,	1		Rock.	Adams,William,	1		Henry	Akers,William,	1	3	Bed.
Adair,Samuel,	1		Rock.	Adams,William,	1	1	Henry	Akers,William,	2		Buck.
Adams,Absalom,	1		Cul.	Adams,William,	1		Brun.	Aiken,James,	1		Henry
Adams,Absalom,	3	1	Cul.	Adams,William,	1		Cul.	Akin,Joseph,	1	2	Camp.
Adams,Andrew,	1	1	Lou.	Adams,William,	1		Lou.	Aiken,Nathaniel,	1		Bot.
Adams,Ben,	1	1	So'n	Adams,William,	1		K.Wm.	Aiken,Nicholas,	1		Henry
Adams,Benjamin,		1	Spots.	Adams,William,	1		Camp.	Akin,Thomas,	1		Henry
Adams,Catarine,		1	Fay.	Adams,William,	1		Camp.	Akin,Thomas,	1		Bot.
Adams,Charles,	1	1	Pr.Wm.	Adams,William,			Cha.Cy.	Ailstock,Michael,			Loui.
Adams,David,	1		Lin.	Adams,William,	1		Loui.	Ailsworth,George,	1	1	Henry
Adams,Elisha,	1		Fau.	Adams,William,	1		Bed.	Aimes,Churchill,	1	3	Acco.
Adams,Ellison,A.	1		K.Wm.	Adams,William,	1		Bed.	Aimes,Elijah,	1	5	Acco.
Adams,Elizabeth,			Brun.	Adams,William,	1		Bed.	Aimes,Elizabeth,	2	8	Acco.
Adams,Elizabeth,		8	Brun.	Adams,William,	1		Lin.	Aimes,John,	1		Acco.

Name			Place
Aimes,Nathaniel,	1	1	Acco.
Aimes,Thomas,Sr.,	3	5	Acco.
Airee,Abraham,	1		Caro.
Aistrop,Robert,	1		Aug.
Alamong,Daniel,			Berk.
Allamong,Jacob,	1		Berk.
Alcock,John,		5	Spots.
Alcock,Robert,	2	16	Cul.
Alcock,Thomas,	1	19	Caro.
Alcock,William,			Cul.
Alcoin,John,	1		Mont.
Alders,Mary,			Spots.
Alderson,Curtis,	1	2	Bot.
Alderson,Jeremiah,	1	2	Lun.
Aldridge,John,	1		Lou.
Aldridge,William,	1	6	Pr.Geo.
Aldridge,William,	1		Bot.
Ale,William,	1		Caro.
Aleet,Thomas,	1		Cul.
Alexander,Andrew,			Aug.
Alexander,Andrew,	1		Aug.
Alexander,Andrew,	2		Aug.
Alexander,Benjamin,	1	8	K.& Q.
Alexander,Elisha,	1	1	K.& Q.
Alexander,Francis,	1	2	Aug.
Alexander,Gabriel,	1	4	Aug.
Alexander,Garrat,	1	15	Berk.
Alexander,George,	1		Cul.
Alexander,Hugh,	1		Bot.
Alexander,James,	2		Aug.
Alexander,James,Sr.,	2	5	Aug.
Alexander,James,Jr.,	1		Aug.
Alexander,James,	1	1	Cul.
Alexander,James,	1		Fay.
Alexander,James,	3	2	Fay.
Alexander,James,	1		Fay.
Alexander,Jane,		1	Rock.
Alexander,Col.John,	1	34	Lou.
Alexander,John,Sr.,	1		Aug.
Alexander,John,Jr.,	1	1	Aug.
Alexander,John,	1	9	Henry
Alexander,John,Jr.,	1		Henry
Alexander,John,	1		Lou.
Alexander,John,	1		Fay.
Alexander,John,	1	1	Fay.
Alexander,John,			Fay.
Alexander,Joseph,	1	3	Rock.
Alexander,Philip,	1	16	Fau.
Alexander,Philip,		41	K.Geo.
Alexander,Capt.Robert,	1	7	Bed.
Alexander,Robert,	1	3	Fay.
Alexander,Robert,	2	3	Aug.
Alexander,Robert,	2	10	Camp.
Alexander,Robert,	3	3	K.Geo.
Alexander,Susanna,	7	5	K.Geo.
Alexander,Thomas,	4	1	K.Geo.
Alexander,Thomas,	1		Bed.
Alexander,Thomas,	1		Rock.
Alexander,Thornton,		36	Pr.Wm.
Alexander,Col.William,	1	41	Pr.Wm.
Alexander,William,	1		Cul.
Alexander,William,			Fay.
Alexander,William,	1		Fay.
Alexander,William,	1	20	Lou.
Alexander,William,	1	1	Henry
Alexander,William,	1		Rock.
Alexander,William,	1	11	Rock.
Alford,Thomas,	1		Mont.
Algier,John,	1		Har.
Algier,Maunus,	2		Har.
Algier,Michael,	2		Har.
Algier,William,	1		Har.
Alin,James,	1		Cul.
Alin,Mary,		4	Cul.
Allegre,Jane,		3	Hen.
Aliff,Thomas,	1		Pr.Wm.
Aliff,William,	1		Lou.
Alfriend,Susanna,		3	Pr.Geo.
Allason,William,	1	12	Fau.
Allason,William,	5	43	Fau.
Albriton,John,	1	1	Lou.
Allen,Allen,			Hen.
Allen,Ann,		1	K.& Q.
Allen,Arthur,	1	4	So'n
Allen,Benjamin,	1		Wash.
Allen,Daniel,	1		Bot.
Allen,Daniel,Jr.,	1		Bot.
Allen,David,	1	9	Hen.
Allen,David,	1	16	Hen.
Allen,David,	2	18	Hen.
Allen,David,	1		Lou.
Allen,Drury,	1		Hen.
Allen,Drury,	1		Bed.
Allen,Drury,	1		Lun.
Allen,Edward,	1	5	E.Cy.
Allen,Elizabeth,		4	Aug.
Allen,Erasmus,	1		Caro.
Allen,Fisher,	1		Cul.
Allen,Francis,	1		Aug.
Allen,George,	1		Henry
Allen,Henry,	1	1	Cul.
Allen,Henry,	1	5	So'n
Allen,Hudson,	1	17	Ja.Cy.
Allen,Hudson,	1	26	York
Allen,Hugh,	1	5	Rock.
Allen,Hugh,	1	2	Bot.
Allen,Hugh,Est.,		2	Aug.
Allen,James,	1	8	Fau.
Allen,James,	1	1	Fau.
Allen,James,			Cul.
Allen,James,Sr.,	1	1	Aug.
Allen,James,	1	7	Aug.
Allen,James,	1	7	Spots.
Allen,James,	2	13	Hen.
Allen,James,	1	1	Gooch.
Allen,John,	1		Rock.
Allen,John,	1		Fau.
Allen,John,	1		Fau.
Allen,John,	1	1	Bot.
Allen,John,	1		Cul.
Allen,John,	1	13	Ja.Cy.
Allen,John,	1		Spots.
Allen,John	1	1	Eli.Cy.
Allen,John,	1		Bed.
Allen,John,	1		Hen.
Allen,John,	1		Hen.
Allen,John,	1	3	Acco.
Allen,John,	1	2	Pr.Geo.
Allen,John,	1	1	Brun.
Allen,John,	1		Gooch.
Allen,John,			Lun.
Allen,John,	1		K.Geo.
Allen,John,	1		Lin.
Allen,John,	1	7	Fay.
Allen,Jones,	1	9	Ja.Cy.
Allen,Joseph,	1	7	Fau.
Allen,Joseph,	1		Ja.Cy.
Allen,Joseph,	1	3	Spots.
Allen,Julius,	1	6	Ja.Cy
Allen,Julius,	1	16	Hen.
Allen,Littleberry,	1	7	Hen.
Allen,Littleberry,	1	6	Hen.
Allen,Malcomb,	½	4	Bot.
Allen,Mary,		1	Fau.
Allen,Mary,	2	17	Buck.
Allen,Mary,			Ja.Cy.
Allen,Moses,	1	3	Bot.
Allen,Peter,	2		Berk.
Allen,Peter,Jr.,	1		Berk.
Allen,Philip,Est.,		7	Buck.
Allen,Richard,	1		Hen.
Allen,Richard,	1	1	Hen.
Allen,Richard,	1		Gooch.
Allen,Robert,	1		Hen.
Allen,Robert,	1	2	Aug.
Allen,Robert,	1	3	Lin.
Allen,Robert,	1	3	Lin.
Allen,Robert,	1		Berk.
Allen,Robert,	1	2	Bot.
Allen,Samuel,	1		Henry
Allen,Samuel,			Buck.
Allen,Thomas,		2	Fau.
Allen,Thomas,	2		Cul.
Allen,Thomas,	1	3	Spots.
Allen,Thomas,	1	5	Spots.
Allen,Thomas,	1	7	Eli.Cy.
Allen,Thomas,	1		Caro.
Allen,Thomas,	1	1	Gooch.
Allen,Thomas,		5	Cul.
Allen,Thomas,	1	3	Cul.
Allen,Thomas,	1		Brun.
Allen,Thomas,	1	4	K.Wm.
Allen,Thomas Hamlin,	1	5	Pr.Geo.
Allen,Ureley,		4	Cul.
Allen,Ursula,		10	Fau.
Allen,Ustey,		4	Cul.
Allen,Vincent,	1		Cul.
Allen,Col.William,	1	58	So'n
Allen,William,	1		Aug.
Allen,William,	1		Fau.
Allen,William,	1		Bot.
Allen,William,	1	5	Bot.
Allen,William,	1	10	Cul.
Allen,William,	1		Aug.
Allen,William,Jr.,	1	10	Ja.Cy.
Allen,William,	1	31	Spots.
Allen,William,	1		Eli.Cy.
Allen,William,	1		Buck.
Allen,William,	1		Mont.
Allen,William,	1		Hen.
Allen,William,	1		Lou.
Allen,William,	1		K.Wm.
Allen,William,	1	8	York
Allen,William,	1		Brun.
Allen,William,	1	8	Brun.
Allen,William,	1	60	Brun.
Allen,William,		41	Brun.
Allen,William,	1		Wash.
Allen,William,	1		Din.
Allen,William Hunt,	1	21	Buck.
Allensworth,William,	1		K.Geo.
Allenton,Jonathan,	1		Har.
Alley,Drury,	1		Pr.Geo.
Alley,Drury,	1		Pr.Geo.
Alley,Erasmus,	1	9	Loui.
Alley,Henry,	1	3	Pr.Geo.
Alley,James,Sr.,	1		Wash.
Alley,Miles,	1	4	Brun.
Alley,Nicholson,	1	7	Bot.
Alley,Samuel,	1	1	Hen.
Alley,Shade,	1	4	Brun.
Alley,Thomas,	1		Wash.
Alley,Thomas,	1		Mont.
Alley,William,	1		Hen.
Alley,William,	1		Pr.Wm.
Allick,Filman,	1		Berk.
Allison,Albert,	1	2	Mont.
Allison,Anderson,	1		Rock.
Allison,Else,		8	Pr.Geo.
Allison,John,	1		Rock.
Allison,John,	1		Wash.
Allison,John,Jr.,	1		Aug.
Allison,John,	1		Lon.
Allison,Robert,	1	1	Wash.
Allison,Peter,	1		Wash.
Allison,Samuel,			West'd.
Allison,William,	1		Aug.
Allison,William,	1		Pr.Wm.
Almand,John,	1		Eli.Cy.
Almand,Thomas,	1		Loui.
Almand,William,	1	3	Eli.Cy.
Almon,John,	1		Har.
Almon,William,	1		Har.
Almond,William,	1	19	Caro.

Name			Place
Alphrey,Joseph,	2		Har.
Alsop,Benjamin,	1	1	Spots.
Alsop,George,	2	9	Caro.
Alsop,John,	1		Mont.
Alsop,Nelly,	2	3	Caro.
Alsop,Sarah,		9	Spots.
Alsup,George,	1		K.Geo.
Allsup,Thomas,Sr.,	1		Henry
Allsup,Thomas,Jr.,	1		Henry
Alstock,Keaser,			Lun.
Alvarez,Israel,	1		York
Alvarez,William,			York
Alverson,John,	1		West'd.
Alverson,John,	1		Cul.
Alvey,William,	1	15	K.Wm.
Alvis,Ashly,	1		Gooch.
Alvis,David,	1		Gooch.
Alvis,Elijah,	1		Gooch.
Alvis,Shadrack,	1	2	Gooch.
Alvison,John,			Bot.
Alvison,John,	2		Bot.
Alvoy,Richard,			Pr.Wm.
Aman,Anthony,	1		Lou.
Amack,Samuel,	1		Bot.
Ambler,Jaquelin,	1	9	Hen.
Ambler,Jacquelin,	1	9	Hen.
Ambler,John,	2	88	Loui.
Ambler,John,		22	Ja.Cy.
Ambler,William,	1		Lou.
Ambrose,Ambrose,	1		Loui.
Ambrose,Henry,	1		Berk.
Ambrose,William,	1		Lun.
Ames,Edmund,	1		Nor.
Ames,John,	1	2	Nor.
Ames,Shadrick,	1	18	Nor.
Amey,Philip,	1		Cul.
Amis,Joseph,	1	10	Cul.
Amiss,Thomas,	1		Cul.
Amiss,William,	1		Cul.
Ammons,Thomas,	1	7	Cul.
Amonet,John,	1		Henry
Amonet,William,	1	1	Buck.
Amos,Francis,	1		Buck.
Amos,Reubin,	1		Buck.
Amos,Thomas,	1		Lou.
Amoss,James,	1	1	Lun.
Amoss,William,	1	5	Henry
Anchrom,Joel,	1	5	K.Geo.
Anderson,Andrew,	2	5	Aug.
Anderson,Andrew,			Fau.
Anderson,Ann,		1	Buck.
Anderson,Armistead,	1		Henry
Anderson,Augustin,			Cul.
Anderson,Bartlett,	1		Bed.
Anderson,Betty,			Pr.Geo.
Anderson,Charles,			Bed.
Anderson,Churchill,	1	3	Brun.
Anderson,Churchill,	1	13	K.&Q.
Anderson,Colebert,	1		Berk.
Anderson,Cornelius,	1		Fau.
Anderson,David,	1	3	Buck.
Anderson,David,	1		Fau.
Anderson,David,	1		Bot.
Anderson,David,	1		Loui.
Anderson,David,	1	1	Spots.
Anderson,Elizabeth,		16	Loui.
Anderson,Garland,	1	22	Caro.
Anderson,George,	6	16	Cul.
Anderson,George,			Cul.
Anderson,George,	2		Cul.
Anderson,George,	1	8	Hen.
Anderson,George,	2		Aug.
Anderson,George,Jr.,	1		Aug.
Anderson,Henry,	1	5	Buck.
Anderson,Henry,	1		Cul.

Name			Place
Anderson,Henry,	1	4	Hen.
Anderson,Isaac,	1	7	Rock.
Anderton,Isaac,	1	8	Brun.
Anderson,Isaac,	1	1	Cul.
Anderson,Jacob,	2	19	Bed.
Anderson,Jacob,			Cul.
Anderson,Jacob,		1	Mont.
Anderson,James,	1	2	Caro.
Anderson,James,	1	1	Aug.
Anderson,James,	1		Mont.
Anderson,James,	1		Rock.
Anderson,James,	1		Loui.
Anderson,James,	1		Bot.
Anderson,James,	1	10	Pr.Wm.
Anderson,James,	1	3	Pr.Geo.
Anderson,James,	1		Aug.
Anderson,James,	1		Fay.
Anderson,James,			Aug.
Anderson,James,	1	4	Lun.
Anderson,John,	1	6	Caro.
Anderson,John,	1		Cul.
Anderson,John,			Cul.
Anderson,John,	1	33	K.Wm.
Anderson,John,	1	1	Pr.Wm.
Anderson,John,	1		Loui.
Anderson,John,	1		Mont.
Anderson,John,	1		Fau.
Anderson,John,	1		Henry
Anderson,John,	2	1	Spots.
Anderson,Jordan,			Din.
Anderson,Joseph,	1		Berk.
Anderson,Joseph,	1		Bot.
Anderson,Judith,		2	Loui.
Anderson,Luke,	1		Ja.Cy.
Anderson,Matthew,	1	3	Buck.
Anderson,Mathew,	1	12	Loui.
Anderson,Michael,	2	46	Loui.
Anderson,Nathan,	1		Har.
Anderson,Nathan,	1	1	Loui.
Anderson,Nathaniel,	1	6	Loui.
Anderson,Nathaniel,	1	1	Buck.
Anderson,Col.Nelson,	1	4	Loui.
Anderson,Nelson,		14	Loui.
Anderson,Nicholas,	2		Fay.
Anderson,Obediah,			Cul.
Anderson,Paulin,		8	K.&Q.
Anderson,Peter,	1		Mont.
Anderson,Phebe,		1	Caro.
Anderson,Presley,	1	2	Fay.
Anderson,Reubin,			Cul.
Anderson,Richard,	2	23	K.&Q.
Anderson,Richard,	1		Loud.
Anderson,Richard,Jr.	1	15	Loui.
Anderson,Col. Robert,		3	Loui.
Anderson,Robert,			Loui.
Anderson,Robert,	1		Loui.
Anderson,Robert,	1	11	Ja.Cy.
Anderson,Robert,	1		Bot.
Anderson,Samuel,	1		Aug.
Anderson,Samuel,	1	2	Aug.
Anderson,Spencer,	1		Pr.Wm.
Anderson,Thomas,	1	58	Buck.
Anderson,Thomas,	1		Aug.
Anderson,Thomas,	1		Spots.
Anderson,Thomas,	1	3	Pr.Wm.
Anderson,Thomas,	1	8	Din.
Anderson,Turner,	1	11	Loui.
Anderson,Uriah,			Cul.
Anderson,Walter,	1	5	Caro.
Anderson,Widdow,			Aug.
Anderson,Capt.William,	1	19	Loui.
Anderson,William,			Lun.
Anderson,William,	1	1	Loui.
Anderson,William,	1	14	Buck.
Anderson,William,	3		Aug.

Name			Place
Anderson,William,	1		Berk.
Anderson,William,	1		Berk.
Anderson,William,	1	5	Bot.
Anderson,William,	1	3	Fay.
Anderson,William,	1	1	Aug.
Anderson,William,	1		Mont.
Anderson,William,	1		Rock.
Anderson,William,	1		Hen.
Anderson,William,	1	1	Gooch.
Anderson,William,	1		Lou.
Anderson,William,	1		West'd.
Andrews,Abraham,	2	3	Lun.
Andrews,Alexander,	1		Brun.
Andrews,Andrew,		4	Nor.
Andrews,Ann,		6	So'n.
Andrews,Annemeriah,		31	Acco.
Andrews,Benjamin,	1	2	Pr.Geo.
Andrews,David,	1		Henry
Andrews,David,	1		Din.
Andrews,David,	1	5	Brun.
Andrews,Drewry,	1	3	So'n.
Andrews,Elizabeth,		2	Pr.Geo.
Andrews,Elizabeth,	1	3	Nor.
Andrews,John,	1	14	So'n.
Andrews,John,	1	2	Pr.Geo.
Andrews,John,	1		Brun.
Andrews,Mark,	1	3	Lun.
Andrews,Moses,	1		Berk.
Andrews,Peter,	1		Lun.
Andrews,Robert,	1	1	Acco.
Andrews,Samuel,	1		Lou.
Andrews,Thomas,	1		Din.
Andrews,Thomas,			Lun.
Andrews,William,	1	9	Pr.Geo.
Andrew,Wills,			Fay.
Aneron,Martin,	1		K.Wm.
Angel,George,	1		Spots.
Angell,George,	1		Fay.
Angel,John,	1	4	Spots,
Angell,John,			Cul.
Angell,John,	1	4	Fay.
Angel,Michael,	2		Berk.
Angell,William,	1		Hen.
Angeler,James,			Hen.
Anglin,Phillip,	2		Henry
Angus,John,	1	1	Pr.Geo.
Annis,William,	1		Pr.Wm.
Ansell,Leonard,	1		Lou.
Ansley,William,	1	5	Lou.
Anthony,James,	1	8	Loui.
Anthony,James,	1	6	Henry
Anthony,John,		4	Bed.
Anthony,John,		9	Bed.
Anthony,John,	1	34	Camp.
Anthony,Joseph,	1		Henry
Anthony,Joseph,Sr.,	1	18	Henry.
Anthony,Joseph,Jr.,	1	7	Henry.
Anthony,Micajah,	1		Henry.
Antler,Henry,	2		Berk.
Antler,Martin,	1		Berk.
Antler,Michael,	1		Berk.
Antler,Philip,	1		Berk.
Applebec,Robert,	1		Cul.
Applegate,Hezikiah,	1		Mont.
Applegate,Jacob,	1		Berk.
Apperson,Daniel,	1		Lun.
Apperson,Francis,	2	6	Cul.
Apperson,George,	1	1	Ja.Cy.
Apperson,James,	1		Lun.
Aperson,John,	1	1	York
Apperson,John,	1	16	Spots.
Apperson,Paul,	1	1	Spots.
Applewhaite,Henry,	1	14	So'n.
Arbuckle,John,	1	2	Lin.
Arbuckle,Samuel,	1		Lin.

Arbuckle,Tabitha,	1	15	Acco.	Arnett,Samuel,	1		Lou.	Ashby,Sarah,	2	5	Acco.
Arbuckle,William,	1	1	Acco.	Arnett,Susanna,	1	14	Loui.	Ashby,Susanah,	1		Acco.
Arburthnot,John,	1		K.Wm.	Arnett,William,			Loui.	Ashby,William,	1		Pr.Wm.
Archer,Edward,	1	8	So'n.	Arnold,Anthony,	1	5	Spots.	Asher,Charles,			Cul.
Atcher,Edward,		3	Din.	Arnold,Benjamin,	1		Fau.	Asher,Jerry,	1		Cul.
Archer,Edward,		3	Din.	Arnold,Benjamin,	1		Fau.	Asher,John,	2	3	Cul.
Archer,Field,		2	Lun.	Arnold,George,	1	2	Spots.	Asher,John,			Buck.
Archer,George,	1	9	Din.	Arnold,Henry,	1	1	Henry	Ashford,John,	1	4	Cul.
Archer,James,	2	2	Cul.	Arnold,Humprhey,	2		Lin.	Ashford,Thomas,	1	3	Cul.
Archer,John,	1		Din.	Arnold,Isaac,	1	2	Loui.	Ashford,William,	1		Bot.
Archer,Stephen,	1		Fay.	Arnold,Isaac,	1	3	Fau.	Ashley,Elizabeth,		3	Ja.Cy.
Archer,Thomas,	1	6	York	Arnold,James,	2	1	Cul,	Ashley,Thomas,	1		Bot.
Archer,William,	1	2	Din.	Arnold,James,	1	1	Caro.	Ashley,William,	1	5	Spots.
Archer,William,	1		Henry	Arnold,John,			Lin.	Ashlin,Thomas,			Hen.
Archer,Zacharias,	1		Fay.	Arnold,John,		1	Spots.	Ashlock,Josiah,	1	3	Ja.Cy.
Archerab,Abraham,	1	9	York	Arnold,Reubin,	1	1	Cul.	Ashman,Thomas,	1	1	Spots.
Archibald,Samuel,	1		Rock.	Arnold,Thomas,			Buck.	Ashmore,William,	1	5	Pr.Wm.
Ardes,Louisa,			Lou.	Arnold,William,			Cul.	Ashten,James,			Bed.
Arginbright,Augusteen,1			Aug.	Arnold,William,	1	3	Loui.	Ashton,Burditt,	1	33	K.Geo.
Arginbright,John,	1		Aug.	Arnold,William,	1	7	Caro.	Ashton,Charles,	1	1	K.Geo.
Ariss,John,	2	21	Berk.	Arnold,William,Sr.,	1		Rock.	Ashton,Charles,Est.		11	K.Geo.
Arler,Henry,	1		Lou.	Arnold,William,Jr.,	1		Rock.	Ashton,A.Henry,		10	K.Geo.
Arlington,John,Sr.,	1	9	Acco.	Arrett,Christopher,	1		Berk.	Ashton,Henry A.	7	4	K.Geo.
Arlington,John,Jr.,	1	1	Acco.	Arrington,Adler,	1	2	Buck.	Ashton,Henry Alexander1		14	Lou.
Armentrout,Christopher3			Har.	Arrington,Jesse,	1	1	So'n.	Ashton,Henry,Jr.,	1		K.Geo.
Armistead,Ann,			Eli.Cy.	Arrington,Samuel,	2		Buck.	Ashton,John,	1	8	West'd.
Armistead,Baker,	1	10	Eli.Cy.	Arrinsbrogh,John,	1		Aug.	Ashton,John,Sr.,	1	29	K.Geo.
Armistead,Bowles,	1	63	Cul.	Artgear,Henry,	1		Lin.	Ashton,John,	1	27	K.Geo.
Armistead,Ellison,	2	16	Nor.	Arthur,Anne,		11	Camp.	Ashton,Laurance,	1	12	K.Geo.
Armistead,Francis,	1	15	Eli.Cy.	Arthur,Barnabas,	1	1	Bed.	Askford,Michael,	1		Lou.
Armistead,Henry,	1	11	Cha.Cy.	Arthur,Benjamin,	1	1	Camp.	Askew,Daniel,	1		Brun.
Armistead,Henry,	1	14	Spots.	Arthur,James,	1		Bed.	Askew,William,	2	1	Berk.
Armistead,Isaac,	1	6	Hen.	Arthur,John,Sr.,			Bed.	Askins,John,	1	1	Fau.
Armistead,James Bray,	1	2	Eli.Cy.	Arthur,Joseph,	1	1	Mont.	Askins,William,	1		Pr.Wm.
Armistead,John,	1	7	Eli.Cy.	Arthur,Samuel,	1		Mont.	Aston,Daniel,	1		Gooch.
Armistead,John,	2	49	Caro.	Arthur,Thomas,	2		Bed.	Atcher,George,	1		Lou.
Armistead,Moss,	1	11	Eli.Cy.	Arthur,Thomas,	1		Bed.	Atchison,James,	1		Fau.
Armistead,Robert,			Eli.Cy.	Arthur,Thomas,	1	3	Bed.	Atchison,John,	1	1	Fau.
Armistead,Robert,	1	64	Loui.	Arthur,Thomas,Jr.,			Bed.	Atchison,Samuel,	1		Har.
Armsted,John,	2	85	Pr.Wm.	Arthur,Thomas,Sr.,	1		Bed.	Atchison,William,Sr.,	3	2	Har.
Armsted,Robert,		4	Camp.	Arthur,William,Jr.,	1		Camp.	Atchison,William,Jr.,	1		Har.
Armistead,Samuel,	1	5	Eli.Cy.	Arthur,William,Sr.,	1		Camp.	Atchley,Abraham,	1		Bot.
Armistead,Thomas,	1	18	Pr.Geo.	Arthurs,John,	1		Wash.	Atchly,Joseph,	1		Bot.
Armistead,Westwood,	1	13	Eli.Cy.	Artis,Absalom,	1		So'n.	Atchley,Martin,	1		Bot.
Armistead,William,	2	43	Eli.Cy.	Artis,Edward,	1	2	So'n.	Atchley,Thomas,	1		Bot.
Armocust,Adam,	1		Aug.	Artis,John,	1		So'n.	Athell,Anthony,	1		Lou.
Armocust,Ann,	1		Aug.	Artis,Lewis,	1		So'n.	Athell,Joseph,			Lou.
Armocust,Michal,	1		Aug.	Arvin,Mary,			Lun.	Athell,Winnifred,	1		Lou.
Armstrong,Able,	1		Aug.	Asberry,George,	1	1	Fau.	Ather,George,	1		Pr.Wm.
Armstrong,Andrew,	2	1	Bot.	Asberry,Hannah,	1	2	Fau.	Athie,John,			Pr.Wm.
Armstrong,Archibald,	3		Aug.	Asberry,Henry,	1		Fau.	Athie,Thomas,	2	8	Pr.Wm.
Armstrong,James,	1		Berk.	Asberry,Henry,	1		Fau.	Athey,William,			Lou.
Armstrong,James,	1		Loui.	Asberry,William,	1	3	Fau.	Atkens,Jacob,	1		Henry
Armstrong,James,	1		Fau.	Asberry,William,	1		Fau.	Atkins,Adam,		6	Brun.
Armstrong,James,	1		Mont.	Asbury,George,	1		Bed.	Atkins,Bartlet,	1		Mont.
Armstrong,James,	1		Fau.	Asburry,Thomas,	1		Bed.	Atkins,Clayton,	1		K.&Q.
Armstrong,James,	2	7	Henry	Asbury,Richard,	1		West'd.	Atkins,Edward,	1		Cul.
Armstrong,Capt.John,	1		Bot.	Ash,Charles,	1		Aug.	Atkins,John,	1		K.&Q.
Armstrong,John,			Bot.	Ash,Elizabeth,		11	Fau.	Atkins,John,	1		K.Wm.
Armstrong,John,	1		K.Geo.	Ash,Francis,	1	4	Fau.	Atkins,John,Jr.,	1	1	K.&Q.
Armstrong,John,Sr.,	1		Lin.	Ash,George,	1	13	Fau.	Atkins,John,	1		Aug.
Armstrong,John,Jr.,	1		Lin.	Ashby,David,			Acco.	Atkins,John,			Brun.
Armstrong,Launcelot,	1	3	Loui.	Ashby,Elias,	1		Pr.Wm.	Atkins,John,	1		Brun.
Armstrong,Richard,	1		Bot.	Ashby,Enoch,	1	3	Fau.	Atkins,Joseph,	1	4	Mont.
Armstrong,Robert,	1		Bed.	Ashby,Ezekiel,			Acco.	Atkins,Owen,	1		Mont.
Armstrong,Robert,	2		Aug.	Ashby,George,			Acco.	Atkins,Richard,	1	1	Brun.
Armstrong,Thomas,	1		K.Geo.	Ashby,Henry,	1		Har.	Atkins,Sherid,	1		Mont.
Armstrong,William,	1		K.Wm.	Ashby,James,	2	3	Acco.	Atkins,William,	1		Brun.
Armstrong,William,	1		Aug.	Ashby,Jesse,			Har.	Atkins,William,	1		Ch.Cy.
Armstrong,William,	1		Loui.	Ashby,John,			York	Atkinson,William,Jr.,	1		So'n.
Armstrong,William,	1		Bed.	Ashby,John,	2	4	Acco.	Atkinson,William,Sr.,			So'n.
Armstrong,William,	1		Aug.	Ashby,John,Jr.,	1	10	Fau.	Atkinson,Daniel,	1		Caro.
Arnett,David,	1	2	Loui.	Ashby,John,Sr.,	1	13	Fau.	Atkinson,George,	1	11	Spots.
Arnett,David,	1	2	Lin.	Ashby,Peter,	1		Har.	Atkinson,Hardy,	1		So'n.
Arnett,James,			Loui.	Ashby,Robert,	1	5	Fau.	Atkinson,Isham,			So'n.

Name			Place
Atkinson,James,	1	1	So'n.
Atkinson,James,	1		Wash.
Atkinson,Jessee,	1	1	Henry
Atkinson,Joel,	1		Henry
Atkinson,John,	1	2	Lun.
Atkinson,John,			Din.
Atkinson,John,	1	1	Spots.
Atkinson,John,	1		Cul.
Atkinson,Joseph,	1		So'n.
Atkins,Joseph,	1		K.&Q.
Atkinson,Joseph,	1	1	So'n.
Atkinson,Josiah,	1		Gooch.
Atkinson,Martha,		5	Ch.Cy.
Atkinson,Martha,		8	Gooch.
Atkinson,Norris,	1		Mont.
Atkinson,Oney,	1		So'n.
Atkinson,Roger,		61	Lun.
Atkinson,Roger,	1	5	Din.
Atkinson,Roger,	2	51	Din.
Atkinson,Samuel,Sr.,	2	1	So'n.
Atkinson,Samuel,Jr.,	1	1	So'n.
Atkinson,Timothy,	1	8	So'n.
Atky,John,	1		Berk.
Atthames,William,	1		Lou.
Atwell,Francis,	1	12	Fau.
Atwell,Mary,		9	West'd.
Atwell,Richard,	2	15	West'd.
Atwell,Col.T.	3	30	Pr.Wm.
Atwell,Thomas,			K.Geo.
Atwood,James,	1	2	Cul.
Atwood,John,	1	1	K.Geo.
Atwoods,William,			Cul.
Audiddle,John,	1		Aug.
Audidle,James,	1		Aug.
Augburns,Edmund,	1	8	Pr.Geo.
Auld,Jacob,	1		Berk.
Aulderson,Benjamin,	1		Wash.
Auldridge,Benjamin,	1	1	Pr.Geo.
Ault,Henry,	1		Har.
Austin,Archelaus,	2	20	Buck.
Austin,Archelaus,	1	1	Hen.
Austin,Elizabeth,			Ja.Cy.
Austin,Frances,			Ch.Cy.
Austin,James,			Hen.
Austin,John,	2		Fau.
Austin,Mary,		3	Hen.
Austin,Mary,		4	Hen.
Austin,Thomas,	1	1	Fau.
Austin,Rush,		1	So'n.
Austin,William,	1		Pr.Wm.
Austin,William,	1	2	Ch.Cy.
Austin,William,	2	21	Bed.
Avent,William,	1	10	Brun.
Avera,Hannah,		1	Eli.Cy.
Avera,Thomas,	1	8	K.W.
Avery,Ann,			Pr.Geo.
Avery,B.Haley,	1	16	Pr.Geo.
Avery,Charles,	1		Brun.
Avery,Edward,	1	2	Brun.
Avery,Edward,Jr.,	1	1	Pr.Geo.
Avery,Edward,	1	6	Pr.Geo.
Avery,Edward,	1	18	Pr.Geo.
Avery,George,	1	9	Brun.
Avery,Isaac,	1	27	Nor.
Avery,Mary,		11	Brun.
Avery,Moses,	1		Wash.
Avery,Richard,	1	2	Pr.Geo.
Aves,Frances,	1		Berk.
Awbrey,Thomas,	1		Lou.
Awbrey,Thomas,Jr.,	1	2	Lou.
Aweny,John,			Fay.
Axline,Adam,	1		Lou.
Axline,John,	1		Lou.
Aylett,Mary,	1	64	K.Wm.
Aylor,Anthony,	1		Aug.
Aylor,Henry,Sr.	2	12	Cul.
Aylor,Henry,Jr.,	1	2	Cul.
Aylor,Jacob,	2		Cul.
Aynes,John,	1		Cul.
Ayres,Charles,	1		Fau.
Ayres,Francis,	1	3	Acco.
Ayres,George,	1		Acco.
Ayres,John,	1	2	Buck.
Ayres,John,	1		Bed.
Ayres,Leven,			Acco.
Ayres,Matthias,	1	2	Buck.
Ayres,Nathan,	1	7	Buck.
Ayres,Richard,	2		Acco.
Ayres,Robert,	1	1	Berk.
Ayres,Samuel,	2	5	Buck.
Ayres,Thomas,	1	5	Caro.
Ayres,Thomas,	2	2	Fau.
Ayres,Thomas,			Acco.
Ayres,William,	1		Acco.
Azburn,John,			Mont.
Azburn,Robert,	1		Mont.
Azburn,Stephen,Sr.,	1		Mont.
Azburn,Stephen,Jr.,	1		Mont.
Azburn,Solomon,	1		Mont.
Baber,Francis,	2	9	Caro.
Baber,George,	1		Buck.
Baber,James,	1	11	Caro.
Baber,Obediah,	1		Fay.
Baber,Robert,	3	8	Camp.
Baber,Robert,	1		Loui.
Baber,Thomas,			Buck.
Baber,William,	1	3	Buck.
Baber,William,Jr.,	1		Buck.
Back,Harmon,	2		Cul.
Back,Harman,	1		Fau.
Back,Henry,	1		Cul.
Back,John,	1		Cul.
Back,Joseph,			Cul.
Backelow,Cornelius,	1		Berk.
Backland,John,	1	1	Berk.
Backorn,John,	2		Har.
Backurst,Bolling,			Ch.Cy.
Bacon,Burwell,			Hen.
Bacon,Izard,	1	17	Hen.
Bacon,Lyddal,	1	5	Lun.
Bacon,Mary,	1	14	Lun.
Bacon,Richard,			Lun.
Bacon,William,	3	15	Hen.
Bacon,William,	1	1	Hen.
Badger,Abel,	1		Acco.
Badger,James,			Acco.
Badger,Nathaniel,	2	7	Acco.
Badget,Thomas,	1		York.
Badgett,John,	1		Loui.
Badgley,Anthony,	1		Har.
Badgley,Anthony,Jr.,	1		Har.
Badgley,David,	1		Har.
Bagby,Henry,	1	9	Buck.
Bagby,John,	1	4	Buck.
Bagby,John,	1	17	K.&Q.
Bagby,John,	1	9	Loui.
Bagby,John,Jr.,	1	3	Buck.
Bagby,Joseph,Joseph,			Buck.
Bagby,Richard,	1		K.&Q.
Bagby,Richard,	1	4	Loui.
Bagby,Robert,	1	8	Buck.
Bagby,Thomas,	1		K.&Q.
Bagby,William,	1	5	Loui.
Bagg,Ann,	1	4	Acco.
Bagg,William,	1	5	Acco.
Baggot,James,	1		Har.
Baggs,Alexander,	2		Rock.
Bagley,John,	1		Loud.
Bagwell,Hickerson,	1	5	K.Wm.
Bagwell,John,	1	5	Acco.
Bagwell,Lundsford,	1		Brun.
Bagwell,Richard,	1	7	Brun.
Bagwell,Sophia,		4	Acco.
Bagwell,Thomas,	1	4	Acco.
Bailer,Jacob,	1		Aug.
Bailes,John,	1		Buck.
Bails,Thomas,	1		Mont.
Bails,William,	1		Mont.
Bailey,Absalom,	1		So'n.
Bailey,Barnaby,	1	12	So'n.
Bailey,Benjamin,	1		Buck.
Bailey,Benjamin,		3	So'n.
Bailey,Benjamin,	1		Mont.
Bailey,Calam,	1	1	Gooch.
Bailey,Charles,	1		Gooch.
Bailey,Charles,	1	3	So'n.
Bailey,Daniel,	1	1	West'd.
Bailey,Francis,	1		K.&Q.
Bailey,George,	1		Fau.
Bailey,Hartwell,	1	2	So'n.
Bailey,Jacob,	1	1	So'n.
Bailey,James,	1	3	Brun.
Bailey,James,	1		Fau.
Bailey,James,	1		K.Geo.
Bailey,James,	1		Henry
Bailey,James,	1		Rock.
Bailey,James,Est.		4	West'd.
Bailey,Jeremiah,	1	5	Din.
Bailey,Jeremiah,	1	19	West'd.
Bailey,Jesse,	1		Bed.
Bailey,John,			Bed.
Bailey,John,	1		Berk.
Bailey,John,	1		Brun.
Bailey,John,			Brun.
Bailey,John,	1		Fau.
Bailey,John,	1	3	K.Geo.
Bailey,John,	2		Loui.
Bailey,John,	1	2	West'd.
Bailey,John,Jr.,	1	3	Lun.
Bailey,John,Sr.,	1		Lun.
Bailey,John,	1	14	So'n.
Bailey,John Edloe,	1		Ch.Cy.
Bailey,Joseph,	1	2	Fau.
Bailey,Joseph,	1		Fau.
Bailey,Joseph,	1	3	Hen.
Bailey,Margaret,		3	Nor.
Bailey,Margarett,	1		Cul.
Bailey,Mary,	1	8	Brun.
Bailey,Matt,			York.
Bailey,Moses,	1	8	Fau.
Bailey,Parker,	1		Ch.Cy.
Bailey,Peter,	1	5	Hen.
Bailey,Rice,			Fau.
Bailey,Richard,	1		Bed.
Bailey,Richard,	1		Fau.
Bailey,Richard,	1	4	Hen.
Bailey,Richard,	1	7	So'n.
Bailey,Robert,	1	8	Brun.
Bailey,Samuel,	1		Buck.
Bailey,Simon,	1		Fau.
Bailey,Stephen,	1		Fau.
Bailey,Stephen,	1	4	K.Geo.
Bailey,Thomas,	1		Henry
Bailey,Thomas,			Loui.
Bailey,Tryal,	1		So'n.
Bailey,W.James,	1	20	K.Wm.
Bailey,Walter,	1	1	So'n.
Bailey,William,	1		Berk.
Bailey,William,	1	8	Buck.
Bailey,William,			Caro.
Bailey,William,			Cul.
Bailey,William,	1		Fau.
Bailey,William,			Henry
Bailey,William,	1	5	York
Bailey,William,	1	1	York
Bailey,Wright,			Fau.

Name			County
Baine,Alexander,	1	35	Bot.
Baine,Robert,			Hen.
Bains,Francis,	1		Cul.
Bains,Henry,	1		Eli.Cy.
Bains,John,	1		Eli.Cy.
Bains,John,	1		Eli.Cy.
Bains,William,	1		Cul.
Baird,Archer,	1		Buck.
Baird,Hannah,		4	Pr.Geo.
Baird,Hardyman,	1		Buck.
Baird,Henry,	1		Buck.
Baird,John,	1	3	Brun.
Baird,John,	1		Buck.
Baird,John,	1	5	Din.
Baird,John,	2	54	Pr.Geo.
Baird,Samuel,	1		Aug.
Baird,Thomas,	1	8	Pr.Geo.
Bairde,Rev.David,	1	2	Lou.
Baise,Nancey,		5	Cul.
Baker,Anthony,	4	1	Har.
Baker,Benjamin,		5	So'n.
Baker,Catharine,	1	2	K.Geo.
Baker,David,	1		Fay.
Baker,David,	1		Mont.
Baker,Edward,	1		Henry
Baker,Elijah,	1		Lin.
Baker,Fennel,	1		Brun.
Baker,Fidkin,	1		Hen.
Baker,George,	1	3	Hen.
Baker,George,	1	3	Hen.
Baker,George,	1		Wash.
Baker,Glover,	1	1	Bed.
Baker,Jacob,	1		Har.
Baker,James,	1		Har.
Baker,James,	1		Henry
Baker,James,	1		Mont.
Baker,John,	1		Bed.
Baker,John,	1	10	Berk.
Baker,John,	1		Berk.
Baker,John,	2		Har.
Baker,John,	1	4	Loui.
Baker,John,	1		Loui.
Baker,Joseph,	1		Henry
Baker,Joseph,	1		Mont.
Baker,Joshua,			Fay.
Baker,Josiah,	1		Mont.
Baker,Moses,	1	1	Fau.
Baker,Moses,	3		Fay.
Baker,Overton,			Loui.
Baker,Philip,	1		Lou.
Baker,Richard,	1		Lin.
Baker,Robert,	1		Mont.
Baker,Robert,	1		Mont.
Baker,Robert,	1		Mont.
Baker,Robert,	1		Wash.
Baker,Richard,	1		Henry
Baker,Robert,	1		Henry
Baker,Samuel,	1		Bed.
Baker,Samuel,	1		Fau.
Baker,Samuel,	2		Har.
Baker,Trent,	1		Cul.
Baker,Walter,	1	17	Berk.
Baker,William,	1		Berk.
Baker,William,	1		Har.
Baker,William,	1		Henry
Baker,William,		8	Loui.
Baker,William,	1	1	Lou.
Baker,William,	1		York.
Balch,Hezekiah,	1	2	Fau.
Baldock,Levi,	2	5	Lin.
Baldwin,Daniel,	1		Spots.
Baldwin,Francis,	1		Berk.
Baldwin,John,	1		Berk.
Baldwin,John,	1		Lou.
Baldwin,Samuel,	1	1	Bot.
Baldwin,William,	2		Berk.
Baldwin,William,	1		Berk.
Baldwin,William,	1		Mont.
Bales,William,	2	3	Pr.Wm.
Baley,Briant,	1		West'd.
Baley,John,	1	2	Lin.
Ball,Benjamin,	1		Fau.
Ball,Benjamin,	2		Fau.
Ball,Benjamin,	1		Lin.
Ball,Burgess,		6	Cul.
Ball,Edward,	2	5	Fau.
Ball,Farling,	1	4	Lou.
Ball,James,	1		Berk.
Ball,James,	1	3	Fau.
Ball,James,	1		Lin.
Ball,John,	2	10	Fau.
Ball,Margaret,		19	West'd.
Ball,Nicholas,	1		Fau.
Ball,Thomas,	1	4	Lin.
Ball,William,	1		Cul.
Ball,William,	2	26	Cul.
Ball,William,	1	3	Fau.
Ball,William,	1	13	Lou.
Ballail,Laurence,Est.,		24	Cul.
Ballantine,John,	1	30	West'd.
Ballard,Bartlett,			Bed.
Ballard,Benjamin,	1	3	Spots.
Ballard,Bland,	1	3	Spots.
Ballard,Edward,	1	2	Eli.Cy.
Ballard,Francis,	1	6	Eli.Cy.
Ballard,John,	1	25	Lun.
Ballard,Micajah,	1		Bed.
Ballard,Richard,	1		Bed.
Ballard,Richard,	1		Bed.
Ballard,Thomas,	1	25	Ch.Cy.
Ballard,William,	1	10	Bed.
Ballard,William,	2	3	Eli.Cy.
Balldick,William,	1		Cul.
Ballen,Leonard,	2	4	Buck.
Ballen,Thomas,	1	5	Buck.
Ballen,William C.	1		Buck.
Ballendine,John,Est.			Lou.
Ballenger,Francis,	1		Lou.
Ballenger,John,			Cul.
Ballenger,John,	1		Pr.Wm.
Ballenger,John,Jr.,			Cul.
Ballenger,John,Sr.,	2		Cul.
Ballenger,Jordan,	1		Pr.Wm.
Ballenger,Samuel,	1		Pr.Wm.
Ballenger,Susanna,			Pr.Wm.
Balley,William,	1		Har.
Ballow,Charles,	1	1	Lin.
Balor,Walker,	1	18	Lin.
Balthrope,Landers,	1	3	K.Geo.
Balthrope,Sharp,	1	1	K.Geo.
Baltue,George,	2		Har.
Bambridge,James,	1		Rock.
Bancroft,William,	1	7	West'd.
Bane,James,	1		Din.
Bandy,George,	1		Bed.
Bandy,John,	1		Bot.
Bandy,Richard,	1	6	Bed.
Bandy,Richard,	1		Bot.
Bandy,Thomas,	1		Bed.
Banister,Col.John,	3	88	Din.
Banker,Adam,			Cul.
Bankhead,James,		23	West'd.
Bankhead,William,	1	33	West'd.
Bankherd,James,	1	27	Caro.
Banks,Adam,	1	8	Cul.
Banks,Andrew,	1	18	Ja.Cy.
Banks,Baylor,	1	3	Cul.
Banks,Gerard,		13	Cul.
Banks,Jacob,	1		Gooch.
Banks,James,	1		York.
Banks,John,	1		Bed.
Banks,John,	1		Eli.Cy.
Banks,Malachi,	1		York
Banks,Mary,		5	Bed.
Banks,Mary,			Ja.Cy.
Banks,Samuel,	1		Bed.
Banks,Samuel,	1	1	Bed.
Banks,Samuel,	1		Berk.
Banks,Thomas,	1	2	Cul.
Banks,Turnstall,		20	K.Wm.
Banks,Turnstall,	1	23	K.&Q.
Banks,William,			Cul.
Bannester,Isaac,	1	1	Bed.
Bannester,James,	1		Bed.
Bannester,William,	1		Bed.
Bannister,Augustin,	1		Fau.
Bannister,James,	1		Fau.
Bannister,James,Jr.,	1		Bed.
Bannister,Thomas,	1		Fau.
Bannister,Williams,	1		Fau.
Banons,Daniel,	1		Fau.
Banta,Samuel,	1	1	Berk.
Benty,Albert,	2		Lin.
Baptist,Edward,			York.
Baptist,Edward,	1	12	York.
Baptist,John,			York.
Baragar,John,	1		Lou.
Baragar,John,	1		Lou.
Barata,Samuel,	1		West'd.
Barb,Henry,	1		Lou.
Barbee,Andrew,Jr.,	1	1	Fau.
Barbee,Andrew,Sr.,	1	10	Fau.
Barbee,Francis,	3	7	Caro.
Barbee,John,	1	2	Caro.
Barbee,John,	1	2	Cul.
Barbee,Joseph,	1	1	Fau.
Barbee,Joseph,	3	4	Fau.
Barber,John,	1		Fau.
Barber,Thomas,	1		Fau.
Barbon,William,		1	K.&Q.
Barbour,Ambrose,	1	15	Cul.
Barbour,James,	1	36	Cul.
Barbour,Sarah,		19	Cul.
Barckman,Christian,	1		Mont.
Barckman,Christian,	1		Mont.
Barclay,Hugh,Jr.,	1	4	Rock.
Barclay,Hugh,Sr.,	1	7	Rock.
Barclay,James,			Rock.
Barcley,John,			Acco.
Barcley,William,		1	Acco.
Barclay,William,	1		Rock.
Bard,William,	1		Aug.
Bare,Peter,	1		Berk.
Bareford,Thomas,	1		Lou.
Baren,William,	1		Bed.
Bare,R.,		1	Pr.Wm.
Bargeman,Christian,	1		Bot.
Bargo,George,	1	2	Cul.
Barham,Charles,	1	14	Ja.Cy.
Barham,Charles,	1	32	So'n.
Barham,James,	1	10	So'n.
Barham,James,	1	7	So'n.
Barham,Joell,	1		So'n.
Barham,John,	1	6	So'n.
Barham,Mary,		8	So'n.
Barham,Moody,	1	1	York.
Barham,Robert,	2	11	Ja.Cy.
Barham,Robert,	1	1	So'n.
Barham,Thomas,	1	4	So'n.
Barifoot,William,	1		K.&Q.
Barker,Alexander,			Hen.
Barker,Burwill,	1	1	Brun.
Barker,Charles,	1		Fau.
Barker,Charles,	1		Henry
Barker,Edward,	1		Aug.
Barker,George,	1		Pr.Wm.
Barker,J.,	1		Pr.Wm.
Barker,James,	1		Aug.

Name			County
Barker,James,	1		Buck.
Barker,John,	1	7	Brun.
Barker,John,	1		Lou.
Barker,John,			Pr.Wm.
Barker,John,	1	7	Fau.
Barker,John,	1	1	Fau.
Barker,John,	2		Henry
Barker,Joseph,	1		Pr.Wm.
Barker,Joshua,	1	4	Pr.Wm.
Barker,Mary,			Gooch.
Barker,Michael,	1		Henry
Barker,Nathaniel,	4	1	Lou.
Barker,Nathaniel,Jr.,	1		Lou.
Barker,Randal,			Lou.
Barker,Thomas,	1		Henry
Barker,William,	1	1	Fau.
Barker,William,	1		Fay.
Barker,William,	1		Gooch.
Barker,William,	1	2	Ja.Cy.
Barker,William,	2		Hen.
Barker,William,	1		Lou.
Barker,William,	1		Wash.
Barkin,Isaac,	1		Wash.
Barksdale,Hickerson,	1	14	Buck.
Barksdale,Stith,	1	3	Buck.
Barksdale,William,	1	2	Buck.
Barksdale,William,			Din.
Barksdill,Henry,	1	2	Henry
Barksdill,John,	1	6	Henry
Barlow,Christopher,	1		Cul.
Barlow,Thomas,	1		Brun.
Barlow,Thomas,	1	10	Nor.
Barlow,William,	1	8	Caro.
Barlow,David,	1		K.Wm.
Barmer,William,	1		So'n.
Barnard,Edward,	1		Har.
Barnard,Richard,	1	23	K.Geo.
Barnard,William,	1	57	K.Geo.
Barner,John,	1	3	Brun.
Barnes,Anderson,			Hen.
Barnes,Bailey,	1	6	So'n.
Barnes,Buxton,	1	4	So'n.
Barnes,George,	1		Bot.
Barnes,George,	1		Rock.
Barnes,Jacob,	1		So'n.
Barnes,Jacob,	1	2	So'n.
Barnes,Jacob,	1	11	So'n.
Barnes,James,	1		Brun.
Barnes,James,	1	1	So'n.
Barnes,John,	1	1	Cul.
Barnes,John,	1		Hen.
Barnes,John,	1	21	Lun.
Barnes,Leonard,	1	16	Cul.
Barnes,Nathan,	1	7	So'n.
Barnes,Thomas,	1		Bot.
Barnes,William,	1		Brun.
Barnes,William,	1	2	Ch.Cy.
Barnes,William,	2		Hen.
Barnet,Alexander,	1		Lin.
Barnet,Isaac,			Fay.
Barnet,John,	1		Brun.
Barnett,Abner,	1		Henry
Barnett,Alexander,	1	1	Wash.
Barnett,Ambrose,	1	15	Fau.
Barnett,Athanatius,	1	1	Loui.
Barnett,Charles,	1		Bot.
Barnett,Edward,	1		Lin.
Barnett,James,		5	Cul.
Barnett,James,	1		Bot.
Barnett,James,Jr.,	1	7	Bot.
Barnett,John,	1		Bot.
Barnett,John,	1		Bot.
Barnett,Nathan,	1		Henry
Barnett,Robert,	1	2	Loui.
Barnett,Thomas,	1		Bot.
Barnett,Thomas,	1	5	Loui.
Barnett,James,	1	8	Loui.
Barnett,John,	1		Gooch.
Barnett,John,	1		Lin.
Barnett,William,	1		Bot.
Barnett,William,	1		Cul.
Barnett,William,	1	8	Gooch.
Barnett,William,	1		Lin.
Barnhizer,Andrew,			Berk.
Barnot,Robert,	1		Lin.
Barns,George,	1		Aug.
Barns,John,			Hen.
Barns,Joseph,	1	1	Berk.
Barns,John,	1		Berk.
Barns,Jesse,	1		Berk.
Barns,Stephen,	1		Berk.
Barns,William,	2		Hen.
Barnutt,James,	1		Mont.
Barr,George,	1		Lou.
Barr,Hugh,	1		Lou.
Barr,Patrick,	1		Wash.
Barr,Richard,	1	1	Hen.
Barr,Robert,	1	11	Fay.
Barrack,David,		1	Ja.Cy.
Barreckonan,Michael,	1		Berk.
Barrer,Richard,	1		Bed.
Barret,David,	1	2	Nor.
barret,Dominack,	1		Aug.
Barret,Edward,	1		Cul.
Barret,George,	1		Bot.
Barret,John,	2	14	Hen.
Barrett,Charles,	1	7	Loui.
Barrett,Charles,	1	7	So'n.
Barrett,Edmund,	1		So'n.
Barrett,Handcock,	1	8	So'n.
Barrett,Jacob,	1		So'n.
Barrett,John,	1		Berk.
Barrett,John,Jr.,	1		So'n.
Barrett,Lewis,	1	18	Loui.
Barrett,Mary,		15	Loui.
Barrett,Robert,	1	25	Loui.
Barrett,Simon,	1		So'n.
Barrett,William,	1	18	Ja.Cy.
Barrett,William,	1	1	So'n.
Barrickman,Jacob,	1		Berk.
Barrier,Jacob,	1	2	Aug.
Barrier,Margaret,		1	Aug.
Barrier,Philip,	1	1	Mont.
Barrington,Charles,	1		Har.
Barrington,Thomas,	1		Berk.
Barritt,Thomas,	1	25	Din.
Barron,David,	1	2	So'n.
Barron,James,	1	3	Eli.Cy.
Barron,John,	1		So'n.
Barron,Richard,	1	8	Eli.Cy.
Barrott,Francis,	1		Henry
Barrott,Miles,	1		Henry
Barrott,William,	1	22	Lun.
Barrow,John,			Brun.
Barrow,John,	1	8	Cul.
Barrow,John,	1	14	So'n.
Barrow,Peter,	1	12	Cha.Cy.
Barrow,Philip,	1		Ch.Cy.
Barrow,William,	1		Brun.
Barry,John,	2	5	Lun.
Barry,Richard,			Lun.
Barry,Richard,	1		Lun.
Barry,William,	2	2	Lun.
Barter,William,	1		Mont.
Bartlet,Harry,	1	12	Spots.
Bartlet,John,	2		Fay.
Bartlet,Thomas,	3	12	Spots.
Bartlet,Nathan,			Fay.
Bartlett,Daniel,			Lou.
Bartlett,Hopkins,	1		K.Geo.
Bartlett,James,	1	2	Henry
Bartlett,James,	1		Loud.
Bartlett,John,	1		Fau.
Bartlett,Nathan,	1		Henry
Bartlett,Richard,	1		Fay.
Bartlett,Robert,			Fau.
Bartlett,Thomas,	1	14	Fau.
Bartlett,William,	1	1	Fau.
Bartlett,William,Jr.,	1		Lou.
Bartlett,William,	2		Lou.
Bartley,John,	1	5	Cul.
Bartley,Joshua,	2	1	Cul.
Bartlys,William,	1		Mont.
Barton,Benjamin,	1		Lou.
Barton,Burr,	1		Fau.
Barton,Cuthbert,			Fau.
Barton,David,	1		Henry
Barton,James,	1		Fau.
Barton,John,			Henry
Barton,Kimber,	1		Fau.
Barton,Levi,	1	1	Fau.
Barton,Theophilas,	1		Berk.
Barton,William,	1		Berk.
Barton,William,	1	1	Henry
Baruhisle,William,	1		Cul.
Barum,Edward,			Hen.
Baryhan,Aris,	1		K.&Q.
Basey,Edward,	2	10	Cul.
Basey,Elizman,	1	3	Cul.
Basey,Isaac,			Cul.
Basey,John,			Cul.
Basham,James,	1		Bed.
Bashaw,Peter,		2	Fau.
Bashaw,Warner,	1	6	West'd.
Basham,William,	1	6	Bed.
Bashford,Samuel,	1		Fay.
Baskiers,Zepheniah,	1	1	Berk.
Baskett,James,	1		K.&Q.
Baskins,Charles,	1	4	Aug.
Bass,Benjamin,	1	6	Brun.
Bass,Charles,	1	1	So'n.
Bass,Hardy,			So'n.
Bass,James,			Brun.
Bass,James,	1	1	Brun.
Bass,Jordan,	1		So'n.
Bass,Partain,	1		Brun.
Bass,Thomas,	3	17	Brun.
Bass,Thomas,	1		So'n.
Bassett,Burwell,	1	29	K.Wm.
Basswell,Susanna,	1	5	Hen.
Baswell,William,	1	6	K.Wm.
Basye,Josias,	1		Fau.
Basye,Richard,	1	3	Fau.
Bateast,John,	1		Lin.
Bateman,George,	1		West'd.
Bateman,John,	1		Bed.
Baten,John,	1	1	So'n.
Bates,Benjamin,		10	York
Bates,Charles,	1	5	Gooch.
Bates,Daniel,	1	11	Gooch.
Bates,Ephraim,	1		Aug.
Bates,Fleming,Est.,		4	York
Bates,Isaac,	1	3	Henry
Bates,James,	1		Ch.Cy.
Bates,James,	2	11	K.&Q.
Bates,Jesse,	1		Lou.
Bates,John,	1		Henry
Bates,John,	1	13	Buck.
Bates,Reuben,	1	1	Loui.
Bates,Reubin,			Cul.
Bates,Richard,		12	Pr.Geo.
Bates,Robert,	1		Cul.
Bates,Thomas T.	1	16	Gooch.
Bates,Thomas,			Cul.
Bates,Thomas,	1		Lou.
Bates,William,			K.&Q.
Bates,William,	2	1	Cul.
Batt,Thomas,	1		Berk.

Name			Loc.
Battail,Hannah,		11	Cul.
Battail,Hay,	2	35	Caro.
Battail,Hay,		24	Cul.
Battail,Lawrence,Est	1	43	Caro.
Battaile,Elizabeth,		4	Spots.
Battaile,Hannah,		14	Caro.
Battaile,Lawrence,Est		14	Spots.
Batte,Robert,	1	35	Pr.Geo.
Batte,William,	1		Brun.
Batten,William,	1	6	West'd.
Batten,Williamson,	1	2	West'd.
Batterton,Henry,	2		Lou.
Batterton,Samuel,			Lou.
Battes,William,	1	9	Pr.Geo.
Batte,William,		7	Brun.
Batteton,Amer,			Fay.
Batteton,Henry,	3		Fay.
Battler,Pearce,	1	7	Berk.
Battom,Francis,	1		Cul.
Batts,Henry,	1	52	Pr.Geo.
Batts,John,	1	14	Pr.Geo.
Batson,Margery,			Lou.
Batson,Mordicai,	2		Har.
Batson,Mordicae,	1		Har.
Baty,James,	1	1	Fay.
Baugh,Adam,	2		Mont.
Baugh,Ann,		5	Pr.Geo.
Baugh,Henry,	1		Berk.
Baugh,Isham,Est.,			Pr.Geo.
Baugh,James,	1	18	Pr.Geo.
Baugh,John,	1		Din.
Baugh,Joseph,			Din.
Baugh,Martha,		2	Din.
Baugh,Michael,	1		Mont.
Baugh,Sarah,		11	Brun.
Baugh,William,	1	3	Brun.
Baughan,Benjamin,	1	4	Caro.
Baughan,James,	1	1	Gooch.
Baughn,Aris,Jr.,	1		K.&Q.
Baughn,Elknah,			Loui.
Baugus,Thomas,	1		Berk.
Baulding,James,			Bed.
Bauldwin,Joseph,	1		Lou.
Baxter,Alexander,	2		Cul.
Baxter,Francis,	1		Lou.
Baxter,German,	2	4	Fay.
Baxter,John,	2	3	Aug.
Baxter,John,	1	12	Pr.Geo.
Baxton,Grisley,			Lin.
Bayley,Francis,	1		Caro.
Bayley,Hannah,		13	Eli.Cy.
Bayley,James,Wallace,			Eli.Cy.
Bayley,William A.	1	5	Eli.Cy.
Bayles,Elijah,			Pr.Wm.
Baylis,Samuel,	1		Pr.Wm.
Baylis,Thomas,	1	9	Eli.Cy.
Baylis,William,	1		Caro.
Baylis,William,	1	4	Fau.
Baylis,William,			Pr.Wm.
Baylor,George,	1	79	Caro.
Baylor,Greggory,		42	Berk.
Baylor,Gregory,	2	36	K.&Q.
Baylor,John,	1	68	Caro.
Baylor,Robert,	2	52	Berk.
Baylor,Walker,	1	24	Caro.
Bayly,Edmund,			Acco.
Bayly,Edmund,Sr.,	2	16	Acco.
Bayly,Ismay,	1	3	Acco.
Bayly,John,	1	5	Acco.
Bayly,John,	1	9	Acco.
Bayly,Joseph,	1		Lou.
Bayly,Major,	1		Acco.
Bayly,Naomi,		8	Acco.
Bayly,Peirce,	1	5	Lou.
Bayly,Richard,	1	4	Acco.
Bayly,Thomas,	3	25	Acco.

Name			Loc.
Bayly,Thomas S.,	1	2	Acco.
Bayhe,Aaron,	1		Lun.
Bayne,Daniel,	1		Lun.
Bayne,Elenor,	1	14	West'd.
Bayne,Elizabeth,	1	7	West'd.
Bayne,Thomas,	2		Lou.
Baynes,William,	1		Lou.
Baynham,Gregory,	1	6	Caro.
Baynham,Joseph,	1	4	Loui.
Baysey,Joseph,	2	1	Cul.
Beach,Joseph,	1		Caro.
Beach,Ruben,		1	Nor.
Beach,Waldern,	1		Rock.
Beachbound,Benjamin,	1		Camp.
Beachum,Levie,	2	1	Acco.
Beadles,Edmond,	1		Loui.
Beadles,James,	1	7	Loui.
Beadles,James,	1	11	K.Wm.
Beadles,Joel,	1		K.Wm.
Beadles,Joseph,	1	9	K.Wm.
Beadles,Justinian,	1	1	K.Wm.
Readles,William,	1	4	Loui.
Beakfield,Jacob,	1		Bot.
Beakman,John,	1		Lou.
Bealand,John,	1		Cul.
Beale,Benjamin,	1		So'n.
Beale,Benjamin,Jr.,	1	1	So'n.
Beal,Burwell,	1	1	So'n.
Beal,Drewry,	1	1	So'n.
Beal,Joshua,	1	1	So'n.
Beal,Ephraim,	1	1	So'n.
Beal,Richard,	1		So'n.
Beal,Sarah,		4	So'n.
Beale,John,	1	1	Hen.
Beale,Lydia,			So'n.
Beale,Priscilla,			So'n.
Beale,Reubin,	1	26	Cul.
Beale,Richard,	1		So'n.
Beale,Thomas,	1		West'd.
Beale,Thomas,	1	5	West'd.
Beale,William,	1		So'n.
Bealey,John,	1		Bot.
Beall,David,	1		Berk.
Beall,Daniel,	1	4	Berk.
Beall,Leonard,	1		Aug.
Bealy,Stephen,	1		Wash.
Bealy,William,	1		Wash.
Beam,John,	1		Berk.
Beam,Michael,			Lou.
Beam,Richard,	1		Lou.
Bean,Benjamin,	1		Har.
Bean,George,	1	1	Spots.
Bean,James,	2	1	Mont.
Bean,James,Jr.,	1		Mont.
Bean,Robert,	1		Rock.
Beane,William,	1	1	West'd.
Beans,Jacob,	1		Aug.
Beard,Adam,	1	1	Bed.
Beard,David,	1	1	Bed.
Beard,David,	1	4	Rock.
Beard,Elizabeth,		1	Mont.
Beard,Elizabeth,		5	Camp.
Beard,Hugh,	1	1	Rock.
Beard,James,	1		Aug.
Beard,Martin,	1		Bot.
Beard,Samuel,			Henry
Beard,Samuel,	1	1	Bed.
Beard,Thomas,	1		Aug.
Beard,William,	1	2	Aug.
Beard,William,	2		Lin.
Bearshears,Phillip,	1		Henry
Bearshears,Robert,	1		Henry
Beasley,Charles,	1		Buck.
Beasley,Edmond,	1	1	Cul.
Beasley,Ephraim,	1		Cul.
Beasley,Ephraim,	1	6	Spots.

Name			Loc.
Beasley,John,	1		Acco.
Beasly,Richard,	2		K.&Q.
Beasley,Robert,	1	18	Lun.
Beasley,Smith,	1		Acco.
Beasley,William,	1		Cul.
Beasly,William,			K.&Q.
Beaty,Arthur,	1		Rock.
Beaty,David,	1		Lou.
Beaty,Robert,	2		Bot.
Beatty,David,	1		Lou.
Beaty,John,			Lou.
Beaty,Robert,	1	2	Lou.
Beaty,Samuel,	1		Lou.
Beaty,William,	2		Lou.
Beaty,William,	1		Lou.
Beaver,Alexander,	1		Bot.
Beaver,Robert,	1		Bot.
Beavers,Benjamin,	1		Pr.Wm.
Beavers,James,	1	1	Henry
Beavers,John,	1		Loui.
Beavers,Joseph,	1		Lou.
Beavers,Mary,	1		Lou.
Beavers,Capt.William,	1		Lou.
Beavers,Sanuel,			Lou.
Beazley,Ann,	1	7	Caro.
Beazley,Anne,		4	Caro.
Beazley,Ben,	1	3	Caro.
Beazley,Ben,	1	2	Caro.
Beazley,Bridget,		6	Buck.
Beazley,Cornelius,	1	2	Caro.
Beazley,Edmund,	1	3	Caro.
Beazley,Elizabeth,		3	Caro.
Beazley,Thomas,	1	4	Caro.
Beazley,John,	1		Buck.
Beazly,William,	1		Buck.
Beatie,David,	1		Wash.
Beatie,Francis,	1	1	Wash.
Beatie,John,	1	2	Wash.
Beatty,Thomas,	1	2	Lou.
Beck,Christopher,	1		Caro.
Beck,George,	2		Har.
Beck,Mrs.Holston,			Henry
Beck,John,	1		Fash.
Beck,Paul,	1		Mont.
Beck,Pereston,	1		Lou.
Beck,Tarnlegent,	1		Bed.
Beck,Vivian,	1		Lou.
Beckham,Elijah,	1		Cul.
Beckham,James,	1	3	Buck.
Beckham,William,	1		Buck.
Beckett,Richard,	1		Bot.
Beckley,John J.,	3	5	Hen.
Becknel,William,	1		Mont.
Bedinger,Abraham,	1		Berk.
Bedinger,Peter,	1		Berk.
Bedingfield,Thomas,	1	2	Lun.
Bedlock,Elizabeth,			Din.
Bedlock,Peter,	1		Din.
Bedsel,John,	1		Mont.
Bedsol,Elisha,	1	1	Mont.
Beech,Ezekiel,	1	1	Acco.
Beech,Fedrick,	1	5	Acco.
Beech,Isiah,			Acco.
Beech,John,	2	4	Acco.
Beech,Kendal,	2	3	Acco.
Beech,Reubin,	1	1	Acco.
Beech,Robert,	1		Berk.
Beegill,Charles,	1		Lou.
Beegill,David,	1		Lou.
Beeler,Benjamin,	1	12	Berk.
Beeler,Joseph,	1		Fay.
Beeler,Samuel,	1	8	Fay.
Beemy,Daniel,	1		Cul.
Beeser,John,			Lou.
Beesley,John,	1		Berk.
Beeson,Edward,	1		Berk.

Name			Place
Beeson,Richard,	2		Berk.
Beezer,John,	1		Lou.
Begley,Henry,	1		Mont.
Begley,John,	1		Mont.
Beheller,David,	1		Henry
Belcher,Thomas,	1		Henry
Bell,Alpheus,	1	2	Cul.
Bell,Archibald,	2		Fay.
Bell,Burwell,	1	11	So'n.
Bell,Charles,	1		Lou.
Bell,David,		7	Camp.
Bell,David,Est.,		9	Aug.
Bell,David,			Buck.
Bell,Frances,		12	Fau.
Bell,George,	1	6	Loui.
Bell,George,	2	1	Mont.
Bell,George,	2	2	Acco.
Bell,Henry,	1	6	Camp.
Bell,Henry,	1	19	Buck.
Bell,Hugh,	1		Berk.
Bell,Isaac,	1	1	Nor.
Bell,Jacob,	1	2	Acco.
Bell,James,	1	3	Cul.
Bell,James,	1		Fay.
Bell,James,	3	3	Aug.
Bell,James,	3		Aug.
Bell,James,	1	19	Fau.
Bell,James,	1		Caro.
Bell,James,Sr.,	1		Aug.
Bell,Capt.James,	1	1	Aug.
Bell,James,	1	1	So'n.
Bell,James,	1		Berk.
Bell,James,	1		Berk.
Bell,Jeremiah,	1		Bot.
Bell,Joab,	1	1	Nor.
Bell,John,	1	11	Ch.Cy.
Bell,John,	1		Mont.
Bell,John,	1	8	K.Wm.
Bell,John,	1		Aug.
Bell,John,	1	3	Din.
Bell,John,			Eli.Cy.
Bell,John,	1		Wash.
Bell,John,	1		Wash.
Bell,John,	1	7	Caro.
Bell,John,	2	18	Caro.
Bell,John,	1		Berk.
Bell,John,			Eli.Cy.
Bell,John Selby,	2	4	Acco.
Bell,John,M.,	2	15	Cul.
Bell,Joseph,	1	4	Aug.
Bell,Joseph,	1		Buck.
Bell,Judith,	2	26	Buck.
Bell,Nathaniel,	1		Eli.Cy.
Bell,Nathaniel,		11	Nor.
Bell,Nathaniel,Sr.,	2	16	Acco.
Bell,Nathaniel,Jr.,			Acco.
Bell,Robert,	1	8	Nor.
Bell,Robert,	1		Mont.
Bell,Robert,	1		Bot.
Bell,Robert,	1		Aug.
Bell,Samuel,	1	4	Loui.
Bell,Samuel,	2	2	Aug.
Bell,Samuel,	1		Aug.
Bell,Samuel,	1		Pr.Wm.
Bell,Samuel,Jr.,			Aug.
Bell,Thomas,	1	1	Loui.
Bell,Thomas,	2	3	Acco.
Bell,Thomas,	1		Buck.
Bell,Victor,	1		Bot.
Bell,William,	1	3	Nor.
Bell,William,	1		Mont.
Bell,William,	2	1	Acco.
Bell,William,	1	7	Acco.
Bell,William,	1	2	Acco.
Bell,William,	1		Aug.
Bell,William,	1		Aug.
Bell,William,	1		Aug.
Bell,William,	1	20	Berk.
Bell,William,	1		Lun.
Bell,William,Est.,	1	2	Spots.
Bell,Zadoc,	1	7	So'n.
Bellamy,John,	1		Gooch.
Bellenger,Edward,	1		Cul.
Bellar,Jacob,	1	1	Berk.
Bellome,Benjamin,	1		Loui.
Belote,Hancock,	1		Acco.
Belote,Hezekiah,	1		Nor.
Belote,John,	2		Acco.
Belote,John,	1	1	Acco.
Belote,Noah,	1	2	Acco.
Belote,William,Sr.,	1		Acco.
Belote,William,	1		Acco.
Belote,William,	1	9	Nor.
Belt,Williamsmith,	1	1	Lou.
Belts,Andrew,	1		Lou.
Belts,Frederick,	1		Lou.
Belvin,William,			York.
Belvin,William,	1		York.
Benditt,Frederick,	1	4	Fau.
Bengs,James,	1	2	Ch.Cy.
Bener,Henry,	1	1	Ch.Cy.
Benham,John,	1		Lou.
Benjay,Sarah,			Fau.
Bennatt,James,	1	3	Gooch.
Bennet,Benjamin,	1		Brun.
Bennet,Benjamin,	1		Rock.
Bennet,Charles,	1	3	K.Geo.
Bennet,Jacob,	1		Aug.
Bennet,James,	1		Mont.
Bennet,James,	1	1	Hen.
Bennet,John,	1		Bot.
Bennet,Moses,	1		Bot.
Bennet,T.,	1		Pr.Wm.
Bennet,Thomas,	1		Mont.
Bennet,William,	1		Hen.
Bennet,William,	1		Acco.
Bennet,William,Sr.,			Mont.
Bennett,Absolum,	1	3	Brun.
Bennett,Alec,		6	K.Wm.
Bennett,Benjamin,	1		Mont.
Bennett,Bartlett,	1	9	Cul.
Bennett,Charles,	1	8	Lou.
Bennett,Daniel,	1	2	West'd.
Bennett,Daniel,	2		Fau.
Bennett,Dozier,			Lou.
Bennett,Frances,		7	Bed.
Bennett,Fisher,	1	1	K.Wm.
Bennett,George,	1		Berk.
Bennett,Henry,	1		Cul.
Bennett,Isaac,	1		Lou.
Bennett,Jacob,	1		Lou.
Bennett,James,	1		Lou.
Bennett,James,	1		K.&Q.
Bennett,Jesse,	1		West'd.
Bennet,John,	1	3	Brun.
Bennett,John,	2		K.Geo.
Bennett,John,	1		Aug.
Bennett,John,	1		Aug.
Bennett,John,	1		So'n.
Bennett,Joseph,	1		Lou.
Bennett,Joseph,	1	4	Brun.
Bennett,Mary,	1		Fau.
Bennett,Michael,	1		Cul.
Bennett,Richard,	1	1	Lou.
Bennett,Richard,	1	1	West'd.
Bennett,Thomas,Sr.,	1		West'd.
Bennett,Thomas,Jr.,	1	1	West'd.
Bennett,Thomas,	1	2	Lou.
Bennett,Samuel,	1	2	K.Wm.
Bennett,Thomas,	1		Bed.
Bennett,William,	1	1	K.Geo.
Bennett,William,	1	1	Eli.Cy.
Bennett,William,	1		Aug.
Bennett,William,	1		Aug.
Benning,John,	1	23	Buck.
Benning,Joseph,	1	10	Buck.
Bens,John,	1		Hen.
Benson,Charles,	1	10	Cul.
Benson,Charles,	1	3	Caro.
Benson,Enoch,	1	1	Cul.
Benson,John,	2	2	Spots.
Benson,Prow,	2	12	Fau.
Benson,William,	2	3	Fay.
Benston,George,	1		Aug.
Benston,Irvin,	1		Aug.
Benston,Matthias,	1	4	Aug.
Benthall,Azel,	2	9	Nor.
Benthall,Caleb,	1	3	Nor.
Benthall,Harrison,	1		Nor.
Benthall,Elisha,		5	Nor.
Bently,Andrew,	1		Lou.
Bentley,John,	1		Lin.
Benton,John,			Hen.
Benton,Thomas,	1		Cul.
Benstone,Ann,	1		Acco.
Benstone,Bradford,	1	3	Acco.
Benstone,George,	2		Acco.
Benstone,Jones,	1	1	Acco.
Benstone,Lazarus,			Acco.
Benstone,Mosses,	2	11	Acco.
Beringham,Edward,	1		Lou.
Berkeley,Edmund,	2	126	K.Wm.
Berkely,Edmund,	1	38	Caro.
Berkely,John,	1		Berk.
Berkeley,William,	1	8	Fau.
Berkley,Barbara,	1	4	Lou.
Berkley,Burgess,			Lou.
Berkley,John,	1	15	West'd.
Berkley,John,	1	10	Lou.
Berkley,Reuben,	2	4	Lou.
Berkley,Scarlet,	1	5	Lou.
Berkley,Mr.,	1	12	Pr.Wm.
Bernard,Charles,	1		Henry
Bernard,John,	3	21	Buck.
Bernard,Johnson,	1		Aug.
Bernard,Robert,	1		Gooch.
Bernard,Walter,	1		Henry
Bernard,William,		35	Henry
Bernard,William,	1	15	Fau.
Berrn,Michael,			Fau.
Berry,Anna,		1	Cul.
Berry,Ane,	1	4	Cul.
Berry,Aron,	1	5	Cul.
Berry,Anthony,	1		Cul.
Berry,Baldwin,	1	4	Lou.
Berry,Charles,	2	8	Aug.
Berry,Edward,	1	4	York
Berry,Edward,	1		Eli.Cy.
Berry,Edward,	1		Fay.
Berry,Elisha,	1	2	Cul.
Berry,Enoch,	2		Brun.
Berry,Ephriam,			Cul.
Berry,George,	1	9	Fau.
Berry,George,	1	2	Fay.
Berry,George,	1	1	Aug.
Berry,George,	1	12	Brun.
Berry,Harry,	1	1	K.Geo.
Berry,Henry,	1	4	Fau.
Berry,Hugh,	1		Wash.
Berry,James,	1		Wash.
Berry,James,	3	1	K.Geo.
Berry,James,	1		York
Berry,James,	1		Rock.
Berry,Joel,	1	13	K.Geo.
Berry,John,	1		Aug.
Berry,John,			Brun.
Berry,John,	1		Lin.
Berry,John,	2	1	Cul.

Name			Co.
Berry,Malckiah,			Cul.
Berry,Malekiah,	3		Cul.
Berry,Mary,			Wash.
Berry,Reuben,	1	1	Har.
Berry,Samuel,	1	1	Spots.
Berry,Thomas,	1	19	K.Geo.
Berry,Thomas,	2	23	Caro.
Berry,William,	1		Aug.
Berry,William,			Loud.
Berry,William,	1	5	Fau.
Berry,William,	1	1	K.Geo.
Berry,William,	1		K.Geo.
Berry,William,	1		Mont.
Berry,William,	2	2	Rock.
Berryhill,John,	1	1	Rock.
Berriman,Jesse,	1		Brun.
Berryman,Benjamin,	1	2	Fau.
Berryman,Isaac,	1	11	Buck.
Berryman,Maximillian,	1	17	Fau.
Berryman,Newton,		3	West'd.
Berryman,Sarah,Jr.,		19	K.Geo.
Berryman,Thomas,	1		Lin.
Berryman,William,	1		Buck.
Berryman,William,	4	26	West'd.
Berson,Hugh,	1		Wash.
Berton,James,	1	5	Lin.
Besore,Barnaby,	1		Berk.
Best,Corneleus,	1		Har.
Best,Francis,	1		Aug.
Best,James,	1		Aug.
Best,James,	1		Lou.
Bethell,Edward,	1		Pr.Wm.
Bethell,Isham,			Hen.
Bethell,John,			Hen.
Bethell,Thomas,	2	3	Hen.
Bethel,Thomas,	1	3	Hen.
Bethell,William,	2	5	Hen.
Bethel,William,	1	6	Hen.
Bethshers,Thomas,	1		Brun.
Bettesworth,Charles,	1		K.Geo.
Bettis,Daniel,	1	1	K.Geo.
Bettis,Thomas,			K.Geo.
Bettisworth,William,	1		West'd.
Betts,Elisha,	1	13	Lun.
Betts,Spencer,	1	1	Lun.
Betts,William,	1	4	Lun.
Betty,John,	1	1	Brun.
Betty,Thomas,	1	3	Brun.
Beuford,James,	1	9	Lun.
Beuford,James,Jr.,	1	7	Lun.
Beuford,Leroy,	1	4	Lun.
Beuford,Thomas,	1	3	Lun.
Beuford,Warren,	1	10	Lun.
Beuford,William,	1	17	Lun.
Bever,Peter,	1		Har.
Beverly,Jean,			Buck.
Beverly,Jean Wily,		14	Caro.
Beverly,Priscilla,			Buck.
Beverley,Robert,	1	60	Caro.
Beverley,Robert,Jr.,	2	28	Caro.
Beverley,Robert,	1	60	K.&Q.
Beverly,Robert,Est.		115	Cul.
Beverly,Silvannus,	1		Buck.
Beverly,William,	1		Buck.
Bevill,John,	1		Lun.
Bevills,(torn),	1	4	Din.
Bibb,Benjamin,			Loui.
Bibb,David,	1	2	Loui.
Bibb,Elizabeth,		17	Loui.
Bibb,Henry,			Loui.
Bibb,Henry,	1	1	Loui.
Bibb,James,			Loui.
Bibb,John,	1	7	Loui.
Bibb,John,	2	6	Loui.
Bibb,Mary,	2	13	Loui.
Bibb,Robert Fleming,	1	7	Loui.
Bibb,Susanna,		12	Gooch.
Bibb,Thomas,			Loui.
Bibb,William,	1	2	Loui.
Bible,Christiain,	1		Har.
Bickley,John,	1	12	Loui.
Bidgood,John,	1	2	So'n.
Bierd,Edward,	1		Bed.
Bigard,James,	1		Lou.
Bigby,Archebel,	1	2	Cul.
Bigbie,Elijah,	1		Pr.Wm.
Biggar,David,	1	4	Loui.
Biggar,James,			Loui.
Biggar,John,	1	3	Loui.
Biggar,Macon,	1		Loui.
Biggar,William,	2	4	Loui.
Biggar,William,Jr.,	1	2	Loui.
Biggins,John,	1	1	Pr.Geo.
Biggins,John,	1		Loud.
Biggins,Richard,	1	10	Pr.Geo.
Biggins,Thomas,	1		Pr.Geo.
Biggis,Benjamin,	1		Lou.
Biggs,Joel,	1		Brun.
Biggs,John,	1		Brun.
Biggs,Stephen,	1		Brun.
Biggs,Tabytha,		6	Nor.
Biggs,Thomas,	1	4	Nor.
Bigman,John,	1		Mont.
Bigs,John,	1		Lin.
Bilbro,William,	1		Bot.
Bill,Henry,	1	1	Henry
Billew,Abram,	1		Aug.
Billups,Christopher,	1	18	Lun.
Billups,Edward,	1	1	Bot.
Billups,John,	1		Bot.
Billups,John,	2	5	Lun.
Billups,Joseph,	1	14	Lun.
Binford,Aquilla,	1		Pr.Geo.
Binford,Chappel,	1	6	Pr.Geo.
Binford,Elizabeth,		2	Hen.
Binford,Elizabeth,		1	Hen.
Binford,Frances,	1	12	Hen.
Binford,James,Est.,		13	Hen.
Binford,James,	1	3	Pr.Geo.
Binford,James,			Hen.
Binford,John,	1	1	Ch.Cy.
Binford,John,	1		Ch.Cy.
Binford,Mary,			Pr.Geo.
Binford,Peter,	1		Pr.Geo.
Binford,Robert,	1	2	Ch.Cy.
Binford,Thomas,			Ch.Cy.
Binford,Thomas,	1	1	Ch.Cy.
Binford,Thomas,	1	9	Pr.Geo.
Binford,Thomas,	2	6	Hen.
Binford,Thomas,	1	5	Hen.
Binford,William,	1	19	Hen.
Binford,William,			Hen.
Binford,William,	1	1	Hen.
Bing,John,	1		Aug.
Bingham,Benjamin,	1		Cul.
Bingham,Stephen,		4	Ja.Cy.
Bingham,Stephen,	1	8	K.Wm.
Bingham,Steven,	1	1	Cul.
Bingham,William,			Buck.
Bingley,Anne,		5	Ja.Cy.
Bingley,Lewis,	1		Ja.Cy.
Bingman,Henry,	2		Mont.
Binian,Martain,	1		Henry
Binne,Charles,	3	11	Lou.
Binne,John,			Lou.
Binnel,James,	2		Cul.
Binns,Charles,	1		Ch.Cy.
Binns,Christopher,	1		Hen.
Binns,Christopher,	1	1	Hen.
Binns,David,			Hen.
Binns,David,Sr.,	1		Hen.
Binns,Dinnis,	1		Hen.
Binns,Joseph,	1		Hen.
Binns,Mary,		5	Ch.Cy.
Bins,Joseph,	1		York
Birch,George,	1		Berk.
Birch,Janard,	1		Henry
Birch,John,	1		Henry
Birch,John,	1		Henry
Birchett,Edward,	2		Din.
Birchett,James,	1		Din.
Birchett,James,	2	13	Pr.Geo.
Birchett,John,	1		Din.
Birchett,Robert,	1	9	Pr.Geo.
Birchett,William,	1	6	Din.
Birchett,William,			Din.
Bird,Adam,	1	13	Ja.Cy.
Bird,Anthony Armistead	1		K.&Q.
Bird,Barbara,		17	K.&Q.
Bird,Baylor,	1	2	K.&Q.
Bird,Benjamin,	1		Lou.
Bird,Jacob,Jr.,	1	1	Acco.
Bird,John,	1	3	So'n.
Bird,John,	1		Lou.
Bird,John,	1		K.&Q.
Bird,John,	3	8	K.&Q.
Bird,John,	1		Loui.
Bird,Levie,	1	4	Acco.
Bird,Levin,			Acco.
Bird,Luke,	1		Lou.
Bird,Mary,		14	K.&Q.
Bird,Philemon,		14	K.&Q.
Bird,Philip,			K.&Q.
Bird,Ralph,			K.&Q.
Bird,Richard,	1		Lou.
Bird,Robert,	1	4	K.&Q.
Bird,Robert,		10	K.Wm.
Bird,Thomas,	1		Gooch.
Bird,Thomas,	2	24	Pr.Wm.
Bird,Thomas,	1		Pr.Wm.
Bird,William,	1	23	K.&Q.
Bird,William,			Pr.Wm.
Bird,William,	1	6	K.Wm.
Birdsong,James,	1	2	Brun.
Birdsong,John,	1	1	Brun.
Birdsong,Merritt,	1		Brun.
Birdsong,William,	1		Brun.
Birk,J.,	1		Pr.Wm.
Birk,John,	1		Lou.
Birkin,John,	1		Lou.
Birks,Charles,Est,		4	Buck.
Birks,George,	1	5	Buck.
Birks,John,	1	1	Buck.
Birks,Sarah,			Buck.
Birt,Harwood,			York
Birt,Harwood,	2	27	York
Biscow,James,	1		Eli.Cy.
Bishong,John,	1		Fay.
Bishop,Adam,	1		Berk.
Bishop,Charles M.,	1	2	Brun.
Bishop,Edmund,	1		Lun.
Bishop,George,	1		Berk.
Bishop,Henry,	1	2	Brun.
Bishop,Henry,	1		Mont.
Bishop,James,	1		Din.
Bishop,James,	1	3	Pr.Wm.
Bishop,Jeremiah,	1		Din.
Bishop,John,	1		Lou.
Bishop,John,	1		Mont.
Bishop,John,	1	3	Nor.
Bishop,John,			So'n.
Bishop,Jonathon,	4	6	Cul.
Bishop,Joseph,			Cul.
Bishop,Josiah,			Cul.
Bishop,Mason,	1	6	Brun.
Bishop,Matthew,	1	1	Brun.
Bishop,Richard,	1		Ch.Cy.
Bishop,Richard,	1		Pr.Geo.

Name			County
Bishop,Samuel,	1		Lou.
Bishop,Thomas,	1		Berk.
Bishop,William,	1		Berk.
Bishop,William,	1	2	Brun.
Bishop,William,	1		Fau.
Bissett,James,	1	6	Hen.
Bissitt,Mrs.Margarett,		2	Din.
Bitting,Anthony,	1	3	Henry
Bittle,Henry,	1	9	So'n.
Bittle,Kirby,	1	7	So'n.
Bittle,Robert,	2	13	So'n.
Bittle,William,			So'n.
Bivin,John,	1	2	Fay.
Blacburus,Col.T.,	1	36	Pr.Wm.
Black,Abraham,	1		Fau.
Black,Alexander,	1		Aug.
Black,Alexander,	1		Bot.
Black,Andrew,	1		Bed.
Black,Cutlip,	1		Aug.
Black,Daniel,	1		Lou.
Black,Elizabeth,			Wash.
Black,George,	1		Wash.
Black,Henry,	1		Rock.
Black,Hugh,	1		Berk.
Black,Hugh,	2		Lin.
Black,James,	1		Berk.
Black,James,	3	2	Bot.
Black,James,	1		Berk.
Black,James,	1		Lin.
Black,James,	1		Wash.
Black,John,	3		Aug.
Black,John,			Mont.
Black,Joseph,	1	1	Lin.
Black,Michael,	1		K.Geo.
Black,Patrick,	1		Lin.
Black,Rebeckak,	1		Aug.
Black,Robert,	1		Mont.
Black,Robert,	1		Rock.
Black,Samuel,	1		Berk.
Black,Samuel,	1	6	Aug.
Black,Thomas,	1		Lin.
Black,Thomas,	1		Rock.
Black,William,	1	2	Aug.
Black,William,	1	8	Aug.
Blackburn,Andrew,			Bed.
Blackburn,Benjamin,		1	Aug.
Blackburn,Christopher,	1	8	Caro.
Blackburn,Col.Thomas,	1	27	Pr.Wm.
Blackburn,Jacob,	1		Mont.
Blackburn,James,	1	5	Buck.
Blackburn,Jesse,	1	2	Hen.
Blackburn,John,	1	1	Berk.
Blackburn,John,	1		Wash.
Blackburn,Joseph,	1		Fay.
Blackburn,Rowland,	1		Hen.
Blackburn,Will,			Hen.
Blackburn,Will,	1		Hen.
Blackburn,William,	1		Har.
Blackerby,Jeduthon,	1	4	Fau.
Blackerby,Joseph,	1	10	Fau.
Blackemore,William,	1		Acco.
Blackey,Jane,		9	Cul.
Blackey,Churchwill,	2	2	Cul.
Blackford,Benjamin,	1	2	Berk.
Blackledge,Icabod,	1		Lou.
Blackley,Acquilla,	1		Henry
Blackley,Robert,	1		Henry
Blackley,Thomas,			Lou.
Blackmore,James,	1	7	Berk.
Blackmore,John,	1	11	Wash.
Blackmore,Joseph,	1	5	Wash.
Blackmore,Thomas,	1		Wash.
Blackmore,William,	1	1	Wash.
Blackwell,David,	1	8	Pr.Wm.
Blackwell,Elizabeth,		8	Fau.
Blackwell,James,	1		Cul.
Blackwell,Jesse,	1	2	Gooch.
Blackwell,John,			Cul.
Blackwell,John,	1		Cul.
Blackwell,John,	2	17	Fau.
Blackwell,John,	1	5	K.Wm.
Blackwell,Joseph,	1	18	Fau.
Blackwell,Joseph,Jr.,		3	Fau.
Blackwell,Micajah,	1	3	K.Wm.
Blackwell,Micajah,	1	16	K.Wm.
Blackwell,Robert,	1	13	Lun.
Blackwell,Robert,	1	9	K.Wm.
Blackwell,Samuel,	1	16	Fau.
Blackwell,Samuel,			Cul.
Blackwood,Samuel,	1		Aug.
Blackwell,Thomas,	1	10	Fau.
Blackwell,Thomas,	1		Fau.
Blackwell,Thomas,	1	12	K.Wm.
Blackwell,William,	1	21	Fau.
Blackwood,Samuel,	1		Lin.
Blades,Jessey,	1		Acco.
Blades,William,			Hen.
Bladsoe,Loveing,	1		Wash.
Blagrave,Henry,	1	18	Lun.
Blaik,Thomas,	1		Aug.
Blaikey,Joseph,		2	Buck.
Blair,William,	1		Aug.
Blair,William,	1		Aug.
Blaikey,William,	1	4	Buck.
Blair,Alexander,	1	1	Berk.
Blair,Archibald,	1	4	Hen.
Blair,James,	1		Rock.
Blair,James,	1		Aug.
Blair,James,	1	2	Rock.
Blair,John,	2		Aug.
Blair,John,	1	13	Ja.Cy.
Blair,John,	1		Lou.
Blair,John,		23	York
Blair,Joseph,	1		Aug.
Blair,Peter,	1		Lin.
Blake,J.,	1		Pr.Wm.
Blake,James,	1	1	So'n.
Blake,John,	1	2	So'n.
Blake,John,	1		K.Wm.
Blake,Samuel,	1	1	So'n.
Blake,Vessams,	2		So'n.
Blake,Thomas,	1	11	So'n.
Blake,Thomas,	1	2	So'n.
Blakeley,Thomas,	1		Aug.
Blakely,Charles,	1		Mont.
Blakeman,Adam,	1		Aug.
Blakeman,Moses,	1		Aug.
Blakey,George,	1	4	Spots.
Blakey,John,			Hen.
Blakey,John,	1		Cul.
Blakey,John,	1		Hen.
Blakey,Morris,	2	4	Hen.
Blakey,Morriss,	1	7	Hen.
Blakey,Pruith,	1	20	Hen.
Blakey,Reuben,	3	4	Hen.
Blakey,Reuben,	1	4	Hen.
Blakey,Smyth,	1	26	Hen.
Blakey,William,			Hen.
Blakley,Churchill,	1	3	Henry
Blaky,George,	1	2	Buck.
Blaky,Robert,Est,		3	Buck.
Blaky,Thomas,	2	14	Buck.
Blalock,Jeremiah,	1		Hen.
Blalock,John,	1		Brun.
Blalock,William,	1		Brun.
Blanchet,Peter,	1		Henry
Bland,Betty Y.		4	K.&Q.
Bland,Edward,	1	12	Pr.Geo.
Bland,Elizabeth,		4	K.&Q.
Bland,Francis,	1		K.&Q.
Bland,Henry,	1		K.&Q.
Bland,James,	1	1	West'd.
Bland,James,	1		K.&Q.
Bland,John,		4	Din.
Bland,John,	1	29	Pr.Geo.
Bland,John,	1	1	K.&Q.
Bland,John,			York
Bland,Mary,		1	Fau.
Bland,Richard,	1	3	K.&Q.
Bland,Richard,	1	41	Pr.Geo.
Bland,S.,	1	1	Pr.Wm.
Bland,Theo.,		8	Pr.Geo.
Bland,Thomas,			Aug.
Bland,Thomas,	1	2	K.&Q.
Bland,Thomas,	1	7	Pr.Wm.
Bland,William,Sr.,	1	2	K.&Q.
Bland,Rev.William,		6	Ja.Cy.
Bland,William,	1	2	K.&Q.
Blane,Alexander,Jr.,			Lin.
Blane,Alexander,Sr.,	2		Lin.
Blane,James,	1		Lin.
Blankenbecker,Jacob,	1	5	Cul.
Blankenbeker,Catharine			Cul.
Blankenbeker,Henry,	1		Cul.
Blankenbeker,John,	1	3	Cul.
Blankenbeker,John,	1		Cul.
Blankenbeker,John,	1		Cul.
Blankenbeker,Michael,	1	4	Cul.
Blankenbeker,Samuel,	1		Cul.
Blankenbeker,Zachariah	2		Cul.
Blankinship,Asa,			Lun.
Blankinship,Elijah,	1		Henry
Blankinship,Isham,	1		Henry
Blankinship,Isham,Jr.,	1		Henry
Blankinship,Isham,Sr.,	1		Henry
Blankinship,Joel,	1		Bed.
Blankinship,Jeremiah,	1		Lun.
Blankinship,John,	1		Lun.
Blankinship,John,	2	1	Lun.
Blankinship,Joseph,	1		Bed.
Blankinship,Leggin,	1		Bed.
Blankinship,Peter,	1		Bed.
Blankinship,Peter,Jr.,	1		Bed.
Blankinship,Thomas,	1	1	Lun.
Blanks,James,			Ch.Cy.
Blanks,John,	1		Lun.
Blanks,Richard,		11	Buck.
Blanks,Shaderis,	1	2	Lin.
Blanks,Thomas,	1		Ch.Cy.
Blanton,Charles,	1		Caro.
Blanton,John,	1	18	Caro.
Blanton,Reubin,	1	1	Brun.
Blanton,Richard,	1		Spots.
Blanton,Richard,	1	15	Caro.
Blanton,Thomas,	2	3	Spots.
Blasingham,John,	2		York
Blassingham,Phillip,	1		Henry
Blasingham,William,			York
Blaydes,William,	1	23	Spots.
Blaymer,Joseph,	1		Berk.
Bleak,George,	1		Aug.
Bleak,James,	1		Aug.
Bleak,Peter,	1		Aug.
Bleak,Thophilus,	1		Aug.
Bledso,Moses,	1	6	Fay.
Bledso,William,	2	8	Cul.
Bledsoe,John,	1	1	Fay.
Bledsoe,Joseph,	1		Lin.
Bledsoe,Joseph,	1	10	Spots.
Bledsoe,Peachey,	1	1	Henry
Bledsoe,William,	1		Lin.
Bleigton,William,	1	2	Ch.Cy.
Blevins,James,	1		Mont.
Blevins,William,	1	10	Henry
Blevins,William,	1		Mont.
Blevins,Willoboy,	1		Mont.
Blick,Benjamin,			Brun.
Blick,George,	1	3	Din.

Name			County	Name			County	Name			County
Blick,James,	2	14	Brun.	Boggs,John,	4	3	Acco.	Bonner,William,	2		Har.
Blick,John,	1		Brun.	Boggs,John,			Acco.	Bonner,William,		2	Pr.Geo.
Blick,John,	1		Din.	Boggs,Levin,			Acco.	Bonner,William,	1	12	Pr.Geo.
Blincoe,Thomas,	2	7	Lou.	Boggs,Robert,	1	1	Fay.	Bonner,William,Jr.,	1	23	Pr.Geo.
Blincoe,William,	1		Lou.	Boggs,Robert,			Bed.	Bonnett,Henry,	1		Har.
Blore,Thomas,	1		Mont.	Boggs,Robert,	2	3	Acco.	Bonnett,William,		3	Berk.
Blow,Martha,	1	9	So'n.	Boggs,William,	2	2	Acco.	Bonry,John,	1	14	Ch.Cy.
Blow,John Thomas,	1	28	So'n.	Boggs,William,			Acco.	Bonwell,Charles,			Acco.
Blow,Richard,	1	16	So'n.	Boggs,William,	2		Berk.	Bonwell,George,	2		Acco.
Bloxum,Ann,		2	Acco.	Boggs,William,	2		Bed.	Bonwell,James,	2	1	Acco.
Bloxom,Richard,	1		Loui.	Bogle,James,	1		Rock.	Bonwell,James.Jr.,			Acco.
Bloxum,Robert,	1		Acco.	Bogle,Joseph,	2		Rock.	Bonwell,John,			Acco.
Bloxum,Southy,	1	5	Acco.	Bohanan,William,	1		Henry	Bonwell,Mary,	2	4	Acco.
Blue,Barnabas,	1		Berk.	Bohannam,Benjamin,	1	2	K.&Q.	Bonwell,McKeel,	2	7	Acco.
Blue,Catherine,			Berk.	Bohannan,Anna,		6	Cul.	Bonwell,McKeel,Jr.,	2	8	Acco.
Blue,Henry,	1		York.	Bohannan,John,	2	9	Cul.	Bonwell,Reubin,	1		Acco.
Blue,Martha,			Berk.	Bohannan,John,	1	5	K.&Q.	Bonwell,Southey,			Acco.
Blue,Michael,	1		Berk.	Bohanon,Henry,	1	3	York	Bonwell,Stephen,	2		Acco.
Blue,Michael,Jr.,	1		Berk.	Bohnan,Joseph,	1		Lun.	Bonwell,Thomas,	1		Acco.
Blue,Uriah,	2		Berk.	Bohoughan,Mordicus,	1		Cul.	Bonwill,James,	1	3	Acco.
Blue,Uriah,Jr.,	1		Berk.	Boid,James,	1		Buck.	Booker,Andrew,	1		Bot.
Blundell,Absalom,	1	4	West'd.	Boiles,Charles,	1		Gooch.	Booker,George,	1	16	Eli.Cy.
Blundell,Elisha,	1		Lou.	Boiles,James,	1		Acco.	Booker,James,	1		Lun.
Blundell,Thomas,		1	West'd.	Boipeau,Daniel,	1	9	Din.	Booker,John,	1	12	Lun.
Blundell,Thomas,Jr.,	1	8	West'd.	Boipeau,John,	1	10	Din.	Booker,John,Jr.,	1	14	Lun.
Blundridge,Solomon,	1		Wash.	Boiser,Peter,	1	2	Din.	Booker,Lowry,	1	12	Lun.
Blunt,Ben,			So'n.	Boisnard,John,	1	8	Acco.	Booker,Marshall,			Din.
Blunt,Benjamin,	2	33	So'n.	Boisseau,Benjamin,	1	14	Din.	Booker,Richard,	1	10	York
Blunt,Charles,			Hen.	Boisseau,Holmes,	1	8	Pr.Geo.	Booker,Richard,	1	13	Lun.
Blunt,John,	2	33	So'n.	Boling,William,	1		Lou.	Bookhout,Charles,			Bed.
Blunt,Priscilla,		14	So'n.	Bolling,Archibald,	2	64	Buck.	Bookhout,Marmer,	1		Bed.
Blunt,William,	2		Hen.	Bolling,Archibald,		23	Camp.	Boon,Jacob,	1		Bed.
Blunt,William,	1	71	So'n.	Bolling,Archibald,			Henry	Boon,Jeremiah,	1		Lin.
Bly,David,	1		Lin.	Bolling,Ellix,Est.,		10	Din.	Boon,John,	2	2	Pr.Wm.
Blyth,John,			So'n.	Bolling,James,	1		Henry	Boon,Joseph,	1		Fay.
Blyth,John,Jr.,	1		So'n.	Bolling,John,	1	71	Gooch.	Boon,Josiah,	1		Lin.
Blythe,James,	1		Fau.	Bolling,Major,	1		Buck.	Boon,Josiah,	1		Cul.
Boans,William,	1		Bot.	Bolling,Mrs.Mary.,		14	Din.	Boon,Samuel,	1		Fay.
Board,James,	1		Bed.	Bolling,Mrs.Mary.		51	Din.	Boon,Samuel,Jr.,	1		Fay.
Board,John,Sr.,			Bed.	Bolling,Robert,Est.,		22	Buck.	Boon,William,	1	22	K.Geo.
Board,John,Jr.,	1		Bed.	Bolling,Robert,Est.,	1	23	Buck.	Booth,Aaron,	1		So'n.
Boarn,John,	1		K.Wm.	Bolling,Robert,	1	23	Din.	Booth,Beverly,	1	6	So'n.
Boaz,Abednego,	1		Buck.	Bolling,Robert,Jr.,	1	5	Din.	Booth,Booz,	1	2	York
Boaz,Daniel,	1		Buck.	Bolling,Robert,		12	Din.	Booth,Caleb,	1		Berk.
Boaz,Mesheck,	1		Buck.	Bolling,Samuel,	1		Henry	Booth,Elijah,	2		Acco.
Bobbet,James,	1		Mont.	Bolling,Susanna,	1	23	Buck.	Booth,George,		13	Din.
Bobbet,William,	1	6	Mont.	Bolling,Thomas,	1	48	Gooch.	Booth,George,	1	1	York
Bobo,G.,	1		Pr.Wm.	Bolling,Thomas,	1		Fau.	Booth,John,	1		Lou.
Bobo,R.,	1		Pr.Wm.	Bolling,William,	1		Buck.	Booth,John,	1	4	Henry
Bobo,Thomas,	1		Pr.Wm.	Bolling,William,	1		Bed.	Booth,John,	1	19	Bed.
Bochman,Henry,	1		Bot.	Bolt,Robert,	1		Henry	Booth,Lucy,		24	K.Wm.
Boden,John,	2		Fau.	Bolton,Robert,	1		Henry	Booth,Mordecai,	1	15	K.Wm.
Bodine,Isaac,	1	2	Lou.	Bolton,Thomas,	1		Henry	Booth,Mordica,	1		Acco.
Bodine,Jacob,	1	1	Lou.	Boly,Benjamin,	1	4	Berk.	Booth,Moses,	1	16	So'n.
Bodine,John,	1		Berk.	Bond,Edward,	1	3	Wash.	Booth,Moses,Jr.,		5	So'n.
Bodkin,John,	1		Aug.	Bond,John,	1		Lou.	Booth,Rebecca,		18	Brun.
Bodine,James,	1		Lou.	Bond,Thomas,	1		Loui.	Booth,Richard,	1	2	Bed.
Bodkin,Hugh,	1		Aug.	Bond,William,	1	7	Wash.	Booth,Sam,	1		York
Bodkin,James,	1		Aug.	Bonds,William,	1		K.&Q.	Booth,Thomas,	1	23	Hen.
Bodkin,Richard,	1		Har.	Bondurant,Darby,	1	1	Buck.	Booth,Thomas,	1		Bed.
Boey,Robert,	3		Berk.	Bondurant,Obediah,	1		Buck.	Booth,William,	1	26	Din.
Bogar,Michael,	1		Lou.	Bomnett,Mrs.,		13	Pr.Wm.	Boothe,Joel,	1		Lun.
Bogard,Ezekiel,	1		Har.	Bonam,Joseph,	1		Lou.	Boothe,Joseph,	1		Aug.
Bogart,Henry,	1		Berk.	Bonard,Henry,	1		Berk.	Boothe,Nathaniel,	1	4	Lun.
Bogart,Nathaniel,	1		Berk.	Bonham,Amariah,	3		Lou.	Booton,John,			Cul.
Bogart,Samuel,	2		Berk.	Bonham,Hezekiah,	2		Har.	Booton,William,	2	11	Cul.
Bogges,Joseph,	1		Cul.	Bonham,Nehemiah,	1		Fau.	Boran,Bazel,	1		Wash.
Bogges,Henry,	1	1	Lou.	Bonham,Peter,			Lou.	Borch,Bridges,			Brun.
Boggess,Jeremiah,	1	1	Fau.	Bonner,Frederick,	1	5	Din.	Bord,John,	1		Berk.
Boggess,Richard,	1		Lou.	Bonner,Henry,	2	9	Pr.Geo.	Bordere,George,	1		Lou.
Boggess,Robert,	1	9	Lou.	Bonner,Jesse,	1	7	Din.	Boreland,John,	3	5	Aug.
Boggess,Vincent,	1	5	Lou.	Bonner,John,	1	5	Pr.Geo.	Borer,Thomas,	1		Har.
Boggs,Frances,	1	1	Acco.	Bonner,Joseph,	1	8	Pr.Geo.	Boron,William,	1	2	Mont.
Boggs,George,			Acco.	Bonner,Joseph,	1		Berk.	Borrah,Adam,	1		Berk.
Boggs,Hancock,			Acco.	Bonner,Marmaduke,	1	7	Pr.Geo.	Borran,William,	1		Wash.
Boggs,James,	1		Fay.	Bonner,Thomas,	1	15	Din.	Borrar,Charles,	1		Har.

Boe,Henry,	1		Loui.	Boutwell,Catherine,	1	19	Caro.	Bowling,Christopher,	1	1	Mont.
Boe,Jemima,		5	Loui.	Boutwell,Edward,	1	2	Eli.Cy	Bowling,Francis,	1		Fau.
Borum,Aaron,	1		Lou.	Boutwell,Edward,	1	2	York	Bowling,James,	1		Mont.
Borum,William,	1		Lou.	Boutwell,Fannie,		4	Caro.	Bowling,John,			Cul.
Borum,William,Jr.,	1		Lou.	Boutwell,Mary,	2	13	Caro.	Bowling,John,	1		K.Geo.
Borum,William,Sr.,	1		Lou.	Boutwell,William,	2	9	Caro.	Bowling,John,	1		Mont.
Bosang,John,	1		Aug.	Bouveman,John,	1		Lou.	Bowling,John,Jr.,			Mont.
Bosell,George,	1	5	Fay.	Bowcock,Elijah,	1		Bed.	Bowling,Joseph,	1		Mont.
Bosher,Charles,	1	1	K.Wm.	Bowcock,John,	1	1	West'd	Bowling,William,	1		Mont.
Boshur,Leonard,			Loui.	Bowcock,Thomas,	1	3	West'd	Bowls,Isaac,			Berk.
Bosman,Edward,	1		Pr.Ge	Bowdin,George,	1		K.&Q.	Bowman,Andrew,	1	4	Berk.
Bost,James,	1		So'n.	Bowdin,Salley,		8	K.&Q..	Bowman,Catherine,	1	8	Acco.
Bostick,John,	1	10	Buck.	Bowdin,Thomas,	1	4	K.&Q.	Bowman,Charles,	1		Hen.
Boston,James,	2		Bot.	Bowdin,William,Jr.,	1	3	K.&Q.	Bowman,James,	1		Hen.
Boswell,Edward,	1		Pr.Wm	Bowdin,William,Sr.,	1	10	K.&Q.	Bowman,John,	1	2	Hen.
Boswell,Elizabeth,		10	Fau.	Bowdoin,Grace,		13	Nor.	Bowman,John,	1		Aug.
Boswell,George,	2		Pr.Wm	Bowdoin,& Hunter,	1	5	Spots.	Bowman,John,	1		Bot.
Boswell,George,	1		Berk.	Bowdoin,John,	1	17	Nor.	Bowman,Robert,	1		Henry
Boswell,Hackett,	1		Aug.	Bowdoin,Preson,	1	14	Spots.	Bowman,William,	1	2	Gooch.
Boswell,John,	1		Berk.	Bowdrie,John,			Gooch.	Bowmer,Peter,			Fau.
Boswell,Col.John,	1	28	Loui.	Bowe,John,	1	10	Spots.	Bowmer,William,	2	1	Cul.
Boswell,Joseph,		5	Lun.	Bowen,James,	1		K.Geo.	Bowner,Peter,			Cul.
Boswell,Thomas,			Lou.	Bowen,James,		2	Fau.	Bowry,Elioner,		3	Eli.Cy.
Boswell,William,	1		Pr.Wm	Bowen,John,	1		Wash.	Bowser,Richard,	1		So'n.
Boswell,William,	1	6	Brun.	Bowen,John,	1	2	K.Geo.	Bowyer,Adam,	1		Camp.
Boswells,Frances Ann,		9	Hen.	Bowen,Thomas,	1		Wash.	Bowyer,John,	1	21	Rock.
Bother,Nicholas,	1		Lou.	Bowen,William,	1		Rock.	Bowyer,Mary,			Camp.
Botorph,Phillip,	1		Rock.	Bower,George,	1		Berk.	Bowyer,Michal,	1	3	Aug.
Bott,John,	1		Mont.	Bower,Henry,	2		Berk.	Bowyer,Thomas,	1	1	Bot.
Bottoms,Francis,	1		Hen.	Bower,James,	1	3	Caro.	Bowyer,William,	1	5	Aug.
Bottoms,Francis,	1		Hen.	Bower,James,	1		Rock.	Boxley,Thomas,	1	13	K.Wm.
Bottoms,Micajah,	1		Hen.	Bowers,Barnett,	1		Lou.	Boxley,William,	1		Lou.
Bottoms,Micajah,	1		Hen.	Bowers,Christian,	1		Pr.Wm.	Boxly,Joseph,	1	18	Loui.
Bottoms,Thomas,	1	3	Hen.	Bowers,Francis,	1		Lun.	Boy,Jacob,	1		Lou.
Bottoms,Thomas,	1	3	Hen.	Bowers,John,	1	2	K.&Q.	Boyce,Richard,	1		Fau.
Bottoms,William,	1	14	Hen.	Bowers,John,	1		Lun.	Boyd,Alexander,	1		Berk.
Bottoms,William,	1	16	Hen.	Bowers,Mary,			K.&Q.	Boyd,Alexander,	1	3	Nor.
Botton,William,	1		Lou.	Bowers,Mary,			So'n.	Boyd,Andrew,	1	19	Mont.
Botts,Archibald,	1		Lou.	Bowers,Mary,		1	Caro.	Boyd,Daniel,	1		Lou.
Botts,Francis,	1	5	Pr.Wm	Bowers,Robert,	1		Lun.	Boyd,Elizabeth,	1		Lou.
Botts,Joshua,	1	8	Lou.	Bowers,Young,	1	1	Lun.	Boyd,George,	1		Mont.
Botts,Moses,			Lou.	Bowes,Peter,	1	10	Fau.	Boyd,George,	1		Lin.
Botts,Sawyer,	1		K.&Q.	Bowie,James,	2	25	Caro.	Boyd,James,	1	1	Lou.
Botts,Seth,	1		Lou.	Bowie,John,	3	24	Caro.	Boyd,James,	1		Lou.
Boudrey,Samuel,	1		Lin.	Bowie,Sarah,		8	Caro.	Boyd,James,	1	6	Bot.
Bough,Jacob,	1		Mont.	Bowin,Joseph,	1		Cul.	Boyd,James,	1	1	K.&Q.
Bougher,Jacob,	1		Mont.	Bowin,Mary,		2	Caro.	Boyd,Jane,			Bed.
Boughman,Andrew,	1		Har.	Bowin,William,	1		Cul.	Boyd,John,	1	1	Fay.
Boughr,Vincent,	1		Cul.	Bowing,Arthur,	1	7	So'n.	Boyd,John,	1	1	Lou.
Boughton,John,	1	12	Camp.	Bowland,Michael,	1		Berk.	Boyd,John,	1		Berk.
Boughton,John,	1	8	K.&Q.	Bowlen,Mark,	2	1	Caro.	Boyd,John,	2		Berk.
Boughton,Thomas,	1	6	K.&Q.	Bowler,Ben,	1	1	Caro.	Boyd,John,	1		Aug.
Bouhannan,Ambrose,	1	3	Cul.	Bowler,Caleb,	1		Caro.	Boyd,John,	1	1	Loui.
Bouldin,Joseph,	1	9	Henry	Bowler,John,	1	1	Caro.	Boyd,John,Sr.,	2		Mont.
Boulson,Thomas,	1		Berk.	Bowler,Mark,	1	4	Caro.	Boyd,Lucy,		31	K.&Q.
Boulware,Richa,	1		Lin.	Bowler,Obediah,	1		Hen.	Boyd,Robert,	1	10	Hen.
Bountain,William,	1		Berk.	Bowler,Richard,			Hen.	Boyd,Samuel,	1	9	Fau.
Bourn,Andrew,	5	19	Cul.	Bowler,Samuel,	1		West'd	Boyd,Samuel,	1		Lou.
Bourn,Andrew,Jr.,			Cul.	Bowler,Thomas,	1		Caro.	Boyd,Thomas,			K.&Q.
Bourn,David,			Loui.	Bowler,William,	2	9	Caro.	Boyd,Thomas,			K.&Q.
Bourn,Elizabeth,	1	2	Loui.	Bowler,William,Jr.,			Caro.	Boyd,Thomas,	1		Lou.
Bourn,Francis,			Cul.	Bowles,Benjamin,	1	2	Hen.	Boyd,Thomas,	1		Lin.
Bourn,Francis,	1	7	Cul.	Bowles,Bartlett,			Loui.	Boyd,Thomas,	1		Aug.
Bourn,John,	1	3	Spots	Bowles,David,	1	9	Hen.	Boyd,William,	1		Berk.
Bourn,John,	1	5	Cul.	Bowles,Elijah,	1	3	Hen.	Boyd,William,	1	1	Berk.
Bourn,Reubin,			Cul.	Bowles,Elizabeth,			Brun.	Boyd,William,	1		Lou.
Bourn,Richard,	1	5	K.&Q.	Bowles,Gideon,	1	5	Gooch.	Boyd,William,	1		Mont.
Bourn,Stephen,Jr.,	1		Loui.	Bowles,Henry,	1	5	Cha.Cy	Boyd,William,	1		Mont.
Bourn,Stephen,Sr.,	1		Loui.	Bowles,Hughes,	1		Gooch.	Boyd,William,	1	5	Henry
Bourn,William,			Cul.	Bowles,Jessee,	1		Hen.	Brock,Thomas,	1	5	So'n.
Bourn,William,			Cul.	Bowles,John,	1		Wash.	Brock,William,	1		Loui.
Bourn,William,	1	4	Caro.	Bowles,John,	1	4	K.Wm.	Brockman,Joseph,	1		Gooch.
Bourn,William,	1		K.&Q.	Bowles,Robert,	1		Bed.	Brockwell,Carter,	1	5	Pr.Geo.
Boush,John,	1	6	Hen.	Bowles,Thomas,	1	3	Hen.	Brockwell,John,	1		Pr.Geo.
Bousman,Henry,	1		Rock.	Bowles,Thomas,	1	1	Hen.	Brockwell,John,Jr.,	1		Pr.Geo.
Boutwell,Ann,	1		Eli.C	Bowles,Thomas,Jr.,	1		Hen.	Brockwell,Joseph,	1	2	Pr.Geo.

Boyd,William,	1		Loui.	Bradham,Thomas,	1		Lou.	Bragg,Joseph,	1	1	Fau.
Boydstone,Benjamin,	1	1	Berk.	Bradley,**eam,	1	1	Lun.	Bragg,Reubin,	1		Fau.
Boydstone,Presley,	1	2	Berk.	Bradley,Absalom,			Cul.	Bragg,Tarpley,	1		Pr.Wm.
Boydstone,Thomas,	1	3	Berk.	Bradley,Andrew,	1			Bragg,William,	1		Cul.
Boyer,John,			Loud.	Bradley,Augustine,			Cul.	Bragg,William,	1		Lun.
Boyer,Martin,	1		Loud.	Bradley,Benjamin,	1	6	Hen.	Braggoner,George,	1		Berk.
Boykin,Arthur,	1	15	Co'n	Bradley,Cornelius,	1		Fay.	Brahan,Lettice,		3	Fau.
Boykin,Daniel,	1		So'n	Bradley,Daney,	1	4	Cha.Cy	Brake,Abraham,	1		Har.
Boykin,Joel,	1	3	So'n	Bradley,Elizabeth,		5	Cha.Cy	Brake,Jacob,Jr.,	1		Har.
Boykin,John,	1	8	So'n	Bradley,Elizabeth,Sr.		4	Cha.Cy	Brake,Jacob,Sr.,	2		Har.
Boykin,John,Sr.,	1	8	So'n	Bradley,George,	1	1	Spots.	Brake,John,	1		Har.
Boykin,Matthew,	1	5	So'n	Bradley,Gideon,	1	3	Cha.Cy	Brame,Nilihz,	1	12	Caro.
Boykin,Simon,	1	17	So'n	Bradley,Gideon,			Cha.Cy	Brame,William,	1	8	Caro.
Boykin,William,	2	15	So'm	Bradley,Gideon,Jr.,		1	Cha.Cy	Bramford,John,	1	8	Buck.
Boyle,George,	1		K.Geo.	Bradley,Hezekiah,	1	5	Caro.	Bramhall,Ignatius,	2		Har.
Boyles,Charles,	1		Rock.	Bradley,Hugh	1	3	Fau.	Bramhall,James,	1		Berk.
Boyles,David,	1		Lou.	Bradley,Jacob,	1	3	Cha.Cy	Bramlett,Ann,	1		Bed.
Boyles,Henry,	1		Berk.	Bradley,James,	1	9	Cha.Cy	Bramlett,Peggy,	2		Fau.
Boyles,James,	1		Mont.	Bradley,James,	2	5	Lun.	Bramlett,Reuben,Sr.,	2		Fau.
Boyles,James,	1		Bot.	Bradley,Jesse,	1		Mont.	Bramlett,Reuben,Jr.,	1		Fau.
Boyles,Stephen,			Berk.	Bradley,Jessie,			Lun.	Brammer,Burgess,	1		Henry
Boyles,William,	1		Berk.	Bradley,John,	1	2	Lou.	Brammer,George,	1		Henry
Boyls,Henry,			Lou.	Bradley,John,	1		Buck.	Brammer,James,	1		Henry
Boyls,Sarah,			Lou.	Bradley,John,	1	4	Cha.Cy	Brammer,John,	1		Henry
Boyls,William,	1		Lou.	Bradley,Jonas,	1		Lou.	Branan,Thomas,	1	1	Caro.
Bozell,Ezekiel,	1		Berk.	Bradley,Joseph,	2		Buck.	Branch,Bailey,	1	2	So'n
Brabson,John,	1		Berk.	Bradley,Joseph,	1	4	Cha.Cy	Branch,Benjamin,	1	10	So'n
Bracey,Ann,			So'n	Bradley,Leonard,	2		Fay.	Branch,Elizabeth,		1	So'n
Bracey,Francis,	1	4	So'n	Bradley,Laurence,			Cul.	Branch,Henry,	1	3	So'n
Bracey,Mary,		4	So'n	Bradley,Mary,			So'n	Branch,John,	1	1	Bed.
Brack,Richard,	1	8	Ja.Cy.	Bradley,Mary,		5	Pr.Geo	Branch,Newsum,	1	7	So'n
Bracken,Rev.John,		11	York	Bradley,Robert,	1	3	Fay.	Branch,Olive,	1	4	Camp.
Bracken,Mr.,		5	Pr.Wm.	Bradley,Sarah,		2	Ja.Cy	Branch,Samuel,	1		Camp.
Bracket,John,	1		Hen.	Bradley,Sarah,	1	9	Cha.Cy	Branch,Susannah,			Berk.
Bracket,John,	1		Hen.	Bradley,Walter,	1	10	Cha.Cy	Branch,William,	1	4	So'n
Bracy,Sack,	1	5	Brun.	Bradley,William,	2	7	Buck.	Branch,William,	1		Bed.
Bracy,Thomas,	1	29	Brun.	Bradley,William,	1		Buck.	Brand,John,	1	1	Caro.
Bradberry,Henry,	1		Henry	Bradley,William,	1		Berk.	Brand,Thomas,	1		Brun.
Bradberry,James,	1		K.Wm.	Bradley,William,	3	16	Cul.	Brand,Vinson,	1		Brun.
Bradberry,Joseph,	1		Henry	Bradley,William,	2	8	Din.	Brandford,Joseph,	1		Cul.
Bradberry,Richard,	1		Henry	Bradley,William,	1	4	Hen.	Branham,Benjamin,			Loui.
Bradburn,Butler,	1	1	Loui.	Bradley,William,	2		Lun.	Branham,Benjamin,Jr.	1		Loui.
Bradburn,Thomas,			Loui.	Bradley,William,			Rock.	Branham,Daniel,	1	12	Cul.
Bradburn,William,	2	5	Loui.	Bradly,Edward,	1		Cha.Cy	Branham,Daniel,	1	10	Spots.
Braden,Robert,	1		Lou.	Bradly,James,	1		Brun.	Branham,David,	1		Mont.
Bradfield,G.,	1		Pr.Wm.	Brads,Daniel,	1		Rock.	Branham,Francis,	2		Cul.
Bradfield,L[eonard]	1		Pr.Wm.	Bradshaw,Benjamin,	1	8	Gooch.	Branham,James,	1	2	Cul.
Bradford,Alexander,	1	11	Fau.	Bradshaw,Benjamin,	3	11	So'n	Branham,John,	1		Henry
Bradford,Arthur,	1	2	Acco.	Bradshaw,Claiborne,			Loui.	Branham,John,	1	1	Fay.
Bradford,Benjamin,	2	8	Fau.	Bradshaw,Elizabeth,			So'n	Branham,John,	1		Spots.
Bradford,Daniel,	1	8	Cul.	Bradshaw,James,	1		Fay.	Branham,Nathaniel,	1		Loui.
Bradford,Daniel,	1	17	Fau.	Bradshaw,John,	1	4	Gooch.	Branham,Tavener,	1	2	Spots.
Bradford,Edmund,	1	1	Acco.	Bradshaw,John,	1	6	Bed.	Branham,Thomas,	1	1	Spots.
Bradford,Enoch,			Cul.	Bradshaw,John,	1	1	Aug.	Branham,Thomas,	1	3	Fay.
Bradford,Enoch,	1		Fay.	Bradshaw,Joseph,	1		So'n	Branham,William,	1		Henry
Bradford,Hugh,	1	6	Rock.	Bradshaw,Josiah,	1	1	Bed.	Brannam,James,	1		Mont.
Bradford,James,	2	5	Acco.	Bradshaw,Learner,	1	2	Gooch.	Brannan,Laurence,	1		Loud.
Bradford,John,	1		Har.	Bradshaw,Martha,			So'n	Brannan,Martin,	1		Bot.
Bradford,John,	2	2	Acco.	Bradshaw,Richard,	1		So'n	Brannon,John,	1	5	Cul.
Bradford,John,	1	1	Cul.	Bradshaw,Thomas,	1		Fay.	Branscomb,John,	1	1	Brun.
Bradford,John,			Fau.	Bradshaw,Thomas,	1		So'n	Branscomb,Richard,	1		Brun.
Bradford,John,	1	4	Fay.	Bradshaw,William,	1		So'n	Branscomb,Sarah,			Brun.
Bradford,Leanna,		5	Acco.	Bradshaw,William,	1		Bed.	Bransgrove,Elizabeth			Bed.
Bradford,Margaret,		2	Acco.	Bradshaw,William,	1	6	Gooch.	Bransom,Benjamin,	1		York
Bradford,Mary,		7	Fau.	Bradshaw,William,	1		Fay.	Bransom,Newyear,	1		West.
Bradford,Rachel,		1	Acco.	Bradwell,Isaac,	1	2	Din.	Branson,Amos,	1		Har.
Bradford,Robert,	1	4	Acco.	Bradwell,Jacob,	1		Din.	Branson,Jarret,	1		Mont.
Bradford,Samuel,	1		Rock.	Brady,Hezekiah,	1		Fay.	Branson,Thomas,	1		Mont.
Bradford,Sarah,		3	Acco.	Brady,Hezekiah,	1	1	Fau.	Branstetter,Michael	2		Mont.
Bradford,Thomas,	1	1	Acco.	Brady,James,	1		Berk.	Brantley,Etheldred,	1	4	So'n
Bradford,Thomas B.,	1	2	Acco.	Brady,James,	1	1	Pr.Wm.	Brantley,James,	1	2	So'n
Bradford,William,	1		Fau.	Brady,Pengrine,	1		Fau.	Brantley,Joshua,	1		So'm
Bradford,William,			Loud.	Brady,William,	3	19	Berk.	Branton, * * *,	1		Din.
Bradford,William H.,	1		Nor.	Brafford,Robert,		1	Aug.	Brasfield,Edward,	1	5	Spots.
Bradford,Zephimah,	1	7	Acco.	Bragg,Dozer,	1	2	Fau.	Brasfield,Leonard,			Spots.
Bradfute,Robert,		2	Bed.	Bragg,John,	1	1	Lou.	Brasfield,Leroy,	1		Cul.
Bradger,Thomas,	2		K.Geo.	Bragg,John,	1		Lun.	Brassington,Samuel,	1	1	Din.

Name			Co.
Braswell,Jesse,	1		Brun.
Bratchy,Thomas,	1	4	Aug.
Bratton,Elizabeth,	1	1	Aug.
Bratton,George,	1	3	Aug.
Bratton,Capt.James,	1	3	Aug.
Brattons,Adam,	1	1	Aug.
Brattons,John,	1		Aug.
Brattons,Robert,	1	5	Aug.
Braughton,James,	1		K.Wm.
Braver,Sarah,			Pr.Wm
Brawford,Samuel,	1	1	Aug.
Brawley,John,	1		Mont.
Brawner,William,	1		Lou.
Brawner,William,	1	1	Lou.
Braxsin,Christian,	1		Fay.
Braxton,Carter,	4	141	K.Wm.
Braxton,George,		118	K.Wm.
Bray,James,	1	2	Fay.
Bray,John,	1		Fau.
Bray,Richard,	1	10	K.& Q.
Bray,Richard Sr.,	1	3	K.& Q.
Bray,William,	1	5	K.& Q.
Brayan,Morgan,Jr.,			Fay.
Brayant,Matthew,			Bed.
Brazeal,Lucy,		10	Hen.
Brazier,Elizabeth,		3	Fau.
Brazor,Ziller,		3	Nor.
Breaden,Edward,		1	Aug.
Bready,John,	1		Mont.
Breckenridge,Lettice,		17	Bot.
Breckenridge,George,	2	2	Mont.
Breden,James,	2		Aug.
Bredin,John,	1		Aug.
Breeding,Caleb,	2	2	K.Wm.
Breeding,David,	1		Hen.
Breeding,John,	1	15	Ja.Cy
Breeding,Joseph,	1		Hen.
Breeding,Moody,	2	2	K.Wm.
Breeding,William,	1		Henry
Breedlove,James,	1		Lun.
Breedlove,James,Jr.,	1		Lun.
Breedlove,John,	1		Lun.
Breedlove,Maramiah,		5	K.Wm.
Breedlove,Mourning,		1	K.Wm.
Breedlove,Phill	1		Cul.
Breedlove,Thomas,	1		Cul.
Breedlove,William,			Cul.
Breedlove,William,	1	6	K.Wm.
Breedwell,William,	1		Cul.
Breeze,John,	2		Wash.
Brockenborough,Austin	1	34	West.
Brener,Philip,	1		Lou.
Brent,Charles,	1	11	Lou.
Brent,Daniel,		12	Pr.Wm
Brent,George,	1	4	Fau.
Brent,Hugh,	1	13	Pr.Wm
Brent,James,	1	7	Aug.
Brent,Thomas,	1	3	Fay.
Brent,William,	2	22	Fau.
Brett,Edward,	2	6	So'n
Brett,William,	1	2	K.Wm.
Bretts,J.	2	11	Pr.Wm
Bretts,John,	1	5	K.& Q
Brewer,George,	1		Brun.
Brewer,Henry,	2	22	Lou.
Brewer,Henry,	1	3	Brun.
Brewer,James,	1		Brun.
Brewer,James,			Brun.
Brewer,James,	2	4	Brun.
Brewer,James,	1		West.
Brewer,Jesse,	1	2	Brun.
Brewer,John,	1	3	Brun.
Brewer,John,	1	11	Brun.
Brewer,John			Lou.
Brewer,John			West.
Brewer,Jordan,	1		So'n
Brewer,Nickolas,			Brun.
Brewer, T.	1	4	Pr.Wm.
Brewer,Thomas,	1	1	Brun.
Brewer,William,	1	7	Brun.
Brewster,Mary,		4	Lou.
Brian,Brumton,	1		Lin.
Brian,Charles,	1		Aug.
Brian,Guy,	1		Cul.
Brian,Josiah,	2		Cul.
Briant,Jeremiah,			Cul.
Briant,John,			Fay.
Briant,John,	2		Fay.
Brice,Samuel,	1	2	Fay.
Bricken,Icicia,	1		Gooch.
Brickey,Jarratt,	1		Bot.
Brickey,Jarrett,Jr.,	1		Bot.
Brickey,John,	1		Bot.
Brickey,Peter,	1		Bot.
Brickey,Peter,	1	12	West.
Brickey,William,	1		Bot.
Brickhouse,George,Sr.	1	14	Nor.
Brickhouse,George,Jr.	1	5	Nor.
Brickhouse,Hezekiah,	2	13	Nor.
Brickhouse,John,Sr.,	3	18	Nor.
Brickhouse,John,Jr.,	1	4	Nor.
Brickhouse,Major,			Nor.
Brickley,John,	1	2	Bot.
Bridges, B.	1	2	Pr.Wm.
Bridges,George,	2	9	Ja.Cy
Bridges,John,	1	6	Lou.
Bridges,Richard,	1	9	Caro.
Bridgforth,Benjamin,	1	12	Lun.
Bridgforth,Benjamin,	1	12	Brun.
Bridgman,Franklin,	1		Hen.
Bridgman,Hezekiah,			Hen.
Bridgwater,Charles,	1	1	Hen.
Bridgwater,Elisha,			Hen.
Bridgwater,Jonathan,	2	5	Hen.
Bridgwater,Jonathan,			Hen.
Bridgwater,Nathaniel,	1	4	Hen.
Bridgwater,William,	2		Hen.
Bridwell,John,	1		Pr.Wm.
Bridwell,William,	1		Fau.
Brigges,John,	1	3	York.
Briggs,Charles,	1	27	So'n
Briggs,Gray,	1	43	Din.
Briggs,Henry,		16	Brun.
Briggs,Henry,estate		17	So'n
Briggs,Howell,	1	6	So'n
Briggs,J.	1		Pr.Wm.
Briggs,John,	1	1	K.&Q.
Briggs,Samuel,	1	1	Brun.
Briggs,William,	1	6	Fau.
Bright,Allentis,		3	Fay.
Bright,Atbert,	1		Mont.
Bright,Charles,	1	1	Bed.
Bright,Edmund,	1	1	Bed.
Bright,Francis,	1	10	York
Bright,George,	2		Aug.
Bright,Henry,	2		Lin.
Bright,Robert,	1	20	Eli.Cy
Bright,Thomas,	1		Wash.
Brightwell, John,	1		K.Wm.
Brigs,Samuel,	3		Lin.
Brilliman,Daniel,	1		Henry
Brink,Samuel,	2		Fay.
Brink,Widow,	2		Har.
Brinning,Daniel,			Hen.
Brinnon,Elizabeth,		3	West.
Brinnon,George,		3	West.
Brinnon,Hannah,		1	West.
Brinnon,John,	1	4	West.
Brisbane,Adam,	1	23	Henry
Briscoe,Casandra,	1		Berk.
Briscoe,Daniel,	1	7	West.
Briscoe,George,	1		West.
Briscoe,George,	1	11	Berk.
Briscoe,James,			Berk.
Briscoe,Dr.John,	1	19	Berk.
Briscoe,John,Jr.,	1	8	Berk.
Briscoe,Reuben,		3	West.
Briscoe,Truman,			Henry
Briscow,James,		2	West.
Brister,Samuel,Sr.,	1		So'n
Brister,Damuel,Jr.,	1		So'n
Brister,Thomas,	1	2	York
Bristoe,Benjamin,	1		Henry
Bristoe,John,	1	1	Din.
Bristoe,John,	1	10	Henry
Bristoe,William,	1		Henry
Briston,James,	1	14	Buck.
Briston,Jedidiah,		1	Buck.
Briston,Thompson,	1	2	Buck.
Bristor,Thomas,	1	5	Ja.Cy.
Bristow,John,	1		Pr.Wm.
Bristow,Thomas,	1		Pr.Wm.
Britian,John,	1		Mont.
Britain,Nathaniel,	1		Mont.
Brition,Robert,	1	1	Camp.
Britt,Benjamin,	1		So'n
Britt,Benjamin,			Brun.
Britt,Britain,	1	6	So'n
Britt,Edward,		9	K.Wm.
Britt,Elizabeth,		9	K.Wm.
Britt,John,	1	3	Gooch.
Britt,John,	1		Mont.
Britt,John,	1		So'n
Britt,John,Sr.,			Bot.
Britt,Joseph,	1	3	So'n
Britt,Martha,		1	So'n
Britt,Matthew,	1	3	So'n
Britt,Nathan,	1		So'n
Britt,Nathan,Jr.,	1	1	So'n
Britt,William,	1	11	Gooch.
Brittain,Bennet,	1		Hen.
Brittian,George,	1		Henry
Brittain,James,	2	11	Hen.
Brittain,Liddall,	1	9	Hen.
Brittain,Samuel,	1	1	Hen.
Brittle,James,	1		Mont.
Brizentine,Isaac,	2	10	Lun.
Brizentine,Leroy,			Lun.
Broach,Benonia,	1		K.&Q
Broach,George,	1		K.&Q
Broach,John,	1		K.&Q
Broadas,Thomas,			Cul.
Broaddus,Edward,	1	4	Caro.
Broaddus,John,	1	21	Caro.
Broaddus,John,Jr.,	1	3	Caro.
Broaddus,Sheldreck,	1	5	Caro.
Broaddus,Shipley,	1	1	Gooch.
Broaddus,Thomas,	1	12	Caro.
Broadus,James,		4	Cul.
Broadus,Richard,	1	1	Cul.
Broadus,Thomas,	1		Cul.
Broadus,Thomas,			K.&Q.
Broadus,William,	1	29	Cul.
Broadhurst,William,	1		Fau.
Broadwater,Charles,	1		Bot.
Broadwater,Cornelis	1		Lou.
Broadwater,Coventon	2	3	Acco.
Brobeck,Bonimus,			Berk.
Brock,Allen,	1		Henry
Brock,Barbara,		1	Spots.
Brock,Elizabeth,		3	Spots.
Brock,Henry,	1	5	Spots.
Brock,Joseph,	2	9	Spots.
Brock,Col.Joseph,	2	29	Spots.
Brock,Joseph,Jr.,	1	4	Spots.
Brock,Joshua,	1		Henry
Brock,Moses,	1		Henry
Brock,Orril,	1		Spots.

Name			Co.	Name			Co.	Name			Co.
Brockwell,Thomas,	1	1	Pr.Geo	Brooks,Zebulon,	1		Nor.	Brown,Hannah,			Buck.
Brockwell,Thomas,	1	1	Pr.Geo	Brothers,John,	1	5	Buck.	Brown,Henry,	1	4	K.&Q.
Brockwell,William,	1	1	Pr.Geo	Brough,William,	1	14	Eli.Cy	Brown,Henry,	3		Cul.
Brockwell,William,	1		Cha.Cy	Broughill,William,	1	1	Caro.	Brown,Henry,			Cul.
Brockwell,William,	1		Pr.Geo	Broughton,Eliza.,	1	3	Lou.	Brown,Henry,	1		Lou.
Brodie,Alexander,	1		York	Broughton,James,	1	2	Acco.	Brown,Henry,	1		Bed.
Brodie,John,	1	8	Eli.Cy	Broughton,William,			Har.	Brown,Henry,			Cul.
Brodie,Lodowick,	1	2	Pr.Geo	Brount,Hannah,	1		Lin.	Brown,Henry,			Cul.
Brodnax,Edward,	2	40	Lun.	Browder,Arthur,	1		Din.	Brown,Henry,	1	24	Ja.Cy.
Brodnax,Henry,	1	23	Din.	Browder,David,	1	4	Din.	Brown,Hezekiah,			Bot.
Brodnax,John,	1	11	Brun.	Browder,Jesse,	1	1	Din.	Brown,Hezekiah,	1		Din.
Brodnax,Thomas Hall,	1	16	Brun.	Browder,John,	1	5	Din.	Brown,Hezeckiah,	1	4	Cul.
Brodnax,William,		7	Brun.	Browder,Joseph,	1	2	Brun.	Brown,Hillary,	1		Hen.
Brodnax,William E.,	1	1	Din.	Browder,Littleberry,	1	3	Din.	Brown,Hugh,	1		Aug.
Bronaugh,Francis,	3	11	Fau.	Browder,Richard,	1	6	Din.	Brown,Hugh,	1	2	Aug.
Bronaugh,George,			Lou.	Browder,Thomas,	1	2	Din.	Brown,Isaac,	1		Lou.
Bronaugh,Mary Ann,		2	Fau.	Browder,Thompson,	1		Din.	Brown,Isaac,	1		Lou.
Bronaugh,Thomas,	1	10	Fau.	Browder,William,	1	20	Din.	Brown,Isham,	1		Buck.
Bronaugh,William,	1	8	K.Geo	Browder,William,	1		Din.	Brown,J.,	1		Pr.Wm.
Bronaugh,Col.William,	2	29	Lou.	Browder,William,	1		Lun.	Brown,James,	1	2	Aug.
Brooke,George,Est.,		23	K.Wm.	Brown,Abraham,	1		Lin.	Brown,James,	2		Lou.
Brooke,Col.George,Est	1	73	K.&Q.	Brown,Abraham,	1	3	Cha.Cy	Brown,James,	1		Buck.
Brooke,Humphrey,	1	15	Fau.	Brown,Abraham,	3		Mont.	Brown,James,	1	1	Pr.Wm.
Brooke,John,	1	11	Hen.	Brown,Alexander,	1	8	Pr.Wm.	Brown,James,	1		Bot.
Brooke,Laurance,	1	6	K.Geo.	Brown,Alice,		2	Din.	Brown,James,	1		Mont.
Brooke,Lawrence,	1	2	Spots.	Brown,Ambras,	1	1	Din.	Brown,James,	1	4	Pr.Wm.
Brooke,Richard,	2	42	Spots.	Brown,Andrew,	1		Lou.	Brown,James,	1	5	Pr.Wm.
Brooke,Richard,			K.&Q.	Brown,Araba,	1		Bed.	Brown,James,	1	2	K.Geo.
Brooke,Robert,	1	39	K.Wm.	Brown,Aron,	1	17	Brun.	Brown,James,	1	4	Spots.
Brooke,Thomas,	1		K.Geo.	Brown,Augustine,	1	1	Henry	Brown,James,	2		Bed.
Brooke,William,	1		Aug.	Brown,Benjamin,	1	3	Lou.	Brown,James,			Cul.
Brooker,Christopher,			K.&Q.	Brown,Benjamin Edward		22	Brun.	Brown,James,	1	3	Cul.
Brooker,Humphrey,		1	Caro.	Brown,Benjamin,			Hen.	Brown,James,			Cul.
Brookes,Edward,	1	2	York	Brown,Benjamin,	1		Aug.	Brown,James,	1	8	Cul.
Brookes,Jarvis,	1		Bot.	Brown,Betty,		4	Brun.	Brown,James,	1		Pr.Wm.
Brookes,Peter,	1		Bot.	Brown,Beverly,	1	33	Brun.	Brown,Jeane,			Cul.
Brookes,Thomas,	1	1	Fau.	Brown,Bond Veal,			Pr.Wm.	Brown,Jehu,	1		Fau.
Brooking,Charles,	2	5	Cul.	Brown,Burwell,	1	3	Pr.Geo.	Brown,Jennings,	1		Buck.
Brooking,Frances,		23	K.&Q.	Brown,Catherine,			K.Geo.	Brown,Jeremiah,	1		Bed.
Brooking,John,			Cul.	Brown,Charles,	1		Pr.Wm.	Brown,Jeremiah,	1	1	Fau.
Brooking,Robert,	1		Cul.	Brown,Charles,	1	1	Fay.	Brown,John,	1	5	West'd.
Brooking,Samuel,			Cul.	Brown,Clayborn,	1		Bed.	Brown,John,	1		Loui.
Brooking,William,	1		Cul.	Brown,Coleman,	1	2	Cul.	Brown,John,	2	30	Cha.Cy.
Brookins,John,	1		K.&Q.	Brown,Coleman,	1	11	Lou.	Brown,John,	1	9	Caro.
Brooks,Bluford,	1	4	Caro.	Brown,Daniel,	1	3	Fau.	Brown,John,	1		Aug.
Brooks,David,	1	1	York	Brown,Daniel,	1	1	Cul.	Brown,John,	1		Aug.
Brooks,Dudley,			Buck.	Brown,Daniel,	1	3	Cul.	Brown,John,	1	7	Aug.
Brooks,Elizabeth,		2	York	Brown,Daniel,	1		Berk.	Brown,John,	1	1	Lou.
Brooks,Elizabeth,			Wash.	Brown,Daniel,	1	4	Bed.	Brown,John,	1		Lou.
Brooks,George,	1		Berk.	Brown,Daniel C.,	1		Cul.	Brown,John,	1		Lou.
Brooks,J.,	1		Pr.Wm	Brown,Daniel,Sr.,	1	5	Bed.	Brown,John,			Buck.
Brooks,James,	1	1	Cul.	Brown,David,	1		Bed.	Brown,John,	2		Buck.
Brooks,James,	1		Fau.	Brown,Dawson,	1		Lou.	Brown,John,	1		Buck.
Brooks,James,	1		Camp.	Brown,Dixon,	1		Fau.	Brown,John,	1		Pr.Geo.
Brooks,James,	1		Camp.	Brown,Dixon,	1		Cha.Cy	Brown,John,	1		Pr.Wm.
Brooks,John,	1		Aug.	Brown,Dudley,	1	2	Din.	Brown,John,	1		Har.
Brooks,John,	1		Lin.	Brown,Eards,	1	4	Lun.	Brown,John,	1		Hen.
Brooks,John,	1		Mont.	Brown,Eards,	1	4	Lun.	Brown,John,	1		Hen.
Brooks,John,	1	2	Camp.	Brown,Edward,	1		Cha.Cy	Brown,John,			Cul.
Brooks,John,	1		Camp.	Brown,Elizabeth,			Din.	Brown,John,			Cul.
Brooks,John,	1	2	Camp.	Brown,Esther,			Rock.	Brown,John,			Brun.
Brooks,John,	1		Camp.	Brown,Francis,			Wash.	Brown,John,	1	1	Lou.
Brooks,John,Sr.,	2	2	Aug.	Brown,Francis,	1	1	Aug.	Brown,John,			Bed.
Brooks,John,Jr.,	1	1	Aug.	Brown,Francis,	2	8	Fay.	Brown,John,	1		Bed.
Brooks,Phebe,		2	West'd	Browder,Frederick,	1	2	Lun.	Brown,John,	1		Cul.
Brooks,Thomas,			York	Brown,Freeman,	1		Cha.Cy	Brown,John,	1		Cul.
Brooks,Thomas,	1		Spots	Brown,G.N.,	1	7	Pr.Wm.	Brown,John,	1	3	Cul.
Brooks,Thomas,	1		Cul.	Brown,Gabriel,			Cul.	Brown,John,	1	1	Cul.
Brooks,Thomas,	1	6	Fay.	Brown,Garfiea,	1		Lin.	Brown,John,	1	1	Henry
Brooks,William,			Bot.	Brown,George,	1		Rock.	Brown,John,	1		Berk.
Brooks,William,	1		Camp.	Brown,George,	1		Fau.	Brown,John,	1		Berk.
Brooks,William,	1		Spots	Brown,George,	2	3	Fau.	Brown,John,	1		Berk.
Brooks,William,	1		Aug.	Brown,George,	1		Berk.	Brown,John,	1		Cul.
Brooks,William,	1	4	Cul.	Brown,George,	1	1	Brun.	Brown,John,	1		Mont.
Brooks,William,	1		Fay.	Brown,George,	1		Bot.	Brown,John,	1		Fau.
Brooks,William,	1	1	Berk.	Brown,Gideon,	1	3	Cul.	Brown,John,	1		Fau.

Name			County
Brown,John,	1		Fau.
Brown,John,	1	1	Fau.
Brown,John,	1		Pr.Wm
Brown,John,	2	16	Ja.Cy
Brown,John,	1	1	Ja.Cy
Brown,John,	1		Lin.
Brown,John,	1		Lin.
Brown,John,	2		Fay.
Brown,John,	1		Berk.
Brown,John,	1	6	Lun.
Brown,John,Sr.,	2		Cul.
Brown,Dr.John,	1		Lou.
Brown,Joseph,	1		Buck.
Brown,Joseph,	1		Buck.
Brown,Joseph,	2	1	Hen.
Brown,Joseph,	1		Bed.
Brown,Joseph,	1		Aug.
Brown,Joseph,			Fau.
Brown,Joseph,	2		Lin.
Brown,Jotham,	1		Bot.
Brown,Law,	1		Mont.
Brown,Lewis,Jr.,	1	14	Brun.
Brown,Lewis,Sr.,	1	8	Brun.
Brown,Marmanduke,	1		Fau.
Brown,Mary,		2	Fau.
Brown,Mary,		7	Ja.Cy
Brown,Mary,	2	1	Cul.
Brown,Micajah,			Hen.
Brown,Mordecai,	1		Cul.
Brown,Moses,	1		Brun.
Brown,Moses,	1		Bot.
Brown,Nathaniel,	1	2	Acco.
Brown,Nicholas,	1	6	Lun.
Brown,Noah,	1	10	Pr.Geo
Brown,Noah,	1	4	Din.
Brown,Patrick,	1		Rock.
Brown,Peter,	1	3	Berk.
Brown,Philip,	1		Lou.
Brown,Prestley,	1		Har.
Brown,R.	1	12	Pr.Wm
Brown,Rachel,			Caro.
Brown,Rebecca,			Din.
Brown,Renna	1	4	Caro.
Brown,Richard,	2		Bed.
Brown,Richard,	1	12	York
Brown,Robert,	1	3	Lun.
Brown,Robert,	1		Cul.
Brown,Robert,			Din.
Brown,Robert,			Wash.
Brown,Robert,			Wash.
Brown,Robert,			Wash.
Brown,Robert,	1	7	Hen.
Brown,Robert,	1	1	Camp.
Brown,Robert Kipling,	1		Eli.C
Brown,Samuel,	1		Spots
Brown,Sarah,		1	Bed.
Brown,Sarah,		1	Bed.
Brown,Sarah,		1	Bed.
Brown,Sarah,	1	19	Pr.Geo
Brown,Sarah,			York.
Brown,Solomon,	1		Mont.
Brown,Stephen,	1		Lun.
Brown,Stephen,	1		Buck.
Brown,Swanson,	1		Fau.
Brown,Thomas,		1	Fau.
Brown,Thomas,	1	4	Fay.
Brown,Thomas,	1	7	Cul.
Brown,Thomas,	1		Cul.
Brown,Thomas,	1	12	Cul.
Brown,Thomas,	1		Cul.
Brown,Thomas,	1		Bed.
Brown,Thomas,	1		Bed.
Brown,Thomas,	1		Spots
Brown,Thomas,	1	3	Spots
Brown,Thomas,	1	15	Lou.
Brown,Thomas,	1		Cul.
Brown,Thomas,	1	2	Cul.
Brown,Thomas,	1	3	Cul.

Name			County
Brown,Thomas,	3		Har.
Brown,Thomas,	1	7	Pr.Geo
Brown,Thomas,	1		Bot.
Brown,Thomas,	1		Lou.
Brown,Thomas,	1	4	Aug.
Brown,Thomas,	1	4	Aug.
Brown,Thomas,			Gooch.
Brown,William,	1	12	West.
Brown,William,	1	11	West.
Brown,William,	1		West.
Brown,William,	1	2	Caro.
Brown,William,	1		Aug.
Brown,William,	1		Lou.
Brown,William,			Lou.
Brown,William,	1		Bot.
Brown,William,	1	5	Pr.Geo
Brown,William,	1	5	Pr.Geo
Brown,William,	2	11	Pr.Wm.
Brown,William,			Hen.
Brown,William,	1	25	Brun.
Brown,William,	1		Brun.
Brown,William,	1	31	Brun.
Brown,William,	1	28	Brun.
Brown,William,	1		Bed.
Brown,William,	1	4	Bed.
Brown,William,	1		Berk.
Brown,William,	1		Henry
Brown,William,	1	2	Henry
Brown,William,	1	2	Cul.
Brown,William,		1	Aug.
Brown,William,			Cul.
Brown,William,	2	3	Cul.
Brown,William,	1	3	Eli.Cy
Brown,William,	1	2	Eli.Cy
Brown,William,	1		Mont.
Brown,William,	1	3	Fay.
Brown,William,	1	2	Rock.
Brown,William,	2		Berk.
Brown,William,	1		Lun.
Brown,William,	1		Wash.
Brown,William,	1	3	K.Geo
Brown,William,Jr.,	1		Bed.
Brown,William,Sr.,			Bed.
Brown,Wilson,	1		Buck.
Brown,Zachariah,	1		Bed.
Browne,William B.	1	75	K.Wm.
Browne,Bennett,	1	25	K.Wm.
Browne,Esther,		1	So'n
Browne,Col.Henry,	1	26	So'n
Browne,Holland,		3	So'n
Browne,John,	1		Ja.Cy
Browne,Mansfield,	1		Ja.Cy
Browne,Olive,		10	So'n
Browne,Samuel,	4	58	So'n
Browne,Samuel,	4		K.Wm.
Browne,Thomas,	5	10	York
Browne,William,	1		So'n
Browning,Archibald,		1	Hen.
Browning,Caleb,			Cul.
Browning,Caleb,	1	1	Fau.
Browning,Charles,	1	2	Cul.
Browning,Charles,	1		Cul.
Browning,Jacob,	2		Fau.
Browning,James,	1		Cul.
Browning,Capt.James,	1	2	Cul.
Browning,John,	1		Cul.
Browning,Nicholas,	1		Cul.
Browning,Reuben,	1	1	Cul.
Browning,Samuel,	1	1	Hen.
Browning,Shadrach,	1		Cul.
Browning,William,	1		Cul.
Brownlee,Alexander,	1		Aug.
Brownlee,Alexander,			Lin.
Brownlee,Alexander,	1		Aug.
Brownlee,James,	1		Aug.
Brownlee,James,Sr.,	1		Aug.
Brownlee,John,	1		Aug.
Brownlee,John,	1		Aug.

Name			County
Brownlee,John,	1		Aug.
Brownlee,John,	1	2	Lin.
Brownlee,John,Sr.,	1		Aug.
Brownlee,John,Jr.			Aug.
Brownlee,Martha,			Aug.
Brownlee,William,	1		Aug.
Brownlee,Capt.Wm.			Aug.
Brownlee,John,	1		Aug.
Brownlow,John,	3		Spots.
Brows,Andrew,	1		Berk.
Broyle,John,	1	2	Cul.
Broyle,Peter,			Cul.
Bruce,James,	1		Cul.
Bruce,James,	1	1	Brun.
Bruce,James,			Cul.
Bruce,Joel,	1	2	K.Geo.
Bruce,John,	2		Cul.
Bruce,Joseph,	1	6	K.Geo.
Bruce,Margaret,		6	Brun.
Bruce,Richard,			K.Geo.
Bruce,William,	2		Cul.
Bruce,William,	1	2	Cul.
Brue,Moses,			Lou.
Bruice,Benjamin,	1	1	Fay.
Bruin,Peter Bryan,	2	13	Berk.
Brumagen,Edward,	1		Camp.
Brumblin,Jesse,	1		Brun.
Brumbly,John,	1		Cul.
Brumfield,Elijah,	1	2	Gooch.
Brumfield,Humphrey,	1		Mont.
Brumfield,James,Jr.,	1		Mont.
Brumfield,John,	1	1	Gooch.
Brumfield,Susanna,		5	K.Wm.
Brumfield,William,	1		K.Wm.
Brumley,Elizabeth,			Caro.
Brumley,John,	1		Lou.
Brumley,John,	1		K.&Q
Brumley,Robert,	1		K.&Q
Brummett,James,	1		Bed.
Brummigam,Edward,	1		Camp.
Brummigan,Edward,	1		Camp.
Brumpton,Bryan,	1		Mont.
Brundidge,Bartlet,	1		Fay.
Brush,Blakenery,	1		Rock.
Brushwood,William,	1		K.&Q
Brux,Henry Robinson,		15	Brun.
Bryan,Batterley,	1	1	Fau.
Bryan,Benjamin,	1	5	Eli.Cy
Bryan,Daniel,	1	2	Fay.
Bryan,Daniel,	1		Berk.
Bryan,David,	1		Wash.
Bryan,David,			Fay.
Bryan,Enoch,	1		Fau.
Bryan,Frederick,	1	4	York
Bryan,Frederick,	1	17	Cha.Cy
Bryan,James,	2		Fay.
Bryan,James,			West.
Bryan,James,	1		Rock.
Bryan,James,	1		Wash.
Bryan,James,	1		Wash.
Bryan,James,	1	3	Bot.
Bryan,James,Sr.,	1		Bot.
Bryan,James,Jr.	1		Bot.
Bryan,John,	1		Mont.
Bryan,John,	1	1	Fau.
Bryan,John,	3	6	Fau.
Bryan,John,	1	2	Berk.
Bryan,John,	1	1	Hen.
Bryan,John,	1	4	York.
Bryan,John,	3		Camp.
Bryan,John,			So'n
Bryan,Martha,		2	Cha.Cy
Bryan,Morgan,	2	3	Fay.
Bryan,Nathan,	1	5	So'n
Bryan,Richard,	1	1	Eli.Cy
Bryan,Simkin,	1		Hen.
Bryan,William,	1	2	Fau.
Bryan,William,			Hen.

Name			County
Bryan,William,Sr.,	2		Bot.
Bryan,William,Jr.,	1	4	Bot.
Bryant,Ann,	1	3	Nor.
Bryant,Ann,		2	Buck.
Bryant,Anderson,	1		Fay.
Bryant,Benjamin,	1		K.Geo.
Bryant,Edmond,	1	5	Spots.
Bryant,Edmond,	1	4	Spots.
Bryant,Elijah,	1		Bed.
Bryant,James,	1		Mont.
Bryant,James,	3	3	Fau.
Bryant,James,	1	1	So'n.
Bryant,Jesse,	1		Pr.Wm.
Bryant,John,	1		Lin.
Bryant,John,	1		Henry
Bryant,John,	1		Henry
Bryant,John,	2	3	Buck.
Bryant,John,			Hen.
Bryant,John,	1		K.Geo.
Bryant,John,	1		Mont.
Bryant,John,	3		Camp.
Bryant,John,Sr.,	1		So'n.
Bryant,John,Jr.,	1		So'n.
Bryant,Jonas,	1	2	So'n.
Bryant,Jonas,	1		So'n.
Bryant,Lewis,	1		So'n.
Bryant,Lewis,Jr.,	1		So'n.
Bryant,Lovell,	1	1	K.Geo.
Bryant,Peter,	1		Fau.
Bryant,Samuel,	2	4	Fay.
Bryant,William,	1	3	K.Geo.
Bryant,William,	2		K.Geo.
Bryant,William,	1		Lin.
Bryn,Cornelius,			Acco.
Bryne,U.,			Pr.Wm.
Bwinley,Ishom,Est.,	1	18	K.Wm.
Buchanan,Alexander,	1		Rock.
Buchanan,Alexander,	1		Mont.
Buchanan,Alexander,			Hen.
Buchanan,Alexander,	3		Aug.
Buchanan,Andrew,	2		Wash.
Buchanan,Ezekiel,	1		Mont.
Buchanan,George,	1		Wash.
Buchanan,James,	1		Rock.
Buchanan,James,	1		Rock.
Buchanan,James,	2	15	Hen.
Buchanan,James,	1		Aug.
Buchanan,James,Sr.,	1		Mont.
Buchanan,John,	1		York
Buchanan,John,			Hen.
Buchanan,John,	1		Wash.
Buchanan,John,	1		Wash.
Buchanan,Joshua,	1	1	Spots.
Buchanan,Moses,	1	1	Wash.
Buchanan,Nathaniel,	1		Mont.
Buchanan,Patrick,	1		Aug.
Buchanan,Robert,	1	1	Mont.
Buchanan,Robert,	1	3	Wash.
Buchanan,Samuel,	1	1	Wash.
Buchanan,David,	1		Aug.
Buchanan,Mary,			Aug.
Buchanan,Spencer,	1	2	Lou.
Buchanan,William,	1		Aug.
Buchanan,William,	1	6	Lou.
Buchannon,John,	1		Berk.
Buck,Benjamin,	1	8	Cha.Cy
Buck,Elizabeth,	1	16	Cha.Cy
Buckalew,Andrew,	1		Lou.
Buckanan,J.,			Pr.Wm.
Buckhannon,William,	3		Berk.
Buckler,Elizabeth,		1	York
Buckles,James,	1		Berk.
Buckles,John,	1		Berk.
Buckles,Robert,	1	1	Berk.
Buckles,Robert,Jr.,	1		Berk.
Buckles,William,	1		Berk.
Buckley,Joshua,	1	1	Lou.
Buckley,Samuel,	1		Henry
Buckley,William,	1	2	Lou.
Buckner,Aylett,	1	22	Fau.
Buckner,Charles,	1		Lun.
Buckner,Elizabeth,		17	Caro.
Buckner,Francis,	1	11	Caro.
Buckner,Francis,		14	Spots.
Buckner,Francis,	1	21	Caro.
Buckner,George,	1	28	Caro.
Buckner,George,Jr.,	1	17	Caro.
Buckner,George,Est.,		9	Cul.
Buckner,Horace,Est.,		11	Cul.
Buckner,Horrace,	1	7	Caro.
Buckner,John,Est.,	1	22	Spots.
Buckner,Lewis,			Hen.
Buckner,Mordicai,	1	11	Spots.
Buckner,Mordicai,	1	11	Spots.
Buckner,Mordicai,	1	26	Spots.
Buckner,Mordecai,	1	2	Caro.
Buckner,Phillip,	3	24	Caro.
Buckner,Richard,	1	25	West'd
Buckner,Richard,	1	22	Caro.
Buckner,Robert,	1	11	Caro.
Buckner,William,	1	21	Caro.
Buckner,William,Jr.,	1	11	Caro.
Bucknor,William,Sr.,	2	35	Caro.
Budd,Major,	1		Acco.
Budd,Mekeel,	1	1	Acco.
Budenot,Ebenezer,	1		Rock.
Budin,William,			Loui.
Buffenberger,Peter,	1		Har.
Buffington,James,	1		Lou.
Buford,Abraham,			Fay.
Buford,Col.Abram,	1	13	Cul.
Buford,Henry,	1	5	Bed.
Buford,James,	1	12	Bed.
Buford,John,	1		Camp.
Buford,John,	1	1	Bed.
Buford,Simion,	1	14	Cul.
Buford,William,	1	8	Bed.
Bugg,John,		2	Brun.
Bugg,Sherrad,	1	1	Bed.
Buheson,Ziles,	2	2	Caro.
Buket,Solomon,	1		Nor.
Bulger,Edmund,	1	1	West'd
Bulitt,Cuthbert,	2	36	Fau.
Bull,Bagwell,	1		Acco.
Bull,Benjamin,	1	1	Acco.
Bull,David,	1	9	West'd
Bull,Elie,	1	1	Acco.
Bull,George,	1	2	Acco.
Bull,John,	1	3	Nor.
Bull,John,	1	4	Berk.
Bull,John,Sr.,	1	6	Acco.
Bull,John,Jr.,	1	5	Acco.
Bull,Major,	1	2	Nor.
Bull,Nicholas,	1	3	Nor.
Bull,Richard,	2	1	Acco.
Bull,Robert,	1		Acco.
Bull,Robert,	1		Berk.
Bull,Southy,	1	2	Acco.
Bull,Tobias,			Acco.
Bull,Tobias,	1	2	Acco.
Bull,William,	1		K.&Q.
Bull,William,	1		Berk.
Bullard,Ambrose,	1	4	Caro.
Bullard,Catherine,		2	Caro.
Bullard,James,	1		So'n.
Bullard,Lewis,	1	7	Caro.
Bullard,Richard,	1	4	Spots.
Bullett,William,	1	1	Har.
Bullifant,James,	1	3	Ch.Cy
Bullifant,James,Jr.,	1		Ch.Cy
Bullifant,John,	1		Ch.Cy
Bullifant,Philip,	1	6	York
Bullington,Josiah,		11	Hen.
Bullington,William,		11	Hen.
Bullitt,Cuthbert,	1	17	Pr.Wm.
Bullitt,Joseph,	1	11	Fau.
Bullman,Thomas,	1	3	K.&Q.
Bullock,David,	1	4	Bed.
Bullock,David,	1	1	Loui.
Bullock,James,	1	6	Eli.Cy.
Bullock,John,	1	21	Loui.
Bullock,John,	1		Spots.
Bullock,Joseph,	1	1	Spots.
Bullock,Nathaniel,	1		Fay.
Bullock,Thomas,	1	4	Nor.
Bulls,Benjamin,	1		So'n.
Bulls,Jesse,	1		So'n.
Bully,Andrew,	1		Eli.Cy.
Bully,John,	1		Eli.Cy.
Bumgarner,Adam,	1		Berk.
Bumgarner,Federick,	1		Cul.
Bumpass,William,	1	5	Buck.
Bunbury,Elizabeth,		10	K.Geo.
Bunbury,John,	1	8	K.Geo.
Bunbury,Thomas,	1	4	K.Geo.
Bunbury,William,	1	3	K.Geo.
Bunbury,William,	1	4	K.Geo.
Bunbury,William,	1	3	K.Geo.
Bunch,Charles,	1		Bed.
Bunch,David,	1		Henry
Bunch,David,			Loui.
Bunch,James,	1	5	Loui.
Bunch,John,	1	3	Loui.
Bunch,Joseph,	1		Bed.
Bunch,Joseph,	1	7	Loui.
Bunch,Polley,		1	Loui.
Bunch,Pouncy,	1	3	Loui.
Bunch,Samuel,	1	3	Loui.
Bunch,William,	1	2	Loui.
Bunch,Zachariah,	1		Bot.
Bundick,John,	1		Acco.
Bundurant,Joel,	1		Camp.
Bundurant,Joel,	1		Camp.
Bundurant,John,	1		Bed.
Bundurant,John,	1	1	Buck.
Bundurant,Joseph,Sr,	1	21	Buck.
Bundurant,Joseph,Jr,	1	1	Buck.
Bundurant,Thomas,	1		Buck.
Buneger,John,	1		Fay.
Bunger,Falter,	1		Cul.
Bunn,Ann,		5	So'n.
Bunn,David,	1		So'n.
Bunn,Hardy,	1		So'n.
Bunnell,William,	1		Spots.
Bunning,Absolum,	1		Hen.
Bunting,Andrew,	1	1	Wash.
Bunting,George,	1	3	Acco.
Bunting,Kendal,	1	2	Acco.
Bunting,Levin,	1	4	Acco.
Bunting,Mary,	1		Acco.
Bunting,Sackor,	1		Acco.
Bunting,Solomon,	1		Acco.
Bunting,Solomon,		4	Nor.
Bunting,William,Jr.,	1	2	Acco.
Bunting,WilliamBlack	1	2	Acco.
Bunton,Moses,	1		Rock.
Bunton,William,	1		Rock.
Burbage,Aron,	1	1	Cul.
Burbage,Moses,	1	1	Cul.
Burbridge,Linchfield	1		Spots.
Burbridge,Mary,		6	Spots.
Burbridge,William,	1		Spots.
Burch,Barnabas,	1	2	Ch.Cy.
Burch,Benjamin,	2	16	Caro.
Burch,Henry,	1	1	K.&Q.
Burch,Henry,	1		K.&Q.
Burch,Henry,Sr.,	1		K.&Q.
Burch,James,	1	5	K.&Q.

Name			County	Name			County	Name			County
Burch,Phillip,	1	2	K.&Q.	Burks,Rowland,	1		Henry	Burt,Philip,		9	York
Burch,Richard,	1	3	Din.	Burn,Thomas,		1	K.Geo	Burt,Richard,	1	8	Eli.Cy.
Burch,Robert,	1		Henry	Burn,William,	1		Lun.	Burt,Thomas,			York
Burch,Vincent,			K.&Q.	Burner,Abraham,	1		Aug.	Burton,Ambrose,	1		Lin.
Burch,William,	1	8	K.&Q.	Burnes,James,	1		Bed.	Burton,Ann,	1	5	Caro.
Burch,William,	1		Mont.	Burnett,Alexander,	1		Berk.	Burton,Benjamin,	1		Acco.
Burcher,John,			York	Burnett,Charles,	1	1	K.Geo	Burton,Daniel,	1	5	Hen.
Burcher,Lucy,		1	York	Burnett,Elijah,	1		Bed.	Burton,Edmund,	1		Aug.
Burchet,Grieff,			Brun.	Burnett,James,	1	3	Buck.	Burton,George,	1		Aug.
Burchett,Drury,	1	20	Pr.Geo	Burnett,Jeremiah,	1	13	Lun.	Burton,Jacob,	1	1	Bed.
Burchett,William,	1	2	Pr.Geo	Burnett,Joseph,	1	10	Din.	Burton,James,	1		K.&Q.
Burchit,Edward,	1	24	Brun.	Burnett,Joseph,	1		Buck.	Burton,Jesse,	1	37	Camp.
Burchitt,***amin,	1		Lun.	Burnett,Joseph,	1		Bed.	Burton,John,	1	7	Hen.
Burchitt,Benjamin,	1		Lun.	Burnett,Reynold,	1		Berk.	Burton,John,	1		K.Geo.
Burchitt,John,	1		Lun.	Burnett,Richard,	1	6	Din.	Burton,John,	1		Mont.
Burd,Benjamin,	1	2	Henry	Burnett,Samuel,	1		Bed.	Burton,John,	1	16	Nor.
Burd,John,			Aug.	Burnett,Thomas,			Din.	Burton,John,	1	2	Buck.
Burden,John,	1		Bed.	Burnett,William,	1		Spots.	Burton,John,Sr.,	2	23	Hen.
Burdet,Humphrey,	1		Mont.	Burnette,William,	1		Camp.	Burton,John,Jr.,			Hen.
Burford,Milton,	1		Buck.	Burnham,John,	1		Eli.Cy	Burton,Martin,	2	19	Hen.
Burdge,Alexander,	1	1	Henry	Burnitt,Charles,	1		Henry	Burton,Nathaniel,	1	9	Buck.
Burdge,Fredrick,	1	10	Brun.	Burnitt,Jeremiah,	1	4	Henry	Burton,Rachal,	1	6	Acco.
Burdge,Nathaniel,	1		Brun.	Burnitt,Jeremiah,Jr.,			Henry	Burton,Robert,	1	9	Bed.
Burdge,Woody,	1	3	Henry	Burnley,James,	1	18	Loui.	Burton,Robert,	1	2	Buck.
Burdine,John,	1	2	Cul.	Burnley,William,			Hen.	Burton,Robert,Sr.,	1	2	Buck.
Burdine,Reginal,	3	3	Cul.	Burns,Alexander,	1		Henry	Burton,Samuel,	1		Lun.
Burdit,Tomkin,			Henry	Burns,Andrew,	1		Henry	Burton,Samuel,		1	K.Geo.
Burditt,Frederick,	1		Lin.	Burns,Charles,	1		Henry	Burton,Seth,	1		Henry
Burditt,Joseph Smith	1		Lin.	Burns,Dinnis,	1		Aug.	Burton,Thomas,	1	16	Acco.
Burditt,Joshua,	1		Lin.	Burns,Ignatius,	1		Lou.	Burton,Thomas,			Din.
Burge,Edward,	2		K.Geo	Burns,John,	1	1	Lou.	Burton,Thomas,Est.,		2	K.&Q.
Burge,James,	1	10	Pr.Geo	Burns,John,	1		Henry	Burton,Walters,	1	7	Gooch.
Burge,Joel,	1		Din.	Burns,John,	1		Aug.	Burton,William,	2	14	Hen.
Burge,John,	1	8	Pr.Geo	Burns,John,	2	4	K.Wm.	Burton,William,	1	1	York
Burge,William,	1	3	Pr.Geo	Burns,Nicholas,	1		Lou.	Burton,William,	1	1	Buck.
Burge,Wood,			Din.	Burns,Phillip,	1		Har.	Burton,William,	1		Buck.
Burges,James,	1		West'd	Burns,Richard,	1		Aug.	Burton,William,	1		Lou.
Burges,Moses,	1	1	K.Geo	Burns,Robert,	1	1	Aug.	Burton,William,	1	16	Ch.Cy.
Burges,William,	1	2	Eli.Cy	Burns,Samuel,	1	1	Henry	Burwell,James,			York
Burgess,William,	1		Aug.	Burns,Thomas,	1	6	Lou.	Burwell,John,	1	42	Din.
Burgess,E.,	1	2	Pr.Wm.	Burns,William,	1		Berk.	Burwell,Lewis,		23	Lun.
Burgess,Edward,	1	1	Bed.	Burnside,Andrew,			Lou.	Burwell,Col.Nath'l,	1	21	Lou.
Burgess,Garner,	1	7	Fau.	Burnside,John,	1	2	Aug.	Burwell,Nathaniel,	1	32	Pr.Wm.
Burges,Rev.Henry John	1	29	So'n.	Burnside,Robert,	3		Lin.	Burwell,Nathaniel,	1	59	K.Wm.
Burgess,Thomas,			Rock.	Burnsides,Walter,	1		Lin.	Burwell,Col.Nath'l,	3	23	York
Burgess,William,			Gooch.	Burr,John,	1		Aug.	Burwell,Nathaniel,	3	65	York
Burgess,William,			West'd	Burras,Edmund,	1		Bed.	Burwell,Nathaniel,	1	36	York
Burk,Alexander,			Cul.	Burras,John,	1		Bed.	Burwell,Nathaniel,	5	47	Ja.Cy.
Burk,Benjamin,	1		Wash.	Burrass,Michael,	1		Cul.	Buryfidge,John,	1		Aug.
Burk,Bob.,			Cul.	Burrell,James,	1		Cul.	Busbey,Matthew,	1		Har.
Burk,David,	1		Wash.	Burris,Bazil,	1		Pr.Wm.	Bush,Abraham,	1	5	Lou.
Burk,George,	1	1	Cul.	Burris,Jacob,	1		Henry	Bush,Absalam,	1		Cul.
Burk,George,	1		Lin.	Burris,Mary,		6	Pr.Wm.	Bush,Ambros,	1	5	Wash.
Burk,Henry,	1		Wash.	Burris,Thomas,	1	1	Fay.	Bush,Ambros,	1	8	Fay.
Burk,Jacob,	1		Berk.	Burron,Thomas,	1	8	Pr.Geo	Bush,Charles,	1		Fay.
Burk,John,	2	29	Caro.	Burrough,John,	1		Mont.	Bush,Francis,	1		Caro.
Burk,John,	1		Aug.	Burroughs,Thomas,	1		Fau.	Bush,John,	1		Cul.
Burk,John,	1		Fau.	Burros,Benjamin,	1		Spots.	Bush,Joseph,	1	4	Ja.Cy.
Burk,Luke,	1		Bed.	Burrow,Henry,	1	11	Din.	Bush,Joshua,	1	6	Cul.
Burk,Michael,	1		Cul.	Burrow,John,	1	12	Din.	Bush,Philip,	1	6	Fay.
Burk,Moses,	1	1	Cul.	Burrow,Martha,		6	Din.	Bush,Philip,	1	2	Wash.
Burk,Richard,	1	1	K.&Q.	Burrow,Philip,	1	2	Din.	Bush,Philip,	1		Bed.
Burk,Robert,	1		Cul.	Burrow,William,	1		Pr.Geo	Bush,Philip,Jr.,	1	8	Fay.
Burk,Samuel,			Cul.	Burrus,Charles,	1	13	Caro.	Bush,Sarah,		2	Fay.
Burk,Thomas,	1	5	K.&Q.	Burrus,Diana,	1	7	Caro.	Bush,Thomas,	1	7	Henry
Burk,Thomas,	1		Mont.	Burrus,John,	1		Caro.	Bush,William,	1	7	Ja.Cy.
Burk,Thomas,	3	3	Mont.	Burrus,Samuel,	2	13	Caro.	Bush,William,	1		Caro.
Burk,Thomas,Jr.,	1		Mont.	Burrus,Thomas,	1		Cul.	Bush,William,	1		Fay.
Burk,William,	1		Cul.	Burrus,William,	1	10	Caro.	Bush,William,	1	3	Fay.
Burk,William,	2		Aug.	Burrwell,Mrs.Mary,	1	44	Pr.Wm.	Bush,William,	1		Lun.
Burk,William,	1	2	K.Wm.	Burson,Benjamin,			Lou.	Bush,William,Sr.,	1		Lun.
Burk,William,	3		Lin.	Burson,George,	1		Lou.	Bush,William,Jr.,	1		Lun.
Burket,Ebinezer,	1	2	Bot.	Burson,James,	1		Lou.	Bushell,John,Sr.,	1		Eli.Cy.
Burkett,Frederick,	1		Aug.	Burson,Jonathon,	1		Lou.	Bushell,John,Jr.,	1		Eli.Cy.
Burkett,Michael,	1	1	Berk.	Burson,Joseph,	1		Lou.	Buskin,Hope,		1	So'n.
Burks,Isham,	1		Bot.	Burt,Philip,			York	Buskirk,Elizabeth,			Lou.
								Bussel,William,	1	4	West'd.

Name			Place
Bussell,George,	1	1	Pr.Wm.
Bustard,John,	1		Mont.
Bustard,William,Sr.,	1	6	Mont.
Buster,David,	1		Mont.
Buster,John,Jr.,	1		Mont.
Butcher,A.,	1	3	Pr.Wm.
Butcher,John,	1	1	Lou.
Butcher,Michael,	1		Hen.
Butcher,Nicholas,	1		Har.
Butcher,Richard,	1		Berk.
Butcher,Samuel,	2		Lin.
Butcher,Samuel,	1		Lou.
Butcher,Susannah,			Lou.
Butcher,William,	1		Lou.
Butler,Ann,		7	Din.
Butler,Beckwith,	1	46	West'd
Butler,Charles,			Pr.Wm
Butler,Christopher,	1	3	West'd
Butler,Dorcas,		7	West'd
Butler,Edward,	1	1	Din.
Butler,George,	1	1	Din.
Butler,Griffin,	1		K.Geo.
Butler,Henry,	1	1	Din.
Butler,Isaac,	1	8	K.Wm.
Butler,Isaac,	1		Din.
Butler,James,	2	4	Din.
Butler,James,Jr.,	1	2	Din.
Butler,Jessee,			Pr.Geo
Butler,John,	1		Cul.
Butler,John,	1	5	Caro.
Butler,John,	1	2	Cul.
Butler,John,	1	4	Din.
Butler,John,			Din.
Butler,John,			Henry
Butler,John,	1	1	K.Geo
Butler,John,	1	1	Din.
Butler,John,	2	8	West'd
Butler,John,	1	5	West'd
Butler,John,	1		Pr.Wm
Butler,John,	1	2	Berk.
Butler,John,Sr.,	1	2	Cul.
Butler,Joseph,	1	9	Lou.
Butler,Joseph,			Lou.
Butler,Joseph,			Lou.
Butler,Joseph,	1	2	Din.
Butler,Joseph,	1	1	Din.
Butler,Joseph,	1	2	Din.
Butler,Joseph,	2	6	Pr.Wm
Butler,Joseph,	1		Fau.
Butler,Joshua,			Fau.
Butler,Josias,	1	1	K.Wm.
Butler,Lawrence,	1	1	Pr.Wm
Butler,Micajah,	1	16	K.Wm.
Butler,Nathan,			Loui.
Butler,Nathaniel,	2	1	West'd
Butler,Nathaniel,	1		West'd
Butler,Peggy,		2	West'd
Butler,Percival,	1	4	Fay.
Butler,Reubin,	1	15	K.Wm.
Butler,Samuel,	1		Fau.
Butler,Sarah,			Pr.Geo
Butler,Spencer,	1		Fau.
Butler,Stephen,	1	1	Din.
Butler,Thomas,	1	3	Brun.
Butler,Thomas,	1	5	Ch.Cy
Butler,Thomas,	1	2	Cul.
Butler,Thomas,	1	6	Din.
Butler,Thomas,	1	27	K.Wm.
Butler,Thomas,	1		Camp.
Butler,Thomas,Sr.,	1	2	West'd
Butler,Thomas,Jr.,	1		West'd
Butler,Wallace,	1	6	Din.
Butler,William,	1		West'd
Butler,William,	1	1	Bed.
Butler,William,	1	5	So'n.
Butler,William,	1		Mont.

Name			Place
Butler,William,			Brun.
Butler,William,	1		Cul.
Butler,William,	1		Cul.
Butler,William,	1		Cul.
Butler,William,	2		Lin.
Butler,William,	1		Henry
Butler,William,			Cul.
Butler,William,	1		Cul.
Butridge,John,			K.Geo
Butt.Archibald,	1		Berk.
Butt,Bazell,	1		Berk.
Butt,Isaac,	1		Berk.
Butt,John,	1		Berk.
Butt,Joseph,	1		Berk.
Butt,Richard,	1		Berk.
Butterworth,Charles,	1	3	Pr.Geo
Butterworth,Nicholas,	1		Din.
Button,Harman,	1		Fau.
Button,Harman,	1	2	Cul.
Button,Jacob,	1		Fau.
Button,John,	1	3	Cul.
Button,William,	1		Cul.
Butts,Benjamin,	1	14	So'n.
Butts,Daniel,		8	So'n.
Butts,James,	1	5	So'n.
Butts,Thomas,	1	3	So'n.
Butts,Thomas C.,	1	4	So'n.
Butts,William,	1	10	So'n.
Buxton,Joice,		5	Buck.
Buzzard,John,	1		Har.
Buzzard,Phillip,	1		Henry
Buzzard,Rudolph,	1		Har.
Byars,Cowroa,	2		Berk.
Byars,Elizabeth,		7	Loui.
Byars,James,	1		Loui.
Byby,Allen,			Bot.
Byerly,Michael,	1		Berk.
Byers,John,	1		Berk.
Byers,William,	1	9	Rock.
Bylee,John,	1		Bot.
Byne,Edmond,	1	18	K.&q.
Byne,John,	1	9	K.&q.
Bynum,Cordall N.,	1		So'n.
Byrom,William,	1	8	Buck.
Byrn,J.,	1	3	Pr.Wm.
Byrn,James,	1		Mont.
Byrn,John,			Lou.
Byrn,Terrence,	1		Lou.
Byrn,William,	1	1	Pr.Wm.
Byrd,Abraham,	1		Henry
Byrd,Ambrose,	1		Din.
Byrd,Arthur,	1	1	So'n.
Byrd,George,	1		Mont.
Byrd,James,	1		So'n.
Byrd,John,	1	33	Ch.Cy
Byrd,John,	1		Aug.
Byrd,Mary,		66	Ch.Cy
Byrd,Moses,	1		So'n.
Byrd,Otway,	1	18	Ch.Cy
Byrd,Richard,	1		Mont.
Byrd,Samuel,	1		Mont.
Byrd,William,	1		Mont.
Bywaters,Robert,	1	3	Cul.
Bywaters,Thomas,			Cul.
Bywaters,Thomas,Jr.,	1		Cul.
Cabell,Col.Joseph,	4	73	Buck.
Cabell,John,	1	23	Buck.
Cad,Charles,	1	2	Fay.
Caddean,Richard,	2	1	West'd
Caddel,Samuel,	1		Rock.
Caffee,James,			Mont.
Caffee,John,	1		Mont.
Caffee,William,Sr.,	2	2	Mont.
Caffee,William,Jr.,			Mont.

Name			Place
Caffell,Phillips,	1	2	Har.
Caffrey,John,	1	2	Camp.
Caffrey,John,	1	2	Camp.
Cahod,John,	1		Pr.Wm.
Caide,Major,	2		Har.
Cail,David,	1		Aug.
Cain,David,	1		Wash.
Cain,Jesse,	1		Wash.
Cain,Richard,			Aug.
Cain,William,	2	5	Pr.Geo.
Cairns,Michael,	1		Bot.
Cairns,Michael,	1		Bot.
Calder,Thomas,	1	3	Hen.
Caldwell,Andrew,	1		Berk.
Caldwell,David,	1	2	Lin.
Caldwel,Robert,	1		Bot.
Caldwell,George,	1	2	Rock.
Caldwell,Hugh,	1		Bot.
Caldwell,James,	3		Berk.
Caldwell,John,	3		Camp.
Caldwell,John,	1		Bot.
Caldwell,John,	2	1	Aug.
Caldwell,John,	2	2	Lin.
Caldwell,Joseph,	1		Rock.
Caldwell,Joseph,	1		Mont.
Caldwell,Moses,			Lou.
Caldwell,Oliver,	1		Camp.
Caldwell,Robert,			Lin.
Caldwell,William,			Bot.
Caldwell,William,	1		Mont.
Caldwill,Joseph,	2	3	Lou.
Cale,David,	1	1	Aug.
Cale,Jacob,	1	1	Aug.
Cale,Peter,	1		Aug.
Caleb,Benjamin,	1	4	Pr.Geo.
Calhoon,William,	1		Mont.
Calhoon,Robert,	1		Mont.
Call,Charles,			Buck.
Carle,Daniel,		12	Brun.
Call,Daniel,	3	17	Din.
Call,Daniel,Jr.,			Lin.
Call,Isaac,	1		K.Geo.
Call,William,	2	3	Pr.Geo.
Callachan,Dinnis,	1	1	Aug.
Callahan,Edward,	1		Wash.
Callaway,Caleb,	1	3	Camp.
Callaway,Charles,	1	6	Bed.
Callaway,Edward,	2	3	Fay.
Callaway,Flanders,	1	1	Fay.
Callaway,James,		2	Camp.
Callaway,John,	1	16	Camp.
Callaway,Micage,	1		Fay.
Callaway,Susannah,		4	Bed.
Callaway,William,	1	15	Bed.
Caller,George,	1		Aug.
Calliham,John,	1	14	Lun.
Calliham,Nicholas,	1		Lun.
Calliham,William,			Spots.
Callis,Emanuel,	1		Lun.
Callis,Emanuel,	1		Lun.
Callis,Henry,	1		Lun.
Callis,James,	1	8	Lun.
Callis,William,	1		Loui.
Callison,James,	1		Aug.
Calloway,Earley,	1	10	Henry
Calloway,James,		9	Henry
Calor,Andrew,			Lou.
Calor,Jacob,	1		Lou.
Calvert,Christopher	1	16	So'n.
Calvert,Elijah,	1		Pr.Wm.
Calvert,Francis,			Pr.Wm.
Calvert,George,	3	5	Cul.
Calvert,James,	1		Bot.
Calvert,John,	1	2	Pr.Wm.
Calvert,John,	1	8	Pr.Wm.
Calvert,L.,	1		Pr.Wm.

Name			County
Calvert,Lydia,			Pr.Wm.
Calvert,Mary,			Cul.
Calvert,Richard,			Pr.Wm.
Calvert,Robert,	3		Bot.
Calvert,Samuel,	1	1	Cul.
Calvert,Sarah,	2	3	Pr.Wm.
Calvert,William,	1	15	Pr.Geo
Calvin,Charles,	1		Fau.
Caldwell,David,	1		Aug.
Caldwell,John,	1		Aug.
Caldwell,Robert,	1		Aug.
Caldwell,William,	1	4	Aug.
Cambern,Leonard,			Lou.
Camell,William,	1		Din.
Cameron,Angus,	1		Fau.
Cameron,Charles,	1		Aug.
Cammeron,John,	1	1	Hen.
Cammeron,Susannah,			Hen.
Cammock,Francis,	1	4	Spots
Cammock,George,	1	9	Spots
Cammock,Henry,	1	1	Spots
Cammock,John,	1	2	Spots
Camp,Henry,	1	6	Cul.
Camp,John,	2	11	Cul.
Camp,Mary,		12	Ja.Cy
Camp,Reuben,	1		Lin.
Camp,Sarah,		7	Ja.Cy
Camp,Thomas,	1	12	Cul.
Camp,William,	1	2	Cul.
Camp,William,	1	1	K.Wm.
Campbell,Alexander	3	1	Rock.
Campbell,Alexander,	1		Fay.
Campbell,Alexander	1	4	K.&Q
Campbell,Alexander,	1		Pr.Wm.
Campbell,Allen,			Fay.
Campbell,Andrew,	1		Aug.
Campbell,Andrew,	1		Berk.
Campbell,Archibald,	1		Fay.
Campbell,Archibald,	1	3	West.
Campbell,Archibald,	1	8	Camp.
Campbell,Arthur,	2		Fay.
Campbell,Charles,	1	2	Rock.
Campbell,Charles,	1	1	Rock.
Campbell,Charles,	1	1	Fay.
Campbell,Charles,	1	2	Lin.
Campbell,Collen,		6	Lou.
Campbell,Colin,	1	2	Brun.
Campbell,Colin,			Pr.Wm.
Campbell,Colin,	1	4	Pr.Wm.
Campbell,Cornelius,	1		Fau.
Campbell,Daniel,	2		Fay.
Campbell,David,	1		Berk.
Campbell,Duncan,	1	1	Berk.
Campbell,Ezekiel,	1		Bot.
Campbell,Elias,	2	8	Cul.
Campbell,Elias,Jr.,	1		Cul.
Campbell,George,	1		Rock.
Campbell,George,	1		Rock.
Campbell,George,	1		Pr.Wm.
Campbell,George,	1		Aug.
Campbell,Henry,	2		Rock.
Campbell,Hugh,	1		Aug.
Campbell,Hugh,	1		Fay.
Campbell,Rev.Isaac,	1	11	Pr.Wm.
Campbell,Isaac,			Mont.
Campbell,Jacob,		2	Wash.
Campbell,James,	1		Cul.
Campbell,James,	1		Aug.
Campbell,James,	1	6	Camp.
Campbell,James,	1	2	K.&Q
Campbell,James,	1		Camp.
Campbell,James,	1	6	Camp.
Campbell,James,	1	7	Mont.
Campbell,James,	1	1	Berk.
Campbell,James,	1	2	Wash.
Campbell,Joanne,		1	Fay.
Campbell,John,	1		Camp.
Campbell,John,			Bed.
Campbell,John,	1	3	Bed.
Campbell,John,	1	2	York
Campbell,John,	1		Cul.
Campbell,John,			Aug.
Campbell,John,			Aug.
Campbell,John,	1	2	Aug.
Campbell,John,	1		Lou.
Campbell,John,Jr.,	2		Aug.
Campbell,John,	1		Rock.
Campbell,John,			Rock.
Campbell,Joseph,Sr.,	1		Rock.
Campbell,Joseph,Jr.,	1		Rock.
Campbell,Joseph,	1		Lin.
Campbell,Joseph,	1		Lin.
Campbell,Joseph,	1		Cul.
Campbell,Joseph,	1		Bed.
Campbell,Joseph,	1	14	Caro.
Campbell,Josias,			Bed.
Campbell,Mary,	1	1	Aug.
Campbell,Mary,			Brun.
Campbell,Owen,	1	4	Cul.
Campbell,Patrick,	2	1	Mont.
Campbell,Patrick,	1		Fay.
Campbell,Priscilla,		1	Eli.Cy
Campbell,Rebecca,		2	Bed.
Campbell,Robert,Sr.,	1	1	Aug.
Campbell,Robert,	1		Berk.
Campbell,Robert,	1		Wash.
Campbell,Robert,	1	1	Aug.
Campbell,Robert,	1		Fay.
Campbell,Samuel,	1	4	Bed.
Campbell,Sarah,		18	K.&Q
Campbell,Thomas,	1	2	Bed.
Campbell,Whitaker,	1	9	K.&Q
Campbell,William,	1	2	Bed.
Campbell,William,	1	18	K.&Q
Campbell,William,	1	4	K.&Q
Campbell,William,	1		Bot.
Campbell,William,	1	2	Bot.
Campbel,William,		3	Bot.
Campbell,William,	1	1	Aug.
Campbell,William,	2		Berk.
Campbell,William,	1	2	Fay.
Campbell,William,	3		Fay.
Campbell,William,	1		Fay.
Campbell,William,			Fay.
Campbell,William,	1		Lin.
Campbell,William,	1		Camp.
Campbell,William,	1		Camp.
Camper,John,	1	1	Lin.
Camper,Tilmon,	1		Fay.
Canaday,Daniel,	1	1	Cul.
Canaday,James,	1		Cul.
Canaday,Leroy,	1	3	Cul.
Canaday,Thomas,	1	1	Cul.
Canady,Daniel,	1	1	Cul.
Canby,Samuel,	1		Lou.
Candler,James,	1		Camp.
Candler,James,	1		Camp.
Candler,John,	1		Camp.
Candler,John,	1		Camp.
Candler,William,	1	1	Bed.
Caner,Matthew,	1		Fau.
Canidy,Philip,	1		Mont.
Cannaday,James,			Henry
Cannaday,John,			Henry
Cannaday,Whorton,	1		Cul.
Cannaday,William,	1		Caro.
Cannaday,William,	1		Henry
Cannaday,James,	1		Ja.Cy
Cannady,William,	1		Cul.
Cannifax,William,	1		Camp.
Cannon,Ellis,	1		Cul.
Cannon,Henry,	1		Fau.
Cannon,J.,	1	9	Pr.Wm.
Cannon,Jesse,			Cul.
Cannon,John,	1		Caro.
Cannon,John,	1	1	York
Cannon,John,	1		Cul.
Cannon,John,	1		Cul.
Cannon,John,			Buck.
Cannon,Joseph,	1		Caro.
Cannon,Mary,			Caro.
Cannon,William,	1		Loui.
Cannon,William,	1	45	Buck.
Canterberry,Samuel,	1		Mont.
Cantrell,Sarah,			Bed.
Cantrell,Stephen,			Wash.
Cantrill,Adam,	1		Henry
Cantwell,John,	1	3	Fau.
Cantwell,John,			Henry
Cap,Rudolph,			Berk.
Capells,William,			Din.
Caple,William,	1		Nor.
Capiday,Michael,			Fay.
Caplenor,Jacob,	1		Har.
Caplinger,John,	1		Har.
Card,Capt.Edmund,	1	12	Gooch.
Carden,Jesse,	1		Gooch.
Carden,Reubin,	1	1	Gooch.
Cardwell,Obedience,		5	Din.
Cardwell,Richard,	1	2	K.&Q
Cardwell,William,	1	2	Ja.Cy.
Carey,Abraham,	1		Wash.
Carey,Miles,	2	14	So'n.
Carey,Samuel,	1		Cul.
Carlile,David,	1	1	Lou.
Carlile,Robert,Jr.,	1		Aug.
Carlin,Daniel,	3	3	Henry
Carlin,Thomas,	2	1	Henry
Carlisle,George,	1		Aug.
Carlisle,John,	1	1	Aug.
Carlisle,John,	1	2	Aug.
Carlisle,Robert,	1	2	Aug.
Carlock,Catharine,			Rock.
Carlock,Catharine,			Rock.
Carlock,Hunkrist,	1		Aug.
Carlton,William,			Bot.
Carlton,Christ'r,Sr	1	2	K.&Q
Carlton,Christopher,	1		K.&Q
Carlton,Daniel,	1		K.&Q
Carlton,Harry,		5	K.&Q
Carlton,Henry,	1	5	K.&Q
Carlton,Humphrey,			K.&Q
Carlton,Isaac,	1	2	K.&Q
Carlton,James,	2	7	K.&Q
Carlton,Joel,	1	1	K.&Q
Carlton,John,	1	1	K.&Q
Carlton,John,	1	5	K.&Q
Carlton,Phillip,	1	1	K.&Q
Carlton,Richard,	1	10	K.&Q
Carlton,Robert,	1	12	K.&Q
Carlton,Robert,Jr.,	1	3	K.&Q
Carlton,Thomas,	1	1	K.&Q
Carlton,Thomas,	1	7	K.&Q
Carlton,Thomas,	1	1	K.&Q
Carlton,William,	1	2	K.&Q
Carmack,Aquila,	1		Wash.
Carmack,Cornelius,	1		Wash.
Carmack,Julius,Sr.,	1		Wash.
Carmack,Julius,Jr.,	1		Wash.
Carmack,William,	1		Wash.
Carmickle,Peter,	1		Berk.
Carmine,John,	1		Acco.
Carmon,John,	2	1	Cul.
Carn,Abraham,	1		Lou.
Carnan,Susanna,		8	Lou.
Carnaham,Adam,	1		Lou.
Carnaham,John,	1		Berk.
Carnell,Moses,	1		Caro.

Name			County	Name			County	Name			County
Carnall,Patrick,	1		Caro.	Carson,David,	1		Wash.	Carter,Joseph,	1	1	Camp.
Carnall,William,	1	6	Caro.	Carson,Isaac,	1	1	Aug.	Carter,Joseph,	1		Wash.
Carner,John,	1		Buck.	Carson,James,	1		Aug.	Carter,Joseph,	2	2	Buck.
Carner,William,			Buck.	Carson,James,	1	1	Camp.	Carter,Josiah,	1	6	Henry
Carnes,Jacob,			Bot.	Carson,John,	2		Wash.	Carter,Landon,		10	Cul.
Carnes,Muhael,	1		Bed.	Carson,John,	1		Rock.	Carter,Landon,		41	Fau.
Carney,John,	1		Bot.	Carson,John,	1		Camp.	Carter,London,	2	62	K.Geo.
Carnot,David,	1		Mont.	Carson,Robert,	1		Rock.	Carter,Landon,	1	120	Pr.Wm.
Carns,Peter,	1		Har.	Carson,Robert,	1		Wash.	Carter,Landon,		24	Lou.
Carpenter,Adam,	1		Lin.	Carson,Samuel,	1		Aug.	Carter,Lunsford,	1		Cul.
Carpenter,Andrew,	1	13	Cul.	Carson,Simon,	1		Aug.	Carter,Mary,	1	4	Bed.
Carpenter,Charles,	2	13	Nor.	Carson,Thomas,	1		Aug.	Carter,Mary,		1	West'd.
Carpenter,Cornelious,	1	1	Cul.	Carson,Thomas,	1		Camp.	Carter,Morris,			Lou.
Carpenter,Conrod,	1		Lin.	Carswell,Andrew,	1		Wash.	Carter,Morris,			Fay.
Carpenter,Elizabeth,		2	Lin.	Carswell,James,	1		Wash.	Carter,N.,	1		Pr.Wm.
Carpenter,George,	1		Spots.	Cartfielder,Jacob,	1		Mont.	Carter,Obadiah,	1		Caro.
Carpenter,Jacob,	1		Har.	Carstarphen,John,	1	8	So'n.	Carter,Parthena,		1	Caro.
Carpenter,John,	1	9	Cul.	Qarter,Aleck,	1		Fau.	Carter,Peter,	1		Caro.
Carpenter,John,Jr.,			Cul.	Carter,Ann,		8	Spots.	Carter,Peter,	1	2	Fau.
Carpenter,John,	1	5	Nor.	Carter,Anne,			York	Carter,Peter,	3	7	Lou.
Carpenter,John,	1	1	K.Wm.	Carter,Bailey,	1		Henry	Carter,R.,	1	38	Pr.Wm.
Carpenter,John,	1		West'd	Carter,Banes,	1		Henry	Carter,Robert,	1	2	Berk.
Carpentar,John,	1	1	Din.	Carter,Benjamin,	1	5	Ch.Cy	Carter,Robert,	1		West'd.
Carpenter,John,	1	2	Loui.	Carter,Benjamin,	1	4	Caro.	Carter,Robert,	2	256	West'd.
Carpenter,Jonathan,	1	2	Spots.	Carter,Burwell,			Din.	Carter,Robert,	2	39	Lou.
Carpenter,Michael,	2	9	Cul.	Carter,Charles,		193	Caro.	Carter,Robert,W.,		15	K.&Q.
Carpenter,Michael,Jr.,	1		Cul.	Carter,Charles	1	59	Pr.Geo	Carter,Robert Worm.	1	20	York
Carpenter,Nathaniel,	1		Caro.	Carter,Charles,	5	188	Fau.	Carter,Sally,			Caro.
Carpenter,Phillip,	1		Loui.	Carter,Charles,	2		Wash.	Carter,Shearwood,	1	6	Hen.
Carpenter,Samuel,	1	1	Cul.	Carter,Charles,			Ch.Cy	Carter,Stephen,	1		Berk.
Carpenter,William,	2	14	Cul.	Carter,Charles,	2	191	Ch.Cy	Carter,Thomas,	1		Wash.
Carper,Jacob,	1	4	Bot.	Carter,Charles,Jr.,	1	2	Ch.Cy	Carter,William,	1	8	Din.
Carper,Nicholass,	1		Bot.	Carter,Charles,		21	West'd	Carter,William,Jr.,	1	3	Din.
Carr,Barbara,	1	25	Loui.	Carter,Edward,	1	2	Caro.	Carter,William,	2		Caro.
Carr,Conrod,	1		Har.	Carter,Edward,	1		Gooch.	Carter,William,	1		Cul.
Carr,Garland,	1	3	Loui.	Carter,Edward,	1	6	Lou.	Carter,William,		3	Cul.
Carr,Henry,Sr.,	3		Har.	Carter,Elijah,	1	1	Spots.	Carter,William,	1		Ch.Cy.
Carr,Henry,Jr.,	1		Har.	Carter,Elizabeth,		5	Spots.	Carter,William,	1		Cul.
Carr,James,	1		Har.	Carter,Elizabeth,		6	Ch.Cy	Carter,William,	1	15	Spots.
Carr,James,	1		Berk.	Carter,George,	1	2	Caro.	Carter,William,	1		Pr.Wm.
Carr,James,	1		Berk.	Carter,George,	1	7	Henry	Carter,William,	2	11	Hen.
Carr,James,	1		Lin.	Carter,George,	1	7	Mont.	Carter,William,			Eli.Cy.
Carr,John,			Har.	Carter,George,	1	11	Fau.	Carter,William,	1		Lou.
Carr,John,	1		Mont.	Carter,George,	1	5	Buck.	Carter,Wormley,	1	10	Lou.
Carr,John,	2		Lin.	Carter,George,	1		Buck.	Carter,Zachry,	1	2	Caro.
Carr,John,Sr.,	2		Lou.	Carter,George,	1	20	Lou.	Cartmel,John,	1		Bot.
Carr,Martha,		24	Gooch.	Carter,George,Est.,		8	Lou.	Cartmil,Henry,	2		Bot.
Carr,Martha,		4	Loui.	Carter,Griffin,	1	2	Caro.	Cartmill,James,	1		Mont.
Carr,Michael,	1		Har.	Carter,Giles,	3	11	Pr.Wm	Cartmill,John,	2		Fay.
Carr,Nathaniel,	1		Lou.	Carter,Giles,	1	8	Hen.	Cartmill,John,	1		Aug.
Carr,Peter Carter,	1	5	Lou.	Carter,Harriss,	1		Din.	Cartmill,Samuel,	1		Aug.
Carr,Robert,	1		So'n.	Carter,Jack,	1		Hen.	Cartmill,Thomas,	1		Aug.
Carr,Thomas,	1		Mont.	Carter,Jacob,	1		Hen.	Cartwright,Robert,	1	1	Berk.
Carr,Titus,	1	13	So'n.	Carter,James,		7	Caro.	Caruthers,Anne,		2	Rock.
Carr,Walter,	1	11	Fay.	Carter,James,	1	1	K.Geo	Caruthers,David,	1		Aug.
Carr,William,	1	14	Pr.Wm.	Carter,James,	1		Lou.	Caruthers,James,	1		Aug.
Carr,William,Sr.,	1		Har.	Carter,Rev.Jesse,	1	15	K.&Q.	Caruthers,James,	1		Rock.
Carr,William,	1		Har.	Carter,John,	1	14	Din.	Caruthers,James,Jr.,	1		Aug.
Carrel,Booker,	1		Gooch.	Carter,John,	1		Caro.	Caruthers,John,	1	2	Rock.
Carrell,Elizabeth,		3	Fau.	Carter,John,	1		Wash.	Caruthers,William,	1		Rock.
Carrel,Jesse,	1	7	So'n.	Carter,John,	1		Ch.Cy	Carver,Joseph,			K.Geo.
Carrel,John,	1	1	Gooch.	Carter,John,	1	3	K.Wm.	Carver,Mary,			K.Geo.
Carrell,Peter,	1		Aug.	Carter,John,			Buck.	Carver,Richard,	1		Buck.
Carrell,Priscilla,			So'n.	Carter,John,			Buck.	Carty,James,	1		Berk.
Carrel,Roger,	1		Gooch.	Carter,John,Est.,	1	18	West'd	Cary,Archibald,Est.,	1	21	Buck.
Carrel,William,	1		Gooch.	Carter,John,	1	20	K.&Q.	Cary,Archibald,		19	Buck.
Carrengton,William,			Lou.	Carter,Capt.John,Sr.	3	32	Spots.	Cary,Edward,	1	9	K.Wm.
Carriel,Jesse,			Bed.	Carter,Capt.John,Jr.	1	9	Spots.	Cary,John,	1		Spots.
Carington,William,	1		Fay.	Carter,John,	1		Spots.	Cary,John,	1	20	Eli.Cy.
Carrigan,Peter,	1		Berk.	Carter,John,			Pr.Wm.	Cary,Obed,	1	2	Nor.
Carrol,Berry,	1		K.&Q.	Carter,John,	4	89	Lou.	Cary,Robert,	1	3	Buck.
Carroll,Cornelius,	1		Henry	Carter,John,			Lou.	Cary,Robert,	2	16	Buck.
Carroll,Dempsey,	1	2	Lou.	Carter,John,	1	5	Hen.	Cary,William,	1	7	Nor.
Carrol,John,	1		West'd	Carter,John,	1	8	Hen.	Cary,William,	1	7	York
Carroll,Rebecca,	1	4	Lou.	Carter,John,	1	2	Eli.Cy	Cary,Wilson,W.,Est.,	1	47	K.&Q.
Carroll,William,	1	1	Lou.	Carter,Joseph,	1	4	Caro.	Casey,Daniel,	1		Henry

Name			County
Casey,James,	1		Bed.
Casey,James,	1		Lin.
Casey,John,	2		Lin.
Casey,Peter,	1	2	Har.
Casey,Robert,	1		York
Casey,William,	1		Lin.
Cash,Archdell,	2		K.Geo.
Cash,James,	1		K.Geo.
Cash,James,	2		Lou.
Cash,John,estate		5	K.Geo.
Cash,Patrick,	1		Mont.
Cash,Peter,			Lou.
Cash,Sarah,		3	K.Geo.
Cashaday,James,	1		Rock.
Cashaday,Michael,	1		Rock.
Cashaday,Peter,	1		Rock.
Cashaday,Simon,	2		Mont.
Cashady,Thomas,	1		Bot.
Cashman, * * *			Har.
Cashman,Matthew,	1		Berk.
Caskas,Michael,	1		Berk.
Casner,Gasper,	1		Fay.
Casner,John,	1		Har.
Cason,Edward,	1		Spots.
Cason,John,	1		Spots.
Cason,Susanna,		3	Spots.
Cason,William,	1	5	Spots.
Cason,William,Jr.,	1		Spots.
Cason,William,			Loui.
Cassaday,William,	1		York
Cassell,John,	1	5	Caro.
Cassells,Mrs.			Din.
Cassells,Rebecca,		1	Din.
Cassells,Sarah,		1	Din.
Cassells,William,		1	Din.
Cassey,Patrick,	1		Acco.
Castle,Hawkins,	1		Spots.
Castle,Jacob,	1		Wash.
Caswell,John,	1		Lin.
Cate,Absalom,	1	4	Cul.
Cate,James,	2	10	Pr.Geo
Catlin,Thomas,			Hen.
Catlett,George,	2	4	Caro.
Catlett,John,	2	18	Caro.
Catlett,John,	1	7	Fau.
Catlett,John,	1	16	K.Wm.
Catlett,Reuben,	1	11	Caro.
Catlett,William,	1		Berk.
Catlive,Charles,	1		Lin.
Cato,John,	1	3	Brun.
Catterman,Daniel,	3		Har.
Cattles,Uraham,	1		York.
Caudrey,John,	1		Lin.
Cauhorn,Samuel,	1		Lin.
Cawood,Thomas,	1		Pr.Wm
Cawthon,Gideon,	1	10	Gooch.
Cayton,Jacob,	1		Henry
Cave,Benjamin,	1	10	Cul.
Cave,David,	1	5	Cul.
Cave,David,	1	3	Cul.
Cave,John,	1	12	Cul.
Cave,John,	2	11	Fay.
Cave,William,	2	8	Fay.
Cave,William,Jr.,	1		Fay.
Cavender,George,	1	6	Wash.
Cavender,John,	1		West.
Cavender,Thomas,		5	West.
Cavender,Williams,	1		Lin.
Cavenough,William,	1		Bed.
Cavenough,William,	1		Mont.
Cavan,William,			Lou.
Caven,William,	1		Lou.
Cavens,John,	2	1	Lou.
Cavens,Joseph,			Lou.
Cavan,Patrick,	2	3	Lou.
Cavens,Thomas,	1	1	Lou.
Cavert,Bergen,	1		Berk.
Caves,Thomas,	1		Pr.Wm
Cavert,Richard,	1		Mont.
Cavin,Edward,	1	1	Fay.
Cavin,Thomas,	1	1	Fay.
Cavins,Edward,	1		Lou.
Caviness,Charles,	1		Lun.
Caviness,John,	2	1	Lun.
Cealey,Merritt,	1	1	Brun.
Cealy,William,	1	2	Brun.
Cecil,John,	1	1	Mont.
Cecil,Samuel,	1	2	Mont.
Ceecil,Saul,	1		Mont.
Cecil,Thomas,	1		Mont.
Cecil,William,	1	2	Mont.
Ceely,William,	1	1	Eli.Cy
Certain,Isaac,	1		Lin.
Certain,Joel,	1		Mont.
Certain,John,	1		Mont.
Certain,John,	1		Mont.
Chaddux,Charles,	1	1	Fau.
Chadwell,David,	1	12	Henry
Chadwell,John,	1		Fau.
Chadwell,William,	1	6	K.Geo
Chaffen,Simon,	1		Bed.
Chalfin,Solomon,	1		Berk.
Chalfant,Robert,	1		Lou.
Chamberlain,John,	1		Lou.
Chamblin,William,	1		Lou.
Chamberlayne,Byrd,	1	21	K.Wm.
Chamberlayne,EdwardP.	1	12	K.Wm.
Chamberlayne,Mary,	1	43	Buck.
Chamberlayne,Thomas,	2	13	K.Wm.
Chamberlayne,William,	2	14	K.Wm.
Chambers,Edmunds,			Acco.
Chambers,Edward,	1	5	Lun.
Chambers,Capt.John,	1	7	Buck.
Chambers,John,Sr.,	2	13	Buck.
Chambers,John,Jr.,	1	2	Buck.
Chambers,John,	1		Rock.
Chambers,John,			Din.
Chambers,Josias,	1	5	Buck.
Chambers,Major,	1	2	Acco.
Chambers,Mary,			Henry
Chambers,Thomas,	1	43	Lun.
Chambers,Thoroughgood	1		Lun.
Chambers,William,	1	17	Lun.
Chambers,William.	1		Lou.
Chambers,William,Sr.,	1	11	Buck.
Chambers,William,	1	3	Buck.
Chambers,William,	1		Henry
Chambless,David	1		Brun.
Chambless,Henry,	2	9	Brun.
Chamblin,Jesse,	1		Bot.
Champ,Robert,			Fay.
Champ,Thomas,	2		Fay.
Champ,William,	1	50	Cul.
Champion,James,	1		Berk.
Champion,John,	3		Berk.
Chapman,George,	1		Berk.
Chapman,Edward,	1	2	Berk.
Champs,John,	1		Har.
Champs,William,	1		Har.
Champs,William,	1		Har.
Chanby,William,	1		Rock.
Chancellor,Robert,	1		Gooch.
Chancellor,Thomas,	1		Gooch.
Chancellor,Thomas,	1	6	West.
Chancey,Elizabeth,		8	Ja.Cy
Chancey,William,	1	12	Cha.C
Chandler,Brittain,	1	1	Din.
Chandler,Elizabeth,		3	Acco.
Chandler,Elizabeth,		5	K.Wm.
Chandler,Fawkes,	1	25	K.Geo
Chandler,George,	1		Din.
Chandler,Hythan,	1		Acco.
Chandler,Isaac,			Buck.
Chandler,John,	1		Din.
Chandler,John,	1	9	Spots.
Chandler,John,	1	1	Henry
Chandler,John,	1		Caro.
Chandler,Levie,	1		Acco.
Chandler,Mitchell,		3	Acco.
Chandler,Patience,		3	Acco.
Chandler,Robert,	1	13	Caro.
Chandler,Sarah,	1		Acco.
Chandler,Timothy,	1		Caro.
Chandler,Thomas,	1		Caro.
Chandler,Thomas,	1	3	West.
Chandler,Thomas,	1	4	Din.
Chandler,Torobable,	1	3	Acco.
Chandler,William,	1		Din.
Chandler,William,	1	13	K.Wm.
Channel,Joseph,	1		Har.
Channel,Joseph,	1		Mont.
Channel,Ralph,	2		So'n
Channellor,Cooper,	1		Pr.Wm.
Channellor,John,			Pr.Wm.
Channellor,John,	3	14	Pr.Wm.
Channellor,Stephen,			Pr.Wm.
Chaplin,Mary,	1		York.
Chapline,Isaac,	2		Berk.
Chapman,Allen,	1	12	York
Chapman,Benjamin,	1		Caro.
Chapman,Benjamin,	1	1	Spots.
Chapman,Cornelious,			Caro.
Chapman,Daniel,	1		Lin.
Chapman,Diana,		2	Fay.
Chapman,Edward,	1		Lin.
Chapman,Elizabeth,		9	K.&Q.
Chapman,George,	1	13	Fau.
Chapman,George,	1	4	Caro.
Chapman,George,	1	4	Caro.
Chapman,George,	1	4	K.&Q.
Chapman,John,	1	13	York
Chapman,John,Jr.,	1	4	York
Chapman,John,	1		Pr.Wm.
Chapman,John,			Lou.
Chapman,John,	1		Cul.
Chapman,John,	1		Caro.
Chapman,John,	1		Aug.
Chapman,John,	1		Lou.
Chapman,John,	1		Mont.
Chapman,Reuben,	1	9	Caro.
Chapman,Richard,	1		Caro.
Chapman,Richard,	1		Mont.
Chapman,Richard,	1		Mont.
Chapman,Richard,	1		Lin.
Chapman,Robert,	1		K.&Q.
Chapman,Robert,	3	11	Caro.
Chapman,Thomas,	1		Pr.Wm.
Chapman,Thomas,	2	15	Pr.Wm.
Chapman,William,	1	4	Caro.
Chapman,William,	1	14	Cul.
Chapman,William,	1		Lin.
Chapman,William,	1		Mont.
Chappell,James,	1	7	So'n
Chappell,John,	1	1	Lun.
Chappel,Mary,	2		Pr.Geo.
Chappell,Thomas,	1	5	Lun.
Chappell,Robert,	1	17	Lun.
Chapple,Agness,	1	16	Pr.Geo.
Chapple,Thomas,	1		Pr.Geo.
Chapple,William,	1	2	Din.
Charles,Henry,		2	York
Charles,James,			Henry
Charles,Jethro,	1	1	So'n
Charles,John,	1		Cha.Cy
Charles,John,	1		Ja.Cy.
Charles,Lewis,	1	(	Brun.
Charles,Lewis			Brun.

Name			Co.
Charles,Lewis,	1	8	Brun.
Charles,Matthew,	1		So'n.
Charles,Philip,	2		Ja.Cy.
Charles,Philip,	1	3	Ch.Cy.
Charles,William,	1		Ch.Cy.
Charles,Willis,	1		Ch.Cy.
Charlton,Jacob,	1		Buck.
Charlton,James,	1		Mont.
Charlton,John,	3		Mont.
Charnack,Abel,	1		Acco.
Charnack,George,			Acco.
Charnack,John,	1		Acco.
Charnack,Sarah,	1		Acco.
Charters,John,	1		Bed.
Charters,Thomas,	1		Bed
Charters,Thomas,	1	21	Ch.Cy.
Chastain,Rane,			Buck.
Chastain,Rane,Jr.,	2	2	Buck.
Chastain,Stephen,			Buck.
Chasteen,John,	1	8	Bed.
Chaudoin,Francis,	2		Buck.
Chaudoin,John,			Buck.
Cheadle,Judith,	1	4	Gooch.
Cheadle,Judith,	1	14	Caro.
Chedwick,Isaac,	1		Bot.
Cheek,Elisha,	1	4	Cul.
Cheek,Francis,	1	1	Cul.
Cheek,George,	1		Berk.
Cheek,Jessee,	1	1	Henry
Cheeke,William,	2		Bed.
Cheek,William,	1	6	Lou.
Cheek,Wyatt,	1		Caro.
Cheely,Joseph,			Brun.
Cheely,Thomas,	1	4	Din.
Cheetwood,Joel,	2		Bed.
Cheetwood,John,	1		Bed.
Cheetwood,William,	1		Bed.
Cheives,Joel,	1		Pr.Geo
Cheives,William,	1	13	Pr.Geo
Chelf,Philip,	1	6	Cul.
Chelton,James,	1	2	Lou.
Chelton,Richard,	2	7	Cul.
Chelton,Steven,			Cul.
Chelton,Thomas,	1		Cul.
Cherfells,John,	1	1	Pr.Geo
Cherr,Joseph,	1	3	Lou.
Cherry,William,	1		Berk.
Cherry,William,	1		Bot.
Cheshire,Baptist,	1		Pr.Wm.
Chesnut,James,	1		Mont.
Chestnutt,John,	1		Aug.
Chestnut,William,	1	5	Aug.
Chevis,David,		4	Spots.
Chewning,George,		3	Loui.
Chewning,Janett,		13	Caro.
Chewning,John,	1	1	Caro.
Chewning,Joseph,	1	1	Loui.
Chewning,Samuel,	1	6	Caro.
Chewning,Samuel,	1	5	K.&Q.
Chewning,Thomas,	1	7	Henry
Chewning,William,	1		Caro.
Chewning,William,	1	6	Caro.
Chews,Capt.John,	1	27	Spots.
Chew,John,Jr.,	1	9	Spots.
Chew,Mrs.Mary,	1	7	Spots.
Chew,Robert,B.,		3	Spots.
Cheyne,Hezekiah,	2	1	Mont.
Chichester,Richard,	1	45	Fau.
Chick,John,	2	3	Fau.
Chicks,Richard,		2	K.&Q.
Chick,Wyatt,	1		K.Wm.
Chiddick,William,	1		Camp.
Chilcott,Eler,	1		Har.
Chilcott,Elihu,	1		Har.
Chinocth,Jonathan,	1		Har.
Chilcott,Joel,	1		Har.

Name			Co.
Childers,Abner,			Hen.
Childers,Frederick,	3		Hen.
Childers,Frederick,Jr			Hen.
Childers,Obediah,	1	1	Hen.
Childers,Zachariah,	1		Hen.
Childers,William,	1		Har.
Childres,Joseph,	1		Gooch.
Childres,Phillip,			Gooch.
Childers,Stephen,	1		Bot.
Childress,Alexander,	1	1	Hen.
Childress,Jacob,	1		Hen.
Childress,John,			Buck.
Childress,John,	1		Hen.
Childress,John,	1		Hen.
Childress,John,	1	1	Buck.
Childress,Francis,	1	1	Buck.
Childress,John,	1		Buck.
Childress,John,	1		Buck.
Childress,Joseph,	1		Buck.
Childress,Robert,	1		Hen.
Childress,Robert,	1		Hen.
Childress,Thomas,	1	1	Hen.
Childress,Thomas,	1		Buck.
Childress,Thomas,	1		Hen.
Childrey,Thomas,	1	8	Hen.
Childrey,Thomas,	1	10	Hen.
Childs,James,	1	1	Cul.
Childs,John,	1		Din.
Childs,William,	1	5	Cul.
Childs,John,	1	1	Pr.Geo
Chiles,Esther,		6	Caro.
Chiles,Henry,	1	7	Caro.
Chiles,Henry,Jr.,	1		Caro.
Chiles,Henry,	1		Henry
Chiles,Henry,	1	2	Spots.
Chiles,Jemima,	1	6	Caro.
Chiles,John,	1	3	Caro.
Chiles,John,	1	12	Caro.
Chiles,John,	1	8	Spots.
Chiles,Capt.John,	1	5	Bed.
Chiles,Mensah,	2	1	Caro.
Chiles,Rowland,	1		Henry
Chiles,Thomas,	1	7	Caro.
Chiles,Walter,	1	11	Spots.
Chiles,William,	1	4	Caro.
Chilton,Charles,	1	19	Fau.
Chilton,John,	1	1	Lou.
Chilton,Steerman,	1	5	Lou.
Chilton,Thomas,	1	2	Lin.
Chinatt,James,	1		Buck.
Chinault,Sarah,	1	1	Caro.
Chinn,Ann,		12	Fay.
Chinn,Charles,	2	12	Fau.
Chinn,Christopher,	1	15	Fau.
Chinn,Christopher,	1	3	Fay.
Chinn,Elijah,	1	1	Fay.
Chinn,Rawleigh,	1	6	Lou.
Chinn,Rawleigh,Jr.,	1	11	Lou.
Chinn,Rawleigh,	1	6	Fay.
Chinn,Thomas,		3	Fau.
Chinn,Thomas,	1	9	Lou.
Chinn,William,	1		Fay.
Chinoweth,Isaac,	1	1	Berk.
Chinoweth,John,	1		Berk.
Chinowith,Joseph,	1		Berk.
Chinowith,William,Sr.	2		Berk.
Chinowith,William,Jr.	1		Berk.
Chisham,John,	1	1	Spots.
Chisholm,Alexander,	2		Lou.
Chism,Elisha,	1		Lin.
Chisman,Mrs.Diana,		9	York
Chisman,Edmund,	1	24	York
Chisman,George,	1	4	York
Chisman,Jacob,	1		Har.
Chisman,John,	1	12	York
Chisman,John,Estate,	1	11	York

Name			Co.
Chisman,Mary,		10	Ja.Cy.
Chisman,Thomas,	1	6	York
Chitty,Britain,	1		So'n.
Chitty,John,	1		So'n.
Chives,David,	1	16	Caro.
Chivers,John,			Caro.
Choate,Augusta,	1		Henry
Choat,Isham,	1		Henry
Chockley,Joseph,	1	1	Lun.
Chopart,Nicholas,	1		Berk.
Choice,Tully,Sr.,	1	2	Henry
Choice,Tully,Jr.,	1		Henry
Chord,Levin,	1	2	Acco.
Chord,William,	1	6	Acco.
Chowning,Charles,	1		Cul.
Christol,***,	1		Mont.
Chrisley,Henry,	1		Mont.
Christian,Allen,	1		Bed.
Christian,Andrew,			Fay.
Christian,Archer,	1		Buck.
Christian,Charles,	1	8	Gooch.
Christian,Charles,	1	15	Ch.Cy.
Christian,Charles,			Ch.Cy.
Christian,Edmond,	1	18	Ch.Cy.
Christian,Francis,		1	Din.
Christian,Gideon,	1	14	Ch.Cy.
Christian,Gilbert,	1	2	Aug.
Christian,Israel,	1	4	Mont.
Christian,James,	1	3	Ja.Cy.
Christian,John,	1		Wash.
Christian,John,	1		Aug.
Christian,John,Jr.,	1		Aug.
Christian,Lewis,	1		Buck.
Christian,Mary,		7	Ch.Cy.
Christian,Michael,	1	35	Nor.
Christian,Patrick,	1		Aug.
Christian,Richard,		3	Ch.Cy.
Christian,Robert,	1	3	Aug.
Christian,Robert,	1	11	Ch.Cy.
Christian,Sampson,	1		Wash.
Christian,Thomas,	1	1	Mont.
Christian,Turner,	1	3	Gooch.
Christian,Turner,	1		Ch.Cy.
Christian,William,		4	Ch.Cy.
Christian,William,	1	33	Ch.Cy.
Christian,William,	1		Aug.
Christian,William,	1	33	Mont.
Christian,William,	1	10	Nor.
Christie,Charles,	1		Fau.
Christie,John,	2	3	K.Geo.
Christmas,Thomas,	1	4	Loui.
Christopher,Morton,	1	1	Cul.
Christopher,William,	1		Bed.
Christy,Patrick,	1		Berk.
Chunaberry,John,			Berk.
Chunn,John Thomas,	1	4	Fau.
Church,Richard,	1		Bed.
Church,Robert,	1		Bed.
Church,Samuel,	2		Acco.
Church,Thomas,			Acco.
Churchhill,Ann,		1	Fau.
Churchhill,Armistead	1	38	Fau.
Churchhill,John,	2	55	Fau.
Churchman,William,	1		Cul.
Churchwell,Richard,	2		Lin.
Churchwide,Richard,	1		Mont.
Cidwell,Charles,			Mont.
Cimball,Adam,	1		Har.
Cimball,John,	1		Har.
Cimbell,Lambert,	1		Har.
Cime,Henry,	2		Lou.
Cime,John,			Lou.
Circle,Peter,	1		Bot.
Cissel,William,	1	4	West'd.
Clack,Charles,	1		Loui.
Clack,John,	1	16	Brun.

Name			County
Clack,John,	1		Henry
Clack,Spencer,	1	1	Henry
Clack,Thomas,	1		Fay.
Claiburne,Col.August.		25	Din.
Claiborne,Augustine,Jr	2	25	Din.
Claiborne,Buller,		28	Din.
Claiborne,Daniel,	1	28	Din.
Claiborne,Elizabeth,		41	K.Wm.
Claiborne,Harbert,	1	32	K.Wm.
Claborne,John,			Lun.
Claiborne,Richard,Est.	1	19	Lun.
Claiborne,Thomas,	1	27	Brun.
Claiborne,Thomas,		7	Brun.
Claiborne,William,	1	7	Din.
Claiborne,Wm.Dandridge	1	62	K.Wm.
Claibrooke,Richard,	2	2	K.Wm.
Claig,Joseph,			Lou.
Clanton,Mark,	1	2	Brun.
Clanton,William,	1		So'n.
Clalerdral,William,	1		Ja.Cy.
Clapham,Josias,	1	41	Lou.
Clardy,Benjamin,	1	2	Bed.
Clark,Andrew,	1		Bot.
Clark,Benjamin,	1		Hen.
Clark,Benjamin,	1		Lou.
Clark,Benjamin,	1	1	Fau.
Clark,Benjamin,	1	10	Loui.
Clark,Bolling,	1	3	Din.
Clark,Charles,	1		Hen.
Clark,Elias,	1	6	Fau.
Clark,Elisha,	2	21	Brun.
Clark,George,			Wash.
Clark,George,	1		Loui.
Clarke,Henry,	1	2	Brun.
Clark,Henry,	1		Lun.
Clark,Henry,	1	2	Henry
Clark,J.,	1		Pr.Wm.
Clark,James,	1		Ja.Cy.
Clark,James,	1	5	Fay.
Clark,James,	3	5	Cul.
Clark,James,			Cul.
Clark,James,	1		Hen.
Clark,James,	1		Hen.
Clark,John,	1	1	Hen.
Clark,John,			Cul.
Clark,John,	1		So'n.
Clark,John,	1	3	So'n.
Clark,John,	1	21	Caro.
Clark,John,	1		Camp.
Clark,John,	1	14	Camp.
Clark,John,	1	8	Loui.
Clark,John,	1		Aug.
Clark,John,	1	1	Fay.
Clark,John,	1		Fay.
Clark,Joseph,	2	5	Buck.
Clark,Joseph,		4	Cul.
Clark,Margaret,			K.Geo.
Clark,Mattew,	1		Ja.Cy.
Clark,Obediah,	2	5	Hen.
Clark,Oliver,	1		Cul.
Clark,Peter,	1	1	Hen.
Clark,Prudence,		2	So'n.
Clark,Reubin,	1	7	Cul.
Clark,Reubin,			Cul.
Clark,Richard,	1		K.&Q.
Clark,Robert,	1	1	Aug.
Clark,Mrs.Temperance,		8	Din.
Clark,Thomas,	1		Bot.
Clark,Thomas,	1		Lou.
Clark,Thomas,	1		Fau.
Clark,Vachal,	1		Bot.
Clark,William,	1	7	Din.
Clark,William,	2	4	Cul.
Clark,Thomas,	1	1	Camp.
Clark,William,	1	16	Loui.
Clark,William,	2	13	Cul.
Clark,Zacheriah,	1		Hen.
Clarke,Abraham,Sr.,	1		Har.
Clarke,Abraham,Jr.,	1		Har.
Clarke,Anthony,	1		Berk.
Clarke,Benjamin,	1		Eli.Cy
Clarke,Benjamin,	1	4	Lun.
Clarke,Benjamin Wil.	1	1	Lun.
Clarke,Daniel,	1		Gooch.
Clarke,David,	1		Hen.
Clarke,David,	1		Har.
Clarke,Edward,	1		Hen.
Clarke,Edward,Jr.,	1	1	Hen.
Clarke,Eleanor,			Pr.Wm.
Clarke,Field,	1	2	Lun.
Clark,Francis,	1	4	Gooch.
Clark,Franklin,	2		So'n.
Clarke,Frederick,	2		Hen.
Clarke,George,	1		Buck.
Clark,George,	1		Berk.
Clarke,Henry,	1		Har.
Clarke,James,	1		Berk.
Clarke,James,	1		Pr.Wm.
Clarke,James,	1		Hen.
Clarke,James,	1	4	Ch.Cy.
Clarke,James,	1	1	Ch.Cy.
Clarke,Jeffrey,	1	4	Gooch.
Clarke,John,	1		Har.
Clarke,John,	1		Lun.
Clarke,John,	1	4	Hen.
Clarke,John,	1		Eli.Cy
Clarke,John,	1	6	Ch.Cy.
Clarke,John,	1		Gooch.
Clarke,John,	1		Roch.
Clarke,Jonathan,	1	12	Spots.
Clarke,Joseph,	1		Gooch.
Clarke,Mecajah,	1		Bed.
Clarke,Michael,	1		Spots.
Clarke,Nicholas,	1		Rock.
Clarke,Robert,Sr.,	1	13	Bea.
Clarke,Robert,Jr.,	1	5	Bed.
Clarke,Robert,	2		Har.
Clarke,Samuel,	1		Har.
Clarke,Shadrack,	1		Lun.
Clarke,Thomas,	1	1	Bed.
Clarke,Thomas,	1	6	Pr.Geo.
Clarke,Turner,	1	1	Gooch.
Clarke,Turner,Jr.,	1		Gooch.
Clarke,Walter,	1	8	Berk.
Clarke,William,	1		Berk.
Clarke,William,	1		Hen.
Clarke,William,			Hen.
Clarke,William,	1		Hen.
Clarkson,Ansalem,	1	10	Loui.
Clarkson,David,	1	1	Henry
Clarkson,Henry,	1	11	Fau.
Clarkson,William,	1	3	Gooch.
Clarkson,William,	1	1	Fay.
Clary,Benjamin,	1		Brun.
Clary,Herod,	1	8	Brun.
Clasby,William,	1	7	Caro.
Class,William,	1	9	Cul.
Clatterbuck,James,			Cul.
Clatterbuck,John,	1		Caro.
Clatterbuck,Richard,	2		Caro.
Clatterbuck,William,	2		Cul.
Claud,John,	1	12	So'n.
Claud,William,	1	9	So'n.
Claughton,Richard,	1	7	Lun.
Clawson,Josias,	1		Lou.
Clawson,Thomas,	1	1	Berk.
Claxton,Jeremiah,	1		West'd
Clusky,Thomas,			West'd
Clutton,William,	1	1	West'd
Claxy,Zachariah,	1		Mont.
Clay,Benony,	1		Nor.
Clay,Rev.Charles,		14	Bed.
Clay,Daniel,	1	1	Lun.
Clay,Jesse,	1		Henry
Clay,John,			Din.
Clay,Mitchell,	1		Mont.
Clay,Obed,	1	3	Lun.
Clay,Thomas,	1	7	Din.
Clay,William,	1	12	Din.
Clay,William,	1		Henry
Clay,William,	1		Nor.
Claybon,John,	1	3	Brun.
Claybor,Samuel,	2	3	Bed.
Claycomb,Conrad,	1		Berk.
Claycomb,Conrad,	2		Berk.
Claypole,Abraham,	1	1	Har.
Claypole,George,	1		Har.
Claypole,James,Sr.,	1		Har.
Claypole,James,Jr.,	2		Har.
Claypole,John,	1		Har.
Claypole,Joseph,	1		Lou.
Clayton,Elizabeth,		8	Spots.
Clayton,Ezekiel,	1		Berk.
Clayton,James,	1		K.&Q.
Clayton,James,	1	15	Spots.
Clayton,John,	1	23	So'n
Clayton,Reuben,	1		K.&Q
Clayton,Samuel,	3	16	Cul.
Clayton,Samuel,Jr.,			Cul.
Clayton,Thomas,	1	5	Spots.
Clayton,Thomas,	1	4	K.&Q.
Clayton,Thomas,	1		Berk.
Clayton,William,	1	2	Caro.
Clayton,William,	1		Lou.
Clayton,William,	1	10	Spots.
Claytor,William,			Spots.
Claywell,Susannah			Acco.
Claywell,Peter,	1		Camp.
Clawson,John,	1		Berk.
Clearwater,Sylvester	1		Lou.
Cleavley,Thomas,	1	1	K.&Q.
Cleck,Jacob,	1		Rock.
Cleck,Mathias,	1		Rock.
Cleek,Michael,	1		Rock.
Cleek,Palser,	1		Rock.
Cleer,George,	1	2	Caro.
Clegg,Clark,	1	3	Nor.
Clegg,Isaac,	1	14	Nor.
Clegg,Isiah,	3	6	K.&Q.
Clement,Adam,	1	18	Camp.
Clement,Adam,	1	18	Camp.
Clements,Ann,		4	K.Wm.
Clements,Benjamin,	1	3	Mont.
Clements,Francis,		7	So'n
Clements,Elizabeth,		9	So'n
Clements,Elizabeth,		15	So'n
Clements,James,	1	2	Gooch.
Clements,Jeremiah,	1		Fau.
Clements,John,	1		Henry
Clements,Jesse,	1		Gooch.
Clements,John,	1		Din.
Clements,John,	1		Gooch.
Clements,John,Jr.,	1		Gooch.
Clements,Katherine,	1		Mont.
Clements,Stephen,			Gooch.
Clements,Thomas,Jr.,	1	10	So'n
Clements,William,	1		Din.
Clemmons,Reubin,	1		Brun.
Clemmons,Robert,	1		Brun.
Clemmons,Thomas,	1		Bot.
Clemonds,Christian,	1	2	Aug.
Clemonds,James,	1	1	Pr.Geo.
Clemmonds,John,	1	1	Aug.
Clemonds,Joshua,	1		Pr.Geo.
Clemons,Elizabeth	1		Fay.
Clemons,Henry,	1		Berk.
Clemens,Robert,	1		Fay.
Clemons,Rodger,	1		Fay.

Name			County	Name			County	Name			County
Clemonts,Gaspert,	1		Aug.	Clyne,Peter,	1		Bot.	Cockram,Edward,	1		Henry
Clendening,John,	1	2	Bot.	Clyon,Peter,	1		Bed.	Cockram,Richard,			Fau.
Clendenning,John,	1	2	Fau.	Coap,William,	1		Mont.	Cockram,William,	1	1	Henry
Clendenning,Samuel,	1		Lou.	Coaps,James,	1		Mont.	Cochran,James,	1		Wash.
Clerk,Daniel,	3	3	Cul.	Coaps,John,	1		Mont.	Cockran,Henry,	1		K.Wm.
Clerk,George,			Cul.	Coaps,William,	1		Mont.	Cockran,James,	1		Fay.
Clerk,Jeremiah,	1		Mont.	Coates,Thomas,	1		Fau.	Cockran,Nathan,	1		Lou.
Clerk,Robert,			Cul.	Coats,Thomas,	2	13	Caro.	Cockran,Robert,	1		Aug.
Cletchers,John,	1		Bed.	Coats,George,			Buck.	Cockran,Thomas,	1	8	Aug.
Cleveland,A.	1	4	Pr.Wm.	Coats,John,	1	9	Spots.	Cochran,Simon,	1	4	Har.
Cleveland,Eli,	3	8	Fay.	Coats,Joshua,	1		Mont.	Cockrell,Anderson,	1		Fau.
Cleveland,James,	1	53	Lou.	Coats,William,		1	Spots.	Cockerill,Benjamin,	1	4	Lou.
Cleveland,William,		1	Lou.	Cobbett,Henry,	1	1	K.Wm.	Cockerill,Christo'r	1	2	Lou.
Cleverius,Benjamin,	2	25	K.&Q	Coberly,James,	2		Har.	Cockerill,Elias,			Lou.
Cleverius,John,	1		K.&Q	Cobler,George,	1		Berk.	Cockerill,George,			Lou.
Cliborn,John,Sr.,	1		Bed.	Cobler,John,	1		Berk.	Cockerill,Hannah,	2		Lou.
Cliborn,John,Jr.,	1		Bed.	Cobler,Thomas,	1		Henry	Cockerill,Jeremiah,			Lou.
Cliborn,Thomas,	1		Bed.	Cobb,Benjamin,	2	4	Lun.	Cockerill,John	1		Lou.
Cliff,Joseph,	1	11	K.Geo.	Cobb,David,	1	6	Caro.	Cockerill,Marmanduke	1		Lou.
Cliff,Robert,	1		Caro.	Cobb,Elizabeth,		1	So'n	Cockerill,Sandford,	1	5	Lou.
Cliff,William,	1	1	Caro.	Cobb,Henry,	1	1	So'n	Cockerill,Jeremiah,		25	Lou.
Cliff,William,	2	2	Caro.	Cobb,James,			Acco.	Cockerell,Thomas,	1	6	Lou.
Clifford,James,	1		Har.	Cobb,John,	1	15	So'n	Cockerell,Wm.Sandford			Lou.
Clift,Benjamin,	1	1	K.Geo.	Cobb,Lazarus,	1		So'n	Coddy,John,	1		Gooch.
Clift,John,	1	2	K.Geo.	Cobb,Nicholas,	1		So'n	Coe,Edward,			Lou.
Clift,Robert,Sr.,	1		K.Geo.	Cobb,Robert,	2	11	Caro.	Cofford,William,	1		Berk.
Clift,Robert,Jr.,	1		K.Geo.	Cobb,Sam,	2		So'n	Cofer,George,			Cul.
Clifton,Benjamin,	1	8	So'n	Cobb,William,	1		Aug.	Cofer,Joel,	1		Cul.
Clifton,Charles,	1	3	Cul.	Cobb,William,	1	1	Nor.	Cofer,Reuben,			Cul.
Clifton,Mildred,			K.Geo.	Cobbs,Edward,	1	14	Bed.	Cofer,Thomas,	2	1	Cul.
Clifton,Richard,	1	9	So'n	Cobbs,Elizabeth,	1	3	York.	Coffee,Ambrose,	2		Fay.
Clifton,Sarah,		12	So'n	Cobbs,John,Jr.,	1	7	Buck.	Coffee,James,	1		Bot.
Clinton,Archibald,	1		Lin.	Cobbs,Roben,	1	7	Bed.	Coffee,William,	1	2	Buck.
Climont,John,	1		Fau.	Cobbs,Thomas,			York.	Coffer,Douglas,			Lou.
Clinch,Jane,		1	Cul.	Cobbs,Thomas,Sr.,	2	20	Buck.	Coffer,Josias,	1		Bed.
Clindenning,Adam,	1		Mont.	Cobbs,Thomas,	1	7	Buck.	Coffelt,Henry,	1		Har.
Cline,David,	1		Lou.	Coburn,John,	1	4	Fay.	Coffenberry,Geo.L.	2		Berk.
Cline,Nicholas,	1		Mont.	Cock,Andrew,	1		Mont.	Coffenberry,Nicholas	1		Berk.
Cline,Joseph,	1		Lou.	Cock,George,	3	11	Camp.	Coffield,Thomas,	1		So'n
Cloak,George,	1	4	Berk.	Cock,James,	1		Mont.	Coffman,Abraham,	1		Har.
Cloar,John,	1		Buck.	Cock,John,	1		Mont.	Coffman,Christopher,	1		Berk.
Cloe,Michael,	1		Henry	Cock,John,	1	11	Camp.	Coffman,Isaac,	1	1	Berk.
Cloey,Cato,	1		Caro.	Cock,John C.		4	Cul.	Coffman,John,	1		Mont.
Clonch,Edmund,			Mont.	Cockburn,Robert,			Berk.	Cogar,Hannah,			Har.
Cloniger,Valentine,	1	4	Aug.	Cocke,Abraham,estate		13	Lun.	Cogar,Henry,	1	1	Henry
Clockenbeard,John,	1		Berk.	Cocke,Acrill,	1	5	Cha.C	Cogar,John,	1		Henry
Clopton,Benjamin,	1	15	Gooch.	Cocke,Allen,estate,		54	Gooch.	Coger,Jacob,	1		Bot.
Clopton,George,	1	6	Hen.	Cocke,Ann,		38	So'n	Coger,Peter,	1		Bot.
Clopton,George,	1	6	Hen.	Cocke,Benjamin,	1		Gooch.	Coghill,Frederick,	1	8	Caro.
Clopton,Walter,	1	5	Gooch.	Cocke,Bowler,	1	29	Hen.	Coghill,Isaac,	1		Lou.
Clore,Adam,	1	1	Cul.	Cocke,Bowler,	1	14	Gooch.	Coghill,James,	1	1	Lin.
Clore,John,	4	5	Cul.	Cocke,Edwrad,	1	3	Char.	Coghill,Thomas,	4	24	Caro.
Clore,John,Jr.,	1	1	Cul.	Cocke,Elizabeth,		53	Pr.Geo	Cogswell,John,	1		Mont.
Clore,Moses,	1		Cul.	Cocke,Francis,	1		Hen.	Cogswell,Joseph,	1	1	Bed.
Clore,Peter,	1		Cul.	Cocke,Hartwell,			Gooch.	Cohagan,William,	1		Lou.
Clore,Michael,	1	1	Cul.	Cocke,James,	1		Gooch.	Cohagaris,Catherine,			Lou.
Close,Michael,	1		Berk.	Cocke,James,estate,		24	Din.	Coker,Henry,	1	6	So'n
Clough,Richard,	1	1	Gooch.	Cocke,James,	1	8	Gooch.	Coker,Jonathan,	1		So'n
Cloud,Isaac,	1		Henry	Cocke,Jane,		12	Cha.C	Coker,Willson,		2	So'n
Cloud,William,	2		Henry	Cocke,John,	1	5	Hen.	Colbert,Richard,	1		York
Clouse,George,	1		Wash.	Cocke,John,	1	12	Caro.	Colborn,Cheeley,	1		K.&Q
Clover,Philip,	2		Berk.	Cocke,John,	1		Gooch.	Colclough,Alexander,	1		Lou.
Cloyd,David,	1	2	Rock.	Cocke,John Hartwell,	1	23	Buck.	Colden,James,	1		York
Cloyd,James,	1		Lin.	Cocke,Pleasant,	1	20	Pr.Geo	Cole,Andrew,	1		West.
Cloyd,John,	1		Mont.	Cocke,Richard,	1	7	Hen.	Cole,Barnett,	1		Berk.
Cloyd,Joseph,	1	5	Mont.	Cocke,Richard,	1	30	Gooch.	Cole,Daniel,	1		Pr.Wm.
Cloyd,Ninian,	1		Mont.	Cocke,Thomas,	1	1	Gooch.	Cole,David,	1		Berk.
Cloyd,Samuel,	1		Mont.	Cocke,William,	1	1	K.Wm.	Cole,Isarel,	1		Wash.
Cloyd,William,	1		Fay.	Cocke,William,	1	10	Lou.	Cole,James,	1		Aug.
Cloynch,Jeremiah,Sr.	1		Mont.	Cocke,William,	1	11	Hen.	Cole,Jane,	1	3	Pr.Wm.
Cloynch,Jeremiah;Jr.	1		Mont.	Cocke,William,	1	8	Hen.	Cole,John,			Pr.Wm.
Cluckenbeard,William	1		Berk.	Cocke,William,Jr.,	1	1	Hen.	Cole,John,	1	2	York
Clui,Jacob,			Lou.	Cockerham,David,			Lun.	Cole,John,	1	8	York.
Clui,John,	2		Lou.	Cockerham,William,	2		Bed.	Cole,John,	1	5	Lun.
Clutton,William,	1		Spots.	Cockerham,William W.	1	3	Lun.	Cole,Joseph,	1		Wash.
Clyde,James,	1		Aug.	Cockram,Abner,	1	1	Henry	Cole,Joseph,	1		Bot.

Connally,Arthur,	1	1	Aug.	Cook,John,	1		Pr.Geo	Cooper,John,	1		Bot.
Connaly,Thomas,	1		Aug.	Cook,John,	1		K.&Q.	Cooper,John,	1		Lun.
Connell,John,Sr.,	1		Lun.	Cook,John,	2	5	K.&Q.	Cooper,John,	1		Rock.
Connell,John,Jr.,	2		Lun.	Cook,John,	1	1	Lin.	Cooper,Joseph,			Loui.
Connell,William,			Lun.	Cook,Jonathan,			Din.	Cooper,Joseph,	1	7	Eli.Cy.
Connely,David,	1		Mont.	Cook,Jonathan,	1	1	Lou.	Cooper,Joseph,	1	8	Henry
Connely,John,	1		Mont.	Cook,Lazarus,	1	9	So'n.	Cooper,Latin,	1		Cul.
Connelley,John,			Lou.	Cook,Lewis,	1		Lou.	Cooper,Mary,		2	Caro.
Connelly,Sandford,	1	6	Lou.	Cook,Mary,			Brun.	Cooper,Michael,	1		Lou.
Conner,Daniel,	1		Har.	Cook,Mary,			Camp.	Cooper,Richard,	1		Fau.
Conner,Daniel,	1		Bot.	Cook,Mary,			Camp.	Cooper,Robert,	1		Aug.
Conner,Edward,	1		Lou.	Cook,Michael,	1		Cul.	Cooper,Samuel,			Lou.
Conner,Edward,	1	11	K.Wm.	Cook,Mordical,		10	West'd	Cooper,Samuel,	2		Fay.
Conner,Frances,	1	20	Caro.	Cook,Peter,	1		Cul.	Cooper,Solomon,	1		So'n.
Conner,James,	1	9	Caro.	Cook,Robert,	1	1	Cul.	Cooper,Thomas,	1	8	Henry
Conner,Jerry,			Lun.	Cook,Thomas,	1		West'd	Cooper,Thomas,	1		Rock.
Conner,John,	1	9	Bot.	Cook,Wiles,	1		Fay.	Cooper,Thomas,	1		Henry
Conner,John,	1		Buck.	Cook,William,	1		Henry	Cooper,William,	1		Lou.
Conner,Lewis,	1	6	Cul.	Cook,William,	1	1	Cul.	Cope,Andrew,	1		Mont.
Conner,Nicholas,	1	2	Buck.	Cook,William,			Brun.	Copeland,Andrew,	2		Lou.
Conner,Owen,	2		Lun.	Cook,William,	1	13	Loui.	Copeland,John,	1		Lou.
Conner,Rice,	1	10	Spots.	Cook,William,			Spots.	Copen,William,	1		Pr.Wm.
Conner,Stephen,	1		Fau.	Cook,William,	1		Wash.	Copes,Charles,	1		Acco.
Conner,William,	2	23	Caro.	Cooke,Alexander,			Fau.	Copes,Capt.Southy,	3		Acco.
Conner,William,	1	2	Cul.	Cooke,Ann,		7	York	Copes,Mary P.,		1	Acco.
Conner,William,	1		Wash.	Cooke,Bennett,	1	3	York	Copes,Southy,Jr.,	1		Acco.
Connor,Phill,	1		Pr.Wm	Cooke,Giles,	1	19	Berk.	Copes,Susannah,	2	9	Acco.
Connello,John,	1	1	Brun.	Cooke,Giles,	1	6	Berk.	Copin,John,			Pr.Wm
Connoway,Nicholas,	1		Hen.	Cooke,John,	1		Berk.	Copin,William,	2	1	Pr.Wm
Conrad,John,	2		Har.	Cooke,John,	1	32	Berk.	Copland,Peter,Est	1	15	Ch.Cy.
Conrade,John,	1		Lou.	Cooke,John,	1	5	Fau.	Copland,Richard,	1	3	Henry.
Conrade,Jonathan,	1		Lou.	Cooksay,Lamaster,	1		Bea.	Cople,James,	1		K.Geo
Conrod,Elender,	1		Cul.	Cooksey,John,	1		Fau.	Cople,William,	1		K.Geo
Conrod,John,	1		Aug.	Cooksey,Philip,	1	2	Fau.	Coppedge,Charles,	1	2	Fau.
Conrod,Wooldrick,	1		Aug.	Cooley,Jabes,	1		Lin.	Coppedge,William,	1	2	Fau.
Conrod,Wooldrick,Jr.,	1		Aug.	Cooley,James,	1		Henry	Copseye,James,			Lou.
Consolver,Jonathan,	1		Bed.	Cooley,Thaadeus,	1		Mont.	Coplan,John,	1		Berk.
Constable,William,	1		Fau.	Cooley,Thadius,	1		Lin.	Copland,David,	1		Lou.
Conte,Frederick,	1		Lou.	Cooley,Thomas,	1		York	Copher,Jessee,	2	2	Fay.
Conaway,James,			Bed.	Coon,Joseph,	1		Berk.	Copher,Reuben,			Fay.
Conway,Cornelius,	1		Berk.	Coon,Michael,	1		Berk.	Copige,Isaac,	2	3	Fay.
Conway,Francis,	1	32	K.Geo	Coons,Henry,	1		Berk.	Copely,Thomas,	1		Mont.
Conway,Jese,	1		Fay.	Coons,Jacob,	1		Berk.	Copenhouser,Thomas,	1		Mont.
Conway,John,	1		Fay.	Coons,Philip,	1		Berk.	Copseye,John,			Lou.
Conway,John,	1	5	Din.	Cookus,Henry,	3		Berk.	Coram,Champ,	1		Fau.
Conway,John,	1		Henry	Copar,William,	1		Berk.	Coram,Richard,	1		Fau.
Conway,Joseph,	1		Fay.	Coones,Frederick,	1		Cul.	Corban,David,	1		Cul.
Conway,Samuel,	1		Fay.	Coones,Joseph,Sr.,			Cul.	Corban,David,	1		Cul.
Conway,Thomas,	1	24	Fau.	Coones,Joseph,	1		Cul.	Corban,Easter,			Cul.
Conway,Thomas,Jr.,	1	12	Fau.	Coons,Henry,	1		Cul.	Corban,Jeremiah,			Cul.
Conway,William,	1	1	Din.	Coons,Jacob,	1		Cul.	Corban,John,			Cul.
Conway,William,	1	8	Fau.	Coons,Auston,		5	Cul.	Corban,John,	1		Cul.
Conyers,David,	3		Fay.	Coones,John,	1	1	Cul.	Corban,Martin,	1		Cul.
Coods,William,		1	Pr.Wm.	Coons,Robert,	1	5	Cul.	Corban,Thomas,	1		Cul.
Cooe,Edward,			Lou.	Coonts,Henry,	1		Rock.	Corban,William,	1		Cul.
Coock,Powel,	1		Aug.	Coosenberry,Moses,	3		Fay.	Corban,William,	1		Cul.
Cook,Abraham,	1		Cul.	Cooper,Appollos,Est.		6	Lou.	Corban,William,Sr.,	2	10	Cul.
Cook,Benjamin,	1	8	Henry	Cooper,Arthur,	1		Bed.	Corban,William,Jr.,	1	1	Cul.
Cook,Benjamin,			K.&Q.	Cooper,Benjamin,	1	1	Lou.	Corbin,Gawin,	1	33	Spots.
Cook,Charles,	1		Cul.	Cooper,Charles,	1		Lun.	Corbin,Gawin,	1	11	West.
Cook,David,	1		Lin.	Cooper,Christopher,	1		Bot.	Corbin,Gawin,	1	74	Caro.
Cook,Edward,			York	Cooper,Christopher,	1		Wash.	Corbin,Godfrey,	1		Lou.
Cook,Foster,	1	5	Din.	Cooper,Daniel,	1		Gooch.	Corbin,Lewis,			Cul.
Cook,George,	1		Spots.	Cooper,Demsey,	1		So'n.	Corbin,Richard,	1	54	Caro.
Cook,Henry,	1	14	Lun.	Cooper,Edmund,	1	2	Din.	Corbin,Richard,	2	68	K.&Q.
Cook,George,	1		Cul.	Cooper,Elizabeth,		1	Rock.	Corbit,Jacob,			So'n.
Cook,Henry,			K.&Q.	Cooper,Frances,			Wash.	Corbit,James,	1		Bot.
Cook,Henry,	2		Lin.	Cooper,Frederick,	1		Lou.	Cordal,James,	1		Mont.
Cook,Henry,	1	1	Lin.	Cooper,Henry,	1		K.&Q.	Cormony,Michael,	1		Mont.
Cook,James,	2	1	K.&Q.	Cooper,James,	1		Bot.	Coughman,David,	1		Mont.
Cook,James,			Cul.	Cooper,James,	1		Brun.	Cove,Robert,	1		Mont.
Cook,Jeremiah,			Lou.	Cooper,Jean,			Rock.	Cowan,William,	1		Mont.
Cook,John,	1	1	Mont.	Cooper,Jesse,	1		So'b.	Cowden,Robert,	1		Mont.
Cook,John,	1		Mont.	Cooper,John,	1	1	Henry	Cordell,George,	1		Fau.
Cook,John,	1	12	Lun.	Cooper,John,	1	45	Ja.Cy.	Corder,James,	1		Fau.
Cook,John,	1		Fau.					Corder,James,	1		Mont.

Name			Place
Cole,Lemander,	6		Loui.
Cole,Robert,	1		Buck.
Cole,Samuel,	1	9	Loui.
Cole,Stephen,	2		Mont.
Cole,Thomas,	1		Wash.
Cole,William,	1	34	Din.
Cole,William,	1	5	York
Cole,William,	1	4	Loui.
Cole,William,	1	13	Brun.
Cole,William,	1		Lou.
Cole,William,Sr.,	1	7	Ja.Cy
Coleburn,Ann,			Caro.
Coleburne,William,	1		Caro.
Colcle,Alexander,	1		Har.
Colder,John,			Din.
Coleman,Ambroase,	1	1	Cul.
Coleman,Caleb,	1	14	Spots.
Coleman,Clayton,	1	21	Spots.
Coleman,Cluerius,		4	Lun.
Coleman,Cuthbert,	1	10	Din.
Coleman,Daniel,	2	21	Caro.
Coleman,Daniel,	1	4	Buck.
Coleman,Daniel,	1		Lou.
Coleman,Daniel,	1		Lou.
Coleman,Edward,	1	3	Spots.
Coleman,Farish,	1	8	Caro.
Coleman,Francis,	1	1	Din.
Coleman,Francis,	1	1	Spots.
Coleman,George,			Camp.
Coleman,Hawes,	1	2	Spots.
Coleman,Henry,	1	2	Bot.
Coleman,Isham,	1		Din.
Coleman,James,	1	6	Buck.
Coleman,James,	1		Bed.
Coleman,James,	2	24	Lou.
Coleman,Jesse,			Buck.
Coleman,Joel,	1		Lou.
Coleman,John,	1		Pr.Wm
Coleman,John,	2	1	Buck.
Coleman,John,	1	5	Din.
Coleman,John,	1		Din.
Coleman,John,	1	11	Caro.
Coleman,Joseph,	1		Lou.
Coleman,Julius,	1	15	Caro.
Coleman,Matthew,	1	16	Din.
Coleman,Mildred,		12	K.&Q
Coleman,Nicey,		10	Spots.
Coleman,Rebecca,		6	Buck.
Coleman,Richard,	1	11	Din.
Coleman,Richard,	1	15	Spots.
Coleman,Richard,Jr.,	1	17	Spots.
Coleman,Richard,	1	7	Spots.
Coleman,Richard,			Brun.
Coleman,Robin,	1		Cul.
Coleman,Robert,			Loui.
Coleman,Robert,	1	1	Spots.
Coleman,Robert,	1	15	Spots.
Coleman,Robert,			Cul.
Coleman,Robert Spils,	1	10	Spots.
Coleman,Samuel,		3	Hen.
Coleman,Samuel,	2	10	Buck.
Coleman,Samuel,	1	10	Caro.
Coleman,Sanuel,	1	14	Caro.
Coleman,Mrs.Sarah,		2	Din.
Coleman,Spilsbe,	1	15	Spots.
Coleman,Thomas,	1	26	K.&Q
Coleman,Thomas,	1		Cul.
Coleman,Thomas,	1	20	Spots.
Coleman,Thomas,	1	6	Caro.
Coleman,Thomas,	1	20	Caro.
Coleman,Thomas,	1	11	Caro.
Coleman,Thomas,Sr.,	1	3	Din.
Coleman,Williamson,	1	17	Din.
Coleman,Wyatt,	1	3	Cul.
Coles,John,	1	10	Din.
Coleson,Jacob,	1		Mont.
Coley,Francis,	1		Brun.
Coley,James,	1		Lou.
Colley,Abraham,	1		Cul.
Colley,John,	1	2	Henry
Colley,Malachi,	1	1	Loui.
Colgan,Daniel,	1	1	Berk.
Colgin,John,	1	6	Cha.Cy
Coll,Timothy,	1		Aug.
Collawne,Thomas,	1	9	Caro.
Collett,John,	4		Berk.
Collier,Aaron,	1		Mont.
Collier,Aaron,	1		Rock.
Collier,Agness,		8	Cha.Cy
Collier,Alexander,	4		Lin.
Collier,Benjamin,	1	5	K.&Q
Collier,Benjamin,	1	5	K.&Q
Collier,Catherine,		12	K.&Q
Collier,Charity,		8	So'n
Collier,Charles,	1		Henry
Collier,Charles,	1	7	K.&Q
Collier,Charles,			Cha.Cy
Collier,Charles,	1	17	Brun.
Collier,Cornelius,	1	17	Lun.
Collier,Francea,		9	K.&Q
Collier,George,	1	2	Brun.
Collier,John,	1	1	Henry
Collier,John,	1	4	K.&Q
Collier,Jonathan,	1		Bot.
Collier,Jonathan,	1		Berk.
Collier,Lewis,	1	10	Brun.
Collier,Lewis,	1		Brun.
Collier,Moses,	1		Rock.
Collier,Richard,			Henry
Collier,Richard,	1		Henry
Collier,Vines,	1	8	Brun.
Collier,William,	1	23	Brun.
Collins,Ambrose,	1		Cul.
Collins,Ambrose,	1		Mont.
Collins,Bartlett,	1	3	Fay.
Collins,Bartlett,	1	1	Spots.
Collins,Christopher,	2	11	West.
Collins,Daniel,	1		Mont.
Collins,David,	1		Mont.
Collins,Edward,	1	7	Spots.
Collins,Edmund,	1	7	Fau.
Collins,Gabriel,			K.&Q
Collins,George,	1	1	Jas.Cy
Collins,George,	1		Mont.
Collins,James,	1	5	Caro.
Collins,James,	1		Cul.
Collins,James,			Fau.
Collins,John,	1		Mont.
Collins,John,	1	1	K.&Q
Collins,John,	1	1	K.&Q
Collins,John,		2	Fau.
Collins,John,	1	2	Aug.
Collins,John,	2	14	Caro.
Collins,Joseph,	1	5	Spots.
Collins,Joyeux,	1	6	K.&Q
Collins,Lewis,	1		Mont.
Collins,Martin,	1		Mont.
Collins,Mary,	1	9	Cul.
Collins,Milton,	1		Mont.
Collins,Richard,	1	4	Spots.
Collins,Robert,	1	4	Fay.
Collins,Robert,	1	2	Spots.
Collins,Sam B.,	1		So'n
Collins,Susanna,		1	Spots.
Collins,Thomas,	1	5	K.&Q
Collins,Thomas,estate		6	Caro.
Collins,William,			Lou.
Collins,William,	1	1	Cul.
Collins,Wyatt,	1		Din.
Collinsworth,Edmund,	1		Mont.
Collinsworth,James,	1		Mont.
Collinsworth,Rubin,	1		Mont.
Collinsworth,Willo'y,	1		West.
Collinsworth,William	1		Brun.
Collis,Thomas,	2	2	Pr.Wm
Coloney,Benjamin,			Acco.
Colony,Edmund,			Acco.
Colony,Major,	1	3	Acco.
Colony,William,	3	8	Acco.
Collons,Francis,			Cul.
Collop,Peter,	1		Mont.
Colson,Thomas,	1	29	Spots.
Colter,James,	1	3	Rock.
Colthrop,Anthony,	1	1	So'n
Colthrop,Henry,	1	1	So'n
Colthrop,James,	1	1	So'n
Colthrop,James,	1	6	So'n
Colthrop,John,	1	2	So'n
Colvert,Samuel,			Cul.
Colvert,John,	1	9	Cul.
Colvin,Benjamin,	1		Cul.
Colvin,Charles,			Cul.
Colvin,Daniel,	1	1	Cul.
Colvin,John,		2	Cul.
Colvin,John,	2		Cul.
Colvin,Joseph,	1		Buck.
Colvin,Mason,	2	1	Cul.
Colvin,William,	1	4	K.Geo.
Colvin,William,	2	3	Din.
Colvin,William,Jr.,			Din.
Colwell,James,			Lou.
Colwell,Mathew,	1		Fay.
Colwell,Robert,	1		Fay.
Colwell,William,	1		Bot.
Comber,Margaret,			Aug.
Combs,Andrew,	1		Lou.
Combs,Benjamin,	1	6	Fay.
Combs,Catherine,	1	3	Fau.
Combs,Edward,	1		York
Combs,Ennis,	1	5	Fau.
Combs,Flewellin,	1		Cha.Cy
Combs,John,	1		Lou.
Combs,Joseph,	2	21	Lou.
Combs,Mary,			Lou.
Combs,Mason,	1		Mont.
Combs,Richard,	1		K.&Q
Combs,Robert,			Lou.
Combs,Robert,	1	1	Fau.
Combs,Samuel,	1		Lou.
Combs,Sarah,		4	Fau.
Combs,Stephen,	1	3	Lou.
Combs,Thomas,	1		York
Combs,William,	1		Mont.
Combs,William,	1		York
Comper,John,	1		Lou.
Comper,Peter,	2		Bot.
Compton,Caleb,	1	1	Bed.
Compton,James,			Cul.
Compton,John,	1	5	Lou.
Compton,John,Jr.,	1		Mont.
Compton,John,	1	3	Din.
Compton,Joseph,	1		Mont.
Compton,Matthew,	1	5	Bot.
Compton,Mathew,	1	1	Cul.
Compton,Philip,			Cul.
Compton,Thomas,	1	10	Cul.
Compton,Walter,	2	6	Cul.
Compton,William,C.	2		Cul.
Compton,Zachariah,	1	3	Cul.
Congleton,John,	1		Fay.
Congleton,William,	1		Wash.
Congrove,William,	1		Fau.
Conine,Richard,	1		Berk.
Conklin,Jacob,	2		Berk.
Con,Michael,	1		Har.
Conley,Bryant,	1		Gooch.
Conley,James,	1		Lou.
Conley,John,	1		Wash.
Conn.Hugh.	1		Lou.

Name	#	#	Place	Name	#	#	Place	Name	#	#	Place
Corder,John,	1		Bot.	Cottrell,Jacob,	1	3	Hen.	Cowan,John,	1		Berk.
Corder,Joseph,	1		Fau.	Cottrell,John,	2	1	Bed.	Cowan,John,	1		Wash.
Corder,William,			Fau.	Cottrell,Peter,	1	3	Hen.	Cowan,William,	1		Wash.
Cordle,Mary,		9	Brun.	Cottrell,Richard,	1	10	Hen.	Cowan,Mary,			Berk.
Cordial,Jacob,	2		Lou.	Cottrell,Richard,Jr.,	1	1	Hen.	Cowan,Robert,	1		Berk.
Cordle,William,	1	12	Brun.	Cottril,Benjamin,	2	20	Buck.	Cowan,Robert,	1	12	Berk.
Core,Zerubable,	1		Nor.	Coulburn,Catherine,	1	10	Acco.	Cowan,Robert,	1	8	Henry
Corely,William,	1	1	Loui.	Coulburn,Geroge,	1	4	Acco.	Cowan,Samuel,	1		Rock.
Corgan,Neal,	1	2	Acco.	Coulburn,George,			Acco.	Cowan,William,	1		Rock.
Corn,George,	1		Henry	Coulburn,James,			Acco.	Cowan,William,	1	5	Lun.
Corn,Jessee,	1		Henry	Coulburn,Revil,	1	5	Acco.	Coward,James,	1		Fay.
Corn,John Peter,	1		Henry	Coulburn,Tabitha,	1	11	Acco.	Coward,Jonathan,	1	1	Cul.
Corn,Samuel,	1		Henry	Coulburn,Thomas,	1	12	Acco.	Coward,William,	1	1	West.
Cornaggey,David,	1		Cul.	Coulburn,William,	3	2	Acco.	Cowardin,John,	1	3	Aug.
Cornaggey,James,			Cul.	Couch,James,	1	7	Buck.	Cowden,James,	1	11	Henry
Cornelius,Absolam,	1	4	Cul.	Couch,John,	1	12	Buck.	Cowden,William,			Henry
Corneilson,John,	1		Lou.	Couchman,Benadick,	2		Berk.	Cowgill,George,	1		Cul.
Cornet,John,	1		Rock.	Coughren,James,	1		Camp.	Cowgill,Jacob,	1		Cul.
Cornett,Frank,	1	1	Hen.	Coulter,Francis,	1		Bot.	Cowgill,John,	1		Cul.
Cornett,Jessee,			Hen.	Coulter,James,	1	1	Aug.	Cowhard,Reuben,	1	2	Bed.
Cornett,John,	1	1	Hen.	Coulter,Joseph,	1		Aug.	Cowles,Edmund,	1	4	Ja.Cy.
Cornet,William,			Hen.	Coulter,Michal,	1	3	Aug.	Cowles,John,	1	8	Ja.Cy.
Cornett,William,	1		Buck.	Council,Amos,	1		So'n.	Cowles,Samuel,	1		Ja.Cy.
Cornhill,John,	1		Pr.Wm.	Council,Charles,	1		So'n.	Cowles,Sarah,	1	16	Ja.Cy.
Cornhill,Noah,	1		Pr.Wm.	Council,Jesse,	1		So'n.	Cowles,Thomas,	1	7	Ja.Cy.
Cornwell,Ezekiel,	1		Pr.Wm.	Council,John,	1		So'n.	Cowles,Thomas,	1	6	West.
Cornwell,Francis,	1		Pr.Wm.	Council,Joshua,	1		So'n.	Cowles,Thomas,	1	14	York
Cornwell,Jarvis,	1	1	Fau.	Counee,Adam,	2		Lou.	Cowles,William,		20	Ch.Cy.
Cornwell,John,	1	1	Fau.	Counee,Henry,	1		Lou.	Cowley,Abraham,Est.,	1	14	Hen.
Cornwell,Joseph,	1	1	Din.	Coupland,David,	3	25	Buck.	Cowley,Francis,	2	2	Gooch.
Cornwell,Mary,			Pr.Wm.	Counsel,Michael,	1	1	Eli.Cy	Cowley,Mary,			Gooch.
Cornwell,Simon,	1		Fau.	Coursey,James,	3	7	Aug.	Cowley,Nathaniel,	1	6	Gooch.
Cornwell,William,	1		Henry	Coursey,William,	1		Nor.	Cowley,Sarah,			Gooch.
Corr,Frances,		5	K.&Q.	Courtney,Charnock,	1	3	West.	Cowley,Thomas,	2		Ch.Cy.
Corr,John,	1		K.&Q.	Courtney,James,	1	1	Fau.	Cowne,Robert,	2	28	K.Wm.
Corr,Thomas,Estate,	1	7	K.&Q.	Courtney,James,	1		Wash.	Cowne,William,	1	12	K.Wm.
Corr,William,	1	1	K.&Q.	Courtney,James,	1	14	West.	Cowper,Edward,	1	11	Eli.Cy.
Corruthers,Thomas,	1		Aug.	Courtney,John,	1	2	K.Wm.	Cowper,Roe,	1	12	Eli.Cy.
Corthorn,John,	1		Spots.	Courtney,John,			Fau.	Cox,Abraham,	1	3	Fau.
Corts,Mary,		15	Cul.	Courtney,John,	1		Fau.	Cox,Amos,	1		Mont.
Cory,Anne,	1	2	Loui.	Courtney,John,	1	2	Fau.	Cox,Anthony,	1		Henry
Cosby,Ann,		8	Loui.	Courtney,John,	1	1	West.	Cox,Benjamin,	1		Mont.
Cosby,Charles,	2	28	So'n.	Courtney,Michael,	1		Lin.	Cox,Charles,	1		Henry
Cosby,Charles,	1	13	Spots.	Courtney,Philip,	1	1	K.&Q.	Cox,David,	1		Mont.
Cosby,Charles,	1	4	Loui.	Courtney,Rebeckah,			Wash.	Cox,Edward,	1	3	Gooch.
Cosby,Charles,	2	1	Loui.	Courtney,Rowlin,			Wash.	Cox,Fleet,	2	57	West.
Cosby,Charles,			Loui.	Courtney,Thomas,	1	3	K.&Q.	Cox,Francis,	1	4	Henry
Cosby,David,	1		Gooch.	Courtney,William,	1	5	K.&Q.	Cox,George,	1		Berk.
Cosby,Hickason,	1		Loui.	Courtney,William,	1	5	Fau.	Cox,George,Estate,	1	58	Hen.
Cosby,John,	1	7	York	Courtney,William,			Fau.	Cox,Harman,	1		Mont.
Cosby,John,Sr.,	1	4	Loui.	Cousins,Adam,	1		Buck.	Cox,Isaac,	1		Mont.
Cosby,John,Jr.,	1	7	Loui.	Cousins,Walter,	1		Gooch	Cox,Isaac,	1		Mont.
Cosby,Thos.Wingfield,			Loui.	Coussins,William,	1	19	Din.	Cox,James,	1		Fau.
Cosby,William,	2	10	Loui.	Couzins,Peter,Est.,		7	Lun.	Cox,James,	1		Mont.
Cosby,Wingfield,	1	11	Loui.	Coutts,Reuben,	3	8	Hen.	Cox,James,	1		Mont.
Cosby,Zacharias,	1		Loui.	Coutts,William,	1	16	Hen.	Cox,Jesse,	1		Mont.
Cosley,Samuel,	1	7	Gooch.	Coutts,William,	1	4	Hen.	Cox,John,	1	6	Mont.
Cosper,Peter,	1		Cul.	Covender,John,	1		Fau.	Cox,John,	1	7	Henry
Coster,William,	1		Rock.	Covenhaver,Joseph,	1		Berk.	Cox,John,	1		Henry
Costin,Abraham,	1	7	Nor.	Covenhover,Lydia,		1	Berk.	Cox,John,	1	4	Gooch.
Costin,Francis,	1	5	Nor.	Copenhaver,Michael,	1		Berk.	Cox,John,		10	Pr.Geo.
Costin,Mathew,	2	3	Nor.	Covenhover,William,	1		Berk.	Cox,John,	1		So'n.
Costin,William,	1		Nor.	Covington,Edmund,	1	2	Lun.	Cox,John,	2	30	Buck.
Cotter,Mary,			Pr.Geo	Coventon,Francis,	1	2	Cul.	Cox,John,	2		Hen.
Cotter,William,	1	2	Pr.Geo	Covington,John,	1		Lun.	Cox,Joseph,	1		Lou.
Cottillin,Edward,	1		York	Covinton,Margeret,		1	Cul.	Cox,M.,	1		Pr.Wm.
Cotton,Drewry,	1	2	So'n.	Covington,Richard,	1	1	Fau.	Cox,Matthew,	2	17	Buck.
Cotton,Henry,	1		Brun.	Covinton,Robert,	1		Cul.	Cox,Phillip,	2		Cul.
Cotten,James,	1		Cul.	Covinton,William,	1	5	Cul.	Cox,Russell,	1		Henry
Cotton,John,	1		Mont.	Cowan,Andrew,	1	1	Wash.	Cox,Major Samuel,	1	1	Lou.
Cotton,John,			Lou.	Cowan,Andrew,			Wash.	Cox,Samuel,	1		Henry
Cotton,William,Sr.,	2	5	Lou.	Cowan,Andrew,	2		Rock.	Cox,Samuel,	1		Fau.
Cotton,William,Jr.,	1	5	Lou.	Cowan,Israel,			Rock.	Cox,Samuel,	1		Mont.
Cowgill,Abraham,	1		Lou.	Cowan,James,			Rock.	Cox,Solomon,	1		Mont.
Cottrel,Charles,	1	6	Buck.	Cowan,James,	1		Berk.	Cox,William,	1		Mont.
Cottrell,Chas.Waddill,	1	4	Hen.	Cowan,John,	4		Berk.	Cox,William,	1		Henry

Name			County	Name			County	Name			County
Cox,William,	1	3	Mont.	Crank,Mathew,	1	8	Caro.	Creel,William,	1		Pr.Wm.
Cox,William,	1		Bot.	Crank,Stephen,	1		K.Geo	Creely,Collin,			Wash.
Coxe,Ayress,	1		Camp.	Crank,Thomas,	1		Gooch.	Creely,John,	1		Wash.
Coxe,Carter,			Bot.	Crank,William,			K.Geo	Creemer,Elizabeth,			Lou.
Coxe,Mathew,	1	4	Bot.	Crannage,Samuel,			K.Geo	Creesay,John,	1		Bed.
Coxwell,Robert,	2		Acco.	Cravat,John,	1		Mont.	Creesay,Thomas,	1		Bed.
Crabb,Edward,	1		Berk.	Crave,Christian,	1		Lou.	Creese,Daniel,			York.
Crabb,Jane,	1	10	West.	Craven,Jeremiah,	1		Bot.	Creighton,Daniel,	1	4	Cha.Cy
Crabb,John,	2	12	West.	Craven,Jeremiah,	1		Berk.	Crenshaw,Benjamin,	1	9	Loui.
Crabb,Vincent,estate,		7	West.	Craven,Michael,	1		Berk.	Crenshaw,Benjamin,	1	9	Gooch.
Crabtree,Jacob,	1		Wash.	Craven,Thomas,	1	1	Lou.	Crenshaw,Cornelius,	1	14	Lun.
Cradock,Robert,			Hen.	Cravens,Jesse,	1		Lin.	Crenshaw,Daniel,	1	1	Lun.
Craddock,Sarah,	1		Cha.Cy	Cravens,Robert,	1	2	Wash.	Crenshaw,David,	1	5	Loui.
Craft,Thomas,	2	15	Brun.	Craw,Thomas,	1		Berk.	Crenshaw,Jessie,	1		Lun.
Craft,Washington,			Brun.	Crawford,Alexander,	1	2	Aug.	Crenshaw,John,	1	2	So'n
Craften,Henry,	1		Bot.	Crawford,Andrew,	1		Bot.	Crenshaw,John,	1		Lun.
Crafford,Archelus,	1		Cul.	Crawford,Andrew,Jr.,	1		Bot.	Crenshaw,Nathaniel,	1		Lun.
Crafford,Gideon,	1	2	Cul.	Crawford,Andrew,	1	9	West.	Crenshaw,Robert,	1	9	Lun.
Crafford,Oliver,			Cul.	Crawford,Archibald,	1		Bot.	Crenshaw,Susanna,		8	K.Wm.
Crafford,William,	2	7	Cul.	Crawford,Christopher,	1		Spots	Crenshaw,Thomas,	1	6	Lun.
Crafton,Anthony,	1	1	Lun.	Crawford,David,	1		Aug.	Crenshaw,William,	1	24	Lou.
Crafton,Elizabeth,		6	K.Wm.	Crawford,Rev.Edward,	1	3	Bot.	Crenshaw,William,	1	8	Loui.
Crafton,James,	1	1	Lun.	Crawford,Edward,	1		Mont.	Creswell,Andrew,	1		Fay.
Crafton,John,	1	5	Lun.	Crawford,George,			Aug.	Cresswell,Hugh,	1		Fay.
Crafton,Kerenhuppuch,		2	Lun.	Crawford,George,)				Cresswell,Robert,	1		Fay.
Crafton,Mary,		3	K.Wm.	Crawford,James,)	3	10	Aug.	Cresswell,Samuel,	1		Fay.
Crafton,Richard,	1	3	Lun.	Crawford,James,	1		Spots	Crews,William,	1		Lin.
Crafton,Richard,	4	5	K.&Q	Crawford,James,Sr.,	1	6	Spots	Crevins,William,	1		Mot.
Crafton,Richard,Jr.,			K.&Q	Crawford,James,	1	5	Aug.	Crew,Andrew,Sr.,	1		Cha.Cy
Crafton,Thomas,	1	1	Lun.	Crawford,James,	1	1	Aug.	Crew,Andrew,Jr.,	1		Cha.Cy
Crafton,Thomas,	1		Lun.	Crawford,James,	1		Mont.	Crew,Benjamin,	1	1	Cha.Cy
Crafford,Mary,		7	So'n	Crawford,James,	1	2	Fay.	Crew,Exon Scott,	1		Cha.Cy
Crage,James,			Lin.	Crawford,James,	1		Rock.	Crew,Jesse,	1	1	Cha.Cy
Crage,John,	1	3	Lin.	Crawford,James,	1		Bot.	Crew,Jacob,	1		Cha.Cy
Craig,Adam,			Hen.	Crawford,John,	1	4	Aug.	Crew,John,Sr.,	1	1	Cha.Cy
Craig,Alexander,	1		Aug.	Crawford,John,	1	1	Bot.	Crew,John,	1		Cha.Cy
Craig,Benjamin,	1		Bot.	Crawford,John,Jr.,	1		Bot.	Crew,Joseph,	1		Cha.Cy
Craig,Elijah,	2	19	Fay.	Crawford,John,	1	5	Loui.	Crew,Robert,	1	1	Cha.Cy
Craig,George,)				Crawford,John,	1	2	Hen.	Crews,Gideon,	1		Buck.
Craig,James,)	2	6	Aug.	Crawford,Josiah,	1		Bot.	Crews,Isaac,	1	8	Camp.
Craig,James,	1	3	Aug.	Crawford,Nathan,	1		Aug.	Crews,James,	1		Buck.
Craig,Rev.James,	1	42	Lun.	Crawford,Patrick,	2	7	Aug.	Crews,Jesse,	1		Bed.
Craig,Rev.James,		10	Fau.	Crawford,Peter,	1	3	Loui.	Crews,John,	1	1	Din.
Craig,James,	2	1	Lou.	Crawford,Presley,	1	1	West.	Crews,Josiah,	1	1	Lun.
Craig,John,			Aug.	Crawford,Rebecca,			Lin.	Crews,Nicholas,	1		Camp.
Craig,John,	1		Fau.	Crawford,Robert,	1		Mont.	Crews,Richard,Sr.,	1		Lun.
Craig,John,	1		Mont.	Crawford,Samuel,	1	2	Bot.	Crews,Richard,Jr.,	1		Lun.
Craig,John,	1		Rock.	Crawford,Samuel,	2		Bot.	Crews,Thomas,	1		Henry
Craig,Robert,			Aug.	Crawford,William,	1	1	Bot.	Cribben,Thomas,	1		Bot.
Craig,Robert,	3	4	Aug.	Crawford,William,			Bot.	Crichton,William,	1	6	So'n
Craig,Robert,	1		Wash.	Crawford,William,	1		Bot.	Crittenden,Jeremiah,	1	1	Lun.
Craig,Samuel,	1	1	Lin.	Crawford,William,	1	4	Aug.	Crittenden,William,	1	1	Lun.
Craig,Toliver,	2	13	Bot.	Crawford,William,			Aug.	Criddle,William,			Brun.
Craig,Toliver,		2	Fay.	Crawford,William,	1		Fau.	Crigler,Aaron,	1		Cul.
Craig,William,			Lou.	Crawford,William,	1		Rock.	Crigler,Christopher,	1	4	Cul.
Craig,William,	1	6	Aug.	Crawford,William,	1		Rock.	Crigler,Nicholas,	1	2	Cul.
Craige,John,	1		Har.	Crawley,Aquila,	1		Cul.	Crigler,Reuben,	1	1	Cul.
Craige,Samuel,	1		Aug.	Crawley,Curtis,	1		Cul.	Crim,Jacob,	1		Cul.
Craighead,George,			Din.	Crawley,Henry,	1		K.Wm.	Crimm,Catherine,		4	Fau.
Craighead,John,	1	2	Bed.	Crawley,Menoah,	1	1	Fau.	Crimm,Harman,	1		Fau.
Craighead,William,	1	17	Lun.	Crawley,John,	1	23	Ja.Cy	Crimm,Jacob,	1		Fau.
Craighton,Robert,	2		Berk.	Crawley,John,	1		Camp.	Crimm,John,	1		Fau.
Cralle,Thomas,	1	8	Lun.	Crawley,Joseph,	1	3	Ja.Cy	Crimm,Joseph,	1		Fau.
Crancy,William,	2	14	Camp.	Crawley,Richard,	1	8	Cul.	Crimm,Peter,	1		Fau.
Crandol,Thomas,	1	1	Eli.Cy	Crawley,Thomas,	1		Henry	Cripper,John,	1	1	Lou.
Crane,James,	1		Cul.	Crawley,William,	1	7	Din.	Critcher,John,	1	21	West.
Crane,James,	1	9	Berk.	Crawley,William,			Camp.	Crystel,Jerry,	1		Cul.
Crane,John,	1	5	Berk.	Craycraft,Charles,	1	4	Har.	Crisel,William,	1		Cul.
Crane,Samuel,	1		Cul.	Creamer,Aaron,	1		Berk.	Crismond,Oswald,	1		K.Geo.
Crane,Samuel,Jr.,	1		Cul.	Creamer,George,	1		Berk.	Crismond,William,	1		K.Geo.
Crane,Ann,			K.&Q	Creamer,John,	1		Berk.	Cristler,Adam,	1		Cul.
Crain,Catherine,		1	K&Q	Creasy,George,	1		Buck.	Cristler,David,	1	1	Cul.
Crain,George,	1		K&Q	Crecher,George,	1		Rock.	Cristler,George,	1	3	Cul.
Crain,John,	1		K&Q	Creel,David,			Pr.Wm.	Cristler,Henry,	1	3	Cul.
Crain,John,	1	4	Fau.	Creel,John,Sr.,	1		Cul.	Cristler,Lenord,	1		Cul.
Crains,William,	1		Cul.	Creel,John,Jr.,	1		Cul.	Criswell,John,			Lou.
Crank,George,	1	2	Loui.					Criswell,Sackerwrite,	1	4	Din.

Name			Loc	Name			Loc	Name			Loc
Crites,Jacob,	1		Har.	Crouch,Joseph,	1		Henry	Cruser,Derrick,	1		Berk.
Crites,Phillip,Jr.,	1		Har.	Crouch,Judith,		1	Gooch.	Crusinburry,George,	1		Mont.
Critten,James,	1		Bot.	Crouch,William,	1		Bed.	Crutcher,Fanny,		10	Cul.
Crittenden,Henry,		10	Brun.	Crouch,Richard,	4	5	Hen.	Crutcher,Henry,	1	3	Caro.
Crittendon,John,	2	9	Cul.	Crouch,Richard,Jr.,			Hen.	Crutcher,Hugh,	1	4	Caro.
Crittendon,Richard,	1		Bot.	Crouch,Stephen,			Hen.	Crutcher,Thomas,	1	13	Caro.
Crittendon,Richard,Sr.,	1	18	K.&Q.	Crouch,Stephen,	1	6	Gooch.	Crutcher,Thomas,	1	14	Spots.
Crittendon,Richard,Jr.,	1	3	K.&Q.	Crouch,Susanna,		4	Gooch.	Crutchfield,George,	1	5	Caro.
Crittendon,William,			Cul.	Croucher,Samuel,	1	2	Henry	Crutchfield,George,	1		Lin.
Crittendon,Zachariah,	1		K.&Q.	Croudus,George,			Gooch.	Crutchfield,John,	1	20	Loui.
Crittington,William,	1	2	Din.	Crow,Anthony,	1	7	K.Wm.	Crutchfield,John,	2		Caro.
Critz,Hamon,Sr.,	3	4	Henry	Crow,Benjamin,	1		Aug.	Crutchfield,Lewis,			Ch.Cy.
Critz,Hamon,Jr.,	1	4	Henry	Crow,David,	1		Har.	Crutchfield,Stap'ton	1	32	Spots.
Crocker,Arthur,	1		So'n.	Crow,Edward,	1		Mont.	Crutchfield,Susanna		3	Ch.Cy.
Crocker,Elijah,	1	4	So'n.	Crow,James,	1		Aug.	Crutchfield,William,	3		Gooch.
Crockett,Andrew,	1	3	Mont.	Crow,James,	2	11	Cul.	Crutchfield,William	3		Gooch.
Crocket,Hugh,	1	4	Bot.	Crow,James,	1		Lin.	Crutchfield,William	1	1	Hen.
Crocket,James,	1	1	Rock.	Crow,John,	1		Cul.	Cubbage,John,	1		Cul.
Crockett,James,	1	5	Mont.	Crow,Robert,Jr.,	1		Mont.	Cubbage,Thomas,	1		Bot.
Crockett,James,	2	3	Fau.	Crow,Robert,	1		Brun.	Cuble,Marcus,	1		Aug.
Crokett,Jessey,			Acco.	Crow,Thomas,	2		Mont.	Cudden,John,	1		Har.
Crockett,John,	1	2	Mont.	Crow,William,	3		Lin.	Culberson,Mary,			Wash.
Crokett,Joseph,	3		Acco.	Crow,William,	2	8	Bot.	Culbreath,Thomas,	1		Aug.
Crocket,Mary,		3	Rock.	Crow,William,	1		Mont.	Cullemy,Lansel,	1		Wash.
Crockett,Samuel,	1	5	Bed.	Crowder,Daniel,	1	8	Din.	Cullen,Charles,	2	1	Caro.
Crokett,Thomas,	1		Acco.	Crowder,Drury,Jr.,	1		Din.	Cullins,James,	1	1	Pr.Wm.
Crockett,Walter,	1	1	Mont.	Crowder,Drury,	1	2	Din.	Cullins,Sarah,		8	Pr.Wm.
Croddy,John,	1		Rock.	Crowder,Henry,			Din.	Culton,Alexander,	2		Rock.
Crofford,John,	1		Lin.	Crowder,Henry,Sr.,	1		Din.	Culton,James,	1	1	Mont.
Croft,James,	1		Mont.	Crowder,James,	1	3	Din.	Culton,James,	1		Rock.
Crook,C.,	1		Pr.Wm.	Crowder,John Wagnon,	1		Din.	Culton,John,	1		Rock.
Crook,George,Sr.,	1	1	Brun.	Crowder,Joseph,	1		Din.	Cumbers,James,	2		Lou.
Crook,George,Jr.,	1		Brun.	Crowder,Phebe,		5	Din.	Cumbo,Jethro,	1		Ja.Cy.
Crook,J.,			Pr.Wm.	Crowder,Richard,	1	10	Din.	Cumbo,Stephen,	1		Ja.Cy.
Crook,James,	2	11	Brun.	Crowder,William,	2	2	Din.	Cummack,William,	1		Bot.
Crook,James,	1		Lou.	Crowder,Zachariah,	1		Din.	Cummings,Anthony,	1		Lou.
Crook,John,	1	3	Lou.	Crowell,David,	1		Lou.	Cummings,Benjamin,	1		Henry
Crook,Joseph,	1	8	Brun.	Crowley,Elizabeth,			Henry	Cummings,Benjamin,	1		Lou.
Crook,Mary,		3	Fau.	Crowson,Charles,	3		Acco.	Cummings,Benjamin,	1		Lou.
Crook,Pennuel,	1	3	Eli.Cy.	Crowson,William,	1	5	Acco.	Cummings,Ellin,			Henry
Crook,William,			Brun.	Crowy,Dennis,	1		Cul.	Cummings,George,	1		Rock.
Crooks,James,	1		Lou.	Cryer,John,	1	36	Din.	Cummings,James,	1		Lou.
Cropper,Col.John,	1	16	Acco.	Cryer,Robert,	1		Din.	Cummings,John,	1		Bot.
Cropper,John,Sr.,	1	5	Acco.	Crymes,George,	2	16	Lun.	Cummings,John,	1		Rock.
Cropper,Laney,		1	Acco.	Crymes,Keziah,		4	Lun.	Cummings,Jonathon,	1		Lou.
Cropper,Sebastian,	1	6	Acco.	Crymes,Thomas,	1	2	Lun.	Cummings,	1		Lou.
Cropper,Thomas,	1	1	Acco.	Crugar,John,	1		Mont.	Cummings,Malachai,	1		Lou.
Crosby,George,	3	4	Fau.	Crugar,Michael,	1		Mont.	Cummings,Robert,	1		Aug.
Crosby,Uriel,	1		Fau.	Crugar,Peter,	1		Mont.	Cummins,Alexander,	1		Fau.
Croson,H.,	1		Pr.Wm.	Crugar,Peter,	1		Mont.	Cummins,George,	1		Lou.
Cross,Christian,	2		Har.	Crumb,Matthias,	1		Mont.	Cummins,James,	1		Lou.
Cross,Drury,			Din.	Crumbar,John,	1		Lou.	Cummins,Thomas,	1		Lou.
Cross,Elizabeth,		5	Lou.	Crumly,George,	1		Berk.	Cummins,John,	1		Fau.
Cross,James,	1	4	K.Geo.	Crumley,William,	1	1	Berk.	Cummins,John,	1		Fau.
Cross,John,	1	24	Lun.	Crum,Margaret,			Lou.	Cummins,Moses,	1		Fau.
Cross,John,	1		Lou.	Crummett,Christopher,	1		Aug.	Cummins,Thomas,	1	1	Fau.
Cross,John,	1		Berk.	Crump,Benjamin,	2	11	Fau.	Cumpton,Philip,	2		Fay.
Cross,Richard,	1		Har.	Crump,George,	1	4	K.Wm.	Cura,Dudley,			Lin.
Cross,Richard,	1	2	Din.	Crump,George,			Cul.	Cushaw,John,	1		Fay.
Cross,Samuel,	1		Rock.	Crump,James,	1	15	West.	Custard,William,	1	1	Fay.
Cross,Solomon,	1		Mont.	Crump,John,		7	York.	Custner,Elizabeth,	1		Fay.
Cross,William,	1	10	Lun.	Crump,Richard,	2	4	Bed.	Cundiff,Benjamin,	1		Bed.
Cross,William,	1	2	Din.	Crump,Thomas,	2		K.Wm.	Cundiff,George,	1		Bed.
Crosthwart,Jacob,	2	5	Fay.	Crump,Thomas,			Bed.	Cundiff,Isaac,	1	1	Fau.
Crosthwart,Samuel,			Fay.	Crump,Thomas,	1		Camp.	Cundiff,James,	1		Fau.
Crot,John Thomas,	1		Camp.	Crump,Turner,	1	1	Fay.	Cundiff,John,	1		Bed.
Crouse,Christopher,	1		Lou.	Crump,William,	1		Fay.	Cundiff,John,			Pr.Wm.
Crouch,Francis,			Fay.	Crumpler,Benjamin,	1		So'n.	Cundiff,John,			Pr.Wm.
Crouch,Jacob,	1		Pr.Wm.	Crumpler,Bezant,	1		So'n.	Cundiff,Valentine,	1		Bed.
Crouch,John,	1		Hen.	Crumpler,John,	1		So'n.	Cundiff,William,	1		Pr.Wm.
Crouch,John,			Fay.	Crumpton,Robert,			Hen.	Cunningham,Ann,	1	1	Aug.
Crouch,John,	1		Bed.	Crumpton,Samuel,	1		Berk.	Cuningham,Ann,		5	Spots.
Crouch,John,	1		Henry	Crumpton,Thomas,	2	2	Hen.	Cunningham,Archib'd,	1		Aug.
Crouch,John,Jr.,	1		Henry	Crunk,John,	2		Berk.	Cunningham,David,	1		Aug.
Crouch,Joseph,	1		Pr.Wm.	Crunk,William,	1		Wash.	Cunningham,Francis,	1		Mont.
Crouch,Joseph,	1		Mont.	Crupper,Richard,	1		Lou.	Cunningham,George,	2	7	Berk.
								Cuningham,James,	1	1	Rock.

Name			Co.	Name			Co.	Name			Co.
Cunningham,James,	3	3	Har.	Curtis,Rice,	2	8	Spots	Dalles,Marmanduke,	1		Bed.
Cunningham,James,	1		Har.	Curtis,Robert,	2	4	K.&Q.	Dallis,James,	1		LLou.
Cunningham,James,	1		Bot.	Curtis,Robert,	1	3	York	Dalles,John,	1		Bed.
Cunningham,James,	1		Aug.	Cussenberry,John,	1		Fau.	Dally,John,	1	3	K.&Q
Cunningham,James,	1		Aug.	Custis,Edmund,	1	27	Acco.	Dally,Thomas,	1		K.&Q
Cunningham,James,	1	2	Eli.Cy	Custis,Col.Henry,	1	18	Acco.	Dalton,Garret,	1		Aug.
Cunningham,James,	1		Buck.	Custis,Henry,	2	10	Acco.	Dalton,James,	2	1	Pr.Wm.
Cunningham,Jane,			Aug.	Custis,Henry,Jr.,			Acco.	Dalton,John,	1	1	Din.
Cunningham,John,	1	1	Henry	Custis,John,	1	13	Acco.	Dalton,Rachel,		5	Pr.Wm.
Cuningham,John,		2	Cul.	Custis,John,	2	29	Acco.	Dalton,Reuben,	1		Mont.
Cunningham,John,	1	1	Aug.	Custis,John,	1	1	Acco.	Dalton,Samuel,	1		Mont.
Cunningham,John,	1	1	Aug.	Custis,John P.,Est.,	1	59	K.Wm.	Dalton,Timothy,	1		Mont.
Cuninghan,John,	1		Lou.	Custis,John,P.,		14	Nor.	Dalton,William,	1		Mont.
Cuningham,Moses,	1		Rock.	Custis,Kassey,		8	Acco.	Dam,William,	1	2	K.&Q
Cunninghame,Patrick,	1		Berk.	Custis,Onley,	1		Acco.	Dam,John,	1	1	K.&Q
Carry,Patrick,	1		Berk.	Custis,Revil,Sr.,	3	5	Acco.	Dameron,Bartholomew	1	9	Brun.
Cunningham,Robert,	1	13	Har.	Custis,Revil,Jr.,	1	13	Acco.	Dameron,Christopher	1	12	Brun.
Cunningham,Samuel B.,			Eli.Cy	Custis,Robinson,	1	9	Acco.	Dameron,Joseph,	1	4	Brun.
Cunningham,William,	1		Eli.Cy	Custis,Thomas,Sr.,	1	6	Acco.	Dameron,Samuel,	1	8	Brun.
Cuningham,Thomas,	1		Rock.	Custis,Thomas,	1	13	Acco.	Dameron,William,	2	1	West.
Cunningham,Thomas,	1		Aug.	Custis,William,S.,	1	24	Acco.	Damron,George,	1		Buck.
Cunningham,Walter,	1	1	Aug.	Cuthburton,James,	1		K.Geo	Damron,Moses,	1		Mont.
Cunningham,William,	1	3	Eli.Cy	Cutlar,Mary,		1	Acco.	Damron,Myke,	1		Buck.
Cunningham,William,			Bed.	Cutlar,Richard,	3	9	Acco.	Danaho,Charles,	1		Camp.
Cunningham,William,	1	4	Har.	Cutlar,Richard,Jr.,			Acco.	Danaho,Hugh,	1	9	Aug.
Cunningham,William,Jr	2	13	Har.	Cutlar,Smith,	1	1	Acco.	Danaho,James,	1	2	Aug.
Cuningham,William,	1		Camp.	Cuttilloe,Abram,	1	1	Lun.	Dance,Drury,	1	2	Din.
Cuper,Valentine,	1		Har.	Cymon,Lewis,			York	Dance,Stephen,	1	4	Din.
Curd,James,	1	21	Gooch.	Cynn,Francis,	1		Pr.Wm	Dancy,Joseph,	1		Hen.
Curd,Col.John,	1	15	Gooch.	Cypher,John,	1		Mont.	Dandridge,Alex.Spot.	1	11	Berk.
Curd,John,		6	Gooch.	Cyphert,Christian,	1		Mont.	Dandridge,Francis,	1	24	K.Wm.
Curd,Joseph,	1	10	Buck.					Dandridge,William,	3	68	K.Wm.
Curd,Sarah,		22	Gooch.	Dabney,Benjamin,	1	11	Din.	Dancy,Benjamin,	1	15	Cha.Cy
Curd,William,	1	9	Buck.	Dabney,Cornelias,	1		Bea.	Dancy,Edward,	1	9	Cha.Cy
Curde,Edward,	1	10	Hen.	Dabney,Cornelius,	1	12	Loui.	Daney,Hardyman,	2	13	Cha.Cy
Curde,Mrs.Mary,		8	Hen.	Dabney,George,	2	28	K.Wm.	Daney,John,	1	14	Cha.Cy
Cureton,James,	1	11	Pr.Geo	Dabney,George,Sr.,	1	24	K.Wm.	Daney,Mary,		1	Cha.Cy
Cureton,James,	1	4	Pr.Geo	Dabney,Isaac,	1	35	K.Wm.	Daney,William,	1	6	Cha.Cy
Cureton,John,Sr.,	1	12	Lun.	Dabney,James,	1	42	Loui.	Danie,Barzilla,	1	5	Din.
Cureton,John,Jr.,	1	7	Lun.	Dabney,John,	1	5	Din.	Danie,Mathew,	1	11	Din.
Cureton,William,	1	23	Pr.Geo	Dabney,Richard,	2	26	K.Wm.	Danie,Thomas,	2	32	Din.
Curevein,Robert,	1	1	Mont.	Dabney,Robert,	2	23	Loui.	Danie,Thomas,Jr.,			Din.
Curl,Jeremiah,	2		Har.	Dabney,Samuel,	1	23	Loui.	Daniel,Andrew,	2		Berk.
Curl,Samuel,	2	1	K.Geo.	Dacus,Nathaniel,	1		Lun.	Daniel,Cary Wells,	1	8	Din.
Curl,William,	1		Har.	Dacus,William,	1	1	Lun.	Daniel,Charles,Jr.,	1	6	Loui.
Curle,Mary,		22	Eli.Cy	Dade,Baldwin,	11	22	K.Geo.	Daniel,Charles,Se.,	1	12,	Loui.
Curle,Mary,		10	Eli.Cy	Dade,Francis,Jr.,	5	4	K.Geo.	Daniel,Christopher,	1	6	Spots.
Curnard,George,	1		Cul.	Dade,Langhom,	1	26	K.Geo.	Daniel,Christopher,	1		Din.
Curpman,Philip,	1		Lou.	Dade,Lenghorn,		6	Cul.	Daniel,David,	1		Berk,
Currie,Doctor,	1	5	Hen.	Dade,Robert,T.,	1	9	Fau.	Daniel,Edmund,	1		Caro.
Currine,Robert,	1		Lou.	Dade,Rose,		19	K.Geo.	Daniel,Elijah,			Cul.
Currinee,John,	1		Lou.	Dade,Rev.Thownshend,	1	1	Lou.	Daniel,George,	1		Henry
Curry,Alexander,	1		Aug.	Dade,Townshend,	29	36	K.Geo.	Daniel,Hugh,	1		Aug.
Curry,James,	1		Fau.	Dade,Townshend,	1	7	Pr.Wm.	Daniel,Ichabua,	1	9	Gooch.
Curry,James,	1		Aug.	Laft,Phillip,	1		Aug.	Daniel,James,	1		Hen.
Curry,John,	1		Pr.Wm	Daggett,Chatten,	1		Bea.	Daniel,James,	1	6	Caro.
Curry,John,	1		Lou.	Dagnall,Richard,	1		Buck.	Daniel,James,	1	2	Caro.
Curry,Mary,			Wash.	Dailey,Frances,			Brun.	Daniel,Jesse,	1		Brun.
Curry,Robt.Master,	1		Aug.	Dailey,Isaac,	1		Mont.	Daniel,John,	1		Spots.
Curry,Samuel,	1		Aug.	Dailey,John,	1		Brun.	Daniel,John,	1	9	Loui.
Curry,Terrence,	1		Berk.	Dailey,Joseph,	1	2	Hen.	Daniel,John,	1	2	Gooch.
Curry,Thomas,	1		Berk.	Dailey,William,	1		Brun.	Daniel,John,	4		Berk.
Curry,William,	2		Aug.	Daingerfield,William	2	56	Spots	Daniel,John,	1		Bea.
Curry,William,Jr.,	1		Aug.	Daingerfield,Wm.,Est.	1	86	Spots	Daniel,John,	1	10	Pr.Geo.
Curtis,Barnabas,			Lou.	Daker,Christopher,	1		Fau.	Daniel,John,	1		Henry
Curtis,Chich,	1	8	Pr.Wm	Dalby,John,	1	6	Nor.	Daniel,John,Sr.,	1	2	Pr.Geo.
Curtis,Cislue,	1		Brun.	Dalby,Spencer,	1	2	Nor.	Daniel,Joseph,			Brun.
Curtis,Edmund,	1	16	York	Dalby,Thomas,Jr.,	1	5	Nor.	Daniel,Joseph,Jr.,	1		Brun.
Curtis,James,	1		West.	Dalby,Thomas,Sr.,	1	15	Nor.	Daniel,Joshua,	1	10	Lou.
Curtis,James,			Lou.	Dale,Alexander,	2		Rock.	Daniel,Lucy,		2	Pr.Geo.
Curtis,Job,Sr.,	1		Berk.	Dale,Peter,	1		Rock.	Daniel,Lumford,	1	3	K.&Q
Curtis,Job,Jr.,	1		Berk.	Dale,Richard,	1		Bea.	Daniel,Marmanduke,	1		Wash.
Curtis,John,			Cul.	Dale,Robert,	1		Wash.	Daniel,Mary,	3		Caro.
Curtis,John,	2	8	Lou.	Dale,William,	1	4	Fau.	Daniel,Mosly,	1	2	Gooch.
Curtis,John,	1		Fau.	Dales,Joseph,	1		So'n.	Daniel,Peter,	1		Camp.
Curtis,Rebecca,			West.	Dalhouse,John,	1	1	Aug.	Daniel,Peter,	1		Camp.

Name			County
Daniel,Peter,	1		Camp.
Daniel,Peter,Jr.,	1		Camp.
Daniel,Peter,Jr.,	1		Camp.
Daniel,Randall,	1	9	Din.
Daniel,Reese,	1	2	Pr.Geo
Daniel,Samuel,	1		Cul.
Daniel,Susanna,			Brun.
Daniel,Thomas,	1	6	Loui.
Daniel,Thomas,	1	2	Din.
Daniel,Thomas,	1	13	Pr.Geo
Daniel,Thomas,	1	1	Brun.
Daniel,William,	1	1	Brun.
Daniel,William,	1	7	Caro.
Daniels,John,	1		Berk.
Dankin,Ebenezer,	1		Fay.
Dannell,Richard,	1		Camp.
Dannell,Richard,	1		Camp.
Danol,Pierce,	1		Bot.
Danzie,JohnJacob,Sr.,			Lun.
Danzie,John Jacob,Jr.,	1	9	Lun.
Darby,Benjamin,	1	4	Acco.
Darby,Custis,	2		Acco.
Darby,John,	1	7	Acco.
Darby,John,	1	11	Nor.
Darby,Owen,	1	4	Acco.
Darby,Patty,		7	Din.
Dare,Edmond,	1	2	Spots
Dark,Mary,			Berk.
Dark,William,	1	1	Berk.
Darling,Robert,	1	1	Har.
Darlington,Abraham,	1		Lin.
Darmitt,Mott,	1		K.Geo
Darnaby,Edward,	1	5	Spots
Darnaby,John,	1	1	Fay.
Darnaby,William,	1	9	Spots
Darnaby,William,Jr.,	1	5	Spots
Darnall,David,	2		Lou.
Darnall,Jeremiah,	1	10	Fau.
Darnall,Joseph,	1	4	Fau.
Darnall,Smith,	1		Fay.
Darnall,Thomas,	1		Fay.
Darnold,Waugh,	1		Cul.
Darr,Boston,	2		Lou.
Darr,George,	1		Lou.
Darricott,Thomas,	1	27	Loui.
Darst,Benjamin,	1	3	Gooch
Darter,Nicholas,	1		Mont.
Darting,Philip,	2		Mont.
Darvell,Edward,	1	8	Pr,Geo
Darville,Mrs.C.		9	Din.
Dashper,Thomas,	1		Loui.
Daughtery,John,	2	2	Lin.
Daugherty,Thomas,	2	4	Bed.
Daugherty,William,	1		Lin.
Daughtery,James,	1		So'n
Daughtery,John,	1		So'n
Doughtery,Mary,			So'n
Daulton,John,	1		Loui.
Davenport,Charles,	2	13	Cul.
Davenport,David,	1	3	Pr.Geo
Davenport,Elizabeth,		7	Pr.Geo
Davenport,Glover,	1		Bed.
Davenport,James,	1	1	Pr.Geo
Davenport,James,	1	1	Spots
Davenport,John,	1	4	Spots
Davenport,Joseph,	1	9	York
Davenport,Joseph,	1		Bed.
Davenport,Martin,	1		Spots
Davenport,Nancy,		2	Pr.Geo
Davenport,William,	1	15	Spots
Daverex,Charles,	1	13	Mont.
Daves,Evan,	1	6	Caro.
Daves,Spilsby,	1	4	Caro.
Davey,William,	1		Caro.
Davice,John,	1		Camp.
Davidson,Edward,			Cha.Cy
Davidson,Elizabeth,			Rock.
Davidson,John,	1		Rock.
Davidson,John,	1		Mont.
Davidson,Jolder,	1		Henry
Davidson,Samuel,	1		Rock.
Davidson,Walter,	1		Mont.
Davidson,William,	2	2	Bot.
Davidson,William,	1		Mont.
Davidson,William,Sr.,	1		Rock.
Davies,Baxter,	1		Mont.
Davies,Charles,	1		Mont.
Davies,Henry,	1	9	Mont.
Davies,Hugh,Sr.,	2		Rock.
Davie,Isaac,	1		Henry
Davies,James,	1		Mont.
Davies,James,	1		Rock.
Davies,James,Jr.,	1	1	Mont.
Davies,James,Sr.,	2		Mont.
Davies,Joseph,	1		Mont.
Davies,Nicholas,	1	42	Bed.
Davie,Peter,	1		Henry
Davies,Robert,	1		Mont.
Davies,Robert,	1	6	Mont.
Davies,Robert,	1		Mont.
Davies,Samuel,	1	9	Din.
Davies,Samuel,	1	1	Mont.
Davies,Thomas,	1		Mont.
Davies,William,	1	1	Mont.
Davies,William,	1		Mont.
Davis,Abel,	1		Lou.
Davis,Abraham,	1		Lun.
Davis,Abraham,	2		Loui.
Davis,Andrew,	2		Wash.
Davis,Ann,			West.
Davis,Ann,			Gooch
Davis,Archer,			York
Davis,Azel,	1	1	Lin.
Davis,Benjamin,	1		Cul.
Davis,Benjamin,	1	3	Brun.
Davis,Benjamin,	1		Buck.
Davis,Benjamin,	1		Lou.
Davis,Benjamin,	1		Bed.
Davis,Benjamin,	1	2	Spots
Davis,Bartlet,			Buck.
Davis,Charles,	1		Aug.
Davis,Cyrus,	1	12	Loui.
Davis,Daniel,	1		Berk.
Davis,Daniel,	1		Berk.
Davis,David,	1		Loud.
Davis,David,	1	2	Loud.
Davis,David,	1	2	Gooch
Davis,Edmund,	1		Gooch
Davis,Edmund,	1		Lun.
Davis,Edward,	1		Berk.
Davis,Eleazer,	1	1	Pr.Wm.
Davis,Eli,	1		Fau.
Davis,Elizabeth,	1	4	West.
Davis,Elizabeth,		4	Lin.
Davis,George,	1		Fau,
Davis,Giles,	1	2	Din.
Davis,Gressitt,	1	5	Din.
Davis,H.	1	4	Pr.Wm.
Davis,Hardaway,		4	Din.
Davis,Hary,		2	Cul.
Davis,Henry,	1		Lin.
Davis,Henry,	1		Wash.
Davis,Henry,	1	3	So'n
Davis,Henry,	1	6	Cul.
Davis,Henry,	1		Cul.
Davis,Hezekiah,	1		Brun.
Davis,Isaac,	1		Bed.
Davis,J.			Pr.Wm.
Davis,Jacob,			Lou.
Davis,James,			Fay.
Davis,James,	1		Eli.Cy
Davis,James,	1		Lin.
Davis,James,	1	1	Wash.
Davis,James,	1		Fau.
Davis,James,	1	2	Spots.
Davis,James,	1		Pr.Wm.
Davis,James,	1		Lou.
Davis,James,	1	3	K.Geo.
Davis,James,	1		Pr.Wm.
Davis,James,	1	1	Cul.
Davis,James,	1		Aug.
Davis,Jane,	1		Lin.
Davis,Jesse,	1		Lin.
Davis,Jesse,	1		West.
Davis,Joel,	1		Buck.
Davis,Joel,	1	3	So'n
Davis,John,	1		Fau.
Davis,John,	1		Spots.
Davis,John,	1		West.
Davis,John,	1		Pr.Wm.
Davis,John,	1		Pr.Wm.
Davis,John,	1	1	Cul.
Davis,John,	1	1	Cul.
Davis,John,	1	11	Ja.Cy
Davis,John,	1		Loui.
Davis,John,	1		Berk.
Davis,John,	1	2	Bed.
Davis,John,	1		Camp.
Davis,John,			Acco.
Davis,John,	1	1	Aug.
Davis,John,	1		Aug.
Davis,John,	1		Bot.
Davis,John,	1		Lou.
Davis,John,			Lou.
Davis,John,	1	1	Lou.
Davis,John,	1	3	K.Wm.
Davis,John,	1		Din.
Davis,John,	1		Lou.
Davis,John,	2		Lou.
Davis,John,	1	1	Lou.
Davis,John,	1	9	So'n
Davis,John,	1		Lun.
Davis,John,	1		Wash.
Davis,John,	1		Lin.
Davis,John,	1		Lin.
Davis,John Lewis,	1	1	Bed.
Davis,Jonathan,	1	1	Lun.
Davis,Jonathan,	2	4	Lou.
Davis,Joseph,			Lin.
Davis,Joseph,			Lun.
Davis,Joseph,			Brun.
Davis,Joseph,			Henry
Davis,Joseph,	1		Henry
Davis,Joshua,			Lou.
Davis,Kiziah,	1	1	Acco.
Davis,Levern,	1	2	Nor.
Davis,Levie,	1		Bed.
Davis,Lydia,			So'n
Davis,Mathew,	1	1	Buck.
Davis,Merritt,			Brun.
Davis,Michael,	1		Berk.
Davis,Morriss,	1	3	Din.
Davis,Nathan,	1		Bot.
Davis,Owen,	1		Berk.
Davis,Owen,	1	1	Brun.
Davis,Peter,	1		West.
Davis,Peter,			Din.
Davis,Philip,	1	4	Caro.
D avis,Philip,	1	6	So'n
Davis,Philip,	1		Henry
Davis,Randle,	1	2	Lun.
Davis,Richard,	1	6	Fay.
Davis,Richard,	1	10	K.Wm.
Davis,Robert,	1		Gooch.
Davis,Robert,	1		Berk.
Davis,Robert,	1	5	Bed.
Davis,Robert,	1	9	K.Wm.
Davis,Robert,	1	1	Brun.
Davis,Robert,	1		Brun.

Name			Place
Davis,Robert,	1	2	Cul.
Davis,Robert,Jr.,	1	2	K.Wm.
Davis,S.	1	3	Pr.Wm
Davis,Samuel,	1		Lin.
Davis,Samuel,	1		Wash.
Davis,Samuel,	1	1	Bot.
Davis,Samuel,	1		Lou.
Davis,Samuel,	1		Lou.
Davis,Samuel,	1	1	Lou.
Davis,Samuel,	1	3	Lou.
Davis,Sarah,			Pr.Wm
Davis,Septimus,			Fay.
Davis,Solomon,	1	7	Din.
Davis,Solomon,	1		Henry
Davis,Stephen,	1	6	Gooch
Davis,Susanna,			Gooch
Davis,Temperence,		1	K.Wm.
Davis,Thomas,	2		Lin.
Davis,Thomas,	1		Lun.
Davis,Thomas,	1		Berk.
Davis,Thomas,	1		Bot.
Davis,Thomas,	1	1	K.Wm.
Davis,Thomas,	1		Har.
Davis,Thomas,	1		Har.
Davis,Thomas,	1		Lou.
Davis,Thomas,	1		Buck.
Davis,W.	1	2	Pr.Wm
Davis,Walter,	1		Aug.
Davis,William,	1	1	Eli.Cy
Davis,William,	1		Fay.
Davis,William,	1		Berk.
Davis,William,	1	1	Acco.
Davis,William,	1		Lou.
Davis,William,	1		Pr.Wm
Davis,William,	1		Pr.Wm
Davis.William,			Cul.
Davis,William,	1		Henry
Davis,William,Sr.,	1	7	Din.
Davis,William,Jr.,	1	11	Din.
Davis,Zachariah,	1		Bed.
Davis,Zachariah,	1	2	Lun.
Davison,Alexander,	2		Camp.
Davison,Andrew,	1		Wash.
Davison,Daniel,	1		Wash.
Davison,Edward,	1		Buck.
Davison,George,	2	4	Lin.
Davison,James,Sr.,	1	1	Wash.
Davison,James,Sr.,	1		Wash.
Davison,John,	1		Henry
Davison,John,	1		Berk.
Davison,John,Sr.,	1		Camp.
Davison,John,Jr.,	1		Camp.
Davison,John,Sr.,	1		Camp.
Davison,John,Jr.,	1		Camp.
Davison,Joseph,	1		Wash.
Davison,William,	1		Henry
Davison,William,	1		Wash.
Davitt,Tully,	1	1	Aug.
Dawd,Philip,	2	2	Pr.Wm
Dawess,Henry,			Bot.
Dawess,Paul,	1		Bot.
Dawess,William,	1		Bot.
Dawkins,John,			Pr.Wm
Dawkins,John,	1	5	Berk.
Dawney,Alexander,	1	9	Cul.
Daws,Hannah,		4	Lun.
Dawson,Abraham,	1		Lou.
Dawson,Benjamin,	1		Spots
Dawson,Frederick,	1		Lou.
Dawson,Jacob,	1		Berk.
Dawson,James,	1		Cul.
Dawson,John,	1		Bed.
Dawson,John,	1		Caro.
Dawson,Mary,		2	Berk.
Dawson,Matthias,	1		Lou.
Dawson,Robert,	1		Spots
Dawson,Samuel,	1	12	Brun.
Dawson,Shadrack,	1		Acco.
Dawson,Thomas,			York
Dawson,William,	1	4	Spots.
Dawson,William,	1		Acco.
Day,Amery,	1		Cul.
Day,Edmund,	1	14	So'n
Day,Edward,	1	3	Lou.
Day,Elizabeth,		8	So'n
Day,Francis,	1		Fau.
Day,Francis,	1	4	Mont.
Day,Hanson,	1		Lou.
Day,Jeremiah,			Lou.
Day,John,	1		Mont.
Day,John,	1	2	So'n.
Day,John,	1		Lou.
Day,John,			Buck.
Day,John,	1		Din.
Day,John,		9	Spots
Day,Joseph,	1		Mont.
Day,Leonard,	1		Fau.
Day,Lewis,			Cul.
Day,Matthew,	1		Lou.
Day,Oliver,	1	7	Brun.
Day,Peter,	1		Buck.
Day,Samuel,	1		Aug.
Day,Thomas,	1		Bed.
Day,William,	1		Lin.
Day,William,	1		Fau.
Day,William,	1		Berk.
Day,William,	1		Cul.
Day,William,	1		Cul.
Day,Zachariah,	1		Lou.
Dayel,Carr,	1		So'n
Dayel,Edmund,	1		So'n
Dayel,Elizabeth,	1		So'n
Dayel,Hardy,	1		So'n
Dayel,Jonah,	1		So'n
Dayel,Richard,	1		So'n
Dayel,William,Sr.,	1		So'n
Dayel,William,Jr.,	1		So'n
Dayley,Charles,	1	6	Lou.
Dayley,John,	2		Berk.
Dayley,Ralph,	1		Lou.
Dayly,Nicholas,	1		Lou.
D'Bell,William,	1	5	Lou.
Deakerson,Francis,	1		Bed.
Deakerson,John,	1		Bed.
Deal,William,	1		Bed.
Dean,Adam,	1	1	Mont.
Dean,Henry Harrison,	1		Henry
Dean,John,			Hen.
Dean,Joshua,	1		Har.
Dean,Martin,	1		Cul.
Dean,Robert,	1		Lin.
Dean,Thomas,	2	3	Har.
Dean,William,			Hen.
Deane,Benjamin,	1		Har.
Deane,Charles,	2	8	Bed.
Deane,Charles,	1	15	West.
Deane,John,	1		Fau.
Deane,Samuel,	1		Lou.
Deane,Thomas,	1		West.
Deane,Thomas,	1		Har.
Deans,Benjamin,	1	3	K.&Q
Deans,Benjamin,			K.&Q
Dear,Andrew,	1		Cul.
Dear,John,	1		Cul.
Dear,Moses,	1		Cul.
Dearing,John,	1		Bed.
Deassonburgh,John,	1		Lou.
Deatterly,Matthew,	3		West.
Debell,John,	1	1	Lou.
Debell,William,			Lou.
Deloach,Solomon,	1	24	So'n
Debell,William,			Lou.
Debon,Abraham,	1		Berk.
Debon,Joseph,	1		Berk.
Debusk,Elisha,			Wash.
Debzel,James,	1		Bot.
Decker,Isaac,	1		Rock.
Decratt,Abraham,	1		Lou.
Dedman,Bartlett,	1		York
Dedman,John,	1		Loui.
Dedman,Nathan,	1		York
Dedman,Philip,	1	1	York
Deel,Daniel,	1		Cul.
Deel,John,	1		Cul.
Deel,Peter,	1		Berk.
Deen,Abraham,	1		Fay.
Deen,Russell,,	1		Cha.Cy
Deer,William,	1	3	K.Geo.
Deering,Jeremiah,	1		Fau.
Deering,John,	1	1	Fau.
Deering,William,	1		Fau.
Defress,James,	1		Rock.
Deglarne, J.		2	Pr.Wm
DeGraffenreidt,Franc.	1	24	Lun.
DeGraffenreidt,Metc.		2	Lun.
DeGraffenreidt,Tsch.	1	28	Lun.
DeGraffenreidt,Wm.	1	12	Lun.
Deham,Samuel,	1		Berk.
Dejarnett,Daniel,	1	1	Lun.
Delaforce, J.	1		Pr.Wm
Delaney,Samuel,	1		Bed.
Delany,Benjamin,	1	2	Cul.
Delany,John,	2	1	Cul.
Delany,John,Sr.,	2	7	Cul.
Delany,Joseph,	1	4	Cul.
Delany,Mary,		2	Cul.
Delay,Henry,	1	1	Fay.
Delbridge,Robert,	1		Rock.
Delbridge,Thomas,	1		Brun.
Delgarn, J.	1		Pr.Wm
Delk,John,	1		So'n
Delkill,John,	1		Lou.
Delling,William,	1		Mont.
Deloach,Benjamin,	1	9	So'n
Deloach,Richard,	1		So'n
Delong,James,	1		Fau.
Delong,Peter,	1		Berk.
Delony,Henry,	1		Berk.
Delony,Henry,	1	9	Brun.
Delozier,Edward,	1		Henry
Delozier,Jesse,	1		Henry
Delp,Conrade,	1		Cul.
Delp,Henry,	1	1	Cul.
Delph,Adam,	1		Cul.
Delph,Samuel,	1	3	Cul.
Demery,John,	1		Lou.
Demory,David,	1		So'n
Demory,John,	1		Lin.
Demoss,Charles,	1		Berk.
Demoss,Peter,	1		Berk.
Demoss,Thomas,	1		Berk.
Dempsey,Barnable,	1		Henry
Dempsey,Thomas,			Henry
Denfey,Samuel,	1	8	Ja.Cy
Denfey,Samuel,	1	8	Ja.Cy
Denheart,Drury,	1	1	Pr.Geo.
Denheart,Rebecca,	1	13	Pr.Geo.
Denison,James,	2	1	Fay.
Dennerson,James,	1		Fau.
Denness,John,	1		Nor.
Denness,Hezekiah,	1		Nor.
Dennett,William C.	1	4	Hen.
Denney,James,	1		Henry
Dennis,John,	1		Lou.
Dennis,Matthew,	1	5	Ja.Cy
Dennis,Nathaniel,	2	4	Hen.
Dennison,John,	1		Aug.
Denny,Joseph,	1		Berk.

Name			Co.
Denny,Patrick,	1		Wash.
Denny,William,Jr.,	1		Aug.
Denos,Augustine,	1	9	York
Denson,Ann,		1	So'n.
Denson,David,	1	1	So'n.
Denson,Jordan,	1	8	So'n.
Denson,Joseph,	1	1	So'n.
Denson,Peter,	1		So'n.
Denson,Tooke,	1		So'n.
Denson,William,	1		Henry
Denson,William,	1	1	So'n.
Denson,William,	1	1	So'n.
Dent,John,	1		Bea.
Dent,Peter,			Bed.
Dent,Shadrack,			Pr.Wm.
Denton,Charles,	1		Buck.
Denton,Jacob,	1		Har.
Denton,Jane,		1	Har.
Denton,Thomas,	1		Har.
Denton,William,	1		Lun.
Depew,John,	1		Bot.
Depew,Samuel,	1		Bot.
Depough,Charles,	1	1	Lin.
Depriest,John,			Henry
Depriest,John,	1		Hen.
Depriest,Randoll,	1		Bed.
Depriest,Tabitha,			Henry
Depriest,William,	1	13	Hen.
Dermont,James,	1		Fau.
Dermont,Michael,	2		Fau.
Derrington,John,	1		Pr.Wm.
Derry,Palser,	1		Lou.
Dervin,William,	1		Loui.
DeSardories,Joseph,	1		Lou.
Deshazo,James,	1	9	K.Wm.
Detheridge,George,			Cul.
Detheridge,John,			Cul.
Deuberry,William,	1		Ja.Cy.
Deuholm,Archibald,			Hen.
Deur,Thomas,			K.&Q.
Deur,William,	2	15	K.&Q.
Devalt,Abraham,	1		Wash.
Devault,John,	3		Har.
Devault,Peter,	1		Har.
Devenport,Abraham,	2	8	Berk.
Devenport,Abraham,Jr.,	1	4	Berk.
Devenport,David,		2	Pr.Geo
Devenport,Julas,	1		Buck.
Deverix,Thomas,	1		Aug.
Devore,William,	1		Har.
Dew,Samuel,	1		Lou.
Dewberry,William,	1	1	Brun.
Dewbry,Rebecca,		4	Eli.Cy
Dewbry,Samuel,	1	4	Eli.Cy
Dewies,Samuel,	1		Fay.
Dewitt,James,	1		Bed.
Dewitt,John Ross,	1		Bed.
Dewitt,Walter,	2	2	Lin.
Diamond,Daniel,	1		Berk.
Dibral,Anthony,	2	13	Buck.
Dibrel,Charles,	2	4	Buck.
Dick,Archibald,	1	21	Caro.
Dick,Charles,	1	12	Spots.
Dicka,Edward,	1		Camp.
Dicken,Benjamin,	1	4	Cul.
Dicken,John,Jr.,	1		Loui.
Dicken,John,Sr.,	1		Loui.
Dicken,Richard,	1		Loui.
Dicken,Richard,	1	7	Cul.
Dickens,Joseph,	1	1	Cul.
Dickens,Norment,	2	4	Caro.
Dickenson,Arthur,	1	1	York
Dickenson,Benjamin,	1	1	Caro.
Dickenson,David,	1	10	Caro.
Dickenson,Griffith,	1	21	Loui.
Dickenson,James,	1	3	Caro.
Dickenson,James,	1		York
Dickenson,John,	1	17	York
Dickenson,Martha,			Caro.
Dickenson,Nath'l Wm,	2	5	Caro.
Dickenson,Thomas,Sr.,	1	7	Caro.
Dickenson,Thomas,Jr.,	1	8	Caro.
Dickenson,William,	2	15	Caro.
Dickerson,Archibald,	1		Fay.
Dickerson,Elijah,	1		Bot.
Dickerson,Elijah,	1		K.Geo.
Dickerson,Griffith,	1	8	Loui.
Dickerson,Griffith,Sr	1		Bot.
Dickerson,Griffith,Jr	1		Bot.
Dickerson,H.C.,	1		K.Geo.
Dickerson,James,	1	31	Loui.
Dickerson,James,	1	2	Henry
Dickerson,James Tutt.	1	5	Fau.
Dickerson,John,	1	3	Henry
Dickerson,John,	1	4	Loui.
Dickerson,Joseph,	1	1	Bea.
Dickerson,Martin,	1		Fay.
Dickerson,Moses,			Bot.
Dickerson,Nathaniel,	1	7	Loui.
Dickerson,Peter,	1	6	Nor.
Dickerson,Richard,	1	12	Spots.
Dickerson,Robert,	1	9	Loui.
Dickerson,Thomas,	1	5	Henry
Dickerson,Thomas,Jr.,	1		Henry
Dickerson,Voluntine,	1		Fay.
Dickerson,William,	1		Fay.
Dickerson,William,	1	2	Loui.
Dickey,James,	1		Lou.
Dickey,William,	1		Aug.
Dickil,James,	1	25	K.&Q.
Dickins,Richard,	1	1	Henry
Dickinson,Elijah,	1		Mont.
Dickinson,Jacob,	2		Har.
Dickinson,John,	1		Har.
Dickinson,Obadiah,	1		Mont.
Dickinson,Thomas,	1		Har.
Dickinson,Thompson,	1	4	Henry
Dickir,John,	1	4	West.
Dickout,Palser,	1		Lou.
Dickson,Archibald,	1	1	Aug.
Dickson,George,	1	2	Bea.
Dickson,James,	2		Rock.
Dickson,John,	1		Bea.
Dickson,Joseph,	1		Bea.
Dickson,William,	1		Bea.
Dicky,James,	1		Aug.
Dicky,John,	1		Aug.
Dicky,Michal,	1	4	Bea.
Didlake,George,	1	4	K.&Q.
Didlake,James,	1	14	K.&Q.
Didlake,John,	1	17	K.&Q.
Didlake,Peggy,	2	4	K.&Q.
Didlake,Robert,	1		K.&Q.
Didlake,Royston,	1	3	K.&Q.
Didlake,William,			K.&Q.
Digges,Cole,	1	11	Ja.Cy.
Digges,Dudley,	1	20	Ja.Cy.
Digges,Edward,	1	33	Fau.
Digges,Thomas,	1	28	Fau.
Diggs,Dudley,	2	84	Loui.
Diggs,Isaac,	1	15	K.&Q.
Diggs,Thomas,	1		Loui.
Diggs,Col.William,	1	72	Din.
Diggs,William,Jr.,	1	74	Loui.
Dihaven,Isaac,	1		Lou.
Dike,John,	1		Bot.
Dill,Francis,	1		Fay.
Dill,James,	1		Bot.
Dill,John,	1		Berk.
Dillard,Ann,		13	K.&Q.
Dillard,Benjamin,	1	9	Camp.
Dillard,David,	1		Caro.
Dillard,Delphia,		4	K.&Q.
Dillard,Edward,			Din.
Dillard,Edward,	1		Din.
Dillard,Elizabeth,		11	K.&Q.
Dillard,George,	2	9	Cul.
Dillard,George,	1		K.&Q.
Dillard,Isabella,		2	Caro.
Dillard,John,	1	10	Henry
Dillard,John,	1	5	Cul.
Dillard,John,			Din.
Dillard,John,	1		Din.
Dillard,Lewis,	1		Caro.
Dillard,Maj.,			Cul.
Dillard,Nicholas,	1	5	K.&Q.
Dillard,Richard,	1	12	Spots.
Dillard,Thomas,	1	4	Spots.
Dillard,Thomas,	1	2	K.&Q.
Dillard,Thomas,	1	4	K.&Q.
Dillard,Thomas,	3	9	Din.
Dillard,Thomas,	1	9	Din.
Dillard,Thomas,	1		Mont.
Dillard,William,	1	8	K.&Q.
Dillard,Winneford,			Caro.
Dillehay,Sarah,			Brun.
Dillen,James,	1		Rock.
Dillin,Samuel,	2		Fay.
Dilling,Thomas,	1	2	Cul.
Dillingham,Michael,	1		Henry
Dillingham,John,	1	1	Henry
Dillingham,Wm.,Sr.,	1		Henry
Dillingham,Wm.,Jr.,	1		Henry
Dillion,Benjamin,	1		Henry
Dillion,Henry,	2	4	Henry
Dillion,James,	1		Henry
Dillion,John,	1		Henry
Dillion,Jonathan,	1		Lou.
Dillion,William,	1		Henry
Dillon,Amos,	1		Lou.
Dillon,Henry,	1		Berk.
Dillon,Josiah,	1		Lou.
Dillon,William,	1		Lou.
Dillon,James,	1		Lou.
Dillon,James,	1		Lou.
Dillon,John,	2		Lou.
Dillon,John,Jr.,			Lou.
Dillman,Jacob,	1		Bed.
Dilly,Aaron,	1		Berk.
Dilly,John,	1		Aug.
Dilman,Daniel,	1		Bed.
Dingus,Peter,	1		Mont.
Dinkins,Benford,	1		Mont.
Dinkins,Ephraim,	1		Mont.
Dinkins,Thomas,	1		Mont.
Dinnis,Joseph,	1		Bot.
Dinsey,William,	1		Bot.
Dinwiddie,James,	1	2	Camp.
Dinwiddie,William,	1		Camp.
Dinwiddie,William,	1		Camp.
Dipors,Joseph,			Pr.Wm.
Dishazo,John,	1	1	K.&Q.
Dishazo,Peter,	1	3	K.&Q.
Dishazo,Richard,	2	10	K.&Q.
Dishazo,William,	1		K.&Q.
Dishazo,William,			K.&Q.
Dishman,David,	1	2	Caro.
Dishman,James,	3	25	K.Geo.
Dishman,Jeremiah,	2	3	Bed.
Dishman,John,	1	7	West.
Dishman,Samuel,	1	3	Caro.
Dishman,Samuel,Sr.,	1	20	K.Geo.
Dishman,Samu'l,Jr.,	3	17	K.Geo.
Dishman,William,	1	4	West.
Dismor,Henry,			Berk.
Dismukes,Benjamin,	2	4	Caro.
Dismukes,Elisha,	1	5	Spots.
Dismukes,James,	1		Lin.

Dismukes,Reuben,	1	6	Caro.	Dodds,William,	1		Henry	Dooly,Volentine,	1		Rock.
Dismukes,William,	1	5	Caro.	Dodson,Daniel,	1	9	Din.	Doran,Jacob,	1		Aug.
Dispain,John,	1		Mont.	Dodson,Daniel,	1	9	Din.	Dorin,Felix,	3		Har.
Divers,John,	1		Lin.	Dodson,Enoch,	1	9	Pr.Wm.	Dorlon,John,	2	12	Din.
Dives,John,	1	4	Bed.	Dodson,George,	1		Berk.	Dorsey,Bates,			Lou.
Divine,William,	1		Bot.	Dodson,John,	1		Cul.	Dorton,Elizabeth,			Wash.
Dix,James,	1	1	Lun.	Dodson,Lamboth,	1		Henry	Dorton,Elizabeth,			Wash.
Dix,John,			Acco.	Doe,William,	1		Acco.	Dorton,William,	1		Wash.
Dix,John,Sr.,	2	1	Acco.	Dogan,Lovewell,			Cul.	Doss,Edward,	1		Buck.
Dix,William,	1	2	Acco.	Dogan,Samuel,Jr.,			Cul.	Doss,James,	1		Buck.
Dixon,Anthony F.,	1	8	Ch.Cy.	Dogan,Samuel,	3	11	Cul.	Doss,Jeremiah,	1		Bea.
Dixon,Edward,	1		Pr.Wm.	Doggett,Bushrod,	3	12	Cul.	Doss,John,	1		Buck.
Dixon,Edmund,	1		Wash.	Doggett,George,			Cul.	Doss,John,	1		Buck.
Dixon,Frank,	1		Ch.Cy.	Doggett,Joel,			Cul.	Doss,Mark,	1	5	Buck.
Dixon,Frank,Jr.,	1		Ch.Cy.	Doggett,Reubin,	1		Cul.	Doss,Stephen,	1		Bed.
Dixon,Frederick,Est,		5	Din.	Dogherty,William,	1		Bot.	Doss,Thomas,Estate,			Buck.
Dixon,Harry,	1	36	Caro.	Dohoda,Moses,	2	1	Fay.	Doss,William,	1		Buck.
Dixon,Harry,	1	26	Caro.	Doherty,William,	1	4	Bot.	Doss,Zacheus,	1		Bed.
Dixon,Harry,Jr.,	1		Ch.Cy.	Doin,Bennett,			Pr.Wm.	Doster,Thomas,	1		Berk.
Dixon,James,	1	18	Eli.Cy	Doin,Daniel,	1		Pr.Wm.	Doudy,John,	1		Bed.
Dixon,James,	1	16	York	Doin,John,	1		Pr.Wm.	Dougherty,Anthony,	1		Rock.
Dixon,John,	1	11	Lun.	Doin,Thomas,			Pr.Wm.	Dougherty,Bryant,	1		Pr.Wm.
Dixon,John,	1	3	Ja.Cy.	Doke,John,	1		Berk.	Dougherty,Charles,	1		Wash.
Dixon,John,	1		Camp.	Dokerie,James,	1		Mont.	Dougherty,Hugh,	1		Aug.
Dixon,John,	1		Berk.	Dolby,Eleshes,	1		Acco.	Dougherty,James,	1		Rock.
Dixon,John,	1	12	Pr.Wm.	Dolby,Peter,	1		Acco.	Dougherty,John,	1		Mont.
Dixon,John,			Pr.Wm.	Doles,Arthur,	2	8	So'n.	Dougherty,Joseph,	1	4	Mont.
Dixon,John,	1	4	Aug.	Doles,Henry,	1	1	So'n.	Dougherty,Michael,	1		Mont.
Dixon,Joseph,	1		Mont.	Dolin,James,	1		Buck.	Dougherty,Nicholas,	1		Mont.
Dixon,Ralph,	1	6	Nor.	Dollard,John,	1	11	Hen.	Dougherty,Robert,	1		Mont.
Dixon,Richard,	1	1	Caro.	Dollard,Amilia,			Bea.	Dougherty,Thomas,	2		Rock.
Dixon,Robert,	1	9	Lun.	Dollin,Thomas,	1		Berk.	Dougherty,William,	1		Rock.
Dixon,Rozell,	1		Cul.	Dolman,Thomas,	1		West.	Doughty,John,			Lou.
Dixon,Sarah,		10	Eli.Cy	Dolman,William,	1	5	West.	Doughty,Reuben,	1		Lou.
Dixon,Solomon,	1		Lou.	Donahoe,Michael,	2	1	Caro.	Douglas,John,	1		Berk.
Dixon,Thomas,	1		Har.	Donakey,William,	1		Berk.	Douglas,John,	1	8	K.&Q.
Dixon,Thomas,	1		Bot.	Donald,Mathew,	1		Rock.	Douglas,Robert,Sr.,			Camp.
Dixon,Turner,	1	37	Caro.	Donald,Thomas,	2		Lin.	Douglas,Robert,Jr.,	1		Camp.
Dixon,Turner,	1	47	Fau.	Donaldson,Alexander,	1		Wash.	Douglas,Sarah,			K.Geo.
Dixon,William,	2		Cul.	Donaldson,Ann,		12	Lou.	Douglas,William,	1	1	Berk.
Dixon,William,	1		Wash.	Donaldson,John,	1	1	Fau.	Douglass,Alexander,	1		Lin.
Dixon,William,	1		Aug.	Donaldson,Robert,	1		Fau.	Douglass,Mrs.Cato,	1	20	Pr.Wm.
Doack,David,	1	4	Aug.	Donaldson,Robert,	1		Aug.	Doughlass,David,	2		Henry
Doack,John,	1		Aug.	Donaldson,Stephen,	1	2	Lou.	Douglass,David,	1	4	Bea.
Doack,Robert,	1	1	Aug.	Donaldson,William,	1		Aug.	Douglass,George,	2		Lin.
Doak,David,Sr.,	1		Mont.	Donaldson,William,	1		Fau.	Douglass,Hugh,			Lou.
Doak,David,Jr.,	1		Mont.	Donally,Christopher,	1		Spots.	Douglass,James,	1	3	Mont.
Doak,James,	1		Mont.	Donathan,Benjamin,	1		Mont.	Douglass,John,	1	5	Buck.
Doak,Samuel,	1		Mont.	Donathan,Elijah,	1		Henry	Douglass,John,	1	3	West.
Doak,William,	1		Mont.	Donathan,William,	1	2	Henry	Douglass,Joseph,	1	3	Fau.
Doan,William,	1		Ch.Cy.	Donelly,William,Jr.,			Lou.	Douglass,Thomas,	1		Aug.
Dobbe,David,	1		Nor.	Doniphan,Alexander,	2	9	K.Geo.	Douglass,William,	3	20	Lou.
Dobbe,Henry,	1	3	Nor.	Doniphon,Joseph,			Fau.	Douglass,William,	1		Ch.Cy.
Dobbe,Isaac,	1		Nor.	Doniphan,Mary,		5	K.Geo.	Douglass,Rev.Wm.,	1	37	Loui.
Dobbe,Jacob,	1		Nor.	Doniphan,Mott,	1	1	K.Geo.	Douthett,John,	5		Har.
Dobbe,John,	1	5	Nor.	Donilson,Isaac,	1		Henry	Doutty,Ann,	1		Acco.
Dobie,Samuel,	1	3	Hen.	Donist,Ruben,	1	3	Henry	Love,Francis,	1		Lin.
Dobie,Samuel,	1	2	Hen.	Donnally,Charles,	2	2	Aug.	Dove,William,	1		Camp.
Dobbins,Charles,	1	6	K.&Q.	Donnelly,William,	2		Lou.	Dowdall,James,	2	10	Fau.
Dobbins,Elizabeth,	1		Mont.	Donnely,James,	1		Mont.	Dowdall,John,	1	3	Lou.
Dobbins,John,	1		Brun.	Donahoe,Charles,	1		Bea.	Dowdall,Thomas,	1	6	Fau.
Dobbins,Moses,	1		Brun.	Donahoe,Edward,Sr.,	1		Bea.	Dowdel,Ann,			K.Geo.
Dobson,Robert,	3		Lin.	Donahoe,Edward,Jr.,	1	1	Bea.	Dowdy,John,	1		Gooch.
Docherty,Michal,	1		Aug.	Donahoe,Robert,			Bea.	Dowles,Elizabeth,		2	K.Wm.
Dodd,Benjamin,	1	1	Fau.	Donkhoe,Samuel,	1		Lou.	Dowles,Elizabeth,		2	K.Wm.
Dodd,James,	1	4	K.Geo.	Donoway,William,			Bea.	Dowling,John,	1	4	K.Geo.
Dodd,John,	1		Lou.	Dooley,Abraham,	1		Mont.	Dowly,Adderson,	1	2	Nor.
Dodd,John,	1	2	Fau.	Dooley,George,	1	1	Bed.	Dowly,Hezekiah,	1	5	Nor.
Dodd,Joseph,	1		West.	Dooley,John,	1		Bed.	Dowly,Peter,	1		Nor.
Dodd,Nathaniel,	2	8	Fau.	Dooley,John,	1		Bed.	Downenan,Ann,	1	18	Pr.Wm.
Dodd,Nathaniel,Jr.,	1	2	Fau.	Dooley,Joseph,	1		Bed.	Downer,Andrew,	1		Bot.
Dodd,Patty,			West.	Dooley,Rebecca,		2	Bea.	Downer,James,	1	16	Caro.
Dodd,William,	1	4	Ja.Cy.	Dooley,Stephen,	1		Bed.	Downes,Benjamin,	1		Lou.
Doad,William,			West.	Dooley,Thomas,	1	2	Henry	Downes,Henry,	1		Lou.
Dodds,Andrew,	1		Lin.	Dooley,Thomas,	1		Bed.	Downes,John,	1		Lou.
Dodds,James,	1		Lin.	Dooley,Thomas,Jr.,	1		Bed.	Downey,Martha,		1	Aug.

Name			County
Downey,Michael,	1	2	K.&Q.
Downing,Andrew,	1		Lun.
Downing,Auther,Sr.,	1	23	Nor.
Downing,Auther,Jr.,	1	15	Nor.
Downing,James,	1	2	Lin.
Downing,John,	1		K.&Q.
Downing,John,	1	2	Lin.
Downing,William,	1		Bed.
Downing,William,	1	5	Nor.
Downing,William,		21	Fau.
Dowman,Rawleigh,	1	21	Fau.
Downman,Rawliegh Pork.		17	Din.
Downman,William,		10	Din.
Downs,John,	1		Berk.
Downs,Joseph J.,	1		Hen.
Downs,Thomas,	1	2	Nor.
Downs,William,	1		Acco.
Downton,Richard,	1	6	Pr.Wm.
Downy,Richard,	1		Berk.
Dowsing,William,	1	22	Lun.
Doyle,Alexander,	1	7	Pr.Wm.
Doyle,Andrew,	1		Mont.
Doyle,Charles,	1		Lou.
Doyl,Thomas,	1		Fay.
Dozard,Abraham,			Hen.
Dozer,James Smith,	1	5	West.
Dozer,Zachariah,	1		Wash.
Dozers,Richard,	1	1	West.
Lozier,Joseph,	2	4	West.
Dozier,Leonard,	1	5	Lun.
Dozier,Richard,	1	3	West.
Dozier,Thomas,	1	9	Lun.
Dozier,Wm.Robinson,	1	5	West.
Dozier,William,	1	6	Lun.
Draifs,Jacob,	1		Har.
Drain,John,	1		Rock.
Drake,Barnaby,	1	2	So'n.
Drake,Benjamin,	1		Lou.
Drake,Benjamin,	1	2	Caro.
Drake,Clapham,	1		Ja.Cy.
Drake,Ephraim,	1		Mont.
Drake,Etheldred,	1		So'n.
Drake,Henry,	1		So'n.
Drake,Jeremiah,	1	5	So'n.
Drake,Joel,	1		So'n.
Drake,John,	1		So'n.
Drake,John,	1		Bot.
Drake,Jonathon,	1		Lou.
Drake,Joseph,	1		Lou.
Drake,Josiah,	1		So'n.
Drake,Margaret,		5	Fay.
Drake,Reve,		6	West.
Drake,Richard,	1		West.
Drake,Robert,	1	3	Ch.Cy.
Drake,Samuel,Sr.,	2		Mont.
Drake,Thomas,	2		West.
Drake,Thomas,	1	3	Lou.
Drake,Thomas,	1	6	So'n.
Drake,Timothy,	1		So'n.
Drake,William,	1		Bed.
Drane,John,	1		Lou.
Draper,Abram,	1		Rock.
Draper,Alexander,	1	11	Pr.Geo.
Draper,Ephraim,	1		So'n.
Draper,Jeremiah,	1	1	So'n.
Draper,Jesse,	1		So'n.
Draper,John,	2		K.&Q.
Draper,John,	2	12	Mont.
Draper,John,	1		Pr.Wm.
Draper,Judith,		3	Din.
Draper,Thomas,			K.&Q.
Draper,Thomas,	1		So'n.
Drenon,Lawrence,	1	2	Aug.
Drenon,Thomas,	1		Aug.
Drew,Ann,		4	So'n.
Drew,Dolphin,	2	17	Berk.
Drew,Dolphin,	1	7	Buck.
Drew,Francis,	1		Din.
Drew,Jeremiah,	1	16	So'n.
Drew,Jesse,Est.,		8	So'n.
Drew,John,	1		Din.
Drew,Mrs.Martha,		3	Din.
Drew,William,	2	7	Berk.
Drewry,Elizabeth,		1	York
Drewry,Elizabeth,			So'n.
Drewry,Humphry,	1		So'n.
Drewry,James,	1	6	York
Drewry,Robert,	1	17	K.Wm.
Drewry,Samuel,Sr.,	1	2	So'n.
Drewry,Samuel,Jr.,	1		So'n.
Drewry,William,	1	2	York
Drewry,William,	1		So'n.
Drighouse,Nathan,	1		Nor.
Driver,John,	2		York
Droddy,William,	1		Wash.
Druen,James,	2	1	Hen.
Druen,Samuel,			Hen.
Druggett,Isaac,Est.,	1		Berk.
Druin,John,	1		Buck.
Drum,George,	1		Lou.
Drum,Philip,	1		Lou.
Drumgold,Edward,	1	7	Brun.
Drummon,Aaron,	1		Lun.
Drummond,Aaron,	1		Fau.
Drummond,David,			Acco.
Drummond,Drake,	2	1	Acco.
Drummond,George,			Acco.
Drummond,Henley,	1	4	Ja.Cy.
Drummond,Henry,	1		Fau.
Drummond,Henry,	1	4	Acco.
Drummond,Henry,	1		Fau.
Drummond,James,	1		Fau.
Drummond,Leah,		3	Acco.
Drummond,Richard,Jr.	1	12	Acco.
Drummond,Robert,	1	1	Acco.
Drummond,Robert,	2	4	Acco.
Drummond,Thomas,	1	1	Fau.
Drummond,Thomas,Sr.,	3	9	K.&Q.
Drummond,Thomas,Jr.,	1	5	K.&Q.
Drummond,William,	1	8	Acco.
Drury,Alford,	1		Loui.
Drury,J.,	1		Pr.Wm.
Drury,William,	1		Pr.Wm.
Dryden,James,	1		Rock.
Dryden,Agness,			Rock.
Dryden,William,	1	4	Lin.
Dubeck,Peter,	1		Pr.Geo.
Dubery,Samuel,	1	1	Ja.Cy.
Dubroe,William,	1		York
Duck,Josiah,	1		So'n.
Ducker,Henry,	1		Acco.
Duckwall,Freder.Sr.,	2		Berk.
Duckwall,Freder.Jr.,	1		Berk.
Dudding,Vol,	1		Rock.
Dudley,Ambrose,	1	2	Caro.
Dudley,Ambrose,	1	11	Spots.
Dudley,Banks,	1	3	K.&Q.
Dudley,Christopher,	1		K.&Q.
Dudley,Gwin,	1		Bed.
Dudley,J.,			Pr.Wm.
Dudley,James,			Lou.
Dudley,Peter,	1	6	Spots.
Dudley,Peter,	1	16	K.&Q.
Dudley,Robert B.,	1	8	K.&Q.
Dudley,Thomas,	1	6	K.&Q.
Dudley,William,	1		Bot.
Dudley,William,	2	3	Ja.Cy.
Dudley,William,Sr.,	1	2	K.&Q.
Dudley,William,Jr.,	1	21	K.&Q.
Dudly,Ambrose,	2	10	Fay.
Dualy,Thomas,			Bot.
Dudly,William,	1		Fay.
Duerson,Henry,	1	9	Spots.
Duerson,Joseph,	1	10	Spots.
Duerson,Thomas,	1	18	Spots.
Duerson,William,	1	7	Spots.
Duff,James,	1	1	Fau.
Duff,Roger,	1		Rock.
Duffy,James,	1		Berk.
Dugan,Alexander,	2		Har.
Dugan,William,	1		Har.
Dugar,Anderson,	1	4	K.Wm.
Dugar,James,	1	1	K.Wm.
Dugar,Robert,	1		K.&Q.
Dugara,Abraham,			Hen.
Dugger,Alexander,			Brun.
Dugger,Daniel,	1	4	Brun.
Dugger,Henry,	1		Brun.
Dugger,James,	1	1	Brun.
Dugger,John,	1		Brun.
Dugger,John,Sr.,	1	7	Brun.
Dugger,John,Jr.,	1	5	Brun.
Duglass,Benjamin,	1	4	Cul.
Duiguid,William,	1	21	Buck.
Duke,Betty,		20	Loui.
Duke,Clevears,	2	65	Loui.
Duke,Clevears,Jr.,	1	9	Loui.
Duke,Henry,			Loui.
Duke,Henry,	1	15	Ch.Cy.
Duke,James,			Caro.
Duke,John,	1		Berk.
Duke,John,Jr.,	1		Berk.
Duke,William,	1		Berk.
Dukin,William,	1	4	Cul.
Dulany,Joseph,	1		Cul.
Dulany,William,	3	1	Cul.
Dulany,Zachariah,	1		Cul.
Dulen,James,	1		Lin.
Dulen,Thadeus,		4	Lou.
Dulen,William,	1	3	Lou.
Dulin,William,	1	3	Fau.
Dulin,William,Jr.,	1	5	Fau.
Dulin,John,	2		Fau.
Duling,Achillis,	1		K.&Q.
Duling,Edmond,	1		Cul.
Duling,Edmond,	1		Cul.
Duling,Joseph,	1		Cul.
Duling,Larkin,	1		K.&Q.
Duling,William,	1	8	K.&Q.
Dullin,William,	1		Berk.
Dulon,James,	1		Fay.
Duly,Jacob,	2		Fay.
Duly,Thomas,	1	2	Fay.
Duly,William,	1		Har.
Dumass,Elizabeth,			Hen.
Dumford,Daniel,	1		Fay.
Dumford,Michael,	1		Fay.
Dummond,Daniel,	1	1	Acco.
Dummond,John,	1	2	Acco.
Dummond,Patience,		1	Acco.
Dummond,Sarah,		4	Acco.
Dummond,Stephen,	1		Acco.
Dummond,Susanah,	1		Acco.
Dupree,John,	1	2	Brun.
Dupree,Joseph,	1	6	Lun.
Dupree,Lewis,	1		Lun.
Dupree,Thomas,	1	1	Lun.
Dupree,William,	1	1	Lun.
Durand,James,	1	5	Spots.
Durand,John,		4	Din.
Durell,James,	1	1	Din.
Durell,William,	1	6	Din.
Durham,George,	1		K.&Q.
Durham,Gregory,	1		Henry
Durham,Joseph,	1		K.&Q.
Durham,Thomas,	1		K.&Q.
Durly,Peter,	1	5	Bot.
Durmant,William,	1		Bot.
Durrett,Francis,	1	4	Caro.

Name			County
Durrett,George,	1	9	Caro.
Durrett,Henry,	1	7	Caro.
Durrett,Joel,	1	6	Caro.
Durrett,John,	2	7	Caro.
Durrett,Richard,	1	13	Caro.
Durrett,Richard,		3	Bed.
Durrett,Robert,	1	4	Spots.
Durrett,William,	1	4	Caro.
Durrett,William,	1	12	Caro.
Dust,John,	1		Berk.
Duty,Thomas,	1		Lou.
Duty,Thomas,Jr.,	1	1	Lou.
Duval,Corneilus,	1	10	Bot.
Duval,Joseph,	1	9	Hen.
DuVal,Philip,			Hen.
Duval,Samuel,	1	24	Gooch.
DuVal,Samuel,	2	27	Hen.
Duval,William,	3	24	Loui.
Duvall,Benjamin S.	1		Bed.
Duvall,Benjamin,			Bed.
Duvall,Henry,	1	9	Cul.
Duvall,James,	1	6	Cul.
DuVall,John,	1	7	Caro.
Duvall,Lewis,	1		Hen.
Duvall,Maran,			Bed.
Duvall,William,	1	4	Spots.
Duvall,William,Jr.,	1	2	Spots.
Dunaway,Benjamin,	1		Fay.
Dunaway,Isaac,			Cul.
Dunaway,Isaac,	1		Cul.
Dunaway,Joseph,			Cul.
Dunbar,David,	1	10	K.&Q
Dunbar,Daniel,	1		Lou.
Dunbar,William,	2		Lou.
Dunbar,William,Jr.,			Lou.
Duncan,Andrew,	1		Mont.
Duncan,Andrew,	1		Wash.
Duncan,Anthony,	1		Mont.
Duncan,Benjamin,			Cul.
Duncan,Charles,	1	11	Fau.
Duncan,Charles,	1	6	Cul.
Duncan,Claburn,	1		Lin.
Duncan,Coleman,	1	5	Lou.
Duncan,Edward,			Buck.
Duncan,Francis,			Cul.
Duncan,Gabriel,	1	1	Camp.
Duncan,George,	1		Lin.
Duncan,George,	1	2	Wash.
Duncan,Gollop,			Cul.
Duncan,Henry,	2		Lou.
Duncan,Howson,	1	2	Fau.
Duncan,Jacob,	1		Buck.
Duncan,James,	1	8	Cul.
Duncan,James,			Cul.
Duncan,James,	1		Lin.
Duncan,Jesse,			Buck.
Duncan,John,	1		Buck.
Duncan,John,			Cul.
Duncan,John,Sr.,	2	5	Fau.
Duncan,John,	1		Wash.
Duncan,Joseph,	2	2	Cul.
Duncan,Joseph,	1	3	Cul.
Duncan,Joseph Marsh,	1		Fau.
Duncan,Joseph,Sr.,	1	14	Fau.
Duncan,Joseph,Jr.,	1	3	Fau.
Duncan,Joshua,			Lou.
Duncan,Marshal,	1		Mont.
Duncan,Martin,			Wash.
Duncan,Matthew,	2		Berk.
Duncan,Robert,	2	13	Cul.
Duncan,Samuel,	2	7	Lin,
Duncan,Samuel,	2	6	Cul.
Duncan,Thomas,	1	1	Berk.
Duncan,Thomas,	1	1	Berk.
Duncan,William,			Fau.
Duncan,William,	2	5	Cul.
Duncan,William,	1	2	Cul.
Duncanson,James,	2	26	Cul.
Duncome,Robert,	1	6	Loui.
Dunces,Lewis,	1		Fay.
Dunevant,William,			Din.
Dunford,Willis,	1	4	Ja.Cy
Dunfrey,Francis,	1	9	Cha.C
Dunge,John,	1		K.Wm.
Dungee,Joseph,	1		K.Wm.
Dungeth,Charles,	1		Berk.
Dunham,Amos,	1	1	Lou.
Dunkin,Charles,	1	5	Lou.
Dunkin,James,	1		Mont.
Dunkin,James,	1		Buck.
Dunkin,James,	1		Fay.
Dunkin,John,	1		Mont.
Dunkin,Robert,	1		Bot.
Dunkley,John,	1		Brun.
Dunkley,Robert,	1		Brun.
Dunlap,Adam,	1		Aug.
Dunlap,Alexander,	1		Aug.
Dunlap,Henry,	1	3	Henry
Dunlap,James,	1		Fay.
Dunlap,John,	1	3	Rock.
Dunlap,Mary,		4	Rock.
Dunlap,William,	1		Aug.
Dunlap,William,	1		Fay.
Dunlop,Daniel,	1		Bed.
Dunlop,Epharim,	1		Wash.
Dunlop,Moses,	1		Bot.
Dunman,James,			Lun.
Dunma,Joseph,	2	6	Lun.
Dunn,Ann,	1	4	Caro.
Dunn,Anthony,	1		Eli.C
Dunn,David,	1	2	Brun.
Dunn,Galewood,	1		Henry
Dunn,Ishmael,	1	10	Brun.
Dunn,James,	1		Berk.
Dunn,John,	1		Lun.
Dunn,John,	1	1	York
Dunn,John,	1		Caro.
Dunn,Martha,	1		Eli.C
Dunn,Michael,	1		Henry
Dunn,Michael,	1		Bot.
Dunn,Capt.Nathaniel,		9	Brun.
Dunn,Richard,	1	2	Henry
Dunn,Robert,	1		Berk.
Dunn,Thomas,	1		Lun.
Dunn,Thomas,	1	3	Camp.
Dunn,Thomas,	1		Mont.
Dunn,Waters,	1	20	Henry
Dunn,Waters,Jr.,	1	1	Henry
Dunn,William,	1		Henry
Dunn,William,	1	3	Eli.C
Dunn,William,	1		Berk.
Dunn,William,	1		Lou.
Dunstill,Joseph,	1		York.
Dunston,Richard,	1	5	Lun.
Dunton,Ailee,	2	14	Acco.
Dunton,Benjamin,	2	4	Acco.
Dunton,Benjamin,	1	8	Nor.
Dunton,Elizabeth,		11	Nor.
Dunton,George,	1	11	Acco.
Dunton,Isabella,		2	Nor.
Dunton,Jacob,	1	10	Nor.
Dunton,Michael,Jr.,	1	4	Nor.
Dunton,Michael,Sr.,	1	4	Nor.
Dunton,Richard,	1	4	Nor.
Dunton,Richard,Jr.,	1	14	Nor.
Dunton,Severn,	1		Nor.
Dunton,Susanna,		10	Nor.
Dunton,Thomas,	1		Lin.
Dunton,William,	1		Nor.
Dunwiddie,Thomas,	1	1	Fay.
Dunwoodie,James,	1		Fay.
Dwyer,John,	1		Din.
Dwyer,William,	1		Din.
Dyche,George,	1		Berk.
Dye,Brown,			Pr.Wm.
Dye,George,		2	Fau.
Dye,George,			K.Geo.
Dye,V.			Pr.Wm.
Dyer,John,	1		Fay.
Dyer,John,	1		Fau.
Dyke,George,	1		Lou.
Dyke,George,	1		Cul.
Dyke,Nathan,	1		Lou.
Dyke,Nathaniel,	1		Cul.
Dykes,Henry,	1	1	Lou.
Dykes,John,	1	8	Loui.
Dykes,John,Jr.,	1		Loui.
Dykes,William,	1		Loui.
Dysart,George,	1		Mont.
Dysart,Maj.James,	2	3	Wash.
Dyson,Aquilla,	1	3	Fau.
Dyson,James,	1		Din.
Dyurnett,Joseph,	1	10	Caro.
Eachoe,Isaac,	1	1	Hen.
Eade,Robert,	1		Berk.
Eades,Carril,	1		Gooch.
Eades,John,	1		Lou.
Eades,Thomas B.	1	4	Gooch.
Eads,Robert,	1		Bed.
Eagle,George,	1		Aug.
Eakin,John,	1		Rock.
Eakin,Samuel,	1		Rock.
Eakin,Samuel,	1		Berk.
Eakin,Thomas,	2	1	Berk.
Eakin,William,	1		Berk.
Eakin,William,	1		Rock.
Eakin,William,	1		Berk.
Eakles,Richard,	1		Berk.
Ealon,Joseph,	1		Berk.
Eanes,Edward,	1	3	Din.
Earington,Daniel,	1	13	K.Geo.
Earington,Farrands,	1	2	K.Geo.
Earl,John,	2		Pr.Wm.
Earley,James Mattin,	1		Aug.
Earley,Jeremiah,	1	14	Cul.
Earley,Jeremiah,	1	1	Henry
Earley,Joseph,	2	23	Cul.
Earley,Sally,		7	Henry
Earls,George,	1		Pr.Wm.
Early,Jacob,	1	26	Bed.
Early,Joel,	2	18	Cul.
Early,Joshua,	1	20	Bed.
Early,Mary,		14	Camp.
Earnest,George,	1		Ja.Cy
Earpe,Daniel,	1		Berk.
Easly,Michael,	1		Berk.
Easley,Miller,	1		Henry
Easley,Robeet,	1	6	Buck.
Easley,Warham,	1	2	Henry
Easley,William,	1	5	Buck.
East,Benjamin,	1		Gooch.
East,David,			Hen.
East,Ezekiel,			Loui.
East,James,	1	1	Loui.
East,James,	1	1	Loui.
East,James,	1		Henry
East,John,	1	5	Henry
East,Josiah,	1		Rock.
East,North,	1		Lin.
East,Servin,	3	1	Acco.
East,Southy,	3		Acco.
Easten,Archillis,	1		Gooch.
Easten,Augustine,	1	5	Gooch.
Easten,Edward,	1		Loui.
Easter,Marshall,	1	4	Cul.
Eastham,Bird,	1	1	Cul.
Eastham,Edward,			Cul.

Eastham, James,	2	3	Cul.	Edmunds, Samuel,	1	20	So'n	Edwards, Joseph,	3	8	Berk.
Eastham, George,	2	3	Fau.	Edmunds, Sterling,	1	27	Brun.	Edwards, Joseph,	1		Fau.
Eastham, Philip,	1	3	Cul.	Edmunds, Thomas,	1	25	Brun.	Edwards, Laban,			Acco.
Eastham, Robert,	1	9	Rock.	Edmunds, Thomas,	1	1	Brun.	Edwards, Mary,			York
Eastham, William,	1	3	Cul.	Edmunds, Thomas,	1	20	So'n	Edwards, Martha,			K.&Q
Easthon, Francis,	1	4	K.&Q	Edmunds, William,	1	15	So'n	Edwards, Micajah,	1	2	So'n
Easton, John,	1		Bed.	Edmundson, Benjamin,	1	10	Lun.	Edwards, Mildred,		1	K.Geo.
Eastus, Elisha,	2	2	Fay.	Edmundson, David,	1	1	Rock.	Edwards, Nathaniel,			So'n
Eaton, Benjamin,	1		Har.	Edmundson, David,			Fay.	Edwards, Nathaniel,	1	7	Brun.
Eaton, Benjamin,	1		Cul.	Edmundson, Humphrey,	1	1	Henry	Edwards, Newit,	1	5	So'n
Eaton, Edward,			York	Edmundson, James,	1	7	Rock.	Edwards, Newit,	1	9	So'n
Eaton, Henry,	1	1	Lou.	Edmundson, James,	1	16	Berk.	Edwards, Peter,	1	2	Mont.
Eaton, Jonathan,	1		Fay.	Edmundson, Richard,	1	9	Henry	Edwards, Peter,			Cul.
Eaton, Joseph,	1		Bed.	Edmundson, Richard, Jr.,	1		Henry	Edwards, Philip,	1		Lou.
Eason, Joseph,			Bot.	Edmundson, Robert,	1		Rock.	Edwards, Philip,	1		Cul.
Eaton, Joseph,	1		Har.	Edrington, Benjamin,		4	K.Geo	Edwards, Reuben,	1	1	Loui.
Eaton, Joseph,	2		Mont.	Edrington, Christopher,	1	15	West.	Edwards, Richard,	2		Har.
Eason, Samuel,	1	1	Bot.	Edrington, John,	1	7	Pr.Wm	Edwards, Richard,	1	11	So'n
Eaton, Thomas,	1		Har.	Edrington, John,			Loui.	Edwards, Sally,			So'n
Eaton, William,	2	9	York	Edwards, Abraham,	1		Mont.	Edwards, Samuel,	1	6	K.Wm.
Eatty, Henry,	1		Berk.	Edwards, Ann,			So'n	Edwards, Sarah,	1	19	So'n
Eave, John,	2		Berk.	Edwards, Abel,	1		Henry	Edwards, Solomon,			Loui.
Echart, Francis,	1		Aug.	Edwards, Acher,			Brun.	Edwards, Thomas,	1	1	Brun.
Eckles, Robert,	1	5	Din.	Edwards, Ambrose, Jr.,	1	2	K.Wm.	Edwards, Thomas, Sr.,		5	Henry
Eckolls, Abner,	1		Henry	Edwards, Ambrose,	1	15	K.Wm.	Edwards, Thomas, Jr.,	1		Henry
Echolls, Jacob,		3	Bed.	Edwards, Amos,	1		Lou.	Edwards, Thomas,	1	1	Fau.
Echolls, John,	1		Bed.	Edwards, Arthur,	1	2	Henry	Edwards, Thomas,	1	13	Lun.
Edds, Samuel,	1		K.Geo.	Edwards, Benjamin,		13	Brun.	Edwards, Torobable,	3		Acco.
Eddings, Anne,		4	Lun.	Edwards, Benjamin,	1	15	Lou.	Edwards, Uriah,		2	Spots.
Eddins, Joseph,	2	2	Cul.	Edwards, Benjamin,	1		So'n	Edwards, Will	1		Hen.
Eddings, Theophilus,			Cul.	Edwards, Benjamin,			Fau.	Edwards, William,	2	10	West.
Eddings, Theophilus,	1	3	Lun.	Edwards, Champ,	1		K.Wm.	Edwards, William,	1		Loui.
Edgar, James,	1		Bed.	Edwards, Charles, Jr.,	1		K.&Q	Edwards, William,	1		Acco.
Edgar, John,	1		Bed.	Edwards, David, Jr.,	1		So'n	Edwards, William,	1		Henry
Edge, Benjamin,	1	1	Caro.	Edwards, David,	3		Acco.	Edwards, William,	1		Brun.
Edge, John,	1		Fau.	Edwards, D.C.,			Buck.	Edwards, William, Jr.,	1	2	Brun.
Edger, George,	1		Wash.	Edwards, Elisha,	1		Lou.	Edwards, William, est.		19	Brun.
Edings, Joseph,	2	2	Cul.	Edwards, Elizabeth, est.		13	So'n	Edwards, William,	2	34	SO'n
Edlen, Thomas,	1	6	Lou.	Edwards, Flemstead,			Buck.	Edwards, William,	1	3	So'n
Edloe, Anne,		10	Cha.Cy	Edwards, Frederick,	1	2	Mont.	Edwards, William,	1		Gooch.
Edloe, Henry,	1	15	Cha.Cy	Edwards, Gallacher,	1		Bot.	Edwards, William,	1		Gooch.
Edloe, John,	2	41	Cha.Cy	Edwards, George,	1		So'n	Edwards, William, Jr.,	1	7	Pr.Geo.
Edloe, John,	1		Cha.Cy	Edwards, Gerard,	1		Fau.	Edwards, William, Jr.,	1	2	Pr.Geo.
Edloe, Rebecca,		1	Cha.Cy	Edwards, Gravel,	1		Loui.	Edwards, William,	1		Cul.
Edloe, William,	1	21	Cha.Cy	Edwards, Gray,	1	11	Brun.	Edwards, Zachariah,			Loui.
Edmiston, John,	1		Wash.	Edwards, Henry,	2	10	Loui.	Edwards, Zachariah,			Loui.
Edmiston, Col.William,	1	5	Wash.	Edwards, Hugh,	1		Lou.	Ege, Samuel,	1	3	Hen.
Edmond, Elinor,			Aug.	Edwards, James,	1	2	K.Geo	Ege, Jacob,	1	1	Hen.
Edmonds, Elias, Sr.,	1	24	Fau.	Edwards, James,	1	33	Spots	Ege, Mrs.,			Hen.
Edmonds, John,	1	35	Fau.	Edwards, James,	1		Henry	Egleton, Thomas,			Henry
Edmonds, William,	1		K.Wm.	Edwards, James,	1		Henry	Eggleston, Francis,		8	Ja.Cy.
Edmonds, William,	1	32	Fau.	Edwards, James,	2		Fau.	Eggleston, Richard,	1	17	Ja.Cy.
Edmondson, Ann,			Wash.	Edwards, Jesse,	1	1	Lou.	Egmon, Lawrence,	1	22	Ch.Cy.
Edmondson, Benjamin,	2	45	Cha.Cy	Edwards, Jesse,	1	1	Brun.	Egnew, James,			Aug.
Edmondson, John,	2	19	Din.	Edwards, Jesse,	1	3	Brun.	Ehart, Abram,			Cul.
Edmondson, Mary,		2	Wash.	Edwards, Joel,	1	1	So'n	Ehart, Michael,	2		Cul.
Edmondson, Matthew,	1	5	Aug.	Edwards, John,	1	10	So'n	Eive, Ansalum,			Brun.
Edmondson, Moses,	2		Wash.	Edwards, John,	1		So'n	Elam, Martin,	1	3	Lun.
Edmondson, Philip Par,	1	5	Cha.Cy	Edwards, John,	1	8	Spots	Elam, Richard,			Camp.
Edmondson, Capt.Robert	1	1	Wash.	Edwards, John,	2		Cul.	Elam, Richard,			Camp.
Edmondson, Samuel,	1	5	Wash.	Edwards, John,	1	2	Cul.	Elbzey, William,	1	20	Lou.
Edmondson, Thomas,			Wash.	Edwards, John,	1		Henry	Elder, Andrew,	1		Wash.
Edmondson, Thomas, Jr.,			Wash.	Edwards, John,			Acco.	Elder, Claiborne,	1		Din.
Edmondson, William, Sr.,	1		Wash.	Edwards, John,			Loui.	Elder, Daniel,			Brun.
Edmunds, Ann,		16	So'n	Edwards, John,	1		Loui.	Elder, Edmund,	1	8	Din.
Edmunds, Charles,	1	20	Brun.	Edwards, John,	1		So'n	Elder, Hannah			Mont.
Edmunds, David,	1	10	Nor.	Edwards, John,	1		Bed.	Elder, John Corban,	1	2	Cul.
Edmunds, Gray,	1	1	Brun.	Edwards, John,	1		Bed.	Elder, John,	1		Din.
Edmunds, Howell,		5	So'n	Edwards, John,	1		Lou.	Elder, Joseph,	1	2	Brun.
Edmunds, Howell,	1	29	So'n	Edwards, John, Sr.,	1	2	Brun.	Elder, Joshua,	1		Lou.
Edmunds, Jonas,	1		So'n	Edwards, John, Jr.,	1	2	Brun.	Elder, Joshua,	1		Brun.
Edmunds, James,	1		Brun.	Edwards, John,	1		Fau.	Elder, Mary,			Din.
Edmunds, John,	1		Berk.	Edwards, John,	1		Fau.	Elder, Mathew,	1	3	Wash.
Edmunds, John Flood,	1	16	Brun.	Edwards, Jonas,	1	2	So'n	Elder, Thomas,	1	4	Din.
Edmunds, Nicholas,	1	34	Brun.	Edwards, Jordan,	1		So'n	Elder, Thomas Jordin,	1	6	Cul.
Edmunds, Sacker,			Acco.								

Name			Loc.
Elder,William,Sr.,	1		Din.
Eldridge,Aristotle,	1	10	Brun.
Eldridge,Horrel,	1	15	Brun.
Eldridge,Rolfe,	1	18	Buck.
Eldridge,Thomas,	1	15	Gooch
Elgin,Francis,	1		Lou.
Elgin,Gustavus,	1		Lou.
Elgin,James,	1	1	Pr.Wm
Elgin,John,	2	15	Buck.
Elgin,Rebecca,	1	9	Lou.
Elgin,Robert,	1		Pr.Wm
Elgin,Samuel,	1	2	Cul.
Elgin,Walter,			Lou.
Elkins,Archibald,	1		Mont.
Elkins,Benjamin,	2	7	Cul.
Elkins,Benjamin,Jr.,	1	2	Cul.
Elkin,David,	2		Cul.
Elkin,Emanuel,	1	3	Cul.
Elkins,Isaah,			Cul.
Elkins,James,	1		Henry
Elkins,Jeremiah,	1		K.Geo
Elkins,Nathaniel,	1		K.Geo
Elkins,Nathaniel,	1		Henry
Elkins,Robert,	1		Wash.
Elkin,Robert,	1		Fay.
Elkins,Ralp,	1		Mont.
Elkins,Zachariah,	1		K.Geo
Ellet,Thomas,	1	2	Camp.
Ellett,Betty,		2	K.Wm.
Ellett,Elizabeth,		7	K.Wm.
Ellett,John,	1	6	K.Wm.
Ellett,John,	1	5	K.Wm.
Ellett,Thomas,	1	19	K.Wm.
Ellett,William,	1	15	K.Wm.
Ellett,William,	1	3	K.Wm.
Ellin,Samuel,	2		Hen.
Ellington,David,	1	12	Lun.
Ellington,Josiah,	1	10	Lun.
Elliot,Benjamin,	1	1	Mont.
Elliot,Faukner,	1		Mont.
Elliot,Isaac,	1		Mont.
Elliot,Jacob,Jr.,	1		Mont.
Eliot,John,	1	1	Nor.
Eliot,John,	1	1	Aug.
Elliot,Richard,	1		Wash.
Elliott,Bernard,	1	6	York
Elliott,Caleb,	1	1	Caro.
Elliott,Charles,	1		Acco.
Elliott,George,		2	Rock.
Elliott,George,	1	21	Din.
Elliott,James,	1	2	Rock.
Elliott,James,	1	1	Aug.
Elliott,John,			K.Geo
Elliott,John,	1		Pr.Wm
Elliott,John,	1	1	Acco.
Elliott,John,	1		Acco.
Elliott,John,	2		Fau.
Elliott,John,	1		Lou.
Elliott,Martin,	1	9	Lun.
Elliott,Martha,			Din.
Elliott,Mary,	1	9	Ja.Cy.
Elliott,Richard,	1		Aug.
Elliott,Richard,	1	45	Brun.
Elliott,Robert,	2	2	Cul.
Elliott,Robert,	1		Rock.
Elliott,Robert,	1		Rock.
Elliott,Robert,	1		Bot.
Elliott,Samuel,	1		Fau.
Elliott,Thomas,		27	K.Wm.
Elliott,Thomas,Sr.,	1	1	Acco.
Elliott,Thomas,Jr.,	1		Acco.
Elliott,Thomazon,			Lou.
Elliott,William,	1		Fau.
Elliott,William,			Lou.
Elliott,William,	2		Fay.
Elliott,William,	1		Caro.
Elliott,William,	1	1	Caro.
Elliot,William,	1		Cul.
Elliott,William,	1	1	Acco.
Ellis,Abraham,	1		Berk.
Ellis,Daniel,		1	York
Ellis,David,	1	3	Hen.
Ellis,Ellison,	1	2	Lun.
Ellis,Enos,			Berk.
Ellis,Henry,			Hen.
Ellis,Hezekiah,	1	7	Spots
Ellis,Jacob,	1	2	Hen.
Ellis,James,	1	4	Aug.
Elliss,James,	1		Fau.
Ellis,Jeremiah,	2	1	So'n.
Ellis,Jesse,Estate,	1	5	Hen.
Ellis,John,	1	2	Lun.
Ellis,John,			York
Ellis,John,	1		Henry
Ellis,John,	1	12	Fay.
Ellis,John,	1	13	Spots
Ellis,John,	1	12	Hen.
Ellis,John,	1	24	Hen.
Ellis,John,	1	3	Hen.
Ellis,John,	2	15	Caro.
Elliss,Jonathan,	1		Fau.
Ellis,Joseph,	1		Gooch
Ellis,Joseph,	2	14	Hen.
Ellis,Joseph,	1		Henry
Ellis,Joseph,	1		Berk.
Ellis,Mordecai,	2		Berk.
Ellis,Robert,	1		Lou.
Ellis,Stephen,	1	2	Gooch
Ellis,Thomas,	1		Fay.
Ellis,Thomas,	1	8	Hen.
Ellis,Thomas,	1		Berk.
Ellis,Thomas,	1	8	Caro.
Ellis,William,Jr.,	1	4	Hen.
Ellis,William,	1	1	So'n.
Ellis,William,	2	6	Fay.
Ellis,William,Jr.,	1	3	Fay.
Ellis,William,	1	6	York
Ellis,William,	1	3	Lun.
Ellis,William,	1		Berk.
Ellis,William,	1	10	Hen.
Ellison,Amos,	1		Bed.
Ellison,Evan,	1		Lou.
Ellison,John,	1		Lin.
Ellison,Robert,	1		Berk.
Ellison,Thomas,	1		Buck.
Ellison,William,	1		Fay.
Elliss,Nathaniel,	1		Fau.
Elliss,Robert,	2		Fau.
Ellmore,John,			Lou.
Ellmore,John,	1		West.
Ellzey,John,	1	1	Lou.
Ellzey,Lewis,	1	11	Lou.
Elmore,Charles,	1	1	Hen.
Elmore,George,	1		Mont.
Elmore,Iaan,		11	Hen.
Elmore,John,	1		Lun.
Elmore,Matthew,	1		Lin.
Elmore,Travis,			Brun.
Elms,Christopher,	1		Wash.
Elswick,John,	1		Mont.
Elswick,Jonathan,	1		Mont.
Elswick,Thomas,Sr.,	1		Har.
Elswick,Thomas,Jr.,	1		Har.
Elsworth,Jacob,	1		Aug.
Ely,Edward,	1	6	Cul.
Ely,Henry,	1	5	Cul.
Emberson,Jesse,	1		Lin.
Emberson,Samuel,	1	8	Lin.
Embree,John,	2	7	Lin.
Embry,Henry,	1	10	Lun.
Emerson,William,	1	1	Spots
Emery,Joseph,	1		Lin.
Emery,Mary,		5	Ch.Cy.
Emmans,William,	2		Bot.
Emmerson,Reuben,	1		Caro.
Emmerson,Thomas,	1		Gooch.
Emmerson,William,	1	2	Caro.
Emmery,Joseph,	3	3	Fay.
Emmet,Richard,	1		Mont.
Emmison,Ash,	1		Fay.
Emmison,Hugh,	1		Fay.
Emmons,James,	1	3	K.&Q.
Emmons,James,	1		Fay.
Emmons,Joseph,	1		Fau.
Emmons,Joseph,			Fay.
Emmons,William,Jr.,	1		Fau.
Emmons,William,		2	Fau.
Emory,John,	1	8	Pr.Geo.
Emrey,George,	1	2	Lou.
Emrey,Jacob,	1		Lou.
Emry,Abigail,			Fau.
Emry,George,	1	1	Fau.
Emry,John,	1		Fau.
Emry,Joseph,	1		Fau.
Emry,Robert,Jr.,	1		Fau.
Emry,Thomas,	2		Fau.
Emry,William,	1	3	Fau.
England,David,	1		Gooch.
England,Joseph,	1	1	Bot.
England,William,	1		Gooch.
Engle,George,	1		Bot.
Engleman,Peter,	1		Aug.
Engleman,Phillip,	1		Aug.
Engleman,William,	1		Aug.
English,Charles,	1		Lin.
English,John,	1		Wash.
English,John,	1		Lin.
English,Nathan,	1	3	So'n.
English,Robert,	1		Rock.
English,Robert,	1		Fau.
English,Stephen,	1	7	Bed.
English,Stephen,	1		Lin.
English,Stephen,Jr.	1		Bed.
Engram,William,	1		Bed.
Ennis,James,	1		Bed.
Enroughty,Edward,	1		Hen.
Enroughty,John,			Hen.
Enroughty,Nathan,	1		Hen.
Eoff,Isaac,	1		Lin.
Eoff,Peter,	3		Lin.
Epes,Amey,		10	Pr.Geo.
Epes,Amy,	1	7	Din.
Epes,Elizabeth,	1	19	Pr.Geo.
Epes,Frances,	3		Pr.Geo.
Epes,Francis,	1	2	Pr.Geo.
Epes,Nathaniel,	1	2	Din.
Epes,Peter,	1	28	Din.
Epes,Peter,	2	38	Pr.Geo.
Epes,Richard,	1	53	Pr.Geo.
Epes,Thomas,			Pr.Geo.
Eplaugh,Jacob,	1		Lou.
Epperson,Anthony,	1	1	Bed.
Epperson,Francis,	1	2	Buck.
Epperson,George,	1	6	Buck.
Epperson,John,	1	1	Buck.
Epperson,John,			Buck.
Epperson,Littleberry			Pr.Geo.
Epperson,Thomas,	1		Buck.
Eppes,Francis,	1		Din.
Eppes,Francis,	1	9	Lun.
Eppes,Joel,	1	10	Pr.Geo.
Eppes,John,	1	3	Lun.
Eppes,John,	1	7	Din.
Eppes,Joshua,	1	8	Din.
Eppes,Mary,		14	Ch.Cy.
Eppes,Peter,	1	20	Din.
Eppes,Peterson,	1	3	Din.
Eppes,Richard,	1	2	Din.

Name			County
Eppes,Richard,		15	Ch.Cy.
Eppes,Temple,Estate,		11	Ch.Cy.
Epps,Francis,	1	11	Din.
Epps,Chratum,	1	1	Camp.
Epps,Peter,	1	2	Din.
Epps,Ruth,			Din.
Epps,Maj.William,	1	28	Din.
Epps,William,	1	15	Din.
Erthin,Reubin,			Cul.
Ervin,Charles,	1		Aug.
Ervin,George,	1		Mont.
Ervin,Joseph,	1		Mont.
Ervin,William,	1	4	Fay.
Ervine,Joseph,	1		Bed.
Ervine,Samuel,	1		Lou.
Erwin,Rev.Benjamin,	1		Aug.
Erwin,Edward,	1		Rock.
Erwin,Edward,	1		Aug.
Erwin,Edward,	1		Aug.
Erwin,Edward,Sr.,	1	5	Aug.
Erwin,Edward,Jr.,	1		Aug.
Erwin,Francis,	1	8	Aug.
Erwin,Henry,	1		Rock.
Erwin,Jared,	1		Aug.
Erwin,Jarret,	1		Har.
Erwin,Jean,			Aug.
Erwin,John,	1	1	Aug.
Erwin,Joseph,			Aug.
Erwin,Lam,	1		Aug.
Erwin,Robert,	1		Rock.
Erwin,Robert,	1		Rock.
Erwin,Robert,Sr.,	2	3	Rock.
Erwin,Samuel,	1		Aug.
Erwin,William,	1		Aug.
Erwin,William,	1		Bot.
Erwin,William,	2		Berk.
Eskins,John,	1		Aug.
Eskridge,Charles,	1	18	Lou.
Estes,Abram,			Lun.
Estes,Ann,		3	Spots.
Estes,Ann,		15	Spots.
Estes,Barttelot,	1	1	Lun.
Estes,Barttelot,	1	2	Lun.
Estes,Benjamin,	1	3	Lun.
Estes,Benjamin,Jr.,	1		Lun.
Estes,Benjamin,	2	11	Bed.
Estes,Elisha,	1	8	Lun.
Estes,Elisha,	1	13	Caro.
Estes,Elisha,	1	1	Henry
Estes,Elisha,Jr.,	1		Henry
Estes,Joel,	1	12	Henry
Estes,John,	1	1	Spots.
Estes,John,	1	10	Caro.
Estes,John,	1		Lun.
Estes,Mary,		6	Henry
Estes,Richard,	1	1	Spots.
Estes,Richard,	1	5	Henry
Estes,Robert,	2	5	Lun.
Estes,Samuel,	1	1	Spots.
Estes,Samuel,	1	2	Lun.
Estes,Thomas,	1	2	Spots.
Estes,William,	1	8	Henry
Estham,James,	1	9	Lun.
Estill,Catherine,		11	Wash.
Estill,Rebecca,		3	Aug.
Estis,Philip,	1	8	Caro.
Etherton,Joseph,	1		Spots.
Etherton,William,			Spots.
Etter,Daniel,	1		Mont.
Etter,John,	1		Mont.
Etter,Peter,	1		Mont.
Etwater,Enos,	1		Aug.
Eubanks,Achilles,	1		Bed.
Eubank,George,	3	7	K.&Q.
Eubank,George,			K.&Q.
Eubank,Henry,	1		K.&Q.
Eubank,James,	2	5	Hen.
Eubank,James,Jr.,			Hen.
Eubank,John,			Lun.
Eubank,Philip,Sr.,	1	2	K.&Q.
Eubank,Philip,	1	1	K.&Q.
Eubank,Rachel,		4	K.&Q.
Eubank,Richard,			K.&Q.
Eubank,Richard,	1	1	K.&Q.
Eubank,Royale,	1		Caro.
Eubank,William,	1	2	K.&Q.
Eubank,William,	1		Hen.
Eubank,William,	4	14	Caro.
Eubank,William,	1	1	Caro.
Eubanks,Richard,Sr.,	1	1	Bed.
Eubanks,Richard,Jr.,	1		Bed.
Eubanks,Thomas,	1		Bed.
Eubanks,William,	1		Bed.
Eubanks,William,	1	15	K.&Q.
Eubanks,William,	1		Bed.
Eustace,Isaac,	1	5	Fau.
Eustace,William,	3	18	Fau.
Evans,Amos,	1		Henry
Evans,Benjamin,	1	5	Lun.
Evans,Benjamin,	1		Lou.
Evans,Clayborne,	1		Hen.
Evans,Daniel,	1		Lou.
Evans,Daniel,	1		Lou.
Evans,Elizabeth,			Lou.
Evans,Elizabeth,			Lou.
Evans,Emanuel,	1		Loui.
Evans,Evan,	2		Lou.
Evans,Evan,	1	11	Brun.
Evans,Francis,		2	So'n.
Evans,Francis,		2	Gooch.
Evans,Francis,			Brun.
Evans,George,	1	3	Henry
Evans,George,	1	4	Henry
Evans,Griffith,	1		Aug.
Evans,Hannah,			Lou.
Evans,Henry,	1		Buck.
Evans,Isaac,			Lou.
Evans,Isaac,Jr.,	1	2	Berk.
Evans,Isaac,	2	3	Berk.
Evans,Isaac,Sr.,	1	9	Berk.
Evans,James,	1		Bot.
Evans,Jesse,	1		Mont.
Evans,Jesse,	1	5	Mont.
Evans,John,	1		Lou.
Evans,John,	1		Lou.
Evans,John,Jr.,	1	2	Berk.
Evans,John,	1		Berk.
Evans,John,	1		Berk.
Evans,John,	1	3	Berk.
Evans,John,	1		Mont.
Evans,John,Jr.,		5	Caro.
Evans,John,	1	12	Caro.
Evans,John,	1		Ch.Cy.
Evans,John,	1		Henry
Evans,Joseph,	1		Berk.
Evans,Littleberry,	1		Ch.Cy.
Evans,Mary,			Lou.
Evans,Matthew,	2	1	Brun.
Evans,Michael,	1		Pr.Wm.
Evans,Nathaniel,	1		Bot.
Evans,Patrick,	1		Bot.
Evans,Peter,	1	7	Bot.
Evans,Peter,	1	11	Pr.Wm.
Evans,Philip,			Spots.
Evans,Rease,	1		Camp.
Evans,Rhoderick,	1		Hen.
Evans,Richard,	1		Berk.
Evans,Robert,	2	2	Caro.
Evans,Robert,	1	4	Caro.
Evans,Robert,	1		Buck.
Evans,Robert,	1		Fau.
Evans,Samuel,	1		Camp.
Evans,Sampson,	1		Camp.
Evans,Susannah,		4	Gooch.
Evans,Theophilus,	1		Mont.
Evans,Theophilus,	1		Mont.
Evans,Thomas,	1		Mont.
Evans,Thomas,	1	8	Pr.Wm.
Evans,Thomas,	1		Henry
Evans,Thomas,	1		Henry
Evans,Thomas,	1	21	Din.
Evans,Thomas,			Bed.
Evans,Thomas,	1	1	Caro.
Evans,William,	1		Lou.
Evans,William,	1		Lou.
Evans,William,	1		Lou.
Evans,William,	1		Mont.
Evans,William,	1		Mont.
Evans,William,	1	1	Din.
Evans,William,	1	12	Lun.
Evans,William,	1	1	Din.
Evans,Wilmoth,		4	Lun.
Evans,Wilmyrth,	1	7	Din.
Evat,Nehemiah,	1		Buck.
Eve,George,	1	5	Cul.
Eve,Thomas,	1	1	Cul.
Evens,Isiah,	2	4	Acco.
Evens,Jacob,	1		Fay.
Evens,Nathan,	1		Acco.
Evens,Nathaniel,	1	4	Acco.
Evens,Phillip,	1		Pr.Geo.
Everart,Joseph,			Lou.
Everengtrum,James,	1		Lou.
Evermont,Michael,	1		Har.
Everrett,Simmons,	1		Bed.
Everitt,Elizabeth,			So'n.
Everitt,Keeton,	1		So'n.
Everitt,Simon,	1		So'n.
Evins,Edward,	1		Lin.
Evins,Jesse,	1		Wash.
Evins,John,	1	9	Nor.
Evins,Johns,	1		Fay.
Evins,Joseph,	1		Buck.
Ewart,Elizabeth,			Fay.
Ewell,Bertrand,	1	2	Pr.Wm.
Ewell,Charles,		1	Pr.Wm.
Ewell,James,	1	24	Pr.Wm.
Ewell,Jesse,		5	Pr.Wm.
Ewell,Margaret,		4	Acco.
Ewell,Solomon,	1	1	Pr.Wm.
Ewers,Jonathon,	1		Lou.
Ewing,Banker,			Bed.
Ewing,Banker,	1	3	Lin.
Ewing,Charles,	1	2	Bed.
Ewing,George,	1	11	Mont.
Ewing,James,	1	6	Aug.
Ewing,James,Jr.,	1		Aug.
Ewing,John,	2		Berk.
Ewing,John,	1		Mont.
Ewing,John,	2		Bed.
Ewing,Martha,		1	Bed.
Ewing,Robert,	1		Bed.
Ewing,Robert,Jr.,	1		Bed.
Ewing,Samuel,			Bed.
Ewing,Samuel,	1	1	Mont.
Ewing,William,	1	5	Mont.
Ewing,William,	1	1	Bed.
Ewing,William,	1	1	Bed.
Ewing,Young,	1		Lin.
Ewis,Thomas,	1		Brun.
Exum,Arthur,	1	3	So'n.
Exum,Benjamin,	1	7	So'n.
Exum,Robert,	1	5	So'n.
Eyre,Margerit,	2	178	Nor.
Ezell,Benjamin,	1	10	Brun.
Ezell,Buckner,	1		Brun.
Ezell,Joseph,	1	1	Brun.
Ezell,William,	1	6	Brun.
Ezell,William,	1	3	Brun.

Name			County	Name			County	Name			County
Ezell,William,	1		Brun.	Farish,Robert,	1	28	Caro.	Feagins,Elizabeth,	1	3	Fau.
				Farish,Stephen,	1	8	Caro.	Feagins,John,	1	1	Fau.
Face,Edward,	1	1	Eli.Cy	Fariss,Carter,			Hen.	Feagins,Rawleigh,	1		Fau.
Fagan,James,	1		Cul.	Fariss,John,	1	5	Hen.	Fear,Edmund,	1		Bed.
Fain,William,	1		Henry	Fariss,Richard,	1		Hen.	Fear,Hamner,	1		Ja.Cy
Faint.George,	1		Har.	Fariss,William,	2	9	Hen.	Fear,William,			Ja.Cy
Fair,Edmund,	1		Fay.	Fariss,William,	1	15	Hen.	Fearn,John,est.,			Buck.
Faircloth,Benjamin,	1	3	So'n	Fariss,William,	1	5	Hen.	Featherston,Charles,			Brun.
Faircloth,Benjamin,Srl,			So'n	Farler,David,	1		Buck.	Featherston,Hezekiah			Brun.
Fairfax,George Wm.,	1	81	Berk.	Farley,Hannah,		21	Din.	Fee,Rachel,			Henry
Faircloth,George,			Lou.	Farley,Seth,	1	5	Lun.	Feehary,James,			Acco.
Fairhurst,Jeremiah,	2		Lou.	Farlor,Daniel,	1		Bed.	Feeter,John,	1		Wash.
Fairhurst,John,	1		Lou.	Farlor,Francis,	1		Bed.	Fegins,Ann,			West.
Fairis,Arthur,	1		Berk.	Farlor,Jeremiah,	1		Bed.	Fegitt,Thomas,	1		West.
Fairis,Davis,	1		Berk.	Farlor,Obediah,	1		Bed.	Feild,James,	1	14	Pr.Geo.
Fairis,Robert,	1		Berk.	Farlour,Henry,	1		Mont.	Felan,Andrew,	1		Lin.
Fairis,William,	2		Berk.	Farlour,Thomas,	1		Mont.	Felan,John,	1		Lin.
Falkner,Jesse,Jr.,	1		Berk.	Farlour,Thomas,Jr.,	1		Mont.	Felan,Thomas,	1	4	Lin.
Falkner,Jesse,Sr.,	1		Berk.	Farmer,Adam,	1		Lou.	Felin,Catherine,			Lin.
Falkner,Thomas,	1	2	K.&Q.	Farmer,Benjamin,	1	5	Lun.	Felin,James,	1	1	Lin.
Falkner,Thomas,	1		Berk.	Farmer,Daniel,	1	6	Cul.	Felkins,John,	1		Fau.
Falls,James,	1		Bot.	Farmer,Gideon,	1		Caro.	Felkins,William,	1		Fau.
Falls,Peter,	1		Bot.	Farmer,Henry,estate,		1	Lun.	Felson,Robert,	1	1	Berk.
Falwell,James,	1		Nuck.	Farmer,Jeremiah,	1		Mont.	Felson,Robert,Jr.,	1		Berk.
Falwell,Richard,	1		Buck.	Farmer,John,	1		Cul.	Felts,Nathaniel,	1	4	So'n
Falwell,William,	1		Buck.	Farmer,Lodowick,	1	3	Lun.	Felts,Philip,	1	1	So'n
Fandal,Philip,	1	7	West.	Farmer,Lodowick,est.		6	Lun.	Felty,Thomas,	1		Fau.
Fanell,John,	1		Henry	Farmer,Ralph,	1		Caro.	Fendley,George,	1		Lin.
Fanning,Bryan,	1		Mont.	Farmer,Sarah,		6	Lun.	Fenn,Thomas,	1	1	Eli.Cy
Fanning,David,	1		Mont.	Farmer,Thompson,	1		Mont.	Fenner,Mary,		9	Pr.Geo.
Fanning,Eckles,Jr.,	1		Mont.	Farmer,William,	1		Mont.	Fenwick,John,			Gooch.
Fanning,Eckles,Sr.,	1		Mont.	Farnsworth,Henry,			Lou.	Ferbus,Alexander,	1		Bed.
Fanning,John,	1		Mont.	Farrar,Barrett,	1	3	Gooch.	Ferganson,Elijah,			Cul.
Fordin,Charles,	1		Lou.	Farrar,Daniel,	1	1	Gooch.	Ferganson,Jesse,			Cul.
Farenholtz,Jacob,	1		K.Wm.	Farrar,John,	1	7	Gooch.	Ferganson,John,	4	3	Cul.
Farenholtz,John,			K.&Q	Farrar,Joseph,	1	2	Gooch.	Ferganson,Lewis,			Cul.
Farganson,Elijah,			Cul.	Farrar,Joseph R.,	1	29	Hen.	Fergerson,J.,	1	3	Pr.Wm.
Farganson,Jesse,			Cul.	Farrar,Perrin,	1	7	Loui.	Ferguson,Andrew,	1		Bot.
Farganson,John,	3	3	Cul.	Farrar,William,		9	Gooch.	Ferguson,Ann,			So'n
Farganson,Lewis,			Cul.	Farrar,William,	1	28	Gooch.	Ferguson,Ann,			Lou.
Farganson,Samuel,	2	25	Cul.	Farrell,George,	1	3	Din.	Ferguson,Briant,	2	20	Fay.
Farganson,William,	1	6	Cul.	Farrell,George,	1	3	Din.	Ferguson,Charles E.,	1		Hen.
Fargerson,Abram,	1	3	Spots.	Farrell,John,	1		Pr.Geo	Ferguson,David,	1		Berk.
Fargeson,William,	1	7	Spots.	Farriss,Elisha,			Wash.	Ferguson,Hannah,			Bot.
Farguson,Alexander,	2	4	Buck.	Farriss,John,	2		Hen.	Ferguson,James,	1		Bot.
Farguson,Horatio,			Lun.	Farrow,Isaac,	1	14	Pr.Wm.	Ferguson,John,	1		Berk.
Farguson,Joel,	2		Buck.	Farrow,John,	1	2	Pr.Wm.	Ferguson,John,	1		Buck.
Farguson,Joel,	2	3	Lun.	Farrow,John,	1	2	Pr.Wm.	Ferguson,John,	1		Fay.
Farguson,John,			Buck.	Farrow,Joseph,	1	6	Lou.	Ferguson,Joseph,			Lou.
Farguson,John,Jr.,	1		Cul.	Farrow,Joseph B.	1	24	Fay.	Ferguson,Peter,	1		Rock.
Farguson,John,	2	11	Henry	Farrow,William,	2	10	Pr.Wm.	Ferguson,Robert,	1		So'n
Farguson,Joseph,Sr.,	1	3	Henry	Farthing,Dudley,	1	1	K.&Q	Ferguson,Robert,	3	1	Har.
Farguson,Obediah,	1		Buck.	Farthing,William,	2	7	Ja.Cy	Ferguson,Samuel,	1		Mont.
Farguson,Robert,			Buck.	Fasler,Nancy,		8	Din.	Ferguson,William,	1		Brun.
Farguson,Robert,			Buck.	Fathery,Matthew,		1	Nor.	Ferguison,Alexander,	1	2	Bed.
Farguson,Thomas,			Lun.	Faudrie,Joseph,			Gooch.	Fergusson,Daniel,			Din.
Farguson,William,	1		Henry	Faught,Casper,	1		Bot.	Fergusson,Henry,	1		Bed.
Faringholtz,David,	1		K.&Q	Faulconer,Samuel,	1	2	Spots.	Fergusson,Isham,	1		Bed.
Faringholtz,William,	1	9	K.&Q	Faulconer,Samuel,Jr.	1		Spots.	Fergusson,John,	1	1	Bed.
Faris,Benjamin,	1		Loui.	Fauley,John,	1		Lou.	Ferigo,Robert,	1		Bed.
Faris,Cager,	1		Lin.	Faulk,Christopher,	1		Berk.	Fernando,Mary,			Pr.Geo.
Faris,Elisha,	1	1	Lin.	Faulkner,Benjamin,	1	1	K.&Q	Fernando,Matthew,	1	8	Pr.Geo.
Faris,Gideon,	1		Wash.	Faulkner,Johnson,	2	17	Caro.	Fernandon,Adam,	1	2	Pr.Wm.
Faris,Isaac,	1		Wash.	Faulkner,Lewis,			Mont.	Ferrell,Martha,			Wash.
Faris,Isaac,	2	2	Lin.	Faulkner,Mary,		5	K.&Q	Ferrell,Gabriel,	1	1	Bed.
Faris,Isam,	1		Lin.	Fauntleroy,Moore,	1	11	Aug.	Ferrell,William,	1		Camp.
Faris,James,Sr.,	1	1	Lin.	Favour,Caleb,	1	7	Cul.	Ferrend,Isaac,	3		Har.
Faris,James,Jr.,	1	4	Lin.	Favour,Isabella,		9	Cul.	Ferrill,Augustine,	1	1	Caro.
Faris,John,	2		Lin.	Fax,Hugh,	1		Henry	Ferrill,Charles,	1		Buck.
Faris,Johnson,	1		Lin.	Fay,John,	1		Berk.	Ferrill,Margaret,			Lin.
Faris,Mary,		4	Loui.	Feagan,Francis,Sr.,	1	8	Pr.Wm.	Ferris,William,			Buck.
Faris,Nathan,	1	1	Lin.	Feagan,Francis,Jr.,			Pr.Wm.	Ferson,Elizabeth,		4	Fay.
Faris,Richard,			Loui.	Feagan,James,			Pr.Wm.	Fewell,John,	1		Fau.
Faris,Robert,	1		Wash.	Feagan,William,	1	6	Pr.Wm.	Fewell,Nathaniel,	1		Fau.
Faris,William,	1		Loui.	Feagan,William,Jr.,	1		Pr.Wm.	Feuner,Windle,	1		Berk.
Farish,John,	1	1	Gooch.	Feagan,Daniel,	1	4	Lou.				
Farish,Joseph,	1	2	Gooch.	Feagins,Edward,	1	2	Fau.				

Name			Loc	Name			Loc	Name			Loc
Fewqua,Giles,	2	1	Ch.Cy.	Finley,George,	1	1	Wash.	Fitchet,Joshua,Jr.,	1		Nor.
Fewqua,Henry,			Ch.Cy.	Finley,James,	2		Mont.	Fitchet,Joshua,Sr.,	1	2	Nor.
Fewqua,Mary,		7	Pr.Geo	Finley,John,	1		Aug.	Fitzgerald,Peter,			Gooch.
Fewqua,Randol,	1	1	Pr.Geo	Finley,John,	1	1	Aug.	Fitzgerald,Elijah,	2		Acco.
Fewqua,Thomas,	1	1	Ch.Cy.	Finley,John,	2	1	Aug.	Fitzgerald,Fred'k,	1		Henry
Ficklin,John,	1	4	K.Geo.	Finley,John,	1		Rock.	Fitzgerald,Henry,	2	3	Acco.
Ficklin,Thomas,	2	2	Fay.	Finley,Robert,Jr.,	1	1	Aug.	Fitzgerald,Harvey,			Henry
Ficklin,William,	2	7	Spots.	Finley,Samuel,	1		Mont.	Fitzgerald,JosephJr			Acco.
Fidler,Benjamin,	1		Loui.	Finley,Thomas,	1		Mont.	Fitzgerald,Jos.,Sr.,	2	2	Acco.
Fidler,Edward,	1		Har.	Finley,William,	1	6	Mont.	Fitzgerald,William,	1	2	Fau.
Fidler,Francis,	1		Loui.	Finley,William,	1	4	Aug.	Fitzgerrald,John,	1		Buck.
Fidler,Frank,	1		Buck.	Finn,Joel,	1		Pr.Geo	Fitzgarrald,John,	1		Berk.
Fidler,Thomas,	1		Fau.	Finn,John,	1		Buck.	Fitzhugh,Battaile J.	1	21	Caro.
Field,Abner,	1	4	Cul.	Finn,John,	1		Pr.Geo	Fitzhugh,Elizabeth,		30	Lin.
Field,Abraham,	1	1	Cul.	Finn,Massenb'g Fra's	1	9	Pr.Geo	Fitzhugh,Elizabeth,	1	17	Pr.Geo.
Field,Mrs.Anne,		17	Brun.	Finn,Thomas,	1	2	Pr.Geo	Fitzhugh,George,		22	Fau.
Field,Daniel,	1	12	Cul.	Finn,William,	1		Henry	Fitzhugh,George,	1	9	K.Geo.
Field,Daniel,Estate,		3	Fau.	Finnell,Benjamin,	1	6	Cul.	Fitzhugh,George,		39	K.Geo.
Field,Elii,		3	Cul.	Finnell,Elijah,	1	4	Cul.	Fitzhugh,Henry,	1	14	Fau.
Field,Henry,	1	12	Cul.	Finnell,John,	3	1	Cul.	Fitzhugh,Henry,	15	19	K.Geo.
Field,Henry,	2	21	Cul.	Finnell,Reubin,	1	2	Cul.	Fitzhugh,Col.Henry,	40	44	K.Geo.
Field,John,	1	14	Cul.	Finney,Elizabeth,		1	Cul.	Fitzhugh,John,	1		Nor.
Field,John,	2	18	Eli.Cy	Finney,James,	1	3	Cul.	Fitzhugh,John,	2	22	Pr.Wm.
Field,Larkin,	1	7	Cul.	Finney,John,	1	3	Cul.	Fitzhugh,John,		18	Pr.Wm.
Field,Reubin,		4	Cul.	Finney,William,	1	10	Acco.	Fitzhugh,John,	1	23	Caro.
Field,Stephen,	4	35	K.&Q.	Finney,William,			Cul.	Fitzhugh,John,	1		K.Geo.
Field,William,	1	2	Lin.	Finnie,John,	1	6	Bed.	Fitzhugh,Martha,	1	6	Ja.Cy.
Fielding,Edward,	1	7	Fau.	Finny,John,	1		Berk.	Fitzhugh,Thomas,	1	14	So'n.
Fielding,John,	1		Bot.	Firestone,Joseph,	1		Lou.	Fitzhugh,Thomas,	1	36	Pr.Wm.
Fields,Anne,	6		Cul.	Firth,Thomas,	1	8	Brun.	Fitzhugh,Thomas,	1	6	Cul.
Fields,Bartlet,	1	7	Eli.Cy	Fish,Thomas,	1		Mont.	Fitzhugh,William,	1	45	Caro.
Fields,Henry,Sr.,	1	11	Cul.	Fishback,Frederick,	1		Cul.	Fitzhugh,William,	1	23	Lou.
Fields,Dr.James,	1	19	Brun.	Fishback,Fredrick,	1	2	Cul.	Fitzhugh,William,	2	36	Fau.
Fields,Jemmima,	1	3	Lou.	Fishback,Harmon,	1	2	Cul.	Fitzhugh,William,	1	49	K.Geo.
Fields,John,	1		Rock.	Fishback,Jacob,	1	5	Cul.	Fitzhugh,William,	1	80	K.Geo.
Fields,John,	1	11	Loui.	Fishback,John,	1	3	Fau.	Fitzhugh,William,		1	Lou.
Fields,John,	2		Caro.	Fishback,John,	1		Berk.	Fitzhugh,William,	1	39	Lou.
Fields,John,	1		Lin.	Fisback,John,	1	7	Cul.	Fitzjarell,William,	2	2	Fay.
Fields,John,	1	1	Fau.	Fishback,Josiah,	1	9	Fau.	Fitzjarrell,John,	1		Lin.
Fields,William,	1	6	Lou.	Fishback,Martin,		6	Cul.	Fitzpatrick,John,	1		Cul.
Fields,Theophilus,Est	1	21	Brun.	Fishback,Philip,	2	1	Fau.	Fitzue,Robert,	1		Bed.
Fieldstad,Marck,	1		Cul.	Fisher,Adam,	3	4	Har.	Fitzue,Robert,Jr.,			Bea.
Fielor,John,	2		Lou.	Fisher,Barbara,	1		Cul.	Fix,Phillip,	1		Aug.
Fiemster,John,	1		Rock.	Fisher,Caleb,	1	7	Nor.	Fizler,Michael,	1		Berk.
Figg,Benjamin,	1		Pr.Geo	Fisher,Daniel,	1		Lou.	Fiztue,Peter,	1		Bea.
Figg,James,		3	K.Wm.	Fisher,Daniel,		5	So'n.	Flanagan,Ambrose,	1		Loui.
Figg,John,	1		Berk.	Fisher,David,	1	5	Lin.	Flanagan,James,	1		Loui.
Figures,Eliz.Lucy,		3	So'n.	Fisher,Edward,	1	3	So'n.	Flanagan,Levi,	1		Bot.
Filler,Andrew,	1		Lou.	Fisher,Frendrick,	1	1	Acco.	Flanders,John,	1		Din.
Fillitson,Francis,	1		Henry	Fisher,George,	3		Har.	Flatcher,William,	1		Wash.
Filwell,John L.,	1	12	Nor.	Fisher,Jacob,	1		Har.	Flathers,Edwards,	1	5	Fau.
Finane,Daniel,	1		Wash.	Fisher,Jacob,	1		Har.	Flax,William,	1		Lin.
Finch,Bernard,	1		Camp.	Fisher,James,	1	18	Brun.	Fleece,Nicholas,	1		Berk.
Finch,Bernard,	1		Camp.	Fisher,James,	1	1	Fay.	Fleeharty,John,	1		Acco.
Finch,Blagdon,	1		Camp.	Fisher,John,	3		Har.	Fleeharty,Levin,	1		Acco.
Finch,Charles,	1	8	Henry	Fisher,John,	1	16	Brun.	Fleeman,Joseph,	1		Loui.
Finch,Edward,	1	13	Ch.Cy	Fisher,John,	1		Berk.	Fleeman,Sarah,			Loui.
Finch,Edward,	1	4	Ch.Cy	Fisher,Martin,		3	K.Geo.	Fleener,Adom,	1		Wash.
Finch,Henry,	1	2	Ch.Cy	Fisher,Michael,	1		Berk.	Fleener,Gasper,	1		Wash.
Finch,Jerry,			Hen.	Fisher,Phillip,	1		Acco.	Fleener,Jacob,	1		Wash.
Finch,John,	1	1	West.	Fisher,Polly,		7	Nor.	Fleener,Nicholas,	1		Wash.
Finch,Thomas,	1		Henry	Fisher,Richard,	1		Fau.	Fleese,Jacob,	1		Berk.
Finch,Thomas,	1	5	Lou.	Fisher,Samuel,	1		Fau.	Fleet,Henry,	1	19	K.&Q.
Finch,William,	1		Henry	Fisher,Thomas,	1		Lun.	Fleet,Peter,	1		Aug.
Finch,William,	1	1	Fau.	Fisher,Thomas Est.,	1	5	West.	Fleming,Carter,	1	1	K.&Q.
Finch,William,	1	8	Brun.	Fisher,Widow,			Har.	Fleming,David,	1		Camp.
Fincham,John,	1		Cul.	Fisher,William,	1		Ja.Cy.	Fleming,David,	1		Camp.
Fincham,Robert,	1		Cul.	Fisher,William,	1	12	Lun.	Fleming,David,	1		Berk.
Fincham,William,	1		Cul.	Fishill,John,	1		Berk.	Fleming,Gardener,	2		Hen.
Fineta,Martin,	1		Berk.	Fitch,Ann,			Berk.	Fleming,George,	1		Rock.
Finigan,Dennis,	1		Lou.	Fitch,Daniel,	1		Berk.	Fleming,James,	1	1	Bot.
Fink,Jacob,	1		Berk.	Fitch,James,	1		Berk.	Fleming,James,	1		Berk.
Fink,Philip,	1		Lou.	Fitch,Samuel,	1		Berk.	Fleming,James,	2		Fay.
Finks,Andrew,	1		Cul.	Fitches,Thomas,	1	4	Buck.	Fleming,James,	1		Har.
Finks,Mark,	1	2	Cul.	Fitchet,Daniel,	1	9	Nor.	Fleming,John,	2	1	Fay.
Finley,Benjamin,	1		Aug.	Fitchet,Grace,		7	Nor.	Fleming,Joseph,	1		Fay.

Name			Place	Name			Place	Name			Place
Fleming,Mrs.Mary,	2	5	Gooch.	Flowers,William,			Fau.	Ford,Francis,	1	4	Spots.
Fleming,Robert,	1		Mont.	Floweru,Daniel,	1	14	Fau.	Ford,Francis,			Din.
Fleming,Samuel,	1	1	K.&Q.	Flowrence,William,	1	3	Fau.	Ford,Francis,	1	2	Din.
Fleming,Samuel,	1	1	Gooch.	Floyd,Benjamin,	1	2	Lin.	Ford,Harwood,	1	1	Hen.
Fleming,Samuel,	1	1	Camp.	Floyd,Charles,Sr.,	1		Nor.	Ford,Henry,	1	2	Din.
Fleming,Col.Tarleton,		80	Gooch.	Floyd,Charles,Jr.,	1	4	Nor.	Ford,Jacob,			Buck.
Fleming,William,	1	2	Aug.	Floyd,David,	2	18	Lin.	Ford,James,	1	2	Caro.
Fleming,Col.William,	2	10	Bot.	Floyd,F.,	1		Pr.Wm	Ford,James,Sr.,		1	Buck.
Fleming,Col.William,		12	Gooch.	Floyd,George,			Lin.	Ford,James,Jr.,	1		Buck.
Flesher,Conrod,	1		Aug.	Floyd,Gideon,	2	10	Caro.	Ford,James,	1		Aug.
Flesher,Henry,	1		Aug.	Floyd,James,	1	1	Caro.	Ford,Jarrall,	1	5	Din.
Flesher,Peter,	1		Aug.	Floyd,James,	1		Din.	Ford,Joel,			Buck.
Flesham,John,	1		Cul.	Floyd,John,			Lun.	Ford,John,			Buck.
Flesham,Michael,	1		Cul.	Floyd,John,	1		Lin.	Ford,John,		1	Caro.
Flesham,Peter,	1		Cul.	Floyd,John,Sr.,		1	Nor.	Ford,John,Jr.,	1		Caro.
Fleshman,Moses,			Cul.	Floyd,John,Jr.,	1	7	Nor.	Ford,John,Jr.,	1		Cul.
Fleshman,Robert,	2		Cul.	Floyd,Josiah,	2	16	Brun.	Ford,John,Sr.,	1		Cul.
Fletcher,Aaron,	1	9	Fau.	Floyd,Mathew,	1	1	Nor.	Ford,Lewis,	3	7	Hen.
Fletcher,Ambros,	1		Wash.	Floyd,Robert,	1		Lun.	Ford,Lucy,		8	Hen.
Fletcher,Benjamin,	1		So'n.	Floyd,Robert,	1		Cul.	Ford,Mary,		1	Spots.
Fletcher,Benjamin,	1		Fau.	Floyd,Thomas,	1		Pr.Geo	Ford,Matthew,Sr.,	1	1	Din.
Fletcher,Christopher,	1		Fau.	Floyd,William,	1	16	Nor.	Ford,Milton,	1	9	Hen.
Fletcher,Drury,			Lun.	Floyd,William,	1		Ch.Cy.	Ford,Nelson,			Hen.
Fletcher,James,			Cul.	Floyed,Benjamin,	2	12	Acco.	Ford,Obediah,	1		Hen.
Fletcher,James,	1	16	Brun.	Floyed,William,	1	6	Acco.	Ford,Peter,	1		Lin.
Fletcher,Joab,	1		Rock.	Flurner,William,	1	4	Bed.	Ford,Peter,	3		Buck.
Fletcher,John,	1	1	Acco.	Flurnoy,David,			Fay.	Ford,Reubin,	1	6	Gooch.
Fletcher,John,	1		Cul.	Flurnoy,Mathew,	3	19	Fay.	Ford,Richard,	1		Buck.
Fletcher,John,	2	4	Cul.	Flutee,John,	2		Fay.	Ford,Ryland,			Hen.
Fletcher,John,	1	3	Henry	Flynn,Michael,	1		Fau.	Ford,Samuel,	1		Hen.
Fletcher,John,	1	4	Brun.	Flynn,Valentine,	1		Fau.	Ford,Samuel,	1		Hen.
Fletcher,Joseph,	1		Mont.	Foalding,James,	1		Bea.	Ford,Samuel,	2	3	Hen.
Fletcher,Joshua,	1	1	Fau.	Fogg,James,	1	6	K.&Q.	Ford,Sherwood,	3		Hen.
Fletcher,Moses,	1		Fau.	Fogg,William,	1		Brun.	Ford,Stephen,			Pr.Wm.
Fletcher,Moses,	1		Fau.	Fogle,John,			Bot.	Ford,William,	1	6	Gooch.
Fletcher,Patterson,	2	2	Cul.	Foley,Bryant,	1		Fau.	Ford,William,	1		Caro.
Fletcher,Peter,	2		Berk.	Foley,James,	1	3	Fau.	Ford,William,	1		Lun.
Fletcher,Rebecca,		21	Pr.Geo	Foley,James,	2	13	Fau.	Ford,William,	1		Fau.
Fletcher,Richard,	1	2	Brun.	Foley,John,	1		Har.	Ford,William,Sr.,	1	4	Din.
Fletcher,Robert,	1		Rock.	Foley,Luke,	1		Henry	Ford,Winny,			Din.
Fletcher,Stephen,	1		Nor.	Foley,Thomas,	1	4	Fau.	Ford,Worrinor,	1		Lin.
Fletcher,Thomas,	1		Fau.	Foley,William,	1	1	Fau.	Foreacres,Hezekiah,	1		Spots.
Fletcher,Thomas C.,			Cul.	Folie,Henry',	1		Mont.	Foreacres,Richard,	1		Spots.
Fletcher,William,	1		Fau.	Folin,George,	1	1	Berk.	Foreman,Henry,	1		Berk.
Fletcher,William,	1		Cul.	Foling,Valentine,	1		Fau.	Foreman,Joseph,	1	4	Berk.
Fletcher,William,	1		Lou.	Foliver,Michael,	1		Berk.	Foreman,Lewis,	1		Lou.
Fletcher,William,	1		Nor.	Folley,Moss,	1		Mont.	Foreman,Peter,	1		Lou.
Flin,George,	1		Berk.	Folston,Swathan,	1		Bot.	Foreman,Reuben,	1	1	Berk.
Fling,Elizabeth,	1		Lou.	Foluo,John,	4	2	Acco.	Forgason,William,	1		Aug.
Fling,William,			Lou.	Foluo,Upshur,			Acco.	Forister,John,	1	1	Cul.
Flinn,John,	1		Fau.	Folwider,John,	1		Aug.	Forker,James,	1		Fay.
Flint,John,	1	1	Cul.	Folwider,Ulrick,	1		Aug.	Forkner,William,	1		Henry
Flint,John,Sr.,	2	2	Cul.	Foney,Charles,	1	5	Buck.	Forman,Robert,	1		Fay.
Flint,Richard,	1		Cul.	Fonler,John,			Camp.	Forrester,Nathaniel,	1		Bed.
Flint,Richard,Sr.,	1	6	Cul.	Fonnicola,Serafluo,	2	11	Hen.	Forson,William,	1	2	Spots.
Flood,John,			Buck.	Fontaine,John,	1	18	Henry	Forsythe,Robert,	1	9	Spots.
Flood,Henry,	1	1	Buck.	Fontaine,Mr.,		12	Pr.Wm.	Fort,Christopher,	1		Fay.
Flood,Thomas,	1		Lou.	Foot,Richard,Estate,	1	16	Pr.Wm.	Fort,John,	1	12	So'n.
Florah,James,	1		Wash.	Foote,George,Estate,		12	Fau.	Fort,John,	1	13	So'n.
Florence,George,		1	Pr.Wm.	Foote,William,	2	13	Fau.	Fort,Joshua,Estate,		19	So'n.
Florence,J.,	1	5	Pr.Wm.	Forbes,Alexander,			Buck.	Fortion,Frederick,			Caro.
Florence,William,	2	5	Cul.	Forbes,David,	1	5	Pr.Wm.	Fortson,Charles,	1	5	K.Wm.
Florence,William,Jr.,			Cul.	Forbes,George,	1	1	Fay.	Fortson,Stephen,	2	3	Caro.
Flourance,G.,	1		Pr.Wm.	Forbis,George,	1	8	Mont.	Fortune,Armistead,	1		Caro.
Flourance,G.,	1		Pr.Wm.	Forbis,John,	1		Mont.	Fortune,Elizabeth,	1	4	Caro.
Flourence,John,	1		Cul.	Forbis,John,	1		Lin.	Fortune,Richard,	1		Caro.
Flourence,M.,	1	8	Pr.Wm.	Forbush,James,	2	5	Lin.	Fosque,John,			Acco.
Flourence,Thomas,	1		Cul.	Ford,Abram,			Din.	Fosque,John,	2		Acco.
Flowers,Andrew,	2		Buck.	Ford,Boaz,	1		Buck.	Fosque,John,Jr.,	2	13	Acco.
Flowers,Andrew,	1		Fau.	Ford,Bartlett,	1		Hen.	Fosque,John,Jr.,	2	13	Acco.
Flowers,Austin,			Buck.	Ford,Daniel,	1		Buck.	Fosque,Nathaniel,			Acco.
Flowers,Edward,	1		Bea.	Ford,Daniel,			Gooch.	Fosque,Nathaniel,			Acco.
Flowers,John,	1		K.Geo.	Ford,Daniel,	1		Henry	Fosh,James,	1		Bot.
Flowers,Ralfe,	3	1	Buck.	Ford,David,	1	1	Hen.	Fosh,James,Jr.,	1		Bot.
Flowers,Valentine,			Buck.	Ford,Elizabeth,		6	Gooch.	Fosh,Jonathan,	1	5	Bot.

Name			Co.	Name			Co.	Name			Co.
Foshee,Abfire,	2	10	Cul.	Foushee,William,	2	18	Hen.	Francis,John,	1		Mont.
Foshee,Benjamin,	1	3	Cul.	Fouty,George,	1		Berk.	Francis,Sterling,	1	6	So'n
Foshee,Daniel,			Cul.	Fowell,William,	1		Pr.Wm	Francis,Thomas,	1		Lou.
Foshee,Elijah,			Cul.	Fowke,Ann,		7	K.Geo	Francis,William,	1		York
Foshee,George,	1		Cul.	Fowke,Enfield,		2	Fau.	Francis,William,	1		Bot.
Foshee,John,	1	2	Cul.	Fowke,George,		2	Fau.	Francis,William,	1		Buck.
Foshee,Joseph,	1	1	Cul.	Fowke,Mary,		2	Fau.	Francis,William,	1		Hen.
Foshee,Thornton,	1	2	Cul.	Fowler,Ben,	1	1	Din.	Francis,William,	1		Hen.
Foshee,William,	1		Cul.	Fowler,Daniel,	1	1	Brun.	Francis,William,			Fay.
Foster,Absalom,	1	1	Acco.	Fowler,Elizabeth,		2	Bed.	Francis,William,	1	10	So'n
Foster,Anthony,	1		Lun.	Fowler,James,	1		So'n	Francisco,George,	1		Aug.
Foster,Arthur,	2	20	So'n	Fowler,John,	1		Wash.	Francisco,Jacob,	1		Bot.
Foster,Asa,			Pr.Wm	Fowler,John,			Lun.	Francisco,Lodowick,	1		Bot.
Foster,Benjamin,			Hen.	Fowler,Joseph,	1	12	Din.	Francisco,Michael,	1		Aug.
Foster,Benjamin,	2		Lou.	Fowler,Sanuel,	1		K.&Q	Francisco,Peter,			Buck.
Foster,Charles,	1	1	Henry	Fowler,Sarah,		6	So'n	Frank,Bedington,	1		K.Geo.
Foster,Christian,	7		K.Wm.	Fowler,William,			K.Wm.	Frank,James,	1		K.Geo.
Foster,Christopher,	1	1	So'n	Fowler,William,	1		Bed.	Frank,John,	1		Bed.
Foster,Edmund,	1	10	Spots	Fowler,William,	1		Din.	Frank,John Martin,	2		Fay.
Foster,Edmond,	1		Loui.	Fowler,William,	1	1	Caro.	Frank,Neremiah,	1		K.Geo.
Foster,Elizabeth,		1	Spots	Fowler,William,	1	1	So'n	Frank,Robert,	1	3	Spots.
Foster,Henry,	1	1	Fay.	Fowlks,Thomas,	1		Brun.	Frank,Robert,	1		K.Geo.
Foster,Henry,	1		Berk.	Fowster,William,	1	3	Bot.	Frank,William,	1		Spots.
Foster,Isaac,	1	2	Pr.Wm	Fox, A.,			Pr.Wm	Franklen,Owen,	1		Bed.
Foster,Isaac,	1	6	Berk.	Fox,Abraham,	1	1	Ja.Cy	Franklin,Abraham,	1	3	Henry
Foster,Isham,	1	1	Lun.	Fox,Ambrose,	1	1	Lou.	Franklin,Benjamin,	1	1	Lun.
Foster,J.	1	2	Pr.Wm	Fox,Amos,	1	1	Lou.	Franklin,Daniel,	1		West.
Foster,James,	1		Aug.	Fox,Ann,		4	Caro.	Franklin,Edmund,	1	5	Camp.
Foster,James,	1		Berk.	Fox,Bryan,	1		Berk.	Franklin,Henry,	1		Camp.
Foster,James,	1		Bed.	Fox,Elizabeth,			Lou.	Franklin,James			Hen.
Foster,Jeremiah,	1	2	Pr.Wm	Fox,Golden,	1		Acco.	Franklin,Lewis,	1	1	Camp.
Foster,John,	1		Berk.	Fox,James,	1		Lou.	Franklin,Lewis,			Henry
Foster,John,	1	2	Caro.	Fox,John,	1	16	Lou.	Franklin,Owen,	1	12	Camp.
Foster,John,	1		Bed.	Fox,John,	1		Cul.	Franklin,Robert,	1		Camp.
Foster,John,	1		Har.	Fox,John,	1	4	K.Wm.	Franklin,Susannah,	3	1	Pr.Wm.
Foster,John,Jr.,	1	3	Lun.	Fox,Joseph,	1		Lou.	Franklin,Thomas,	1	1	Camp.
Foster,John,Sr.,	1	12	Lun.	Fox,Joseph,	1	30	K.Wm.	Franklin,Thomas,	1	1	Camp.
Foster,Joshua,	1	1	Pr.Wm	Fox,Joseph,	1	18	West.	Frankling,Elisha,	1		Hen.
Foster,M.	1	4	Pr.Wm	Fox,Levina,		8	K.Wm.	Frankling,Francis,	1	14	Hen.
Foster,Mark,	1		Bot.	Fox,Nathaniel,	1	4	K.Wm.	Frankling,Lachariah,	1		Hen.
Foster,Mark,Jr.,	1		Bot.	Fox,Samuel,	1	7	Fau.	Frankling,Peter,			Hen.
Foster,Moses,	1	4	So'n	Fox,Thomas,	1	8	K.Wm.	Frankling,Thomas,	1		Hen.
Foster,Moses,			Lou.	Fox,Thomas,	1	33	Spots	Frazer,Jackson,	1	4	Hen.
Foster,Nat,			Pr.Wm	Fox,William,	1		Lou.	Frasher,James,	1		Cul.
Foster,Nimrod,	1		Pr.Wm	Fox,William,	1	2	Spots	Frazer,Anthony,	1	9	Spots.
Foster,Reuben,	1		Cul.	Foxworthy,John,	1		Pr.Wm	Frazer,George,	1	1	Bot.
Foster,Richard,	1	1	K.Wm.	Fram,John,	1		Lun.	Frazer,James,	1		Wash.
Foster,Robert,	1		Bot.	Frame,David,	1		Aug.	Frazer,James,	2		Lou.
Foster,Robert,	1	6	Caro.	Frame,Jeremiah,	2		Fay.	Frazer,James,	1	12	Spots.
Foster,Samuel,	1	2	Lou.	Frame,Jeremiah,	1		Aug.	Frazer,Jesse,	1	5	Hen.
Foster,Susanna,		5	Lun.	Frame,John,	1		Rock.	Frazer,John,	1	7	K.Wm.
Foster,Thomas,	2		Mont.	Frame,John,	1		Fay.	Frazer,John,	1		Wash.
Foster,Thomas,	1		Berk.	Frame,Joseph,	1		Henry	Frazer,John,	1		Aug.
Foster,Thomas,	2	10	K.&Q	Frame,Susanna,	1		Fay.	Frazer,Joseph,	1	3	Bot.
Foster,Thomas,	1	6	Fau.	Frame,Thomas,	1	10	Aug.	Frazer,Robert,			Henry
Foster,William,	1	7	K.Wm.	Frame,William,	1		Rock.	Frazer,Samuel,	1		Aug.
Foster,William,			Mont.	France,Henry,	1	7	Henry	Frazer,Samuel,Sr.,	1		Aug.
Foster,William,	1		Mont.	France,John,	1		Lou.	Frazer,William,	1		Bot.
Foster,William,	1	8	So'n	France,John,	1		Lou.	Frazer,William,	1	13	Hen.
Foster,William,			Cul.	France,Lawrence,	1		Lou.	Frazer,William,	1		Wash.
Foster,William,			Cul.	France,Mary,		9	Henry	Frazer,William,	2	30	K.Wm.
Foster,William,			Pr.Wm	France,Nicholas,	2		Lou.	Frazer,William,Jr.,	2	29	K.Wm.
Foster,William,	1		Pr.Wm	France,Peter,	1	1	Henry	Frazier,Alexander,	1	1	Din.
Foster,William,& Thomas	2	3	Aug.	France,Peter,	1	1	Berk.	Frazier,Ann,			Eli.Cy.
Fothergill,Thomas,	1		Har.	Franceway,Joseph,	1	1	Berk.	Frazier,Ann,			Fau.
Fouch,Abraham,	1		Lou.	Francies,Thomas,	1	3	Hen.	Frazier,Collin,	1	1	Spots.
Fouch,Isaac,			Lou.	Frances,Abraham,	1		York	Frazier,George,	1		Rock.
Fouch,Isaac,			Lou.	Francis,Christopher,	1	1	York	Frazier,James,	1		Rock.
Fouch,Jacob,	2		Lou.	Francis,Elizabeth,		8	So'n	Frazier,John,	1	5	Din.
Fouch,Thomas,	1	1	Lou.	Francis,Evan,	2		Fay.	Frazier,John,	1	1	Eli.Cy.
Foulger,John,			Berk.	Francis,Henry,	1		Mont.	Fraizier,Mary,		4	Gooch.
Foulkes,William,	1	8	Cha.Cy	Francis,Henry,	1		Mont.	Frazier,William,	1	4	Fay.
Fountain,Aaron,	1	23	Loui.	Francis,John,	1		Aug.	Fred,John,			Fay.
Fouracres,James,	1		Berk.	Francis,John,			Fay.	Fredd,Joseph,		1	Lou.
Foure,George,	1		Lou.	Francis,John,	1	6	So'n	Freel,Jeremiah,		1	Aug.
Foushee,Charles,		2	Cul.	Francis,John,	1		So'n				

Name			County
Freeland, Isaac,	1		Brun.
Freeland, Mace,	1	8	Buck.
Freeland, Mary,		4	Buck.
Freeman, Abraham,	1		Hen.
Freeman, Abram,	1		So'n.
Freeman, Elisha,	1	2	Lin.
Freeman, Gideon,	1	7	Din.
Freeman, Hamlen,	1	8	Brun.
Freeman, Harris,	1	4	Cul.
Freeman, Harris,			Cul.
Freeman, Herod,	2	2	Cul.
Freeman, Henry,	1	6	Lun.
Freeman, Isaac,	1		Loui.
Freeman, Isham,	1	8	Hen.
Freeman, James,			Hen.
Freeman, James,	1		Hen.
Freeman, James,			Hen.
Freeman, James,			Bed.
Freeman, Jesse,	1		Brun.
Freeman, John,	1		Loui.
Freeman, John,	1	1	Cul.
Freeman, John,			Cul.
Freeman, John, Jr.,			Cul.
Freeman, Jonathan,	1		Cul.
Freeman, Mingo,	1		Hen.
Freeman, Nat,	1		So'n.
Freeman, Olive,			So'n.
Freeman, Richard,	1		Hen.
Freeman, Robert,	1	1	Loui.
Freeman, Robert, Sr.,	2		Cul.
Freeman, Robert, Jr.,	1	3	Cul.
Freeman, Samuel,			K.Geo.
Freeman, Thomas,	1	3	Cul.
Freeman, William,			So'n.
Freeman, William,	1		Buck.
Frees, Frederick,	1		Berk.
Freestone, Jacob,	1		Lou.
French, Daniel,	1		Bed.
French, Dr.George,	1	11	Spots.
French, George,	1		Berk.
French, George,	1		Fau.
French, Hugh,	1	4	Gooch.
French, J.,	1	2	Pr.Wm.
French, Jacob,	1		Berk.
French, Jacob,	1		Berk.
French, James,	1	22	Din.
French, John,	2	5	Fau.
French, John,			Bed.
French, John,			Mont.
French, John,	1		Lin.
French, John,	1		Berk.
French, Matthew,	1		Mont.
French, William,	1		Henry
French, William,	1		Bea.
Frenklin, William,	1	4	Bot.
Frenter, Richard,	1		Bot.
Fresh, Casper,	1		Fay.
Freshover, Windle,	1		Berk.
Freshwater, William, Sr	1	12	Nor.
Freshwater, William, Jr	2		Nor.
Fretwell, John,	1	3	Loui.
Friel, Daniel,	1	1	Aug.
Friensley, Simon,	1	2	Spots.
Frier, Robert,	2		Fay.
Friley, Frederick,	1		Wash.
Fristoe, Robert,	1		Mont.
Fritz, Kelly,	1		Berk.
Fritz, Michael,	1		Berk.
Frogmorton, John,			Hen.
Frogmorton, Josiah,	1		Hen.
Frogmorton, Richard,	2		Hen.
Froman, Elijah,	1	1	K.Wm.
Frost, John,	1		Wash.
Frost, Joseph,	1		Wash.
Frost, Joseph,	1		Lou.
Frost, Ruben,	1		Nor.
Frost, Simeon,	1		Wash.
Frost, Thomas,	1		Berk.
Frost, Thomas,	1		Wash.
Frowman, Temple,	1		K.Wm.
Fry, George, Sr.,	1		Mont.
Fry, George, Jr.,	1		Mont.
Fry, Henry,	3	45	Cul.
Fry, Henry, Jr.,	1		Har.
Fry, Jacob,	2		Berk.
Fry, Lodawick,	2	2	Berk.
Fry, William,	3		Fay.
Fryar, J.,	2	1	Pr.Wm.
Fryatt, Bartholemew,	2	1	Berk.
Fryatt, John,	1	1	Berk.
Frye, Jacob,	1		Lou.
Fryer, Alexander,	1		Berk.
Fryer, Alexander, Jr.,	1		Berk.
Fryer, Matthew,	1		Berk.
Fryer, Robert,	1	1	Lou.
Fudge, John,	1	1	Aug.
Fugate, Benjamin,			Wash.
Fugate, James,	1		Mont.
Fugate, Josias,	1	2	Mont.
Fugate, Nancy,			Wash.
Fugate, Randal,	1		Mont.
Fugate, Zachariah,	1		Wash.
Fuklin, Charles,		2	Fau.
Fulcher, Cason,	1		Henry
Fulcher, Sarah,			Caro.
Fulkison, Abraham,	1		Wash.
Fulkeson, Benjamin,	1		Lou.
Fulkerson, Frederick,	1	4	Henry
Fulkineer, Jacob,	1		Lou.
Fulkison, James,	1	7	Wash.
Fulkerson, James,			Henry
Full, George,	1		Har.
Fullelove, Anthony,	1		Lun.
Fullelove, William,	1		Lun.
Fullen, Charles,	1		Mont.
Fuller, Elizabeth,		2	York
Fuller, Henry,			Rock.
Fuller, Joseph,	1		Berk.
Fullerton, Robert,	1		Berk.
Fullilove, Anthony, Jr	1		Lun.
Fullin, William,	1		Lin.
Fullin, William,	1		Lin.
Fulling, Francis,	1		Rock.
Fulton, David,	1	1	Mont.
Fulton, David,	1		Wash.
Fulton, David,	1		Berk.
Fulton, Davis,			Lou.
Fulton, Hugh,	1		Lou.
Fulton, Hugh,	1		Aug.
Fulton, James,	1	1	Aug.
Fulton, James,	1		Berk.
Fulton, James,			Fay.
Fulton, John,	1		Aug.
Fulton, John,	3		Aug.
Fulton, John,	2	3	Wash.
Fulton, Mary,			Aug.
Fulton, Robert,	2		Lou.
Fulton, Thomas,	1		Aug.
Fulton, William,	1		Mont.
Fulton, William,	1		Berk.
Fulton, William,	1		Aug.
Funk, Joseph,	1		Lun.
Funk, Peter,	1		Camp.
Funkhouser, Christ'er	1		Wash.
Funkhouser, John,	1		Wash.
Fuqua, Isham,	1		Bed.
Fuqua, John,	1	3	Bea.
Fuqua, Joseph,	1		Bed.
Fuqua, Joseph,	1	1	Buck.
Fuqua, Thomas,	1	6	Bea.
Fuqua, William,	1	3	Buck.
Furgeson, Abraham,	1	4	Fay.
Furgeson, Larkin,	2		Fay.
Furgeson, William,	1	1	Pr.Geo.
Furgusson, Daniel,	1		Din.
Furgusson, Richard,	1	5	Din.
Furist, Christian,	1		Lou.
Furlong, John,	1		Gooch.
Furnis, Thomas,			Cul.
Furqueran, John,	1	5	Bed.
Furqueran, Peter,	1	9	Bed.
Fursythe, David,	1		Berk.
Furr, Charity,			Lou.
Furr, Edwin,	1	1	Lou.
Furr, Enoch,	1	3	Lou.
Furr, Ephraim,	2	2	Fau.
Furr, Jeremiah,			Lou.
Furr, Moses,	1	1	Lou.
Furr, Thomas,			Fau.
Furr, William,	1		Lou.
Furrer, John,	1		Lou.
Furrer, Matthias,	1		Lou.
Fusel, Soloman,			Hen.
Fusell, Thomas,			Hen.
Fuson, John,	1		Henry
Fuson, John, Jr.,			Henry
Fuson, William,			Henry
Fussel, John,			Hen.
Gaar, Adam,	1	3	Cul.
Gaar, Andrew,	1		Cul.
Gaar, Benjamin,	1	2	Cul.
Gaar, John,	1	1	Cul.
Gaar, Michael,	1	8	Cul.
Gabbert, George,	1		Rock.
Gabbert, Jacob,	1		Aug.
Gabbart, Mathias,	1		Rock.
Gadberry, John,	1		Rock.
Gadberry, Thomas,	1		Henry
Gadberry, William,	1		Henry
Gaddis, Thomas,	1		Spots.
Gaddy, Bartholomew,	1		Bed.
Gaddy, George, Sr.,	1	1	Bed.
Gaddy, George,	1		Bed.
Gaddy, Richard,	1	2	Ja.Cy.
Gaddy, Sherod,	1		Bed.
Gaddy, William,	1		Bed.
Gaddy, William,	1		Bed.
Gaddy, William,	1	2	Ja.Cy.
Gaddy, William, Jr.,	1	5	Ja.Cy.
Gaether, Ephraim,	1	1	Berk.
Gafford, Thomas,	1		Lun.
Gaines, Benjamin,	1	6	Cul.
Gains, Bernera,	1		Fay.
Gaines, Betty,		11	K.&Q.
Gaines, Edmona,	1	4	Cul.
Gaines, Francis,			Cul.
Gaines, George,			Cul.
Gaines, Harry,	2	41	K.&Q.
Gaines, Henry,	1		Cul.
Gaines, Henry,	1	6	Cul.
Gaines, Henry,	2	1	Cul.
Gains, James,	1	3	Loui.
Gaines, James,	2	6	Cul.
Gaines, James,	1		Cul.
Gaines, John,			Cul.
Gaines, Joseph,	1	1	Cul.
Gaines, Pendleton,			Cul.
Gaines, Reubin,			Cul.
Gaines, Richard,	1		Cul.
Gaines, Richard,	1	4	Cul.
Gaines, Richard,	2	5	Cul.
Gaines, Robert,	1	15	K.&Q.
Gaines, Robert, Jr.,	1		K.&Q.
Gaines, Sarah,		4	Cul.
Gaines, Thomas,	1		Cul.
Gaines, Thomas,	1	13	Cul.
Gains, William,	2	15	Pr.Wm.

Gaines,William,	1	2	Cul.	Garlick,Mary,		36	K.Wm.	Garrott,Ambrose,	1		Cul.
Gains, R.			Pr.Wm.	Garlick,Mary,	1	11	K.Wm.	Garrott,Carrington,			Lun.
Gains,William,	1		Spots.	Garlick,Samuel,		2	K.Wm.	Garrott,Charles,est.	1	15	Buck.
Gaits,William,	1	3	Buck.	Garlick,Samuel,		11	K.&Q.	Garrott,Humphrey,	1		Lun.
Galbraith,Agness,			Rock.	Garner,Benjamin,	1		Fau.	Garrott,Isaac,			Buck.
Galbraith,Alexander,	1		Camp.	Garner,Charles,	1		Fau.	Garrott,Isaac,	1		Buck.
Galbreath,James,	1		Rock.	Garner,Charles,Jr.,	1		Fau.	Garrott,James,	2		Lun.
Galbraith,John,	1		Rock.	Garner,George,	2	31	West.	Garrott,John,	1		Buck.
Gale,Joseph,	1	7	Berk.	Garner,James,	1		Fau.	Garrott,John,	1	3	Buck.
Gale,Josiah,	1		Fay.	Garner,Jesse,	1		So'n	Garrott,John,	1		Lun.
Gale,William,	1	3	K.&Q.	Garner,Jonas,	1		Fau.	Garrott,Jonathan,	1		Caro.
Galford,Thomas,	1		Aug.	Garner,John,est.,		8	So'n	Garrott,Robert,	1		Lun.
Gallahorn,John,	1		Henry	Garner,John,		1	Rock.	Garrott,Stephen,	1	1	Buck.
Gallahue,Charlotte,			Pr.Wm.	Garner,Nathaniel,	1		West.	Garrett,Stephen,Jr.	1		Buck.
Gallahue,Rachel,			Pr.Wm.	Garner,Richard,	1	1	Spots.	Garrott,Thomas,	1		Cul.
Gallimore,William,	1		Henry	Garner,Thomas,	1		Cul.	Garrott,Thomas,	1	6	Lun.
Galloway,Benjamin,	1	2	Camp.	Garner,Thomas,	1		Fau.	Garrott,Richard,	1		Din.
Galloway,David,	1	9	Spots.	Garner,Vincent,	2	6	Fau.	Garrott,William,	1		Buck.
Galloway,David,Jr.,	1	15	Spots.	Garner,William,	1	4	Brun.	Garrott,William,	1		Henry
Galloway,James,	1		Bot.	Garnes,Lewis,			Lou.	Garvin,Hugh,	1	1	Camp.
Galloway,John,	2		Bed.	Garnett,Anthony,	1	8	Cul.	Garvin,Isaac,	1		Lin,
Galloway,Tary,	1		Buck.	Garnett,Austin,		5	Caro.	Garwin,John,	1		Aug.
Galloway,William,	1		Bot.	Gernett,Benjamin,			Cul.	Garwin,Thomas,	1		Aug.
Gallyhorn,Edward,	1		Lou.	Garnett,Edmond,			Cul.	Garwood,John,	2		Cul.
Galt,Gabriel,	2	8	Henry	Garnett,James,	1	6	Caro.	Garwood,James,	1		Bot.
Galt,Hugh,			Din.	Garnett,James,	2	6	Cul.	Gary,Boyce,		15	Pr.Geo.
Gamble,George,	1		Wash.	Garnett,John,	1	5	K.&Q.	Gary,Boyce,	1	3	Pr.Geo.
Gamble,John,	1	7	Aug.	Garnett,John,	1	2	K.&Q.	Gary,Elizabeth,		8	Pr.Geo.
Gamble,Robert,		3	Aug.	Garnett,John,	2	6	Cul.	Gary,Josiah,	1	4	Pr.Geo.
Gannaway,Edmund,	1	1	Buck.	Garnett,Muscoe,	1	4	Spots.	Gary,William,	1	13	Pr.Geo.
Gannaway,Grigory,	1	4	Buck.	Garnett,Nathaniel,			Buck.	Gasaway,Nicholas,	1		Berk.
Gannaway,John,	1	5	Buck.	Garnett,Reuben,	1	2	Cul.	Gasaway,Thomas,	1		Berk.
Gannaway,Mary,		5	Buck.	Garnett,Robert,	1	7	Cul.	Gassaway,Thomas,Jr.	1		Berk.
Gannaway,Robert,	1	2	Buck,	Garnett,Thomas,	2	7	Cul.	Gascorn,Sarah,	1	5	Nor.
Gannaway,Thomas,	1	2	Buck.	Garnett,Thomas,	1	7	Caro.	Gascoyne,Rachel,	2	11	Acco.
Gannaway,William,	1	6	Buck.	Garnett,Whiscoe,		26	Caro.	Gash,Martin,	1		Wash.
Gansau,Jacob,			Har.	Garrard,Anthony,	1		Fau.	Gash,Michael,Sr.,	1	1	Bed.
Gant,Joseph,	1		Lou.	Garratt,James,			Pr.Wm.	Gash,Michael,Jr.,	1	1	Bed.
Gantt,John,	1	20	Berk.	Garratt,Richard,	1	6	Pr.Wm.	Gaskins,Job,	1		Aug.
Gardner,Ann,		1	So'n	Garrell,Richard,		2	York	Gasney,Henry,	1		Berk.
Gardner,Francis,	1		Aug.	Garrett,Humphrey,	1	13	K.&Q.	Gaston,Alexander,	1		Lin.
Gardner,Hanson,	1	4	Mont.	Garret,Rosanna,			Bot.	Gates,Elijah,	1		Bed.
Gardner,Jacob,	1		Lou.	Garrison,Abel,	1	6	Nor.	Gates,Gen.Horatio,		7	Berk.
Gardner,James,	1	4	So'n	Garrison,Abraham,	1		Lin.	Gates,Jacob,	1		Berk.
Gardner,James,	3	3	K.&Q.	Garrison,Archibald,	1	1	Nor.	Gates,John,	1		Pr.Wm.
Gardner,James,	1	8	So'n	Garrison,Elizabeth,		4	Acco.	Gates,William,	1		Henry
Gardner,Jesse,	1	1	So'n	Garrison,George,	2	14	Acco.	Gatewood,Chaney,	1	16	K.&Q
Gardner,John,	1		Aug.	Garrison,Isiah,	1	3	Acco.	Gatewood,Dudley,	1	20	Bed.
Gardner,John,	1	3	Loui.	Garrison,John,	1		Har.	Gatewood,Henry,Sr.,	2	1	Spots.
Gardner,Joseph,	1		Lou.	Garrison,Jonathan,	1	5	Acco.	Gatewood,Henry,	1	7	Spots.
Gardner,Joseph,Jr.,	1	1	Lou.	Garrison,Jonathan,Jr			Acco.	Gatewood,James,	2	18	Caro.
Gardner,Luke,	1		Lou.	Garrison,Richard,	1		Acco.	Gatewood,James,	1	23	Bed.
Gardner,Matthew,	1	7	So'n	Garrison,William,	2	8	Acco.	Gatewood,John,	1	11	Caro.
Gardner,Samuel,	1		Lou.	Garriss,George,	1	3	Nor.	Gatewood,John,	1	22	K.Wm.
Gardner,Silvester,	1	5	Lou.	Garrity,James,	1	6	So'n	Gatewood,John,	1	3	K.&Q.
Gardner,Thomas,	1		Spots.	Garrow,John,	1	11	York.	Gatewood,John,	1	7	K.&Q.
Gardner,William,	1	3	Henry	Garrow,William,	1	4	York	Gatewood,Joseph,	1	7	K.&Q.
Gardner,William,	1		Acco.	Garth,David,	1	4	Lou.	Gatewood,Joseph,	1	7	K.&Q.
Gardiner,Anthony,	1	14	K.&Q.	Garth,David,	1	4	Lou.	Gatewood,Pinchpy,	1	24	Caro.
Gardiner,James,	2	35	K.&Q.	Garth,John,	1	9	Loui.	Gatewood,Rachel,		26	Caro.
Gardiner,John,	1	37	K.&Q.	Garret,Benjamin,	1		Mont.	Gatewood,Thomas,			York.
Gardinhire,Jacob,	2		Pr.Wm.	Garrett,Elizabeth,		7	Loui.	Gatewood,William,		1	K.&Q.
Gardous,John,	1		West.	Garrett,Henry,	1	18	Loui.	Gatewood,William,			K.&Q.
Garland,Charles,	1	1	Loui.	Garrett,John,	1		Lou.	Gatewood,William,	1		K.&Q.
Garland,James,			Loui.	Garrett,John,			K.Wm.	Gathright,Agness,		7	Hen.
Garland,Jesse,	1	11	Buck.	Garrett,Joseph,	1		Lou.	Gathright,Anselem,	1	6	Hen.
Garland,Mary,	1	27	Lun.	Garrett,Richard,Sr,	3		K.&Q.	Gathright,Benjamin,			Hen.
Garland,Nathaniel,	1	10	Loui.	Garrett,Thomas,	1		Lou.	Gathright,Benjamin,	1	9	Hen.
Garland,Peter,	1	17	Lun.	Garrett,William,	1		Lou.	Gathright,Epharim,	1	25	Hen.
Garland,Robert,	2	19	Loui.	Garrett,William,	1	11	Loui.	Gathright,Epharim,Jr	1	3	Hen.
Garland,Samuel,	1	28	Lun.	Garrett,William,est.		11	K.&Q.	Gathright,John,	2	11	Hen.
Garland,Thomas,	1	1	Loui.	Garriott,Benjamin,			Cul.	Gathright,John,			Hen.
Garland,Thomas,	1	5	Lun.	Garriott,Catherine,	1		Cul.	Gathright,Joseph,			Hen.
Garlick,Camm,		14	K.Wm.	Garriott,John,	1		Cul.	Gathright,Miles,	1	1	Bed.
Garlick,Camm,est.		8	K.&Q.	Garriott,Reuben,	1		Cul.	Gathright,Samuel,	1		Bed.
Garlick,John,	2	19	Caro.	Garriott,Reuben,			Cul.	Gathright,Samuel,	5	28	Hen.

Gathright,William,			Henry	George,James,	1	6	Gooch.	Gibson,James,	1		Berk.
Gathright,William,	1	11	Hen.	George,John,	1		Lou.	Gibson,John,	1		Aug.
Gathright,William,	1	35	Hen.	George,John,	1	4	Henry	Gibson,John,			Wash.
Gathright,William,	1	16	Hen.	George,John,Sr.,	1	17	Caro.	Gibson,John,	1	2	Lun.
Gatson,Peter,	1		Bed.	George,John Ch.,	1	6	Caro.	Gibson,John,	1		Loui.
Gaul,George,	1		Rock.	George,Joseph,	1		Har.	Gibson,John,	1	1	Caro.
Gault,Leah,		5	Nor.	George,Lucy,		9	Caro.	Gibson,John,	1	5	K.&Q.
Gaumers,Jacob,	1		Berk.	George,Margaret,		8	Fau.	Gibson,John,	1		Lou.
Gaunt,John,	1	4	Caro.	George,Michael,	1		Lou.	Gibson,John,	1	1	Buck.
Gaunt,Lunsford,			Cul.	George,Nicholas,	1	2	Fay.	Gibson,John,	1		Bed.
Gaunt,Mary,	1	1	Cul.	George,Parnach,	1	7	Fau.	Gibson,Joseph,	1		Lou.
Gaunt,Sarah,	1	3	Caro.	George,Reuben,	1	18	Caro.	Gibson,Jonathan,	2	30	Fau.
Gautier,Anthony,	1	5	West.	George,Reuben,	2	5	Hen.	Gibson,Lightfoot,			Loui.
Gazaway,Thomas,	1		Henry	George,Robert,	1	3	Gooch.	Gibson,Mary,			Fay.
Gavens,Thomas,	1		Har.	George,Solomon,	1		Bot.	Gibson,Miles,	1	8	Buck.
Gay,Charles,	1	1	Hen.	George,Thomas,	1	3	Lou.	Gibson,Moses,			Lou.
Gay,Elizabeth,			Rock.	George,Whitun,	1		Fay.	Gibson,Nathan,	1		Loui.
Gay,Henry,	1		Rock.	George,Capt William,	1		Lou.	Gibson,Patrick,	1		Camp.
Gay,John,	1	7	Rock.	George,William,			Gooch.	Gibson,Patrick,	1		Camp.
Gay,John,	1		Rock.	George,William,	1	6	Gooch.	Gibson,Richard,	1	2	K.&Q.
Gay,Martha,	1		Rock.	George,William,	1		Bot.	Gibson,Robert,	1		Fau.
Gay,Robert,	1	1	Rock.	George,William,	1	10	Henry	Gibson,Robert,	1		Aug.
Gay,Robert,	1		Rock.	George,William,		6	***	Gibson,Samuel,	1		Aug.
Gay,William,	1		Rock.	Gerrard,David,	1		Berk.	Gibson,Samuel,	1		Spots.
Gay,Thomas,			Acco.	Gerrard,John,	1		Berk.	Gibson,Thomas,	1		K.&Q.
Gayle,John,	1	2	Caro.	Gerrard,Justice,	1		Berk.	Gibson,Thomas,	1		Lou.
Gayle,John,	1	7	K.&Q.	Gervis,George,	1	2	York	Gibson,Thomas,	1	1	Berk.
Gayle,Matthew,	2	7	K.&Q.	Gest,George,	1		Har.	Gibson,Thomas,	1		Berk.
Gayle,Mathew,	1	11	Lun.	Gest,Joseph,	1		Berk.	Gibson,William,	1		Aug.
Gayle,Mathew,Jr.,	2	2	Lun.	Gholson,William,	1	1	Spots.	Gibson,William,	1	1	Fau.
Gaylor,Edward,	1		Rock.	Gholston,Thomas,	1	11	Brun.	Gibson,William,Jr.,	1		Fau.
Gearton,George,	1	1	K.Wm.	Gibbeans,Thomas,	1		Loui.	Gibson,William,	1		Loui.
Gearton,James,	2		K.Wm.	Gibbons,George,			York	Gibson,William,	1		Bed.
Geday,James,	3	16	Din.	Gibbons,John,	1	1	York	Gibson,William,	1		Rock.
Gee,Benjamin,	1	1	Lun.	Gibbons,Lawrence,			York	Gibson,William,	1		Fay.
Gee,Benjamin,	1		Bot.	Gibbons,Mary,	2	14	York	Gibson,Wyatt,	1		K.&Q.
Gee,Charles,	2	11	Pr.Geo	Gibbons,Morgan,	1		Berk.	Giacomb,Joseph,	1		Lin.
Gee,Charles,	1	1	Lun.	Gibbons,Roger,	3		Berk.	Gidean,Francis,	1	3	Loui.
Gee,David,	1	2	Lun.	Gibbons,Robert,	1	4	York	Gidens,Ishmael,	1	2	York
Gee,Edward,	2		Bot.	Gibb,William,	2	9	Acco.	Giddens,John,	1		Cul.
Gee,George,	1		Lun.	Gibbs,Alexander,	1		Bed.	Gidean,William,	1		Loui.
Gee,Henry,	1	9	Lun.	Gibbs,David,	1		Bed.	Giadins,Thomas,	1		Acco.
Gee,James,Sr.,	2		Lun.	Gibbs,Elizabeth,			Brun.	Gidion,John,	1	4	Nor.
Gee,James,Jr.,			Lun.	Gibbs,Francis,	2	7	Cul.	Giffy,John,	1		Berk.
Gee,Jessie,	1	6	Lun.	Gibbs,James Lenen,	1	4	Lou.	Gilburt,Charles,	1		Spots.
Gee,Jessie,Jr.,	1	4	Lun.	Gibbs,John,	1	1	Din.	Gilberts,John,	1		Rock.
Gee,John,			Brun.	Gibbs,John,	1	9	Cul.	Gilbert,John,	1	2	Gooch.
Gee,John,	1		Pr.Geo	Gibbs,Julias,	1	1	Cul.	Gilbert,Joseph,	1		Lou.
Gee,Nevil,	1	4	Lun.	Gibbs,Julius,	1	1	Fay.	Gilbert,Nathan,	1		Berk.
Gee,Parker,	1		Bot.	Gibbs,Mary,			Brun.	Gilbert,Robert,	2	9	Hen.
Gee,Rachel,		5	Pr.Geo	Gibbs,Stephen,	1		Brun.	Gilbert,Silas,	1	1	Lou.
Gee,Robert,	1		Brun.	Gibbs,Thomas,	1	2	York	Gilbert,William,	1	2	West.
Gee,Robert,	1		Bot.	Gibbs,William,	1	2	Brun.	Gilbraith,John,	1		Berk.
Gee,Thomas,	1		Berk.	Gibbs,William,	1		York	Gilbraith,Mrs.,			Berk.
Gee,Thomas,	1		Bot.	Gibbs,William,			Cul.	Gilchrist,Robert,	1	20	Caro.
Gee,William,	2	10	Brun.	Gibbs,Zachery,	1	9	Cul.	Gilchrest,Robert,	1	30	Caro.
Geer,Aquela,	1	1	Bed.	Gibson,Abraham,	1	1	Fau.	Gilding,Charles,	1	5	Nor.
Gegery,John,	1		Henry	Gibson,Alexander,	2		Aug.	Giles,Elizabeth,	1	7	Hen.
Gelasple,William,	1		Fay.	Gibson,Alice,	1		Lou.	Giles,John,		1	Lou.
Gemmills,David,	1		York	Gibson,Andrew,	1		Mont.	Giles,John,			Lou.
Gemmills,James,	1		York	Gibson,Archibald,	1	1	Aug.	Giles,John,	1	11	York
Gemmills,John,	1		York	Gibson,Churchill,	1	3	Lun.	Giles,William,	1	5	Hen.
Gemmills,Nathan,	1		York	Gibson,David,	1		Mont.	Giles,***,	1	6	Hen.
Gennet,Thomas,Jr.,	1		Hen.	Gibson,David,	1		Aug.	Gilham,William,	1	1	Aug.
Genn,James,	1	5	Fau.	Gibson,Edward,	1	4	Buck.	Gilkison,Hugh,	1	1	Aug.
Gentry,David,	1	3	Caro.	Gibson,George,	1		Fau.	Gilkison,James,	1		Fay.
Gentry,James,	1	13	Loui.	Gibson,George,	2		Loui.	Gilkison,William,	1	1	Aug.
Gentry,John,	1		Loui.	Gibson,George,	1	4	Caro.	Gill,David,	1		Ch.Cy.
Gentry,Martin,	1		Loui.	Gibson,Gidean,	1		Loui.	Gill,Edward,	1		West.
Gentry,Nathan,	1		Loui.	Gibson,Henry,	2		Bot.	Gill,Elizabeth,	1	8	Ch.Cy.
Gentry,Nicholas,	1	6	Loui.	Gibson,Isaac,	1		Lou.	Gill,George,	1	7	West.
Geoghegan,Anthony,	1	1	Hen.	Gibson,James,	1		Wash.	Gill,Henry,	1	1	Lun.
George,Ann,		3	So'n.	Gibson,James,	1		Lou.	Gill,Ingram,	1	2	Ch.Cy.
George,Elizabeth,		3	Caro.	Gibson,James,	2		Loui.	Gill,Ingram,	1		Ch.Cy.
George,Enoch,	1	5	Brun.	Gibson,James,	1		Eli.Cy	Gill,James,	1		Eli.Cy.
George,Fred'k Eppes,	1	2	Din.	Gibson,James,	1	1	Bed.	Gill,James,	1		Berk.

Name			County
Gill,John,			Pr.Wm.
Gill,John,	2	7	Pr.Wm.
Gill,Prissley,	1		Rock.
Gill,Richard,	1		Rock.
Gill,Richard,	1		Ch.Cy
Gill,Samuel,	1	2	Bot.
Gill,Samuel,	2	3	Lin.
Gill,Thomas,	1		Ch.Cy
Gill,William,	1	2	Lun.
Gill,William,			Ch.Cy
Gill,William,Jr.,	1		Ch.Cy
Gillan,William,			Pr.Wm.
Gillaspey,Thomas,	1		Aug.
Gillespy,William,	1	5	Aug.
Gillaspy,Simon,	1	2	Bot.
Gillaspy,William,	1		Bot.
Gillet,Peggy,	1	9	Acco.
Gillett,Peter,Sr.,	1	2	York
Gillet,Peter,Jr.,	1	2	York
Gillett,Reubin,	1		York
Gillett,Simon,		3	York
Gillespy,Daniel,	1		Aug.
Gillespy,Jacob,	1		Aug.
Gillespy,James,	1		Aug.
Gilliland,James,	1		Bot.
Gillispy,John,	1	2	Aug.
Gillaspey,Samuel,	1		Aug.
Gilliam,Arthur,	1	10	So'n.
Gilliam,Charles,	1	1	Camp.
Gilliam,Charles,	1	1	Camp.
Gilliam,David,			Buck.
Gilliam,Deverix,	1		Henry
Gilliams,Edgecomb,	1		Henry
Gilliam,Elizabeth,	1	41	Pr.Geo
Gilliam,Epaphaoditus,	1	2	Buck.
Gilliam,Jeffry,	1		Ch.Cy
Gilliam,John,			Buck.
Gilliam,John,	1	24	Gooch.
Gilliam,John,	1		So'n.
Gilliam,John,	1	91	Pr.Geo
Gilliam,Penelope,			So'n.
Gilliam,Peter,	1	6	Henry
Gilliam,Richard,	1	6	Bed.
Gilliam,Richard,	1	5	Lun.
Gilliam,Robert,	1	17	Gooch.
Gilliam,Robert,		31	Pr.Geo
Gilliam,Robert,	2	46	Pr.Geo
Gilliam,Susannah,		7	Buck.
Gilliam,Thomas,	1	20	So'n.
Gilliam,Thomas,Jr.,	1	10	So'n.
Gilliam,Thomas,	1		Bot.
Gilliam,William,	1	1	Buck.
Gilliam,William,	3		Buck.
Gilliam,William,	1	2	Camp.
Gillison,James,	1		Fau.
Gillison,John,		17	Cul.
Gillison,Mary,		9	Fau.
Gillis,James,	1		Bot.
Gilly,Charles,	1		Henry
Gilley,Francis,	1		Henry
Gillock,James,	1	2	Cul.
Gillum,Hinche,	1		Brun.
Gillum,John,	1	26	Brun.
Gilly,George,	1		Henry
Gilly,Richard,	1		Henry
Gimblett,Richard,	1		Berk.
Gilmer,Richard,			K.&Q.
Gilmon,Warrick,	1		Pr.Geo
Gilmore,James,	2	8	Rock.
Gilmore,James,	1	4	Rock.
Gilmore,James,	1		Mont.
Gilmore,James,	1	2	Lin.
Gilmore,James,Sr.,	1	1	Aug.
Gilmore,James,	1		Aug.
Gilmore,John,	1		Aug.
Gilmore,John,	1		Rock.
Gilmore,John,	1	3	Rock.
Gilmore,John,Jr.,	1		Rock.
Gilmore,Robert,			Lou.
Gilmore,Samuel,	1	1	Lin.
Gilmore,Sarah,		3	Har.
Gilmore,William,	1	7	Wash.
Gilmore,William,			Lin.
Ginkins,Anthony,	1		Cul.
Ginkins,Henry,	1		Cul.
Ginkins,Jerimiah,	1		Bot.
Ginkins,Joseph,	1		Bot.
Ginkins,Thomas,	1		Cul.
Ginn,Thomas,	3		Cul.
Ginn,Thomas,	1	2	Ja.Cy
Ginther,John C.,	1	3	York.
Gipson,John,	1	13	Fay.
Gipson,John,Jr.,	1		Fay.
Gipson,William,	1	1	Buck.
Gist,Hanson,			Lou.
Gist,John,	1	6	Lou.
Gist,John,	2	6	Lou.
Gist,William,	1	8	Lou.
Gittens,Evan,	1		Rock.
Give,John,	2		Berk.
Givans,George,	1	2	Aug.
Givans,James,			Aug.
Givans,James,		2	Aug.
Givans,Capt.John,	1	3	Aug.
Givans,John,	3	5	Aug.
Givans,Samuel,			Aug.
Givans,William,	1	1	Aug.
Givens,Daniel,	1		Bot.
Givens,James,	1	2	Lin.
Givens,Robert,	1	1	Lin.
Givens,Samuel,	1		Fay.
Givoden,John,	1		Buck.
Glacee,Matthew,	2		Fay.
Gladdan,Jerard,	1		Bot.
Gladden,George,	1		Acco.
Gladdish,John,	1	1	Brun.
Glanville,Edmund,	1	14	Nor.
Glascock,George,	1	7	Fau.
Glascock,Gregory,	1	1	Fau.
Glascock,Hezikiah,	1	2	Fau.
Glascock,John,	2		Fau.
Glascock,John,Jr.,	1		Fau.
Glascock,Peter,	2	8	Fau.
Glascock,Thomas,	1	2	Fau.
Glascock,Travis,	2		Fau.
Glasgow,Arthur,	1		Rock.
Glasgow,Robert,	1		Rock.
Glass,Charles,	1		Camp.
Glass,Charles,	1		Camp.
Glass,Henry,	1	3	Spots
Glass,James,			Gooch
Glass,John,	1		Gooch
Glass,Thomas,	1		Gooch
Glass,Vincent,	1	1	Cul.
Glass,Vincent,	1	3	Camp.
Glass,Vincent Sr.,	1	3	Camp.
Glass,Vincent Jr.,			Camp.
Glasscock,Elijah,	1		Lou.
Glasscock,James,	1		Lou.
Glasscock,Jesse,	1	1	Lou.
Glasscock,Peter,	1	11	Lou.
Glassell,Andrew,	2	14	Cul.
Glasson,George,			Buck.
Glaves,Michael,	1		Mont.
Glaves,William,	1	2	Mont.
Glazebrook,James,	1		Ja.Cy
Glean,John,	1		Bot.
Gleason,John,	1	1	Nor.
Glen,Daniel,	1		Buck.
Glen,George,	1		Aug.
Glen,John,	1		Loui.
Glen,John,	1		Hen.
Glenn,Andrew,	1		Mont.
Glenn,James,	1		Wash.
Glenn,Jeremiah,			Hen.
Glenn,Jeremiah,	1	14	Lun.
Glenn,John,	1	10	Lun.
Glenn,Joseph(James),	1		Berk.
Glenn,Matthew,	1		Hen.
Glenn,William,	1	10	Lun.
Glenn,William,	1	1	Berk.
Glover,Anthony,	1	8	Buck.
Glover,Chesley,			Buck.
Glover,Edmund,	1	5	Buck.
Glover,John,	1	14	Buck.
Glover,John,	1	7	Lin.
Glover,John,	1	12	Fay.
Glover,Joseph,	1	1	Lin.
Glover,Joseph,	1	12	Pr.Geo.
Glover,Robert,	2	15	Buck.
Glover,Samuel,	1	1	Buck.
Glover,Samuel,Jr.,	1	18	Buck.
Glover,Thomas,	1		Fau.
Glover,Thomas,	1	1	K.&Q.
Glover,William,	1	2	Lin.
Glover,William,	1	5	K.Wm.
Glover,William,			Pr.Geo.
Goad,Abraham,	1		Mont.
Goad,William,	1		Mont.
Gobble,Frederick,	1		Wash.
Gobble,George,	1		Wash.
Godard,James,	1		Henry
Godbey,John,	1	1	Caro.
Goden,John,	1	3	Ja.Cy
Goddwin,Gabriel,	1		Berk.
Goday,William,	1	3	York
Godfrey,Edward,	1		Har.
Godfrey,John,	1		Buck.
Godfrey,John,	1		Har.
Godfrey,William,	1		Har.
Godman,John,	1		Berk.
Godsey,Austin,	1		Buck.
Godsey,Henry,	1		Buck.
Godwin,Anthony,		20	So'n.
Godwin,Archibald,	1	10	Nor.
Godwin,Daniel,	1	2	Nor.
Godwin,Devorax,	1	15	Nor.
Godwin,William,	1		Brun.
Goff,Abrose,	1		Bed.
Goff,Jesse,	1		Lou.
Goff,John,	1		Buck.
Goff,John,	1	1	Bed.
Goff,John,	1		Mont.
Goff,Joseph,	1	1	Bed.
Goff,Joshua,	1		Fau.
Goff,Michael,	1		Lou.
Goff,Thomas,	1	4	Henry
Goff,Thomas,	3	2	Har.
Goff,William,	1		Lou.
Goff,William,	2	1	Buck.
Gofferd,John,	1		Bot.
Goffigon,Nathaniel,	1	5	Nor.
Goffigon,Southey,	1	8	Nor.
Goforth,William,	1		Wash.
Goft,Andrew,	1	1	Wash.
Goggin,Stephen,	1		Camp.
Goggins,John,	1	4	Lin.
Goggins,Stephen,	1	1	Bed.
Goggins,Richard,	1		Camp.
Goggins,William,	1		Lin.
Gohlson,William,	1		Din.
Going,Daniel,	1		Bed.
Going,David,	2		Henry
Going,Jason,	1		Lou.
Going,John,	1		Henry
Going,John,	1		Henry
Going,Joseph,	1	1	Bed.
Going,Luke,	2		Lou.

Name			County
Going,Moses,	1		Henry
Going,William,Sr.,	1		Bed.
Going,William,	1		Bed.
Going,William,	1		Buck.
Gold,John,	1	1	Brun.
Gold,John,	1	3	Berk.
Gold,Joseph,	1		Lou.
Golden,John,	1		Pr.Geo
Golding,John,	2		Pr.Wm.
Golding,Mary,			Henry
Golding,William,	1		Fau.
Goldman,Martin,		1	K.&Q.
Goldsberry,Benjamin,	1		Berk.
Goldsberry,Robert,	1		Berk.
Goldsberry,Thos.Mayn'd	1		Berk.
Goldsmith,Vincent,	1		Berk.
Goldsmith,William,	1		Loui.
Goldsmith,William,Jr.,	1		Loui.
Goldsburg,John B.,	1	1	Brun.
Golsby,Daniel,	1		Henry
Gooch,Claibourn,	1		Loui.
Gooch,James,	1	1	K.Wm.
Gooch,Linah,	1		Loui.
Gooch,Lovinah,		4	Loui.
Gooch,Rowland,	1		Loui.
Gooch,Stephen,	1	2	Loui.
Gooch,Thomas,	1	3	Loui.
Gooch,William,	1	4	Eli.Cy.
Good,Edmund,	1		Bed.
Good,John,	1		Buck.
Goodall,Charles,	1	4	Ja.Cy.
Goodall,John,	1	9	Ja.Cy.
Goodbar,Joseph,	1		Rock.
Goodby,William,	1	3	Mont.
Goody,John,	1		Lou.
Goode,Benjamin,			Hen.
Goode,Benjamin,			Hen.
Goode,John,	1		Hen.
Goode,Joseph,	1	9	Hen.
Goode,Joseph,Jr.,	1		Hen.
Goode,Samuel,	1	4	Hen.
Goode,Thomas,	2	8	Hen.
Goode,Thomas,	2	10	Hen.
Goode,Thomas,	1		Din.
Goodden,Abraham,	1		Mont.
Goodin,Benjamin,	1		Henry
Goodin,Lewis,	1		Fay.
Goodloe,Harry,	1	13	Spots.
Goodloe,Henry,		8	Caro.
Goodloe,Robert,	1	23	Spots.
Goodloe,Thomas,	1	6	Spots.
Goodman,Anselam,	1		Bed.
Goodman,Bartlett,	1		Loui.
Goodman,Charles,	1		Gooch.
Goodman,James,	1		Bot.
Goodman,John,	1		Loui.
Goodman,John,	1		Bed.
Goodpasture,Abraham,	1		Aug.
Goodrich,Briggs,	1	19	Brun.
Goodrich,Edward,Sr.,	1	4	Brun.
Goodrich,Edward,Jr.,	1		Brun.
Goodrich,William,	1	6	Brun.
Goodrum,John,	1	3	Brun.
Goodrum,William,	1	3	Brun.
Goodson,Thomas,	1		Bot.
Goodson,Thomas,	1		Bot.
Goodson,William,	1		Bot.
Goodwin,Abraham,	1		Fau.
Goodwin,Amos,	1		Lou.
Goodwin,Ann,		2	York
Goodwin,Armistead,			Din.
Goodwin,Bozwell,	3	9	Din.
Goodwin,Coleman,		7	Caro.
Goodwin,Daniel,	1		Bot.
Goodwin,James,	1	10	Eli.Cy.
Goodwin,John,	2	32	York

Name			County
Goodwin,Joseph,	1		Henry
Goodwin,Mark,	1		Din.
Goodwin,Peter,			York
Goodwin,Peter,	1	15	Caro.
Goodwin,Rebecca,		19	K.Wm.
Goodwin,Rebecca,	1	9	York
Goodwin,Robert,	1	4	Loui.
Goodwin,Robert,	1	15	Loui.
Goodwin,Stephen,			Din.
Goodwine,Solomon,	1		Har.
Goodwyh,John,	1	9	Lun.
Goodwyn,Braddock,	1	7	Din.
Goodwyn,Hannah,		6	Din.
Goodwyn,Harwood,	1	11	Din.
Goodwyn,Joseph,	1	14	Din.
Goodwyn,Peterson,	1	10	Din.
Goolsby,William,	1	12	Buck.
Goore,Peter,	2		Fay.
Gorden,Albin,	1	3	K.Wm.
Gorden,Alexander,	1	3	Cul.
Gordgame,David,	1	10	Pr.Geo
Gordin,John,	1	1	Cul.
Gordin,William,			Cul.
Gordon,Alexander,	1	3	Din.
Gordon,Ann Isham,		49	Pr.Geo
Gordon,Churchell,	1	10	Cul.
Gordon,Elizabeth,	2		K.Geo.
Gordon,George,		7	West.
Gordon,George,	1	2	Fay.
Gordon,Hugh,	1		K.Geo.
Gordon,James,	1		Hen.
Gordon,John,	2	5	K.Geo.
Gordon,John,			Cul.
Gordon,John,	1	1	Brun.
Gordon,John,	1		Rock.
Gordon,John,	1	4	Gooch.
Gordon,John,	1		Berk.
Gordon,John,	1		Har.
Gordon,John,	1		K.&Q.
Gordon,John,			Fay.
Gordon,John,Estate,		27	Pr.Geo
Gordon,Levin,	1	2	Acco.
Gordon,Moses,	1		Mont.
Gordon,Mary,	1	16	Pr.Geo
Gordon,Richard,		5	Ch.Cy.
Gordon,Thomas,	2	37	Pr.Geo
Gordon,Notty,	1		Buck.
Gordon,Obediah,	1		Hen.
Gordan,Richard,	3	2	Hen.
Gordon,Thomas,	1		Hen.
Gordon,William,	1	1	Hen.
Gordon,William,	2	16	Lun.
Gore,Benjamin,			Cul.
Gore,John,	1		Cul.
Gore,John,	1		Lou.
Gore,Michael,	1		Bot.
Gorham,Thomas,	1	5	Lou.
Gorrell,John,	1		Fay.
Gorrell,William,	2	2	Berk.
Gorring,Frederick,	1		Berk.
Gorshow,Isaac Spice,	1		Camp.
Gorster,Henry,	1		Berk.
Gose,Stephen,	3		Mont.
Goss,Henry,	1		Caro.
Goss,James,	1	4	Buck.
Gossley,William,	1	7	York
Gosset,James,	1		Mont.
Gossett,Matthias,	1		Berk.
Gothera,John B.,	1		Buck.
Gotner,Frederick,	1		Lin.
Gottea,William,	1		Rock.
Gouge,Benjamin,	1		Cul.
Goulman,Robert,	1		Caro.
Goure,Joshua,	1		Lou.
Goure,Joshua,Sr.,	1	9	Lou.
Goure,Thomas,	1	1	Lou.

Name			County
Gower,Standley,	1	2	Bed.
Gowin,Alexander,	1		West.
Gozney,Richard,	1		Cul.
Graceham,Laurance,	1		Lin.
Grady,John,	1		Cul.
Grady,Jonathan,	1		Lun.
Grady,William,	2		Caro.
Grady,William,	1		Cul.
Grafton,James,	1	2	K.&Q.
Grafton,James,	1		K.&Q.
Grafton,Thomas,	1	4	K.&Q.
Grafton,William,	1		K.&Q.
Grag,John,	1		Fay.
Graham,Arthur,	1		Rock.
Graham,Christopher,	1		Aug.
Graham,Christopher,	1	4	Aug.
Graham,Duncan,	2	12	Caro.
Graham,Elisabeth,		2	Aug.
Graham,Elizabeth,		8	Lou.
Graham,Francis,	1	2	Bot.
Graham,George,	1		Pr.Wm.
Graham,George,	1	1	Pr.Wm.
Graham,James,	1		Aug.
Graham,James,	1		Berk.
Graham,James,	1		Berk.
Graham,John,)	3		Pr.Wm.
Graham,John,Jr)			
Graham,John,	2		Aug.
Graham,John,	1		Aug.
Graham,John,	1		Aug.
Graham,John,	1		Aug.
Graham,John,	1		Wash.
Graham,John,	1		Lin.
Graham,Mary,		9	Fau.
Graham,Richard,	1	14	Pr.Wm.
Graham,Robert,	1		Pr.Wm.
Graham,Sarah,		11	Caro.
Graham,Thomas,	1		Pr.Wm.
Graham,Thomas,Sr.,	1		Aug.
Graham,Thomas,Jr.,	1		Aug.
Graham,Rev.William,	1	4	Rock.
Graham,William,	1		Bot.
Graham,William,	1		Bot.
Graham,William,	1		Aug.
Grainge,Stephen,	1		Gooch.
Grallige,John,	1		Lou.
Grammer,Andrew,	1		Lou.
Grammer,John,	1	5	Pr.Geo.
Grammer,John,	1	1	Pr.Geo.
Grammer,John,	1		Henry
Grammer,Peter,	1		Din.
Grammor,Tim,	1	5	Pr.Geo.
Grammer,William,Est		9	Pr.Geo.
Gramshaw,David,	1	5	West.
Granger,John,	1	3	Lun.
Grainger,Elizabeth,			West.
Grant,Abram,	1	6	Din.
Grant,Alexander,	1		D.Geo.
Grant,James,	1		West.
Grant,James,	1		Fau.
Grant,John,	2	7	Din.
Grant,John,	1	5	Acco.
Grant,John,	1		Lou.
Grant,John,	1		Lou.
Grant,John,	1		Bed.
Grant,John,			Rock.
Grant,Malcom,	1	6	Ch.Cy.
Grant,Mary,		23	K.Geo.
Grant,Peter,	1	11	Fau.
Grant,Samuel,	1	6	Fay.
Grant,Stephen,			Din.
Grant,William,	1	4	Din.
Grant,William,	1	18	Fau.
Grant,William,	1	2	Pr.Wm.
Grantum,David,			Gooch.
Grantum,John,	1		Berk.

Name			County
Grantum, Joseph,	1	5	Berk.
Grantum, William,	2		Berk.
Grass, Jacob,	1		Aug.
Grass, Jacob, Jr.,	1		Aug.
Grass, Petre,	2		Aug.
Grasty, George,	1	14	Fau.
Granthan, James,	1	9	Pr.Geo
Grantlin, Michael,	1	2	Hen.
Gratt, Margaret,		22	K.Geo.
Graves, Ann,	1	10	Spots.
Graves, Beverley,	1	8	Caro.
Graves, Charles,			York
Graves, Charles,	2	2	York
Graves, Dangerfield,	1	6	Caro.
Graves, Edward,	1	5	Cul.
Graves, Edward,	1	3	K.&Q.
Graves, Francis,	1	3	K.Wm.
Graves, Francis,	1	1	Hen.
Graves, Henry,		7	York
Graves, James,	1		Cul.
Graves, Joel,			Cul.
Graves, John,	1	2	Fay.
Graves, John,	1		Fay.
Graves, John,	1		Nor.
Graves, John,	2	12	Spots.
Graves, John,	1	8	Cul.
Graves, John,	2	10	Cul.
Graves, John,			Cul.
Graves, John,	1	1	K.&Q.
Graves, Joseph,		6	Loui.
Graves, Joseph,	1	1	Caro.
Graves, Joseph,	1	18	Spots.
Graves, Lewis,	1	2	Cul.
Graves, Ralph,	1	16	York.
Graves, Richard,	1		Loui.
Graves, Richard,	1	3	Caro.
Graves, Richard,	1	6	Din.
Graves, Rice,	2	10	Loui.
Graves, Thomas,			Loui.
Graves, Thomas,	1	11	Loui.
Graves, Thomas, Sr.,	1	11	Cul.
Graves, Thomas, Jr.,	1	9	Cul.
Graves, Thomas,	3	8	Cul.
Graves, Thomas,		3	Fay.
Graves, Thomas, Jr.,	1	6	Fay.
Graves, William,	1	2	Loui.
Graves, William,	1	3	Loui.
Graves, William, Estate,		8	Ja.Cy.
Graves, William,			Cul.
Graves, William,	1	2	Henry
Graves, William,			Henry
Graves, William,	1	10	Henry
Graves, William,	1		Nor.
Gravely, John,	1		Henry
Gravely, Joseph,	1		Henry
Gravett, George,			Spots.
Gravet, Obediah,	1		Henry
Gravitt, John,	1	1	K.Geo.
Gray, Ann,		1	So'n.
Gray, Benjamin,	1		Cul.
Gray, Benjamin,	1		So'n.
Gray, David,	1		Rock.
Gray, David,	1	5	Din.
Gray, David,	1		Berk.
Gray, Col.Edwin,	1	23	So'n.
Gray, Edwin,		5	So'n.
Gray, Elizabeth,		5	So'n.
Gray, Gabriel,	1	13	Cul.
Gray, Garrett,	2		Fau.
Gray, George,		10	Cul.
Gray, George,	1	13	Cul.
Gray, Henry,	1	5	Gooch.
Gray, Hugh,			Berk.
Gray, Isaac,	1		Mont.
Gray, Isaac,	1		Mont.
Gray, Capt.James,	1	23	So'n.
Gray, James,	1		Bot.
Gray, Jenus,	1		Mont.
Gray, Jesse,	1		Mont.
Gray, Jesse,	1		Mont.
Gray, James,	1	1	Caro.
Gray, John,	1	4	So'n.
Gray, John,	1	3	Caro.
Gray, John,	1	4	Din.
Gray, John,	1		Berk.
Gray, John,	1		Henry
Gray, John,		1	Gooch.
Gray, John,	1	24	Cul.
Gray, John,	1		Rock.
Gray, Jonathan,	1		Berk.
Gray, Joseph,	1	2	Din.
Gray, Joseph,	1		Wash.
Gray, Joseph,	1	14	Mont.
Gray, Levin,	2		Acco.
Gray, Margaret,			Wash.
Gray, Nathaniel,	1		West.
Gray, Samuel,	1		Henry
Gray, Thomas,	1		Loui.
Gray, Travis,	1		Pr.Wm.
Gray, Walter,	1		Bot.
Gray, William,		2	K.Wm.
Gray, William,	1	1	West.
Gray, William,	1		So'n.
Gray, William,	2	18	Cul.
Gray, William,	1		Rock.
Gray, William,			Rock.
Gray, William,	1		Berk.
Gray, William,	1	12	Caro.
Gray, William, estate,		5	Caro.
Grays, John,			Mont.
Grayham, Archibald,	2	16	Henry
Grayham, Francis,	1		Henry
Grayham, Jacob,	1		Har.
Grayham, James,	1		Lin.
Grayham, John,	1		Lou.
Grayham, John,	1		Henry
Grayham, John,	1		Cul.
Grayham, Peter,	1		Lou.
Grayham, Sally,			Bea.
Graypeal, Peter,	1		Bed.
Grayson, Benjamin,		8	Lou.
Grayson, John,			Fay.
Grysom, Moses,	1		Mont.
Grayson, Robert,	1		Mont.
Grayson, Rev.Spence,		13	Lou.
Grayson, Col.William,	1	8	Lou.
Grayson, Col.William,	1	21	Pr.Wm.
Grayson, William,	1	2	Spots.
Grayson, William,	1		Cul.
Grearheart, Peter,	2		Henry
Grebill, Peter,	1		Bot.
Green, Alexander,W.,	1	7	Ja.Cy.
Green, Ambrose,	1	4	K.Wm.
Green, Ann,		9	Cul.
Green, Ann,		10	Fau.
Green, Armistead,	2	9	Cul.
Green, Bartlet,			Mont.
Green, Benjamin,	1		Lou.
Green, Clement,			Brun.
Green, Edward,	1	5	Bot.
Green, Eleanor,		5	Cul.
Green, Elijah,	1		Pr.Wm.
Green, Filmer,	1	6	Ja.Cy.
Green, Filmer,Jr.,	1		Ja.Cy.
Green, Forrest,	1	3	Loui.
Green, Francis B.,		13	Pr.Geo
Green, Fredrick,	2	11	Brun.
Green, George,	1	17	Pr.Wm.
Green, George,Jr.,	1	1	Pr.Wm.
Green, George,	1	2	Fau.
Green, George,			Har.
Green, Green Berry,	1	1	Buck.
Green, Hugh,	1		Aug.
Green,	1	10	Lou.
Green, James,	1	3	Brun.
Green, James,	1		Lun.
Green, James,	1	13	Cul.
Green, James, Jr.,	1	7	Cul.
Green, James,	1		Bot.
Green, James,	1		Henry
Green, James,	1	2	Henry
Green, Jesse,	1		Pr.Wm.
Green, John,	1		Gooch.
Green, John,	1	3	Brun.
Green, John,	1	4	Lou.
Green, John,	1	2	Bot.
Green, John,	1		Aug.
Green, John,	1		Spots.
Green, John,	1	14	Cul.
Green, Joseph,	1	3	K.Geo.
Green, Judith,		3	Brun.
Green, Lewis,	1		Wash.
Green, Malichi,	1		Loui.
Green, Mary Ann,		9	Caro.
Green, Moses,			Henry
Green, Nathan,	1		Mont.
Green, Pheobe,			Lou.
Green, Philomen,	1		Henry
Green, Richard,	1		Cul.
Green, Richard,	1		Bed.
Green, Richard,	1	1	Mont.
Green, Rignall,	1		Berk.
Green, Sarah,		6	Pr.Wm.
Green, Thomas,	1		Bea.
Green, Thomas,	1		Lun.
Green, Thomas,	1	1	West.
Green, Thomas,	1	1	Fau.
Green, Thomas,	1		Henry
Green, William,	1		Mont.
Green, William,	1		Berk.
Green, William,	1		Aug.
Green, William,	1	15	Pr.Geo.
Green, William,	1	16	Cul.
Green, William,	1	1	Cul.
Green, William,	1	10	Cul.
Green, Willis,	1	7	Lin.
Greengilpin, Francis,	1		Lou.
Greenhill, Joseph,	2	18	Brun.
Greenhill, Samuel,	1	8	Din.
Greening, Thomas,	1		Fau.
Greenlaw, William,			K.Geo.
Greenlee, Alexander,	1		Bot.
Greenlee, David,	1	3	Rock.
Greenlee, Edward,	1		Bot.
Greenlee, John,	1	8	Rock.
Greenlee, William,	1		Bot.
Greenlee, James,			Lou.
Greenock, John R.,			Brun.
Greenshaw, John,	2	1	Brun.
Greenshaw, John,			Brun.
Greenstreet, James,	1		Mont.
Greenup, John,	1		Mont.
Greenway, Dr.James,	1	29	Din.
Greenwood, Daniel,	1	2	Fau.
Greenwood, Philip,	1	1	Berk.
Greenwood, Samuel,	1		K.&Q
Greer, Acquilla,	1	6	Henry
Greer, Ann,		4	Bed.
Greer, Benjamin,	1	7	Bed.
Greer, James,	1	3	Bed.
Greer, James,	1	1	Bed.
Greer, Moses,	1	1	Bed.
Greer, Thomas,	1		Lou.
Greer, Thomas,	1		Wash.
Greer, Vincent,	1		Bed.
Greer, William,	1	3	Henry
Greer, William,	1	5	Henry
Greer, William, Sr.,	1		Wash.

Name			County
Greer,William,Jr.,	1		Wash.
Greever,William,	1		Aug.
Gregg,Aaron,			Lou.
Gregg,Abner,	1		Lou.
Gregg,Elijah,	1		Lou.
Gregg,George,	1		Lou.
Gregg,George,Sr.,	1		Lou.
Gregg,George,Jr.,	1		Lou.
Gregg,Henry,	1		Aug.
Gregg,Henry,	1		Mont.
Gregg,John,	2		Lou.
Gregg,John,			Lou.
Gregg,John,			Lou.
Gregg,Robert,Sr.,	1		Aug.
Gregg,Robert,	1		Aug.
Gregg,Samuel,	1		Aug.
Greeg,Samuel,	2		Lou.
Gregg,Samuel,	1		Lou.
Gregg,Stephen,			Lou.
Gregg,Thomas,			Lou.
Gregg,Thomas,	1		Lou.
Gregg,Thomas,Sr.,	1		Lou.
Gregg,Thomas,	1		Aug.
Gregg,Thomas,	1		Aug.
Gregory,Edward,	1		Berk.
Gregory,Elizabeth,		4	Cha.Cy
Gregory,James,Sr.,	3		West.
Gregory,James,Jr.,	1		West.
Gregory,James,	1	1	Caro.
Gregory,James,	1	11	Cha.Cy
Gregory,James,	1	1	Lun.
Gregory,James,	1		Aug.
Gregory,John,	1	12	Cha.Cy
Gregory,John,	1		Aug.
Gregory,Joseph,	1		West.
Gregory,Margaret,		10	Pr.Geo
Gregory,Mary,	2		Pr.Geo
Gregory,Nathaniel,	1	7	Brun.
Gregory,Richard,	1	21	Din.
Gregory,Richard,			Pr.Wm.
Gregory,Roger,	2	9	Hen.
Gresham,Ambrose,	1		K.&Q
Gresham,Ambrose,			Din.
Gresham,Isaac Spice,	1		Camp.
Gresham,Job,	1	3	K.&Q
Grisham,Dr.John,	1	4	K.&Q
Gresham,John,	1	4	K.&Q
Gresham,Henry,	1		Henry
Gresham,Leonard,			K.&Q
Gresham,Machin,	1		K.&Q
Gresham,Phillip,	1	5	K.&Q
Gresham,Ruth,		4	K.&Q
Gresham,Samuel,	1	6	K.&Q
Gresham,Thomas,	1	9	K.&Q
Gresham,Thomas,	1		Din.
Gresham,William,	1		K.&Q
Gresson,Assa,	1	6	Brun.
Gressel,William,			Buck.
Greswit,James,	1		So'n
Grey,David,	2		Fay.
Grey,George,	1	1	Eli.Cy
Grey,George,	1	1	Fay.
Grey,George,			Fay.
Grey,John,	1		Fay.
Grey,Patrick,	1		Fay.
Grey,Samuel,			Fay.
Grier,Alexander,	1	1	Rock.
Grier,Robert,	1		Wash.
Grieves,Benjamin,	1		Brun.
Griffe,John,	1		Lou.
Griffin,Anthony,	1	1	Lun.
Griffin,Anthony,	1		Cul.
Griffin,Corbin,	2	25	York
Griffin,Edward,	1	1	So'n
Griffin,Henry,			Pr.Wm.
Griffin,Henry,		3	Pr.Wm.
Griffin,Henry,	1	3	Fau.
Griffin,John,	1	8	Caro.
Griffin,John,	1		Aug.
Griffin,John	1	3	Pr.Geo
Griffin,John T.	3	39	Gooch.
Griffin,Leroy,est.		29	West.
Griffin,Micajah,	1	4	So'n
Griffin,Obediah,	1		Hen.
Griffin,Olive,		1	So'n
Griffin,Pierce,	1		Hen.
Griffin,Roy,	1	3	Caro.
Griffin,Samuel,	1	7	Ja.Cy
Griffin,Thomas,	2	3	So'n
Griffin,Thomas,	1		Pr.Geo
Griffin,William,	1	56	K.&Q
Griffin,William,	1	1	Pr.Geo
Griffin,Zachariah,	1		Buck.
Griffin,Zachary,	1	1	Cul.
Griffith,Abel,	1		Aug.
Griffith,Benjamin,	1		Berk.
Griffith,Benjamin,	1		Bed.
Griffith,Catherine,		1	Nor.
Griffith,Daniel,	1	2	Nor.
Griffith,Evan,	1	2	Fau.
Griffith,George,	1	1	Henry
Griffith,George,Sr.,	1		Bed.
Griffith,James,			Aug.
Griffith,John,			Bed.
Griffith,John,	1	1	Mont.
Griffith,John,	1	1	Nor.
Griffith,John,	2		Cul.
Griffith,John.	1		Fau.
Griffith,John,	1		Nor.
Griffith,Laban,	1		Nor.
Griffith,Luke,	1	1	Nor.
Griffith,Moses,	1	6	Nor.
Griffith,Thomas,	1		Aug.
Griffith,Thomas,	1	6	Cha.Cy
Griffith,William,	1		Bed.
Griffith,William,			Bot.
Griffis,John,	1		Brun.
Griffis,Thomas,	1		Brun.
Griffy,Thomas,	1		Lou.
Grigg,Abner,	1	1	Din.
Grigg,Jesse,	1	1	Din.
Grigg,Ruth,		2	Din.
Griggs,James,			West.
Griggs,John,	1		Henry
Griggs,Lee,	1	6	West.
Griggs,Mary,		9	West.
Griggs,Thomas,	1	8	Berk.
Grigor,John,	1		Bot.
Grigory,John,			Bot.
Grigory,Thomas,	1	2	Buck.
Grigory,William,	1	15	Buck.
Grigsby,Ann,		13	Fau.
Grigsby,Benjamin,	1		Fau.
Grigsby,Betrey,	1	12	Fau.
Grigsby,James,	1	22	Fau.
Grigsby,James,	1	1	Cul.
Grigsby,James,	3	8	Rock.
Grigsby,John,	1	10	Fau.
Grigsby,John,Jr.,	1		Fau.
Grigsby,John,	1	4	K.Geo
Grigsby,John,	1	9	Rock.
Grigsby,John,	1	1	Cul.
Grigsby,Mott,		2	K.Geo
Grigsby,Nathaniel,	2	8	Lou.
Grigsby,Nathaniel,			Lou.
Grigsby,Redmon,	2	8	Pr.Wm.
Grigsby,Richard,	1	1	Cul.
Grigsby,William,	1		Fau.
Grigsby,William,		3	Cul.
Grinds,James(?)			Pr.Wm.
Grimes,Amos,	1		Bot.
Grimes,Charles,		34	Cul.
Grimes,Felix,	1		Berk.
Grimes,Henry,	1		Wash.
Grimes,Jacob,			Bot.
Grimes,James,	1	1	Pr.Wm.
Grimes,James,	1		Henry
Grimes,James,			Fay.
Grimes,James,			Fay.
Grimes,Jonathan,	1		Bot.
Grimes,Mark,	1		Har.
Grimes,Nicholas,	2	15	Lou.
Grimes,Philip,	3	13	Fay.
Grimes,Phillip,Jr.,	1		Lou.
Grimes,William,	1		Fay.
Grimes,William,			Lou.
Grimmit,John,	3		Henry
Grimmit,Robert,	1		Henry
Grimsley,James,	1		Cul.
Grimsley,James,Jr.,	1		Cul.
Grimsley,John,			Cul.
Grimsley,Joseph,	1		Cul.
Grimsley,Lefton,			Cul.
Grimsley,Thomas,	1		Cul.
Grimsley,William,	1	1	Fau.
Grimsley,William,			Cul.
Grimsley,William,			Cul.
Grimstead,Henry,	1		K.Wm.
Grimstead,John,	1		Pr.Wm.
Grinell,Ambrose,		9	K.Wm.
Griner,David,	1		Aug.
Grinley,John,	1		Bot.
Grinnalds,Richard,	4	3	Acco.
Grinnalds,William,	1	1	Acco.
Grinnan,Daniel,	1	9	Cul.
Grinnell,William,	1	14	Lou.
Grinstead,Daniel,			Hen.
Grinstead,James,			Hen.
Grinstead,Jesse,	1		Hen.
Grinstead,Jesse,	1		Hen.
Grinstead,John,			Hen.
Grinstead,John	1		Hen.
Grinstead,Tapley,	1		Caro.
Griver,Philip,	1		Wash.
Grizard,Harvey,	1	3	So'n
Grizard,Jeremiah,	1	1	So'n
Grizard,Mary,			So'n
Groce,Isaac,			Mont.
Groce,Jacob,			Mont.
Groce,Richard,			Mont.
Grogan,John,	1		Henry
Groom,Barbary,		3	K.&Q
Groom,Mary,		4	K.&Q
Groom,Robert,	1	2	K.&Q
Groom,Henry M.	1		Gooch.
Groom,William,	1	4	Gooch.
Groom,William,Jr.,	1		Gooch.
Groon,Jonathan,	1		Bed.
Crosclose,Peter,	1		Mont.
Grosclose,Peter,Jr.,	1		Mont.
Gross,Charles.	1		Lou.
Gross,John,	1		Wash.
Grotten,Amey,	2	7	Acco.
Groten,Jonathan,			Acco.
Groten,Margery,			Acco.
Grotten,Severn,	2	3	Acco.
Groten,Thomas,			Acco.
Groten,Torobable,	2	7	Acco.
Grove,Jacob,	1		Lou.
Grove,John,Jr.	1	1	Berk.
Grove,Joseph,	1		Lou.
Grove,William,	2		Lou.
Grove,Windle,	1		Aug.
Groves,Peter,	1		Nor.
Groves,Philip,	1		Fau.
Groves,William,	1		Fau.
Groves,William,	1		Rock.
Groveham,William,	1		K.Wm.
Grub,Henry,	1		Mont.

Name			Co.	Name			Co.	Name			Co.
Grubbs,Bennage,	1		Fau.	Guy,Robert,	3	3	Acco.	Haggert,David,	1		Fay.
Grubbs,Daniel,	1		Gooch.	Guy,Samuel,	1		Fau.	Haggert,James,	1		Fay.
Grubbs,Nancy,			Lou.	Guy,Samuel,	1		Pr.Wm.	Haggert,Martin,	1		Fay.
Grubbs,Richard,		2	Pr.Wm.	Guy,Samuel,Sr.,			Lou.	Haggler,Postean,	4		Har.
Grubs,Benjamin,	1	1	Loui.	Guy,Samuel,Jr.,	1		Lou.	Haggler,William,	1		Har.
Grubs,John,	1	9	Loui.	Guy,Thomas,	2		Acco.	Hagney,George,	1	10	Berk.
Grubs,Thomas,	1		Brun.	Guy,Thomas Terry,	1	8	Caro.	Hagood,Benjamin,	1	4	Brun.
Gruisload,James,	2	4	Pr.Wm.	Guy,William,			Pr.Wm.	Hagood,Gressom,	1	3	Brun.
Gruisload,Peter,			Pr.Wm.	Gwaltney,Michael,	1		Brun.	Hagood,Randol,	1	1	Brun.
Grulus,Peter,	1	4	Fau.	Gualthmey,***,	1	20	K.&Q.	Hague,John,	1	3	Hen.
Grun,Elizabeth,			K.&Q.	Gwathmey,Ann,		5	K.Wm.	Hail,Nicholas,	1	1	Berk.
Grun,Mary,			K.&Q.	Gwathmey,Hannah,		2	K.Wm.	Hail,Thomas,	1		Bot.
Grun,Rose,	1	7	Nor.	Gwathmey,Joseph,	2	18	K.Wm.	Haile,Abednegoe,	1	2	Bed.
Grun,Thomas,	1		Nor.	Gwathmey,Molley,		2	K.Wm.	Haile,Adra,	1		Bed.
Grymes,Benjamin,	1	28	K.Wm.	Gwathmey,Owen,	1	19	K.Wm.	Haile,Lewis,			K.&Q.
Grymes,Pricilla,		8	Spots.	Gwathmey,Temple,	8	29	K.&Q.	Haile,Richard,	1	7	Bed.
Guerrant,Maj.John,	1	8	Gooch.	Gwathney,William,	1	1	So'n.	Hailey,Bartlett,	1		Loui.
Guerrant,John,	1	14	Gooch.	Gwatkins,Charles,	1	11	Bed.	Hailey,Benjamin,	1		Loui.
Guerrant,John,	1		Buck.	Gwatkins,Charles,			Fay.	Hailey,John,	1	8	Fau.
Guerrant,Peter,	1	6	Buck.	Gwin,David,	1	1	Aug.	Hailey,Stephen,	1		Bed.
Guffin,Thomas,	1		Mont.	Gwin,Joseph,	1		Aug.	Hailey,Thomas,	1	3	Brun.
Guffy,Alexander,	1		Rock.	Gwin,Morris,	1		Rock.	Hails,John,	1		K.Geo.
Guffy,James,	1		Rock.	Gwin,Thomas,	1		Rock.	Hails,Thomas,	1		K.Geo.
Guill,John,	1		Fay.	Gwins,George,	1	4	Lin.	Hailsworth,George,			Hen.
Gulick,Ferdinando,	1		Lou.	Gwins,James,	1		Lin.	Haines,Carlile,	1		Cul.
Gulley,John,	1		Cul.	(Gwin),Robert,Sr.,	1		Aug.	Haines,Jacob,	2		Cul.
Gully,Sarah,		2	Cul.	Gwin,John,	1		Wash.	Haines,Jasper,	1	1	Cul.
Gulliford,Allen,	1		Bot.	Gwin,Robert,	1		Aug.	Haines,John,	1		Lou.
Gullion,Barney,	1		Mont.	Gwin,William,Sr.,	1		West.	Haines,Mary,			Caro.
Gullion,John,	1		Mont.					Haines,Thomas,	1		Lou.
Guir,Mary,			Loui.	Hack,George,	1	18	Acco.	Hainey,Charles,	1	5	Cul.
Gumm,John,Sr.,	1		Aug.	Hack,Peter,Sr.,	1	21	Acco.	Hainey,Richard,	2	5	Cul.
Gun,William,	1	11	Brun.	Hack,Peter,Jr.,	1	14	Acco.	Hainey,William,	1	2	Cul.
Gunn,Daniel,	1	12	Lun.	Hacket,Baissell,	1		Aug.	Hains,Nicholas,	1		Bot.
Gunn,John,	1		Lou.	Hackett,Martin,	1	4	Caro.	Hains,Peter,	1		Berk.
Gunn,Lucy,		2	Hen.	Hackett,Thomas,	1	5	Caro.	Hair,James,	2		Berk.
Gunnel,John,			Loui.	Hackley,Francis,	1	2	Cul.	Hair,John,	1		Aug.
Gunnell,Robert,			Fay.	Hackley,James,	1	4	Spots.	Hair,John,	1		Berk.
Gunter,Charles,	1		Caro.	Hackley,Joseph,	1	2	Cul.	Hairston,George,	1	29	Henry
Gunter,Charles,	1		Acco.	Hackley,Lott,	1	9	Fau.	Hairston,Peter,	1	18	Henry
Gunter,Edward,	2		Acco.	Hackley,Richard,	1	1	Cul.	Hairston,Peter,		6	Henry
Gunter,John,	1	2	K.Wm.	Hackleys,James,	1	10	Cul.	Hairston,Robert,	1	19	Henry
Gunter,John,	1	5	Loui.	Hackney,Benjamin,	1	16	West.	Haiste,John,	1		Cul.
Gunter,Stephen,			Acco.	Hackney,Bozwell,	1		Din.	Haisty,Benjamin,	1	5	So'n.
Gunter,William,	1		K.Wm.	Hackney,Jacob,	1	10	Berk.	Haisty,James,	1		So'n.
Gurley,Rev.George,	1	9	So'n.	Hackney,John,	1	9	Caro.	Haisty,John,	1		So'n.
Gurr,Daniel,	1	4	Pr.Geo	Hackney,John,Jr.,	1	4	Caro.	Haisty,Joshua,	1		So'n.
Gusler,Henry,	1		Mont.	Hackney,Thomas,	1		Spots.	Haisty,Moses,	1	2	So'n.
Gusman,Abraham,	1		Berk.	Hackney,William,	1	1	Har.	Haisty,Robert,	1		So'n.
Gussett,John,	1		Henry	Hackney,William,	1	1	Pr.Geo	Halbert,Michael,	1		Lou.
Guterage,Thomas,			K.Geo.	Hacksworth,George,	1		Bed.	Halbert,William,	1	8	Henry
Guthery,Henry,	1	4	Bed.	Hacksworth,George,Jr	1		Bed.	Halcomb,Richard,	1		So'n.
Guthery,William,	1		Aug.	Hacksworth,John,	1		Bed.	Halcomb,Richard,	1		So'n.
Gutrey,William,	1		Bot.	Haddax,Samuel,	1		Wash.	Halcome,J.,	1		Pr.Wm.
Gutridge,Ann,			West.	Hadden,Dorothy,			Rock.	Haldane,James,	1	3	Din.
Guthrie,James,	1	6	K.&Q.	Hadden,William,	1		Rock.	Haldimand,Christian,			Bot.
Guthrie,Major,	1	1	K.&Q.	Haddin,Goodrich,	1	7	Din.	Hale,Benjamin,	1	1	So'n.
Guthrie,Mary,		5	K.&Q.	Haddocks,John,	1		Lou.	Hale,Dan,	1		Har.
Guthrie,Mary,Jr.,			K.&Q.	Haddon,Francis,	1	8	Pr.Geo	Hale,James,	1		Lou.
Guthrie,Richard,	1		K.&Q.	Haddon,Samuel,	1		Lin.	Hale,Job,	1	1	Bot.
Guthry,Frances,	2		Bot.	Haddon,William,	1		Lin.	Hale,John,Sr.,	1		Bot.
Guttridge,Allen,	1	1	Fau.	Haddox,Ezekiel,	1		Fau.	Hale,John,Sr.,	1		Henry
Guy,Ann,	1	6	Acco.	Haden,Benjamin,	1	2	Camp.	Hale,John,Jr.,	1		Bot.
Guy,Charles,	1		Pr.Wm.	Haden,George,	1		Loui.	Hale,Joseph,	1		Bot.
Guy,George,	2	20	Caro.	Haden,John,	1	12	Camp.	Hale,Joseph,	1		Henry
Guy,George,	1	6	Caro.	Hadlock,Robert,	1		Acco.	Hale,Nicholas,	1		Har.
Guy,Henry,	1	60	Nor.	Hadlock,Robert,	1		Berk.	Hale,Thomas,	1	3	Henry
Guy,Hezekiah,	1		Lou.	Hagan,Thomas,	1		Fay.	Hales,John,	2	27	Hen.
Guy,James,	1		Aug.	Hagarman,Aram,	2		Lou.	Hales,John,Jr.,			Hen.
Guy,James,	1		Aug.	Hagarman,James,			Lou.	Hales,Peter,	1		Buck.
Guy,John,	1		Aug.	Hagely,George,	2		Berk.	Haley,Benjamin,	1	2	Spots.
Guy,John,	1		Acco.	Hager,John,	1		Henry	Haley,David,	1		Henry
Guy,Jonathan,	1		Acco.	Hagg,J.,	1		Pr.Wm.	Haley,Henry,	1	1	Lun.
Guy,Major,	1	4	Acco.	Haggaman,John,	1	7	Nor.	Haley,Henry,	1		Lun.
Guy,Moses,	1		Pr.Wm.	Haggard,Benjamin,	1		Lin.	Haley,Humphy,	3	13	Caro.
Guy,Nicholas,			Acco.	Haggard,William,	2		Lin.	Haley,John,	1		Henry

Name			County	Name			County	Name			County
Haley,John,est.		14	Caro.	Hall,Thomas,	1		Cul.	Hamilton,R.,			Pr.Wm.
Haley,Peter,	1	1	York	Hall,Thomas,	1	2	Berk.	Hamilton,Richard,	1	1	Caro.
Haley,Samuel,	1		Eli.Cy	Hall,Thomas,	1		Har.	Hamilton,Robert,	1		Cul.
Halfacre,George,	1		Wash.	Hall,Wanes,			Lou.	Hamel,Robert,	1		Rock.
Halfacre,Jacob,	1		Mont.	Hall,William,	1	2	K.Wm.	Hamilton,Robert,	3		Rock.
Halfacre,Michael,	1		Wash.	Hall,William,	1		Mont.	Hamilton,Robert,			Berk.
Haliot,William,	1	8	Nor.	Hall,William,	1		Mont.	Hamilton,Samuel,	1	2	Buck.
Halk,John,	1		Har.	Hall,William,	1	6	Mont.	Hamiltom,Samuel,	1		Rock.
Halk,Martin,	1		Har.	Hall,William,	1		Loui.	Hamilton,Samuel,	1	1	Wash.
Hall,Alexander,	1		Fay.	Hall,William,	1		Buck.	Hamilton,Barah,		6	Loui.
Hall,Andrew,	1	1	Rock.	Hall,William,	1		Lou.	Hamilton,Thomas,	1		Mont.
Hall,Anthony,	1		Berk.	Hall,William,	1	3	Pr.Geo	Hamilton,Thomas,	2		Lin.
Hall,Ashton,			West.	Hall,William,	1		Bed.	Hamilton,Thomas,	1		Har.
Hall,C.			Camp.	Hall,William,	1		Bed.	Hamilton,Walter,			Brun.
Hall,Caleb,	1	2	Bed.	Hall,William,	1		Berk.	Hamilton,William,	1	4	Brun.
Hall,Charles,	1	6	Camp.	Hall,William,	1		Berk.	Hamilton,William,	1		Rock.
Hall,Charles,	1		Acco.	Hall,William,	1		Lin.	Hamilton,William,	1		Fau.
Hall,Corbin,	1		K.&Q	Hall,William,	1		Henry	Hamilton,William,	1		Aug.
Hall,Cornelius,	1		Lou.	Hall,William,	1		Fau.	Hamlet,George,	1		Cha.Cy
Hall,Daniel R.,	1	25	Nor.	Hall,William,	1		Lou.	Hamlet,John,	1		Cha.Cy
Hall,David,	1		Loui.	Halliard,William,	1	6	K.&Q.	Hamlett,Carter,	1		Din.
Hall,David,	1		Camp.	Halling,John Wilcox.	1	3	Lou.	Hamlett,James,	1	10	Lun.
Hall,Edward,	2	8	Aug.	Halloway,William,			Hen.	Hamlett,William,	1	10	Lun.
Hall,Edward,	1		Fay.	Hally,William,	1		Pr.Wm.	Hamlin,Charles,	1	8	Lun.
Hall,Edward,	2		Fay.	Haly,Benjamin,	1	10	Fay.	Hamlin,Daniel,	1	3	Wash.
Hall,Edward,Jr.,			Fay.	Haly,William,	1		Fay.	Hamlin,John,	1	3	Pr.Geo.
Hall,Elizabeth,			So'n	Ham,Edward,	1		Cul.	Hamlin,Stephen,	1	30	Din.
Hall,Ephrim,	1		Acco.	Ham,Jacob,	1		Berk.	Hammack,William,	1	3	Lun.
Hall,George,	1		Berk.	Ham,Jacob,Jr.,	1		Berk.	Hammell,Hugh,	1	1	Pr.Wm.
Hall,George,	1		Acco.	Ham,James,			Cul.	Hammer,Paulser,	1		Aug.
Hall,Henry,	1		Aug.	Hamblet,Gideon,			Hen.	Hammet,George,	1		Lou.
Hall,Hezekiah,	1		Bed.	Hambleton,Alexander,	1		Fay.	Hammet,John,	1		K.Geo.
Hall,Instance,	1	3	Pr.Geo	Hambleton,David,			Fay.	Hammett,Daniel,	1		Cul.
Hall,Instance,	1	7	Din.	Hambleton,George,	1		Fay.	Hammit,William,	1		Henry
Hall,Isaac,			Pr.Wm.	Hambleton,John,	1		Lin.	Hammitt,George,	1		Cul.
Hall,Isaac,	1	14	Pr.Geo	Hambleton,Richard,	1		Bed.	Hammock,John,	1	8	Lun.
Hall,Isaac,			Wash.	Hambleton,Thomas,	1		Bed.	Hammon,Ares,	2		Har.
Hall,Isham,	1		Henry	Hambleton,Thomas,	3		Fay.	Hammon,George,	1		Lou.
Hall,James,	1	13	Brun.	Hambleton,William,	1		Lin.	Hammon,Robert,	1		Mont.
Hall,James,	1	1	Rock.	Hambleton,William,	1		Bot.	Hammon,Thomas,	1		Lun.
Hall,John,	1	6	Caro.	Hamblett,Turner,	1	1	Din.	Hammon,Thomas,			Bot.
Hall,John,	1	1	Camp.	Hambrick,Joseph,	1		Bed.	Hammond,John,	1		Aug.
Hall,John,	1		Mont.	Hambrick,Mary,			Lou.	Hammond,John,			Brun.
Hall,John,	1	11	Lou.	Hamersly,Robert,	1		Berk.	Hammond,Merriman,	1	1	K.&Q
Hall,John,	1	5	Aug.	Hamilton,Agness,			Rock.	Hammond,William,	1	1	Brun.
Hall,John,	2	5	Fay.	Hamilton,Alexander,	1		Aug.	Hammons,Sylvester,	1		Brun.
Hall,John,	1		Fay.	Hamilton,Alexander,	1	1	Aug.	Hammons,William,	1		Henry
Hall,John,	2	1	Lin.	Hamilton,Alexander,	1	7	Berk.	Hammons,William,	1	1	Brun.
Hall,John,	1		Berk.	Hamilton,Alexander,	1		Lou.	Haman,Stevin,			Cul.
Hall,John,	1		Berk.	Hamilton,Andrew,	2	8	Pr.Geo	Hamore,John,	1		Brun.
Hall,John,	1		Henry	Hamilton,Andrew,Jr.,	1		Aug.	Hampliton,Allen,	1		Nor.
Hall,John,	1		Henry	Hamilton,Andrew,Sr.,		3	Aug.	Hampliton,John,	1	1	Nor.
Hall,John,	2	19	Pr.Geo	Hamilton,Archibald,	1		Rock.	Hampson,Elizabeth,			Berk.
Hall,John,Jr.,	1		Bed.	Hamilton,Archibald,	1		Lou.	Hampton,Ambrose,	1		Brun.
Hall,John,Sr.,	1	6	Bed.	Hamilton,Arthur,	1		Aug.	Hampton,David,	1	1	Fay.
Hall,Joseph,	1		Lin.	Hamilton,Audley,	1	2	Aug.	Hampton,George,	1	8	Caro.
Hall,Joseph,	1		Berk.	Hamilton,Charles,	1		Aug.	Hampton,Henry,	1		Brun.
Hall,Lamford,	1		Henry	Hamilton,Effey,		1	Lou.	Hampton,Henry,	2	12	Pr.Wm.
Hall,Leonard,	1		Lin.	Hamilton,Francis,	1		Mont.	Hampton,Jeremiah,	2		Lou.
Hall,Leonard,	2	13	Bed.	Hamilton,Francis,	1	5	Berk.	Hampton,John,	1	26	Caro.
Hall,Lyman,	1	30	Aug.	Hamilton,George,	1	5	Henry	Hampton,John,	1	5	Bed.
Hall,Mary,			Har.	Hamilton,Godfrey,	1		Bot.	Hampton,Joseph,			Lou.
Hall,Moses,	1		Fay.	Hamilton,Henry,	1		Har.	Hampton,Moses,	1		Brun.
Hall,Nathan,	1	8	Henry	Hamilton,Henry,	1		Berk.	Hampton,Robert,	1		Henry
Hall,Nathaniel,	1		Rock.	Hamilton,James,	1		Lin.	Hampton,William,	1	10	Pr.Wm.
Hall,Owen,	1		Bed.	Hamilton,James,	1		Rock.	Hamrick,Isaac,	1		Pr.Wm.
Hall,Patrick,	1	1	Brun.	Hamilton,Jean,		1	Lou.	Hamrick,John,	1		Fau.
Hall,Patrick,	1	3	Aug.	Hamilton,John,	1	1	Aug.	Hamrick,Silas,	1	2	Pr.Wm.
Hall,Presly,			West.	Hamilton,John,	1		Aug.	Hamrick,William,	1		Fau.
Hall,Randolph,			Henry	Hamilton,John,	1		Aug.	Hamrick,William,	1		Fau.
Hall,Richard,	2		Fay.	Hamilton,John,	2	3	Aug.	Hanback,Jacob,	1		Cul.
Hall,Richard,	1	1	Mont.	Hamilton,John,	1		Lin.	Hanback,Jacob,Jr.,	1		Cul.
Hall,Richard,	1		Lou.	Hamilton,John,	1		Har.	Hanback,John,	1		Cul.
Hall,Robert,	1		Bed.	Hamilton,Joseph,	1	5	Brun.	Hanby,John,	1		Lou.
Hall,Robert,	1	14	Din.	Hamilton,Morris,	1		Buck.	Hanby,Jomathan,	1	4	Henry
Hall,Robert,	1		Fau.	Hamilton,Osburn,	1		Aug.	Hanby,Joseph,	1		Nor.

Name			Place
Hanby,William,	1		Nor.
Hancher,William,	1	9	Berk.
Hancock,Austin,	2	1	Loui.
Hancock,Benjamin,			Loui.
Hancock,Benjamin,	1	6	Brun.
Hancock,Benjamin,	1		Henry
Hancock,Edward,	1		Bed.
Hancock,Elijah,	1	1	Acco.
Hancock,George,	1		Acco.
Hancock,George,	1	17	Bot.
Hancock,John,	1	2	Loui.
Hancock,John,	1	7	So'n.
Hancock,Richard,	1		Henry
Hancock,Robert,	1	8	Brun.
Hancock,Samuel,	1		Bed.
Hancock,Simon,	1	7	Bed.
Hancock,Thomas,	1		Henry
Hancock,William,	1	1	Bed.
Hancock,William,	1	7	Bed.
Hancocke,George,	1	26	Lou.
Hancocke,George,	1	2	Gooch.
Hancocke,Maj.,	1	2	Gooch.
Hancocke,Simon,	1	10	Lou.
Hancocke,Stephen,	1	1	So'n.
Hand,Aaron,	1		Har.
Hand,Christopher,	1		Aug.
Hand,Henry,	1		Cul.
Hand,James,	1		Berk.
Handcocke,Sam,	1	1	So'n.
Handley,John,Jr.,			Aug.
Handley,Nancy,	2		Bot.
Handy,John,	1		Henry
Handy,William,	1		Bed.
Hanell,William,	1		Henry
Haner,Harmon,	1	1	Spots.
Haney,Antony,	1		Cul.
Haney,Jenkins,	1		Spots.
Haney,William,	1	9	Lou.
Hanger,Frederick,Jr.,			Aug.
Hanger,Peter,	2	5	Aug.
Hanke,William,	1		Lou.
Hankin,William,	1	20	Ja.Cy.
Hankins,Charles,	1	9	Ja.Cy.
Hankins,John,	1	13	Ja.Cy.
Hankins,John,	1		Lun.
Hankins,Richard,	1		Mont.
Hankins,William,	1		Mont.
Hanks,Abram,	1		Pr.Wm.
Hanks,John,	1		Cul.
Hanks,Luke,	1		Pr.Wm.
Hanks,Peter,	3		Fay.
Hanky,Frederick,	1		Lin.
Hanlan,Stephen,	1		Henry
Hanley,John,	1	3	Aug.
Hanley,William,	1		Aug.
Hanna,John,	1		Berk.
Hanna,William,	2	5	Berk.
Hannaford,John,	4	8	Acco.
Hannaford,Joseph,			Acco.
Hannaford,William,	2	3	Acco.
Hannah,Alexander,	1	5	Bot.
Hannah,Alexander,	1		Lin.
Hannah,Alexander,	1		Rock.
Hannah,Charles,			Hen.
Hannah,George,	1		Bot.
Hannah,James,	3		Berk.
Hannah,Robert,	1		Aug.
Hannan,Eason,	1		Bot.
Hannon,Thomas,	1		Bot.
Hanny,Michael,	1		Bed.
Hansbrough,Mannic,	2	4	Lin.
Hansbrough,Peter,	1	4	K.Geo.
Hansbrough,William,	1	8	Fau.
Hansel,Phillip,	2		Aug.
Hansford,Alexander,	1	5	K.Geo.
Hansford,Ben,	1	6	York

Name			Place
Hansford,Elizabeth,		2	K.Geo.
Hansford,Richard,	1	4	York
Hansford,Stephen,	1	3	K.Geo.
Hansford,Thomas,	1		York
Hansford,Thomas,Jr.,	1	2	York
Hansford,William,	2		Buck.
Hansil,William,	1	2	Ch.Cy.
Hansill,Lawrence,	1		Berk.
Hansill,Philip,	1		Berk.
Hensley,Benjamin,			Mont.
Hansley,Charles,	1		Mont.
Hansley,Chrisley,	1		Mont.
Hansley,Samuel,	1		Wash.
Hanson,Nimrod,			Lun.
Happy,James,	1		Fay.
Harbert,Amos,	1		Lin.
Harbert,Elisha,	1		Lin.
Harbert,Elisha,Sr.,	2		Lin.
Harbinson,David,	1		Mont.
Harbinson,Margaret,			Cul.
Harbour,David,	1		Henry
Harbour,Isaias,	1		Henry
Harbour,Joel,	1		Henry
Harbour,Joyce,			Henry
Harbour,Lesphia,	1		Henry
Hardaway,Ainsworth,	1	11	Din.
Hardaway,Henry,	1	9	Din.
Hardaway,James,	1	10	Din.
Hardaway,John,	1	9	Din.
Hardaway,Mary,		8	Brun.
Hardaway,Robert,	1	10	Din.
Hardaway,Samuel,	1	14	Din.
Hardaway,Stith,	1	13	Din.
Hardaway,Thomas,	1	16	Din.
Hardaway,Thomas,	1	19	Din.
Hardaway,William,	1	15	Din.
Hardaway,William,Jr.	1	6	Din.
Hardaway,William,	1	4	Brun.
Hardege,Will,	1		Lin.
Harden,Elixious,	1		Bed.
Harden,Vangelis,	2		Har.
Hardey,Andrew,			Bed.
Hardey,Joseph,	1		Bed.
Hardey,Robert,	1	3	Bed.
Hardia,John,	2	3	Spots.
Hardige,William,	1		Fau.
Hardin,Charles,	1	3	Lou.
Hardin,Erasmus,	1	7	Din.
Hardin,James,	1		Berk.
Hardine,Anthony,		3	Lou.
Harding,Edward,	1		Pr.Wm.
Harding,Giles,	1	8	Gooch.
Harding,Joseph,	1		Lou.
Harding,Joseph,	1	5	Din.
Harding,Phebe,		10	Lun.
Harding,Robert,	1	6	Lun.
Harding,Thomas,	1	9	Gooch.
Harding,William,	1	1	Lun.
Hardman,Charles,			Henry
Hardman,John,			Buck.
Hardman,John,	1	2	Henry
Hardmant,William,	1		Henry
Hardonan,Frederick,	1		Berk.
Hardwich,William,	1	3	Fau.
Hardwick,John,	1	9	Bed.
Hardwick,John,			Bed.
Hardwick,Robert,	1		Bed.
Hardwick,Robert,	1	8	Bed.
Hardwick,Thomas,	2	2	Buck.
Hardwick,Thomas,	1		Wash.
Hardwick,Younger,	1	2	Din.
Hardwood,John,Jr.,Est		15	Hen.
Hardy,Andrew,	1		Din.
Hardy,Covington,	1	7	Lun.
Hardy,Curtis,	1		Lun.

Name			Place
Hardy,George,	1		Lou.
Hardy,John,	1	6	Lun.
Hardy,John,Jr.,	1	4	Lun.
Hardy,Parott,	1		Din.
Hardy,Richard,	1	2	Lun.
Hardy,Samuel,	1	1	Hen.
Hardy,Solomon,	1		Lou.
Hardy,Thomas,	1	12	Lun.
Hardy,William,	1	13	Lun.
Hardyman,Francis,	1	11	Ch.Cy.
Hardyman,Littleberry	1	19	Ch.Cy.
Hardyman,Stith,	1	21	Ch.Cy.
Hardyman,William,	1	4	Ch.Cy.
Hardyman,Wm,Estate,		47	Ch.Cy.
Hare,William,	1	9	K.&Q.
Hangar,John,	1		Loui.
Harget,Peter,			Fay.
Hargrader,Coonrod,	1		Bed.
Hargrader,Phillip,	1		Bed.
Hargrass,Bagwell,	1	1	Acco.
Hargrass,Eburn,	2		Acco.
Hargrass,John,	1		Acco.
Hargrave,Humphrey,	1	3	Caro.
Hargrave,Jesse,	1	12	Caro.
Hargrave,Silas,	1	1	So'n.
Hargrove,Samuel,	1	3	Caro.
Harkins,Edward,	1		Rock.
Harkleroad,Lawr'ce,	1		Wash.
Harklerode,John,	1		Lou.
Harlan,Elijah,	2		Berk.
Harlan,Jehue,	1		Berk.
Harlan,Moses,	2		Berk.
Harlan,Stephen,	2		Berk.
Harless,Ferdinand,	1		Bot.
Harless,Martin,	1		Bot.
Harlin,George,	1		Lin.
Harlis,Henry,	1		Mont.
Harlow,John,	1	4	Hen.
Harlow,Maximilian,		4	Hen.
Harlow,William,	1		Loui.
Harly,John,	1		Berk.
Harman,Bayly,	1	1	Acco.
Harman,Cornelius,	1		Acco.
Harman,Daniel,	1		Mont.
Harman,George,	2	3	Nor.
Harman,Henry,Sr.,	1		Acco.
Harman,Henry,Jr.,	3	8	Acco.
Harman,Jacob,	1		Mont.
Harman,Jacob,Jr.,	1		Mont.
Harman,John,	1		Bed.
Harman,John,	1	1	Bed.
Harman,John,			Acco.
Harman,John,	1		Acco.
Harman,Kandel,	1		Acco.
Harman,Matthias,	1		Mont.
Harman,Nicholas,	1		Berk.
Harman,Peter,	1		Bed.
Harman,Peter,	2	2	Lou.
Harman,Peter,	1		Mont.
Harman,Torobable,	1	1	Acco.
Harman,Torobable,	1		Acco.
Harman,William,	1		Brun.
Harman,William,	1		Mont.
Harman,William,	2	5	Acco.
Harmanson,Henry,	1	25	Nor.
Harmanson,John S.,	1	29	Nor.
Harmanson,John,Sr.,	1	15	Nor.
Harmanson,William,	1	10	Nor.
Harmison,James,	1		Berk.
Harmison,Matthew,	1		Berk.
Harmison,Thomas,	1		Berk.
Harmon,David,	1		Har.
Harmon,Edward,	1		Buck.
Harmon,George,	1		Brun.
Harmon,Israel,	1		Lin.
Harmon,Jacob,	2		Lin.

Name			County	Name			County	Name			County
Harrison,Rebecca,		5	Pr.Geo	Hart,Joseph,	1	5	So'n.	Harwood,William,	1	1	Ch.Cy.
Harrison,Richard,	1	13	So'n.	Hart,L.,	2		Pr.Wm.	Harwood,William,	1	5	Hen.
Harrison,Robert,	1		Cul.	Hart,Lenard,	1		Wash.	Hasby,John,			Cul.
Harrison,Robert,	1	12	Pr.Geo	Hart,Robert,	1	7	K.&Q.	Hasey,John Anthony,	1	2	Mont.
Harrison,Robert,Jr.,	1	7	Pr.Geo	Hart,Robert,	1	1	So'n.	Hash,John,	1		Mont.
Harrison,Samuel,			West.	Hart,Robert,	1	24	Spots.	Hash,Thomas,	1		Mont.
Harrison,Samuel,	1		Berk.	Hart,T.,	2		Pr.Wm.	Hash,William,	1		Mont.
Harrison,Sarah,		18	Pr.Geo	Hart,Thomas,	1	2	Berk.	Haskew,Gallemon,	1		K.&Q.
Harrison,Seth,	1	24	Pr.Wm.	Hart,Thomas,	1	6	Ja.Cy.	Haskew,John,	1		K.&Q.
Harrison,Solomon,	1	1	So'n.	Hart,Thomas,			Lin.	Haskins,Aron,Estate,		15	Brun.
Harrison,Solomon,	1		Mont.	Hart,Thomas,Jr.,	1		Berk.	Haskins,Christ'er,	1	12	Brun.
Harrison,Susanna,		3	Pr.Geo	Hart,Vallentine,	2		Cul.	Haskins,Edmond,			K.&Q.
Harrison,Thomas,		1	Brun.	Hart,William,	1		K.&Q.	Haskins,John,	1	18	K.&Q.
Harrison,Thomas,	1	2	Pr.Geo	Hart,William,	1		K.&Q.	Haskins,John,	1	18	Brun.
Harrison,Thomas,	1	3	Pr.Geo	Hart,William,	1		Lou.	Haskins,Samuel,	1	2	K.&Q.
Harrison,Thomas,	1		Rock.	Hart,William,	1	2	Ja.Cy.	Hastings,Rees,	1		Berk.
Harrison,Thomas.Ellzey	1		Lou.	Hartford,Adam,			Fay.	Hatch,John,	1	1	K.Wm.
Harrison,William,	1	11	West.	Hartgrove,Benjamin,	1		Mont.	Hatch,Susanna,		6	Pr.Geo.
Harrison,William,	1	4	Pr.Geo	Hartgrove,George,	1		K.Wm.	Hatcher,Achibald,	1		Buck.
Harrison,William,	1	1	Din.	Hartgrove,John,	1	1	Mont.	Hatcher,Drury,	1		Gooch.
Harrison,William,Jr.,	1	3	Brun.	Hartgrove,John,	1		Lin.	Hatcher,Elijah,	1		Bed.
Harrison,William,	1	14	Brun.	Hartgrove,William,	1	9	K.Wm.	Hatcher,Farlor,	1	1	Bed.
Harrison,William,	1	3	Nor.	Hartless,Peter,	1		Caro.	Hatcher,George,	1		Lou.
Harrison,William,	1	17	Caro.	Hartley,James,	3	1	K.Geo.	Hatcher,Capt.Gidn,	1	11	Gooch.
Harrison,William,	1	1	York	Hartly,Daniel,	1		Berk.	Hatcher,James,	1		Lou.
Harrison,William,	1		Acco.	Hartman,Henry,	1		Har.	Hatcher,Jeremiah,	1	8	Bed.
Harrison,Rev.William,	1	15	Din.	Hartman,John,	1		Bot.	Hatcher,John,	2		Lou.
Harrison,William,Sr.,	1	2	Pr.Geo	Hartman,Marvils,	1		Berk.	Hatcher,Joshua,			Lou.
Harriss,Arthur,	1		Fau.	Hartness,Robert,	1		Fay.	Hatcher,Josias,	1		Buck.
Harriss,Edward,	1	6	Ja.Cy.	Harton,James,	1		Mont.	Hatcher,Julius,	1	7	Bed.
Harriss,Elisha,	1	1	Fau.	Hartwell,John,	1		Henry	Hatcher,Richard,	1	2	Bed.
Harriss,George,	1		Har.	Hartwell,Paul,	2	17	Brun.	Hatcher,Samuel,	1	2	Bed.
Harriss,Hardy,	1	9	So'n.	Hartwell,Richard,	1	7	Brun.	Hatcher,Sarah,		2	Bed.
Harriss,James,	1		Fau.	Harvey,Daniel,	1		Rock.	Hatcher,Thomas,	1		Lou.
Harriss,James,			Cul.	Harvey,Francis,			Cul.	Hatcher,William,	1		Lou.
Harriss,John,	1		Bed.	Harvey,John,	1		Caro.	Hatchett,Edward,	1	6	Lun.
Harriss,John,	1		Har.	Harvey,Jonathan,	1	4	Acco.	Hatchett,Edward,Jr.	1	1	Lun.
Harriss,John,	1	17	Ja.Cy.	Harvey,Robert,	1	10	Bot.	Hatchett,William,	1	15	Lun.
Harriss,John,	1		Fau.	Harvey,Thomas,	1		Brun.	Hatfield,Andrew,	1		Mont.
Harriss,Micajah,	2	12	So'n.	Harvey,William,	2	8	Spots.	Hatfield,Sarah,		1	So'n.
Harriss,Micajah,	1		Din.	Harvey,William,	3	1	Cul.	Hatfield,Jemima,	1		So'n.
Harriss,Moses,	1	4	Bed.	Harvey,William,			Cul.	Hathaway,David,	1		Fay.
Harriss,Richard,	1	1	Fau.	Harvy,Elijah,			Cul.	Hathaway,James,	1	15	Fau.
Harriss,Ruth,		4	So'n.	Harvy,Ellison,	1	3	Buck.	Hatthaway,John,	1	7	Fau.
Harriss,Samuel,	1	4	Fau.	Harvy,Thomas,Jr.,	1		Buck.	Hathcock,Joseph,	1		Brun.
Harriss,Simon,	1	5	So'n.	Harvy,William,	1	4	Buck.	Hatten,Adam,	2		Fay.
Harriss,Thomas,	1	42	Pr.Geo	Harwell,Buckner,	1	8	Brun.	Hatton,Elizabeth,		2	Ja.Cy.
Harriss,Thomas,	1		Pr.Wm.	Harwell,George,		5	Brun.	Hatton,George,	1		Ja.Cy.
Harriss,Thomas,		1	Ja.Cy.	Harwell,Grieff,	1	3	Brun.	Hatton,Jane,			Lou.
Harriss,Thomas,			Fau.	Harwell,Ishmael,	1	6	Din.	Hatton,John,	1		Caro.
Harriss,William,	1		Fau.	Harwell,James,	1	10	Din.	Hatton,Mark,	1		Aug.
Harriss,William,	1	9	Bed.	Harwell,James,	1	3	Brun.	Hatton,Samuel,	1		Eli.Cy.
Harriss,William,	1		Cul.	Harwell,John,			Brun.	Hatton,Samuel,	1		Lou.
Harriss,William,	1	12	Din.	Harwell,Mark,	1	1	Pr.Geo	Hatton,Thomas,	1	1	Eli.Cy.
Harrisson,John,Sr.,			Bot.	Harwell,Richard,			Din.	Hatton,William,	1		Bed.
Harrisson,John,Jr.,	1		Bot.	Harwell,Samuel,Sr.,	1	14	Brun.	Hatton,William,	1	1	Eli.Cy.
Harrold,Gilbert,	1		Camp.	Harwell,Samuel,Sr.,	1	17	Din.	Hauck,John,	2		Har.
Harrold,Housand,	1		Bed.	Harwell,Samuel,Jr.,	1	4	Brun.	Hatzell,Malka,	1		Lou.
Harrold,Jesse,	1		Camp.	Harwell,Samuel,Jr.,	1	8	Din.	Hauke,John,	1		Bea.
Harrow,James,	1		Fay.	Harwell,Thomas,	1	1	Pr.Geo	Havelick,Frederick,	1		Berk.
Harrow,John,	1		Fay.	Harwood,Agnes,	1	7	K.&Q.	Haven,Howard,	1		Mont.
Harshman,Jacob,	1		Har.	Harwood,Christopher,	2	23	K.&Q.	Haven,James,	1		Mont.
Hart,Anthony,	1	1	K.&Q.	Harwood,Edward,	1	14	York	Haven,James,Sr.,	1		Mont.
Hart,Daniel,	1		Lou.	Harwood,Elisha,	1	12	Hen.	Haven,John,	1		Mont.
Hart,Edward,	1		Caro.	Harwood,Elizabeth,		5	Hen.	Haven,John,			Bot.
Hart,Henry,	1	1	So'n.	Harwood,Humphrey,		5	Ja.Cy.	Haven,John,			Bot.
Hart,Israel,.	1	2	Lin.	Harwood,John,	1	33	K.&Q.	Havens,William,	1		Caro.
Hart,James,	1		Mont.	Harwood,John,	1	14	Ch.Cy.	Hawes,Isaac,	1	1	Caro.
Hart,James,	1		K.&Q.	Harwood,John,	1	13	Hen.	Hawes,John,	1	3	K.Wm.
Hart,James,	1		Berk.	Harwood,Joseph,	1	9	K.&Q.	Hawes,Samuel,	1	54	Caro.
Hart,Jesse,	1	2	So'n.	Harwood,Samuel,	1	16	Ch.Cy.	Hawes,Thomas,	1	10	Caro.
Hart,Jesse,	1	2	So'n.	Harwood,Thomas,		1	Ch.Cy.	Hawey,Richard,			Fay.
Hart,John,	1		Caro.	Harwood,Thomas,			Ch.Cy.	Hawk,Henry,			Aug.
Hart,John,	1	6	So'n.	Harwood,Thomas,	1	13	Hen.	Hawkes,John,	1		Henry
Hart,John,	1		Spots.	Harwood,William,			K.&Q.	Hawkes,William,	1		Henry
Hart,John,	1		Berk.	Harwood,William,	1		Lin.	Hawkin,John,	1		Berk.
								Hawkins,Aaron,	1		West.

Name			Co.	Name			Co.	Name			Co.
Harmon,Jacob,	1		Lin.	Harris,James,	1		Buck.	Harris,William,	1	25	K.Wm.
Harmon,John,	1	3	Din.	Harris,James,	1		Mont.	Harris,William,			Loui.
Harmon,Philip,	1		Lin.	Harris,James,	1		So'n	Harris,William,	2	7	Loui.
Harmon,Thomas,	1		Din.	Harris,James,	1		Lun.	Harris,William,	1		York
Harmon,Thomas,Sr.,	1	10	Din.	Harris,James,	1		Rock.	Harris,William,	1		Aug.
Harmon,Valentine,	1	2	Lin.	Harris,James,	1	7	Caro.	Harrison,Alexander,	1		Lou.
Harmon,William,	1		Din.	Harris,James,Jr.,	1		So'n	Harrison,Alexander,			Acco.
Harness,Christy,	1		Bot.	Harris,James,Jr.,	1		Cha.Cy	Harrison,Andrew,est.		18	Caro.
Harness,Elizabeth,			Har.	Harris,Job,	1		Loui.	Harrison,Ann,		4	Din.
Harness,George,	3		Har.	Harris,Job,	1		Spots.	Harrison,Ann,		7	Pr.Geo.
Harness,George,	2	3	Har.	Harris,Joel,	1		So'n	Harrison,Anslem,	1	1	So'n
Harness,Jacob,	3	10	Har.	Harris,John,	1		Cha.Cy	Harrison,Arthur,	1	10	Brun.
Harness,John,	3	2	Har.	Harris,John,	1	11	Buck.	Harrison,Gov.Benja.	1	13	Hen.
Harness,Michael,	1		Har.	Harris,John,	1	2	Buck.	Harrison,Gov.Benja.	1	17	Hen.
Harness,Peter,	1		Har.	Harris,John,	1	3	Caro.	Harrison,Gov.Benja.		1	Hen.
Harper,Adam,	1		Har.	Harris,John,	1		Mont.	Harrison,Col.Benja.	2	53	Fau.
Harper,Ebenezer,	1		Berk.	Harris,John,	1		Loui.	Harrison,Benjamin,Sr.	1	16	Brun.
Harper,Elizabeth,			Pr.Wm.	Harris,John,	1		So'n	Harrison,Benjamin,Jr.	1	25	Brun.
Harper,George,	1	17	Din.	Harris,John,			Pr.Wm.	Harrison,Benjamin,	1	20	Pr.Geo.
Harper,Isaac,	1		Pr.Wm.	Harris,John,	1		West.	Harrison,Benjamin,	4	104	Pr.Geo.
Harper,James,	1		Lou.	Harris,John,	1	5	Lun.	Harrison,Benjamin,	1	5	Brun.
Harper,James,	1		K.&Q	Harris,John,	1		Lou.	Harrison,Benjamin,	1	10	Hen.
Harper,John,	1		Lou.	Harris,John,	1		Lou.	Harrison,Benjamin,	2	90	Cha.Cy
Harper,John,	2	4	So'n	Harris,Henry,			Henry	Harrison,Burr,	1	20	Fau.
Harper,John,			Lou.	Harris,Col,John,		5	Buck.	Harrison,Burr,	3	13	Pr.Wm.
Harper,John,	3		Berk.	Harris,John,Sr.,	1	6	Buck.	Harrison,Caleb,	1	2	Acco.
Harper,John,	1		Berk.	Harris,Jones,	1		Fay.	Harrison,Charles,	1	5	Brun.
Harper,John P.	1	8	Din.	Harris,Joseph,	1		Buck.	Harrison,Collier,&			
Harper,Joseph,			Brun.	Harris,Joseph,	1		Brun.	Harrison,Braxton,		13	Cha.Cy.
Harper,Joseph,	1	18	Din.	Harris,Joseph,	1		Lin.	Harrison,Collier,	1	4	Cha.Cy
Harper,Nathaniel,	1	23	Din.	Harris,Joshua,	1	7	So'n	Harrison,Cuddy,	1	4	So'n
Harper,Nicholas,	1		Aug.	Harris,Joshua,	1	1	Lou.	Harrison,Cuthbert,	1	15	Lou.
Harper,Nicholas,	2		Lou.	Harris,Judah,		2	Caro.	Harrison,Daniel,	1	1	Brun.
Harper,Peter,	1		Fay.	Harris,Landon,	1		So'n	Harrison,Edward,	1		Din.
Harper,Robert,	1	1	Berk.	Harris,Lewis,	1	8	So'n	Harrison,Eleanor,			West.
Harper,Sarah,		2	West.	Harris,Mary,			Lin.	Harrison,Elizabeth,		9	Pr.Geo.
Harper,Scarlet,	1		Pr.Wm	Harris,Micajah,	1		Loui.	Harrison,Frances,		1	York.
Harper,Thomas,	1		Lou.	Harris,Micajah,	1		Loui.	Harrison,George,	1	14	Fau.
Harper,Thomas,	1		Fau.	Harris,Moses,	1	1	Loui.	Harrison,George,	1	14	Fau.
Harper,William,	1		Caro.	Harris,Nancy,		1	Brun.	Harrison,George,			Cul.
Harper,William,	1		Lou.	Harris,Narrilles,			Mont.	Harrison,Harmon,	1		Brun.
Harper,William,	1		Cul.	Harris,Nathan,	1	12	Brun.	Harrison,Henry,		10	Pr.Geo.
Harper,William,Jr.,	1	5	Din.	Harris,Nathan,	1	15	So'n	Harrison,Henry,	1	6	So'n
Harper,William,Sr.,	1	19	Din.	Harris,Nathaniel,	1	1	Bed.	Harrison,Henry,	1	8	Brun.
Harpole,Adam,	1		Har.	Harris,Nathaniel,	1		Loui.	Harrison,Hezekiah,	2	4	Fay.
Harpole,Adam,Jr.,	1		Har.	Harris,Nathaniel,			Gooch.	Harrison,Hiram,			Fay.
Harpole,Adam,Jr.,	3		Har.	Harris,Nathaniel,	1	4	Cul.	Harrison,J.	1		Pr.Wm.
Harpole,Nicholas,	2		Har.	Harris,Nelson,			Loui.	Harrison,James,	1	9	Brun.
Harracks,Richard,	1		Gooch	Harris,Obed,	1		Pr.Wm.	Harrison,James,			Pr.Geo.
Harrell,Samuel,	1		Cul.	Harris,Peter,	1	2	Henry	Harrison,Jane,		8	Din.
Harrill,Daniel,	1		Fau.	Harris,Randal,	1		Gooch.	Harrison,Jane,	1	2	Fau.
Harrington,Charles,	1		Aug.	Harris,Randall,	1	5	So'n	Harrison,Jeremiah,	1		West.
Harris,Amos,	1	5	So'n	Harris,Robert,	1		Aug.	Harrison,John,	1		Mont.
Harris,Archalaus,	1	1	Loui.	Harris,Robert,	1	13	Loui.	Harrison,John,			Brun.
Harris,Benjamin,	1	5	So'n	Harris,Robert,Jr.,	1	2	Bot.	Harrison,John,	1		Brun.
Harris,Carter,	1		So'n	Harris,Rowe,	1	11	Brun.	Harrison,John,	1	14	Pr,Geo.
Harris,Charles,	1		So'n	Harris,Sterling,	1	3	Brun.	Harrison,John,	1	11	Spots.
Harris,Cornelius,	1		Loui.	Harris,Maj.Thomas,	1	12	Gooch.	Harrison,John Peyton,		2	Fau.
Harris,Daniel,		3	Loui.	Harris,Thomas,	1	2	Caro.	Harrison,John Peyton,	1	6	Lou.
Harris,Daniel,	1		Lou.	Harris,Thomas,	1		Bot.	Harrison,Jonathan,	1		Bot.
Harris,Drury,	1	4	So'n	Harris,Thomas,		7	Camp.	Harrison,Josiah,	1		Acco.
Harris,Edward,	1	25	So'n	Harris,Thomas,	1	1	Buck.	Harrison,Joseph,			Loui.
Harris,Edward,	1	5	Loui.	Harris,Thomas,	1		Loui.	Harrison,Lemuel,	1	8	Pr.Geo.
Harris,Francis,	1	3	Buck.	Harris,Thomas,	1	15	Brun.	Harrison,Levin,			Acco.
Harris,Frederick,	1	13	Loui.	Harris,Thomas,	1		Berk.	Harrison,Lovell,		3	West.
Harris,Gideon,	1	5	Brun.	Harris,Thomas,	1		Fay.	Harrison,Matthew,	1	4	Pr.Wm.
Harris,Hardy,		14	So'n	Harris,Thomas,	2		Lou.	Harrison,Nathaniel,		28	Brun.
Harris,Hardy,	1	10	So'n	Harris,Thomas,	1		Lou.	Harrison,Nathaniel,	1	16	Brun.
Harris,Harmon,	1	9	So'n	Harris,Capt.William,	1	10	Loui.	Harrison,Nathaniel,	1	6	Brun.
Harris,Harrison,	1	12	Gooch	Harris,William,			Henry	Harrison,Nathaniel,	1	23	Din.
Harris,Henry,	1	1	Henry	Harris,William,	1		Henry	Harrison,Nathaniel,	1	68	Pr.Geo.
Harris,Henry,	1	4	So'n	Harris,William,	1		Henry	Harrison,Peter,	1		West.
Harris,Howel,	1	3	Brun.	Harris,William,	1		Henry	Harrison,Philip,	2		Acco.
Harris,Howell,	2	32	So'n	Harris,William,			Loui.	Harrison,Rebecca,		4	Pr.Geo.
Harris,Isham,	1		Mont.	Harris,William,	1	1	Buck.	Harrison,Rebecca,			Din.
Harris,James,	1		Aug.	Harris,William,	1		Caro.	Harrison,R.			Pr.Wm.

Name			County	Name			County	Name			County
Hawkins,Benjamin,	1		Henry	Hayes,William,	1		Fau.	Hazlerigg,William,		2	West.
Hawkins,Benjamin,	2		Cul.	Hayes,William,	2	10	Lun.	Hazlerigg,William,	1	3	Pr.Wm.
Hawkins,Giles,	1		Bot.	Hayle,John,	1		Berk.	Hazlewood,James,			Din.
Hawkins,Hamilton,			Din.	Hayles,Richard,	1	2	Ja.Cy	Hazlewood,John,	2		Lun.
Hawkins,Henry,	1		Pr.Wm.	Hayley,Benjamin,	2	1	Acco.	Hazlewood,Luke,			Lun.
Hawkins,Isham,	1		Din.	Hayley,Benjamin,			Acco.	Hazlewood,Mary,	1	3	Ja.Cy
Hawkins,James,	1	8	Eli.Cy	Hayley,William,	2	1	Acco.	Hazlewood,Richard,	1	1	Ja.Cy
Hawkins,Jane,			Din.	Haymore,Britian Jones,	2	3	Brun.	Hazlewood,Thomas,	1		Ja.Cy
Hawkins,John,	1	11	Bot.	Haymore,Mark,			Brun.	Head,Alexander Spen,	1	15	Spots.
Hawkins,John,	1		Bot.	Hayn,Christopher,	1		Bot.	Head,David,	1	4	Spots.
Hawkins,John,			Lou.	Haynar,Thomas,	1	6	Bed.	Head,Francis,	1		Cul.
Hawkins,John,	1	12	Spots.	Haynes,Andrew,	1	9	Brun.	Head,Hadley,	1	3	Cul.
Hawkins,John,	1	3	Spots.	Haynes,Benjamin,	1		Bot.	Head,Henry,	1	5	Spots.
Hawkins,John,	1	15	Caro.	Haynes,George,	1	4	Henry	Head,Henry,	1	8	Spots.
Hawkins,John,	1		Cul.	Haynes,Henry,	1	3	Bed.	Head,Isaac,	1		Spots.
Hawkins,John,	1		Fau.	Haynes,Henry,	1		Bed.	Head,John Alfred,	1	2	Cul.
Hawkins,John,	1		Din.	Haynes,Henry,	1	8	Henry	Head,Jonathan,	1	7	Har.
Hawkins,John,Sr.,	1	3	Lun.	Haynes,Henry,Jr.,	1		Henry	Head,Mary,			Wash.
Hawkins,John,Jr.,	1	5	Lun.	Haynes,Humphrey,			Lun.	Headon,Elijah,	1		Lou.
Hawkins,Jonathan,	1		West.	Haynes,James,			Bed.	Headon,George,	1	1	Lou.
Hawkins,Joseph,	1	8	Bot.	Haynes,John,	1	5	Bed.	Headon,George,Jr.,	1		Lou.
Hawkins,Joseph,	1	11	Spots.	Haynes,John,	1	3	Bed.	Headon,John,	1		Lou.
Hawkins,Joseph,	2		Lin.	Haynes,John,	1		Bot.	Headon,Richard,	1	2	Lou.
Hawkins,Manoa,			Cul.	Haynes,Joseph,	1		Bot.	Headon,Samuel,	1	6	Lou.
Hawkins,Mathew,	1	1	Cul.	Haynes,Parmeanas,	1	5	Bed.	Headrick,Capt.Peter			Aug.
Hawkins,Nathan,	1	10	Spots.	Haynes,Stephen,	1	4	Caro.	Headsheath,George,	1		Mont.
Hawkins,Nicholas,Jr.,	1	1	Spots.	Haynes,Stephen,	1		Cul.	Headspeath,William,	2	7	Henry
Hawkins,Phillamon,	1		Din.	Haynes,Thomas,	2	15	Brun.	Heady,Abraham,	1		Mont.
Hawkins,Robert,			Camp.	Haynes,William,	1	3	Henry	Heale,George,	1	22	Fau.
Hawkins,Robert,			Camp.	Hayns,Nathan,	1	1	Berk.	Heale,George,	3	55	Fau.
Hawkins,Sarah,		6	Bot.	Hays,Andrew,	1		Mont.	Heale ,George,	1	22	Fau.
Hawkins,Thomas,	1	2	Bot.	Hays,Andrew,	1	11	Rock.	Heale,Philip,	1	26	Fau.
Hawkins,Thomas,	1		Lou.	Hays,Andrew,	1		Berk.	Heale,William,	2	29	Fau.
Hawkins,William,	1	2	Eli.Cy	Hays,Charles,	1		Mont.	Heard,Jessee,	1	8	Henry
Hawkins,William,	1		Fau.	Hays,Charles,	1	1	Wash.	Heard,John,	1		Henry
Hawkins,William,	1	4	Cul.	Hays,Charles,	1	4	Rock.	Heard,John,	1	3	Henry
Hawkins,William,	2	1	Cul.	Hays,Hugh,	1		Aug.	Heard,Stephen,	1	3	Henry
Hawkins,William,	1		Camp.	Hays,Hugh,	1		Camp.	Heard,Thomas,	1	8	Henry
Hawkins,William,	1		Camp.	Heys,James,	1	2	Rock.	Heard,William,	1	2	Henry
Hawks,Frederick,	1		Din.	Hays,James,	1		Rock.	Heard,William,	1		Henry
Hawks,John,			Din.	Hays,John,	1		Mont.	Hearn,John,	1		Brun.
Hawks,Thomas,	1		Brun.	Hays,John,	1	1	Mont.	Hearndon,William,	1	9	Pr.Wm.
Hawley,John,	2	1	Lou.	Hays,John,			Bot.	Heath,Abram,	1	15	Pr.Geo.
Hawler,Peter,	1		Lou.	Hays,John,		6	Rock.	Heath,Andrew,	1		Lou.
Hawley,William,			Lou.	Hays,John,	2		Berk.	Heath,Asahel,	1		Har.
Haulrey,William,	1		Fay.	Hays,John,Sr.,	1		Berk.	Heath,Bridget,		3	Nor.
Hawrick,P.,	1		Pr.Wm.	Hays,Lewis,	1		Mont.	Heath,Daniel,	1		Pr.Geo.
Hawrick,Benjamin,	1		Pr.Wm.	Hays,Luke,	1		Mont.	Heath,Drury,	1	15	Pr.Geo.
Haws,Francis,	1		Bed.	Hays,Moses,	1	5	Aug.	Heath,Edmund,	3	1	Acco.
Haws,Samuel,	1		Aug.	Hays,Patrick,	1		Aug.	Heath,Fletcher,			Acco.
Hawthorn,James,	1	1	Aug.	Hays,Samuel,	1		Aug.	Heath,Henry,	2	5	Acco.
Hawthorn,Peter,	1	7	Brun.	Hays,Thomas,Sr.,	2		Berk.	Heath,James,	1	2	Nor.
Hawthron,William,	1		Gooch.	Hays,William,	1		Camp.	Heath,Joel,	1	4	Pr.Geo.
Hay,Anne,		2	York	Hays,William,	1		Camp.	Heath,John,	1		Pr.Geo.
Hay,Charles,			Hen.	Hays,William,	1		Mont.	Heath,Joseph,	1	7	Pr.Geo.
Hay,David,	1	2	Rock.	Hays,William,	1		Aug.	Heath,Joseph,	1	2	Pr.Geo.
Hay,Dimack,	1	1	K.Wm.	Hays,William,	1	1	Fay.	Heath,Joseph,	2	5	Acco.
Hay,Doro,		9	Hen.	Hays,William,	1		Berk.	Heath,Josiah,	1	6	Nor.
Hay,John,	1		Har.	Hayse,Hugh,	1		Lin.	Heath,Josiah,	1	4	Din.
Hay,John,	1	6	York	Hayse,James,	1		Lin.	Heath,Richard,	1	15	Pr.Geo.
Hay,Sabret,	1		Cul.	Hayse,William,	1		Henry	Heath,Sarah,		6	Acco.
Hay,William,	1		So'n.	Hayslett,Andrew,	1		Berk.	Heath,Teackle,		1	Acco.
Hay,William,	1		Lin.	Hayslett,Robert,	1		Berk.	Heath,Thomas,	1	4	Pr.Geo.
Hay,William,	1	9	Hen.	Hayslop,George,			Acco.	Heath,Thomas,	1	6	Din.
Hay,William,	2	10	Gooch.	Hayslop,Levin,	1		Acco.	Heath,Thomas,	1		K.Wm.
Hayden,Zachariah,	1	9	Gooch.	Hayslop,Smith,			Acco.	Heath,William,	1	1	K.&Q.
Haydon,Ezekel,	1		Spots.	Haywood,George,	2	2	Cul.	Heath,William,	1		K.Wm.
Haydon,Jessee,	1	5	Spots.	Hayth,Thomas,	2	3	Camp.	Heath,William,	2	12	Pr.Geo.
Haydon,Thomas,	1	17	Spots.	Hazel,Daniel,	1		Wash.	Heaton,Isaac,	2		Berk.
Hayes,Edmund,			Fau.	Hazle,Elisha,			Lou.	Heaton,John,	1		Lou.
Hayes,Henry,	1	9	Lun.	Hazelrig,Charles,	1		Fay.	Heaton,Thomas,	1		Berk.
Hayes,Jacob,	1	1	Fau.	Hazelrig,James,	2	3	Fay.	Heaton,William,	1		Fau.
Hayes,John,			Fau.	Hazelrig,John,	1		Fay.	Heatore,John,	1		Lou.
Hayes,Richard,	1	8	Lun.	Hazelrig,Joshua,	1		Fay.	Hedge,Benjamin,	1		Berk.
Hayes,Richard,Jr.,	2	9	Lun.	Hazelrig,William,	1		Fay.	Hedger,John,	1		Har.
Hayes,Susanna,			Pr.Wm.	Hazelrigg,J.	1	1	Pr.Wm.	Hedger,Joseph,			Cul.

Name			Co.	Name			Co.	Name			Co.
Hedger,Stephen,	1		Har.	Henderson,Joseph,	1		Aug.	Henshaw,John,	1	8	Cul.
Hedger,Thomas,	2		Cul.	Henderson,Joseph,	1		Rock.	Hensley,Fielding,			Buck.
Hedges,James,	1		Berk.	Henderson,Mary,			Wash.	Hensley,Elizabeth,			Cul.
Hedges,John,	1		Berk.	Henderson,Richard,	1		Wash.	Hensley,Enoch,			Cul.
Hedges,Jonas,	2		Berk.	Henderson,Robert,	1		Wash.	Hensley,George,	1	2	Spots.
Hedges,Joseph,	1		Berk.	Henderson,Robert,	1	2	Nor.	Hensley,John,	1		Henry
Hedges,Joshua,	1	3	Berk.	Henderson,Robert,	1	1	Bot.	Hensley,Joseph,	1	1	Wash.
Hedges,Joshua,Jr.,	1		Berk.	Henderson,Samuel,	1		Bot.	Hensley,Richardson,	1		Spots.
Hedges,Robert,	1	2	Pr.Wm.	Henderson,Samuel,	1	7	Bed.	Hensley,Robert,	1		Cul.
Hedges,Robert,Sr.,	1	1	Pr.Wm.	Henderson,Samuel,	1		Lou.	Hensley,Samuel,	1		Bed.
Hedges,Samuel,	1		Berk.	Henderson,Samuel,Sr.,	3	9	Aug.	Hensley,Sarah,	1	1	Spots.
Hedges,Solomon,	1		Berk.	Henderson,Samuel,Jr.,	1		Bed.	Hensley,William,	1	3	Cul.
Hedgman,John,	1	22	Fau.	Henderson,Thomas,	1	8	Spots.	Hensley,William,	2		Buck.
Hedgpett,George,	1		Mont.	Henderson,William,	1		Fay.	Henson,John,	1		Mont.
Hedley,John,	1		Mont.	Henderson,William,			Aug.	Henson,Richard,	1		Loui.
Hedrick,Charles,	1		Berk.	Henderson,William,	1	13	Camp.	Henson,Samuel,	1	1	Loui.
Heeth,David,	1	12	Pr.Geo	Henderson,William,	1		Rock.	Henson,William,	1		Henry
Hefferlin,William,	1		Fau.	Henderson,William,	1		Aug.	Henson,William,	1		Cul.
Heflin,Simon,	1		Fau.	Henderson,William,	1		Lou.	Hensy,William,	1	3	Pr.Wm.
Hegarty,John,	1		Aug.	Henderson,William,	1	1	Pr.Wm.	Hepburn,Elizabeth,		5	Caro.
Hegins,Peter,	1		Lin.	Henderson,William,	1		Wash.	Hepburne,John,	1	1	Lou.
Heit,J.,	1		Pr.Wm.	Henderson,Zerubable,	1	1	Nor.	Heppingstall,Joseph,	1		Berk.
Heldreth,John,	1		Mont.	Hendley,Thomas,	1	1	K.&Q.	Herald,Rubin,	1		Mont.
Heldrup,Samuel,	1		Spots.	Hendrick,Bird,			Loui.	Heraldson,William,	1		Mont.
Hellir,Richard,			K.&Q.	Hendrick,Gustavus,	1	6	Lun.	Herbert,Edward,			Hen.
Helm,John,	1		Camp.	Hendrick,William,	1	4	Loui.	Herbert,John,	1		Lou.
Helm,John,	1	6	Lou.	Hendrick,William,	2	4	Loui.	Herbert,Matthew,	4	11	Hen.
Helm,Lynaugh,	3	22	Pr.Wm.	Hendricks,Daniel,	1		Berk.	Herbert,Pascon,	1	10	Eli.Cy.
Helm,Martin,	1		Berk.	Hendricks,James,	2	3	Berk.	Herbert,Peter,	1	2	Lou.
Helm,Sarah,		1	Camp.	Hendrickson,Jacob,	1		Cul.	Herbert,Samuel,	1		Hen.
Helm,Thomas,	1	14	Fau.	Hendrickson,Thomas,	2		Wash.	Herbert,Thomas,			Hen.
Helm,William,			Pr.Wm.	Hening,Elenor,		7	Cul.	Herbert,William,			Hen.
Helmedollar,Michael,	1		Lou.	Hening,David,	2	10	Cul.	Herbert,William,	4	8	Hen.
Helmick,John,	1		Har.	Hening,George,			Cul.	Herbert,William,	1		Mont.
Helmik,Jacob,	1		Har.	Henington,Christ'er,			Henry	Herbison,David,	1		Aug.
Helms,George,	1		Lin.	Henington,James,	1		Henry	Herd,Edward,	2		Berk.
Helms,Joseph,	1	2	Lin.	Henley,Archer,	1	7	Ja.Cy.	Herd,George,	1		Mont.
Helms,Joseph,	1	2	Lou.	Henley,Elizabeth,		6	Ja.Cy.	Hermon,Thomas,	1		Bot.
Helms,Leonard,	1		Lin.	Henley,Hezekiah,	1	3	Hen.	Herndon,Benjamin,	1	6	Caro.
Helms,Margins,	1		Lin.	Henley,Leonard,	1	10	Loui.	Herndon,David,	1	2	Fay.
Helson,James,	1		Bed.	Henley,Leonard,	1	11	Hen.	Herndon,David,	1	8	Caro.
Helvey,Abraham,	1		Mont.	Henley,Richardson,	1	3	Loui.	Herndon,Edward,	2	1	Cul.
Hemingway,Daniel,	1	20	K.&Q.	Henley,William,	1	2	Buck.	Herndon,Edward,	1	23	Spots.
Hemingway,John,	1	1	K.&Q.	Henley,William,			Buck.	Herndon,Edward,		13	Spots.
Hemphill,James,	3	11	Mont.	Henline,George,	2		Fay.	Herndon,Edward,Jr.,	1	5	Spots.
Henage,George,	1	1	West.	Henline,John,			Fay.	Herndon,Henry,	1	5	Fay.
Hencher,John,	1		Aug.	Henly,Peter,			Lou.	Herndon,John,	1	2	Gooch.
Henderson,Abraham,	1		Mont.	Henry,Andrew,	1	1	Bot.	Herndon,John,	1	7	Fau.
Henderson,Alexander,	1	1	Bot.	Henry,George,	1		Fau.	Herndon,John,	1	13	Spots.
Henderson,Alexander,	2		Rock.	Henry,Hugh,	1		Bed.	Herndon,Joseph,	1	28	Spots.
Henderson,Alexander,	1		Pr.Wm.	Henry,Hugh,	1		Bot.	Herndon,Lewis,	1	2	Gooch.
Henderson,Alex'er,Jr.,	1		Rock.	Henry,James,	1		Bot.	Herndon,Thomas,	1	3	Fay.
Henderson,Andrew,	1		Wash.	Henry,James,		11	Acco.	Herndon,William,	2	7	Cul.
Henderson,Ann,			Loui.	Henry,James,	1	23	K.&Q.	Herndon,William,			Cul.
Henderson,Archibald,	1		Rock.	Henry,James,			Eli.Cy	Heron,James,			Hen.
Henderson,Daniel,		1	Camp.	Henry,James B.Smith,	1	2	Aug.	Herons,Samuel,	1		Fay.
Henderson,Daniel,		1	Camp.	Henry,James Weaver,	3		Aug.	Herral,Jeremiah,	1		Wash.
Henderson,David,	1	4	Aug.	Henry,John,	1		Har.	Herrald,Peter,	1		Buck.
Henderson,David,	1	1	Fay.	Henry,John,			Fau.	Herrald,James,	1		Wash.
Henderson,David,Sr.,	3	5	Aug.	Henry,John,	1		Bot.	Herrin,Isaac,	2	2	Cul.
Henderson,Elisabeth,		1	Aug.	Henry,John,	1		Bot.	Herring,Arthur,	1	12	Lun.
Henderson,Elizabeth,		1	Loui.	Henry,John,	1		Bot.	Herring,Elias,	1	22	So'n.
Henderson,James,	1		Fay.	Henry,John,	2		Lou.	Herring,Stephen,	1	1	Lun.
Henderson,James,			Aug.	Henry,John,Sr.,	1		Fau.	Herring,William,	1	3	Lun.
Henderson,James,Sr.,	1	3	Aug.	Henry,John,Sr.,	2		Lou.	Herrison,Amos,	1		Wash.
Henderson,Joans,	2	2	Aug.	Henry,Joseph,	1		Fau.	Herrison,Isaiah,	1		Wash.
Henderson,John,	1		Wash.	Henry,Patrick,		11	Henry	Herrison,Jeramiah,	1	1	Wash.
Henderson,John,	1	2	Henry	Henry,Patrick,	2	64	Henry	Heskett,Benjamin,	1		Lou.
Henderson,John,	1		Mont.	Henry,Peter,	1		Berk.	Heslop,William,	1	4	Spots.
Henderson,John,	1		Cul.	Henry,Samuel,	1	3	Aug.	Hess,Andrew,	1		Lou.
Henderson,John,	1	1	Gooch.	Henry,Watson,			Lin.	Hess,John,	1		Lou.
Henderson,John,	1		Bot.	Henry,William,	1		Bot.	Hess,Palser,	1		Lou.
Henderson,John,	1	1	Bot.	Henry,William,	1		Bot.	Hess,Peter,	1		Lou.
Henderson,John,	1		Bed.	Henry,William,	1	2	Cul.	Hess,William,	1		Lou.
Henderson,John,	1	2	Aug.	Henry,William,	1		Lin.	Hesser,Conrod,	1		Lou.
Henderson,Joseph,	1	7	Cul.	Henry,William,	1	4	Fay.	Hessong,Peter,	1		Berk.

Hester,Charles,	1	3	Loui.	Hicks,Moses,	1	6	Gooch.	Hill,Joseph,	1	1	Cul.
Hester,Heril,	1		Mont.	Hicks,Pewett,	1	3	Loui.	Hill,Joseph,	1	1	Fay.
Hester,John,	1	5	Loui.	Hicks,Robert,	1	20	Brun.	Hill,Leroy,	1		Cul.
Hetcher,Henry,	1		Lou.	Hicks,Thomas,	1		Har.	Hill,Michael,	1	1	Pr.Geo.
Hetricks,Peter,	1		Mont.	Hicks,William,	1		Eli.Cy	Hill,Mildred,			Ch.Cy.
Hetcher,Philip,Jr.,	1		Lou.	Hicks,William,	1		Caro.	Hill,Reuben,	1	1	So'n.
Hewell,Joseph,	1	4	Spots.	Hicks,William,	1	1	Gooch.	Hill,Richard,			Mont.
Hewell,William,	1		Spots.	Hicks,William,		1	Gooch.	Hill,Richard,	1		Mont.
Hewitt,John,	1		Bot.	Hider,Adam,	2	2	Har.	Hill,Richard,	1	34	Din.
Hewitt,William,	1	4	Fau.	Hier,Jacob,	1		Har.	Hill,Richard,			Cul.
Hewlet,Martin,	1		Ch.Cy.	Hier,Peter,	1		Har.	Hill,Robert,	3		Bot.
Hewlet,Thomas,	1		Henry	Hieronymus,Francis,	1		Lou.	Hill,Robert,	1		Brun.
Hewlett,John,	1	4	Caro.	Hiers,Henry,	1		Rock.	Hill,Robert,	1	16	Spots.
Hewlett,Richard,	2	1	Caro.	Higgason,Samuel,	1	3	Loui.	Hill,Robert,	1	19	K.&Q.
Hewlett,William,	1	1	Henry	Higgins,Aaron,	1	1	Fay.	Hill,Russil,	2	9	Cul.
Hewlett,William,	2	12	Caro.	Higgins,Alexander,	1		Fau.	Hill,Samuel,			Loui.
Hews,James,	1		So'n.	Higgins,C.,			Hen.	Hill,Swinfield,	1		Henry
Hewton,George,	1		Lin.	Higgins,James,	1	2	Caro.	Hill,Thomas,	1		Lun.
Hezer,Henry,	1		Lou.	Higgins,Joel,			Caro.	Hill,Thomas,			Henry
Hiat,John,	3	5	Lin.	Higgins,John,	1		Fau.	Hill,Thomas,			Pr.Wm.
Hiatt,Benjamin,	1	1	Spots.	Higgins,John,	3		Har.	Hill,Thomas,	2	8	K.&Q.
Hiatt,George,	1	1	Berk.	Higgins,John,	2		Fay.	Hill,Wearing,	1	1	Cul.
Hiatt,Simson,	1		Berk.	Higgins,John,	1		Fay.	Hill,William,	1	10	Cul.
Hiatt,William,	1		Berk.	Higgins,Nelley,			K.Geo.	Hill,William,			Bot.
Hibbons,John,	1		Berk.	Higgins,Peter,	1	4	Har.	Hill,William,	1		Fau.
Hibbs,Isaac,	1		Bed.	Higgins,Robert,	2	9	Har.	Hill,William,	1	21	Brun.
Hibbs,Joseph,Sr.,	1		Lou.	Higgins,William,	2	2	Fay.	Hill,William,	2	23	Din.
Hibbs,Joseph,Jr.,	1		Lou.	Higgins,William,	2	10	Caro.	Hill,William,	2	21	K.&Q.
Hibbs,William,	1		Lou.	Higgins,William,	1		Fau.	Hill,William,	1		Fay.
Hibdon,William,			Hen.	Higgins,William,Jr.,	1	4	Caro.	Hill,William,		21	K.&Q.
Hick,Lewis,	1		Bot.	High,David,	1	2	Brun.	Hilliard,Daniel,	1		West.
Hickenbottom,William,			Henry	High,Martha,		1	Din.	Hilliard,John,	1		Ch.Cy.
Hickerson,John,	1	1	Fau.	Highlander,George,	1		Pr.Wm.	Hilliard,Levy,	1		West.
Hickerson,John,	1	1	Pr.Wm.	Hight,Richard,	1	9	Lun.	Hillis,Ann,			Fay.
Hickerson,Nathaniel,	1		Fau.	Hightower,George,	1	6	Lun.	Hillis,John,	1		Berk.
Hickerson,Thomas,	1		Henry	Hightower,John,	1	9	Lun.	Hillis,Robert,	1		Fay.
Hickerson,William,	1		Fau.	Hightower,John,Jr.,	1	6	Lun.	Hillary,William,	1		Fau.
Hickey,John,			Henry	Hightower,Joseph,	1	9	Lun.	Hillton,Jonathan,	1		K.Geo.
Hickey,Simon,			Fay.	Hightower,Joshua,	1	5	Brun.	Hilton,Abraham,	1		Mont.
Hickland,John,	1		Aug.	Hightower,Rawleigh,	1	5	Brun.	Hilton,Elijah,	1		Bot.
Hickland,Capt.Thomas,	1	1	Aug.	Hightower,Thomas,	1	10	Brun.	Hilton,Jessee,	1		Henry
Hickland,Thomas,Jr.,	1		Aug.	Highwarden,John,	1	1	Pr.Wm.	Hilton,Jessey,	1		Lin.
Hicklin,Hugh,			Fay.	Higs,Jeremiah,	2		Pr.Wm.	Hilton,John,	1		Henry
Hicklin,Hugh,	1		Aug.	Higs,Samuel,			Pr.Wm.	Hilton,Mary,		4	West.
Hickman,Ann,		4	K.Wm.	Hilburn,Christopher,	1		Fau.	Hilton,Samuel,			Henry
Hickman,Conrod,	1		Lou.	Hilchacock,Thomas,	1		K.&Q.	Hilton,Solomon,	1		Henry
Hickman,David,	1	1	Cul.	Hiler,Henry,	1		Lou.	Hillyard,Joseph,	2	38	K.Wm.
Hickman,Edward,	1		Acco.	Hiler,Michael,	1		Lou.	Hinche,Obediah,	1		Loui.
Hickman,Henry,			Cul.	Hill,***,	1		Mont.	Hind,Samuel,	1		Aug.
Hickman,James,	2	8	Cul.	Hill,Baylor,	1	29	K.Wm.	Hind,William,	1	4	Aug.
Hickman,James,Jr.,			Cul.	Hill,Charles,	1		Cul.	Hindman,Alexander,	*	*	***
Hickman,Joel,			Cul.	Hill,Charles,	1		Cul.	Hinds,James,	3		Lin.
Hickman,John,	1	1	Fau.	Hill,Charles,	1	1	Brun.	Hinds,Samuel,			Lin.
Hickman,John,	2	20	K.Wm.	Hill,Clemuel,	1		Lin.	Hine,Thomas,	1		Aug.
Hickman,John,	3	31	K.Wm.	Hill,Daniel,	2		Har.	Hines,David,	1		So'n.
Hickman,John,	2	3	Rock.	Hill,Durham,	1		So'n.	Hines,John,	1	7	Gooch.
Hickman,Joseph,	1	1	Fau.	Hill,Edward,	1	55	K.&Q.	Hines,John,	1	9	So'n.
Hickman,Peter,	1		Berk.	Hill,Frances,			Brun.	Hines,Peter,	1		So'n.
Hickman,Richard,	1	7	Fay.	Hill,Francis,	1	4	Ch.Cy.	Hines,Richard,	1		So'n.
Hickman,Richard,	1		Acco.	Hill,Hannah,			Brun.	Hines,Stephen,	1		So'n.
Hickman,Roger,	1		Aug.	Hill,Henry,	1		Camp.	Hines,Thomas,	1		So'n.
Hickman,Samuel,	1	1	Mont.	Hill,Henry,	1	17	Cul.	Hines,William,			K.Wm.
Hickman,Selby,	2	2	Acco.	Hill,Humphrey,	1		K.&Q.	Hines,William,	1	24	So'n.
Hickman,Thomas,	1	1	Acco.	Hill,Isaac,	1	9	Ch.Cy.	Hines,William,	1	10	So'n.
Hickman,William,	1		Lou.	Hill,James,		4	York	Hiniker,Christian,	1		Har.
Hicks,Agnes,			Lin.	Hill,James,	1		Aug.	Hinkle,Benjamin,	1		Har.
Hicks,Charles,	1	6	Brun.	Hill,James,	1		Buck.	Hinkle,John,			Har.
Hicks,Daniel,	2		Buck.	Hill,James,	1	22	K.Wm.	Hinson,Charles,	1		Cul.
Hicks,George,	2	7	Brun.	Hill,John,			Brun.	Hinson,George,	1		Fau.
Hicks,James,	1		Cul.	Hill,John,	1		Fau.	Hinson,John,			Buck.
Hicks,James,	1	25	Brun.	Hill,John,	1		Cul.	Hinson,Robert,	1		Fau.
Hicks,Jeremiah,	1		Brun.	Hill,John,	1		Rock.	Hinson,Thomas,	1	6	K.&Q.
Hicks,John,	1	8	Brun.	Hill,John,	1	1	Buck.	Hinton,Samuel,	1	11	Din.
Hicks,John,	1		Eli.Cy	Hill,John,	1		Bed.	Hipis,Nikils,	1		Bot.
Hicks,Lewis,	1	13	Brun.	Hill,John,	1		K.Wm.	Hipkins,John,	2	8	Caro.
Hicks,Mary,		2	Brun.	Hill,John,	3	49	K.Wm.	Hipkins,Richard,	2	41	West.

Name			County
Hire,John,	1		Har.
Hire,Leonard,	1		Har.
Hire,Lewis,	1		Har.
Hire,Mary,	1		Har.
Hirchins,John,	1		Mont.
Hisle,John,	3	1	Cul.
Hitch,Christopher,	1	2	Fau.
Hitchcock,John,	1	3	Din.
Hitchens,William,	1		Acco.
Hite,Abraham,	1	7	Har.
Hite,Frances,		21	Berk.
Hite,Henry,	1		Bot.
Hite,Howel,	1		Brun.
Hite,John,	1	2	Berk.
Hite,Mathias,	1		Har.
Hite,Sarah,		7	Berk.
Hith,Col.William,		4	Din.
Hitt,Charles,	1		Fau.
Hitt,Elias,	1	1	Fau.
Hitt,Harman,	1	7	Fau.
Hitt,Jesse,	1	1	Fau.
Hitt,John,	1		Fau.
Hitt,Joseph,	1		Cul.
Hitt,Lazarus,	1		Fau.
Hitt,Mary,	1	2	Fau.
Hitt,Peter,	1	7	Fau.
Hix,Hickerson,	1		Buck.
Hix,Isaac,	1		Lun.
Hix,John,	1	5	Lun.
Hix,John,Jr.,	1	5	Lun.
Hix,Joseph,	1		Lun.
Hix,Joseph,	1		Ja.Cy
Hix,Joseph,	1	1	Mont.
Hix,Kimble,	1		Fau.
Hix,Mesheck,	1	3	Gooch.
Hix,Nathaniel,	1		Lun.
Hix,Phillip,	1		Bed.
Hix,William,	1		Bed.
Hixon, B.	1		Pr.Wm.
Hixon,Donald,	1		Bot.
Hixon,Matthew,			Lou.
Hixon,Timothy,	1		Lou.
Hixon,William,	2		Lou.
Hobbs,Amey,		9	Pr.Geo
Hobbs,Benjamin,	1	13	Pr.Geo
Hobbs,Benjamin,	1		Pr.Geo
Hobbs,Bernard,	1	3	Pr.Geo
Hobbs,David,	1	13	Pr.Geo
Hobbs,Drury,	1	2	Pr.Geo
Hobbs,Elizabeth,		3	Pr.Geo
Hobbs,Ethal,	1	2	Pr.Geo
Hobbs,Howel,			Brun.
Hobbs,Hubbard,		7	Brun.
Hobbs,James,	1		Brun.
Hobbs,Jesse,	1		Din.
Hobbs,Jessee,	1	3	Pr.Geo
Hobbs,Joel,	1		Wash.
Hobbs,John,	1	17	Pr.Geo
Hobbs,L'dowick,	1	3	Pr.Geo
Hobbs,Nathaniel,	1	16	Din.
Hobbs,Rebecca,		3	Pr.Geo
Hobbs,Robert,	1	4	Pr.Geo
Hobbs,Susanna,			Pr.Geo
Hobbs,Thomas,			Wash.
Hobbs,Thomas,	1	5	Pr.Geo
Hobbs,Vinson,Sr.,	1		Wash.
Hobbs,Vinson,Jr.,	1		Wash.
Hobbs,William,	1	9	Pr.Geo
Hobbs,William,	1	2	Pr.Geo
Hobs,Ezekiel,	1		Wash.
Hobson,Benjamin,			Hen.
Hobson,Joseph,	1	2	Lun.
Hobson,Matthew,	1	11	Hen.
Hobson,Nicholas,	1	16	Lun.
Hobson,William,	3	15	Hen.
Hobson,William,Jr.,			Hen.
Hock,Elijah,	2		Berk.
Hode,Howson,	2	8	Fau.
Hode,Peter,	2		Fau.
Hode,Elinor,			Rock.
Hodge,James,			Rock.
Hodge,John,	1	6	Aug.
Hodge,Milly,	1	29	West.
Hodges,Abednigh,	1		Henry
Hodges,Enoch,			Henry
Hodges,Francis,	2	6	Caro.
Hodges,Jesse,	1	3	Gooch.
Hodges,John,	1		Berk.
Hodges,John,	1	17	Pr.Wm.
Hodges,John,	1	2	Gooch.
Hodges,Josiah.	1	1	Henry
Hodges,Lucy,		1	Gooch.
Hodges,Sarah,		4	K.&Q
Hodges,William,	1	5	Lou.
Hodges,William,	1		Gooch.
Hodgson,James,	1		Berk.
Hodikins,Samuel,	1		Fay.
Hodnett,John,	2	11	Buck.
Hodnett,Philip,			Buck.
Hoe,Gerrard,		14	Cul.
Hoeman,John,	1		Lou.
Hoff,Charles,	1		Lou.
Hogan,Isham,	1	8	Din.
Hogan,James,			Loui.
Hogan,John,	1		Loui.
Hogan,John,	1	2	Fau.
Hogan,John,	2		Fau.
Hogan,Joseph,	1		Lin.
Hogan,Rawleigh,	1		Fau.
Hogan,Thomas,	1	5	Fau.
Hogan,William,	2	3	Loui.
Hogan,William,	1	3	Pr.Wm.
Hogard,Jesse,			Loui.
Hoggatt,Anthony,	1	1	Buck.
Hoggatt,John,			Buck.
Hogbin,John,	2		Har.
Hogg,James,	1		Mont.
Hogge,James,	1		Aug.
Hogg,Jane,		6	K.Wm.
Hogg,Richard,	1	8	Hen.
Hogin,James,	2	3	Fay.
Hogshare,John,	1		Acco.
Hogshead,Ann,			Aug.
Hogshead,David,	1		Aug.
Hogshead,David,	1		Aug.
Hogshead,Elizabeth,			Aug.
Hogshead,James,	1	1	Aug.
Hogshead,John,	2		Aug.
Hogshead,Michael,	2		Aug.
Hogshead,Robert,	1		Aug.
Hogue,David,	1		Har.
Hogue,Moses,	1	2	Har.
Hogue,Solomon,	1		Lou.
Hogue,Solomon,	1		Lou.
Hogue,William,	1		Lou.
Holaway,George,		40	Caro.
Holdcroft,Dionissus,	1		Ja.Cy
Holdcroft,Norvel,	1		Cha.Cy
Holdaway,Charles,	1		Cul.
Holdcroft,William,	1		Cha.Cy
Holden,Ann,		13	Acco.
Holden,Davis,	1	1	Cul.
Holder,Benjamin,	1		Cul.
Holder,Francis,			Fay.
Holder,Francis,			Lou.
Holder,John,	7	20	Fay.
Holder,Luke,	2	2	Lou.
Holder,Luke,			Fay.
Holderby,William,		8	K.&Q
Holdercroft,Edward,	1	1	Cha.Cy
Holdern,Bartholomew,			Lou.
Holdern,Cornelius,	2		Lou.
Holdman,William,	1		Rock.
Holderby,Betty,			K.&Q
Holdsworth,Charles,	1	4	Cha.Cy
Holdsworth,John,	1	2	Cha.Cy
Holdsworth,William,	1	3	Cha.Cy
Hole,Charles,	2		Lou.
Hole,George,	1		Aug.
Hole,Jacob,			Lou.
Hole,Capt.Peter,	1		Aug.
Holeman,William,	2	7	Gooch.
Holmes,Benjamin,	1		Hen.
Holmes,Thomas,	1		Hen.
Holemes,William,	1		Hen.
Holenback,Daniel,	1		Cul.
Holens,William,	1		Mont.
Holhane,Daniel,	1		Wash.
Holladay,Benjamin,	1	15	Spots.
Holladay,Benjamin,	1	1	Spots.
Holladay,Dinnis,	1		Din.
Holladay,George,	1		West.
Holladay,James,	1	1	Spots.
Holladay,Joseph,	2	15	Spots.
Holladay,Joseph,Jr.,	1		Spots.
Holladay,Lewis,	1	16	Spots.
Holladay,Mildred,		10	Spots.
Holland,Ann,		1	Nor.
Holland,Asa,			Bed.
Holland,George,	1		Mont.
Holland,George,	2	16	Loui.
Holland,George,Jr.,	1	4	Gooch.
Holland,Jacob,	1	2	Mont.
Holland,James,			Loui.
Holland,John,	1	2	Gooch.
Holland,John,	1	1	Nor.
Holland,Peter,Sr.,	1		Bed.
Holland,Peter,Jr.,	1	2	Bed.
Holland,Thomas,	1		Wash.
Holland,Thomas,	1		Lou.
Holland,William,	1	2	Loui.
Holland,William,	1	6	West.
Holland,William,			Bed.
Hollendine,Anthony,	1		Mont.
Hollaway,Frank,	1	3	Din.
Hollaway,Nathan,	1	2	Caro.
Holley,Abel,	1	2	Acco.
Holley,Francis,	2	7	Bed.
Holliday,Banes,	1		Henry
Holliday,Mary,	1		Pr.Wm.
Holliday,John,	2		Pr.Wm.
Holliday,James,	1	2	Berk.
Holliday,James,			Pr.Wm.
Holliday,Robert,	1	1	Henry
Holliday,Samuel,	1		Fau.
Holliday,Thomas,	1	20	So'n
Hollier,Simon,	1	20	Eli.Cy
Holliman,Benjamin,	1	1	So'n
Holliman,Micajah,	1	13	So'n
Holliman,William,Jr.,	1		So'n
Holliman,William,Sr.,	1	6	So'n
Hollings,John,	1		K.Wm.
Hollings,William,	1		K.Wm.
Hollins,Benjamin,	1	3	Loui.
Hollinsworth,James,	1		Henry
Hollinsworth,John,	1	2	Pr.Geo.
Hollinsworth,Thomas,	1		Henry
Hollinsworth,Thomas,	1	10	Pr.Geo.
Holloday,David,	1		Bed.
Holloday,John,	1		Bed.
Holloway,Asai,			Brun.
Holloway,Assa,			Brun.
Holloway,Betty,	1	43	Caro.
Holloway,Daniel,	1	3	Brun.
Holloway,David,			Brun.
Holloway,Edward,		3	Brun.
Holloway,George,	1		Cul.
Holloway,George,	1	35	K.&Q

Name			County	Name			County	Name			County
Holloway,Henry,	1		Cul.	Hood,Richard,est.,	2	2	K.Geo.	Horn,Frederick,	1		Berk.
Holloway,James,	1	2	York	Hood,Seymour,	11	12	K.Geo.	Horn,George,		1	Berk.
Holloway,Jesse,	1	1	Brun.	Hood,Thomas,			York.	Horn,Sheroa,		1	Spots.
Holloway,John,	1	5	Din.	Hood,William,	1	8	K.Geo.	Hornback,Abraham,	1		Fay.
Holloway,John,	1	19	Pr.Geo	Hoode, H.	1	30	Pr.Wm.	Hornback,Anthony,	1		Har.
Holloway,Joseph,	1		Bed.	Hoods,William,	1	7	Pr.Wm.	Hornback,James,	1		Har.
Holloway,Lewis,	1	3	Brun.	Hooe,Bernett,		9	Lou.	Hornback,John,	1		Har.
Holloway,Major,	1	1	Gooch.	Hooe,John,			Lou.	Hornback,Michael,	1		Har.
Holloway,N.			Hen.	Hoof,Moore,	1		Pr.Wm.	Hornback,Samuel,	4		Har.
Holloway,Peter,	1		York	Hoof, P.	2		Pr.Wm.	Hornback,Simon,	1		Har.
Holloway,Thomas,	1		York	Hooff,P.,Jr.,	1		Pr.Wm.	Hornbarrier,Jacob,	1		Mont.
Holloway,William,	2	14	Brun.	Hook,John,	1	7	Bed.	Hornbarrier,Philip,	1		Mont.
Holloway,William,	1	7	Caro.	Hook,John Adam,	1		Berk.	Hornbuckle,G.,			Pr.Wm.
Holloway,William,	1	1	Bed.	Hook,John & George,	2		Aug.	Horner,Isaac,	1		Cul.
Hollowway,Charles,	1		Cul.	Hooker,John,	1		K.&Q	Hornsby,Argal,	1	1	Acco.
Holly,William,	1		Bot.	Hooker,Robert,	1		Mont.	Hornsby,Eli,	2	7	Acco.
Holman,***,	1	17	Hen.	Hoomes,Benjamin,	1	7	K&Q	Hornsby,Elisha,	2	3	Acco.
Holman,James,	1	13	Gooch.	Hoomes,John,		21	Caro.	Hornsby,John,Sr.,	1	5	Acco.
Holmes,Benjamin,	1		Henry	Hoomes,John,	4	69	Caro.	Hornsby,Joseph,	1	27	Ja.Cy.
Holmes,Edward,	1		Lou.	Hoomes,David,			K.Wm.	Hornsby,Major,	1	8	Acco.
Holmes,John,	2		Lou.	Hoomes,William,	1	8	K.Wm.	Hornsby,Thomas,	1		Henry
Holmes,John,Jr.,			Lou.	Hooper,George,	1	18	Buck.	Hornsby,William,			Acco.
Holmes,Lewis,			Din.	Hooper,James,	1		Hen.	Horoine,Jacob,	1		Lin.
Holmes,Solomon,	1	6	So'n.	Hooper,James,	1	4	Lun.	Horoine,Michael,	1	2	Lin.
Holms,Edward,	1		Nor.	Hooper,John,	1		Hen.	Horseman,Abram,			Lou.
Holmes,Gab.,	1		Rock.	Hooper,Joseph,	1	1	Buck.	Horseman,William,	3	2	Lou.
Holrelaro,Joseph,	1		Cul.	Hooper,Obediah,	1	7	Lun.	Horsey,Isaac,			West.
Holt,Ambrose,	1		Henry	Hooper,Richard,	1	4	Hen.	Horslentine,Jacob,	1		Wash.
Holt,Etheldred,	1		So'n.	Hooper,Richard,Sr.,	1		Hen.	Horst,George,	2		Har.
Holt,Frederick,	1	4	So'n.	Hooper,Thomas,	1	1	Lun.	Horst,Peter,	1		Har.
Holt,Jerdonez,		3	Ch.Cy.	Hooper,William,	1		Lun.	Horton,James,	1		Fau.
Holt,John,	1	5	Ja.Cy.	Hoote,Elizabeth,			Lou.	Horton,John Peyton,	1		Pr.Wm.
Holt,John,			Acco.	Hoover,Mackis,	1		Berk.	Horton,Mary,	1	6	Pr.Wm.
Holt,John,W.,		5	Bed.	Hope,George,	1	13	Eli.Cy	Horton,Rhueben,			Pr.Wm.
Holt,Micajah,	1	2	So'n.	Hope,Henry,	1		Pr.Wm.	Horton,Sarah,			Pr.Wm.
Holt,Nicholas,	1		Ch.Cy.	Hopewell,John,	1		Lou.	Horton,Snowdon,	1	9	Pr.Wm.
Holt,Phillip,	1		Bed.	Hopkins,Elizabeth,		4	Loui.	Horton,William,	1		Cul.
Holt,Richard,	1	10	K.&Q.	Hopkins,Francis,	1	3	Bed.	Hory,Samuel,	1		K.&Q.
Holt,Richard,	1		Henry	Hopkins,Francis,	1		Lin.	Hoskins,Robert,	1	6	K.&Q.
Holt,Stephen,	1		Mont.	Hopkins,George,	1		Mont.	Hoskins,William,	1	1	Henry
Holt,Stewart,	1	8	Nor.	Hopkins,James,	1		Berk.	Hossey,Isaac,			K.Geo.
Holt,Thomas,	1	8	So'n.	Hopkins,John,	1	20	Gooch.	Houchens,Bernard,	1	2	K.Wm.
Holt,William,	2	39	Ja.Cy.	Hopkins,John,Jr.,	1	1	Hen.	Houchens,Charles,	1		Gooch.
Holt,William,	1		Buck.	Hopkins,Nehamiah,	1		Wash.	Houchens,Edward,	1		Gooch.
Holt,William,	1		Acco.	Hopkins,Peter,	1	1	Loui.	Houchens,Frances,	1	2	Gooch.
Holton,William,	2		Fau.	Hopkins,Reuben,	1		Hen.	Houchens,James,	1		Gooch.
Holtzclaw,Archibald,			Fau.	Hopkins,Richard,	1		Lou.	Houqeshell,Jacob,	1		Lin.
Holtzclaw,Benjamin,	1	1	Fau.	Hopkins,Stephen,	1		Acco.	Hough,James,	1		Lou.
Holtzclaw,Catey,		3	Fau.	Hopkins,Thomas,			Lou.	Hough,John,	1		Lou.
Holtzclaw,Jacob,	1		Fau.	Hopkins,William,		1	Wash.	Hough,John,	2		Lou.
Holtzclaw,Josiah,	1		Fau.	Hopkins,William,	1	1	Lin.	Hough,John,	1		Lou.
Holycross,John,	1		Din.	Hopper,Elizabeth,			Cul.	Hough,John,Sr.,	1		Lou.
Homan,John,	1		Har.	Hopper,James,	1		Lou.	Hough,Joseph,	1		Lou.
Homan,Sithman,	1		Har.	Hopper,John,	1	5	Gooch	Hough,Mahlon,	1		Lou.
Homas,Joseph,	1		Bot.	Hopper,John,	1		Fau.	Hough,Philip,	1		Lou.
Home,Spilsby,	1	2	Pr.Wm.	Hopper,John,Sr.,			Fau.	Hough,Samuel,	1		Lou.
Homes,Christopher,	1	19	Cul.	Hopper,Joseph,	1		Fau.	Hough,William,	1		Lou.
Homes,Dunkin,	1		Loui.	Hopper,Mary,			Fau.	Hough,William,			Lou.
Homes,Edmund,	1		Fau.	Hopper,Thomas,	1		Henry	Hough,William,Sr.,	1		Lou.
Homes,George,	1		Fau.	Hopper,Thomas,		3	Cul.	Houghman,Anthony,	1		Lou.
Homes,James,	1	1	Fau.	Hoppn,Robert,	1		Fau.	Houghman,Jacob,	1		Lou.
Homes,John,	1		Lin.	Hopson,John,	1		York	Houghman,John,	1		Lou.
Homes,John,	1		Lin.	Hopson,John,Estate,		8	Buck.	Houghman,Peter,	2		Fay.
Homes,Mary,		1	York	Hopson,William,	1	1	Spots.	Houke,George,	1		Mont.
Hon,Jonas,	2		Fay.	Hopwood,James,	1		Pr.Wm.	Houlstone,James,	2		Acco.
Honey,James,	1		Ch.Cy.	Hopwood,Moses,	1	1	Pr.Wm.	Houlstone,John,	2		Acco.
Honiman,Samuel,			Lou.	Hopwood,Christopher,	1		Pr.Wm.	Hounds,Edward,			Pr.Wm.
Hood,B.,	2	27	Pr.Wm.	Hord,Charles,			Lin.	Hounds,Thomas,Sr.,	1	4	Pr.Wm.
Hood,Charles,	1		K.Wm.	Hord,James,	1	11	Cul.	Hounds,Thomas,Jr.,	1		Pr.Wm.
Hood,David,	1	1	Din.	Hord,John,	1	34	Caro.	Hounds,Thomas,Jr.,	1		Pr.Wm.
Hood,Gerrard,	2	12	K.Geo.	Hord,Lucy,Estate,		24	Caro.	Hounds,Uth,	1	6	Pr.Wm.
Hood,Giles,	2	2	Cha.Cy	Hord,Mordecai,	1	21	Henry	House,Drury,			Brun.
Hood,John,			Cha.Cy	Hore,J.,	1	30	Pr.Wm.	House,Henry,	2	3	Brun.
Hood,John,	1		Din.	Horkins,Joseph,	1		Mont.	House,Isham,	1	5	Brun.
Hood,John,			Lou.	Horley,James,			Cul.	House,Jacob,	1		Har.
Hood, R.	1	11	Pr.Wm.	Horley,Matthew,	2		Cul.	House,John,	1		Brun.

Name			Co.	Name			Co.	Name			Co.
House,Jordan,	1	7	Brun.	Howell,James,	1		Mont.	Hudson,James,	1		Cul.
House,Lawrence,	2	7	Brun.	Howell,Jesse,	1	2	Nor.	Hudson,Jesse,	1		Bot.
House,Mary,		1	Brun.	Howell,John,		8	Nor.	Hudson,Joel,	1		Bed.
House,Mary,	1		Brun.	Howell,(Jno.)	1		K.&Q.	Hudson,John,	1		Har.
House,Mary,			Eli.Cy	Howell,John,	1		Hen.	Hudson,John,	1		Mont.
House,Matthias,	2		Cul.	Howell,John,	1		Lou.	Hudson,John,			Buck.
House,Miles,			Brun.	Howell,John,	1		Bed.	Hudson,John,			K.Geo.
House,Suckey,		2	Brun.	Howell,John,	1	6	Din.	Hudson,Joshua,	1		Henry
House,William,	1	3	Brun.	Howell,Samuel,	1		Lou.	Hudson,Joshua,	1		Fay.
Householder,Matthias,	1		Berk.	Howell,Timothy,	1		Lou.	Hudson,Joshua,	1		K.Geo.
Householove,Adam,	1		Lou.	Howell,Thomas,	1		Bot.	Hudson,Obediah,	1		Henry
Houseman,George,	1		Berk.	Howell,William,	1		Mont.	Hudson,Peter,	1		Henry
Houseley,Robert,	1		Mont.	Howerton,Ambrose,			K.&Q.	Hudson,Richard,Est.		3	Lun.
Housling,James,	1	1	Hen.	Howerton,Charles,	1	2	K.&Q.	Hudson,Ruel,	1	1	Spots.
Houseman,David,	2		Berk.	Howerton,James,Sr.,	1		Brun.	Hudson,Thomas,	1		Rock.
Housman,Martin,	1		Berk.	Howerton,James,Jr.,	1		Brun.	Hudson,Tuttle,			Din.
Houston,Ann,			Caro.	Howerton,John,	1		Mont.	Hudson,Vall,	1	3	K.Geo.
Houston,Hugh,	1		Caro.	Howerton,Thomas,	1	1	Brun.	Hudson,Ward,	1	8	Lun.
Houston,James,	1	1	Rock.	Howerton,Thomas,	1		Hen.	Hudson,William,	2	11	Din.
Houston,Jennet,			Caro.	Howett,J.,	1	13	Pr.Wm.	Hudson,William,	1		K.&Q.
Houston,John,	1	3	Caro.	Howser,Christian,	1		Lou.	Hudson,William,	1		K.&Q.
Houston,John,	2		Rock.	Howson,Benjamin,	1		Cul.	Hudson,William,	1	6	Lun.
Houston,John,	1		Rock.	Hoy,Thomas,	1		Henry	Hudson,William,	1		Caro.
Houston,Mary,		1	Rock.	Hoyles,Elizabeth,		6	K.Geo.	Hudson,William,	1		Bot.
Houston,Robert,	1	1	Caro.	Hoylman,Stophel,	1		Rock.	Hueston,Benjamin,	1		Lou.
Houston,Robert,	1	3	Caro.	Hubank,Major,	1	2	K.&Q.	Huff,Daniel,	1	4	Brun.
Houston,Samuel,	1	1	Rock.	Hubank,Widdow,		9	K.&Q.	Huff,Francis,	2		Aug.
Houston,William,	1		Rock.	Hubard,Jack,			York	Huff,Henry,	1		Bed.
Hout,George,	1		Berk.	Hubard,Patty,		4	York	Huff,James,	1		Brun.
Houton,Elijah,	1		Lou.	Hubard,Absolam,	1	5	York	Huff,John,	1		Bot.
How,Edward,	1		Rock.	Hubbard,Benjamin,	1		Henry	Huff,John,	2		Bot.
How,John,	1		Berk.	Hubbard,Cuthbert,	2	5	York	Huff,Joseph,	1		Bot.
How,Joseph,	1		Mont.	Hubbard,Daniel,	1	1	Loui.	Huff,Leonard,	1		Bot.
How,Samuel,	1		Berk.	Hubbard,Ephraim,	1	16	Fau.	Huff,Mary,			Henry
Howard,Allen,	1		Bed.	Hubbard,Eusebus,	1	6	Henry	Huff,Peter,	1		Henry
Howard,Drury,	1		Bed.	Hubbard,Harrison,	2	2	Henry	Huff,Philemon,		1	Brun.
Howard,Edwrad C.,	1	15	York	Hubbard,Mary,			York	Huff,Phillip,	1		Bot.
Howard,Henry,est.		33	York	Hubbard,Matthew,	1		Lun.	Huff,Reubin,			Brun.
Howard,James,	1		Wash.	Hubbard,Ralph,	1	9	Lun.	Huff,Thomas,	1	1	Mont.
Howard,James,	1		Fay.	Hubbard,Samuel,	1		Camp.	Huff,William,	1	1	Brun.
Howard,James,	1		Gooch	Hubbard,Samuel,	1		Camp.	Huff,William,	1		Bot.
Howard,John ,	1	8	Gooch	Hubbard,Thomas,	1		Henry	Huff,William,Estate,		2	Brun.
Howard,John,	1	11	Bot.	Hubble,Thomas,	1		Lou.	Huffman,Christopher,	2		Har.
Howard,John,	1	4	Fay.	Huber,George,	1		Pr.Wm.	Huffman,Gaypert,	1		Aug.
Howard,Michael,	1		Lou.	Huckaby,John,	1		Henry	Huffman,George,	1		Berk.
Howard,Mordecai,	1	4	Brun.	Huckerby,Joshua,	1		Bed.	Huffman,George,	1		Aug.
Howard,Robert,	1	20	York.	Huckerby,Thomas,	1		Bed.	Huffman,Jacob,	1		Bot.
Howard,Samuel,	1		Aug.	Huckstep,John,	1		Fay.	Huffman,Jacob,	1		Mont.
Howard,William,	1	22	York.	Huckstep,Solomon,	1	1	K.Wm.	Huffman,John,	1		Bot.
Howard,William,	1		Brun.	Hucky,Daniel,	1		Berk.	Huffman,John,	1		Fau.
Howard,William,	1		Spots	Huddleston,Robert,	1	1	Buck.	Huffman,John,	1		Henry
Howard,William,est.,		3	Bed.	Huddleston,Robert,Jr.	1		Buck.	Huffman,Leonard,	1		Har.
Howart,Edward,	1		Bot.	Huddlestone,Samuel,			Buck.	Huffman,Margaret,	2		Fau.
Howart,Ezekiel,	1		Bot.	Huddlestone,Thomas,	2	4	Buck.	Hufman,Ambrose,	1		Cul.
Howdershell,Jacob,			Bed.	Huagen,Daniel,	1		Lin.	Hufman,Benjamin,			Cul.
Howdershell,Michael,	2		Lou.	Hudgens,Moses,	1		Buck.	Hufman,Benjamin,	1		Cul.
Howdershell,Michael,			Lou.	Hungin,Aaron,	1		Lun.	Hufman,Charles,			Cul.
Howdischild,Henry,	1		Cul.	Huagin,Samuel,	1		Brun.	Hufman,Daniel,	1		Cul.
Howe,James,	1	2	Buck.	Hudleston,Abraham,	1		Bed.	Hufman,Frederick,	1	1	Cul.
Howe,Stophel,	1		Aug.	Hudleston,Daniel,	1		Bed.	Hufman,George,	1		Cul.
Howel,Abner,	1		Bot.	Hudleston,William,	1		Bed.	Hufman,Harmon,			Cul.
Howel,Benjamin,	1		Bot.	Hudnall,Joseph,Jr.,	1		Fau.	Hufman,Henry,			Cul.
Howel,Charles,	1		Bot.	Hudnall,William,	1		Bed.	Hufman,Henry,	1		Cul.
Howel,David,			Bot.	Hudnell,John,	1	6	Cul.	Hufman,Henry,	1		Cul.
Howel,Donold,	1		Bot.	Hudson,Abraham,	1	2	Bed.	Hufman,Henry,	3	3	Cul.
Howel,Frances,		1	Brun.	Hudson,Alexander,	1		Bed.	Hufman,Henry,Jr.,	1		Cul.
Howel,John,	1		Bot.	Hudson,Benjamin,	1		Henry	Hufman,Henry,Jr.,			Cul.
Howel,Joshuae,	1		Bot.	Hudson,Charles,	1	2	Lun.	Hufman,Jacob,	1	3	Cul.
Howel,Thomas,	1		Rock.	Hudson,Christopher,	1	4	Loui.	Hufman,James,	1		Cul.
Howell,***,	2		K.&Q.	Hudson,David,	1	1	Lun.	Hufman,James,	1		Cul.
Howell,Andrew,	1		Lou.	Hudson,David,	1	21	Loui.	Hufman,James,			Cul.
Howell,Daniel,	1	4	Lou.	Hudson,David,	1		Har.	Hufman,John,	1	1	Cul.
Howell,George,	1		Mont.	Hudson,David,Jr.,	1		Cul.	Hufman,Joseph,	1		Cul.
Howell,Hezekiah,	1		Lou.	Hudson,George,	1		Aug.	Hufman,Joseph,			Cul.
Howell,James,			K.&Q.	Hudson,Hall,	1		Henry	Hufman,Joseph,	1		Cul.
				Hudson,Irby,	1	9	Din.	Hufman,Martin,	1		Cul.

Name			County
Hufman,Michael,	2	1	Cul.
Hufman,Nicholas,	4	1	Cul.
Hufman,Peter,	1		Cul.
Hufman,Powl,	1	1	Cul.
Hufman,Samuel,			Cul.
Hufman,Tilman,	1		Cul.
Hufman,Tilman,	4	5	Cul.
Hufman,William,Sr.,	1	1	Cul.
Hufman,William,Jr.,	1		Cul.
Hufty,Benjamin,	1		Lou.
Hugeley,Abraham,	2		Lou.
Hugeley,Charles,	3		Lou.
Hugeley,Jacob,	2		Lou.
Hugeley,Job,	1		Lou.
Huges,Daniel,			York
Huggins,Luke,	1		Bea.
Huggins,Philip,	1		Bed.
Hughart,James,	1	1	Aug.
Hughart,Thomas,	1	5	Aug.
Hughes,Absalom,	1		Ch.Cy.
Hughes,Annis,		5	Ch.Cy.
Hughes,Archelous,	1	14	Henry
Hughes,Benjamin,	1	7	Gooch.
Hughes,Billey,	1		Loui.
Hughes,Blackmore,	1	1	Henry
Hughes,Blackmore,	1	3	Henry
Hughes,Daniel,	1		York
Hughes,David,	1		Bed.
Hughes,David,	1		Aug.
Hughes,Elias,	1	1	Wash.
Hughes,Mrs.Euph,			Aug.
Hughes,Evin,	1		Har.
Hughes,George,	1		Camp.
Hughes,Isaac,	1		Lou.
Hughes,James,			Rock.
Hughes,James,	1	10	York
Hughes,James,	1		Har.
Hughes,James,	1		Ja.Cy.
Hughes,James,	1	1	K.Wm.
Hughes,Jeremiah,	1	1	Ch.Cy.
Hughes,John,	1	3	Cul.
Hughes,John,	1	6	Bed.
Hughes,Joshua,	1		Loui.
Hughes,Neil,	1		Aug.
Hughes,Philip,		1	K.Wm.
Hughes,Reade,	1		K.Wm.
Hughes,Robert,	1	2	Camp.
Hughes,Robert,	2	8	Buck.
Hughes,Robert,	1	1	Hen.
Hughes,Russell,	1	1	Loui.
Hughes,Thomas,	1	2	Aug.
Hughes,Thomas,	1	9	Cul.
Hughes,Thophilius,	1		Lou.
Hughes,William,	1		K.Geo.
Hughes,William,		1	Pr.Wm.
Hughes,William,	1	3	Pr.Wm.
Hughes,William,	1	4	Lun.
Hughes,William,	1	5	Gooch.
Hughes,William,	2	1	York
Hughes,William,	1		Camp.
Hughes,William,	1	4	Cul.
Hughes,Capt.William,	1	7	Loui.
Hughmoody,Henry,	1		Fau.
Hughs,Anthony,	1	9	Cul.
Hughs,David,	1		Wash.
Hughs,James,	1		Fay.
Hughs,John,			Brun.
Hughs,John,	1	1	Nor.
Hughs,John,	1		Wash.
Hughs,John,	1		Lin.
Hughs,Jonathan,	2		Berk.
Hughs,Martha,		3	Ja.Cy.
Hughs,Stevens,	1		Bot.
Hughs,Thomas,	1		Lou.
Hughs,William,	1	7	Cul.
Hughs,William,	1		Wash.
Hughsmith,Jacob,	1		Berk.
Hughston,Thomas,	1		Bed.
Hulett,Hannah,		2	York
Hulitt,William,	1		Fau.
Hull,Francis,	1		Aug.
Hull,George,	1	1	West.
Hull,John,		5	Fau.
Hull,Joseph,	1		Din.
Hull,Nathaniel,	1		Berk.
Hull,Samuel,	1		Lou.
Hulse,Elizabeth,		1	Berk.
Hulse,James,	1	1	Bot.
Hulse,John,	1		Berk.
Hulse,Paul,	1	1	Berk.
Hulse,Robert,	1	1	Berk.
Hulse,William,	1		Berk.
Humble,Uriah,	1		Fay.
Humber,John,	1	11	Gooch.
Hume,A.,	1	1	Pr.Wm.
Hume,Charles,	1	3	Cul.
Hume,George,	1	1	Cul.
Hume,George,	2	6	Cul.
Hume,James,	1		Fau.
Hume,James,	1		Cul.
Hume,James,			Cul.
Hume,John,	1		Fau.
Hume,John,	1		Fau.
Hume,John,	2		Cul.
Hume,Robert,	1		Fau.
Hume,William,	1		Fau.
Hume,Andrew,	1		Fau.
Humes,Francis,	1	9	Cul.
Humes,John,	2		Cul.
Humler,Charles,	1	19	Lun.
Hummer,Michael,	1		Lou.
Hummer,William,	1		Lou.
Humon,Jonathan,	1		Mont.
Humphlet,King,	1	1	Eli.Cy
Humphrey,Benjamin,	2		Cul.
Humphrey,George,	1		Cul.
Humphrey,James,	2		Cul.
Humphrey,Jesse,	1		Cul.
Humphrey,Jonathan,	1		Cul.
Humphrey,Thomas,	1	4	Lou.
Humphrey,Thomas,	1		Cul.
Humphreys,David,	1		Aug.
Humphreys,John,	1		Bot.
Humphreys,Uriah,	1	10	Bot.
Humphries,Anderson,	1		K.Geo
Humphries,William,	1	32	Lou.
Humphris,Sisler,			Loui.
Humphriss,Morriss,	1		Henry
Humphry,Edmond,	1		Loui.
Hums,Garret,	1		Fay.
Hums,George,	1		Fay.
Humston,Edward,	1	13	Fau.
Humston,Edward,Jr.,	1	13	Fau.
Hun,Benjamin,	1		Cul.
Hundley,James,	1	1	Buck.
Hundley,John,	1	3	K.&Q.
Hundley,Josiah,	1	3	Camp.
Hundley,Richard,	1	12	Caro.
Hungate,Charles,	1		Bot.
Hungate,John,	1		Bot.
Hungate,William,	1		Bot.
Hungerford,Ann,		21	West.
Hungerford,Thomas,	2	13	West.
Hunley,Joseph,	1		Bed.
Hunnicutt,Benjamin,	1	8	Pr.Geo
Hunnicutt,John,	1	5	Pr.Geo
Hunnicutt,Robert,	1	11	Pr.Geo
Hunnicutt,Robert,	1	7	Pr.Geo
Hunicutt,William,	2	4	Pr.Geo
Hunnicut,William,	1	1	Din.
Hunnicutt,Wyke,	1	9	Pr.Geo
Hunt,Cary,	1	9	K.Wm.
Hunt,Charles,	1		Aug.
Hunt,James,	1		Henry
Hunt,John,		4	K.Wm.
Hunt,John,	1	3	Fay.
Hunt,John,	1		Mont.
Hunt,Joshua,	1		So'n.
Hunt,Julius,	2		Cul.
Hunt,Julius,			Cul.
Hunt,Levi,	1		Fay.
Hunt,Richard,	1		Lin.
Hunt,Stephen,	1		Lou.
Hunt,Thomas,	1	11	York
Hunt,Thomas,	1		Bed.
Hunt,Thomas,	1		Lou.
Hunt,Turner,		11	Brun.
Hunt,William,	1	12	K.&Q.
Hunter,Alexander,	1	7	Henry
Hunter,Andrew,	1		Bea.
Hunter & Banks,	4	4	Hen.
Hunter,Eliphalet,			Lou.
Hunter,Francis,	1		Fay.
Hunter,George,	1		Loui.
Hunter,Henry,			Fay.
Hunter,Mrs.Israel,	1		Lou.
Hunter,Jacob,	4		Fay.
Hunter,James,	1	47	Cul.
Hunter,James,			Camp.
Hunter,James,	2	10	Hen.
Hunter,James,	1	26	Fau.
Hunter,John,	1	9	Camp.
Hunter,John,	1	5	Eli.Cy.
Hunter,John,			Fay.
Hunter,John,	1		Henry
Hunter,John,			York
Hunter,John,	1	1	Aug.
Hunter,Jonathan,	1		Lou.
Hunter,Malcomb,	1		Bot.
Hunter,Moses,	1		Berk.
Hunter,Patrick,	1		Fay.
Hunter,Peter,	1		Bed.
Hunter,Peter,	1		Fay.
Hunter,Rebecca,	1		Fay.
Hunter,Robert,	1		Mont.
Hunter,Samuel,	1	8	Aug.
Hunter,Stephen,	1	3	Loui.
Hunter,Thomas,	1		Har.
Hunter,Thomas,	1		Mont.
Hunter,William,	2	2	Fay.
Hunter,William,	1	2	Henry
Hunton,William,	1	19	Fau.
Huntsman,Joseph,	1	4	Lin.
Huntsman,Peter,			Lou.
Hurley,Leonard,	1	19	Ja.Cy.
Hurst,Edward,	1		Eli.Cy.
Hurst,Henry,	1		Fau.
Hurst,James,	1		Mont.
Hurst,John,	1		Lou.
Hurst,John,	1		Lou.
Hurst,John,		13	Lou.
Hurst,Lewis,	1		So'n.
Hurst,Martha,			Lou.
Hurst,Robert,	1	2	So'n.
Hurst,Rosanna,			Fau.
Hurst,William,	1	6	So'n.
Hurt,***,	1	1	K.&Q.
Hurt,Ann,	2	8	Caro.
Hurt,Elisha,	1		Bed.
Hurt,James,	1	4	Ch.Cy.
Hurt,James,	1	3	Cul.
Hurt,James,	1		Bed.
Hurt,John,	1	5	Caro.
Hurt,Joseph,	1		Henry
Hurt,Moses,	1	2	Bed.
Hurt,Nathan,	1		Bed.
Hurt,William,	1		Bed.
Hurt,William,	1		Cul.

Name			County
Hunsecker,Christian,	1		Berk.
Husk,Michael,	1		Fay.
Husky,Fredrick,	1	1	Brun.
Husky,John,	1	2	Brun.
Husky,William,	1		Brun.
Huson,Elizabeth,			Eli.Cy
Huson,William,	1		York
Huson,William,	1		Eli.Cy
Huson,William,			Eli.Cy
Hussey,Isaac,	1		Lou.
Hussey,Thomas,	1	3	Lou.
Hust,Christopher,	2		Bot.
Hust,Miller,			Bot.
Hustleman,Michael,	1		Lou.
Huston,Nathan,	1		Lin.
Huston,Robert,	1		Wash.
Huston,Samuel,	1		Wash.
Huston,Stephen,	1	1	Lin.
Huston,William,	1		Aug.
Huston,William,	1	1	Wash.
Hutchens,Benjamin,	1	3	Gooch
Hutchens,John,	2		Hen.
Hutchens,Strang,		2	Gooch
Hutcherson,Charles,	1	1	Spots
Hutcherson,James,	2	3	Spots
Hutcherson,John,	1	2	Spots
Hutcherson,Thomas,	1		Spots
Hutcherson,William,	1	3	Spots
Hutcherson,William,	1		Spots
Hutcheson,Charles,	1	11	K.&Q.
Hutcheson,James,	1		Bot.
Hutcheson,John,			Bot.
Hutcheson,John,	2	2	Caro.
Hutcheson,John,Jr.,	1	1	Acco.
Hutcheson,John,Sr.,	1	10	Acco.
Hutcheson,Joseph,			Lou.
Hutcheson,Margaret,		2	Acco.
Hutcheson,Peter,	1		Mont.
Hutcheson,Robert,	1		Bot.
Hutcheson,Robert,	2	2	Acco.
Hutcheson,Thomas,	1		Bot.
Hutcheson,William,	2	4	Lou.
Hutcheson,William,	1		Camp.
Hutchings,Ambrose,	1		Henry
Hutchings,Bozwell,	1		Din.
Hutchings,Charles,	1		Din.
Hutchings,Mrs.Eliz.,		4	So'n.
Hutchings,John,	1	2	Gooch
Hutchings,John,	1	6	West.
Hutchings,Strange,	1	4	Gooch
Hutchins,Robert,			Lou.
Hutchinson,Paul,	1		Henry
Hutchinson,Richard,	1		Henry
Hutchinson,Sarah,	1		Henry
Hutchinson,Andrew,	1	1	Lou.
Hutchison,B.,	1		Pr.Wm
Hutchison,Benjamin,Jr	1	1	Lou.
Hutchison,Benjamin,Sr	2	1	Lou.
Hutchison,George,			Aug.
Hutchison,Isaac,	1	2	Lou.
Hutchison,Jeremiah,Jr	1		Lou.
Hutchison,Jeremiah,Sr	1	8	Lou.
Hutchison,John,Jr.,	1		Lou.
Hutchison,Joseph,			Lou.
Hutchison,Joseph,	1	10	Lou.
Hutchison,Joseph,		2	Lou.
Hutchison,Lewis,	1	2	Lou.
Hutchison,R.,	1	2	Pr.Wm
Hutchison,Robert,	1		Aug.
Hutchison,S.,			Pr.Wm
Hutchison,Samuel,	1	1	Lou.
Hutchison,Sarah,			Aug.
Hutchison,Thomas,	1		Lou.
Hutchison,Thomas,	1		Lou.
Hutchison,Thomas,	1	2	Lin.
Hutchison,William,	1	1	Aug.
Hutchison,William,			Lou.
Hutchison,William,	1	5	Lou.
Hutson,Jesse,	1	2	Nor.
Hutson,Richard,	1	6	Caro.
Hutt,Caty,	1	16	West.
Hutt,Garrard Robinson	1	6	West.
Hutt,Joseph,	1	1	K.Geo.
Hutt,William,	1	14	West.
Hutten,Isaac,	1	1	Har.
Hutten,Moses,	3	10	Har.
Hutton,Jacob,	1	1	Har.
Hutton,James,	1		Wash.
Hutton,John,	1		Berk.
Hutton,Joseph,	1		Lou.
Huyford,John,Sr.,	2	8	Lou.
Huyford,John,Jr.,			Lou.
Hyde,Richard,	1	5	Brun.
Hyde,Robert,			York
Hylton,Daniel L.,	2	31	Hen.
Hylton,John,	1	20	Ch.Cy
Hyzer,John,	1		Aug.
Iddings,David,	1		Bot.
Iddings,James,	1		Bot.
Iden,Jacob,			Lou.
Iden,John,	1		Lou.
Iden,Samuel,Sr.,	2		Lou.
Iman,Christopher,	2		Har.
Inman,Elisha,	1		Bed.
Inman,William,	1		Bed.
Immerson,Walter,	1		Acco.
Inge,Betty,			Din.
Inge,Elizabeth,		9	K.Wm.
Inge,Vincent,	1		Din.
Ingle,John,	1		Berk.
Ingle,Michael,	1		Berk.
Ingle,Michael,	1		Berk.
Ingle,Philip,	1		Berk.
Ingle,Rachel,	3		Buck.
Ingledove,William,	1		Mont.
Ingledue,Blackstone,	1		Lou.
Ingleman,Jacob,	1		Lin.
Ingles,John,	1		Mont.
Inglis,Thomas,	1	2	Mont.
Inglis,William,	1	10	Mont.
Ingram,Abraham,Sr.,	1		Aug.
Ingram,Andrew,	1		Mont.
Ingram,Bartholomew,	1	9	Brun.
Ingram,Benjamin,	1	21	Brun.
Ingram,Charles,	1		Lun.
Ingram,James,	1	1	Henry
Ingram,Jonathan,	1		Mont.
Ingram,John,	1	11	Lun.
Ingram,John,	1		Henry
Ingram,John,Sr.,	1	16	Brun.
Ingram,John,	2	2	Brun.
Ingram,John,	1	6	Brun.
Ingram,Joseph,	1	3	Brun.
Ingram,Joseph,	1	9	Brun.
Ingram,Joseph,Jr.,	1	1	Brun.
Ingram,Moses,	1	12	Brun.
Ingram,Richard,	1	11	Lun.
Ingram,Robert,Estate,		5	Lun.
Ingram,Thomas,	2	5	Brun.
Ingram,William,	1		So'n.
Innes,Harry,	1	13	Bed.
Innes,Hugh,	1	15	Henry
Innis,John,			Lin.
Innis,William,	1		Caro.
Innis,John,	1	7	Din.
Inskeep,William,	1		Cul.
Inskip,Abraham,	2		Har.
Inscip,James,	1		Har.
Insminger,John,Sr.,	1		Bot.
Irby,Douglas,	1		Camp.
Irby,Elizabeth,		4	Ch.Cy.
Irby,Francis,	1	20	Ch.Cy.
Irby,Hardyman,	1	2	Ch.Cy.
Irby,John,	1	7	Ch.Cy.
Irby,John,		4	Ch.Cy.
Irby,Littleberry,	1	1	Ch.Cy.
Ireson,Elizabeth,			K.&Q.
Ireson,Frances,			K.&Q.
Ireson,Lucy,			K.&Q.
Ireson,Mary,			K.&Q.
Ireson,Reubin,			K.&Q.
Ireson,William,			K.&Q.
Irion,Philip Jacob,	1	5	Bed.
Iron,Charles,	1		Henry
Ironmonger,John,	1	1	Caro.
Ironmonger,Robert,	1		Fau.
Ironmunger,Jacob,	1		Acco.
Irvin,Joseph,	1		Fay.
Irvin,James,	1		Aug.
Irvine,Christopher,	1		Camp.
Irvine,David,	1	18	Camp.
Irvine,Jonas,	1		Bea.
Irvine,Miss Nancy,		3	Bea.
Irving,Charles,	3	3	Hen.
Irwin,Francis,	1	9	Cul.
Irwin,Richard,	1		Berk.
Irwin,William,	1		Berk.
Isaac,Luckett,			Pr.Wm.
Isaacs,Isaiah,	2	5	Hen.
Isaacs,John,	1		Lin.
Isbell,Christopher,	1		Gooch.
Isbell,George,	1		Berk.
Isbell,George,		5	Caro.
Isbell,James,	1		Gooch.
Isbell,Joseph,	1	3	Loui.
Isbell,Lewis,	1		Gooch.
Isbell,William,	1	9	Gooch.
Iseman,George,	1		Lou.
Isham,Jonathan,	1	1	Mont.
Islor,Henry,	1		Berk.
Islor,Jacob,	1		Berk.
Islor,Jacob,	1		Berk.
Ison,William,	1		Henry
Ivey,George,	1	9	So'n.
Ivey,Henry,	1	15	So'n.
Ivey,John,	1		Lou.
Ivey,John,	1		So'n.
Ivey,John,	1	4	So'n.
Ivey,Joshua,	1	7	Pr.Geo.
Ivey,Philip,	1		Lou.
Ivey,Robert,	1	1	So'n.
Ivey,Sarah,		1	So'n.
Ivy,Benjamin,Sr.,	2	1	Brun.
Ivy,Benjamin,Jr.,	1	1	Brun.
Ivy,Francis,			Brun.
Ivy,Peter,			Brun.
Ivy,William,	1		Brun.
Jack,Samuel,	1		Bea.
Jack,James,	1		Berk.
Jack,James,Jr.,	1		Berk.
Jackman,Jane,		1	Lin.
Jackman,John,	1		Lin.
Jackman,Joseph,	1	3	Fau.
Jackman,Richard,	1	5	Lin.
Jackman,Thomas,	1		Fau.
Jackman,William,	1		Fau.
Jacks,Richard,	1		Henry
Jackson,Abell,	1		Bed.
Jackson,Abner,	1	4	Din.
Jackson,Ambrose,	1	2	K.Wm.
Jackson,Ann,		2	York
Jackson,Anne,		23	Cul.
Jackson,Benjamin,	1		Brun.
Jackson,Charles,	1	6	Loui.
Jackson,Chris-Mac.,	2		Bot.
Jackson,Congrave,	1	8	Bed.

Jackson,Daniel,	1	3	Din.	Jacob,Vinaine,	1		Bot.	Janney,Jonas,	1		Lou.
Jackson,David,	1		Aug.	Jacobs,William,	1	1	Fau.	Janney,Joseph,	1		Lou.
Jackson,David,	1		Ch.Cy.	Jacoby,Francis,	1		Cul.	Janney,William,	1		Lou.
Jackson,Druery,	1		Cul.	Jactn,Samuel,	1		Rock.	January,James,	1		Fay.
Jackson,Edward,	1		Din.	Jactn,William,	1		Rock.	Jarmans,Michael,	1		Fau.
Jackson,Ephraem,	1	3	Brun.	Jameison,Benjamin,	1	2	Pr.Wm.	Jarrall,Stith,			Ch.Cy.
Jackson,Ephram,	1	1	Brun.	Jameison,David,Sr.,	1	7	Pr.Wm.	Jarrard,William,	1	4	Fau.
Jackson,Fips,	1	3	K.Wm.	Jameison,David,Jr.,	1	1	Pr.Wm.	Jarrell,Alexander,	1		Cul.
Jackson,Frances,		5	West.	Jameison,William,	1	2	Pr.Wm.	Jarrell,Daniel,	1	1	Cul.
Jackson,Francis,Sr.,	1	2	Pr.Wm.	James,Cary,	1	1	Brun.	Jarrell,James,		2	Caro.
Jackson,George,	1	1	Pr.Wm.	James,Daniel,	1		Bed.	Jarrell,JarrellFitz	1		Bed.
Jackson,Henry,Sr.,			Brun.	James,David,	1		Lou.	Jarrell,Joshua,	1		Cul.
Jackson,Henry,Jr.,	2	29	Brun.	James,Dinah,		19	Fau.	Jarrell,Mrs.Mary,		21	So'n.
Jackson,Jacob,			Wash.	James,Elias,	1		Lou.	Jarrell,William,	1		Cul.
Jackson,James,	1	1	Din.	James,Elisha,	1		York	Jarrett,Rev.Deveraux	1	24	Din.
Jackson,James,	1		Hen.	James,Francis,	1		Fau.	Jarrill,Elizabeth,			Cul.
Jackson,James,	1		Lou.	James,George,	1	2	Cul.	Jarriott,Archelus,	1	8	Gooch.
Jackson,Jarvis,	1	2	Bed.	James,George,	1	5	Fau.	Jarriott,David,	1	3	Gooch.
Jackson,Joel,	1	3	Din.	James,Hezekiah,	1	11	Nor.	Jarriott,Devereux,	1	4	Gooch.
Jackson,John,	1	3	Aug.	James,Jacob,	1	1	Lou.	Jarrott,Adah,			Lun.
Jackson,John,	1		Bed.	James,John,	2		Berk.	Jarrott,John,			Lun.
Jackson,John,	1	2	Berk.	James,John,	1	4	Caro.	Jarrott,Thomas,Sr.,	1	1	Lun.
Jackson,John,	1		Berk.	James,John,	1	3	Fau.	Jarrott,Thomas,Jr.,	1		Lun.
Jackson,John,	1		Ch.Cy.	James,John,	1	8	Fau.	Jarvis,Alexander,	1		Henry
Jackson,John,	1		Cul.	James,John,			Hen.	Jarvis,George,	1	2	Eli.Cy.
Jackson,John,	1	3	Din.	James,John,	1	16	Ja.Cy.	Jarvis,John,	1	2	York
Jackson,John,	1	1	Din.	James,John,	1	10	Lin.	Jarvis,Thomas,	1		Aug.
Jackson,John,	2	1	Lin.	James,John,	1	5	So'n.	Jasper,John,	1		Aug.
Jackson,John,	1		Lou.	James,John,Sr.,	1		Mont.	Javiss,William,	1	13	Nor.
Jackson,John,	1		Lou.	James,Jonathon,	1		Lou.	Jean,John,	1		Pr.Geo.
Jackson,John,	1		So'n.	James,Joseph,	2	11	Cul.	Jean,Luvisa,			Pr.Geo.
Jackson,John,	1	2	Pr.Wm.	James,Joseph,	2	9	Fau.	Jeeter,Henry,	1	1	Bed.
Jackson,Jonathan,	1	5	West.	James,Joseph,	1		Lou.	Jeffers,James,	1		Ja.Cy.
Jackson,Joseph,	1	4	Din.	James,Mary,	1	12	Cul.	Jefferies,Sarah,			Buck.
Jackson,Joseph,	1	2	Fau.	James,Mary,			K.&Q.	Jefferies,William,			Buck.
Jackson,Joseph,	2	8	Lin.	James,Mary,			So'n.	Jefferson,Elizabeth	1	8	Lun.
Jackson,Joshua,	1	2	Cul.	James,Micheal,	1		Nor.	Jefferson,Luke,	1		Har.
Jackson,Mark,	1	12	Brun.	James,Peter,	1		York	Jefferson,Randolph,		30	Buck.
Jackson,Mary,		2	Din.	James,Richara,	1		Lou.	Jefferson,Thomas,		31	Bed.
Jackson,Nathan,	1		So'n.	James,Col.Richard,	1	7	Loui.	Jefferson,Thomas,	1	37	Gooch.
Jackson,Patience,	2		So'n.	James,Richard,	1	5	Nor.	Jefferson,William,	1		Fau.
Jackson,Ralph,	1	7	Din.	James,Sarah,	1		Acco.	Jeffries,Alexander,	1	1	Fau.
Jackson,Ralph,Jr.,	1	3	Din.	James,Sherid,	1		Mont.	Jeffries,Alex.,Jr.,	1		Fau.
Jackson,Richard,	1		Lou.	James,Thomas,	1		Berk.	Jeffries,Ambrose,	1	12	K.&Q.
Jackson,Richard,	1	20	West.	James,Thomas,	1		Fau.	Jeffries,Andrew,	1		Brun.
Jackson,Robert,	1		Berk.	James,Thomas,	1	1	Fau.	Jeffries,Bowker,	1		K.&Q.
Jackson,Robert,	1		Berk.	James,Thomas,	1	21	Nor.	Jeffries,Edward,	1		K.&Q.
Jackson,Robert,	1	3	Din.	James,Walter,			West.	Jeffries,Edward,Jr.	1		K.&Q.
Jackson,Robert,	1		Lou.	James,William,	1		Acco.	Jeffries,James,	1	2	Fau.
Jackson,Samuel,	1		Berk.	James,William,	1	3	Brun.	Jeffries,James,	1	1	Lun.
Jackson,Samuel,	1	10	Pr.Wm.	James,William,	1	16	Ja.Cy.	Jeffries,John,	1		Brun.
Jackson,Samuel,Jr.,	1	4	Pr.Wm.	James,William,	1		Lou.	Jeffries,Joseph,	2	7	Fau.
Jackson,Samuel,Estate		1	West.	Jameson,Benjamin,	1		Lou.	Jefferies,Moses,	1		Berk.
Jackson,Sarah,		1	Lun.	Jameson,David,	2	3	Cul.	Jeffries,Moses,	1	5	Pr.Wm.
Jackson,Thomas,	1	7	Brun.	Jameson,David,	1		Fay.	Jeffries,Mourning,			K.&Q.
Jackson,Thomas,	1	10	Brun.	Jameson,James,	1	1	Fay.	Jeffries,Nathaniel,	2	7	Buck.
Jackson,Thomas,	2	19	Loui.	Jameson,John,	1		Fay.	Jeffries,Thomas,			K.&Q.
Jackson,Thomas,Jr.,			Loui.	Jameson,Robert,	1	1	Fay.	Jeffries,Thomas,		2	Lun.
Jackson,William,	1	3	Ch.Cy.	Jameson,Robert,	1		Rock.	Jelks,Richard,	1	7	So'n.
Jackson,William,	1	4	Din.	Jameson,Thomas,	2	10	Fay.	Jenings,Charles,	3	6	Eli.Cy.
Jackson,William,	1		Lou.	Jamison,David,	2	29	York	Jenings,Thomas,	1	6	Eli.Cy.
Jackson,William,	1	7	Loui.	Jamison,David,Jr.,	1	23	Caro.	Jenings,William,	1	3	Eli.Cy.
Jackson,William,	2	48	Spots.	Jamison,George,	1	2	Aug.	Jenkins,Aaron,	1		Lou.
Jackson,William,	1	2	Spots.	Jamison,James,	1		Ja.Cy.	Jenkins,Christian,			So'n.
Jacob,William,	1	12	Nor.	Jamison,John,	1	1	Henry	Jenkins,Edward,	1		Henry
Jacobs,Ann,			Cul.	Jamison,John,	1	1	Henry	Jenkins,Ezechiel,	2		Lou.
Jacobs,George,	1		Fau.	Jamison,John,	1		Rock.	Jenkins,George,	1		Berk.
Jacob,Hancock,Jr.,	1	13	Nor.	Jamison,Thomas,	1	2	Henry	Jenkins,Henry,	1	9	Eli.Cy.
Jacob,Hancock,Sr.,	1	9	Nor.	Jamison,William,	1	1	Henry	Jenkins,Henry,	1	6	Lou.
Jacobs,Jacob,	1		Lou.	Jamison,William,	1		Rock.	Jenkins,Isaac,	1		Lou.
Jacobs,John,		1	Fau.	Jams,John,	1		Berk.	Jenkins,James,	1		Eli.Cy.
Jacobs,Price,			Cul.	Jane,Joseph,	1		Har.	Jenkins,James,	1		Lou.
Jacobs,Samuel,	1		Har.	Janel,Richard,	1		Cul.	Jenkins,John,	1		Berk.
Jacobs,Thomas,	2	21	Acco.	Janney,Amos,	1		Lou.	Jenkins,John,	1		Buck.
Jacobs,Thomas,	1	3	Fau.	Janney,Israel,	1		Lou.	Jenkins,John,	1	3	Lou.
Jacob,Thomas,	1		Nor.	Janney,Jacob,Sr.,	1		Lou.	Jenkins,Obediah,			Buck.

Name			Loc.	Name			Loc.	Name			Loc.
Jenkins,Richard,	1		Eli.Cy	Jewill,William,	1		Cul.	Johnson,Benjamin,	1		Camp.
Jenkins,Richard,	1	1	Lou.	Jiles,Frederick,			Lou.	Johnson,Benjamin,	1		Fay.
Jenkins,Robert,	1		Lou.	Jinkins,Abraham,			Cul.	Johnson,Benjamin,	1	4	Gooch.
Jenkins,Rollin,	1		Wash.	Jinkins,Amos,	1		Bed.	Johnson,Benjamin,	1	7	Gooch.
Jenkins,Samuel,	1	1	Lou.	Jinkins,Charles,	1		Spots.	Johnson,Benjamin,			Gooch.
Jenkins,Spencer,	1	8	So'n.	Jinkins,Gipson,	1	1	Spots.	Johnson,Benjamin,	1	11	Hen.
Jenkins,Stephen,	1		Lou.	Jinkins,Jeremiah,	1		Bed.	Johnson,Benjamin,Jr			Hen.
Jenkins,Thomas,	1		Fau.	Jinkins,John,	1		Cul.	Johnson,Benjamin,	1	14	K.Geo.
Jenkins,Thomas,	1		Lou.	Jinkins,John,	1	2	Cul.	Johnson,Benjamin,	1	13	K.Wm.
Jenkins,Thomas,	1		West.	Jinkins,John,	1		Henry	Johnson,Benjamin,	2		Lou.
Jenkins,Timothy,	1		Cul.	Jinkins,John,	1		Mont.	Johnson,Benjamin,	1	2	Loui.
Jenkins,Valentine,	1	4	So'n.	Jinkins,John,	1	8	Spots.	Johnson,Charity,		5	So'n.
Jenkins,William,	3		Fay.	Jinkins,John,Jr.,			Spots.	Johnson,Charles,	1		Camp.
Jenkins,William,	1		Lou.	Jinkins,Jonas,	1		Cul.	Johnson,Charles,	1	9	Gooch.
Jenkins,William,			Lou.	Jinkins,Lewis,	1	4	Henry	Johnson,Charles,	1	6	Gooch.
Jenkins,William,	1	1	Lou.	Jinkins,Richard,	1		Cul.	Johnson,Charles,	1	1	Pr.Wm.
Jenkins,William,	1	1	Lou.	Jinkins,Richard,	1		Cul.	Johnson,Charles,Jr.	1	1	Gooch.
Jenkins,William,	1	1	West.	Jinkins,Richard,Jr.,	1		Cul.	Johnson,Christopher,	1		Camp.
Jennet,James,	1		Hen.	Jinkins,Richard,Sr.,	1		Cul.	Johnson,Christopher,	1		Camp.
Jennett,Thomas,	1	5	Hen.	Jinkins,Thomas,	1		K.Geo.	Johnson,Christopher,	1	8	Loui.
Jenney,William,	1	1	Har.	Jinkins,William,	1	1	Henry	Johnson,Council,	1		So'n.
Jenney,William,	2	15	Nor.	Jinkins,William,	1	1	Spots.	Johnson,Daniel,	1	1	Caro.
Jennings,Augustin,	1	7	Fau.	Jinkins,William,			Spots.	Johnson,Daniel,	1	2	Gooch.
Jennings,Bales,	1	4	Fau.	Jinkins,William,Sr.,	1		Spots.	Johnson,David,	1	7	Brun.
Jennings,Daniel,	2	7	Lou.	Jinnings,Augustine,	1		Cul.	Johnson,David,	1		Camp.
Jennings,James,	1	10	Din.	Jinnings,Joshua,	1	5	Cul.	Johnson,David,	1		Fau.
Jennings,James,	1	15	Lou.	Jinnings,Thomas,	1	3	Spots.	Johnson,David,	1	2	Gooch.
Jennings,Jesse,	1		Camp.	Jock,George,	1		Har.	Johnson,David,Jr.,	1	4	Gooch.
Jennings,Jesse,	1		Hen.	Jock,Jeremiah,	1		Har.	Johnson,David,	1		Hen.
Jennings,Lewis,	1	10	Fau.	Joel,Ann,			Berk.	Johnson,David,	1	40	Loui.
Jennings,Miles,	2	10	Henry	John,James,	1		Berk.	Johnson,David,	2	3	Lun.
Jennings,Moody,Estate,	1	15	Loui.	John,Martha,			Lou.	Johnson,David,	1	1	Pr.Wm.
Jennings,William,	1		Buck.	John,Moses,	1		Henry	Johnson,David,	1		So'n.
Jennings,William,	1		Hen.	John,Samuel,	1		Berk.	Johnson,Densey,	1	1	So'n.
Jennings,William,	1	10	Fau.	John,William,	1		Berk.	Johnson,Edmund,	1		Lun.
Jennings,William,	1		Mont.	Johnes,John,	1		Hen.	Johnson,Edmund,	1	2	Nor.
Jerdone,Francis,			Loui.	Johns,Edmona,		4	Camp.	Johnson,Elijah,	1		Loui.
Jerdone,Sarah,	3	42	Loui.	Johns,Edmund,		4	Camp.	Johnson,Elizabeth,		6	Loui.
Jerdone,Sarah,		8	Loui.	Johns,Isiah,	1		Buck.	Johnson,Elizabeth,		6	Loui.
Jervis,James,	1		Wash.	Johns,James,	1	3	Buck.	Johnson,Fredrick,	1		Brun.
Jervis,K.,			Pr.Wm.	Johns,Jesse,			Buck.	Johnson,Gabriel,	1		K.Geo.
Jesup,Thomas,	1		Mont.	Johns,Jesse,	1	9	Buck.	Johnson,George,	1		Bed.
Jeter,Elijah,	2	14	Caro.	Johns,Jesse,	1	9	Camp.	Johnson,George,	1	3	Cul.
Jeter,Elizabeth,	2	7	Caro.	Johns,Jesse,	1	7	Camp.	Johnson,George,	1		Fau.
Jeter,Joseph,	1	2	Lun.	Johns,Jesse,	1	9	Camp.	Johnson,George,	1		Fau.
Jeter,William,	1	4	Caro.	Johns,John,	1	13	Buck.	Johnson,George,	1	3	K.Geo.
Jett,Catharine,		18	West.	Johns,Joshua,	1		Pr.Geo	Johnson,George,	2		Lou.
Jett,Edgar,			Cul.	Johns,Mary,	1	5	Caro.	Johnson,George,	1	8	Loui.
Jett,Francis,	1	1	Fau.	Johns,Robert,	1		Camp.	Johnson,George,			Loui.
Jett,Francis,	1	15	K.Geo.	Johns,Stephen,	1		Gooch.	Johnson,Gideon,			York
Jett,James,	1	5	Cul.	Johns,William,	1	9	Buck.	Johnson,Giles,	1		Ch.Cy.
Jett,James,	1	4	Fau.	Johnson,Abraham,	1	4	So'n.	Johnson,Giles,	1	1	So'n.
Jett,James,			Cul.	Johnson,Alexander,	1	1	Fau.	Johnson,Hannah,			Gooch.
Jett,John,			Cul.	Johnson,Alexander,	1		Spots.	Johnson,Hannah,			Lou.
Jett,John,	1		Cul.	Johnson,Amos,	1		Mont.	Johnson,Hardy,	1	1	So'n.
Jett,John,	2		Cul.	Johnson,Anderson,	1		K.Wm.	Johnson,Harris,	1	3	So'n.
Jett,John,	1		Fau.	Johnson,Anna,		1	Gooch.	Johnson,Henry,	1		Hen.
Jett,John,	1		Henry	Johnson,Anne,			Lun.	Johnson,Henry,	1	12	Spots.
Jett,John,	1	3	K.Geo.	Johnson,Anthony,	1		Aug.	Johnson,Isaac,	1		Berk.
Jett,John,Jr.,	1		K.Geo.	Johnson,Aquilla,	2	21	Spots.	Johnson,Isaac,			Brun.
Jett,Peter,	1	4	K.Geo.	Johnson,Aquilla,Jr.,	1	9	Spots.	Johnson,Isaac,			Fau.
Jett,Peter,	1	11	K.Geo.	Johnson,Archibald,	2	2	K.&c.	Johnson,Isaac,	1	12	Lun.
Jett,Steven,			Cul.	Johnson,Arwalker,			Fay.	Johnson,Isaac,	2		So'n.
Jett,Thomas,	1		Pr.Wm.	Johnson,Arthur,	1		Brun.	Johnson,Isham,	1		Gooch.
Jett,Thomas,	2	43	West.	Johnson,Ashley,	1		Camp.	Johnson,Jacob,	1		Cul.
Jett,William,	1		Cul.	Johnson,Bailey,	2	8	Fau.	Johnson,Jacob,	1		Fau.
Jett,William,	3	7	Cul.	Johnson,Baldwin,		1	West.	Johnson,Jacob,	1		Gooch.
Jett,William,	1		Fau.	Johnson,Barthuell,	1		Acco.	Johnson,Jacob,	1		Henry
Jett,William,	1		Fau.	Johnson,Beede,	1	3	Fau.	Johnson,Jacob,	1	2	So'n.
Jett,William,	1		Fau.	Johnson,Benjamin,	1	8	Bed.	Johnson,Jacob,	1	3	So'n.
Jett,William,Jr.,	1	8	West.	Johnson,Benjamin,Jr.	1		Bed.	Johnson,James,	1		Berk.
Jewel,Tabby,		1	Aug.	Johnson,Benjamin,			Brun.	Johnson,James,	2		Brun.
Jewell,Ewell,	1	1	Pr.Wm.	Johnson,Benjamin,	1	5	Brun.	Johnson,James,	1	3	Brun.
Jewell,George,			Pr.Wm.	Johnson,Benjamin,	1	14	Brun.	Johnson,James,	1		Camp.
Jewell,Presly,	1		Pr.Wm.	Johnson,Benjamin,	1	2	Camp.	Johnson,James,	1		Ch.Cy.
Jewell,William,	1		Pr.Wm.					Johnson,James,	1	10	Din.

Name			Place	Name			Place	Name			Place
Johnson,James,	3	2	Fay.	Johnson,Obediance,Sr.	1	12	Nor.	Johnston,Benjamin,	1	3	Caro.
Johnson,James,	1		Gooch.	Johnson,Pabuck,			Bed.	Johnston,Daniel,	1	1	Caro.
Johnson,James,	1		Gooch.	Johnson,Patrick,	1		Mont.	Johnston,David,	1		Mont.
Johnson,James,	1	12	K.Wm.	Johnson,Philip,	1	28	Ja.Cy.	Johnston,David,	1		Mont.
Johnson,James,Jr.,	1	6	K.Wm.	Johnson,Philip,	1	1	K.Wm.	Johnston,Elizabeth,		4	Caro.
Johnson,James,	1	6	Loui.	Johnson,Pricilla,		8	Nor.	Johnston,Emanuel,	1		Hen.
Johnson,James,	1	13	Loui.	Johnson,R.,			Pr.Wm.	Johnston,Eneas,	1		Mont.
Johnson,James,	1	1	Lun.	Johnson,Rebecca,		3	Ja.Cy.	Johnston,George,	1	6	Brun.
Johnson,James,			Mont.	Johnson,Richard,	1	8	Gooch.	Johnston,Hugh,			Wash.
Johnson,James,	1		Pr.Wm.	Johnson,Richard,	1		K.Wm.	Johnston,J.,	1		Pr.Wm.
Johnson,James,	1		So'n.	Johnson,Richard,	1	14	Loui.	Johnston,James,	1	12	Caro.
Johnson,James,	1	1	York	Johnson,Richard,	1	2	Loui.	Johnston,James,	1		Mont.
Johnson,Jane,		4	Nor.	Johnson,Roland,			Lun.	Johnston,James,	1		Rock.
Johnson,Jeffrey,Sr.,	1		Fau.	Johnson,Robert,	1		Bed.	Johnston,James,	1		Rock.
Johnson,Jesse,	1		So'n.	Johnson,Robert,	1		Har.	Johnston,James,	1		Wash.
Johnson,Jessie,	1		Lun.	Johnson,Robert,	1		Fay.	Johnston,Jedediah,	2	5	Caro.
Johnson,Joannas,	1		Nor.	Johnson,Robert,	1		Lou.	Johnston,John,	2	3	Bot.
Johnson,John,	1		Acco.	Johnson,Robert,	1	16	Fay.	Johnston,John,	2	14	Caro.
Johnson,John,	1		Aug.	Johnson,Samuel,	1		Aug.	Johnston,John,	1		Mont.
Johnson,John,	1		Bed.	Johnson,Samuel,	1		Bot.	Johnston,John,	1	2	Mont.
Johnson,John,	1	1	Berk.	Johnson,Samuel,	2	5	Fay.	Johnston,Joseph,	1		Fay.
Johnson,John,	1		Berk.	Johnson,Samuel,	1	4	Henry	Johnston,&Lindsey,	2	17	Caro.
Johnson,John,			Bot.	Johnson,Samuel,	1	9	K.Geo.	Johnston,Moses,	1		Bot.
Johnson,John,	1	4	Brun.	Johnson,Samuel,	1	8	Nor.	Johnston,Patrick,	1		Har.
Johnson,John,			Cul.	Johnson,Samuel,	1	8	Nor.	Johnston,Phillip,	1	12	Caro.
Johnson,John,	1	5	Cul.	Johnson,Sarah,		3	Gooch.	Johnston,Reuben,	2		Caro.
Johnson,John,	1	1	Fau.	Johnson,Shadrach,	1		So'n.	Johnston,Reuben,	1		Wash.
Johnson,John,	3		Fay.	Johnson,Silas,	2		Fay.	Johnston,Richard,	1	20	Caro.
Johnson,John,	1		Fay.	Johnson,Smith,	1	3	Fau.	Johnston,Robert,	1	11	Caro.
Johnson,John,	1	8	Gooch.	Johnson,Stephen,	1		Lun.	Johnston,Robert,	1		Lou.
Johnson,John,	2		Har.	Johnson,Stephen,	1	2	So'n.	Johnston,Samuel,	1	1	Lin.
Johnson,John,	1	5	Hen.	Johnson,Stephen,	2	30	Spots.	Johnston,William,	1		Bot.
Johnson,John,			Hen.	Johnson,Susanah,		7	Lun.	Johnston,William,	1	4	Bot.
Johnson,John,	1	1	K.Geo.	Johnson,Tabitha,		2	Nor.	Jolley,Benjamin,	2		Fau.
Johnson,John,	1		K.Geo.	Johnson,Maj.Thomas,	1	17	Loui.	Jolly,David,	1		Fay.
Johnson,John,	1		Lin.	Johnson,Thomas,	1	3	Acco.	Jolly,Edward,	1		Din.
Johnson,John,	1		Lin.	Johnson,Thomas,	2		Brun.	Jolly,John,	1		Din.
Johnson,John,	1		Loui.	Johnson,Thomas,	1	6	Brun.	Jolly,Thomas,	1	1	Hen.
Johnson,John,	1		Pr.Wm.	Johnson,Thomas,	1	11	Cul.	Jonas,Sturdy,	1		Bot.
Johnson,John,	1		Spots.	Johnson,Thomas,	1	2	Din.	Jones,Aaron,	1	3	Cul.
Johnson,John,	1	10	So'n.	Johnson,Thomas,	1		Fau.	Jones,Abraham,	1		Ja.Cy.
Johnson,John,	1	2	So'n.	Johnson,Thomas,	1	37	Loui.	Jones,Abraham,	1		Mont.
Johnson,John,	1		So'n.	Johnson,Thomas,	1	37	Loui.	Jones,Abraham,	1		Mont.
Johnson,John,	1	1	So'n.	Johnson,Thomas,	1		Loui.	Jones,Abraham,Sr.,	4		Buck.
Johnson,John,			York	Johnson,Thomas,	1	14	Loui.	Jones,Abraham,Jr.,	1		Buck.
Johnson,John,Jr.,	1		So'n.	Johnson,Thomas,	1		Mont.	Jones,Albrigton,	1	26	So'n.
Johnson,John,Sr.,		1	K.Geo.	Johnson,Tunis,	1	3	Fau.	Jones,Albrigton,		11	So'n.
Johnson,Johnson,	1		Mont.	Johnson,Col.William,			Loui.	Jones,Allen,	1	6	York
Johnson,Jonathan,	1		Spots.	Johnson,William,	1		Aug.	Jones,Ambrose,	4	6	Caro.
Johnson,Jordan,	1		So'n.	Johnson,William,	1		Bed.	Jones,Ambrose,	1	2	Cul.
Johnson,Joshua,	1	4	Lun.	Johnson,William,	1		Berk.	Jones,Ambrose,	1	5	Henry
Johnson,Labin,	1	1	Acco.	Johnson,William,	1	1	Brun.	Jones,Aniel,			Hen.
Johnson,Laban,	1	5	Nor.	Johnson,William,	1		Berk.	Jones,Ann,		29	Caro.
Johnson,Larkin,			Cul.	Johnson,William,	1		Camp.	Jones,Ann,		10	Loui.
Johnson,Lemon,	1		So'n.	Johnson,William,	1		Camp.	Jones,Anne,		1	Loui.
Johnson,Manark,	1		Gooch.	Johnson,William,	1		Cul.	Jones,Anselmn,	1		So'n.
Johnson,Martin,	1		Fay.	Johnson,William,		1	Fau.	Jones,Baalam,	1	2	Brun.
Johnson,Mary,		2	Lou.	Johnson,William,	1	1	Gooch.	Jones,Barnabus,	1	4	Brun.
Johnson,Mary,			So'n.	Johnson,William,	1		Henry	Jones,Benjamin,	1	20	Brun.
Johnson,Mason,	1		Lou.	Johnson,William,	2	10	K.Wm.	Jones,Benjamin,	1		Gooch.
Johnson,Mathew,	1		Loui.	Johnson,William,	1		Lou.	Jones,Benjamin,	2		Hen.
Johnson,Michael,	1	14	Hen.	Johnson,William,	1		Lou.	Jones,Benjamin,	1		Hen.
Johnson,Michael,	1		Lun.	Johnson,William,	1	4	Loui.	Jones,Benjamin,	1	7	Lun.
Johnson,Mooreman,	1		Camp.	Johnson,William,	1		Lun.	Jones,Berryman,	1		Aug.
Johnson,Mooseman,	1		Camp.	Johnson,William,	1	4	Lun.	Jones,Betty,		23	Din.
Johnson,Morris,			Lun.	Johnson,William,Jr.,	1	1	Lun.	Jones,Brereton,	1	2	Fau.
Johnson,Moses,	1	4	Fau.	Johnson,William,Jr.,	1		Lun.	Jones,Briton,			Brun.
Johnson,Moses,	1		So'n.	Johnson,William,Sr.,	1		Lun.	Jones,Brooke,	2	4	Cul.
Johnson,Moses,	1	3	So'n.	Johnson,William,	1	1	So'n.	Jones,Cadwallader,	1	12	Brun.
Johnson,Moses,			So'n.	Johnson,William,	1		So'n.	Jones,Catherine,	1	8	Cul.
Johnson,Moses,Jr.,	1	6	Brun.	Johnson,William,Jr.,	1		Brun.	Jones,Catesby,	1	18	West.
Johnson,Moses,Sr.,	2	14	Brun.	Johnson,Wm.Murrel,	1		Brun.	Jones,Charles,	1	2	West.
Johnson,Nathan,			Brun.	Johnson,Yellis,	1	2	Fau.	Jones,Chas,Grigsby,	1	3	K.Geo.
Johnson,Nathan,	1		So'n.	Johnson,Zachariah,	1	4	Aug.	Jones,Clayton,	1		K.&Q.
Johnson,Noel,	1	9	Lin.	Johnston,Andrew,	1		Mont.	Jones,Calvert,	1	1	K.Geo.
Johnson,Obediance,Jr.	1	19	Nor.	Johnston,Benjamin,	1	2	Camp.	Jones,David,	1		Berk.

Jones,David,	1	5	Din.	Jones,John,	1		Berk.	Jones,Peter,	1	40	Brun.
Jones,David,	1		Henry	Jones,John,	1		Bot.	Jones,Peter,	1		Din.
Jones,David,			K.Geo.	Jones,John,	1	7	Brun.	Jones,Peter,	2		Fau.
Jones,David,	1	2	Loui.	Jones,John,			Camp.	Jones,Peter,	1	20	Lun.
Jones,David,	1	3	Nor.	Jones,John,	1		Camp.	Jones,Peter,	1	2	Pr.Geo.
Jones,David,	1	3	So'n.	Jones,John,	1		Caro.	Jones,Phillip,	1	6	Caro.
Jones,Daniel,	1		Bot.	Jones,John,	1		Caro.	Jones,Phillip,	1	20	Din.
Jones,Daniel,	1	3	Ja.Cy.	Jones,John,	1		Din.	Jones,Phillip,		12	Din.
Jones,Edmund,	2	3	Caro.	Jones,John,	1	11	Eli.Cy	Jones,Pressley,	1	1	K.Geo.
Jones,Edmund,	1	11	Caro.	Jones,John,	1		Fau.	Jones,Prudence,		4	So'n.
Jones,Edward,	1		Mont.	Jones,John,	1	9	Fau.	Jones,Rachel,			Henry
Jones,Elizabeth,	1		Fay.	Jones,John,			Fau.	Jones,Richard,	1		Henry
Jones,Elizabeth,		5	K.&Q.	Jones,John,	1	1	Gooch.	Jones,Richard,			Mont.
Jones,Elizabeth,		5	Lun.	Jones,John,	1		Har.	Jones,Richard,	1		Rock.
Jones,Elizabeth,	1		So'n.	Jones,John,	1		Hen.	Jones,Robert,	1		Aug.
Jones,Elliott,			Fay.	Jones,John,	1		Henry	Jones,Robert,	1		Berk.
Jones,Elsey,		4	Ja.Cy.	Jones,John,	1		Henry	Jones,Robert,	1	11	Buck.
Jones,Emanuel,	1	33	K.Wm.	Jones,John,	1	1	Ja.Cy.	Jones,Robert,	2	1	Cul.
Jones,Enes,	1		Aug.	Jones,John,	1		K.Geo.	Jones,Robert,	1		Henry
Jones,Evan,	1		Mont.	Jones,John,	1		K.Geo.	Jones,Robert,	1		Henry
Jones,Evin,	1		Fay.	Jones,John,	1		Lin.	Jones,Rodger,	1		Fay.
Jones,Evin,	1		Fay.	Jones,John,	1	12	Lin.	Jones,Rowland,	1	14	Ja.Cy.
Jones,Francis,			Fay.	Jones,John,	1	12	Lou.	Jones,Samuel,	1		Berk.
Jones,Frederick,	1	29	Din.	Jones,John,	1		Lou.	Jones,Samuel,	1		Din.
Jones,George,			Aug.	Jones,John,	1		Lou.	Jones,Samuel,	1	3	Eli.Cy.
Jones,George,	1	1	Bed.	Jones,John,	1		Mont.	Jones,Samuel,	1		Fau.
Jones,George,	1		Berk.	Jones,John,			Pr.Wm.	Jones,Samuel,	1		Fau.
Jones,George,			Henry	Jones,John,	1		Rock.	Jones,Samuel,	1		Har.
Jones,George,	1		K.Geo.	Jones,John,	1		Rock.	Jones,Samuel,	1	3	Hen.
Jones,George,			K.Wm.	Jones,John,	1		Wash.	Jones,Samuel,	1	5	Hen.
Jones,George,	1		Pr.Wm.	Jones,John Anthony,	1	18	Buck.	Jones,Sarah,			Ja.Cy.
Jones,George,Sr.,	1		Pr.Wm.	Jones,Col.John,	1	30	Brun.	Jones,Sarah,			Lun.
Jones,Giles,	1		Fay.	Jones,Col.John,	1	12	Din.	Jones,Shardrack,			Lun.
Jones,Grace,	3	9	Fay.	Jones,John,Sr.,	2	24	Buck.	Jones,Solomon,	1	8	Pr.Wm.
Jones,Henry,	1		Brun.	Jones,John,Jr.,	1	11	Buck.	Jones,Stephen,	1	7	Brun.
Jones,Henry,	1		Fau.	Jones,John,Jr.,	3	69	Din.	Jones,Stephen,	1		Mont.
Jones,Henry,	1	4	Fau.	Jones,John Robt.Est.		9	Brun.	Jones,Thomas,	1	21	Camp.
Jones,Henry,	1	6	Henry	Jones,Jonathan,	1		Cul.	Jones,Maj.Thomas,	1	21	Camp.
Jones,Henry,			Lou.	Jones,Jordan,	1	4	So'n.	Jones,Thomas,	1	7	Caro.
Jones,Henry,	1	3	So'n.	Jones,Joseph,	2	10	Caro.	Jones,Thomas,	1	1	Caro.
Jones,Hannah,			Wash.	Jones,Joseph,	1		Cul.	Jones,Thomas,	1	11	Caro.
Jones,Harrison,	1	1	Gooch.	Jones,Col.Joseph,	1	10	Din.	Jones,Thomas,	1	12	Caro.
Jones,Isaiah,	1		Lou.	Jones,Joseph,	1	15	Din.	Jones,Thomas,			Cul.
Jones,Jabee,	1		Lou.	Jones,Joseph,	1		Henry	Jones,Thomas,	1		Bed.
Jones,Jabesh,	1		Mont.	Jones,Joseph,	1	25	K.Geo.	Jones,Thomas,	1	13	Brun.
Jones,James,	1	8	Brun.	Jones,Joseph,	1		Mont.	Jones,Thomas,	1		Buck.
Jones,James,	1	8	Caro.	Jones,Joseph,		19	Spots.	Jones,Thomas,	1		Fay.
Jones,James,	1	2	Caro.	Jones,Joshua,	1		Lou.	Jones,Thomas,	1		Henry
Jones,James,			Din.	Jones,Josias,	1	19	Buck.	Jones,Thomas,	1	1	Henry
Jones,James,	1		Fau.	Jones,Julias,	1		Bed.	Jones,Thomas,			K.Geo.
Jones,James,	1		Fay.	Jones,Kennon,	1	30	Din.	Jones,Thomas,			K.&Q.
Jones,James,	1		Ja.Cy.	Jones,Leah,		1	K.Wm.	Jones,Thomas,	1	15	K.Wm.
Jones,James,	1		Ja.Cy.	Jones,Lemuel,	1	7	So'n.	Jones,Thomas,	1		Loui.
Jones,James,	1		K.Geo.	Jones,Levy,	1		Henry	Jones,Thomas,			Lun.
Jones,James,	1	9	K.&Q.	Jones,Lewis,	1		Caro.	Jones,Thomas,	1	14	Lun.
Jones,James,Estate,		10	K.&Q.	Jones,Lewis,	1	4	Din.	Jones,Thomas,	1		Mont.
Jones,James,	1		K.Wm.	Jones,Lucretia,	1	8	Lun.	Jones,Thomas,	1		Spots.
Jones,James,	1	1	Lou.	Jones,Lucy,			Ja.Cy	Jones,Thomas,	1	1	Spots.
Jones,James,	1	3	Loui.	Jones,Munitree,	1	1	Mont.	Jones,Taviner,			Cul.
Jones,James,	1		Lun.	Jones,Margarett,	1		K.Geo.	Jones,Theophiles,			Cul.
Jones,James,	1	4	Lun.	Jones,Mary,		1	Din.	Jones,Thomas,Sr.,	1	15	Camp.
Jones,James,	1		Pr.Wm.	Jones,Mary,			Lou.	Jones,Thomas,Sr.,	1	15	Camp.
Jones,James,	1	10	So'n.	Jones,Mrs.Mary,		2	So'n.	Jones,Valentine,			Aug.
Jones,James,	1	1	So'n.	Jones,Matthew,	1		Brun.	Jones,William,	1		Aug.
Jones,James,Sr.,	1	1	So'n.	Jones,Matthew,	1	4	Din.	Jones,William,	1	2	Bed.
Jones,James,		8	Spots.	Jones,Matthew,	1		So'n.	Jones,William,	1		Berk.
Jones,James,	1	1	Spots.	Jones,Matthew,	1	1	So'n.	Jones,William,	1		Brun.
Jones,Jesse,	1	7	Brun.	Jones,Merit,	1		Hen.	Jones,William,	1	9	Brun.
Jones,Jesse,	1	7	Camp.	Jones,Michael,		4	Buck.	Jones,William,	1	7	Camp.
Jones,Jesse,	1		K.Geo.	Jones,Michael,	1		Cul.	Jones,William,	1	7	Camp.
Jones,Joel Walker,	1		Buck.	Jones,Mordica,	1	11	Brun.	Jones,William,	1		Caro.
Jones,John,	1		Aug.	Jones,Moses,	1		Caro.	Jones,William,	1	3	Cul.
Jones,John,	1		Bed.	Jones,Mosess,	1		Cul.	Jones,William,	1	1	Cul.
Jones,John,	1		Bed.	Jones,Natt,	1	1	K.Geo	Jones,William,	1		Cul.
Jones,John,	1		Berk.	Jones,Paul,	1	42	Ch.Cy.	Jones,William,	1		Cul.
Jones,John,	1		Berk.	Jones,Maj.Peter,	1	5	Brun.	Jones,William,	2		Din.

Name			Loc.
Jones,William,	1	2	Fau.
Jones William,	1		Fau.
Jones,William,	1		Fay.
Jones,William,	1	16	Hen.
Jones,William,	1	1	Henry
Jones,William,	1		K.Geo.
Jones,William,	1	10	K.&Q
Jones,William,	1		K.&Q
Jones,William,	1	24	K.Wm.
Jones,William,			K.Wm.
Jones,William,	1	1	Lin.
Jones,William,	1		Lou.
Jones,William,			Lou.
Jones,William,	1	1	Loui.
Jones,William,	1		Mont.
Jones,William,	1	20	Pr.Geo.
Jones,William,	1	6	Pr.Geo.
Jones,William,	1		Pr.Wm.
Jones,William,	1		Rock.
Jones,William,	3	36	Spots.
Jones,William,Sr.,	1	4	Buck.
Jones,William,Sr.,	2	17	Buck.
Jones,William,Jr.,			Buck.
Jones,William,Sr.,	1	3	Fau.
Jones,William,Jr.,	1		Fau.
Jordan,Angel,			Lou.
Jordan,Benjamin,	1	8	Hen.
Jordan,Charles,	1	3	Camp.
Jordan,Edward,	1	14	Lun.
Jordan,Edward,Sr.,	1	6	Lun.
Jordan,Elizabeth,		4	Gooch.
Jordan,Fleming,	1		Hen.
Jordan,Fleming,			Hen.
Jordan,Freeman,	1	6	Brun.
Jordan,Henry,	1	1	Hen.
Jordan,James,	1	3	Brun.
Jordan,John,	1	5	Lun.
Jordan,John,	1	2	Pr.Wm.
Jordan,Josiah,	1	6	Pr.Geo.
Jordan,Lyddia,		6	Hen.
Jordan,Noble,	1	1	Hen.
Jordan,Rachel,		1	K.&Q.
Jordan,Samuel,	1	26	Buck.
Jordan,Samuel,	1	11	Lun.
Jordan,Thomas,	1	6	Hen.
Jordan,Thomas,	1		Lou.
Jordan,William,	1	7	Camp.
Jordan,William,	1	7	Camp.
Jordan,William,	1	1	K.&Q.
Jorden,Robert,	1		Caro.
Jordin,George,	1		Cul.
Jordin,Sharshell,	1	1	Cul.
Jordin,William,	1		Cul.
Jordon,Absalam,	1		Bed.
Jordon,Andrew,	1		Aug.
Jordon,George,	1		Har.
Jordon,Hezikiah,	1		Mont.
Jordon,John,			Aug.
Jordon,Jonas,	1	1	Bed.
Jordon,Joshua,	1		Har.
Jordon,William,	1		Aug.
Jordon,William,Sr.,	1		Aug.
Jordon,William,			K.&Q.
Jordone,Francis,Est.,		38	Spots.
Joslin,Benjamin,	1		Mont.
Jossling,John,	1	2	Lin.
Jossling,Will,	1		Lin.
Jouitt,John,	1	1	Gooch.
Journican,John,	1		Henry
Jourpouke,David,			Har.
Joyce,Alexander,	1	11	Henry
Joyne,Charles,	1	3	Nor.
Joyne,John,Jr.,	1	1	Nor.
Joyne,John,Sr.,	1	5	Nor.
Joy,Richard,	1		Lou.
Joyne,Sarah,		4	Nor.
Joyne,Watkins,	1	80	Nor.
Joyne,William,	1		Nor.
Joyner,Absalom,	1	1	So'n.
Joyner,Amos,	1	2	So'n.
Joyner,Ann,			So'n.
Joyner,Ann,		7	So'n.
Joyner,Bridget,		1	So'n.
Joyner,Giles,	1	10	So'n.
Joyner,Henry,	1	3	So'n.
Joyner,Hope,			So'n.
Joyner,Jacob,	1	6	So'n.
Joyner,Jesse,	1	5	So'n.
Joyner,Jethro,	1	5	So'n.
Joyner,John,		1	So'n.
Joyner,John,Jr.,	1		So'n.
Joyner,John,Sr.,	1		So'n.
Joyner,Joseph,	1	1	So'n.
Joyber,Joshua,Sr.,	1		So'n.
Joyner,Joshua,Jr.,	1		So'n.
Joyner,Joshua,Jr.,	1		So'n.
Joyner,Lawrence,	1	7	So'n.
Joyner,Lewis,Jr.,	1	1	So'n.
Joyner,Lewis,Sr.,	1	8	So'n.
Joyner,Martha,		2	So'n.
Joyner,Matthew,	1		So'n.
Joyner,Mary,		1	So'n.
Joyner,Moses,	1		So'n.
Joyner,Sarah,		1	So'n.
Joyner,Toomes,	1	1	So'n.
Joyner,William,	1	5	So'n.
Joynes,Levin,	1	16	Acco.
Joynes,Margaret,	1	10	Acco.
Joynes,William,			Acco.
Judd,John,	1	3	Brun.
Jude,Frederick,	1		Hen.
Jude,George,		6	Gooch.
Jude,George,	1	1	Hen.
Jude,Mary&Jude,Jane,		19	Gooch.
Judkins,Jordan,	1	3	So'n.
Judkins,William,	1		So'n.
Judy,Henry,	1		Har.
Judy,Margaret,			Har.
Judy,Nicholas,	1		Har.
Julian,Dr.John,	1	4	Spots.
Julian,Phebe,		5	Spots.
Jumper,Richard,	1		Din.
Jurdan,Thomas,	1	3	K.Geo.
Jury,Abner,	1		Berk.
Jury,David,	1		Lou.
Justice,Moses,	1		Mont.
Justice,William,	1		Brun.
Kabler,Frederick,			Cul.
Kabler,Ione,	2	7	Cul.
Kabler,Nicholas,	1	3	Cul.
Kabler,William,	1		Cul.
Kadwallader,Moses,	1		Lou.
Kairns,George,	1		Bot.
Kallam,Abraham,	2	1	Acco.
Kallam,Argil,Sr.,	3	8	Acco.
Kallam,Bable,	1		Acco.
Kallam,Custis,			Acco.
Kallam,Elizabeth,	2		Acco.
Kallam,Feddrick,	1	9	Acco.
Kallam,George,	1	1	Acco.
Kallam,Hezekiah,	3		Acco.
Kallam,Housen,			Acco.
Kallam,James,	1		Acco.
Kallam,John,	1	2	Acco.
Kallam,John,	1	9	Acco.
Kallam,Joseph,			Acco.
Kallam,Joseph,	2	6	Acco.
Kallam,Kandal,	1		Acco.
Kellum,Keziah,			Acco.
Kallam,Keziah,	1	7	Acco.
Kallam,Margaret,		1	Acco.
Kellum,Mitildah,		2	Acco.
Kallam,Reubin,	2		Acco.
Kallam,Robert,			Acco.
Kallam,Sackor,	1		Acco.
Kallam,Severn,			Acco.
Kallam,Shadrick,			Acco.
Kallam,Shadrick,	1	5	Acco.
Kallam,Smith,	1	3	Acco.
Kallam,Solomon,	1		Acco.
Kallam,Spencer,			Acco.
Kallam,Torobable,	2	15	Acco.
Kaller,George,	2		Aug.
Kamp,John,	1		Henry
Kamper,Frederick,	1	1	Fau.
Kamper,Henry,	1	1	Fau.
Kamper,Jacob,	1	2	Fau.
Kamper,James,	1		Fau.
Kamper,John,Sr.,	1	6	Fau.
Kamper,John,	1		Fau.
Kamper,John,	1	1	Fau.
Kamper,John,	1	1	Fau.
Kamper,Peter,Sr.,	1	2	Fau.
Kamper,Peter,Jr.,	1	4	Fau.
Kamper,Sarah,			Fau.
Kamper,Solomon,	1		Fau.
Kamper,Tilman,	1		Fau.
Kandal,John,	1	4	Acco.
Kane,Jacob,	1	1	Mont.
Kane,John,	1		Mont.
Kane,Susannah,			Berk.
Karcher,Elizabeth,			Berk.
Karnel,William,	1		Caro.
Kauffman,George,	1	14	K.&Q.
Kauffman,John,	3	11	K.&Q.
Kauffman,John,	1	3	K.&Q.
Kay,James,	1	14	Caro.
Kay,James,	1	5	K.Geo.
Kay,Robert,	1	11	Cul.
Kay,William,	1		Caro.
Key,George,			K.&Q.
Kayes,Frederick,	1		Berk.
Kays,Christopher,	1	4	K.&Q.
Keal,Jacob,	1		Berk.
Keamer,James,	1		So'n.
Kearby,John,	1		Henry
Kearby,Richard,	1	2	Henry
Kearsy,George,			Brun.
Keatts,Curtis,	1	7	Lun.
Keatts,James,	1	3	Lun.
Keatts,William,	1	2	Lun.
Keegley,George,	1		Mont.
Keel,James,	1		Wash.
Keel,John,	1		Henry
Keel,Robert,	1		Wash.
Keeling,William,	1		K.&Q.
Keemer,James,	1		York
Keen,Elisha,	1		Henry
Keen,Francis,	2	8	Lou.
Keen,James,	1		Wash.
Keen,John,	1		Henry
Keen,Jorceel,	1		Berk.
Keen,Joseph,	1		Berk.
Keen,Josiah,	1		Berk.
Keen,Matthias,	1		Berk.
Keen,Matthias,	1		Mont.
Keen,William,	1		Ja.Cy.
Keenum,James,	1		Bed.
Keep,James,	1		Bot.
Keep,Samuel,	1		Bot.
Keep,William,	1		Bot.
Keer,David,	1		Bed.
Keer,Hannah,			Wash.
Keer,James,	1		Wash.

Name			Place
Keer,James,	1		Bed.
Keer,William,	1		Bed.
Keer,William,	1		Bed.
Keer,William,	1		Wash.
Keer,William,	2	2	Wash.
Keerhart,Abraham,	1		Mont.
Keersley,John,	1	3	Berk.
Kees,John,	1	12	Fau.
Keesicker,Andrew,	1		Berk.
Keesicker,John,	2		Berk.
Keeth,Conelius,	1	1	Henry
Keeth,Nicholas,	1	2	Bed.
Keeton,John,	1		Spots.
Keewood,Berry,	1		Wash.
Keewood,John,	1		Wash.
Keewood,Moses,	1		Wash.
Keewood,Stephen,	1		Wash.
Kegan,John,	1		Caro.
Keho,Morriss,	1		Har.
Keif,Thomas,	1		Mont.
Keirns,Daniel,	1		Fau.
Keirns,Robert,	1		Fau.
Keith,Alexander,	1	3	Pr.Wm.
Keith,Alexander,	1	9	Fau.
Keith,Daniel,	1		Mont.
Keith,Isham,	1	10	Fau.
Keith,John,	1	12	Fau.
Keith,Thomas,	1	10	Fau.
Keivnes,John,	1		Fau.
Kekele,Jacob,	1		Fay.
Kekele,John,	2		Fay.
Kekele,Jacob,Jr.,	1		Fay.
Kelburn,Elijah,	1		Mont.
Kell,James,	1		Fay.
Keller,George,	1		Har.
Keller,Henry,	1		Bed.
Kelley,Barnabas,	1		Henry
Kelley,Bealas,	1		Fay.
Kelley,Emmanuel,	1		Fay.
Kelley,Ephrim,	1		Acco.
Kelley,Ezekiel,	1		Wash.
Kelley,George,	1		Bot.
Kelley,James,			Lou.
Kelley,Jesnima,		1	Acco.
Kelley,John,	1		Henry
Kelley,John,	1		Cul.
Kelley,Joseph,	3	6	Lou.
Kelley,Michael,	1		Henry
Kelley,Thomas,	2		Caro.
Kelley,William,	1		Acco.
Kelley,William,	2	1	Caro.
Kelley,William,Jr.,	1		Cul.
Kelley,William,	1		Cul.
Kelly,***,	2		Hen.
Kelly,Benjamin,	1		Bot.
Kelly,Benjamin,	1		Bot.
Kelly,Daniel,			Lou.
Kelly,David,Sr.,			Brun.
Kelly,David,	1		Brun.
Kelly,G.,	1		Pr.Wm.
Kelly,George,Jr.,	1		Hen.
Kelly,George,	1		Rock.
Kelly,Giles,	1	3	Brun.
Kelly,Henry,	1		Bot.
Kelly,Isaiah,	2		Acco.
Kelly,James,	1		Brun.
Kelley,James,	1		Cul.
Kelly,James,	1		Bed.
Kelly,John,	1		Aug.
Kelly,John,	1		Bot.
Kelly,John,	1		Wash.
Kelly,John,	2		Fau.
Kelly,John,	1		Hen.
Kelly,John,	1		Pr.Wm.
Kelly,John,	2		Hen.
Kelly,Joseph,	1		Fay.
Kelly,Judy,			Bot.
Kelly,Moses,	1		Brun.
Kelly,Oan,	1		Aug.
Kelly,Patrick,	2		Lou.
Kelly,Patrick,			Hen.
Kelly,Valentine,			Hen.
Kelly,William,	1		Hen.
Kelly,S.,	1		Pr.Wm.
Kelly,Samuel,	1	2	Brun.
Kelly,Susannah,		6	Acco.
Kelly,Thomas,	2		Berk.
Kelly,Thomas,	1		Fau.
Kelly,William,	1	1	Berk.
Kelly,William,	1		Henry.
Kelly,William,Jr.,	1		Henry
Kello,Col.Richard,	3	19	So'n.
Kello,Sam,	1	12	So'n.
Kellow,William,	1	11	So'n.
Kelsey,James,	1		Mont.
Kelshan,John,	1		Ch.Cy
Kelshan,John,Jr.,	1		Ch.Cy
Kelso,Hugh,	1	2	Rock.
Kelso,John,	1		Rock.
Kemmvilin,Jacob,	1		Berk.
Kemp,John,	1	7	K.&Q.
Kemp,John,	1	2	K.&Q.
Kemp,William,			Hen.
Kemper,Henry,	3	1	Fay.
Kamper,Peter,	1		Cul.
Kemper,William,			Fay.
Kenary,Christian,	1		Lin.
Keneard,Mary,			Fau.
Kendal,Thomas,	1		Fau.
Kendall,Adah,		2	Nor.
Kendall,Benjamin,	1		K.Geo
Kendall,Boudoin,	1	11	Nor.
Kendall,Capt.Custis,		12	Nor.
Kendell,Elizabeth,			K.Geo.
Kendell,Francis,	1		Cul.
Kendall,George,Sr.,	1	13	Nor.
Kendall,George,Jr.,	1	8	Nor.
Kendall,John,	1		K.Geo
Kendall,John,Jr.,	1	20	Nor.
Kendall,John,Sr.,	2	30	Nor.
Kendall,Littleton,		1	Nor.
Kendall,Moses,	1		K.Geo.
Kendall,Thomas,	1	10	Nor.
Kendall,William,	1	24	Nor.
Kendall,Samuel,Jr.,	1		K.Geo.
Kendall,Samuel,Sr.,	1	10	K.Geo.
Kendall,Wofinael,	1	8	K.Geo.
Kendrick,Benjamin,			Cul.
Kendrick,Jacob,	1	2	Cul.
Kendricks,John,	1		Lou.
Kendrick,Miriam,			Wash.
Kenly,James,	1		Lin.
Kensley,Coonrod,	1		Cul.
Kenn,William,	1		Berk.
Kenady,Andrew,	1	2	Rock.
Kenady,James,	1		Rock.
Kennady,Alexander,	1	1	Spots.
Kennady,Charles,		5	Loui.
Keneday,Connel,	1		Mont.
Kennaday,Esther,		2	Bed.
Kennaday,Esther,		3	Bed.
Kennaday,James,	1	1	Bed.
Kennedy,John,	1		Berk.
Keneade,Robert,	3		Rock.
Kennedy,Daniel,	1		Berk.
Kennedy,David,	1	2	Berk.
Kennady,Davinport,	1	9	Loui.
Kennedy,Robert,	1		Berk.
Kennedy,Robert,	1		Brun.
Kennedy,Samuel,	1		Berk.
Kennedy,Samuel,	1		Har.
Kenneday,Thomas,	1		Berk.
Kennedy,William,	1		Aug.
Kennedy,William,	2		Wash.
Kenner,George,	1	2	Fau.
Kenner,Margaret,	1	10	Fau.
Kenner,Rodham,		9	K.Geo.
Kennerly,James,	2	7	Aug.
Kennerly,James,Jr.,	1	5	Aug.
Kennerly,Ruben,			Aug.
Kennerly,Samuel,	1		Bot.
Kennerly,William,	1		Aug.
Kennihorn,John,	2		Acco.
Kennon,Benjamin,	1	3	Henry
Kennon,Samuel,	1		Henry
Kennon,Thomas,	1	6	Lou.
Kenny,Brian,	1		Aug.
Kenny,Christopher,	1		Berk.
Kenney,James,	1		Fay.
Kenny,James,	1		Aug.
Kenny,John,			Loui.
Kenny,John,	1		Berk.
Kenny,Matthew,	1	2	Aug.
Kenny,Richard,	2	1	Spots.
Kenny,Robert,	1	1	Aug.
Kent,David,	1		Fay.
Kent,John,	1	3	Bot.
Kent,Mary,		13	Bot.
Kent,S.,			Pr.Wm.
Kent,Mary,			Fau.
Kenty,Thomas,			Loui.
Kenworthy,John,	1		Mont.
Kenworthy,Thomas,	1		Mont.
Kephart,John,			Fay.
Kerby,David,	1		Henry
Kearby,Francis,	1		Henry
Kearby,Jessee,Sr.,	1		Henry
Kearby,Jessee,	1		Henry
Kearby,John,	1		Henry
Kearby,Joseph,	1		Henry
Kerchevall,Benjamin,	1		Berk.
Kerchevall,James,	1		Berk.
Kerchival,Charles,	1	1	K.&Q.
Kerk,Joseph,	1		Berk.
Kerney,James,	1	11	Berk.
Kerney,William,	3		Berk.
Kernot,James,	1		Mont.
Kerny,Alexander,	1		Berk.
Keri,Edward,	4	34	Acco.
Ker,George,	2	2	Acco.
Ker,John,	1		Acco.
Kerr,Alexander,			Pr.Geo.
Kerr,Gilbert,	1		Aug.
Kerr,James,	1	3	Aug.
Kerr,James,			Hen.
Kerr,James,	1		Mont.
Kerr,Lucy,			Bot.
Kerr,Margaret,			Bot.
Kerr,Samuel,	1		Bot.
Kerr,Thomas,	1		Aug.
Kerr,William,	2		Aug.
Kerrick,Henry B.,	1		Lou.
Kerrick,Walter,	1		Lou.
Kerrigan,Patrick,	1		Bot.
Kersey,Edward,	1		Buck.
Kersey,George,	1	5	Loui.
Kersey,Katherine,			Buck.
Kersey,Thomas,	1		Loui.
Kersey,Thomas,	1		Bot.
Kersey,William,	1		Bot.
Kersey,William,	1		So'n.
Kerton,Anthony,	1	3	K.Geo.
Kesee,George,	1	1	Wash.
Kesee,John,	1	1	Wash.
Kesey,John,	1		Bot.
Kesey,Samuel,	2		Bot.
Kester,John,	1		Lou.
Kesterson,William,	1	6	Fau.

Name			County
Kessinger,John,	1	2	Lin.
Kettering,Jacob,	1		Mont.
Kettering,Jacob,	5		Mont.
Kettering,Lawrence,	2		Mont.
Kew,John,			West.
Key,James,	1	7	Fau.
Key,John,	1	6	Bed.
Key,John Waller,			Bed.
Key,Price,	1		Fau.
Key,William,	1	2	Loui.
Keyes,Frances,	1		Berk.
Keyes,Humphry,	1	1	Berk.
Keyes,John,	1		Berk.
Keyes,Robert,	2		Pr.Wm.
Keyes,Ruth,		2	Berk.
Keyes,Thomas,	1		Pr.Wm.
Keyes,Thomas,Jr.,	1		Pr.Wm.
Keyes,William,	1		Pr.Wm.
Keyes,William,	2		Pr.Wm.
Keys,David,	1		Fau.
Keys,George,	1		Lin.
Keys,James,			Wash.
Keys,John,	1	2	Wash.
Keys,Rawleigh,			Pr.Wm.
Keys,Samuel,	1		Rock.
Keys,Sarah,			Rock.
Keyser,Joseph,	1		Mont.
Keyton,Hezekiah,	1		Cul.
Kezekiah,Lodewick,	1		Henry
Kibble,John,	1		Fau.
Kibble,William,	1	1	Fau.
Kibreth,Hugh,	1		Lin.
Kidd,Bartholomew,	1	3	K.&..
Kidd,Daniel,	1	1	Aug.
Kidd,John,	1	11	K.&Q.
Kidd,John,	1	4	Buck.
Kidd,Lewis,	1		Buck.
Kidd,Moses,	1	5	Buck.
Kidd,Samuel,	1		Buck.
Kibb,Thomas,			Lou.
Kidd,Thomas,	1	5	Caro.
Kidd,William,	1		Mont.
Kidd,William,	1		Buck.
Kidd,William,	2	10	Caro.
Kidd,William,	1		Buck.
Kidner,George,	2		Har.
Kidner,Nicholas,	1		Har.
Kidwell,John,	2		Fau.
Kihon,William,	1		Fau.
Kilbreak,Evan,	1		Lin.
Kilbry,James,	1		Cul.
Kilburn,Henry,	1		Lin.
Kilgore,Charles,	1	2	Wash.
Kilgore,George,	1	1	Lou.
Killgore,Robert,	1		Wash.
Killavane,John,	1		Rock.
Killey,Alexander,		2	Nor.
Killey,Isaac,	1		Bot.
Killum,Jonathan,	1		Nor.
Killum,Stephen,	1		Nor.
Kilpatrick,Andrew,			Aug.
Kimberlin,Jacob,	1		Bot.
Kimberlin,Martin,	1		Mont.
Kimberlin,Michael,	1		Bot.
Kimberlin,Paulser,	1	4	Bot.
Kimbrow,John,			Loui.
Kimbrow,Robert,	1	6	Loui.
Kimbrow,Samuel,	1	3	Loui.
Kinard,David,	1		Cul.
Kinard,George,	1		Cul.
Kincaid,Andrew,	1		Lin.
Kincaid,John,	1		Fay.
Kincaid,John,	2	1	Aug.
Kincaid,John,	1		Aug.
Kincaid,Robert,	1		Lin.
Kincaid,Capt.William,	1	3	Aug.

Name			County
Kincaid,William,	1		Aug.
Kinkead,David,	1		Wash.
Kinkead,Capt.John,	1		Wash.
Kinnais,Andrew,	1		Aug.
Kincannon,Andrew,	1		Wash.
Kincannon,Francis,Sr	1		Wash.
Kincannon,Francis,Jr	1	3	Wash.
Kincannon,James,	1	1	Wash.
Kincannon,Mathew,	1		Wash.
Kincaole,Thomas,	1		Rock.
Kincheloe,C.,	1	12	Pr.Wm.
Kincheloe,John,	1	13	Fau.
Kinnchorn,William,	1	1	Acco.
Kincart,Samuel,	1		Wash.
Kinder,Gasper,	1		Berk.
Kinder,Geroge,	1		Mont.
Kinder,Jacob,	1		Mont.
Kinder,Peter,	1		Mont.
Kinder,Peter,	1		Rock.
Kindred,Benjamin,	1	4	So'n.
Kindred,John,	1	3	So'n.
Kindred,Samuel,	1	3	So'n.
Kinarick,Bennony,	1		Cul.
Kindrick,Daniel,	1		Cul.
Kindrick,John,Sr.,	1	2	Wash.
Kindrick,John,Jr.,	1		Wash.
Kindrick,Preston,	1		Henry
Kindrick,Thomas,	1		Wash.
Kinarick,William,	1		Cul.
King,Andrew,	1	4	Pr.Geo
King,Avery,	1		Bed.
King,Baker,	1		Henry
King,Benjamin,	1	9	Lou.
King,Charles,	1	5	Brun.
King,Charles,Jr.,	1	2	Brun.
King,Edward,	1		Brun.
King,Elizabeth,		2	Caro.
King,G.,	1	13	Pr.Wm.
King,George,	1		Berk.
King,George,	1		Mont.
King,George,	1	2	Brun.
Kipheart,Godfrey,	2		Lou.
King,Henry,	1		Aug.
King,James,	1		Cul.
King,James,	1		Bed.
King,James,	1		Spots.
King,James,	1		Din.
Kirk,Jeremiah,	1	6	K.Geo.
King,John,	1		Brun.
King,John,	1		Bed.
King,John,	1		Berk.
King,John,	1		Cul.
King,John,	1	1	Lin.
King,John,Sr.,	1	3	Aug.
King,John,	1		Aug.
King,John,	1		Bot.
King,John,Sr.,	1	6	Lou.
King,John,	1	13	K.Wm.
King,John,	1		Aug.
King,John,	1		Mont.
King,John,	1	10	Henry
King,Joseph,	1		Henry
King,Marimiat,		6	K.Wm.
King,Martain,	1	6	Bed.
King,Martha,		1	Din.
King,Mary,		3	Din.
King,Michael,	1	8	Eli.Cy
King,Miles,	1	12	Eli.Cy
King,Nathaniel,	2	6	Brun.
King,Nathaniel,Jr.,			Brun.
King,Osborn,	1		Lou.
King,Philip,	1		Berk.
King,Philip,	1		Henry
King,Richard,	1	9	K.Wm.
King,Robert,	1	1	Bot.
King,Robert,	1		Cul.

Name			County
King,Robert,	2	37	K.Wm.
King,Robert,	2		Fau.
King,Samuel,	1	1	Berk.
King,Smith,	1	3	Lou.
King,Smith,	2		West.
King,Stephen,	1		Henry
King,Thomas,	1	16	K.Wm.
King,Thomas,	1	3	Lou.
King,Timothy,	1		Pr.Wm.
King,Thomas,Sr.,	1	4	Loui.
King,Thomas,Jr.,	1		Loui.
King,Thomas,	1		Berk.
King,Thomas,	2	4	West.
King,William,	1	9	K.Wm.
King,William,	1		Fau.
King,William,	1	1	West.
King,William,	1	10	Brun.
King,William,	1	15	Hen.
King,William,	1	5	Eli.Cy
King,William,	1	5	Mont.
Kingny,Jacob,			Rock.
Kingny,Peter,			Rock.
Kingny,Tobias,	1		Rock.
Kington,Francis,	1		Henry
Kington,John,			Din.
Kinner,Rodham,		13	Caro.
Kinkey,Simon,	1		Aug.
Kinney,John,	1		Bot.
Kinser,George,	1		Mont.
Kinser,Jacob,	1		Mont.
Kinser,Walter,	1		Mont.
Kinsey,Henry,	1		Bed.
Kinsey,John,	1		Bot.
Kimzey,Benjamin,	1		Henry
Kirby,Benjamon,	1	4	So'n
Kirby,Bennett,	1	8	Din.
Kirby,Miss Fanny,		5	Din.
Kirby,Hawkins,	1		Bot.
Lirby,John,	1	4	York.
Kirby,John,	1	9	So'n
Kirby,John,	1	10	Ja.Cy
Kirby,John,	2	13	So'n
Kirby,John,	1	9	Din.
Kirby,Margaret,		8	York.
Kirby,Moody,	1	2	So'n
Kirby,Silas,	1	6	So'n
Kirby,Thomas,		2	Din.
Kirby,Thomas,	1	24	Eli.Cy
Kirby,Turner,	1	9	So'n
Kirby,William,	1	7	Din.
Kirk,Alexander,	1		Aug.
Kirk,Hezeliah,	1	2	K.Geo.
Kirk,James,	1		Aug.
Kirk,James,	2	5	Brun.
Kirk,James,	1	9	Lou.
Kirk,John,	1		Aug.
Kirk,John,			Brun.
Kirk,John,	2		Fau.
Kirk,John,Jr.,	1		Fau.
Kirk,John,	1		West.
Kirk,Randal,	1		West.
Kirk,Thomas,	1		Bot.
Kirkham,Rosana,			Rock.
Kirkland,Benjamin,	1		Brun.
Kirkland,Benjamin,			Pr.Geo.
Kirkland,Elizabeth,			Pr.Geo.
Kirkland,John,			Pr.Geo.
Kirkland,Joseph,	1	10	Pr.Geo.
Kirth,Reuben,	1		Mont.
Kirtland,John,	1		Lun.
Kirkpatrick,Charles,	3		Rock.
Kirkpatrick,Charles,	1		Rock.
Kirkpatrick,James,	1	2	Lin.
Kirkpatrick,James,	1	2	Mont.
Kirkpatrick,James,	1		Rock.
Kirkpatrick,John,	1		Aug.

Name			Location
Kirkpatrick,John,	1		Aug.
Kirkpatrick,John,	1		Rock.
Kirkpatrick,John,	1		Rock.
Kirkpatrick,Robert,	1	1	Rock.
Kirkpatrick,Robert,	1		Lou.
Kirkpatrick,Samuel,	1		Rock.
Kirkpatrick,Thomas,	1		Rock.
Kirkpatrick,Thomas,			Rock.
Kirkpatrick,William,	1		Aug.
Kirtley,Elijah,	1	6	Cul.
Kirtley,Francis,	1	2	Cul.
Kirtley,Jemima,		8	Cul.
Kirtley,Jemima,	1	7	Cul.
Kirtly,Thomas,	1	1	Cul.
Kirtley,Thomas,	1	13	Cul.
Kirtley,William,	1	15	Cul.
Kirtley,William,	1	6	Cul.
Kisee,John,		2	Caro.
Kitchen,Bohannah,	3		Buck.
Kitchen,Daniel,			Lou.
Kitchen,Fred,	1		So'n
Kitchen,George,	1	3	Pr.Wm.
Kitchen,Jesse,			So'n
Kitchen,John,	1	1	Lou.
Kitchen,John,	1		Henry
Kitchen,John,	1		Camp.
Kitchen,John,	1		Buck.
Kitchen,Natan,	1		So'n
Kitchen,Thomas,	1		Buck.
Kitchen,William,	1		So'n.
Kitchen,William,	1		Henry
Kittering,Michael,	1		Mont.
Kitts,William,	1		Wash.
Klug,Michael,	1	3	Cul.
Knave,Michael,	1		Mont.
Knibb,John,	2	15	Cha.Cy
Knibb,Joshua,			Cha.Cy
Knight,Effee,			Spots.
Knight,Epharim,	1		Spots.
Knight,James,	1		Aug.
Knight,John,	1	1	Nor.
Knight,Joseph,	1	4	Lun.
Knight,Peter,	1	10	Lun.
Knight,William,	1	2	Nor.
Knight,Woodson,	1	13	Lun.
Knighton,William,	1		Lou.
Knowland,John,	1	1	K.Geo.
Knox,David,	1		Fay.
Knox,James,	1	20	Henry
Knox,Robert,est.,	1	11	Fau.
Knox,Robert,	1		Fay.
Knox,Thomas,	1		Bot.
Knox,William,	1	19	Fau.
Knox,William,	2	31	Cul.
Kock,James,	1		Cul.
Kogar,Jacob,	1		Henry
Kogar,Nicholas,	1		Henry
Kogle,Christian,	1		Berk.
Kortz,Michael,	1		Lou.
Krantz,Michael,	1		Bed.
Kraton,William,	1		Henry
Kruke,Jacob,	1		Berk.
Kyle,David,	2	11	Buck.
Kyle,Joseph,	1		Berk.
Kyle,Joseph,	1	9	Bot.
Kyle,William,	1	8	Bot.
Kyzer,John,	1		Berk.
Labant,John,		13	Cha.Cy
Lacee,James,	1		Rock.
Lacewell,Moses,	1		Lou.
Lacey,John,			Cul.
Lacey,John,	1		Pr.Wm.
Lacey,John,	1		Hen.
Lackey,Adam,	1		Henry
Lackey,John,	1		Henry
Lackey,Thomas,	2		Rock.
Lackke,Andrew,	1		Aug.
Lackland,James,		1	Buck.
Lackland,John,	1		Rock.
Lackland,Joseph,Sr.,	1		Rock.
Lackland,Joseph,Jr.,	1		Rock.
Lackland,Margory,		12	Buck.
Lackland,Tadock,	1	1	Buck.
Lacock,Nathan,	1		Lou.
Lacy,Capt.,		3	Pr.Geo
Lacy,Elliott,	2		Gooch.
Lacy,Jesse,	1	3	Loui.
Lacy,Matthew,	1	3	Gooch.
Lacy,Noah,	1		Buck.
Lacy,Sarah,		8	Gooch.
Lacy,Thomas,			York
Lacy,Thomas B.,est.,		4	Cha.Cy
Lacy,William,		4	Pr.Geo
Ladd,Amos,	1		Cha.Cy
Ladd,James,	1		Cha.Cy
Ladd,Jess,	1	1	Cha.Cy
Ladd,John,	1		Cha.Cy
Ladd,Judith,		8	Cha.Cy
Ladd,Samuel,	1		Cha.Cy
Ladd,Thomas,	1	2	Lun.
Ladd,Thomas,	1		Cha.Cy
Lafon,Francis,	1	4	K.&Q
Lafon,Nicholas,		1	K.&Q
Lafevre,Henry,	1		Lou.
Lafferty,John,	1		Berk.
Lafferty,Thomas,	1	4	Berk.
Laffoon,John,	1		Lun.
Laffoon,Mathew,	1		Brun.
Laffoon,Nathaniel,Sr.	1		Lun.
Laffoon,Nathaniel,Jr.	1		Lun.
Lail,George,	1		Fay.
Laing,Alexander,			Fau.
Lainheart,Isaac,	1		Bed.
Larid,David,	1		Rock.
Lake,David,			Lou.
Lake,Thomas,	1		Lou.
Lake,Vincent,	1		Fau.
Lake,William,	1		Fau.
Lamb,Archibald,	1		Bed.
Lamb,John,	1		Berk.
Lamb,John,			Din.
Lamb,John,		2	Din.
Lamb,Nicholas,	1	3	Din.
Lamb,Richard,	2	13	Brun.
Lamb,Thomas,	1	11	Din.
Lamb,Walter,	1		Henry
Lamb,William,	1	2	Din.
Lambag,Anthony,	1		Lou.
Lambert,Charles,Sr.,	1	3	Bed.
Lambert,David,	1	3	Hen.
Lambert,Henry,	2		Mont.
Lambert,Lewis,	1	8	Lun.
Lambert,Lewis,			Brun.
Lambert,Philip,	1		Mont.
Lambert,Richard,	2	6	Brun.
Lambert,Thomas,	1		K.&Q
Lambett,John,	1	13	K.Wm.
Lambett,Meredeth,	1	3	K.Wm.
Lame,John,	1	1	Wash.
Lamkin,Ashton,	1	4	West.
Lamkin,Chattin,	1		Fau.
Lamkin,George,	2	8	Pr.Wm.
Lamkin,George,Jr.,			Pr.Wm.
Lamkin,James,	1	4	Fau.
Lamkin,James,	1	1	West.
Lamkin,Peter,	1	5	West.
Lamkin,Peter,	1	1	Pr.Wm.
Lamm,James,	1	2	Aug.
Lamm,Samuel,	1	1	Aug.
Lamme,Nathan,	1		Lin.
Lampkin,Edward,	1		Cul.
Lampton,John Wood,	1	6	Camp.
Lampton,Joshua,	1		Fau.
Lampton,Samuel,	1		Fau.
Lampton,William,			Spots.
Lampton,William,	2		Lin.
Lancaster,Etheldred,	1	5	So'n
Lancaster,James,	1	6	So'n
Lancaster,Joseph,	1	5	So'n
Lance,Bernet,	1		Aug.
Lance,Conrod,	1		Aug.
Lance,Joseph,	1		Aug.
Lanciska,Henry,	4		Har.
Land,John,	1	3	Buck.
Land,Richard,	1		Cul.
Land,William,	1		Bot.
Landers,Henry,Jr.,	1		Har.
Landers,Henry,Sr.,	3		Har.
Landers,Kimbrow,	1		Loui.
Landers,Nathaniel,			Lou.
Landers,William,	1		Mont.
Landrum, S.		9	Pr.Wm.
Lane,Aaron,	1	9	Cul.
Lane,Ben,			Brun.
Lane,Benjamin,		4	Brun.
Lane,Daniel,	1	3	Loui.
Lane,David,	1		David, Spots.
Lane,Gilmon,	1		Spots.
Lane,Hardage,	3	14	Lou.
Lane,Henry S.,			Lou.
Lane,James,			York
Lane,James,	1	7	Lou.
Lane,James,Jr.,	1	3	Lou.
Lane,James Hardage,	2	9	Lou.
Lane,John,	1	1	Lou.
Lane,John,	1	6	Camp.
Lane,John,	1	6	Camp.
Lane,Joseph,			K.Geo.
Lane,Maj.Joseph,		2	Brun.
Lane,Simon,	1		Brun.
Lane,William,Sr.,	1	13	Lou.
Lane,William,Jr.,	4	24	Lou.
Lane,William,	1		Fau.
Landman,Griffin,	1		Cul.
Landram,Mark,			Cul.
Landrum,Francis,	1	2	Lun.
Landrum,Hawkins,	1	4	Buck.
Landrum,James,	1	4	K.Wm.
Landrum,Lunsford,	1	1	Buck.
Landrum,Martha,	1	1	Lun.
Landrum,Nelly,	2	18	Caro.
Landrum,Richard,			Lun.
Lang,Daniel,	1		Lou.
Lang,James,	1		Cul.
Lang,John,	1		Din.
Lane,Thomas,	1	9	So'n
Langard,David,			Loui.
Langbourn,William,	1	62	K.Wm.
Langdon,Jonathan,	1		Wash.
Langfitt,John,	1	4	Pr.Wm
Langford,Benjamin,			Lin.
Langford,Mary,		2	Lin.
Langford,Stephen,	1	1	Lin.
Langham,John,			K.&Q
Langham,Ransom,			K.&Q
Langham,William,	1	4	K.&Q
Langhorne,Maurice,		20	Buck.
Langley,Elizabeth,		1	Eli.Cy
Langley,James,	1		Wash.
Langley,Robert,	1	26	Din.
Langley,Wilson,	1	1	Eli.Cy
Langley,William,	1		Eli.Cy
Langstone,John,	1	7	Brun.
Langstone,Mary,		3	York

Name			County
Lanier,Benjamin,	2	11	Brun.
Lanier,Buckner,	1	9	Brun.
Lanier,Clement,	1	4	Brun.
Lanier,David,	1	10	Henry
Lanier,Drury,	1		Brun.
Lanier,John,	1	1	Brun.
Lanier,John,	1	4	Brun.
Lanier,Lemuel,	1	3	Brun.
Lanier,Lewis,	1	4	Din.
Lanier,Lewis,	1	7	Din.
Lanier,Nicholas,			Brun.
Lanier,Nicholas,			Brun.
Lanier,Richard,	1	3	Brun.
Lanier,Robert,	1		Brun.
Lanier,Samuel,	1	8	Henry
Lanier,William,	1	12	Brun.
Lanoir,Fisher,	1	9	Din.
Lanford,Sarah,		1	Caro.
Lanford,William,	1		Caro.
Langford,Harry,	1		K.&Q.
Lankaster,Joseph,	1		Hen.
Lankford,Edward,	1		Ja.C.
Lankford,Elisha,			So'n.
Lankford,Elizabeth,		9	So'n.
Lankford,John,	1	1	So'n.
Lankford,Joseph,	1	1	Caro.
Lankford,Stephen,	1		So'n.
Lankford,Thomas,	1	1	K.&Q.
Lashbrooke,John			Pr.Wm.
Lans,Zachariah,			Eliz.C
Lanter,Rubeon,	1		Rock.C
Lanthorpe,Alexander,	1	1	Pr.Geo
Lanthorpe,John,	1	1	Pr.Geo
Lantroop,Mary,		1	Pr.Geo
Lapsley,John,		1	Bot.
Lapsley,John,	1	2	Lin.
Lapsley,Joseph,Sr.	1	5	Rock.
Lapsley,Joseph,Jr.	1		Rock.
Lapsley,Samuel			Rock.
Lard,John,	1		Camp.
Lare,Andrew,	2		Lin.
Lare,George,	1		Lin.
Laremore,John,	1		Rock.
Larimon,James,	1		Berk.
Lark,Tenison,			York.
Larkin,Hugh,	1		Berk.
Larrance,Edward,	3	18	Fau.
Larrance,Edward,,	1	4	Fau.
Larrance,Peter,	1	3	Fau.
Larrone,Abraham,	3		Lou.
Larrowe,Isaac,			Lou.
Larrowe,Peter,			Lou.
Lashley,Benjamin,	2	7	Brun.
Lasley,John,	1		Loui.
Lasley,Manoah,	1		Loui.
Lasley,Patrick,	2	1	Lou.
Lason,William,			Wash.
Latham,Frances,	3	19	Cul.
Latham,George,			Cul.
Latham,Philip,			Cul.
Latham,Robert,			Cul.
Latham,Dukie,	1	13	Cul.
Latham,Jonathan,	1		Pr.Wm
Latham,Robert,	1	12	Cul.
Latham,Thomas,	2	11	Cul.
Latham,Thomas,			Cul.
Lathey,John,	1		Fau.
Lathim,John,	1	1	Wash.
Latimer,George,	1	14	Eli.C.
Latimer,Rosea,		7	Eli.C.
Latimer,Thomas,	1		Eli.C.
Latimer,William,	1	19	Eli.C.
Latimore,John,	1	5	Brun.
Lattimore,William,	1		Lou.
Laughland,James,	1		Berk.
Laughland,James,	1		Har.
Laughlin,Jeremiah,		6	K.&Q.
Laughlin,Peter,	1		Mont.
Laughlin,Jeremiah,		6	K.&Q.
Laughlin,Peter,	1		Mont.
Laughlin,Thomas,	1	9	K.Wm.
Laughlin,Thomas,	1	20	Caro.
Laughorn,Henry,	1		Bed.
Launders,Benjamin,	1		Henry
Laurance,John,	2		Har.
Laurance,Samuel	1		Rock.C
Laurence,Charles,	1		West.
Laurence,John,	1		West.
Laurence,John,		8	So'n.
Laurey,Giles,	1		Cul.
Laury,Melvin,	1		Rock.C
Loury,John,	1	33	Eliz.C
Laverty,Ralph,	1		Augu.
Lavy,Joseph,	1	1	West.
Law,Michael,	1		Rock.
Law,Morris,	1		Rock.
Law,Nathaniel,	1		Henry
Law,William,	1		Henry
Lawell,Thomas,			Acco.
Lawins,Francis,	2	7	Cul.
Lawins,Benjamin,	1	8	Cul.
Lawler,John,	2	14	Cul.
Lawler,Michael,			Cul.
Lawler,Nicholas,	1		Fau.
Laws,John,Sr.	1		Mont.
Laws,John,Jr.	1		Mont.
Laws,Joseph,	1		Mont.
Laws,Shedrack,	1		Mont.
Lawson,David,	1		Henry
Lawson,Drury,			Mont.
Lawson,Gavin,	1	34	Cul.
Lawson,Gavin,		8	Fau.
Lawson,Isaac,	1		Rock.
Lawson,Isham,			Cha.C
Lawson,Jacob,	1		Henry
Lawson,James,			Mont.
Lawson,John,	1	10	Fau.
Lawson,John,	1	24	West.
Lawson,Mourman,	1		Henry
Lawson,Phillip,			Henry
Lawson,Robert,	1		Acco.
Lawson,Susannah,		2	Henry
Lawson,Thomas,	1	33	Pr.Wm.
Lawson,Thomas,	14	37	Pr.Wm.
Lawson,William,	1		Mont.
Lawson,William,	1		Mont.
Lawson,William,	1		Henry
Lawrence,Henry,	1	1	Gooch.
Lawrence,Isham,	1		Brun.
Lawrence,Ishmael,	1	2	Hen.
Lawrence, J.			Hen.
Lawrence,Jacob,	1		Lin.
Lawrence,James,	2	1	Lun.
Lawrence,James,Jr.			Lun.
Lawrence,John,	1	1	Loui.
Lawrence,Joshua,	1	1	Acco.
Lawrence,Robert,		4	So'n.
Lawrence,Thomas,	1		So'n.
Lawrence,Wood,	1		Brun.
Lax,James,			Buck.
Lax,Timothy,	1		Wash.
Lax,William,Sr.			Lun.
Lax,William,Jr.	2	5	Lun.
Lay,Abraham,	1	10	Loud.
Lay,Abraham,Jr.	2	1	Loud.
Lay,Emanuel,	1		Lou.
Lay,Gideon,	1		Camp.
Lay,Israel,			Lou.
Lay,Joseph,	1	1	Lou.
Lay,Joseph,	1	1	Lou.
Lay,Stephen,	1	1	Lou.
Laybrrok,Paulser,	1		Mont.
Laycock,Thomas,	1	1	West.
Laylor,Bable,	1	9	Acco.
Layman,George			
Layman,George,		2	Cul.
Layman,George,			Cul.
Layne,Ayres,	1	6	Gooch.
Layne,Caty,			Henry.
Layne,Charles,	2		Buck.
Layne,Davis,	1		Gooch.
Layne,Edward,			Buck.
Layne,Henry,	1	5	Spots.
Layne,Henry,	1		Gooch.
Layne,John,	1		Gooch.
Layne,Jesse,	1		Buck.
Clayton,Robert,	1	2	Fau.
Layton,Stephen,	1		Henry
Lazenia,John,	1		Bed.
Lemore,James M.	1		So'n.
Lea,John,	1	14	Loui.
Leach,Absolom,	1		Pr.Wm.
Leach,Bartlett,	1	1	Pr.Wm.
Leach,George,	1		Fau.
Leach,James,	1		Fau.
Leach,James,	1	8	Din.
Leach,John,			Lou.
Leach,John,		1	Lou.
Leach,John,	1	1	Din.
Leach,Thomas,	1		Fau.
Leach,William,	1		Fau.
Leach,William,		5	Pr.Wm.
Leachman,L.	1		Pr.Wm.
Leachman,T.	2		Pr.Wm.
Leachman,Thomas,	1		Fau.
Leachman,William,	1		Fau.
Leaderdale,William,Sr	1		Bot.
Leak,Peter,	1	4	Henry
Leak,Thomas,	1		Henry
Leake,Capt.Elisha,	2	12	Gooch.
Leake,John,	1		Fau.
Leake,Josias,	1	18	Gooch.
Leaman,Joseph,	1		Bot.
Leaper,Hugh,	1	1	Lin.
Lear,Susanna,			Cul.
Lear,William,	1		Bed.
Learwood,John,	1		Buck.
Leaser,Joseph,	1		Augu.
Leaster,Robert,	1		Augu.
Leath,Charles,	1	6	Brun.
Leather,John,	1	5	Cul.
Leather,Joshua,	1	5	Cul.
Leather,Nicholas,	1		Cul.
Leather,Paul,	1	9	Cul.
Leatherbury,Charles,	1	3	Acco.
Leatherbury,George,			Acco.
Leatherbury,Peggy,		11	Acco.
Leatherbury,Thomas,	1		Acco.
Leatherbury,William,	1		Acco.
Leathers,George,	1		Cul.
Leavell,Benjamin,			Spots.
Leavell,Benjamin,	1	3	Spots.
Leavell,James,	1	1	Cul.
Lebe,John,	1	1	York
Lecatt,Shadrick,	3	7	Acco.
Ledardale,James,Sr.	1		Bot.
Ledardale,James,Jr.	1	5	Bot.
Ledardale,William,Jr	1		Bot.
Ledbetter,Drury,	1	2	Din.
Ledbetter,Henry,	1	12	Brun.
Ledbetter,Isaac,	1	9	Brun.
Ledbetter,James,	1	1	Brun.
Ledbetter,Joseph,	1	5	Pr.Geo.
Ledbetter,Nathan,	1	3	Din.
Ledbetter,Richard,	1	1	Brun.
Ledbetter,Wood,	1	2	Pr.Geo.
Leady,Christian,	1		Berk.
Ledford,John,	1	1	Caro.
Ledford,Joseph,	1	1	Caro.
Ledfoure,Daniel,	1		Pr.Wm.
Ledger,William,	1		York

Name			County	Name			County	Name			County
Ledgerwood,William,	2		Fay.	Lee,William,	3		Har.	Leprade,John,	1	7	Gooch.
Lee,Abram,			Pr.Wm.	Leech,John,	1		Rock.	Leprade,John,	1	18	Gooch.
Lee,Alexander,	1		Lou.	Leetch,Benjamin,	1		Cul.	Lerew,Abram,	2		Augu.
Lee,Ann,	1		Acco.	Lefoe,Daniel,	1	1	Caro.	Lerew,Jacob,	1		Augu.
Lee,Anthony,	1		Berk.	Leeforce,Randol,	1	2	Fay.	Lerount,Charles,	1		Fay.
Lee,Burwell,	1		Pr.Geo.	Leforce,Samuel,	1	1	Bot.	Lest,Michael,			Mont.
Lee,Gen.Charles,	2	6	Berk.	Leek,Nicholas,	1		Augu.	Lesley,John,			Mont.
Lee,Clement,	1		Mont.	Lees,John,	1		Lou.	Lesley,John,	1		Mont.
Lee,D.	1		Pr.Wm.	Leftwich,Augustin,Sr.	1	15	Bed.	Lesley,Samuel,	1		Augu.
Lee,Daniel,	1		Pr.Geo.	Leftwich,Augustin,Jr.	1	3	Bed.	Lesley,Sarah,			Augu.
Lee,Daniel,			Lou.	Leftwich,Elijah,	1	28	K.Wm.	Lesner,John,	1		Berk.
Lee,Edward,			Pr.Wm.	Leftwich,Littleburry,	1	3	Bed.	Lessly,Thomas,	1		Augu.
Lee,Flora,	1	18	West.	Leftwich,Thomas,	1	7	Bed.	Lessenberry,John,	1	8	Pr.Geo.
Lee,Francis,	2	6	York.	Leftwich,Uriah,	1	1	Bed.	Lesnur,Robert,	1		Berk.
Lee,George Fairfax,	1	37	West.	Leftwich,Col.William,	1	24	Bed.	Lester,Alexander,	1		Lun.
Lee,Gresham,	1	6	Buck.	Leewright,John,	1	11	Pr.Wm.	Lester,Andrew,	1	5	Brun.
Lee,Hancock,	1	19	Fau.	Leewright,John,			Pr.Wm.	Lester,Benjamin,	1	4	York
Lee,Col.Henry,	1	47	Pr.Wm.	Legate,George,	1		Har.	Lester,Bryan,	1	15	Lun.
Lee,Col.Henry,Jr.,			Lou.	Legate,John,	1		Har.	Lester,Bryan Jr.	1	1	Lun.
Lee,Henry,	1	4	West.	Legerwood,William,	1	4	Augu.	Lester,Frances,		11	Jas.C.
Lee,Henry,Jr.,	2	48	West.	Legg,Ambrose,	1		Pr.Wm.	Lester,Henry,	1		Henry
Lee,Henry,	1	14	Fau.	Legge,Elijah,			Pr.Wm.	Lester,John,	1	2	Lun.
Lee,Henry,			Pr.Wm.	Legge,Fortunaus,	1		Pr.Wm.	Lester,Nat,			York
Lee,Henry,	1	42	Lou.	Legge,James,	1		Pr.Wm.	Lester,Samuel,	1		Mont.
Lee,James,	1		Camp.	Legg,Capt.John,	1	4	Spots	Lester,Timothy,	1	5	Jas.C.
Lee,James,	1	1	Buck.	Legge,Thomas,Sr.	1		Pr.Wm.	Lester,William,	1	3	K.Geo.
Lee,James,	1		Camp.	Legg,Thomas,Jr.			Pr.Wm.	Lester,William,	1	16	Jas.C.
Lee,Jesse,	1	16	Din.	Legg,William,	1		Pr.Wm.	Lestley,William,	1		Mont.
Lee,Jesse,	1		Mont.	Leidy,Andrew,	1	1	Wash.	Lesusur,Chastain,	1	6	Buck.
Lee,Jessee,	1		Pr.Geo.	Leith,Arthur,	1	10	Pr.Geo.	Lesure,Peter,	1	4	Buck.
Lee,John,	1		K.Geo.	Leith,Charles,	1	8	Pr.Geo.	Lesure,Samuel,	1	3	Buck.
Lee,John,			Hen.	Leith,James,Sr.,	1	3	Lou.	Letcher,John,	1	5	Rock.
Lee,John,	1		Fau.	Leith,James,Jr.,	1	1	Lou.	Letcher,Stephen,G.	1	6	Gooch.
Lee,John,	1		Bed.	Leith,Peter,	1		Din.	Lett,James,	1		Brun.
Lee,John,	1		Berk.	Leith,Stephen,	1		Pr.Geo.	Lett,John,	1	10	Brun.
Lee,John,	1		Pr.Geo.	Leivesey,Amos,	1		Pr.Geo.	Letter,John,	1		Lin.
Lee,John,	1	6	Pr.Geo.	Leivesay,Jessee,	1	1	Pr.Geo.	Letter,William,	1		Berk.
Lee,John,est.,		3	Gooch.	Lemaders,Richard,	1		Berk.	Lettiston,Elijah,	1	8	Acco.
Lee,Joseph,	1		Mont.	Leman,John,	1		Bot.	Lettiston,Thomas Sr.	1	2	Acco.
Lee,Lewis,	1	2	Pr.Wm.	Leman,Robert,			Spots	Lettiston,Thomas,Jr.	1		Acco.
Lee,M.,			Pr.Wm.	Lemar,Charles,	1		Berk.	Lettiston,Tully,	1	6	Acco.
Lee,Nathaniel,	1	8	Pr.Geo.	Lemare,Gallant,	1		Wash.	Lettiston,William,	1	3	Acco.
Lee,Peter,	1		Pr.Geo.	Lemare,James,	1		Wash.	Lettiston,Wittet,	2		Acco.
Lee,Peter,	1		Wash.	Lemare,John,	1		Wash.	Leveston,Aaron,	1		Bed.
Lee,Peter,	1		Pr.Geo.	Lemare,Luke,	1		Wash.	Levey,Ann			K.Geo.
Lee,Peter,			Pr.Wm.	Lemare,William,	1		Wash.	Levil,Edward,			Cul.
Lee,Phill		1	Gooch.	Lemaster,John,	1		Bot.	Levingstone,Jacob,	1		Berk.
Lee,Philip,est.		9	West.	Lemay,John,	1		Loui.	Levingston,John,	1		Wash.
Lee,Philip,est.,	2	31	Lou.	Lemay,John,	1	2	Lun.	Levingston,Peter,	1	4	Wash.
Lee,Richard,			Hen.	Lemay,Samuel,	1	5	Gooch	Levingston,Samuel,	1		Wash.
Lee,Richard,	1	9	Buck.	Lemert,Lewis,	1		Lou.	Levingston,William,	1		Augu.
Lee,Richard,			Buck.	Lemmon,George,	1		Augu.	Levingston,William,	1	2	Wash.
Lee,Richard,	1	28	West.	Lemons,John,	1		Lou.	Lewis,Abraham,	1	1	Lou.
Lee,Richard,	4	89	West.	Lemmon,William,	1		Camp.	Lewis,Alexander,	1		Bot.
Lee,Richard,E.	1	5	Eliz.C	Lemmon,William,	1		Camp.	Lewis,Andrew,	2	18	Bot.
Lee,Richard Henry,	1	43	West.	Lemur,Alexander,	1	1	Berk.	Lewis,Benjamin,	1	11	Hen.
Lee,Stephen Sr.	3	10	Pr.Wm.	Lemur,John,	1		Berk.	Lewis,Benjamin,		20	Hen.
Lee,Stephen,	1		Fau.	Lemur,William,	1	1	Berk.	Lewis,Benjamin,	1	16	So'n.
Lee,Stephen,	1		Lou.	Lendray,Joshua,	2	2	Cul.	Lewis,Benjamin,			Din.
Lee,Stephen,	1	7	Henry	LenenWeaver,Philip,	1		Lou.	Lewis,Benjamin,		6	So'n.
Lee,Thomas,	1	2	Pr.Geo.	Lener,Mordecai,	1		Lou.	Lewis,Charles,			Lou.
Lee,Thomas,	1		Pr.Geo.	Lenn,James,	1		Berk.	Lewis,Charles,	3	26	Hen.
Lee,Thomas,			Wash.	Lennocks,John,			Hen.	Lewis,Christopher,	1	1	K.& Q.
Lee,Thomas,			K.Geo.	Lenry,Miajah,	1		Caro.	Lewis,Dan,	1		Rock.
Lee,Thomas,	1	1	Pr.Geo.	Lenry,John,	2		Caro.	Lewis,Daniel,	2	5	Lou.
Lee,William,			K.Geo.	Lensey,James,	1		Cul.	Lewis,David,			Lou.
Lee,William,	1		Camp.	Lenvil,Morgan,	1		Fay.	Lewis,David Sr.,	1		Berk.
Lee,William,Sr.	1		Camp.	Leonard,Adam,	1		Berk.	Lewis,David,Jr.,	1		Berk.
Lee,William,Jr.	1		Camp.	Leonard,Benjamin,	1		Hen.	Lewis,Edward,	1		Din.
Lee,William,	1		Camp.	Leonard,Martin,	1		Har.	Lewis,Elizabeth,	1		Acco.
Lee,William,		11	Lou.	Leonard,Nicholas,	1		Berk.	Lewis,Fielding,est.,		42	Spots.
Lee,William,	1		Pr.Geo.	Leonard,Noble,	1	1	Pr.Geo.	Lewis,Francis,			Hen.
Lee,William,est.,	4	93	Jas.C.	Leonard,Samuel,	1	1	Cha.C	Lewis,Francis,	1	3	Hen.
Lee,William,			Buck.	Leonard,Vanduvan,	1	3	Pr.Geo.	Lewis,Francis,	1	3	Din.
Lee,William,	1	1	Wash.	Leonard,William,	1	12	Cha.C	Lewis,George,	1		Fay.
Lee,William,	1		Mont.	Lenore,Robert,	1	12	Brun.	Lewis,George,	1	5	West.

Name			County
Lewis,George,	1		Har.
Lewis,George,	1	13	Lou.
Lewis,George,	2		Lou.
Lewis,Gilley,			Hen.
Lewis,Griffin,	1	10	Camp.
Lewis,Henry,	2	1	Acco.
Lewis,Henry,	3	17	Cul.
Lewis,Henry,	1	1	Caro.
Lewis,Henry,	1	4	Spots.
Lewis,Howell,	3	35	Loui.
Lewis,Iveson,	1	13	K.&Q.
Lewis,Jacob,	1		Wash.
Lewis,James,			Cul.
Lewis,James,	1		Din.
Lewis,James,			Lou.
Lewis,James,	1		Bed.
Lewis,James,	1	2	Fau.
Lewis,James,	1	8	Lou.
Lewis,James,	1	17	Spots.
Lewis,Jehu,	1		Lou.
Lewis,Jeremiah,			York.
Lewis,Joel,	1		Lou.
Lewis,Joel,	1	7	Spots.
Lewis,John,	2	11	Lou.
Lewis,John,	1	7	Lou.
Lewis,John,			Cha.C.
Lewis,John,			Cha.C.
Lewis,John,	1		Din.
Lewis,John,	1	9	Din.
Lewis,John,	1		Har.
Lewis,John,F.,	1	13	Spots.
Lewis,John,Z.,	1	18	Spots.
Lewis,John,	1	4	Cul.
Lewis,John,	2	13	Jas.C.
Lewis,John,	2	5	Lin.
Lewis,John,	2	35	Caro.
Lewis,John,	1	1	Camp.
Lewis,John,Jr.	1		Eliz.C.
Lewis,John,	1	26	Pr.Geo.
Lewis,John,	1	8	Gooch.
Lewis,John,	1		Gooch.
Lewis,John,	1		Berk.
Lewis,John,	1		Berk.
Lewis,Capt.Joseph,	2	10	Lou.
Lewis,Capt.Joseph,	1	20	Hen.
Lewis,Joseph,	2		Din.
Lewis,Joseph,	2	1	Cul.
Lewis,Joseph,	1		Rock.
Lewis,Joseph,	1		Henry
Lewis,Joseph,	1		Lin.
Lewis,Joseph,	1		Gooch.
Lewis,Joseph,	1	1	Gooch.
Lewis,Joseph,Sr.	1	15	Gooch.
Lewis,Joseph,Jr.,	1	13	Gooch.
Lewis,Major,			Buck.
Lewis,Matthew,	1		Eliz.C.
Lewis,Mrs.Mary,	1	56	Gooch.
Lewis,Miles,	1		Lin.
Lewis,Nathaniel,	1		West
Lewis,Nicholas,	1	26	Spots.
Lewis,Rebecca,		2	Hen.
Lewis,Richard,	1		Caro.
Lewis,Richard,	2		Acco.
Lewis,Robert,	1	3	Hen.
Lewis,Robert,			Hen.
Lewis,Robert,	1	41	Gooch.
Lewis,Robert,	1	10	Spots.
Lewis,Samuel,		10	Spots.
Lewis,Sarah,			So'n.
Lewis,Sarah,		8	Augu.
Lewis,Shadrach,	1	2	So'n.
Lewis,Shadrick,	1		Nor.
Lewis,Solomon,	1		Nor.
Lewis,Stephen,	1		Lou.
Lewis,Susanna,		1	Hen.
Lewis,Thomas,	1		Bot.

Name			County
Lewis,Thomas,	2	17	Camp.
Lewis,Thomas,	2	17	Camp.
Lewis,Thomas,	1		Eliz.C.
Lewis,Thomas,	1		Lin.
Lewis,Thomas,	1	17	Fay.
Lewis,Thomas,	1		Din.
Lewis,Thomas,			Lou.
Lewis,Thomas,			Lou.
Lewis,Thomas,	1	1	Lou.
Lewis,Thomas,	1	6	Lou.
Lewis,Thomas,Jr.,	1		Acco.
Lewis,Vincent,	4	13	Lou.
Lewis,Waller,	1	14	Loui.
Lewis,Warer,	1	25	Spots.
Lewis,Capt.William,	1	15	Din.
Lewis,William,	1		Lou.
Lewis,William,			Spots.
Lewis,William,			Lou.
Lewis,William,		2	Hen.
Lewis,William,	1	1	Eliz.C.
Lewis,William,	1	1	Gooch.
Lewis,William J.,	1	5	Jas.C.
Lewis,William,			Din.
Lewis,William,	1		Henry
Lewis,William,			Fay.
Lewis,William,	1		Lin.
Lewis,Capt.Zachariah,		8	Pr.Wm.
Lewis,Zacharias	1	9	Fau.
Lewis,Zachary,	1	35	Spots.
Lewis,Zaciariah,	1	2	Caro.
Lewis,Zebulon,	1	16	Brun.
Lewellen,Alex.McG.,	1		Buck.
Lewellin,Frances,		2	Eliz.C.
Lewellin,Thomas,	1		Lou.
Lewellin,Shadruck,	1		Lou.
Leweling,Thomas,	1		Bot.
Lewellings,Alexander,	1		Eliz.C.
Leyburn,George,	1		Augu.
Licker,Conrad,		1	Lou.
Ligget,Alexander,	1		Rock.
Ligget,John,	1		Lin.
Liggit,James,	1		Rock.
Liggit,John,			Rock.
Liggon,John,			Buck.
Liggon,John,	1	1	Hen.
Liggon,Matthew,	1	1	Din.
Liggon,Samuel,	1		Hen.
Liggon,Samuel,Jr.,	1		Hen.
Liegh,John,	1	3	K.&Q.
Liegh,Richard,	1	15	K.&Q.
Light,Peter,	7		Berk.
Lightfoot,Goodrich,			Cul.
Lightfoot,John,	1	2	Brun.
Lightfoot,John,	1	4	Cul.
Lightfoot,John,	2	10	Cul.
Lightfoot,Mary,		8	Brun.
Lightfoot,Mary,	1	3	Jas.C
Lightfoot,Milly,	1	34	Brun.
Lightfoot,Philip,	2	37	Caro.
Lightfoot,Philip,	1	6	Cul.
Lightfoot,William,	2	98	Cha.C.
Lightfoot,William,	1	15	Cul.
Liking,Marquis,	1		Bot.
Liking,William,	1		Bot.
Likings,John,	1		Har.
Lilburn,Andrew,	1		Berk.
Lilburn,Elizabeth,		1	York
Lilburn,Mary,		1	Berk.
Lillard,Benjamin,	1	3	Cul.
Lillard,James Sr.,	1	3	Cul.
Lillard,James,Jr.,	1		Cul.
Lillard,John,		5	Cul.
Lillard,Thomas,	2		Cul.
Lillard,William,	1		Cul.
Lille,William,	2	12	Berk.
Lilly,John,	1		Augu.

Name			County
Lilly,Thomas,	1	8	York
Limit,John,	1		K.Geo.
Lin,Joseph,	1		Lin.
Lincey,John,	1	2	Cul.
Linche,Barbery,		1	Hen.
Linder,Jacob,	1		Wash.
Linder,Jacob,	1		Berk.
Linder,Jacob Jr.,	1	1	Berk.
Linder,Lawrence,	1		Berk.
Lindsay,Daniel,	1	20	Spots.
Lihosay,Lucy,	1	3	Caro.
Lindsay,William,	1	21	Caro.
Lindsey,James,			Hen.
Lindsey,James,	1		Henry
Lindsey,John,	1		Lou.
Lindsey,John,	1		Hen.
Lindsey,John,	1	15	Henry
Lindsey,Moses,	1		Hen.
Lindsey,William,			Hen.
Lindsey,William,	1		Mont.
Liner,Henry,	1		Augu.
Linger,Nicholas,	1		Har.
Lingnocker,Archibald			Bot.
Lingoe,Caleb,	1		Acco.
Lingoe,John,	1		Acco.
Lingoe,Joshua,	3		Acco.
Lingoe,Ralph,	1		Acco.
Lingoe,Robert,	1		Acco.
Lingoe,Robinson,	1		Acco.
Lingoe,Thomas,	1		Acco.
Link,Jacob,	2		Lou.
Link,John,			Lou.
Link,Mathias,	1		Augu.
Linn,Joseph,	1		Augu.
Linney,William,	1	11	Loui.
Linsay,Samuel,	1		Bot.
Linsay,Walter,	1		Bot.
Linsay,Widow,		2	Bot.
Linsday,William,	1		Brun.
Linsey,Anthony,	1		Fay.
Linsey,Edward,	1		Pr.Geo.
Linsey,Edward,	1	2	Jas.C.
Linsey,James,	1		K.Wm.
Linsey,James,	1		Fay.
Linsey,Jesse,	1	1	Jas.C.
Linsey,John,	1	1	Jas.C.
Linsey,John,	1		Fay.
Linsey,Matthew,	1		Mont
Linsey,William,	3	1	Fay.
Linsey,William Jr.			Fay.
Linthicum,Edward,	1	3	Buck.
Linthicum,Edward,			Buck.
Linton,Capt.John,	1	6	Lou,
Linton,John,	1	18	Pr.Wm.
Linton,William,	1		Fau.
Linton,William,	1	8	Pr.Wm.
Lip,Henry,	2		Cul.
Lipford,Pear,			Buck.
Lips,John,	1		Berk.
Lipscomb,Ambrose,	1	15	K.Wm.
Lipscomb,Ambrose,	2	13	K.Wm.
Lipscomb,Ambrose,	1	7	K.Wm.
Lipscomb,Ann,	1	11	K.Wm.
Lipscomb,Anderson,	1	10	K.Wm.
Lipscomb,Benoney,	1	6	K.Wm.
Lipscomb,Bernard,.	1	7	K.Wm.
Lipscomb,Charles,	2	1	K.Wm.
Lipscomb,Charles,	1	5	K.Wm.
Lipscomb,Colonel,	1	8	Buck.
Lipscomb,Daniel,	1		K.Wm.
Lipscomb,Daniel,Jr.		11	K.Wm.
Lipscomb,David,			Loui.
Lipscomb,Elizabeth,		18	K.Wm.
Lipscomb,Elizabeth,		6	K.Wm.
Lipscomb,Francis,	1	8	Loui.
Lipscomb,George,	3	14	K.Wm.

Name			Loc	Name			Loc	Name			Loc
Lipscomb,Henry,	1	1	K.Wm.	Lock,Richard,			Lou.	Long,James,			Cul.
Lipscomb,James,	1	7	K.Wm.	Lock,Sarah,	1		Mont.	Long,John,	1		Lou.
Lipscomb,James,	1	11	K.Wm.	Lock,William,	1		Berk.	Long,John,	2	8	Cul.
Lipscomb,Jane,		5	K.Wm.	Locker,Thomas,	1		Lou.	Long,John,	1	1	Caro.
Lipscomb,John,	1	6	Loui.	Lockert,James,	2		Fay.	Long,John,	1		Cul.
Lipscomb,John Pem.	2	9	K.Wm.	Locket,David,	1	9	Buck.	Long,John,	1		Cul.
Lipscomb,Josiah,	1	2	K.Wm.	Lockhart,Andrew,	1		Mont.	Long,John,	1		Cul.
Lipscomb,Joseph,	1	11	Loui.	Lockhart,Thomas,	1	2	Henry	Long,John,	2	9	Caro.
Lipscomb,Kesiah,			K.Wm.	Lockhart,Thomas,			Rock.	Long,John,	1	6	Caro.
Lipscomb,Major,,	1		K.Wm.	Lockhart,Patrick,	1	8	Bot.	Long,John,	1	15	Caro.
Lipscomb,Mary,		3	K.Wm.	Lockhart,William,	1		Mont.	Long,John,	1	1	Bed.
Lipscomb,Mourning,	1	5	K.Wm.	Lockhart,William,	1		Augu.	Long,John,	1		Bot.
Lipscomb,Nunn,	2	14	K.Wm.	Lockhart,William,	1		Mont.	Long,John,	1		Mont.
Lipscomb,Pemberton,	1	8	K.Wm.	Lockridge,Robert,	1		Rock.	Long,John,Read,	1	7	Cul.
Lipscomb,Philip,	1	6	Spots.	Locky,Thomas,	1		Bot.	Long,Joseph,	1		Augu.
Lipscomb,Thomas,	1	13	Spots.	Lodge,Francis,H.			K.& Q.	Long,Levie,	1	2	Acco.
Lipscomb,Thomas,	1	1	K.Wm.	Lodge,Jacob,			Lou.	Long,Nicholas,	1	6	Caro.
Lipscomb,William,	3	17	Loui.	Lodge,Josabed,	2		Lou.	Long,Reubin,	2	16	Cul.
Lipscomb,William Jr.,			Loui.	Lodge,William,	1		Lou.	Long,Richard,	1		Wash.
Lipscomb,William,	1	1	Hen.	Lofflin,Daniel,	1	2	Lou.	Long,Samuel,			Cul.
Lipscomb,William,	1	7	Loui.	Logan,Anthony,	1		Fay.	Long,Samuel,	1	2	Acco.
Lipscomb,William,			K.Wm.	Logan,Benjamin,	1	8	Lin.	Long,Samuel,	1	3	Augu.
Lipscomb,Yancy,	1	13	K.Wm.	Logan,Charles,	1	29	Hen.	Long,Sarah,	1	2	Cul.
Lipscomb,Yancey,		10	K.Wm.	Logan,David,	2		Lin.	Long,Thomas,	1		Lou.
Liptrap,Isaac,	1		Rock.	Logan,David,	1	2	Rock.	Long,Ware,	2		Cul.
Lister,Sarah,est.,		6	York	Logan,David,	1		Fay.	Long,Warr,	1		Bot.
Litchford,John,	3	1	Jas.C.	Logan,David,	2		Har.	Long,William,	1	1	Lin.
Litchworth,Benjamin,	1		Loui.	Logan,George,	1		Fay.	Long,William,	1	3	Caro.
Litchworth,Thomas,	1	3	Loui.	Logan,Hugh,	1		Fay.	Long,William,	1		Cul.
Littel,James,	1		Mont.	Logan,James,	1	2	Wash.	Long,William,	1		Henry
Litter,Thomas,	1		Har.	Logan,James,	5	1	Lin.	Long,William,	1		Wash.
Litteston,Jacob,			Acco.	Logan,James,	1	1	Rock.	Longbottom,John,	1		Brun.
Litting,Matthias,	1		Mont.	Logan,James,	1		Rock.	Longdon,Samuel,	2	4	Spots.
Little,David,	1		Bot.	Logan,James,	1		Fay.	Longest,Dorothy,		6	K.& Q.
Little,Isaac,	1		Mont.	Logan,James,Jr.,	1	2	Lin.	Longest,Caleb,	1	1	K.& Q.
Little,James,	1		Fay.	Logan,John,	1	3	Bot.	Longest,John,	1		K.& Q.
Little,Joseph,	1		Rock.	Logan,Marget,		2	Lin.	Longest,Lewis,	1		K.& Q.
Little,Thomas,	1		Rock.	Logan,Nathaniel,	1		Lin.	Longest,Richard,	1	2	K.& Q.
Little,Thomas,	1		Bot.	Logan,Samuel,	1		Fay.	Longley,Joseph,	2		Lou.
Litlegow,Alexander,	1	8	Pr.Wm.	Logan,Thomas,	1		Rock.	Longley,William,			Lou.
Littlejohn,Daniel,	1		Berk.	Logan,William,	1	6	Lin.	Longley,William,	1		Mont.
Littlejohn,John,	1		Berk.	Logan,William,	3		Fay.	Longwith,Thomas,	1		Har.
Littlejohn,John,	2	1	Lou.	Logan,William,	2	3	Rock.	Lonohenay,Ezekiel,			Lou.
Littlejohn,William,	1		Berk.	Logan,William,	2		Bot.	Look,James,	1		Din.
Littleton,Charles,	1		Lou.	Loggan,William,	2		Augu.	Lord,Frances,	1		K.Geo.
Littleton,John,	1	2	Lou.	Logwood,Edmund,		3	Bed.	Lord,J.,	1		Pr.Wm.
Littleton,Thomas,			Lou.	Logwood,Thomas,	1	15	Bed.	Lord,William,			Pr.Wm.
Littleton,William,	2		Lou.	Lohead,David,	1		Fay.	Lorrain,Barn,			Hen.
Littlepage,Thomas,	1	25	K.Wm.	Loller,James,	1		Fau.	Lorton,Israel,	1	1	Mont.
Litz,William,			Mont.	Loman,James,	1	1	Lun.	Lorton,Jacob,	1	1	Mont.
Lively,David,	1		Jas.C.	Lomax,Thomas,	1	79	Caro.	Lorton,Sarah,		1	Cha.C.
Lively,James,	1	2	Jas.C.	Long,Adam,	2		Lou.	Losh,Boston,	1		Lou.
Lively,Richard,	1	3	Jas.C.	Long,Adam,	2		Lou.	Losh,Daniel,	1		Lou.
Liverett,Thomas,	1	5	Lun.	Long,Alexander,	1		Augu.	Lott,Jesse,	1	7	Berk.
Livesey,B.			Pr.Geo.	Long,Armistead,			Cul.	Lott,J.,	1	2	Caro.
Livesey,George,	1		Henry	Long,Benjamin,	3	11	Cul.	Lott,Robert,	1		Berk.
Livesey,John,	1		Henry	Long,Bromfield,	1	2	Cul.	Lowry,James,	1		K.Geo.
Livesey,Thomas,	1	3	Henry	Long,Brum,			Cul.	Lowry,John,	1		Augu.
Livesey,Thomas Jr.,	1		Henry	Long,Christopher,	1		Bot.	Lowry,Richard,	1	17	Spots.
Livesey,Thomas,	2	2	Pr.Geo.	Long,Christopher,	1		Mont.	Love,Allen,	4	34	Brun.
Livesey,William,	1	7	Pr.Geo.	Long,Daniel,	1		Cul.	Love,Augustin,	1	17	Fau.
Livesy,Thomas,	1	23	Pr.Geo.	Long,David,	1		Augu.	Love,Charles,	1		Lou.
Livingstone,Samuel,			K.& Q.	Long,Edward,	1		Lou.	Love,Charles,	2	7	Pr.Wm.
Loaden,John,	1	3	Bea.	Long,Elisabeth,		1	Augu.	Love,Charles,			Pr.Wm.
Loan,John,	1		Berk.	Long,Erant,	1	4	Cul.	Love,Charles,	1	1	Lun.
Loan,John,	1		Rock.	Long,Francis,	1		Augu.	Love,Elias,			So'n.
Loans,James,	1	2	K.& Q.	Long,Gabriel,	1	6	Cul.	Love,Henry,	1		So'n.
Lochridge,Andrew,	1	4	Augu.	Long,Gabriel,	1	15	Cul.	Love,Hugh,est.,	1	21	Brun.
Lochridge,John,	1		Augu.	Long,Gabriel,			Cul.	Love,James,	1		Lou.
Lochridge,John,	1		Augu.	Long,Gabriel,			Cul.	Love,John,	1	1	Bot.
Lochridge,Samuel,	1		Augu.	Long,Gabriel,			Cul.	Love,John,			Pr.Wm.
Lochridge,William,	1		Augu.	Long,Henry,	1		Mont.	Love,John,	1	1	Mont.
Lock,Charles,	1	4	Din.	Long,Henry,	1		Lou.	Love,Joseph,	1	2	Mont.
Lock,George,	1	1	Berk.	Long,Jacob,	1		Lou.	Love,Phillip,	1	3	Bot.
Lock,John,	1	4	Lun.	Long,James,	1	1	Augu.	Love,Robert,	1		Mont.
Lock,John,	1	1	Berk.	Long,James,	2	7	Cul.	Loving,David,	1		Bea.

Name			County
Love,Robert,	1		Berk.
Love,Robert,	1		Lin.
Love,Samuel,	2	24	Lou.
Love,Samuel,	1	9	West.
Love,Samuel,	1	5	Lun.
Love,Samuel,			Pr.Wm
Love,Samuel,	1	30	Pr.Wm
Love,Silas,	1		So'n
Love,Thomas,	1		So'n
Love,Thomas,	1	5	Pr.Wm
Love,William,	1	8	Lun.
Love,William,	1	1	Mont.
Loveall,John,	1	6	Gooch.
Lovelace,James,	1		Cul.
Lovelass,John,	1		Cul.
Loveless,Thomas,	1		Lou.
Lovell,John,	1	9	K.Geo.
Lovell,Markham,	1	3	Henry
Lovell,William,	1	4	Henry
Lovett,Daniel,	1		Lou.
Lovet,William,	1	2	K.Wm.
Lovin,John,	1		Lin.
Loving,Christopher,	1		Caro.
Loving,James,	1		Caro.
Loving,John,	1		Caro.
Loving,Richard,	1		Hen.
Loving,Thomas,	1		Caro.
Loving,Thomas,Jr.,	1		Caro.
Loving,William,	1		Caro.
Lovingood,Hermon,	1		Aug.
Low,Daniel,	1	1	Buck.
Low,Daniel Johnson,	1	7	Buck.
Low,Edward,	1		Lin.
Low,Elizabeth,			Lin.
Low,Samuel,	1		Lin.
Low,William,	1	13	Buck.
Lowe,Benjamin,	1		Lou.
Lowe,Harry,	1	6	Lou.
Lowe,John,	1	3	Spots.
Lowe,John,	1	1	Pr.Wm
Lowe,John,	1		West.
Lowe,Ledbetter,	1		So'n
Lowe,Levi,	1		So'n
Lowe,Lightborne,	1		So'n
Lowe,Richard,	1	11	West.
Lowe,Thomas,	1		Henry
Lower,John,	1		Berk.
Lower,William,			Hen.
Lowery,James,	2		Berk.
Lowery,Martha,		21	Berk.
Lowery,Robert,	1		Berk.
Lowman,George,	1		Berk.
Lowman,George,	1		Mont.
Lowry,Aaron,	1		Loui.
Lowry,Absalom,	1		Loui.
Lowry,Alexander,	1		Aug.
Lowry,George,	1	13	Fau.
Lowry,James,	1		Wash.
Lowry,Capt.John,	1		Wash.
Lowry,Joseph,	1		Gooch.
Lowry,Lewis,	1		Gooch.
Lowry,Martha,	1	21	Caro.
Lowry,Matthew,	1	3	Gooch.
Lowry,Samuel,	1		Aug.
Lowry,Samuel,	1		Har.
Lowry,Stephen,	1		Caro.
Lowry,Stephen,	1		Fay.
Lowry,Thomas,est.,		20	Lun.
Lowry,William,	1	16	Lun.
Lowry,William,	2		Bed.
Lowther,James,	1		Mont.
Lowther,John,	1		Mont.
Lowther,Ruth,			Har.
Loyd,Elisha,			Lou.
Loyd,George,	1	2	Din.
Loyd,Henry,	1		Lou.
Loyd,James,	1		Brun.
Loyd,James,	1		Bot.
Loyd,John,	1		Buck.
Loyd,John,	1	1	Din.
Loyd,John,	1	1	Henry
Loyd,Kennon,	1		Din.
Loyd,Lewis,	1	8	Din.
Loyde,Robert,	1		Lou.
Loyd,Thomas,	1	1	Din.
Loyd,Thomas,	1		Wash.
Loyd,William,	1	6	Din.
Loyd,Thomas,	1		Spots
Lucas,A.,	1	2	Pr.Wm
Lucas,Aaron,	1		Hen.
Lucas,Charles,	1		Mont.
Lucas,Dozy,			Lou.
Lucas,Edmund,			Caro.
Lucas,Edward,	1	1	Berk.
Lucas,Francis,			Cul.
Lucas,Francis,Jr.,	1		Cul.
Lucas,Frederick,	1	10	Brun.
Lucas,Col.James,	1	5	Brun.
Lucas,John,		2	Caro.
Lucas,John,Sr.,	1	11	Lun.
Lucas,John,Jr.,	1	1	Lun.
Lucas,John,	1		Hen.
Lucas,John,	1		West.
Lucas,John,	1	1	Bot.
Lucas,John,	1		Mont.
Lucas,Joseph,	1		Hen.
Lucas,Leonard,	1		K.Geo
Lucas,Parker,	1		Mont.
Lucas,Samuel,	1		Hen.
Lucas,Susannah,			Lou.
Lucas,Thomas,	1	2	Lou.
Lucas,William,	1	2	Berk.
Lucas,William,	1		Berk.
Lucas,Zachary,	1	1	Spots.
Lucus,William,	1		Cul.
Luck,Nathan,	2	1	Caro.
Luck,Richard,	1		Spots.
Luck,Samuel,	1	9	Spots.
Lucy,Joshua,			Brun.
Lucy,Robert,	1	7	Brun.
Luiton,William,	1	3	Pr.Wm
Lukart,John,	1		K.Wm.
Luke,Daniel,	1	4	Nor.
Luke,Isaac,	1	1	Nor.
Luke,John,	1		Lou.
Luke,William,	1		Berk.
Luker,John,	1		Acco.
Lukie,Andrew,	1	7	Caro.
Lumpkin,Anthony,	1	3	K.&Q
Lumpkin,Anthony,	1	6	K.&Q
Lumpkin,Henry,	1	15	K.&Q
Lumpkin,Jacob,	1	16	K.&Q
Lumpkin,John,	1	1	K.&Q
Lumpkin,Joice,		6	K.&Q
Lumpkin,Mary,		10	K.&Q
Lumpkin,Nimrod,	1	2	K.&Q
Lumpkin,Philip,	1	3	Lin.
Lumpkin,Richard,	1	9	K.&Q
Lumpkin,Robert,	1	8	K.&Q
Lumpkin,Robert,	1	10	K.&Q
Lumpkin,Robert,	1	4	K.&Q
Lumpkin,Sarah,	1	6	K.&Q
Lumpkin,Thomas,	1	6	Bed.
Lumpkin,William,			K.&Q
Lumpkin,William,	1	10	K.&Q
Lumsden,Charles,	1		Henry
Lumsden,George,	2	5	Lou.
Lumsden,John,	1		Loui.
Lumsden,John,	1		Henry
Lumsden,William,			Loui.
Lundy,Elizabeth,		8	So'n
Lundy,James,	1	6	So'n
Lundy,John,	1	17	So'n
Lundy,Pheobe,		9	So'n
Lundy,Robert,	1	4	So'n
Luney,Absalom,	1		Bot.
Luney,John,	1	1	Bot.
Luney,Joseph,	1	5	Bot.
Lundie,Thomas,	1	10	Brun.
Lunn,William,	1	1	Cha.Cy
Lunsford,Amos,	1	2	Fau.
Lunsford,Isaac,	1		Din.
Lunsford,Jemima,	1	1	Fau.
Lunsford,Richard,	1	3	Din.
Lurtee,John,	1	7	K.Geo.
Lurton,James,	1		Acco.
Lurton,John,	1		Acco.
Lurton,Labin,	1		Acco.
Luscoleet,John,	1		Bot.
Lusk,Hugh,			Rock.
Lusk,John,Sr.,	1		Rock.
Lusk,John,Jr.,	1		Rock.
Lusk,Samuel,	2		Fay.
Lusk,Samuel,	1		Rock.
Lusk,William,	1		Rock.
Luster,John,	1		Bot.
Lut,Stephen,	1	9	Bot.
Luter,John,	1		So'n
Luts,Michael,	1		Lou.
Lutti,John,	1		Cul.
Luttrell,Edward,	1		Fau.
Luttrell,John,	1		Fau.
Luttrell,Richard,			Fau.
Luttrell,Richard,	1	3	Fau.
Luttrell,Richard,	1		Fau.
Luttrell,Robert,	1	1	Fau.
Luttrell,Robert,	1	6	Pr.Wm.
Luttrell,Simon,	1	5	Pr.Wm.
Luwedge,Edward,	1	1	Spots.
Lyall,Joseph,	1	10	Brun.
Lyall,Thomas,			Brun.
Lyburn,Richard,	1	2	Caro.
Lyburn,Stafford,	3	9	Caro.
Lydea,Joseph,	1		Mont.
Lyle,Agness,			Rock.
Lyle,Daniel,	2		Rock.
Lyle,Hugh,	3	4	Berk.
Lyle,James,	1	4	Rock.
Lyle,James,			Rock.
Lyle,John,	1		Rock.
Lyle,John,	1	1	Berk.
Lyle,John,	1		Rock.
Lyle,John,	1		Rock.
Lyle,Robert,	1		Rock.
Lyle,Samuel,	2	8	Rock.
Lyle,William,	1	1	Rock.
Lyles,Hugh Isaac,	1		Mont.
Lyles,Joseph,	1		Lou.
Lyles,Manasses,	1		Lou.
Lyles,Zachariah,	1		Lou.
Lylse,David,	1		K.Wm.
Lynch,Elijah,	1		Camp.
Lynch,H.James,	1	17	Caro.
Lynch,James,	1		Brun.
Lynch,James,	1		Mont.
Lynch,Jesse,	1		Mont.
Lynch,John,	1		Brun.
Lynch,John,	1		Camp.
Lynch,Patrick,	1	2	Han.
Lynch,Peter,	1		Har.
Lynch,William,	1		Brun.
Lynch,William,	1		Henry
Lyndsey,William,	1	7	Pr.Wm.
Lyne,Henry,	2	8	Henry
Lyne,John,	1	1	Hen.
Lyne,John,	1	15	K.&Q
Lyne,Thomas,	1		Lou.
Lyne,William,	1	35	K.&Q

Lynn,John,	1		Pr.Wm.	Madison,John,	1		K.Wm.	Mallory,Roger,	1	19	Brun.
Lynn,William,	2		Fau.	Madison,John,est.		50	Bot.	Mallory,William,	1	1	Loui.
Lynn,William,			Pr.Wm.	Madison,Richard,	1	1	Augu.	Mallory,William,	1	20	Eliz.C.
Lyon,Alexander,	1		Cul.	Madison,Thomas,		1	K.Wm.	Mallory,William,	1		Brun,
Lyon,Andrew,	1	2	Caro.	Madison,Thomas P.,	1	9	K.Wm.	Mallory,William,	1	11	York
Lyon,Charles,	1		Har.	Madison,William,			K.Wm.	Mallow,Adam,	1		Har.
Lyon,David,	1		Lin..	Madison,William,Jr.,	1		K.Wm.	Mallow,Henry,	1		Har.
Lyon,Diana,	1	3	Caro.	Madison,William,est.		19	Bot.	Mallow,Michael,	1		Har.
Lyon,Dixon,	1	1	K.& Q.	Maddox,George,	1	6	Pr.Wm.	Malone,Daniel,	1	8	Lun.
Lyon,Enoc,	1	1	York	Maganan,Darby,	1		Cul.	Malone,George,	2	12	Brun.
Lyon,Jacob,			Cul.	Magby,Matthew,	1		Berk.	Malone,John,	1		Lou.
Lyon,James,	2	12	Henry	Magee,Robert,	1		Mont.	Malone,Lewis,			Brun.
Lyon,John,	2		Jas.C.	Maget,James,	1	6	So'n.	Malone,Michael,	1	2	Din.
Lyon,Sarah,		3	Acco.	Maget,Nicholas,	1	18	So'n.	Malone,Nancy,	1	6	Din.
Lyon,Stephen,	1	3	Henry	Maget,Samuel,			So'n.	Malone,Nathaniel,			Din.
Lyon,Stephen,	1		Rock.	Magill,Robert,	1		Berk.	Malone,Richard,	1	2	Din.
Lyon,William,	1	3	Cul.	Magradah,Jacob,			Bed.	Malone,William,	1	8	Din.
Lyon,Zachariah,	1	1	Lou.	Magrath,Brian,	2		Cul.	Man,William,	1		Lin.
Lyons,Abram,	1		Cul.	Magruder,Thomas,	1	4	Cul.	Manfee,Elizabeth,			Cul.
Lyons,Andrew,	1		Pr.Wm.	Mahawney,James,	1	1	Lou.	Manford,William,	1		Berk.
Lyons,Peter,		15	K.Wm.	Mahue,James,	1		Lou.	Mangram,Elizabeth,		1	Din.
Lyre,Bartholomew,	1		Camp.	Maidlin,Frederick,	1		Din.	Manifee,Henry,	1		Cul.
Lyre,Nicholas,	1		Camp.	Maidlin,Michal,	1		Din.	Manifee,Henry,	2	7	Cul.
Lytle,John,	1		Fay.	Maidlin,Richard,	1		Din.	Manifee,Shenur,	1		Cul.
Lytle,William,	2		Fay.	Main,John,	1		Berk.	Manifee,William,	1		Lin.
Lytle,William,	1		Bot.	Main,Sebeer,			Wash.	Manifee,William,	1	4	Henry
Lyton,Sarah,			Loui.	Main,William,			Lin.	Manion,Ambrose,	1		Bed.
Mabry,George,	1	6	Henry	Mainyard,Nancy,		2	Hen.	Manion,Thomas,	1		Bed.
Mabry,Isaac,	1		Henry	Mairs,Hugh,	2		Mont.	Mankin,Mark,	2	1	Pr.Wm.
Macallister,Robert,	1		Cul.	Mairs,James,	1		Mont.	Mankins,James,	1		Henry
Macallistor,John,	1		Cul.	Mairs,John,	1		Mont.	Mankloe,Elizabeth,		1	Loui.
Maccandlish,Robert,	1	3	K.& Q.	Mais,Joseph,	2		Augu.	Manlove,Dr.C.	1	14	Din.
Macgoan,John,			Acco.	Maise,William,	1		Pr.Wm.	Mann,Augustine,	1	8	K.& Q.
Machan,Mary,			Pr.Geo	Maith,Christopher,			Rock.	Mann,Barnet,	1		Lou.
Machan,Thomas,	1		Fay.	Major,Anne,		3	Cha.C.	Mann,Charles,	3		Lin.
Machem,Thomas,	1	2	Lou.	Major,Barnett,	1		Din.	Mann,Charles,	1	4	Lun.
Machens,Thomas,	1	4	Pr.Geo	Major,Bernard,	1	16	Cha.C.	Mann,Francis,	1	1	Lin.
Machin,George,	1		Pr.Geo	Major,Christianna,		14	Din.	Mann,George,	1		Lou.
Mackay,William,	1		Pr.Wm.	Major,Francis,	1	5	Cul.	Mann,James,	1		Camp.
Macke,Robert,	1		Fay.	Major,Humphrey,	1		Cul.	Mann,John,	1	1	K.Wm.
Mackee,Alexander,	1		Camp.	Major,James,	1		Henry,	Mann,Joseph,	1	3	West.
Mackey,John,	1	1	West.	Major,John,	1	5	Cul.	Mann,Mary,			Gooch.
Mackey,Mary,		5	Rock.	Major,John,	1	11	Cha.C.	Mann,Nathaniel	1		Mont.
Mackey,Walter,	1		Camp.	Major,John,		1	Pr.Geo	Mann,Thomas,	1	1	Loui.
Macksbury,Samuel,	2	4	Lin.	Major,Lodw,	1	5	Cul.	Mann,William,	1		York.
Macky,Doctor Robert,	1		Din.	Major,Mary,		6	Cha.C.	Mannan,John,	1		K.Geo.
Maclin,Frederick,	1	30	Brun.	Major,Mary,		4	K.& Q.	Mannan,Robert,	1	1	K.Geo.
Maclin,Henry,	1	9	Brun.	Major,Rev. Richard,	1	1	Lou.	Manning,Caleb,	1	3	Brun.
Maclin,James,	1		Brun.	Major,Richard,	1	2	Cul.	Manning,Davis,			Henry,
Maclin,John,	1		Din.	Major,Samuel,	1	5	Cul.	Manning,Henry,	1		Henry
Macrae,John,			Pr.Wm.	Major,Samuel,Jr.,	1	8	Cul.	Manning,Joel,	1		Brun,
Made,Thomas,	1		Mont.	Major,Thomas,	1		Mont.	Manning,John,	1		Henry
Madden,Michael,	1		Mont.	Major,William,	2	20	Nor.	Manning,Mary,		4	Berk.
Madden,Scarlet,	1	4	Pr.Wm.	Major,William,	1		Brun.	Manning,Samuel,	1		Berk.
Madderson,John,	1	3	Loui.	Majors,Feddrick,	1		Acco.	Manning,Samuel,	1		Henry
Madduin,Patrick,	1		Berk.	Majors,George,	1	1	Cul.	Manning,Stephen,	1		Jas,C.
Maddocke,James,	1	20	Gooch.	Majors,John,	1		Henry	Mansfield,William,	1		K.& Q.
Maddocks,William,		2	Buck.	Majors,John,	2	11	Fay.	Manson,John,			Din.
Maddox,Benjamin,	1		Gooch.	Majors,John,	1	12	Acco.	Manson,John,	1	10	Din.
Maddox,Jesse,	1		Cul.	Majors,William,	1		Lin.	Manson,Nathaniel,	1	9	Bed.
Maddox,John,	1		Gooch.	Malahome,Rawley,			Pr.Wm.	Manson,Peter,	1	19	Din.
Maddox,Michael,	1		Buck.	Malcom,John,	3		Augu.	Manson,Robert,	1	11	York
Maddox,Michail,	1	2	Cha.C.	Malcom,Joseph,	1		Augu.	Manspoile,Jacob,	1	2	Cul.
Maddox,Notly,	2	10	Cul.	Malcom,Samuel,	1		Augu.	Mapp,Housen,Sr.,	2	4	Acco.
Maddox,Thomas,	1	2	Cul.	Maller,George,	1		Lou.	Mapp,John,	1	14	Nor.
Maddox,William,	1	1	Hen.	Mallore,John,			Bed.	Mapp,Rachal,	1	4	Acco.
Maddox,Willia m,	1	11	Buck.	Mallory,Clement P.,	1	7	Brun.	Mapp,William,	1	7	Nor.
Maddux,George,			Fau.	Mallory,Edward,	1	16	Eliz.C	Marable,George,	1	6	Lun.
Maddux,Thomas,Sr.,			Fau.	Mallory,Francis,	1	6	Brun.	Marable,John,	1	8	Lun.
Maddux,Thomas,	2	11	Fau.	Mallory,John,	1	4	Lun.	Marbes,John,	1		Cul.
Madison,Francis,	1	21	Cul.	Mallory,John,			Loui.	March,Philip,	1		Lou.
Madison,George,	1	18	Caro.	Mallory,Mary,		30	Eliz.C	Marchant,Richard,	1		Berk.
Madison,Henry,Sr.,	2	10	K.Wm.	Mallory,Peter,			Caro.	Marck,Mathais,	1		Cul.
Madison,Henry,Jr.,	2	9	K.Wm.	Mallory,Philip,	2	19	K.Wm.	Marck,Nepew,	2	1	Pr.Geo.
Madison,James,		28	Cul.	Mallory,Roger,	1	2	Fay.	Marcum,John,	1		Mont.
Madison,John,		2	K.Wm.	Mallory,Roger,	1	4	Loui.	Marcum,William,	1		Mont.

Name			County
Marders,James,	1		K.Geo.
Marders,Moses,	1		K.Geo.
Marders,Rowley,	1	6	K.Geo.
Marders,Samuel,		5	K.Geo.
Mare,George,	1		Lin.
Mare,Nicholas,	1		Har.
Mare,Will.,	1		Lin.
Mares,Alexander,	1		Mont.
Mares,Joseph,	1		Mont.
Mares,Samuel,	1		Mont.
Margerum,H.,	1	2	Pr.Wm.
Mark,John,	1	1	Berk.
Mark,Ubrie,		20	Pr.Geo
Markam,Thomas,	1		Bed.
Marken,Samuel,	1		Lou.
Markham,James,	1	5	Fau.
Markham,John,	1	9	Fau.
Markland,William,	1		Wash.
Marks,Abel,			Lou.
Marks,Edward,	1	8	Brun.
Marks,Edward,	1		So'n.
Marks,Edward,	1	8	Pr.Geo
Marks,Elisha,	1	6	Lou.
Marks,Israel,	1		So'n.
Marks,John Sr.,	2		Lou.
Marks,John,	1		Lou.
Marks,Joseph,	1	2	So'n.
Marks,Nathaniel,	1		Pr.Geo
Marks,Richard,	1		So'n.
Marmaduke,Daniel,	1	2	West.
Marmaduke,John,	1	10	West.
Marmaduke,Sampson,	1	1	West.
Marmaduke,Vincent,	1	4	West.
Marmaduke,William,	1	8	West.
Marmon,Mary,			K.&Q
Marmon,William,	1		K.&Q
Marpole,George,	1		Camp.
Marquart,Nicholas,	1		Berk.
Marques,John,	1	3	K.Geo.
Marr,Daniel,	1		Fau.
Marr,Elizabeth,			Fay.
Marr,John,	3	25	Henry
Marrable,Abraham,	1	2	Cha.Cy
Marrable,Anne,		13	Cha.Cy
Marrable,Edward,	1	6	Cha.Cy
Marrable,Hartwell,	1	14	Brun.
Marrable,William,	1	10	Cha.Cy
Marrow,Francis,	1	2	Aug.
Marrs,Barnabas,	1		Har.
Marrs,Henry Monday,	1	1	Har.
Marrs,Stephen,	1		Berk.
Marsdon,Lucy M.,		13	Cul.
Marsh,John,			Cul.
Marsh,Richard,	1		Berk.
Marsh,William,	1		Cul.
Marshal,Thomas,	1		Mont.
Marshal,William,	1	7	Lin.
Marshall,Benjamin,		1	K.Geo.
Marshall,Benjamin,	1	5	Brun.
Marshall,Edward,	1		Berk.
Marshall,Elizabeth,		12	Caro.
Marshall,Enoch,	1		Cul.
Marshall,Ezekiel,			Brun.
Marshall,George,	1	19	K.Geo.
Marshall,George,	1		Aug.
Marshall,George,	1		Brun.
Marshall,Henry,	1		Fay.
Marshall,Ichabud,	1	3	Brun.
Marshall,Jacob,	1	2	Pr.Wm.
Marshall,James,	1	9	K.Geo.
Marshall,James,	1	12	Brun.
Marshall,James,	1		Berk.
Marshall,James,	2		Lou.
Marshall,John,	1	5	Cul.
Marshall,John,	3	1	Aug.
Marshall,John,	1		K.Geo.
Marshall,John,	1		Fay.
Marshall,John,	1		Lin.
Marshall,Lindsey,	1		Berk.
Marshall,Margaret,		11	Caro.
Marshall,Mark,	1	6	Lin.
Marshall,Mary,	1	2	K.Geo.
Marshall,Robert,	1	3	Fay.
Marshall,Robert,	1		Cul.
Marshall,Rush,	1	2	K.Geo.
Marshall,Samuel,			Lou.
Marshall,Samuel,	1		Camp.
Marshall,Thomas,	1	8	Lou.
Marshall,Thomas,	2	20	Fau.
Marshall,William,	1	1	K.Geo.
Marshall,William,	1		Brun.
Marshall,William,	1	28	Caro.
Marshall,William,	2	6	Caro.
Marshall,William,Jr.,	1	3	Caro.
Marshall,William,	1		Lou.
Marshell,Thomas,	1	1	Cul.
Marshell,Thomas,	1		Cul.
Marshil,John,	1		K.&Q
Marson,Christopher,	1		Mont.
Marstin,Thomas,	1	15	Cul.
Martain,Andrew,	1	1	Acco.
Martain,Caleb,	1		Acco.
Martain,Edward,			Acco.
Martain,Gideon,	1		Bed.
Martain,Henry,	2		Acco.
Martain,John,	2		Acco.
Martain,William,	1	1	Bed.
Martain,William,	1		Acco.
Martin,Aaron,	1		Pr.Wm.
Martin,Adam,	1		Aug.
Martin,Ann,		1	Caro.
Martin,Asaac,	1		Spots.
Martin,Benjamin,	1		Fay.
Martin,Benjamin,	1		Fau.
Martin,Blackley,	1		Cul.
Martin,Brice,	1	2	Henry
Martin,Charles,	1	1	Fau.
Martin,Charles,	1	12	Fau.
Martin,Christian,	1		Mont.
Martin,David,	1		Camp.
Martin,David,	1		Gooch.
Martin,Elizabeth,			Acco.
Martin,Elizabeth,		6	Caro.
Martin,George,Sr.,	2		Mont.
Martin,George,	1		Mont.
Martin,George,	1	1	Berk.
Martin,George,	1	3	Henry
Martin,George,			Lou.
Martin,George,			Cul.
Martin,George,	1		Mont.
Martin,Hugh,	1	2	Henry
Martin,Hugh,	1		Fay.
Martin,Jacob,	1	8	West.
Martin,Jacob,	1		Rock.
Martin,James,	2	18	K.Wm.
Martin,James,	1		K.Geo.
Martin,James,	1		Henry
Martin,James,	1		Caro.
Martin,James,	1		Camp.
Martin,James,	1		Camp.
Martin,James,		1	So'n
Martin,James Green,	1		Pr.Wm.
Martin,Jeremiah,	2	8	Ja.Cy
Martin,John,	1		Lou.
Martin,John,	1	2	Acco.
Martin,John,	1	12	Henry
Martin,John,	1		Henry
Martin,John,	1		Mont.
Martin,John,	1		Lin.
Martin,John,			Aug.
Martin,John,			Caro.
Martin,John,	1		Caro.
Martin,John,	1	7	Caro.
Martin,John,	1	13	Caro.
Martin,John,Jr.,	2	1	Caro.
Martin,John,	1	1	Gooch.
Martin,John,	1	18	Gooch.
Martin,John,	1		Gooch.
Martin,John,Sr.,	1		Gooch.
Martin,John,Jr.,			Gooch.
Martin,John,	1		Fau.
Martin,John,	2	2	Fau.
Martin,John,	1	1	K.&Q
Martin,John,	1		Fau.
Martin,Jonathan,	1		Bot.
Martin,Jonathan,	1		Lou.
Martin,Joseph,	1		Fau.
Martin,Joseph,	1		Lou.
Martin,Joseph,	1		Lou.
Martin,Joseph,	1		Lun.
Martin,Joseph,		7	Henry
Martin,Joseph,	1		Camp.
Martin,Joseph,	1		Aug.
Martin,Joseph,	1		Mont.
Martin,Joshua,	1		Bot.
Martin,Leonard,	3		K.Geo.
Martin,Levin,			Acco.
Martin,Lewis,	1		Aug.
Martin,Martha,			Camp.
Martin,Martin,	1		Cha.Cy
Martin,Mary,		3	Camp.
Martin,Mary,		3	Camp.
Martin,Mary Ann,			Fau.
Martin,Mary Ann,		9	West.
Martin,Orion,	2	2	Fay.
Martin,Peter,	2		Berk.
Martin,Philip,	1		Mont.
Martin,Reuben,	1		Fau.
Martin,Samuel,	1		Fay.
Martin,Samuel,	1		Gooch.
Martin,Samuel,	1		Camp.
Martin,Samuel,	1		Camp.
Martin,Samuel,	1		Camp.
Martin,Samuel,	1		Camp.
Martin,Sarah,		6	Bed.
Martin,Smith,	1	3	Acco.
Martin,Susanna,		5	K.&Q
Martin,Taddock,	1		Bot.
Martin,Thomas,	1	1	Bed.
Martin,Thomas,			Buck.
Martin,Thomas,	1		Bot.
Martin,Thomas,	1	7	K.&Q
Martin,Thomas,	1	1	Pr.Wm.
Martin,Thomas,	1		Berk.
Martin,Volentine,	3		Bot.
Martin,William,	1		Fay.
Martin,William,	1		Rock.
Martin,William,	1		Buck.
Martin,William,	1		Henry
Martin,William,	1		Henry
Martin,William,		6	Brun.
Martin,William,			Mont.
Martin,William,	1	13	Camp.
Martin,William,	1		Lou.
Martin,William,	1		Pr.Wm.
Marton,George,	1	5	K.Geo.
Marton,John,	1	4	K.Geo.
Marton,Lucy,		3	K.Geo.
Marts,John,	1	1	Lou.
Marx,Michael,	1	6	Cul.
Marye,James,est.,		28	Spots.
Mask,Page,			Bed.
Mason,Babel,	1		Acco.
Mason,Benjamin,	1	2	Lou.
Mason,Burgess,	1	2	Lou.
Mason,Charles,	1	17	Caro.
Mason,Christopher,	1	2	Brun.
Mason,Crosha,		4	Caro.
Mason,Daniel,		8	Brun.
Mason,Daniel,	1	22	Din.

Name			County
Mason,Daniel,		16	Lun.
Mason,David,	1	8	Caro.
Mason,Edward,	1		Berk.
Mason,Edward,	1		Mont.
Mason,Elizabeth,			Bed.
Mason,Elizabeth,	2	2	Caro.
Mason,George,	1	1	Caro.
Mason,George,	1	6	Lou.
Mason,James,	1		Bot.
Mason,James,	1		Lin.
Mason,James,	1		Berk.
Mason,James,	1		Henry
Mason,James,	1	2	Spots.
Mason,James,	2	16	Brun.
Mason,John,	1	2	Caro.
Mason,John,	2	17	Fay.
Mason,John,	1	1	K.Wm.
Mason,John,	1		Camp.
Mason,John,	1		Berk.
Mason,John,	1	13	Spots.
Mason,Joseph,	1		Bot.
Mason,Joseph,	1	13	Brun.
Mason,Louisa,		3	York
Mason,Martin,	1		Camp.
Mason,Mary,			Camp.
Mason,Mary,		7	Brun.
Mason,Nathan,	1		Lun.
Mason,Nathaniel,			Lou.
Mason,Nathaniel,	2	4	Lun.
Mason,Nehemiah,	11	6	K.Geo.
Mason,Nevin Thompson,			Lou.
Mason,Peter,	1		Lou.
Mason,Peter,	1	3	Spots.
Mason,Peter,			Lou.
Mason,Peter,			Lun.
Mason,Richard,	1	3	Din.
Mason,Richard,	1		Brun.
Mason,Robert,	1	2	Henry
Mason,Thomson,	2	57	Lou.
Mason,William,	1	6	Caro.
Mason,William,	1		Brun.
Mason,William,	1	2	Lun.
Mason,William,	1	2	Cul.
Mason,William,est.,	1	29	Brun.
Mason,William,	1		Lin.
Mason,William,	1		Lin.
Mason,Winfield,	1	40	Din.
Masoner,John,	1		Mont.
Massee,Nathaniel,	1	1	Fay.
Massenburg,Robert,	1	3	Eliz.C
Massey,Charles,	11	16	K.Geo.
Massey,Edward,	2		K .Geo
Massey,Elizabeth,		5	West.
Massey,Harris,	1		Loui.
Massey,Patty,		2	West.
Massey,Rueben,	1	1	Spots.
Massey,Robert,	1	7	K.Geo.
Massey,Robert,	1	4	K.Geo.
Massey,Segis,	6	6	K.Geo.
Massey,Thomas,	1	14	Loui.
Massey,Thomas,est.	1	2	K.Geo.
Massey,Thomas,	1	3	Fau.
Massey,Thomas,	1	9	K.Geo.
Massey,William,	2	4	Spots.
Massie,Charles,	1	6	Gooch.
Massie,Capt.Nathaniel	1	26	Gooch.
Massie,Nathaniel,	1	1	Fay.
Massie,Thomas,	1	7	Gooch.
Massie,William,	1	2	Gooch.
Masters,Gerard,	1		Pr.Wm.
Masters,James,	1		Henry
Masters,Thomas,	1		Rock.
Masterson,Hugh,	2		Fay.
Masterson,James,	1		Fay.
Masterson,Richard,	1	13	Fay.
Masterson,Thomas,	1	19	Pr.Geo
Masterson,Zacharias,	1		Fay.
Mastin,Benjamin,	1		Spots.
Mastin,Jo.			Pr.Wm.
Mastin,John,	1	3	Spots.
Mastin,John,			Spots.
Mastin,Thomas,	1		Spots.
Maston,Peter,			Fay.
Mateers,William,	1		Augu.
Mathew,N.	1	6	Pr.Wm.
Mathews,Bristol,	1		Bot.
Mathews,Custis,	1	5	Nor.
Mathews,Frances,		3	Rock.
Mathews,Hutchings,	2	10	Hen.
Mathews,James,	1		Bot.
Mathews,John Jr.,	1		Brun.
Mathews,John,	1		Henry
Mathews,Jonathan,	1	5	Nor.
Mathews,Kendall,	1		Nor.
Mathews,Leven,	1	6	Nor.
Mathews,Martha,		6	Nor.
Mathews,Richard,	1		Loui.
Mathews,Samuel,			Camp.
Mathews,Samuel,			Camp.
Mathews,Sherod,			Loui.
Mathews,William,	1		Camp.
Mathews,William,	1		Pr.Wm
Mathews,William,	1	7	Pr.Wm.
Mathis,Arthur,			Brun.
Matison,William,	1		Pr.Wm.
Matlock,John,	1	4	Loui.
Matlock,John,	1		Henry
Matlock,Zachariah,	1	2	Loui.
Matson,J.,	2	7	Pr.Wm.
Mattews,Samuel,	1		Hen.
Matthew,Benjamin,	2		Fau.
Matthew,Edward,	1		Fau.
Matthew,Edward,	1	4	Pr.Wm
Matthew,Harrison,	1		Fau.
Matthew,Nathan,	1		Fau.
Matthewis,William,	1		Bed.
Matthews,Abraham,	1		So'n.
Matthews,Aquila,	1		Cul.
Matthews,Benjamin,	1		Cul.
Matthews,Charles,	1	3	Hen.
Matthews,Daniel,	1		Brun.
Matthews,David,			Hen.
Matthews,Edward,	1	13	Gooch
Matthews,Col.George,	1	11	Augu.
Matthews,George,			Augu.
Matthews,Grigory,	1	3	Buck.
Matthews,J.,	1		Pr.Wm
Matthews,James,	1		Buck.
Matthews,John,	1		Cul.
Matthews,John,	1	11	Brun.
Matthews,John,Sr.,	1		Brun.
Matthews,John,	1		Cul.
Matthews,John,	1		Pr.Wm.
Matthews,John,	1		Lin.
Matthews,John,	1		Lou.
Matthews,Jonathan,	1		Fau.
Matthews,Richard,	1		Augu.
Matthews,Sampson,	1	14	Augu.
Matthews,Sampson,			Augu.
Matthews,Samuel,	1		So'n.
Matthews,Simon,	1		Lou.
Matthews,Thomas,	1		Lou.
Matthews,Thomas,	1	4	Cha.C
Matthews,Thomas,	2		Buck.
Matthews,Thomas,	2		Hen.
Matthews,William,	1		West.
Matthews,William,	1	3	K.Geo.
Matthews,William,	1	1	Augu.
Matthews,William,	1		Camp.
Matthews,William,	1		So'n.
Matthews,William,	1		Gooch
Matthews,William,	1		Berk.
Matthis,Cornelius,	1		Brun.
Matthis,Luke,	1	7	Brun.
Matthis,Patty,		2	Lun.
Matthis,William,	1		Lun.
Matthiss,Drury,	1	7	Brun.
Mattinglee,Richard,	1		Mont.
Mattinglee,Walter,	1		Mont.
Mattison,Benjamin,	1		Pr.Wm.
Mattison,Jenny,			Pr.Wm.
Mattison,John,	1		Pr.Wm.
Mattison,Thomas,	1		Pr.Wm.
Mattocks,William,	1		Pr.Geo.
Mattox,Joseph,	1	6	Pr.Geo.
Mattox,Lazarus,	1	6	Lun.
Mattox,Sukey,			Buck.
Mattox,Thomas,	1	11	Pr.Geo.
Mattox,Wilfred,	1	3	Lun.
Mattox,William,	1		Pr.Wm.
Mattox,William,	1	2	K.Wm.
Mavis,Richard,	1		Brun.
Mavity,Robert,	1		Henry
Mavity,William,	1		Henry
Maupin,Jessee,	1		Henry
Maury,Abraham,	1	10	Lun.
Maury,Matthew,	1	9	Lun.
Mauzey,Henry,	1	3	Cul.
Mauzey,Peter,	3	1	Hen.
Mauzy,Betty,		4	Fau.
Mauzy,Henry,	2	9	Fau.
Mauzy,John,	1	9	Fau.
Mauzy,John,	1	3	Fau.
Maxcey,Jerimiah,	1		Bed.
Maxcey,Josiah,	1		Bed.
Maxcey,Walter,	1	2	Bed.
Maxey,Bede,		7	Buck.
Maxey,Charles,	1	3	Buck.
Maxey,Edward,	1		Buck.
Maxey,Edward,Jr.,	1		Buck.
Maxey,John Jr.,	1		Buck.
Maxey,Nathanial,	1	1	Buck.
Maxey,Sampson,	1		Buck.
Maxey,Walter,	1	1	Henry
Maxey,William,	1		Buck.
Maxfield,James,	1		Cul.
Maxill,John Jr.,	1	1	Lin.
Maxwell,Alexander,	1		Fay.
Maxwell,Bazleel,	1		Mont.
Maxwell,Elisha,	1		Mont.
Maxwell,Elisha,	1		Loui.
Maxwell,George,	1		Mont.
Maxwell,James,	1		Cul.
Maxwell,John,			Rock.
Maxwell,John,	2		Berk.
Maxwell,John,	1		Berk.
Maxwell,John,	2	2	Fay.
Maxwell,John,	1	2	Mont.
Maxwell,Thomas,	1		Cul.
Maxwell,Thomas,	2		Fay.
Maxwell,Thomas,			Fay.
Maxwell,William,			Fay.
Maxwell,William,	2		Mont.
Maxwell,William,	1		Mont.
Maxwell,William,	1		Mont.
May,Benjamin,	1		K.& Q.
May,Benjamin,	1		Buck.
May,Col.Charles,	2	14	Lou.
May,Daniel,	1		Lou.
May,Francis,	1		Lou.
May,George,	1		Cul.
May,George,	1		Fau.
May,James,	1	3	Henry
May,John,	1		Lou.
May,John,	1		Henry
May,John,	1		Buck.
May,John,	1		Berk.
May,Joseph,	1		Bed.
May,Thomas,	1		Spots.
May,Thomas,	1		Mont.

Name			County
May,William,			Henry
Mayburry,Frederick,	1		Bed.
Mayburry,George,	1		Bed.
Mayburry,Henry,	1		Bed.
Mayes,Daniel,	1		Din.
Mayes,Matthew,	1	9	Din.
Mayes,William,	1	1	Din.
Mayhall,Samuel,	1		Aug.
Mayhall,Stephen,	1		Aug.
Mayhue,John,	1		Lou.
Mayfield,George,	1	1	Lin.
Mayfield,Isaac,	1		Lin.
Mayfield,John,	1		Spots.
Mayfield,James,	1		Mont.
Mayfield,Southerland,	1		Mont.
Maynard,Ambrose,			Cha.C.
Maynard,Edward,	1	4	Cha.C.
Maynard,Mary,	1	2	Cha.C.
Maynard,William,	1	5	Cha.C.
Mayo,Jacob,	1	4	Loui.
Mayo,Joseph,		37	Hen.
Mayo,Valentine,	1	6	Henry
Mays,James,	1		Bed.
Mays,James,	1		Bed.
Mayse,David,	1		Henry
Mayse,Littleberry,	1		Henry
Mayse,Sherwood,	1		Henry
Mayson,Adam,	1		Acco.
Mayson,Caleb,	2		Acco.
Mayson,George,			Acco.
Mayson,Henry,	1		Acco.
Mayson,Thomas,	3		Acco.
Mayson,William,	2		Acco.
Mayton,David,	1		Lun.
Mayton,John,	1	3	Lun.
Mazant,John,		7	West.
Maze,Michael,	1		Pr.Wm.
Maze,Richard,	1	1	Bot.
Maze,William,	1		Bot.
Mazingo,George,	1		Cul.
Mazzingo,Charles,Sr.,	1		Cul.
Mazzingo,Charles,	1		Cul.
McAboy,Thomas,	1		Pr.Wm.
McAlexander,William,	1		Henry
McAlister,James,	1		Camp.
McAlister,James,		1	Camp.
McAllister,Garland,	1	2	Loui.
McAllister,George,	1		Camp.
McAllister,John,	1	1	Camp.
McAltrice,Phillip,	1		Har.
McAnair,Daniel,	2	1	Augu.
McAndrows,Richard,	1		Augu.
McAntire,John,	1	6	Bot.
McArthur,James,	1		Har.
McArthur,James,Jr.,	1		Har.
McBride,Charles,	1		Lou.
McBride,Daniel,	1		Henry
McBride,Daniel,	1		Lou.
McBride,Edward,	1	4	Gooch.
McBride,Edward,	1		Gooch.
McBride,James,	1		Henry
McBride,James,	1		Lou.
McBride,Miner,	1		Gooch.
McBride,Thomas,	1		Wash.
McBride,William,	2		Fau.
McBrown,Alexander,	1	2	Cha.C.
McCaa,Sarah,		2	Eli.C.
McCabe,Henry,	1	1	Lou.
McCackie,William,	1		So'n.
McCade,James,	1		Fau.
McCaffery,James,	1		Lou.
McCaffery,John,	1		Wash.
McCaffery,William,	1		Lou.
McCain,Mathew,	1		Wash.
McCahan,Hugh,	1		Berk.
McCahone,Major,	1		Jas.C.

Name			County
McCallan,Robert	1		Berk.
McCallaster,Peter,	1	1	Bot.
McCalley,Charles,	1		Spots.
McCalley,John,	2	6	Spots.
McCalister,James,	1	6	Berk.
McCallister,Benjamin,	1		Rock.
McCallister,George,			Rock.
McCallister,James,	1		Cul.
McCallister,John,	1		Loui.
McCallister,Joseph,	1		Rock.
McCallister,William,	1	2	Loui.
McCallister,William,	1		Caro.
McCallum,John,	1		Bot.
McCampbell,Andrew,	1		Rock.
McCampbell,Andrew,	1	1	Rock.
McCampbell,Andrew,	1	1	Rock.
McCampbell,James,	2		Rock.
McCampbell,James,	1	4	Rock.
McCampbell,John,	1		Rock.
McCampbell,Robert,	1	1	Rock.
McCampbell,Samuel,	1	1	Rock.
McCampbell,Soloman,	1		Rock.
McCampbell,William,	1	2	Rock.
McCamy,William,	1	2	Augu.
McCann,Joseph,	1	1	Fay.
McCann,Neel,	3	1	Fay.
McCanol,James,	1		Bot.
McCapin,John,	1		Wash.
McCappin,Robert,	1		Rock.
McCappin,Robert,	1		Rock.
McCarnish,Thomas,	1		Camp.
McCarroll,John,	1		Berk.
McCartey,Thomas,	3	1	Har.
McCartie,David,	3		Caro.
McCarty,Andrew,	1		Lou.
McCarty,Billington,	1	1	Cul.
McCarty,Daniel,	3	94	West.
McCarty,Daniel,		23	West.
McCarty,Daniel,	7	5	K.Geo.
McCarty,Daniel,	1	31	Lou.
McCarty,James,	1		Augu.
McCarty,Jeremiah,	1		Lou.
McCarty,John,	1		Cul.
McCarty,Prisy,		1	K.Geo.
McCarty,Thaddeus,	1	8	Lou.
McCarty,Timothy,	1		Berk.
McCarty,William,			Lou.
McCarrer,Archibald,	1		Henry
McCarrer,John,	1		Henry
McCaslin,Andrew,	1		Augu.
McCaslin,John,	1		Augu.
McCaul,Alexander,	1	6	Hen.
McCaul,James,	2		Bot.
McCaul,Stoakes,	1	11	Gooch.
McCave,Ross,	1		Har.
McCawn,Alexander,	1		Rock.
McCawn,James,	1		Rock.
McCawn,James,	1		Rock.
McCawn,John,	2	1	Rock.
McCawn,John,Jr.,	1		Rock.
McCawn,Joseph,	1		Rock.
McCay,Archibald,	1		Rock.
McCenachan,Alexander,	1	14	Augu.
McChesney,Isabella,			Rock.
McChesney,James,		4	Rock.
McChesney,James,	1	4	Augu.
McChesney,Robert,	1	2	Augu.
McChesney,Samuel,	1	6	Rock.
McChesney,William,	1		Berk.
McChesney,William,	2		Har.
McCiery,James,	1		Bot.
McCillip,Gilbert,	1		Berk.
McCinney,Charles,	1		Bed.
McCitchell,Gabriel,	1	6	Jas.C
McClain,Alexander,	1		Fay.
McClain,Daniel,	1		Fay.

Name			County
McClain,Francis,	1		Lou.
McClain,James,	1		Lou.
McClain,James,	1		Augu.
McClain,James,	1		Bot.
McClain,John,	1		Rock.
McClain,John,	1	1	Lou.
McClain,Susanna,			Jas.C.
McClaland,Benjamin,	1		Fay.
McClanahan,Absalam,	1		Bed.
McClanahan,Andrew,	1		Fau.
McClanahan,David,	1		Fau,
McClanahan,James,	1	10	Fau.
McClanahan,James,	1		Lou.
McClanahan,John,	1	6	West.
McClanahan,John,	1		Bed.
McClanahan,Magdalen,	1	6	West.
McClanahan,Moore,	1		Fau.
McClanahan,Thomas,	1	6	Cul.
McClanahan,William,	2	12	Cul.
McClanahan,William,Jr.			Cul.
McClanahan,William,	1	1	Cul.
McClanahan,William,	1	3	West.
McClary,John,	1	5	York
McClaughlin,James,	1		Lun.
McClellan,William,	2	1	Lou.
McClenachan,Alexander	1	1	Rock.
McClenachan,David,	1		Bot.
McClenachan,Samuel,	1		Bot.
McClenahan,William,	1	17	Bot.
McClenahan,William,	1		Bot.
McClanahan, **	1		Rock.
McClennahan,Alex.	1		Bot.
McClennahan,William,	1		Bot.
McCline,Halbert,	2		Wash.
McCling,James,	1		Bot.
McClintock,William,	1		Augu.
McClintock,William,	1		Augu.
McClond,John,	1		Lou.
McClonds,John,	1		Pr.Geo.
McCloud,Charles,	1		Mont..
McCloud,William,	1		Spots.
McCloy,Archibald,	1		Bot.
McCluir,Andrew,	1	2	Fay.
McCluir,Andrew,	1		Fay.
McCluir,Samuel,	1	1	Fay.
McClun,Alexander,	1		Rock.
McClune,John,	1	4	Aug.
McClung,Henry,	1	1	Rock.
McClung,James,	1		Rock.
McClung,James,	2		Rock.
McClung,John,	1		Aug.
McClung,John,	2	5	Rock.
McClung,William,	1		Rock.
McClung,William,			Rock.
McClung,William,	1		Rock.
McClure,Alexander,	1	2	Rock.
McClure,Andrew,	1		Aug.
McClure,Andrew,	3		Aug.
McClure,Arthur,	1		Rock.
McClure,David,	1	1	Rock.
McClure,Elisabeth,	2	1	Augu.
McClure,Halbert,	1		Rock.
McClure,Isble,		1	Rock.
McClure,James,	1		Augu.
McClure,James,	1		Bot.
McClure,James,	1		Bed.
McClure,John,	1		Augu.
McClure,John,	1		Augu.
McClure,Josiah,	1		Augu.
McClure,Michal,	1		Augu.
McClure,Nathaniel,	1		Wash.
McClure,Samuel,	1		Augu.
McClure,William,	1		Augu.
McClure,William,	1	1	Rock.
McClure,William,	1		Rock.
McClurg,Walter,	1	8	Eli.C.

Name			Place
McCollam, John,	1		Rock.
McCollam, Patrick,	2	2	Rock.
McCollach, John, Sr.,	1		Rock.
McColloch, John, Jr.,	1		Rock.
McCollock, D.,			Din.
McCollock, David,	1	1	Din.
McCollock, John,	3		Din.
McCollock, John, Jr.,			Din.
McCollum, John,	1		Aug.
McComb, Andrew,	1	1	Aug.
McComb, William,	1		Aug.
McCombs, John,	1		Mont.
McConica, Christopher	1	7	Pr.Geo.
McConnal, Richard,	1		Aug.
McConnel, Abraham,	1	1	Bot.
McConnell, Abraham,	1		Berk.
McConnell, Adam,	1		Fay.
McConnell, James,	1		Rock.
McConnell, James,			Bot.
McConnell, Joseph,	1	1	Lin.
McConnell, Moses,	1		Bot.
McConnell, Patrick,	1		Rock.
McConnico, Jared,	1	4	Lun.
McConnico, John,			Din.
McCord, Benjamin,	1		Wash.
McCorkall, Andrew,			Aug.
McCorkall, Samuel,	1		Aug.
McCorkle, James,	1		Mont.
McCorkle, Samuel,	1		Rock.
McCorkle, William,	1		Rock.
McCormac, John,	1	2	Fau.
McCormac, Stephen,	1	18	Fau.
McCormack, David,	1		Buck.
McCormack, Hugh,			Lin.
McCormack, Joshua,	1	1	Wash.
McCormack, Micajah,	1		Bed.
McCormack, Sherwood,	1		Buck.
McCormack, Thomas,	1		Buck.
McCormick, Andrew,	1		Berk.
McCormick, Chrnelius,	1		Berk.
McCormick, Daniel,	2	4	Lin.
McCormick, Edward,	1	1	Berk.
McCormick, James,	1	2	Berk.
McCormick, John,	1	6	Berk.
McCormick, John,	1		Lin.
McCormick, Robert,	1		Rock.
McCormick, Robert,	1		Berk.
McCormick, William,	1		Berk.
McCormick, William,	1		Lin.
McCoskry, James,	1		Rock.
McCosky, John,	2		Rock.
McCoskry, Samuel,	1		Rock.
McCrosky, John,	1		Rock.
McCoun, George,	1		Mont.
McCoun, James,	1		Mont.
McCowan, Daniel,	1		Gooch/Wash.
McCoy, Daniel,	1		Berk.
McCoy, Daniel,			Pr.Wm.
McCoy, Daniel,	1		Bot.
McCoy, Edward,	1		Lin.
McCoy, James,	1		West.
McCoy, John,	1	4	Fau.
McCoy, John,	1		Mont.
McCoy, Joseph,	1		Berk.
McCoy, Joseph,	1		Bed.
McCoy, Thomas,	1		Berk.
McCoy, William,	1		Bed.
McCoye, John,	1	3	Henry
McCoye, Walter,	1		Henry
McCoyle, Benjamin,	1	1	Spots.
McCutchan, James,	1		Wash.
McCutchan, John,	1		Wash.
McCutchan, Patrick,	1		Wash.
McCutchan, Samuel,	1		Wash.
McCrae's, est.,	1	18	Pr.Wm.
McCraken, John,	1		Bot.
McCran, Dancy,			Buck.
McCraw, Edward,	1		Bed.
McCray, Alexander,	1	2	Loui.
McCray, James,	1		Rock.
McCray, Joseph,	1		Rock.
McCray, Robert,	1		Aug.
McCready, Ezekiel,	1	1	Nor.
McCreery, John,	1		Aug.
McCreery, Robert,	1	2	Aug.
McCrevie, Archibald,	1		Bot.
McCrory, James,	1	1	Rock.
McCrosky, David,	1		Rock.
McCrosky, John,	1		Rock.
McCrosky, John,	1		Wash.
McCrosky, Samuel S.,		21	So'n
McCrosky, Rev. Samuel,		20	Nor.
McCrull, Niel,	1	16	Spots.
McCruit, Thomas,	1		Lou.
McCulloch, Thomas,	1	1	Aug.
McCullock, Alexander,	1		Berk.
McCullock, John,			Wash.
McCullock, Joseph,	1		Berk.
McCullock, William,	1		Berk.
McCullough, Lowry,			Pr.Wm.
McCully, Robert,	1		Lou.
McCun, John,	1		Rock.
McCune, Samuel,	2	2	Aug.
McCurdey, Archibald,	1		Mont.
McCurdey, Henry,	1		Mont.
McCutchan, James, Sr.,			Aug.
McCutchan, John,	1	1	Aug.
McCutchan, John,	1		Aug.
McCutchan, Joseph,	1		Aug.
McCutchan, Robert,	2	1	Aug.
McCutchan, Capt. Samuel,	1		Aug.
McCutchan, Samuel E.,	3		Aug.
McCutchan, William,	2		Aug.
McCutchan, William,	1		Aug.
McCutlow, William,	1	9	Ja.Cy
McDade, John,	1	3	Berk.
McDaniel, Alexander,	1		Cul.
McDaniel, Alexander,	1		Bed.
McDaniel, David,			Cul.
McDaniel, Francis,	1		Fay.
McDaniel, George,	1		Lou.
McDaniel, Hugh,	1		Fay.
McDaniel, Henry,	2		Fay.
McDaniel, Henry,	1	1	Spots.
McDaniel, James,	1		Fay.
McDaniel, John,	1	1	Fay.
McDaniel, John,	1		Fay.
McDaniel, John,	1	2	Cul.
McDaniel, John, Jr.,			Cul.
McDaniel, John,	1		Aug.
McDaniel, John,	1		Buck.
McDaniel, Mathias,	1		Cul.
McDaniel, Michael,	1		Henry
McDaniel, William,	1	9	Pr.Wm.
McDaniel, William,			Fau.
McDaniel, William, Jr.	1		Fau.
McDavid, Patrick,	1		Aug.
McDavit, James,	1		Har.
McDarment, Joseph,	1		Lou.
McDonnal, Randolph,	1		Rock.
McDonald, Alexander,	2		Wash.
McDonald, Andrew,	2	2	Berk.
McDonald, Arthur,	1		Lou.
McDonald, Edward,	1	3	Bot.
McDonald, Gerrard,	1		Fau.
McDonald, Hugh,			Camp.
McDonald, John,	1		Pr.Wm.
McDonald, John,	1		Loui.
McDonald, John,	1		Camp.
McDonald, Reubin,			Wash.
McDonald, Walter,	1		Bot.
McDonald, William,	1		Bot.
McDonald, William,	1		K.Geo.
McDonald, William,	1		Wash.
McDonnald, Bryen,	1	2	Mont.
McDonnald, James,	2		Mont.
McDonnald, James,	1	1	Mont.
McDonnald, John,	1		Aug.
McDonnald, Joseph,	1		Mont.
McDonnald, Magnus,	1		Mont.
McDonnald, Samuel,	1		Aug.
McDougall, James,	1	13	Pr.Geo.
McDougall, John,	1	4	Aug.
McDoul, William,			Buck.
McDowell, Daniel,	1		Lin.
McDowell, Elizabeth,		10	Rock.
McDowell, George,	1		Bot.
McDowell, Hugh,	1		Aug.
McDowell, James,	1	3	Fay.
McDowell, James,	1	1	Rock.
McDowell, James,	1	12	Ja.Cy
McDowell, John,			Rock.
McDowell, John,	1	5	Fay.
McDowell, Michael,	1		Bot.
McDowell, Samuel,	2	4	Rock.
McEdloe, William,	2	4	So'n
McEllery, James,	1		Aug.
McEleery, Samuel,	1	1	Aug.
McElhany, Francis,	1		Bot.
McElhany, John,	1		Rock.
McElhany, Robert,	1		Bot.
McElhany, Robert,	1		Rock.
McElhany, Robert,	1	8	Rock.
McElhany, Samuel,	1		Bot.
McElhany, William,	1		Rock.
McElhanney, Patrick,	1		Mont.
McEliver, William,	1		Lin.
McEllorry, Richard,	1		Bed.
McElroy, Alexander,	1		Aug.
McElroy, John,	1	2	Buck.
McElroy, William,	2		Rock.
McElroy, William,	1		Mont.
McElroy, William,			Rock.
McEntosh, James,	1	5	K.Geo.
McEntosh, John,	1		Rock.
McEttymar, * * *,	2		Har.
McEver, James,	1		Camp.
McFadden, Hugh,	1		Rock.
McFaggin, Hugh,	2		Lin.
McFaggin, James,	1		Lin.
McFall, John,	2		Fay.
McFall, John,	1		Rock.
McFarland, ***,			Bed.
McFarland, Benjamin,	2	7	Bed.
McFarland, Duncan,	1		Aug.
McFarland, Mary,			Lou.
McFarland, Robert,	1		Wash.
McFarlane, Alexander	1	1	Mont.
McFarlane, Elizabeth		1	West.
McFarlane, John,	1		Mont.
McFarelane, Joseph,			Mont.
McFarlane, William,	1		Mont.
McFarlin, Robert,	1	1	Rock.
McFarlin, Thomas,	1		Rock.
McFarlin, William,	1		Rock.
McFarling, James,	1		Lou.
McFarling, John,	1		Lou.
McFarling, William,	1		Lou.
McFarran, James,	2	1	Bot.
McFerran, Martin,	1		Bot.
McFerran, Samuel,	1		Bot.
McFerran, Samuel,	1		Berk.
McGahey, Manassey,	1		Lou.
McGahy, John,	1		Berk.
McGall, Robert,	1		Berk.
McGarr, Terrence,			Fay.
McGarrah, Matthew,	1		Berk.

Name			County
McGaughlin,John,	1		Berk.
McGaughlin,Lemon,	1		Berk.
McGavock,James,	1	14	Mont.
McGeach,John,	1	3	Lou.
McGrach,Joseph,	1		Lou.
McGeath,James,	1		Lou.
McGee,Ann,		17	Caro.
McGee,David,	3		Fay.
McGee,David,			Bot.
McGee,James,	1		Bot.
McGee,James,	2		Fay.
McGee,John,	1		Fau.
McGee,Joseph,	1	6	Caro.
McGee,Ralph,	1	1	So'n
McGee,Richard,			Rock.
McGee,Samuel,	1		Spots.
McGee,William,			Fay.
McGeehe,Augustine,	1	2	Loui.
McGeehe,Edward,			Loui.
McGehee,James,	1	9	Loui.
McGehee,Samuel,	1	22	Loui.
McGehee,William,	1	14	Loui.
McGehee,William,	1	2	Loui.
McGehee,William,Sr.,	1	16	Loui.
McGehee,William,Jr.,	1	1	Loui.
McGehe,John,Sr.,	2	19	Loui.
McGehe,John,	1	2	Loui.
McGehe,Samuel,	1		Fay.
McGill,Charles,	1		Berk.
McGill,James,	1		Fay.
McGill,John,	2		Lin.
McGill,Robert,	1		Berk.
McGill,Will,	2		Lin.
McGilvery,William,	4		K.Geo
McGimsey,John,	1		Aug.
McGinnes,John,	1		Bed.
McGinty,James,	1		Fay.
McGlammery,John,	1		Aug.
McGlasgow,Philip,	1		Gooch.
McGlasson,Judith,	1	5	Buck.
McGlasson,Matthew,	1	4	Buck.
McGlauchland,Edward,	1		Rock.
McGlaughlin,James,	1		Aug.
McGleester,Niel,	1		Mont.
McGloucklin,Charles,			Bed.
McGlochin, J.	1		Pr.Wm
McGloghlin,John,	1		Har.
McGown,David,	1		Henry
McGowan,James,	1		Berk.
McGown,Samuel,	1		Henry
McGraday,Laughland,	1		Bed.
McGrady,James,	1	3	Lou.
McGraugh,John,	1		Caro.
McGraugh,Finley,	1		Berk.
McGraw,John,	1		Lin.
McGregor,John,	1		Pr.Wm.
McGrew,John,	1		Berk.
McGriff,John,	1		Mont.
McGriff,Thomas,	1		Mont.
McGriff,Thomas,	1		Mont.
McGuffy,Henry,	1		Henry
McGuhee,Holden,	1		Henry
McGuhee,Samuel,	1		Henry
McGuire,Alexander,	1		West.
McGuire,Allegonia,	1		Henry
McGuire,Francis,Sr.,	1		Mont.
McGuire,James,			Bot.
McGuire,John,	1		Mont.
McGuire,John,			Fay.
McGuire,John,		4	West.
McGuire,John,	1		Bed.
McGuire,Lawrence,	1		Bed.
McGuire,Margat,	1		Fay.
McGuire,William,	1		Mont.
McGuier,Zachariah,	1		Henry
McHan,Thomas,	1	2	Pr.Geo
McHeely,William,	1		Bot.
McHenry,John,	1		Wash.
McHolland,William,	1	1	Eli.Cy
McHollams,John,	1	5	Nor.
McIllhaney,James,	1		Lou.
McIlhaney,John,	2	3	Lou.
McIlhaney,John,	2	3	Lou.
McIllhatton,Alexander	1		Berk.
McIlvaine,Moses,	1	5	Bed.
McIntire,David,	1	1	Berk.
McIntire,Daniel,	1		Berk.
McIntire,Daniel,			Pr.Wm.
McIntire,James,	1		Fay.
McIntire,John H.,			Pr.Wm.
McIntire,Nicholas,	2	5	Berk.
McIntire,Thomas,	1		Berk.
McIntosh,Abel,	1		Berk.
McIntosh,Alexander,	1		Berk.
McIntosh,Alexander,			So'n
McIntosh,James,	1	1	Lou.
McIntosh,Daniel,	1		Berk.
McIntosh,John,	1		Lin.
McIntosh,Thomas,			Lou.
McIntosh,William,	1	1	K.&Q
McIntyre,Alexander,	1	6	Lou.
McInvale,James,	1	3	Brun.
McKain,Alexander,	1		Henry
McKain,Hugh,	1		Henry
McKain,Thomas,	1		Henry
McKamy,James,	1		Aug.
McKamy,John,	1	2	Aug.
McKane,Robert,	1		Lin.
McKay,James,	1		Lin.
McKeachy,James,	1		Bot.
McKean,Betha,			Lou.
McKeand,John,	3	14	Hen.
McKee,Esther,		1	Rock.
McKee,James,	1		Rock.
McKee,John,	3	5	Rock.
McKee,Joseph,	1		Lou.
McKee,Lydia,		3	Rock.
McKee,Richard,	1		Mont.
McKee,Robert,	1		Rock.
McKee,Samuel,	1		Aug.
McKee,William,	1	1	Rock.
McKemy,Alexander,			Rock.
McKemy,James,	1		Rock.
McKemy,John,	1		Rock.
McKemy,Robert,	1	1	Rock.
McKemy,Samuel,	1		Rock.
McKemy,William,	3		Rock.
McKemy,William,Jr.,			Rock.
McKenal,John,	1		Har.
McKenley,Daniel,	1		Cul.
McKenney,David,	1		Fay.
McKenney,John,	2		Fay.
McKenney,John,	1		Fay.
McKenney,John,Jr.,	3		Fay.
McKenney,John,	1		Har.
McKenney,Robert,			Fay.
McKennie,John,	1		Berk.
McKenny,Andrew,	1		Berk.
McKenny,Arch,	1		Lin.
McKenny,Charles,	1	1	Cha.Cy
McKenny,Daniel,	2		Lin.
McKenny,Daniel,	1	5	West.
McKenny,Duke,	1		West.
McKenny,Edward,	1		Berk.
McKenny,Garrard,	1	12	West.
McKenny,George,	1	2	West.
McKenny,James,	1	1	Lin.
McKenny,James,	1		Berk.
McKenny,Jesse,	2	2	K.Geo
McKenny,John,	1		Brun.
McKenny,John,	1		Brun.
McKenny,John,Jr.,	1		Brun.
McKenny,John,	1		Lin.
McKenny,John,	1		Spots.
McKenny,John,	1	1	Aug.
McKenny,John,	1		Rock.
McKenny,Matthew,	1	3	So'n
McKenny,Morris,	1		Brun.
McKenny,Moses,	1	2	So'n
McKenny,Rodham,	4	1	West.
McKenny,Stephen,	2	1	Lin.
McKenny,Thomas,	1		Brun.
McKenny,Thomas,	1		Spots.
McKenny,William,	1		Brun.
McKensy,Alexander,	1		Pr.Wm.
McKenzy,James,	1		Lou.
McKerman,Peter,	2		Berk.
McKesee,John,	1	24	Caro.
McKetrick,Robert,	2		Aug.
McKewn,Gilbert,	1		Berk.
McKewn,James,	1		Berk.
McKewn,John,	1		Berk.
McKewn,Michael,	1	4	Berk.
McKewn,Robert,	1		Berk.
McKey,Elias,	1		Wash.
McKie,Daniel,			Lun.
McKie,Michael,	2	16	Lun.
McKillup,Hugh,	1	1	Pr.Wm.
McKim,Alexander,	1	5	Lou.
McKindley,Ralph,	2		Fau.
McKindred,John,			Pr.Wm.
McKinley,Andrew,	1	2	Lin.
McKinley,James,	1		Lou.
McKinley,William,	1		Fau.
McKinnie,Duke,	1		Camp.
McKinnie,Duke,	1		Camp.
McKinnymDavid,	1		Rock.
McKinny,Dinnis,	1		Aug.
McKinny,James,	1		Lou.
McKinny,James,	1	3	Caro.
McKinny,John,	1	7	Camp.
McKinny,Joseph,	1		Camp.
McKinny,William,	1		Fay.
McKinney,Alexander,	1		Aug.
McKinney,Alexander,	1		Aug.
McKinney,Collin,	1		Wash.
McKinney,John,	1		Cul.
McKinney,John,	1	2	Mont.
McKinney,William,	1		Bot.
McKinnie,Duke,	1		Camp.
McKinnie,Duke,	1		Camp.
McKinnis,Lampkin,			Camp.
McKinny,David,	1		Rock.
McKinny,Dennis,	1		Aug.
McKinny,James,	1		Lou.
McKinny,James,	1	3	Caro.
McKinny,John,	1	7	Caro.
McKinny,Joseph,	1		Camp.
McKinny,William,	1		Fay.
McKinsey,Daniel,	1		Henry
McKinsey,James,	1	2	Lou.
McKinsey,Murdock,	1		Mont.
McKinsey,Rolly,	1		Lin.
McKinter,Robert,	1		Lin.
McKinzie,John,	3		Lin.
McKnight,Benjamin,	1		Lin.
McKnight,Charles,	1		Berk.
McKnight,Eli,			Lou.
McKnight,George,	1		Bot.
McKnight,Robert,	1		Berk.
McKnight,William,	3		Lou.
McKonkie,Alexander,	1	5	Fau.
McKoy,Cornelius,	1	5	Spots.
McKoy,Daniel,	1		Camp.
McLachlen,Mary,		5	Eli.Cy
McLary,Hugh,	1		Aug.
McLaughlin,Charles,	1		Mont.
McLaughlin,William,	1		Mont.

Name			Loc.
McLean,John,	1		Berk.
McLeer,Frizzell,	1	2	Lun.
McLeer,Samuel,	1		Rock.
McLemore,William,	1	2	So'n.
McLenachan,Elijah,	1		Augu.
McLenachan,Robert,	1	6	Augu.
McLure,James,	1		Lin.
McLure,John,Sr.,	2		Lin.
McLure,John,	1		Lin.
McLure,John,			Lin.
McLure,Nathan,	1		Lin.
McLure,Robert,	1		Lin.
McLure,William,	1		Lin.
McMachen,James,	1		Berk.
McMachen,James,			•Fay.
McMahan,Robert,	1		Fay.
McMahan,Roger,	1		Pr.Wm
McMahon,Barnabas,	1		Har.
McMahon,Conatant,	1		Har.
McMahon,John,	2		Augu.
McMahon,Samuel,	1		Wash.
McMakin,Alexander,	1	2	Lou.
McMananey,Peter,	1		Lou.
McManimy,Tarlton,	1		Lou.
McMannamy,Katren,			Camp.
McMannaway,John,	1		Buck.
McManners,James,	1		Cha.C
McMasters,Thomas,	1		Lou.
McMath,James,	1		Rock.
McMath,John,	1		Acco.
McMatron,William,	1		Wash.
McMekins,Joseph,	1		Hen.
McMial,Andrew,	2	1	So'n.
McMial,Frederick,			So'n.
McMial,Jacob,	1		So'n.
McMillian,John,	1		Fau.
McMillian,John,	1	14	Pr.Wm
McMillian,Mrs.Seth,		11	Pr.Wm
McMillion,Robert,	1	1	Fay.
McMillion,William,	1	1	Wash.
McMillon,Abraham,	1		Mont.
McMorn,Domnick,			Wash.
McMorris,David,	1		Lou.
McMott,William,			Fay.
McMullan,Robert,	1		Augu.
McMullen,Alexander,	1		Loud.
McMullen,Robert,	1		Loud.
McMullen,William,	1		Mont.
McMullen,William,	1		Bot.
McMullin,Henry,	1		Wash.
McMullin,James,	1		Fay.
McMullin,James,	2		Fay.
McMullin,John,	1		Rock.
McMullin,Samuel,	1	4	Fay.
McMullin,Thomas,	1		Fay.
McMurray,William,	1	1	Bot.
McMurry,Thomas,	1		Lin.
McMustree,Joseph,	1	3	Fay.
McNabb,John,	1		K.Wm.
McNabb,Samuel,	2		Rock.
McNabb,William,	1		Lou.
McNaile,Hugh,			Bot.
McNamara,Joseph,	1		Fau.
McNamara,Philip,	1		Fau.
McNarie,Hugh,			Fay.
McNarie,John,	1		Fay.
McNarie,William,	2	1	Fay.
McNeal,Archibald,	1		Buck.
McNeally,David,	4		Lin.
McNeally,George,	1		Lin.
McNeally,John,	1		Lin.
McNear,John,	1		Fay.
McNeel,Daniel,	1		Bot.
McNeely,David,	1		Bot.
McNeely,David,	1		Bot.
McNeely,George,	1		Bot.
McNeely,James,	1		Rock.
McNeely,William,	1		Bot.
McNeil,Dan,	3	3	Har.
McNeil,Hector,			Din.
McNeil,John,	1	3	Har.
McNella,John,	1		Lin.
McNew,Edward,	1		Wash.
McNew,Elisha,	1		Wash.
McNew,John,	1		Har.
McNew,Shederick,	1		Wash.
McNew,William,	1		Wash.
McNight,John,	2		Rock.
McNight,Timothy,	1	1	Rock.
McNut,Thomas,	1		Rock.
McNutt,Alexander,			Rock.
McNutt,Alexander,	1		Wash.
McNutt,George,	1		Mont.
McNutt,James,		1	Augu.
McNutt,John,	1		Mont.
McNutt,John,	1		Rock.
McNutt,Robert,	1		Augu.
McOffutt,William,	1	2	Lou.
McPeak,James,	1		Henry
McPeak,William,	1		Henry
McPhearson,Alexander,	1		Bot.
McPhearson,Daniel,	1	2	Bot.
McPhearson,Richard,	1		Bot.
McPhearson,Murdock,	1		Lou.
McPheeters,Alex.Sr.,	1	4	Augu.
McPheeters,Alexander,	1	1	Augu.
McPheeters,John,	1	9	Augu.
McPheeters,William,	1	6	Augu.
McPherson,Daniel,	4		Berk.
McPherson,Dun,	1		York
McPherson,Samuel,	1		Pr.Wm
McPherson,Samuel,			Lou.
McPherson,Stephen,	1		Lou.
McPherson,Stephen,Jr.,	1		Lou.
McPherson,William,	1		Berk.
McQueen,Alexander,	1	5	Cul.
McQueen,Charles,	1	1	Fau.
McQueen,John,	1		Cul.
McQueen,Samuel,	1		Cul.
McQueen,William,	1	1	Cul.
McQuerry,John,	1		Lin.
McQuerry,William,	2		Lin.
McQuilky,John,			Hen.
McQuin,Henry,	1		Cul.
McQuity,Samuel,	1		Lou.
McQuitty,James,	1	1	Spot.
McQuitty,Mary,	1		Spot.
McRabster,Daniel,			Hen.
McRae,Philip,	1		Hen.
McRanels,John,	1	1	Wash.
McRanels,Joseph,	1		Wash.
McReynolds,James,	1	7	Camp
McRoberts,Alexander,	1	1	Hen.
McRoberts,Alexander,	1		Bot.
McRoberts,John,	1		Bot.
McRoberts,John,	1		Augu
McRoberts,Samuel,	1		Bot.
McShane,Nehemiah,	1	8	Buck
McShane,Richard,			Buck
McSpadden,Archibald,	1		Wash
McSpadden,Moses,	1		Wash
McSpadden,Thomas,	1		Wash
McTire,John,	1	1	Jas.
McVe,John,	1		Augu
McVee,Matthew,	1	2	Hen.
McVey,James,	1	2	Bed.
McVicker,John,	1		Lou.
McWane,Alexander,	1		Augu
McWharter,Robert,	1		Fau.
McWhort,John,	1	1	Spot
McWilliams,Benjamin,		4	Spot
McWilliams,David,	2		Berk
McWilliams,David,	1		Rock.
McWilliams,Hugh,	1		Henry.
McWilliams,William,	1	6	Spots.
Meachum,Paul,	1	16	Gooch.
Mead,Abel,	1		Henry
Mead,Benjamin,	1		Lou.
Mead,Henry,	1		Lou.
Mead,John,	1	10	Bed.
Mead,Nicholas,	1	2	Bed.
Mead,Mahland,	1		Bed.
Mead,Robert,	1		Bed.
Mead,Samuel,			Bed.
Mead,Col.William,	1	29	Bed.
Mead,William,	1		Lou.
Mead,William,	1	1	York.
Meade,Andrew,	1	63	Brun.
Meade,David,	1	36	Pr.Geo.
Meaden,Benjamin,	1		Wash.
Meadors,Ambrose,	1		Bed.
Meadors,Isham,			Bed.
Meadors,James,	1	3	Bed.
Meadors,Jarris,			Bed.
Meadors,Jeremiah,	1	1	Bed.
Meadors,Jeremiah,	1	1	Bed.
Meadors,Jesse,	1		Bed.
Meadors,John,	1		Bed.
Meadors,John,Jr.,	1		Bed.
Meadors,John,	1	4	Bed.
Meadors,Joel,	1	8	Bed.
Meadors,Joel,Jr.,	1		Bed.
Meadors,Joel,Jr.,	1		Bed.
Meadors,Thomas,	1		Bed.
Meadors,William,	1		Bed.
Meanley,Richard,	1	12	Din.
Meanley,Samuel,	1	1	Lun.
Meanley,William,	1	11	Din.
Meanly,Archer,	1		Cha.Cy.
Meanly,D.Q.,			Din.
Meanly,Elizabeth,		2	Gooch.
Meanly,John,	1		Lun.
Meanly,Samuel,Jr.,	1		Lun.
Meanly,William,			Buck.
Meard,John,	3	10	Acco.
Mears,Mary,	2		Acco.
Mears,Richard,			Acco.
Medcalf,Thomas,	1		Henry
Medley,Ambrose,	1	3	Cul.
Medley,Jacob,	2	13	Cul.
Medley,John,			Fau.
Medley,Reubin,			Cul.
Medley,Reubin,		4	Cul.
Medley,Reubin,	1	1	Lun.
Medlock,John,	1		Bot.
Meek,Ann,	1		Wash.
Meek,Daniel,	1		Aug.
Meek,John,	1		Aug.
Meek,Joseph,	1		Wash.
Meeke,Moses,			Lou.
Meeks,Thomas,	1	3	Aug.
Meek,Thomas,	1		Wash.
Meeks,Alethe,	1		Mont.
Meers,Arthur,	1		Acco.
Meers,Coventon,	2	4	Acco.
Meers,Daniel,			Acco.
Meers,Elisha,	2	9	Acco.
Meers,George,	3		Acco.
Meers,Hellery,			Acco.
Meers,John,	1	1	Acco.
Meers,John,			Acco.
Meers,John,	1	8	Acco.
Meers,Levin,Sr.,	3		Acco.
Meers,Levin,	1		Acco.
Meers,Levern,	1		Acco.
Meers,Richard,	2	2	Acco.
Meers,Solomon,			Acco.
Meers,Southy,	2	8	Acco.

Name			County
Meers,Spencer,	2	4	Acco.
Meers,William,			Acco.
Meers,William,	1	4	Acco.
Meers,William,	1	4	Acco.
Meets,John,	1		Lou.
Mefford,Jacob,	1	1	Bot.
Megann,John,	1		Cul.
Megee,Thomas,Sr.,	1	10	Spots
Megee,Thomas,Jr.,	1	10	Spots
Meggison,William,est.,		4	Buck.
Meglamere,John,	1	4	So'n
Mehomer,Dennis,	1		K.Geo
Mehomer,Enuch,	1		K.Geo
Mehoney,Henry,	1		K.Geo
Mehorn,Robinson,	1		Acco.
Mehorney,Benjamin,	2		K.Geo
Mehurin,Samuel,	1		Mont.
Meldrom,John,			Lun.
Melear,Richard,	1	1	Bed.
Melona,Raulin,	1	2	Brun.
Melone,Wynnie,	1	2	Lun.
Meloyd,David,	1	9	Buck.
Melson,Charles,	1		Buck.
Melson,Daniel,	2		Acco.
Melson,Kendal,	1		Acco.
Melson,Levin,	1	1	Acco
Melson,Ruth,	2		Acco.
Melson,Shadrick,	1		Acco.
Melson,Smith,Sr.,	2	1	Acco.
Melson,Smith,Jr.,	1	1	Acco.
Melson,William,			Acco.
Melson,William,	1		Bed.
Melton,Absalom,	1		Bed.
Melton,Elisha,	1		So'n
Melton,George,	1		Hen.
Melton,James,	1		Henry
Melton,James,	1		Loui.
Melton,Josiah,	1		So'n
Melton,R.,		2	Pr.Wm
Melton,William,	1		Loui.
Melvin,George,	1		Acco.
Melvin,John,	1	1	Berk.
Melvin,John,	1	1	Berk.
Melvin,Thomas,	1		Berk.
Memory,George,	1	1	West.
Mendinghall,James,	1		Berk.
Mendinghall,James,	2		Berk.
Menifee,Jerrett,	1		Mont.
Mennis,Callohill,	1	6	York
Mercer,Edward,	2		Berk.
Mercer,Edward,	1		Lou.
Mercer,Isabella,		5	Spots
Mercer,James,	2	55	Spots
Mercer,James,	1	3	So'n
Mercer,James,	1	11	Lou.
Mercer,James,	1		Berk.
Mercer,John,		1	K.Geo
Mercer,John,	1	2	So'n
Mercer,John,	1		Berk.
Mercer,John Francis,	2	40	Fau.
Mercer,Richard,	1		Lou.
Mercer,Robert,	1		Berk.
Merchant,Philip,	1		Lou.
Meredith,David,	1		Henry
Meredith,Gough R.,	1	7	K.&Q
Meredith,James,Sr.,	1		Henry
Meredith,James,Jr.,	1		Henry
Meredith,John,	1		Henry
Meredith,John,	1	3	Din.
Meredith,John,	1	18	K.&Q
Meredith,Junor,	1		Henry
Meredith,Samuel,	1	10	K.Wm.
Meredith,Samuel,	1		Henry
Meredith,Samuel,est.	2	35	K.&Q
Meredith,William,	1	4	Din.
Meredith,William,Sr.,	1	24	K.&Q

Name			County
Meredith,William,	1	14	Buck.
Merewether,Francis,	2	37	Spots.
Merewether,John,	1	8	Spots.
Merewether,Zachary,	2	13	Spots.
Meredith,Bradley,	1		Mont.
Meredith,David,	1	1	Brun.
Meredith,David,Jr.,	1	1	Brun.
Meredith,William,	1	5	Brun.
Meriwether,James,	1	19	Loui.
Meriwether,William,	1	36	Loui.
Merrett,Thomas,	1	1	Bed.
Merrick,Hannah,			Lou.
Merrick,James,	1		Lou.
Merrill,Nicholas,	1		Lou.
Merrin,Ann,			Gooch.
Merrin,Bartholomew,	1		Gooch.
Merriott,Thomas,	1	9	Brun.
Merritt,Henry,	1	22	Brun.
Merritt,William,	1	9	Brun.
Merry,David,	1	8	Cha.Cy
Merry,William,	1	19	Cha.Cy
Merrymoon,David,	1		Din.
Merrymoon,Francis,	1	6	Din.
Mershen,Joseph,	1	1	Lou.
Mershett,William,	1		Lou.
Mershon,Abram,	1		Cul.
Mershon,Andrew,	1		Cul.
Mershon,Cornelius,	2		Cul.
Messersmith,Barney,	1		Mont.
Messersmith,John,	1		Mont.
Messham,Abraham,	1		Fau.
Metcalf,Allen,	1		Berk.
Metcalf,Amos,	1		Berk.
Metcalf,John,	1	6	Fau.
Metcalf,Margaret,			Berk.
Metcalf,Thomas,	2	8	K.&Q
Metcalf,Vachell,	2		Berk.
Metcalf,William,	1		Fau.
Meteer,James,	1		Aug.
Mews,Thomas,			West.
Michael,Daniel,	1		Fau.
Michael,John,Sr.,	1	40	Nor.
Michael,John,Jr.,	1	8	Nor.
Michael,Philip,	1		Lou.
Michael,Philip,Jr.,	1		Lou.
Michel,Henry,	1		Lou.
Michel,Archer,Bryce& William,	2	31	Gooch.
Michulm,John,	1		Camp.
Mickie,George,	1	5	Loui.
Mickie,Elizabeth,	1	17	Loui.
Mickie,John,	1	1	Loui.
Mickie,Robert,	1	22	Loui.
Mickel,Ann,		1	Gooch.
Mickel,David,	1		Gooch.
Mickins,John,	2		Fay.
Micou,Harry,	1	12	Caro.
Micou,John,	1	34	Caro.
Micou,Richard,	1	24	Caro.
Midcalf,John,	1		Acco.
Midcalf,Mark,	2		Acco.
Midcalf,Sarah,		6	Acco.
Midcalf,Thomas,	1	2	Acco.
Middlemast,Archibald,	1	4	Din.
Middleton,Benedict,	2	17	West.
Middleton,Benjamin,	1		West.
Middleton,Billy,			Lou.
Middleton,George,	1		Acco.
Middleton,Jacob,	1		Bot.
Middleton,John,	1	5	West.
Middleton,John,	1		Bot.
Middleton,John,	1		Mont.
Middleton,Major,			Acco.
Middleton,Tamer,			Acco.
Middleton,Thomas,	1	2	Bot.
Middleton,Thomas,Jr.,	1		Bot.

Name			County
Middleton,Thomas,	1	1	Berk.
Middleton,Thomas,	1	1	West.
Middleton,Walter,	1		Bot.
Middleton,William,	1	2	West.
Middleton,William,	1	30	West.
Middleton,William,	1		Lou.
Middleton,William,	2		Acco.
Miers,Benjamin,	1		Henry
Miers,Henry,	1		Bot.
Miers,Michael,	1		Bot.
Miflin,Anthony,	1		K.Geo
Miflin,George,	1	2	K.Geo
Milam,Ann,		1	Bed.
Milam,Elizabeth,			Bed.
Milam,Moses,	1	1	Bed.
Milam,Rush,	1		Bed.
Milam,Samuel,	1		Henry
Milam,William,	1		Bed.
Milam,Zachariah,	1		Bed.
Milby,John,	2	9	Acco.
Milby,Patience,		8	Acco.
Miles,Charles,			Cul.
Miles,Charles,	2	6	York.
Miles,Charles,Jr.,			York
Miles,David,	1		Mont.
Miles,David,	2		Har.
Miles,Elizabeth,	2	4	Cul.
Miles,Isham,	1	6	Buck.
Miles,James,	1		Din.
Miles,John,	1		Mont.
Miles,John,	1		Cul.
Miles,John,	1		Din.
Miles,Jonadab,	1		Lou.
Miles,Jonah,	1		Lou.
Miles,Samuel,	1		Henry
Milhanke,David,	1		Henry
Milinor,Smith,	1	3	Acco.
Millam,Thomas,	1	8	Lou.
Millan,William,	1		Lou.
Millar,Edward,	1		Lou.
Millard,Elizabeth,			Fau.
Millburn,Jonathan,	1		Lou.
Millar,Andrew,	1	4	Lin.
Millar,Andrew,	1		Wash.
Millar,John,	1		Lin.
Miller,Abraham,	1		Lin.
Miller,Agness,	2	6	Berk.
Miller,Aminadab,	1	1	Hen.
Miller,Andrew,	1		Har.
Miller,Anthony,	1		Har.
Miller,Archibald,	1		Lou.
Miller,Beaverly,	1		Mont.
Miller,Calep,	1		Henry
Miller,Christian,	1		Berk.
Miller,Christian,	1		Lou.
Miller,Conrod,	1		Berk.
Miller,Dabney,	1	18	Hen.
Miller,Daniel,	1		Rock.
Miller,David,	1		Lou.
Miller,David,	1		Bot.
Miller,David,	2		Berk.
Miller,Edward,	1	7	Hen.
Miller,Eleanor,			Lin.
Miller,Elijah,			Camp.
Miller,Ellen,	1		Berk.
Miller,Francis,	1		Cul.
Miller,Frederick,	1		Buck.
Miller,Frederick,			Mont.
Miller,George,	1		Henry
Miller,George,	1		Har.
Miller,George,	1		Har.
Miller,George,	2		Lin.
Miller,Henry,	1		Berk.
Miller,Henry,	2		Berk.
Miller,Henry,	1		Berk.
Miller,Henry,	1		Har.
Miller,Henry,	1		Har.

Name			County
Miller,Henry,	1		Cul.
Miller,Henry,			Bot.
Miller,Henry,	2		Rock.
Miller,Hugh,	1		Berk.
Miller,Hugh,	1		Berk.
Miller,Isaac,	1		Lou.
Miller,Isom,	1	3	K.&Q
Miller,Jacob,	1		Berk.
Miller,Jacob,	1		Berk.
Miller,Jacob,	1	2	Brun.
Miller,Jacob,	2	3	Har.
Miller,Jacob,	1		Lou.
Miller,Jacob,	2		Cul.
Miller,Jacob,	2		Lou.
Miller,Jacob,Jr.,			Lou.
Miller,Jacob,	1		Bed.
Miller,Jacob,	1		Har.
Miller,James,	1	1	Berk.
Miller,James,	1		Berk.
Miller,James,	1		K.&Q
Miller,James,	1		Mont.
Miller,James,	1		Cul.
Miller,James,	1		Mont.
Miller,James,	1		Fau.
Miller,James,	4	5	Caro.
Miller,John,	1		Berk.
Miller,John,	1		Berk.
Miller,John,	1		Berk.
Miller,John,	1	2	Berk.
Miller,John,	1		Berk.
Miller,John,		6	Hen.
Miller,John,	1	2	Hen.
Miller,John,	1		Mont.
Miller,John,	1		Fau.
Miller,John,	1	2	Buck.
Miller,John,	1	1	Aug.
Miller,John,	1		Henry
Miller,John,	1		Henry
Miller,John,	1		Cul.
Miller,John,	2		Har.
Miller,John,	1		Fay.
Miller,John,			Cul.
Miller,John,	1		Fau.
Miller,John,	1		Bot.
Miller,John,	2		Mont.
Miller,John,	1		Mont.
Miller,John,	1	3	Camp.
Miller,John,			Bed.
Miller,John,est.	3	44	Caro.
Miller,John Daniel,	1		Lou.
Miller,Joseph,	1		Mont.
Miller,Joseph,	1		Lou.
Miller,Judith,			Berk.
Miller,Lodowick,	1		Lou.
Miller,Mark,			Cul.
Miller,Martin,	1		Berk.
Miller,Martin,	1		Berk.
Miller,Mary,		11	Gooch.
Miller,Mary Ann,		3	Buck.
Miller,Michael,	2		Har.
Miller,Michael,	1		Bed.
Miller,Nathaniel,	1	2	Hen.
Miller,Patrick,	2		Aug.
Miller,Peter,	1		Lou.
Miller,Peter,	1		Lou.
Miller,Philip,	1		Berk.
Miller,Richard,	1		Hen.
Miller,Robert,	2		Berk.
Miller,Robert,			Cul.
Miller,Robert,	1		Mont.
Miller,Samuel,	1		Rock.
Miller,Sarah,		21	So'n
Miller,Simon,Sr.,	2	30	Cul.
Miller,Simon,Jr.,		8	Cul.
Miller,Simon,Sr.,	1	15	Bed.
Miller,Simon,Jr.,	1	3	Bed.

Name			County
Miller,Stephen,	1		Har.
Miller,Capt.Thomas,	2	23	Buck.
Miller,Thomas,	1	18	K.&Q
Miller,Thomas,	1	2	Spots.
Miller,Thomas,	1	10	Gooch.
Miller,Thomas,	1		Bot.
Miller,Thomas,	1		Bot.
Miller,Will,	1	2	Lin.
Miller,William,	1	17	Hen.
Miller,William,	1		Hen.
Miller,William,	1		Fau.
Miller,William,	1	1	Bed.
Miller,William,	2	1	Caro.
Miller,William H.,	1	12	Gooch.
Miller,William,	1		Henry
Miller,William,	1		Henry
Miller,Zachariah,	1		Berk.
Miller,Zachariah,	1		Berk.
Milles,Jasper,	1		Aug.
Millgr,Christy,	1		Berk.
Milliam,William,	1		Pr.Wm.
Millikin,John,	1		Berk.
Millikan, John,	1		Rock.
Millikan,John,	1		Rock.
Millikan,William,	1		Rock.
Mills,Blaney,			Bot.
Mills,Hannah,		2	York.
Mills,Hugh,			Bot.
Mills,James,	1		Bed.
Mills,James,	1	1	Caro.
Mills,John,	1	8	Bot.
Mills,John,		3	K.Wm.
Mills,John,	1		Aug.
Mills,John,	2	9	Lun.
Mills,John,	1		Hen.
Mills,Norwich,	2	28	Hen.
Mills,Robert,	1		Aug.
Mills,Thompson,	1	2	Caro.
Mills,William,	1	8	Spots.
Milner,Thomas,	1		So'n
Mims,David,	1	9	Gooch.
Mims,Drury,	2	17	Buck.
Mims,Elizabeth,		8	Gooch.
Mims,Gideon,	1	6	Gooch.
Mims,Martin,	1	4	Gooch.
Mims,Sarah,			Gooch.
Minate,Richard,	1		Mont.
Minate,William,	1		Mont.
Minatred,Paul,	1	1	Pr.Wm.
Minegar,John,	1		Lou.
Minegar,Michael,	1		Lou.
Miner,John,	1	10	Cul.
Miner,Owen,	1	6	Cul.
Mines,Thomas,	1		Aug.
Minge,Christiana,	2	96	Cha.Cy
Minge,Elizabeth,	1	4	Cha.Cy
Minge,John,			Cha.Cy
Minge,John,	1		Pr.Geo
Minge,Mary,		10	Cha.Cy
Minge,Mary,			Pr.Geo
Minge,William,	1	1	Pr.Geo
Minger,Henry,	1		Aug.
Miniard,Joshua,	1	11	So'n
Minifee,John,	2	13	Cul.
Minner,Armistead,	1	8	Cul.
Minnis,Mary,		1	York.
Minitree,Ann,	1	20	Cha.Cy
Minnitree,Archibald,	2	5	Din.
Minitree,Jacob,	1	9	Pr.Wm.
Minitree,John,			Cha.Cy
Minitree,William,	1	2	Din.
Minor,Cyrus,	1	4	Lun.
Minor,Maj.Garrett,	1	22	Loui.
Minor,James,		1	Loui.
Minor,Capt.John,est.		18	Lou.
Minor,John,	1	37	Caro.

Name			County
Minor,Joseph,	1	3	K.&Q
Minor,Joseph,	2	12	Lun.
Minor,Joseph,Jr.,			Lun.
Minor,Col.Nicholas,	2	9	Lou.
Minor,Peggy,		1	Spots.
Minor,Peter,	2	1	Din.
Minor,Spence,	1	5	Lou.
Minor,Stewart,			Lou.
Minor,Thomas,	1	26	Spots.
Minor,Thomes,	1	13	Spots.
Minor,Thomas,	1	10	Loui.
Minor,Thomas,	1	3	Lou.
Minor,Thomas,		9	Caro.
Minor,Vivion,	1	20	Caro.
Minor,William,			Hen.
Minox,Charles,	1		Lou.
Minson,Euphan,	1	14	Eli.Cy
Mintall,Christopher,	1		Lou.
Minter,John,	1	2	Henry
Minter,Joseph,	1	8	Fau.
Minter,Mary,		5	Fau.
Minter,William,	1		Lin.
Minton,John,	1		Wash.
Minton,Mills,		14	So'n
Minton,Richard,	1		Lou.
Minx,John,	1	16	Bot.
Miras,Jacob,	2		Bot.
Mires,Ludwick,	1		Aug.
Mischell,John,	1	5	Din.
Mitcham,Benjamin,	1		Bed.
Mitcham,Elizabeth,		2	Spots.
Mitcham,James,	1	3	Spots.
Mitcham,John,	1	9	Spots.
Mitchell,Abraham,	1		
Mitchell,Abraham,	1		Bed.
Mitchell,Adam,	2	4	Lou.
Mitchell,Alexander,			Buck.
Mitchell,Aquilla,	1		Bed.
Mitchell,Barnett,	1	3	Loui.
Mitchell,Benjamin,			Lou.
Mitchell,Cary,	1	7	K.Wm.
Mitchell,Daniel,	1		Bed.
Mitchell,David,	1		Bot.
Mitchell,David,	2		Fay.
Mitchell,Edward,	1	16	Din.
Mitchell,Edward,	1	1	Eli.Cy
Mitchell,Enos,	1		Bed.
Mitchell,George,	1		West.
Mitchell,Henry,	1	1	Din.
Mitchell,Henry,	1	8	Mont.
Mitchell,Hezekiah,	1	2	Caro.
Mitchell,Hood,			Brun.
Mitchell,Ignatius,	1		Pr.Wm.
Mitchell,Ignatious,	1	1	Fay.
Mitchell,Isaac,			K.Wm.
Mitchell,Jack,	1	5	K.Wm.
Mitchell,James,	1	12	Bot.
Mitchell,James,			Fay.
Mitchell,James,	1	5	Aug.
Mitchell,James,Jr.,	1	3	Aug.
Mitchell,James,	1	10	K.Wm.
Mitchell,James,	1		Bed.
Mitchell,John,	1	18	Din.
Mitchell,John,	1		Har.
Mitchell,John,	1	8	So'n
Mitchell,John,	1		Hen.
Mitchell,John,	1		Pr.Wm.
Mitchell,John,	1	9	Brun.
Mitchell,John,	1		Fau.
Mitchell,John,	1	3	Lou.
Mitchell,John,	1	2	Bed.
Mitchell,John,			Bed.
Mitchell,John,	1	1	K.Wm.
Mitchell,John,	1	8	K.&Q
Mitchell,John,			Hen.

Name			Co.
Mitchell,John,	1		Rock.
Mitchell,John,	1	5	Loui.
Mitchell,John,	1	7	Caro.
Mitchell,Joseph,	1	1	Berk.
Mitchell,Moses,	1		Fay.
Mitchell,Ralph,	1		Henry
Mitchell,Richard,	1	2	Henry
Mitchell,Richard,	1	1	Caro.
Mitchell,Robert,	1	8	Henry
Mitchell,Robert,	1		Berk.
Mitchell,Robert,	1	11	Din.
Mitchell,Robert,Sr.,	1		Bed.
Mitchell,Robert,Jr.,	1		Bed.
Mitchell,Robert,Jr.	1		Bed.
Mitchell,Robert,	1		Aug.
Mitchell,Robert,	1	7	Hen.
Mitchell,Robert,		4	Hen.
Mitchell,Robert,			Pr.Geo
Mitchell,Ross,	1	1	Eli.Cy
Mitchell,Ruben,	2	9	Eli.Cy
Mitchell,Samuel,	1	1	Fay.
Mitchell,Samuel,	1		Mont.
Mitchell,Samuel,	1		Bed.
Mitchell,Stephen,			York
Mitchell,Sue,	1	1	K.&Q
Mitchell,Susanna,		5	K.&Q
Mitchell,Thomas,	1		Fay.
Mitchell,Thomas,	1	8	Cul.
Mitchell,Thomas,	1	1	Ja.Cy
Mitchell,Thomas,	1		Berk.
Mitchell,Thomas,	1		Pr.Wm
Mitchell,Thomas,	1		Aug.
Mitchell,Thomas,	1	8	Loui.
Mitchell,Wyatt,	1		Cul.
Mitchell,William,	1	1	Din.
Mitchell,William,	1		Henry
Mitchell,William,	1	3	Henry
Mitchell,William,	1		Cul.
Mitchell,William,	2	4	Pr.Wm
Mitchell,William,	1	13	Brun.
Mitchell,William,	1		Lou.
Mitchell,William,	1		Aug.
Mitchell,William,	1	20	York
Mitchell,William,	1		Rock.
Mitchell,William,	1		Caro.
Mitchell,William,	1		Lin.
Mitihell,George,	1	1	Mont.
Mitholland,Patrick,	1		Lou.
Mitthorn,George,	1		Berk.
Mittinger,Daniel,	2		Lou.
Mittinger,Reynold,			Lou.
Mitts,Adam,	1		Har.
Miur,Francis,	1	47	Din.
Mize,Avis,			Lun.
Mize,John,	1		Lun.
Mize,John,	1		Lun.
Mize,Mary,			Lun.
Mize,Stephen,	1		Lun.
Mize,Sylvania,			Lun.
Mize,William,	1		Lun.
Mobley,James,	1		Lin.
Mobley,James,	1	2	Wash.
Mobley,James,	1		Wash.
Mobley,John,	1		Wash.
Modecit,Charles,			Pr.Wm
Moffett,Henry,	1		Lou.
Moffett,Jesse,	1		Fau.
Moffett,John,	1	17	Fau.
Moffett,Josiah,	2	2	Lou.
Moffett,Robert,	1		Mont.
Moffitt,Col.George,	1	16	Aug.
Moffitt,James,	1		Aug.
Moffitt,John,	1	5	Aug.
Moffitt,William,			Aug.
Mohorne,John,	1	1	Lun.
Moler,Adam,	1		Berk.

Name			Co.
Moler,Henry,	1		Berk.
Moler,Jacob,	1		Berk.
Moles,Samuel,	1	2	West.
Molton,William,	1	4	Pr.Wm.
Monaele,George,	1		Berk.
Monday,George,			Cul.
Monday,John,	1	11	Fau.
Monday,Robert,	1	5	Fau.
Monday,William,	1	4	Fau.
Money,James,			Fay.
Money,Nicholas,	1		Lou.
Money,William,	1		Lou.
Monjay,Thomas,	1		Cul.
Monks,John,	1		Har.
Monson,Archibald,	1		Mont.
Montague,Clement,	1	11	Spots
Montague,Thomas,	1	5	Spots
Montenay,Isaac,	1		Lou.
Monteith,James,	1	6	Lou.
Montgomery,Alexander,	1		Rick.
Montgomery,Alexander	1	2	Hen.
Montgomery,Alexander,	1		Wash.
Montgomery,F.			Pr.Wm
Montgomery,Humphrey	1	1	Aug.
Montgomery,James,	1		Wash.
Montgomery,James,	1		Mont.
Montgomery,James,	1		Gooch
Montgomery,James,	1		Mont.
Montgomery,James,	1		Aug.
Montgomery,James,	1		Rock.
Montgomery,James,	1	8	Mont.
Montgomery,John,Sr.,	1		Wash.
Montgomery,John,	1		West.
Montgomery,John,	1		West.
Montgomery,John,	1		Aug.
Montgomery,John,Sr.,	1	4	Mont.
Montgomery,John,Jr.,	1		Mont.
Montgomery,Joseph,	1		Mont.
Montgomery,Joseph,	1	2	Mont.
Montgomery,Robert,	1		Wash.
Montgomery,Robert,			Rock.
Montgomery,Robert,	1		Mont.
Montgomery,Robert,Jr	1		Mont.
Montgomery,Robert,	1	1	Lin.
Montgomery,Robert,	1	1	Lin.
Montgomery,Sam'l,Sr.,	2		Mont.
Montgomery,Sam'l,Jr.,			Mont.
Montgomery,Samuel,	1		Mont.
Montgomery,Thomas,	1	1	Wash.
Montgomery,Thomas,	1	1	Mont.
Montgomery,Thomas,	1	1	Lin.
Montgomery,Thomas,	1	1	Lin.
Montgomery,William,	1		Mont.
Montgomery,William,	2	7	Pr.Wm
Montgomery,William,	1		Rock.
Montgomery,William,	1	3	Lin.
Montgomery,William,	1		Lin.
Monroe,Alexander,	1		Fau.
Monroe,Andrew,	1	4	West.
Monroe,Benjamin,	1	12	West.
Monroe,David,	1	9	West.
Monroe,Elliott,	1	18	West.
Monroe,Hugh,	1		Pr.Wm
Monroe,James,	1	1	Hen.
Monroe,James,	1	3	West.
Monroe,John,	1	3	West.
Monroe,John,	1	10	West.
Monroe,John,	1	36	West.
Monroe,John,	2	1	Fau.
Monroe,William,	1	6	West.
Monroe,William,	1	2	K.Geo
Monrow,James,	1	1	Cul.
Mooberry,Andrew,	1		Spots
Mooberry,John,	1		Spots
Moody,Andrew,	1		Aug.

Name			Co.
Moody,Andrew,	1		Aug.
Moody,Francis,		7	Pr.Ge
Moody,Giles,			York
Moody,Henry,	1		Brun.
Moody,John,	1	6	Lun.
Moody,John,	1	2	Din.
Moody,Matt,	1	6	York
Moody,Matthew,	1	1	Hen.
Moody,Philip,	1		Din.
Moody,Philip,		4	So'n
Moody,Philip,	1	4	So'n
Moody,Robert,	1		Aug.
Moody,Thomas,	1	2	Lun.
Moody,Thomas,	1		Caro.
Moody,William,	2	11	York
Moody,William,	1	17	York
Moon,Alexander,	2	1	Rock.
Moon,Andrew,	1	1	Rock.
Moon,Gideon,	1	13	Lun.
Moon,Jacob,	1	6	Bed.
Moon,Jacob,	1		Berk.
Moon,James,	1	5	K.&Q
Moon,John,	1	2	Rock.
Moon,Joseph,	1	4	Rock.
Moon,Nanny,	1	5	Bed.
Moon,Thomas,	1		Berk.
Moon,Warner,	1		Lou.
Moon,Turner,	1	8	Bed.
Moon,William,Sr.,	1	3	Rock.
Moon,William,	1		Rock.
Mooney,James,	1		Fay.
Mooney,Nicholas,	1		Fau.
Moor,Eliab,	1		Wash.
Moor,James,	1		Bot.
Moor,James,	2		Bot.
Moor,John,	1		Bot.
Moor,John,	1		Bot.
Moor,John,	1	1	Berk.
Moor,Samuel,	1	6	Fau..
Moor,William,			Acco.
Moore,Abraham,			Henry
Moore,Alexander,	1	2	Lun.
Moore,Amos,	1		Gooch
Moore,Andrew,	1	3	Rock.
Moore,Andrew,Jr.,	1		Rock.
Moore,Andrew,	1		Mont.
Moore,Anthony,	1		Har.
Moore,Arlin,	1	6	Lun.
Moore,Augustine,	2	19	York
Moore,Augustine,	1	7	Eli.C.
Moore,Benjamin,	1		Berk.
Moore,Benjamin,	1	3	Din.
Moore,Benjamin,	2	3	Din.
Moore,Cato,	1	11	Berk.
Moore,David,	1		Rock.
Moore,David,	1		Lun.
Moore,David,	1	16	Lun.
Moore,David,	1		Aug.
Moore,Drury,	1		Brun.
Moore,Edward,	1		Lin.
Moore,Edward,	1		Lun.
Moore,Eliab,	4		Wash.
Moore,Elijah,	1		Pr.Wm.
Moore,Elizabeth,		9	So'n
Moore,Frederick,	1		Mont.
Moore,Garland,	1	4	West.
Moore,Harbin,	1	1	Lou.
Moore,Harbin,	1	11	Cul.
Moore,Henry,	1		Henry
Moore,Isaac,Sr.,	1	7	Nor.
Moore,Isaac,Jr.,	1	2	Nor.
Moore,Jacob,	1		Nor.
Moore,Jacob,	2	3	Lou.
Moore,James,	1		Lou.
Moore,James,	1		Mont.
Moore,James,	1	1	West.

Name			County
Moore,James,	1		Rock.
Moore,James,			Brun.
Moore,James,			Din.
Moore,Jary,	1		Brun.
Moore,Jeremiah,	1		Lun.
Moore,Jesse,	1	1	Lou.
Moore,Jessie,	1	.	Lun.
Moore,Jessie,	1		Lun.
Moore,Joanna,	1	24	K.Wm.
Moore,John,	1		K.Geo.
Moore,John,	1		Camp.
Moore,John,	1	1	K.&Q
Moore,John,			Din.
Moore,John,	1		Berk.
Moore,John,	1		Berk.
Moore,John,	1		Berk.
Moore,John,	1		Caro.
Moore,John,	1	4	Nor.
Moore,John,	1		Lun.
Moore,John,	1		Lun.
Moore,John,	1		Lou.
Moore,John,	1	10	Pr.Geo
Moore,John,	1		Mont.
Moore,John,	1		Brun.
Moore,Johnson,	1		Berk.
Moore,John,Sr.,	2	1	Rock.
Moore,John,Jr.,	1	1	Rock.
Moore,John,	1		Rock.
Moore,John Samuel,	1		K.Wm.
Moore,Joseph,	1		Caro.
Moore,Joseph,Sr.,	1		Lin.
Moore,Joseph,	1		Lin.
Moore,Katherine A.,	2	90	K.Wm.
Moore,Levi,	1		Aug.
Moore,Mary,	1	2	West.
Moore,Mary,			Brun.
Moore,Mary,		11	York,
Moore,Merritt,	1	8	Eli.C.
Moore,Merritt,	1	29	York
Moore,Moses,			Aug.
Moore,Philip,	1		K.&Q
Moore,Phillip,	1		Din.
Moore,Reubin,	1	6	Cul.
Moore,Richard,	1		Hen.
Moore,Richard,	1	1	Wash.
Moore,Richard,Sr.,			K.&Q
Moore,Richard,Jr.,	1		K.&Q
Moore,Robert,	2	2	Rock.
Moore,Robert,	1	1	Buck.
Moore,Robert,	1		Lun.
Moore,Robert,	1		Lin.
Moore,Robert,	1	1	Berk.
Moore,Robert,			West.
Moore,Sammy Lampkin,	1		Camp.
Moore,Sammy Lampkin,	1		Camp.
Moore,Sampson,	1		Camp.
Moore,Samuel,	1		Rock.
Moore,Samuel,	1		Rock.
Moore,Samuel,	1		Rock.
Moore,Samuel,	3		Rock.
Moore,Samuel,	1		Fay.
Moore,Sarah,	1	8	So'n
Moore,Starkey,	1	11	Din.
Moore,Stephen,	3		Acco.
Moore,Thomas,	1	1	K.Wm.
Moore,Thomas,	1	3	K.&Q
Moore,Thomas,	1	2	Camp.
Moore,Thomas,	1		Camp.
Moore,Thomas,	1	2	Camp.
Moore,Thomas,	1	1	West.
Moore,Thomas,	1	5	Caro.
Moore,Thomas,	1	2	Din.
Moore,Thomas,	1		Din.
Moore,Thomas,	1		Lun.
Moore,Thomas,	1	1	Lou.
Moore,Thomas,	1		Lou.
Moore,Thomas,	1		Mont.
Moore,Ussery,	1		Lun.
Moore,Vincent,	1	1	West.
Moore,Widow,	1	10	Lou.
Moore,William,	1	3	Rock.
Moore,William,	1		Hen.
Moore,William,	1		Spots
Moore,William,	1	1	Caro.
Moore,William,	1		Lou.
Moore,William,			So'n
Moore,William,	1		Lou.
Moore,William,	2	16	Eli.C
Moore,William,	1		Fau.
Moore,William,	1		Henry
Moore,William,	1	2	Brun.
Moore,William,			Brun.
Moore,William,	1		Brun.
Moore,William,	1	1	Lun.
Moore,William,			Lun.
Moore,William,Jr.,	1		Lun.
Moore,William,	1	1	Nor.
Moore,William,			York
Moore,William,	1		Aug.
Moore,William,	1		Aug.
Moore,William,	1		Rock.
Moore,William,	1		Mont.
Moore,William,			Wash.
Moore,William,Jr.,	1		Lin.
Moorey,John,	1		Fau.
Moorman,Charles,	1	4	Bed.
Moorman,Charles,	1	3	Bed.
Moorman,Thomas,	1	8	Loui.
Mooseman,Aihiles,	1	4	Caro.
Mordecai,Jacob,			Hen.
More,Peter,			Fay.
More,Samuel,	1		Fay.
More,Samuel,	1		Fay.
Moreass,Robert,		7	Brun.
Morecock,Edward,	1		Cha.C
Morecodk,Mildred,		21	Cha.C
Morecock,Thomas,	1	10	Cha.C
Morehead,Alexander,	1	5	Fau.
Morehead,Charles,	1	5	Fau.
Morehead,John,	1	18	Fau.
Morehead,Matthew,	1		Aug.
Morehead,Presley,	2	11	Fau.
Morehead,Samuel,	1	7	Fau.
Morehead,Turner,	1	7	Fau.
Morehead,William,	1	3	Fau.
Morein,James,	1	2	Lou.
Moreland,Francis,	1	12	Din.
Moreland,John,	1	2	Din.
Moreland,John,	1		Lou.
Moreland,Joseph,	1	9	Din.
Moreland,Richard,	1	5	York
Moreland,Robert,	1	3	Din.
Moreland,Wright,	1		Gooch
Morelats,Abraham,	1		Berk.
Morents,Jacob,	1		Cul.
Morgan,Abel,	1	1	Berk.
Morgan,Abel,	1		Fau.
Morgan,Abraham,	1		Mont.
Morgan,Benjamin,	1		Berk.
Morgan,Calia,		1	So'n
Morgan,Charles,	1	5	Fau.
Morgan,Charles,	1		Mont.
Morgan,Charles,	1	9	Fay.
Morgan,Daniel,	2	18	West.
Morgan,David,	1		Bed.
Morgan,Enoch,	1		Fau.
Morgan,Esther,			Bed.
Morgan,Evan,	1		Bed.
Morgan,Francis,	1	6	Cul.
Morgan,Isaac,	2		Berk.
Morgan,Jane,			Berk.
Morgan,Jarrett,	1	4	So'n
Morgan,John,	1		So'n.
Morgan,John,	1		Berk.
Morgan,John,	1		Fau.
Morgan,John,	1		West.
Morgan,John,			Henry
Morgan,John,	1		Henry
Morgan,John,	1	1	Fay.
Morgan,John,Jr.,	1		Fay.
Morgan,Joseph,	1	4	Fau.
Morgan,Mordicai,	1	1	Fay.
Morgan,Morgan,	2	1	Berk.
Morgan,Nathan,	1		Mont.
Morgan,Nathaniel,	1		Mont.
Morgan,Reece,	1		Bed.
Morgan,Richard,			Berk.
Morgan,Simon,	1	4	Fau.
Morgan,Thomas,	1		Mont.
Morgan,Thomas,	1		Lun.
Morgan,Thomas,	1		Lun.
Morgan,William,	1	13	Fau.
Morgan,William,	1	5	Fau.
Morgan,William,	1	4	Berk.
Morgan,William,	1	3	Berk.
Morgan,William,Jr.,	1		Berk.
Morgan,William,	1		So'n.
Morgan,William,	1	1	So'n.
Morgert,Katharine,			Lou.
Morgert,Peter,	1		Lou.
Morgon,Thomas,	1	3	Din.
Morning,Thomas,	1		Caro.
Morran,Arthur,	1	9	Cul.
Morrell,Nathaniel,	2	1	So'n.
Morris,Baldwin,Shep.	1	2	Eli.C
Morris,Benjamin,	1	6	Cha.C
Morris,Benjamin,	1	7	Buck.
Morris,Benjamin,			Lou.
Morris,Charles,	1	7	West.
Morris,Chislon,	1	7	So'n.
Morris,Christopher,	1		Eli.C
Morris,David,	1		Lou.
Morris,Elizabeth,		1	Fay.
Morris,Elizabeth,	1	1	Hen.
Morris,Evans,	1		Spots
Morris,George,	1	8	Loui.
Morris,George,	1		Brun,
Morris,Giles,	1		York
Morris,Henry,	1		So'n.
Morris,Henry,Sr.,	1	10	Brun.
Morris,Henry,			Brun.
Morris,Henry,	1	2	Buck.
Morris,Isaac,	1		Fau.
Morris,Jacob,	2		Lou.
Morris,James,	1	4	So'n.
Morris,James,	1	1	Berk.
Morris,James,Jr.,		1	Berk.
Morris,Jesse,			Lin.
Morris,John,	1		Wash.
Morris,John,			Camp.
Morris,John,	2	12	Camp.
Morris,John,	1		Lou.
Morris,John,	1	1	So'n.
Morris,John,	1	7	Lou.
Morris,John,	1	17	Jas.C.
Morris,John,	1	1	Gooch
Morris,John,			Brun.
Morris,Joseph,			Cul.
Morris,Joshua,	1	5	Jas.C.
Morris,Joshua,	2	15	Hen.
Morris,Joshua,	2		Cul.
Morris,Lester,	1	8	Brun.
Morris,Mark,	1		Rock.
Morris,Mary,		11	Jas.C.
Morris,Moses,	1	1	Spots.
Morris,Nathaniel,	1	6	Buck.
Morris,Nathaniel,			Brun.
Morris,Nicholas,	1	2	Buck.
Morris,Nicholas,	1	3	So'n.

Morris,Nimrod,			Lou.	Moseley,Charles,	1	10	Buck.	Mott,Moses,	1		Mont.
Morris,Col.N.G.	1	8	Gooch.	Moseley,Hillary,	1	9	Pr.Geo	Moudy,William,			Pr.Wm.
Morris,Obadiah,	1	1	Lou.	Moseley,Isaac,	1	5	Brun.	Mouldrough,Hugh,	1		Bot.
Morris,Pahnan,			Hen.	Moseley,John,	1	9	Buck.	Mouldrough,John,	1		Bot.
Morris,Col.Richard,	1	40	Loui.	Moseley,John,Jr.,			Buck.	Mounce,Mary,	2	1	Lin.
Morris,Robert,	1		Berk.	Mosely,Arthur,	1	13	Bed.	Mounger,Henry,			So'n.
Morris,Robert,			Din.	Mosely,Benjamin,	1	13	Buck.	Mount,Elijah,	1		Lou.
Morris,Robert,			Hen.	Mosely,Benjamin,	3	22	Buck.	Mount,Ezekiel,			Lou.
Morris,Samuel,	1	1	Loui.	Mosely,Edward,	1		Bed.	Mount,Thomas,	2		Lou.
Morris,Steven,	1	7	Cul.	Mosely,Francis,	2	23	Buck.	Mountague,John,	1	13	Caro.
Morris,Thomas,	1		Rock.	Mosely,Robert,	1	12	Buck.	Mountague,John,	1		Cul.
Morris,Thomas,	1		Rock.	Mosely,Thomas,Jr.	1		Buck.	Mountcastle,Ann,	1	8	Cha.C.
Morris,Thomas,	1		Cul.	Mosley,Avy,	1	3	Gooch.	Mountcastle,Benjamin,		1	Cha.C.
Morris,William,	1		Wash.	Mosley,Benjamin,Sr.,	1		Brun.	Mountcastle,Henry,	1		Cha.C.
Morris,William,		11	Loui.	Mosley,Benjamin,Jr.,	1		Brun.	Mountcastle,Joseph,	1	8	Cha.C.
Morris,William,	1		York	Mosley,Clemons,	1		Fay.	Mountcastle,Richard,	1	2	Cha.C.
Morris,William,	1	7	Eli.C.	Mosley,Jacob,	1		Fay.	Mountfort,Joseph,	1	11	So'n.
Morris,William,	1		Cul.	Mosley,John,	1		Brun.	Mountfort,Thomas,	2	6	So'n.
Morris,William,	1		Bed.	Mosley,Joseph,	1	8	Brun.	Mouring,William,	2	28	K.Wm.
Morrison,Alexander,	1	25	Brun.	Mosley,Joseph,	1		Gooch.	Mouse,Daniel,			Har.
Morrison,Archibald,	1	3	Lou.	Mosley,Nathan,	1		Brun.	Mowra,Lewis,	1		Augu.
Morrison,Archibald,	1	3	Lou.	Mosley,Samuel,	1	2	Brun.	Mowry,Harry,	1		Augu.
Morrison,Ezekeil,	1		Henry	Mosley,Thomas,Sr.,	1		Brun.	Mowry,Peter,	1		Augu.
Morrison,Hugh,	2		Fau.	Mosley,Thomas,Jr.,	1		Brun.	Moxley,Alvin,		14	Pr.Wm
Morrison,Hugh,	1	1	Cul.	Mosley,Walter,	1	4	Bed.	Moxley,Alvin, est.		11	West.
Morrison,James,			Buck.	Mosley,William,	1	1	Bed.	Moxley,Augustine,	1	9	West.
Morrison,James,	1		Berk.	Mosley,William,	1		Brun.	Moxley,Daniel,	1	6	Lou.
Morrison,John,	1	12	Pr.Geo	Mosley,William,Sr.	1		Brun.	Moxley,Elizabeth,		10	West.
Morrison,John,	2		Fay.	Moss,Ben,	3	3	York.	Moxley,John,	1	2	West.
Morrison,Joseph,	1		Berk.	Moss,Benjamin,	1	5	Loui.	Moxley,Joseph,Sr.	1	14	Lou.
Morrison,Nathaniel,	1		Berk.	Moss,Benjamin,	3	24	York.	Moxley,Joseph,Jr.,	1	4	Lou.
Morrison,Thomas,	1		Henry	Moss,David,	1	5	Brun.	Moxley,Joseph,	1	11	West.
Morriss,Benjamin,			Cul.	Moss,David,			Brun.	Moxley,Joseph,Jr.,	1		West.
Morriss,Ezekiel,	1		Henry	Moss,Edward,Jr.,	1	7	York	Moxley,Robert,	1	1	West.
Morriss,George,	1		Nor.	Moss,Edmund,Jr.,	1		Buck.	Moxley,Rodham,	1	9	West.
Morriss,Henry,	1	2	Din.	Moss,Francis,			York.	Moxley,William,			Lou.
Morriss,Hercules,	1	9	Din.	Moss,Gideon,	1	2	Lou.	Moxley,William,	1	7	Spots
Morriss,James,	1		K.& Q.	Moss,James,		2	Buck.	Moyer,Christopher,	1		Cul.
Morriss,John,			Cul.	Moss,James,	1	4	Buck.	Moyers,Peter,	1		Mont.
Morriss,John,	1	3	Din.	Moss,John,	1	7	York.	Moylee,James,	1		K.Wm.
Morriss,Joseph,	1	6	Henry	Moss,John,	1	4	York	Moythan,Benjamin,	1		Rock.
Morriss,John,			Har.	Moss,John,			York	Mucgregor,Thomas,	1		Augu.
Morriss,Joshua,	1		Bot.	Moss,John,	1	16	York	Mucklehatan,John,	1		Fay.
Morriss,Sam'l,Coleman	1	5	Henry	Moss,John,	4	1	K.Geo.	Muffett,Walter,	1	2	Berk.
Morriss,Thomas,	1	7	Brun.	Moss,John,	2	8	Loui.	Muir,George,	1		Fay.
Morriss,William,	1	6	Hen.	Moss,John,		5	Lou.	Muir,Phebe,			Lou.
Morriss,William,	1		K.&Q.	Moss,John,	1	11	Gooch.	Muire,Ann,	1	18	Acco.
Morron,John,	1	4	Buck.	Moss,John,Jr.,	1	5	Gooch.	Muire,John,	1	7	K.& Q
Morrow,Adam,	1		Wash.	Moss,John,	1	2	Brun.	Muire,Richard,	1	3	K.& Q
Morrow,Charles,	1		Berk.	Moss,John,			Brun.	Muirhead,Andrew,	1		Lou.
Morrow,George,	1		Augu.	Moss,Meredith,	1		Pr.Wm.	Muirhead,William,	1		Lou.
Morrow,James,	1		Har.	Moss,Moses,	2	9	Pr.Wm.	Mukleberry,Robert,	1	15	Caro.
Morrow,James,	1	3	Fay.	Moss,Nathaniel,	1		Lou.	Mulbery,Jacob,	1		Fay.
Morrow,John,	1	3	Berk.	Moss,Nathaniel,			Gooch.	Mull,David,	1		Lou.
Morrow,Patrick,	1		Mont.	Moss,Randolph,	1	1	York.	Mullenix,John,	1		Augu.
Morrow,Richard,	1		Har.	Moss,Samuel,	1	1	Gooch.	Mullican,John,		1	Spots
Morrow,Thomas,			Henry	Moss,Shelden,	1	12	Eli.C.	Mullican,William,	1		Bed.
Mortimer,Dr.Charles,	1	7	Spots	Moss,Thomas,			Buck.	Mullikin,Burton,	1	2	Fau.
Morton,David,	1		Wash.	Moss,Thomas,Jr.,	1	1	Buck.	Mullin,James,	1	5	Caro.
Morton,James,	1	6	Henry	Moss,Thomas,	1	8	Buck.	Mulliner,Nathaniel,	1		Berk.
Morton,Jeremiah,	1	1	Bed.	Moss,Thomas,	5	8	K.Geo.	Mullins,Ann,			West.
Morton,John,	1	4	Bed.	Moss,Thomas,	1	3	Caro.	Mullins,Connerly,		2	Buck.
Morton,Thomas,			Fay.	Moss,Thomas,	1	1	Fau.	Mullins,Connerly,			Buck.
Morton,William,	3	1	West.	Moss,Thomas,	1	2	Lou.	Mullins,David,	1	5	Gooch.
Morton,William J.	1	10	Gooch.	Moss,Triplett,	1		Pr.Wm.	Mullins,Henry,	1	20	Gooch.
Mosbey,Joseph,	1		Hen.	Moss,William,			York	Mullins,John,	1	5	Gooch.
Mosbey,Robert,	1		Hen.	Mossom,David,	1	1	Eli.Cy	Mullins,John,	1	3	West.
Mosby,Benjamin,	1	13	Loui.	Motes,Jacob,	1		Aug.	Mullins,William,	1		Henry
Mosby,David,	1	6	Fay.	Mothershead,Alvin,	1		West.	Mullins,William,	1		Henry
Mosby,Hezekiah,	1		Hen.	Mothershead,George,	1		West.	Mumford,William,	1		K.Geo.
Mosby,John,	1	9	Hen.	Mothershead,John,	3		West.	Mumpower,Peter,	1		Wash.
Mosby,Josiah,	2	11	Hen.	Mothershead,John,Jr.,		1	West.	Muncey,Francis,	1		Mont.
Moses,Adam,	2		Har.	Mothershead,Nathaniel,	1		West.	Muncey,Luke,	1		Mont.
Moses,Samuel,	1		Aug.	Mothrel,George,			Aug.	Muncey,Samuel,	1		Mont.
Moseley,Abraham,	1		Fay.	Motley,Edwin,	1	13	K.&Q	Muncey,Samuel,Jr.,	1		Mont.
Moseley,Arthur,		5	Cha.Cy	Motley,William,	1		Caro.	Muncey,Skidmore,	1		Mont.

Muncey,William,	1		Mont.	Murrill,Wilkerson,	1		Buck.	Nail,Frederick,	1		Berk.
Muncy,Holton,	1		Mont.	Murry,Alexander,		10	So'n.	Nail,Thomas,	1		Aug.
Muncy,Obediah,	1		Mont.	Murry,Anthony,	1	9	Buck.	Naile,William,	1		Lou.
Munday,Edmond,	1	3	Caro.	Murry,Charles,	1	1	Berk.	Nalle,Francis,	2	8	Cul.
Mundell,John,Sr.,	1	12	So'n	Murry,David,			Bed.	Nalle,John,	2	5	Cul.
Mundell,John,Jr.,	1	1	So'n	Murry,Enoch,	1		Fau.	Nalle,Mary,		7	Cul.
Munford,William Green	1	30	Cha.Cy	Murry,James,	1	5	Fau.	Nalls,James,	1	1	Cul.
Munge,Catherine,	1	1	Acco.	Murry,James,	1	1	Cul.	Nalls,Martin,	1	8	Cul.
Munger,Cornelius J.	1	1	Acco.	Murry,John,	1		Fau.	Nalls,Richard,	1	2	Cul.
Munger,George,	1	3	Acco.	Murry,John,	1	1	Fau.	Nalls,William,	1		Fau.
Munger,Thomas J.,	1		Acco.	Murry,Ralph,	1	1	Fau.	Nance,Eaton,	1	4	Cha.C.
Mungle,Jacob,	1		Wash.	Murry,Thomas,	1		Bed.	Nance,Frederick,			Din.
Munroe,James,	1	4	K.Geo.	Murry,William,	1	1	Fau.	Nance,Frederick,	1	24	Lun.
Munroe,John,			Lun.	Murry,Zachariah,	2	3	Berk.	Nance,John,	1	3	Henry
Munroe,Johnson,	1		Lun.	Mury,William,		3	K.Geo.	Nance,John,	1	5	Cha.C.
Munroe,Mary,	1		Lun.	Muschett,James,	1	19	Fau.	Nance,Thomas,	1	10	Bed.
Munrony,Silvester,	1		Lin.	Muse,Ann,			West.	Nance,William,	1		Cha.C.
Munson,Samuel,	1		Mont.	Muse,Battaile,			Lou.	Nance,William,	1		Lun.
Muracken,Thomas,	1		Lou.	Muse,George,	1		West.	Nanny,Amos,	1	1	Brun.
Murdoch,Joseph,est.,	1	13	Fau.	Muse,George,	2	14	Caro.	Nanny,James,	1		Brun.
Murdock,John,	1		Wash.	Muse,James,	1	11	West.	Nanny,John,	1		Brun.
Murdock,Mary,		23	K.Geo.	Muse,James,	1	20	West.	Nanny,Uriah,	1	3	Brun.
Murfee,Elizabeth,			So'n	Muse,Jeremiah,	1	2	West.	Napscott,James,	1		York
Murfey,Thomas,	1		Lou.	Muse,Nicholas,	2	15	West.	Napier,Ashford,	1	1	Buck.
Murfey,William,	1	1	Pr.Geo	Muse,Richard,	2	4	Mont.	Napier,Nene,	1	3	Gooch
Murphee,James,	1	6	So'n	Muse,Richard,		5	K.Geo.	Napier,Rene,	1	2	Gooch
Murphee,Richard,est.			So'n	Muse,Richard,	1	10	West.	Naples,George,	1		Lou.
Murphee,Simon,	1	2	So'n	Muse,Samuel,	1	5	West.	Nash,George,	1		West.
Murphey,John,			Buck.	Muse,Sanford,		2	West.	Nash,Henry,	1	2	Gooch
Murphey,John,	1		Wash.	Muse,Thomas,	1	8	West.	Nash,James,	1	3	Cul.
Murphey,John,	1		Lin.	Muse,Thomas,	1	8	West.	Nash,John,	1	3	K.Wm.
Murphey,Richard,	1		Buck.	Muse,William,	1	2	West.	Nash,John,	1	1	K.&Q
Murphey,Thomas Truman	2		Buck.	Muser,Peter,	1		Mont.	Nash,John,	2	6	West.
Murphey,Truman,			Buck.	Musgrove,Henry,	1		Bed.	Nash,John,	1	4	Cul.
Murphy,Edmund,	1		Gooch.	Musgrove,Penketh,	1	4	York	Nash,John,	1		Mont.
Murphy,Isaac,	1		Pr.Wm.	Musgrove,Pinkethman,	1	1	Jas.C.	Nash,John,	1		Lin.
Murphy,James,	1		Cul.	Musgrove,Samuel,	1		Henry	Nash,Larkin,	1		Cul.
Murphy,James,	1	1	Pr.Wm.	Musick,Elexous,	1		Henry	Nash,Marvil,	1		Lin.
Murphy,James,	1	1	Henry	Mustin,Thomas,	2	2	K.Geo.	Nash,Maxwell,	2	14	Fau.
Murphy,John,	1		Berk.	Mustoe,Anthony,	1		Augu.	Nash,William,	1	1	Lin.
Murphy,John,	1		Bed.	Mutlow,Benjamin,	1	3	Jas.C.	Naughan,Sarah,		4	Pr.Geo
Murphy,John,	1		Berk.	Myer,John,	1		Berk.	Naughton,Samuel,	1		Pr.Geo
Murphy,John,	1		Rock.	Myers,Adam,	1		Berk.	Nave,Henry,	1		Har.
Murphy,John,	1	1	Lou.	Myers,Andrew,	1		Lou.	Nave,Michael,	1		Har.
Murphy,John,	1		Bot.	Myers,Charles,	1		Har.	Nawkirk,Tunis,	1	2	Berk.
Murphy,Josiah,	1		Pr.Wm.	Myers,Francis,	2		Har.	Nay,John,	1		Cul.
Murphy,Michael,	1		Bed.	Myers,George,	1		Lou.	Nay,Jacob,	1		Cul.
Murphy,Thomas,	1		Cul.	Myers,Isaiah,	1		Lou.	Naylor,Jane,		19	Eli.C.
Murphy,Timothy,	1		Mont.	Myers,Jacob,	1		Lin.	Neal,Basil,	1		Henry
Murphy,Valentine,	1		Berk.	Myers,John,	2		Lou.	Neal,Benjamin,	1	1	Henry
Murrah,Gavan,	1		Caro.	Myers,John,	1		Lou.	Neal,Benjamin,			Fau.
Murrah,Mark,	1	1	Caro.	Myers,John,	2		Berk.	Neal,Christopher,	1		Fau.
Murrall,Thomas,	1	7	Cha.Cy	Myers,John,	1		Har.	Neal,John,	2	17	Cul.
Murrall,Thomas,Jr.,	1		Cha.Cy	Myers,Joseph,	1		Lou.	Neal,John,	2		Cul.
Murray,Ann,	1	28	Pr.Geo	Myers,Lewis,	1		Lin.	Neal,Mycajah,	1	6	Cul.
Murray,David,	1	18	Bed.	Myler,George,	2		Berk.	Neal,R.,	1	7	Pr.Wm.
Murray,James,	1	2	Din.	Myles,Richard,	1		Berk.	Neal,Thomas,	1	6	Lun.
Murray,James,	2		Lou.	Myley,Jacob,	2		Lou.	Neal,Walter,	1		Bed.
Murray,James,Jr,			Lou.	Myley,Jacob,Jr.,			Lou.	Neal,William,			Fay.
Murray,John,	3		Caro.	Myrick,Ann,		20	So'n.	Neal,William,	1	1	Lin.
Murray,John,	1	9	Pr.Wm.	Myrick,Howell,	1	12	So'n.	Neal,Zachariah,	1	4	Bed.
Murray,Samuel,	1	1	Lou.	Myrick,John,	1	15	So'n.	Neal,Zaphaniah,	1		Bed.
Murray,William,			Lou.	Myrick,John,	2	10	Brun.	Neale,Behjamin,	1	6	Fau.
Murray,William,	2	28	Pr.Geo	Myrick,Owen,	1	17	So'n.	Neale,Charles,	1	19	K.Wm.
Murray,William,	1	11	Caro.	Myrick,Owen,	1	48	Brun.	Neale,Christopher,	1	7	Lou.
Murrell,Drury,	1		Lun.	Myrick,Owen,Jr.,			Brun.	Neale,Daniel,	1		Lou.
Murrell,Drury,	1	5	Gooch.	Myrtle,William,	2		Cul.	Neale,John,	1	8	West.
Murrell,Gardiner,	1	1	Din.	Myster,Benjamin,	1		Acco.	Neale,John,	1		Lou.
Murrell,George,	1		Lin.	Myster,John,	1		Acco.	Neale,John,	1		Har.
Murrell,Jeffery,	1		Lun.	Myster,William,Sr.,	2		Acco.	Neale,Joseph,	1	5	Fau.
Murrell,Jeffery,	1		Henry	Myster,William,Jr.,			Acco.	Neale,Joseph,	1		Fau.
Murrell,John,	1	1	Din.					Neale,Mary,			Lou.
Murrell,Mary,		3	Din.	Nafe,Jacob,	1		Bed.	Neale,Matthew,	1		Fau.
Murrell,Robert,	1		Din.	Naff,George,	1		Har.	Neale,Moses,	1		Har.
Murrell,Thomas,	1		Henry	Naff,Jacob,	1		Har.	Neale,Presley,	1	8	West.
Murrell,William,	1	8	Din.	Naffzingus,John,est.		1	Berk.				

92

Neale, Presley,	1	4	West.	Nelson, William,	3	13	Lou.	Newman, Thomas,	1	1	York
Neale, Richard,	1	8	West.	Nelson, William,	1	1	Hen.	Newman, Thomas,	1		Bot.
Neale, Rodham,		3	West.	Nelson, William,	1	18	Caro.	Newman, Thomas,	2	9	Cul.
Neale, Thomas,	2	14	Lou.	Nelson, William,	1	9	K.Wm.	Newman, William,	3		Hen.
Neall, John,			Brun.	Nervsam, William,	1		Camp.	Newman, William,		1	K.Wm.
Neall, John,		4	Brun.	Nesbit, Samuel,	1		Rock.	Newport, Richard,	1		Henry
Neaves, Christian,		4	Gooch.	Nesbit, William,			Rock.	Newsum, Benjamin,	1	7	So'n.
Neaves, Daniel,	2	9	K.Wm.	Ness, Henry,	1		Berk.	Newsum, Francis,	1	3	So'n.
Neaves, James,	1	1	K.Wm.	Nester, Fredrick,	1		Mont.	Newsum, Jacob,	1	7	So'n.
Neaves, John,	1	8	Gooch.	Nettles, John,	1	2	Eli.C.	Newsum, Joel,	1	10	So'n.
Neavil, Thomas,			Fau.	Nettles, Vicanious,	1	15	Eli.C.	Newsum, John,	1		So'n.
Neblitt, Edward,	1	12	Pr.Geo	Nettles, Vicanious,			Eli.C.	Newsum, Patience,		8	So'n.
Needham, Joseph,	1	11	Eli.C.	Neurstep, Edward,	1	2	Jas.C.	Newsum, Randall,	1		So'n.
Needy, David,	1		Berk.	Neutre, Gollfred,			Cul.	Newsum, Randolph,	1	8	So'n.
Neel, Daniel,	2		Fay.	Neverson, John,	1	5	Nor.	Newsum, Robert, Jr.,	1	1	So'n.
Neel, George,	1		Lin.	Nevil, James,	2		Lin.	Newsum, Tabitha,		16	So'n.
Neel, Thomas,			Hen.	Nevill, Joseph,	2	4	Har.	Newsum, Thomas,	1	1	So'n.
Neeley, Alexander,	1		Mont.	Nevills, John,	1		Henry	Newsum, William,	1		So'n.
Neelly, William,			Berk.	New, Anthony,	1	18	Caro.	Newsum, William,	2		So'n.
Neels, John,	1		Cul.	New, Hannah,			Cha.C.	Newton, Abraham,	1	5	Fau.
Neely, James,	2	2	Bot.	New, James,	1	8	K.Wm.	Newton, Benjamin,	1		So'n.
Neely, James, Jr.,	1	9	Bot.	New, James,			Cha.C.	Newton, Henry,	1	1	Spots.
Neely, James,			Rock.	New, James,	1		Cha.C.	Newton, Joseph,	3		Augu.
Neely, John,	3	8	Bot.	New, Jess,	1		Cha.C.	Newton, Mary,	1	9	Caro.
Neely, John,	1		Rock.	New, John,			Hen.	Newton, Patty,		1	So'n.
Neely, William,	1	14	Bot.	New, John,	1	1	Cha.C.	Newton, Richard,	1		Bot.
Neer, Philip,	1		Lou.	New, Richard,	1		Cha.C.	Newton, Richard,	1		Mont.
Neerheart, Jacob,	1		Lou.	New, William,	3	13	Hen.	Newton, Samuel,	1	2	Loui.
Neeri, Devault,	1		Lou.	New, William, Jr.,	1	1	Hen.	Newton, Shadrach,	1		So'n.
Nees, Henry,	1		Wash.	Newall, Adam,	1	7	Cul.	Newton, Shederick,	1		Wash.
Neff, Henry,	1		Lin.	Newberry, Robert,		1	West.	Newton, Thomas,	1		Eli.C.
Neighbours, Francis,	2		Buck.	Newberry, Samuel,	1		Mont.	Newton, William,	1	2	Cul.
Neighbours, John,			Buck.	Newbill, George,	1	9	K.& Q.	Newton, William,	1	2	So'n.
Neil, Arthur,	1		Wash.	Newby, Betty,			Fau.	Newton, Willoughby,	1	7	West.
Neil, Arthur, Jr.,	1		Wash.	Newcomb, Benjamin,	2		K.& Q.	Niblett, Elizabeth,			Lun.
Neil, Francis,	1		Wash.	Newcomer, Henry,	2		Augu.	Niblett, John,	1	3	Lun.
Neil, Capt.William,	1		Wash.	Newell, Camp,	1	5	Pr.Geo	Niblett, Sterling,	1	7	Lun.
Neilson, John,	1		Lou.	Newell, Edward,	1	9	Pr.Geo	Niblett, William,	1	2	Lun.
Nelson, Alexander,			Hen.	Newell, James, Sr.,	1		Mont.	Niblett, William,	1	3	Pr.Geo.
Nelson, Andrew,			Augu.	Newell, James, Jr.,	1	4	Mont.	Niblock, John,	1	1	Fay.
Nelson, Edward,	1		Fay.	Newell, John,	1	3	Pr.Geo	Nicholas, Anne,		11	Hen.
Nelson, Elisha,	1		Wash.	Newell, John,	1		Mont.	Nicholas, Benjamin,	1		Wash.
Nelson, Elizabeth,		6	Nor.	Newell, John,	1	1	K.& Q.	Nicholas, George,	1		Augu.
Nelson, Elizabeth,		2	Loui.	Newell, Sarah,			Lou.	Nicholas, John,	1		Wash.
Nelson, Gen.,		115	Pr.Wm.	Newell, William,	1		Mont.	Nicholas, John,	1	15	Din.
Nelson, Hugh,			Lou.	Newgent, Ann,	1	6	Fau.	Nicholas, John, Jr.,			Buck.
Nelson, Hugh,	2	27	York	Newgent, Edward,	1	2	Fau.	Nicholas, John,	3	45	Buck.
Nelson, Hugh,	1		Augu.	Newgent, Thomas,	1	29	Fau.	Nicholas, John,	1	3	Buck.
Nelson, James,	1		Lou.	Newhouse, Isaac,	1		Fau.	Nicholas, Peter,	1		Wash.
Nelson, James,	1		Buck.	Newhouse, Jonathan,	1		Fau.	Nicholas, Robt, Carter	1	41	Hen.
Nelson, James, Sr.,	2	5	Spots.	Newland, Abraham,	1		Wash.	Nicholls, Archibald,	1		Bed.
Nelson, James, Jr.,	1	2	Spots.	Newland, Isaac,	1		Wash.	Nicholls, Basill,	1	1	Bed.
Nelson, John,			Buck.	Newland, James,	1		Berk.	Nicholls, Flail,	1		Bed.
Nelson, John,			Buck.	Newland, John,	1		Berk.	Nicholls, Isaac, Jr.	1		Lou.
Nelson, John,	1		Rock.	Newly, John,	1		Lun.	Nicholls, James,	1		Bed.
Nelson, John,	1	3	Nor.	Newman, Abner,			Cul.	Nicholls, John,	1		Bed.
Nelson, John,	1		Fau.	Newman, Alexander,	1	1	Cul.	Nichols, Amos,	1		Berk.
Nelson, John,	1	3	Spots.	Newman, Coonrad,	1		Bed.	Nichols, Frederick,	1	2	Lou.
Nelson, John,	1	4	Fau.	Newman, Daniel,	1		Henry	Nichols, Joseph,	1	4	Eli.C.
Nelson, John,	1	2	Fau.	Newman, Edward,	1		Lou.	Nichols, Matthias,	1		Buck.
Nelson, Col.John,	1	26	Loui.	Newman, Edward,	1	1	Hen.	Nichols, Matthias,	1		Berk.
Nelson, Joseph,	1		Augu.	Newman, Elth,	1	11	Pr.Wm.	Nichols, Samuel,	1	1	Fau.
Nelson, Joseph,	1	5	Spots.	Newman, George,	1	7	Cul.	Nichols, Thomas,	1		Fau.
Nelson, Joseph,	2	8	Fau.	Newman, Henry,	1		Mont.	Nicholas, William,	1		Cul.
Nelson, Mary,		23	West.	Newman, James,	1	6	Cul.	Nicholson, Henry,	1	2	Brun.
Nelson, Moses,			Fay.	Newman, John Posey,	1	8	Pr.Wm.	Nicholson, John,	1	5	Brun.
Nelson, Peter,	1	1	K.& Q.	Newman, John,			Henry	Nicholson, John,	1		Cul.
Nelson, Robert,			Hen.	Newman, Jonathan,	1		Bot.	Nickens, Benjamin,			Pr.Wm.
Nelson, Spencer,	1		Acco.	Newman, Joseph,	1		Henry	Nickle, John,	2		Augu.
Nelson, Tamer,			Acco.	Newman, Lottin,	2	29	K.Wm.	Nickolls, George,	1		Lou.
Nelson, Thomas,	6	134	K.Wm.	Newman, Michael,	1		Mont.	Nickolls, Isaac, Sr.,	1		Lou.
Nelson, Thomas,	2	6	Fau.	Newman, Nash,	1		Lou.	Nickolls, Isaac, Jr.,	1		Lou.
Nelson, Thomas, Jr.,	1	31	York	Newman, Nimrod,	1		Bed.	Nickolls, James,	1		Lou.
Nelson, Thomas,	1	5	Augu.	Newman, Robert,			Pr.Wm.	Nickolls, John,	1		Lou.
Nelson, William,	1	17	West.	Newman, Shepherd,	1		Hen.	Nickolls, Samuel,	1		Lou.
Nelson, William,	2		Lin.	Newman, T.,	1	9	Pr.Wm.	Nickolls, William,	1		Lou.

Name			Co.	Name			Co.	Name			Co.
Nickolson,George,	1		Lou.	Norment,Samuel,Jr.,	1	9	Caro.	Nunnelly,Thomas,	1		Din.
Nickthonger,Jacob,	1		Mont.	Normon,John,	1		Cul.	Nuse,Philip,	1		Mont.
Nicolson,Henry,		6	Jas.C.	Normon,Ruebin,	1		Cul.	Nutt,Jonathan,	1		Lou.
Nicolson,Mark,	1	14	So'n.	Normon,William,	1		Cul.	Nuval,William,	2	6	Pr.Geo.
Nicolson,Mary,		6	So'n.	Normon,William,	1		Cul.	Oage,Robert,	1	2	Nor.
Nicolson,Robert,		5	York	Norris,James,	1		Pr.Wm	Oakes,Henry,Sr.,	2	3	K.&Q
Nicolson,Samuel,	1	8	So'n.	Norris,John,	1		Wash.	Oakes,Isaac,	1	2	K.Wm,
Nicolson,Sarah,		3	So'n.	Norris,William,	1	7	Fau.	Oakley,George,	1		Lou.
Nictor,Frederick,	1	5	Cha.C.	Norriss,John,	1		Fau.	Oakley,James,	1		Henry
Niecly,Samuel,	1		Cul.	Norriss,Joseph,	1		Pr.Geo	Oakley,Thomas,Sr.,	1		Henry
Niegley,Jacob,	1		Lou.	North,Abraham,	1	14	Bed.	Oakley,Thomas,	1		Henry
Niel,William,	1		Bot.	North,John,Sr.,	1	10	Din.	Oar,John,	1		Fau.
Nimme,Robert,	1		Bed.	North,John,Jr.,	1	4	Din.	Oats,Nicholas,	1		Lou.
Nipp,Adam,			Mont.	North,Richard,	1	2	Buck.	Oats,William,	2		Acco.
Nivels,Henry,	1		Rock.	Northam,Southy,	2	1	Acco.	Obanion,Bryan,	1	1	Berk.Obannon
Nixon,Barnaby,	1	2	Pr.Geo.	Northcut,Ben.,	1		Pr.Wm	Obannon,Andrew,	1	5	Fau.
Nixon,George,	1	1	Loud.	Northcut,Jeremiah,	1		Fau.	Obanon,Benjamin,	1	1	Fau.
Nixon,Henry,	1		Lun.	Northup,Daniel,	1	1	Bot.	Obanon,John,	4	12	Fau.
Nixon,Hugh,	1		Buck.	Norton,Henry,	1		Mont.	Obanon,Samuel,	1	1	Fau.
Nixon,James,	1		Lou.	Norton,John,	1		Fay.	Oberry,Henry,	1		So'n
Noble,Anthony,	1	1	Berk.	Norton,John,	1	4	Jas.C.	Oberry,John,	1		So'n
Noble,Cornelius,	1	1	Eli.C.	Norton,John,	1		Lou.	Obryan,Patrick	3		Buck.
Noble,David,	1		Bot.	Norton,John Hatley,	1	11	Fau.	Obryan,Patrick,Jr.,			Buck.
Noble,David,	4	1	Fay.	Norton,Thomas Sr.,	1		Din.	O'Bryan,Thomas,	1		Bot.
Noble,George,	1	10	Pr.Geo.	Norton,Thomas Jr.,	1		Din.	Obryan,William,			Buck.
Noble,William,	1	3	Din.	Norton,William,	1		Mont.	O'Bryant,Dennis,	1		Henry
Noblets,Thomas,	1		Mont.	Norvell,James,	1	9	Gooch.	Oburn,Sarah,			Berk.
Nock,Benjamin,	2	5	Acco.	Norvell,Thomas,	1	1	Gooch.	Ochiltree,Michael,	1		Bot.
Nock,George,	1	2	Acco.	Norvell,William,	2	38	Jas.C.	O'Dair,Cornelius,	1		Aug.
Nock,John,	1	4	Acco.	Norvells,James,		2	Mont.	Odear,David,	1		K.&Q.
Nock,Levie,	2	2	Acco.	Norvill,Aguila,	1	1	Pr.Wm	O'Dear,Laban,	1	2	Nor.
Nock,Robert,	1	3	Acco.	Norwood,John,	1		West.	O'Dear,Major,	1	1	K.&Q.
Nock,Solomon,			Acco.	Notherland,Jane,		1	K.Wm.	O'Dear,Rosamond,			K.&Q.
Noe,Basil,	1	6	Cul.	Nottingham,Abel,	1	6	Nor.	O'Dear,Stephen,	1	1	K.&Q.
Noe,Bennett,			Cul.	Nottingham,Jacob,	1	13	Nor.	O'Dear,William,	1		Nor.
Noe,John,	1		Henry	Nottingham,Mary,		6	Nor.	Odell,Thomas,	1		Berk.
Noe,John,			Cul.	Nottingham,Richard,	1	4	Nor.	Oden,Jesse,	2		Pr.Wm.
Noe,Mary,	2	6	Cul.	Nottingham,Robert,	1	3	Acco	Oden,Thomas,	1	6	Lou.
Noe,Randal,	1		Lou.	Nottingham,Robert,	1	4	Nor.	Odenwald,Jacob,	1		Berk.
Noe,Samuel,	1		Henry	Nottingham,Severn,	1	7	Nor,	Odor,Joseph,Sr.,	1		Fau.
Noe,Thomas,	1		Cul.	Nottingham,Thos.Sr.,	1	17	Nor.	Odor,Joseph,Jr.,	1		Fau.
Noe,Zaphaniah,	1	6	Cul.	Nottingham,Thos.Jr.,	1	10	Nor.	Odor,Thomas,	1		Fau.
Noel,Daniel,	1		West.	Nottingham,William,	1	10	Nor.	Offill,John,	1		Aug.
Noel,Nicholas,	1		Har.	Nourse,James,	1	11	Berk	Ofreel,Manus,	1		Aug.
Noell,Francis,	1	1	K.& Q.	Nourse,James Jr.,	1	1	Berk	O'Gullion,Duncas,	1		Mont.
Nofsiger,John,	1		Bed.	Nowe,Jesse,	1		Buck	Ogburn,Benjamin,	1	5	Brun.
Nokes,Benjamin,	1		Lin.	Nowland,James,	1	1	Gooch	Ogburn,Charles,	1		Brun.
Nokes,George,Sr.,	2		Lin.	Nowland,Martin,	1		Mont	Ogburn,David,	1	3	Berk.
Noland,Pearce,	1		Berk.	Nowland,Stephen,	1	1	Gooch	Ogburn,Enouch,	1		Mont.
Noland,Philip,	2	9	Lou.	Nowland,William,	1		Berk	Ogburn,James,	1	1	Brun.
Noland,Philip,Jr.,	1	3	Lou.	Nowling,Elizabeth,			Henry	Ogburn,Jonathan,	2		Berk.
Noland,Samuel,			Lou.	Nox,Enoch,	1		Fay.	Ogburn,William,	1	4	Berk.
Noland,Thomas,	1	1	Berk.	Nox,James,	2		Fay.	Ogburn,William,	1	1	Brun.
Noland,William,	1		Cul.	Nuckolds,James,	2	12	Loui	Ogdon,Joseph,	1		Berk.
Nolles,Joshua,	1		Lou.	Nuckolds,John,	1	2	Loui	Ogdons,Cornelius,	1		Lou.
Nolly,Nathan,	1		Brun.	Nuckolds,Keziah,	1	14	Loui	Ogle,Benjamin,	1	23	Berk.
Noningmacker,Lewis,	1		Cul.	Nuckolds,Thomas,	1		Loui	Ogle,Hercules,	1	1	Bot.
Nowell,Cornelius,	1	22	Bed.	Nuckolds,William,			Loui	Ogle,Hercules,	1		Mont.
Nowell,Thomas,	1	2	Bed.	Nuckolos,Charles,	1	1	Gooch	Ogle,John,	1		Mont.
Nowland,Philip,	1		Berk.	Nuckolos,Molley,		1	Gooch	Ogle,Thomas,	1		Mont.
Norfleet,Cordall,	1	29	So'n.	Nuckolos,Pouncy,	1	4	Gooch	Ogleby,Thomas,	1		Fau.
Norman,Clement,	2		Fau.	Nuckolos,Samuel,	1	1	Gooch	Oglesby,David,	1		Buck.
Norman,Coteny,	1		Cul.	Nuckolos,Thomas,	1	1	Gooch	Oglesby,Elisha,	1		Wash.
Norman,Ezekiel,	1		Fau.	Nuckolos,William,	1	1	Gooch	Oglesby,Richard,	1	3	Camp.
Norman,Isaac,	1		Fau.	Nugent,John,	1		Pr.Geo	Ogletree,Thomas,	1		Lun.
Norman,Jesse,	1		Fau.	Nunn,Ingram,	1	2	Henry	O'Hair,Michael,	1		Bot.
Norman,John,	1		Fau.	Nunn,James,	1	4	K.& Q.	O'Harro,Richard,	1		West.
Norman,Joseph,	1		Loui.	Nunn,John,	1		Caro.	Okely,Henry,			Cul.
Norman,Joseph,	2	5	Cul.	Nunn,Moses,	1	8	K.&.Q.	Old,Edward,	1	8	Din.
Norman,Samuel,	1		Hen.	Nunn,Thomas,	1		Caro.	Old,James,	1	14	Din.
Norman,Samuel,	1	1	Hen.	Nunn,Thomas,	1	1	Henry	Old,John,	1	2	Din.
Norman,William,	1		Cul.	Nunn,Thomas,	1	5	K.& Q.	Oldacre,Abraham,	1		Lou.
Norman,William,	1		Fau.	Nunn,William,	1	4	K.&Q.	Oldacre,Henry,	1		Lou.
Norman,William,			Pr.Wm.	Nunnelly,John,Sr.,	1	1	Din.	Oldacre,Henry,			Lou.
Norment,John,	1	5	Caro.	Nunnelly,John,Jr.,	1		Din.	Oldacre,Isaac,	1		Har.
Norment,Samuel,Sr.,	1		Caro.	Nunnelly,Thomas,	1		Din.				

Name			Co.
Oldacre, Jacob,	1		Henry
Oldacre, John,	1		Lou.
Oldacre, William,	1		Har.
Oldham, Charles,	1		Brun.
Oldham, George,	1	6	Acco.
Oldham, George,	1	1	Lou.
Oldham, John,	1		Henry
Oldham, Samuel,	1	34	K.Geo.
Oldham, Samuel,	1	7	Berk.
Oldhauser, Emery,	1		Rock.
Oley, Capt.John,	1	15	Bed.
Oleson, Martin,	1		Lou.
Oliff, James,	1		West.
Olinger, Philip,	1		Aug.
Olinger, Stofal,	2		Aug.
Oliphant, Ephraim,	1	1	Lou.
Oliphant, Samuel,	1		Lou.
Oliver, Benjamin,	1	5	Lun.
Oliver, James,	1		Aug.
Oliver, James,	1		Berk.
Oliver, John,	2	1	Caro.
Oliver, John,	1	1	K.&Q.
Oliver, John,	1		K.Geo.
Oliver, John,	1	5	Caro.
Oliver, John, Jr.,	1	3	Caro.
Oliver, John,	1		Aug.
Oliver, John,	1	2	Aug.
Oliver, John,	1		Fay.
Oliver, Joseph,	1		Berk.
Oliver, Nicholas,	1	2	Caro.
Oliver, Peter,	1		Pr.Wm.
Oliver, Richard,	2	2	Caro.
Oliver, Stephen,	1	4	Caro.
Oliver, Thomas,	1	5	K.Wm.
Oliver, Thomas,	1	3	K.Geo.
Oliver, Thomas,	1		Spots.
Oliver, Thomas,	1	5	Gooch.
Oliver, Vincent,	1		Hen.
Oliver, William,	1	2	Caro.
O'Mohundro, James,	1		West.
O'Mohundro, John,	1	2	West.
O'Mohundro, Thomas,	1	4	West.
Onail, James,	1		Aug.
Onail, John,	1		Aug.
O'Neal, Bryant,	1	1	Lin.
Oneal, Daniel,	1		Bed.
Oneal, Diarus,			Cul.
Oneal, John,	1		Cul.
Oneal, John,	1	6	K.&Q.
Oneal, Lodowick,	1	13	Spots.
O'Neal, Thomas,	1	13	Caro.
O'Neale, Conn,			Lou.
O'Neale, Edward,	1	1	Lou.
O'Neale, Gregory,	1	4	K.Wm.
O'Neale, Jean,	1		Lou.
O'Neale, John,	1		Lou.
Oney, Benjamin,	1		So'n
Oney, Lucy,		1	So'n
Oney, Thomas,	1		So'n
Ong, Jeremiah,	1		Berk.
Onley, Edmund,	1		Acco.
Onley, Fairfax,	1		Acco.
Only, John, Jr.,	1	4	Acco.
Onstott, John,	1		Wash.
Oran, James,	2		Lou.
Orchards, James,	1		Bed.
Ore, James,		1	Loui.
Ore, Joseph,	1		Loui.
Orear, Benjamin,	2	1	Fau.
Orear, Daniel,			Pr.Wm.
Orear, Jeremiah,	2	1	Fau.
Orear, John,	2	6	Pr.Wm.
Organ, Sarah,			Pr.Wm.
Organ, Samuel,	1	2	Fau.
Organ, William Derby,	1	2	Brun.
Orichord, Alexander,	2		Har.
Orr, James,	1		Berk.
Orr, John,	3	10	Hen.
Orr, John,	4	12	Hen.
Orr, John,	3	26	Lou.
Orr, John,	1	1	Bed.
Orr, Joshua,	1		Fay.
Orrick, Mary,		7	Berk.
Orrick, Nicholas,	1	5	Berk.
Orrill, John,	2	1	K.&Q.
Orrill, Lawrence,			K.&Q.
Orrill, William,	1		K.&Q.
Orrison, Andrew,	3		Lou.
Orrison, Andrew, Jr.,			Lou.
Orrison, Arthur,	1		Lou.
Orrison, John,	1		Lou.
Orrison, Mathew,			Lou.
Orten, Robert,	1		Har.
Osborne, Abner,			Lou.
Osborne, John,	2	5	Lou.
Osborne, Nickolls,	2	2	Lou.
Osborne, Nicholas,	1		Lou.
Osborne, Richard,	1		Lou.
Osborne, William,	1	3	Fau.
Osborne, William,			Lou.
Osborns, John,			Bed.
Osburn, James,	1		Wash.
Osburn, Josiah,	1		Har.
Osburn, Stephen,	1		Wash.
Osburn, Thomas,	1		Wash.
Osburn, William,	1		Cul.
Osburn, Zerab,	1		Har.
Osheal, David,	1	14	So'n
Oshwall, Mich,	1		Lin.
Oslin, Martha,	1	1	Cha.Cy
Oslin, Samuel,			Cha.Cy
Osmore, William,	1		Din.
Otey, William,	1	7	Cha.Cy
Ott, John,	1		Aug.
Ott, John, Jr.,	1		Aug.
Ott, John,	1		Berk.
Outten, Mary,		7	Acco.
Outten, Matthias,	3	2	Acco.
Outten, Purnal,	1	2	Acco.
Outten, Samuel,	1	9	Acco.
Overby, Anthony,	1	2	Din.
Overby, Freeman,	1		Brun.
Overby, Jeremiah,	1	7	Din.
Overby, Jeremiah,	1		Din.
Overby, John,			Brun.
Overby, John,	1		Din.
Overby, Richard,	1	11	Din.
Overby, Robert,	1		Din.
Overby, William,	1		Lun.
Overfelt, Benjamin,	1		Lou.
Overfelt, Peter,	2		Lou.
Overly, Peter,	1		Berk.
Overly, Valentine,	1		Berk.
Overstreet, Gabriel,	1	12	K.&Q.
Overstreet, James,	1	1	Gooch.
Overstreet, John,			Bed.
Overstreet, Thomas, Sr.,	1	6	Bed.
Overstreet, Thomas, Jr.,	1		Bed.
Overstreet, Thomas,	1		Bed.
Overstreet, William,	1		Bed.
Overton, Caleb,	1		Din.
Overton, James,	1	18	Loui.
Overton, James,	1		Mont.
Overton, John,	1	10	Loui.
Overton, John,	1	4	Lun.
Overton, Richard,			Loui.
Overton, Waller,	1	1	Loui.
Owan, Dennis,	1		Berk.
Owen, Augustine,	1	2	K.&Q.
Owen, Barnett,	1		Gooch.
Owen, Barnett,	1		Lun.
Owen, David,	1		Lun.
Owen, Elias,	1		Bot.
Owen, Elisha,	1	7	Hen.
Owen, Elizabeth,		3	Hen.
Owen, Fountain,			Hen.
Owen, Hobson,	2	24	Hen.
Owen, James,			Brun.
Owen, Jemima,		1	Hen.
Owen, Joseph,	1	1	Lun.
Owen, Mary,			Gooch.
Owen, Robertson,	1	1	Brun.
Owen, Robertson,			Hen.
Owen, Robertson,	1		Hen.
Owen, Thomas,	1	20	Hen.
Owen, Thomas, Jr.			Hen.
Owen, Valentine,	2	3	Brun.
Owen, William,	1		Hen.
Owen, William,	1		Lun.
Owen, William,	1	4	Brun.
Owens, David,	1	6	Bot.
Owens, David,	1	7	Spots.
Owens, John,	1		Bed.
Owens, John,	1	1	Wash.
Owens, John,	1		Fau.
Owens, John,	1	6	Fau.
Owens, Johnston,	1		Pr.Wm.
Owens, Joshua,	1		Fau.
Owens, Nathaniel,	1		Fau.
Owens, Owen,	1	1	K.&Q.
Owens, Owen,	1		Bed.
Owens, Owen,	1		Aug.
Owens, Patrick,	1		Fay.
Owens, Philip,	1		Camp.
Owens, Rawleigh,			Pr.Wm.
Owens, Reuben,	1	3	K.Geo.
Owens, Samuel,	1	1	K.Geo.
Owens, Thomas,	1	2	Berk.
Owens, William,	1		Spots.
Owens, William,	1	3	Fau.
Owens, William,	1		Mont.
Owins, Joshua,	1		Fay.
Owings, Thomas,	1	1	Nor.
Owings, William,	1		Lin.
Owney, Joseph,	1		Mont.
Ownsbey, John,	1	1	Lin.
Ownshull, John,	2		Mont.
Ousley, Anthony,	1	1	Lou.
Owsley, Anthony,	1	2	Lin.
Owsley, Henry,	1		Lou.
Owsley, Jonathan,	1	8	Lin.
Owsley, Jonathan,	1	1	Lou.
Owsley, Payne,	1		Lou.
Owsley, Thomas,	1		Lou.
Owsley, Thomas,	1	20	Lou.
Owsley, Thomas, Sr.,	2	18	Lin.
Owsley, Thomas,	1	1	Lin.
Owsley, William,	1	5	Lou.
Owsley, William,	1		Fay.
Owsley, William,	1	4	Lin.
Oxer, George,	1		Wash.
Oxer, Simon,	1		Wash.
Oxford, Elizabeth,		5	Cul.
Oxley, Brittain,	1		Lou.
Oxley, Clear,	1		Lou.
Oxley, Henry,	1		Lou.
Oxley, John,	1		Lou.
Oyler, Melcher,	2		Wash.
Paage, James,	1		Rock.
Paage, John,	2	1	Rock.
Paage, Jonathan,	1		Rock.
Pace, Buckner,	1	6	Gooch.
Pace, Edward,			Gooch.
Pace, Francis,	1	3	Din.
Pace, Jesse,	1		Gooch.
Pace, John,	1	1	Gooch.

Name			County
Pace,John,	1	1	Lun.
Pace,Joseph,	1		Gooch.
Pack,Thomas,	1		Mont.
Packwood,Samuel,	1		Henry
Pacter,John,	1		Rock.
Padgett,Francis,	1	3	Lou.
Padgett,Moses,	1		Lou.
Padgett,Samuel,	1		K.& Q.
Padgett,Timothy,			Lou.
Pagan,David,			Din.
Page,Alexander,	1		Mont.
Page,Benjamin,	1		Gooch.
Page,Edward,	1	1	Lun.
Page,George,	1	1	K.Wm.
Page,George,	2	4	Caro.
Page,James,			Gooch.
Page,John,	1		Gooch.
Page,John,	1		Lun.
Page,Col.John,	1	25	Lou.
Page,John,	2	82	Caro.
Page,Joseph,	1		Gooch.
Page,Mann,	4	157	Spots.
Page,Mann,	1	32	Pr.Wm.
Page,Mann,est.	1	24	Pr.Wm.
Page,Mrs,	2	42	Lou.
Page,Robert,Sr.,	1	8	Gooch.
Page,Robert,Jr.,	1		Gooch.
Page,Robert,	1		Gooch.
Page,William,	1		Gooch.
Page,William,	1		Gooch.
Page,William,	1	1	Camp.
Paget,Edward,	1		Fau.
Paggette,James,	1		Bed.
Pain,George,	2		Berk.
Pain,Henry,	2		Berk.
Pain,Jesse,	1		Berk.
Paine,Benjamin,	1		Buck.
Paine,Reubin,	1		Cul.
Paine,Samuel,	1	2	Cul.
Painter,George,	1		Berk.
Painter,Jacob,	1		Berk.
Painter,Thomas,	1		Berk.
Pair,Chitwood,	1	4	Caro.
Pair,James,	1		So'n.
Pair,John,	1	1	Caro.
Palmer,Ann,		3	K.Wm.
Palmer,Jeffery,	1	4	K.Wm.
Palmer,George,			Augu.
Palmer,George,	1		K.Wm.
Palmer,Isaac,	1		Buck.
Palmer,James,	1		So'n.
Palmer,John,	1		Fau.
Palmer,John,Sr.,	1	9	Buck.
Palmer,John,Jr.,	1	1	Buck.
Palmer,Jonathan,	1		Lou.
Palmer,Joseph,	1		Spots.
Palmer,Joseph,	1		Buck.
Palmer,Lydia,			Eli.C.
Palmer,Mildred,	1	6	Caro.
Palmer,Nixon,	1		Buck.
Palmer,Samuel,	1		Lou.
Palmer,Thomas,	1		Lou.
Palmer,William,	1		Lou.
Palmer,William,	1		K.Wm.
Palmer,William,	1	3	Buck.
Palmer,William,	2		Augu.
Palmore,James,	2		Buck.
Palmore,John,			Buck.
Pallack,James,	1		Rock.
Pallack,Samuel,	1		Rock.
Pallitt,Lewis,	1		Berk.
Pamplin,Henry,	1	1	Lun.
Pamplin,John,Sr.,	1	9	Lun.
Pamplin,John,Jr.,	1	2	Lun.
Pamplin,William,Sr.,	1	6	Lun.
Pamplin,William,Jr.,	1		Lun.
Pancake,Andrew,	2		Har.
Pancake,John,	1		Har.
Pane,John,	1		Wash.
Pancoust,Israel,	1		Lou.
Paninger,Henry,	1		Augu.
Pankey,John,	2	2	Buck.
Pannel,David,	3	13	K.Wm.
Panner,Peter,	1		Mont.
Pare,Thomas,	1		Brun.
Pareton,Samuel,	1		Rock.
Parfeet,Christopher,	1	2	Lou.
Parfeet,Robert,	1	2	Lou.
Parham,Ephram,	1	3	Brun.
Parham,Haddon,	1	2	Pr.Geo.
Parham,James,	1	9	Pr.Geo.
Parham,Joanna,		3	Din.
Parham,Lewis,	1	20	Brun.
Parham,Stith,	1	15	Din.
Parham,Thomas,			Din.
Parham,William,	1	2	Brun.
Paris,David,	1		Loui.
Paris,George,	1	1	Mont.
Parish,Humphry,	1	3	Loui.
Parish,James,	1		Loui.
Parish,James,	1	5	Spots.
Parish,Jane,		5	Eli.C.
Parish,Joel,	1	8	Spots.
Parish,Joel,		3	Spots.
Parish,John,			Eli.C.
Parish,John,	1	1	Eli.C.
Parish,John,	1		Loui.
Parish,Joseph,	1		Bed.
Parish,Mary,			Din.
Parish,Mary,		2	Eli.C.
Parish,Nathaniel,	1		Eli.C.
Parish,Robert,	1		Fay.
Parish,Sarah,		3	Eli.C.
Parish,Thomas,			Brun.
Parish,William,	1	1	Brun.
Parish,William,	1		Bed.
Park,Jonathan,	2	7	Hen.
Park,Rodger,	1		Lou.
Park,Thomas,			Brun.
Park,William,	1		Berk.
Parker,Alexander,	1	14	Lou.
Parker,John,	1	3	Loui.
Parker,Capt.Alexander,	1	7	West.
Parker,Alexander,	1	11	Fau.
Parker,Alexander,	1	13	Caro.
Parker,Ann,	1	1	Acco.
Parker,Charles,		3	Acco.
Parker,Drewry,	1	17	So'n.
Parker,Eli,	1		Lin.
Parker,Frances,		5	Cha.C.
Parker,George,	1	14	Acco.
Parker,Jane,	1	6	Brun.
Parker,Jeff,			Hen.
Parker,John,	1	3	K.& Q.
Parker,Jeremiah,	1	1	Lin.
Parker,John,	1		Bed.
Parker,John,	1		Acco.
Parker,John,R.,	3	4	Acco.
Parker,John,	1		Lou.
Parker,John,	2		Har.
Parker,John,	1	1	Hen.
Parker,Joseph,	1		Fau.
Parker,Joseph,	1	8	Hen.
Parker,Joseph,	1		Lou.
Parker,Mary,		1	Acco.
Parker,Michal,	1		Acco.
Parker,Peggy,	1	1	Acco.
Parker,Richard,	1	9	Acco.
Parker,Richard,	1	3	Fau.
Parker,Richard,	1	3	Fay.
Parker,Richard,	2	20	West.
Parker,Richard,		5	Cul.
Parker,Robert,	1	6	Acco.
Parker,Robert,	1	1	Acco.
Parker,Samuell,	1		Acco.
Parker,Sarah,		16	Acco.
Parker,Thomas,	2	7	Acco.
Parker,Thomas,	1	17	Acco.
Parker,Thomas,	1		Bed.
Parker,William,	2	11	Caro.
Parker,William,	2	22	Spots.
Parker,William,	1	16	West.
Parker,William,	1		Acco.
Parker,Winslow,	1	6	Spots.
Parkhust,Ezekiel,	1		Fay.
Parks,John,	2	4	Berk.
Parks,John,	1	1	Rock.
Parks,Richard,	1	13	Cul.
Parks,William,	1		Henry
Parks,Samuel,	1	2	Berk.
Parks,William,	1		Mont.
Parks,William,	1		Lin.
Parks,William,	2	1	Cul.
Parlor,Adam,	1		Cul.
Parmer,Betty,		8	K.& Q.
Parmer,Daniel,			Cul.
Parmer,Joseph,	1	1	Cul.
Parmer,Joseph,	1		Fay.
Parr,James,	1	1	Fau.
Parr,John,	1	2	Henry
Parr,Michael,	1		Berk.
Parradise,John,		15	Jas.C.
Parramore,Ezra,	1	4	Nor.
Parramore,Thomas,	2	12	Acco.
Parramore,Thomas,			Acco.
Parramore,William,	3	10	Acco.
Parret,Thomas,			Wash.
Parris,John,	1		Augu.
Parrish,Aaron,	1	3	Gooch.
Parrish,Alexander,			Bed.
Parrish,Booker,	1	8	Gooch.
Parrish,Charles,	1	7	Lun.
Parrish,David,	1	1	Lun.
Parrish,David,	1	1	Gooch.
Parrish,Elizabeth,		3	Cha.Cy
Parrish,Capt.Humphrey	1	12	Gooch.
Parrish,James,	1		Lun.
Parrish,Joel,	1		Lun.
Parrish,Joel,	1	3	Gooch.
Parrish,John,	1	7	Gooch.
Parrish,Jolly,	1	10	Gooch.
Parrish,Joseph,	1	9	Cha.Cy
Parrish,Julius,	1		Bot.
Parrish,Mary,		3	Gooch.
Parrish,Meredith,			Gooch.
Parrish,Moses,	1	3	Gooch.
Parrish,Peter,	1	1	Gooch.
Parrish,Robert,			Gooch.
Parrish,Robert,	1		Lun.
Parrish,Sherwood,	1	7	Gooch.
Parrish,Timothy,	1	9	Caro.
Parrish,William,Sr.,	1	3	Cha.Cy
Parrish,William,Jr.,	1		Cha.Cy
Parrish,William,	1	5	Gooch.
Parron,Daniel,	1	7	Camp.
Parron,Stephen,	2	4	Camp.
Parrott,Curtis,	1		Loui.
Parrott,Tharp,	1		Henry
Parrott,William,B.,	1	6	Lun.
Parrow,Daniel,	1	7	Camp.
Parrow,Stpehen,	2	4	Camp.
Parsley,Moses,			Mont.
Parsley,Thomas,	1		Henry
Parsonet,John,	1		Spots.
Parsons,George,	1	4	Cul.
Partan,John,	1		Mont.
Partlock,Mrs.Ann,		3	Din.
Parks,John,			Acco.

Name			County
Parsons,James,	2	12	Har.
Parsons,James,	1	8	York.
Parsons,John,	1		Fau.
Parsons,John,	2	9	Eli.Cy
Parsons,John,	2	10	Nor.
Parsons,Joseph,	1	3	Din.
Parsons,Samuel,			Hen.
Parsons,Sarah,		8	Nor.
Parsons,Sarah,	1	5	Cul.
Parsons,Thomas,	1	5	Eli.Cy
Parsons,Thomas,	1		Lun.
Parsons,Thomas,	1		Mont.
Parsons,Thomas,	1	22	Nor.
Parsons,William,	1	41	Pr.Geo
Parsons,Wm.Aplomas,			Eli.Cy
Parsons,Woodson,	1	10	Hen.
Partin,Charles,	1		Henry
Partin,William,	1		Henry
Partloe,Benjamin,	1	2	Cul.
Partlow,David,	2	1	Fau.
Partlow,Samuel,	1	6	Spots.
Partlow,John,	1	6	Caro.
Pash,John,	1		Lou.
Pasteur,Bloust,	1		Eli.Cy
Pasteur,Dr.William,	2	18	Gooch.
Pasteur,William,	2	25	York
Paston,Joseph,	1		Bot.
Pate,Anthony,	1	3	Bed.
Pate,Capt.Jeremiah,	1	4	Bed.
Pate,Matthew,	1	4	Bed.
Pate,Thomas,	1		Bed.
Pate,Thomas,	1	10	Ja.Cy
Paten,Jeremiah,	1		Cul.
Paterson,John,	1		Fay.
Paterson,Joseph,	1		Fay.
Paterson,Mathew,	1		Fay.
Pates,Rance,	1	1	K.Geo.
Pates,Reuben,			K.Geo.
Pates,Richard,	1	1	K.Geo.
Pates,William,	1	1	K.Geo.
Patman,William,	1	1	Hen.
Patrick,Curtis,	2	9	York
Patrick,Edmond,	1	8	York
Patrick,John,			York
Patrick,Hugh,	1	2	Mont.
Patrick,James,	1		Mont.
Patrick,Jeremiah,	1		Mont.
Patrick,John,	1		Brun.
Patrick,John,	1	12	York
Patrick,John,	1	14	Aug.
Patrick,Thomas,			York.
Patrick,Thomas,	1		Fay.
Patrick,William,	2	8	York.
Patterson,David,	1		Berk.
Patterson,David,	1		Berk.
Patterson,George,	1	5	Pr.Geo
Patterson,George,	1		Bot.
Patterson,Hannah,		4	Berk.
Patterson,James,	1	1	Rock.
Patterson,James,	1		Aug.
Patterson,James,	1	2	Aug.
Patterson,James,	1	1	Hen.
Patterson,James,	1		Har.
Patterson,John,	1		Bot.
Patterson,John,	1		Lou.
Patterson,John,	1	6	Aug.
Patterson,John,	1		Loui.
Patterson,Jonathan,	1	5	Lun.
Patterson,Joseph,	1		Aug.
Patterson,Joseph,	1	1	Pr.Geo
Patterson,Joseph,	1		Bed.
Patterson,Mary,			Pr.Wm.
Patterson,Nathaniel,	2		Camp.
Patterson,Robert,	1		Berk.
Patterson,Robert,	1		Aug.
Patterson,Samuel,	1	1	Rock.
Patterson,Thomas,	1		Camp.
Patterson,Thomas,	1		Camp.
Patterson,Thomas,	1	6	Aug.
Patterson,Thomas,	1		Berk.
Patterson,Thomas,	1		Har.
Patterson,Thomas,	1		Mont.
Patterson,Turner,	1		Loui.
Patterson,William,	1		K.&Q
Patterson,William,	1		Buck.
Patterson,William,	1	3	Mont.
Patterson,William,	1		Har.
Patterson,William,	1		Berk.
Patterson,William,	2		Berk.
Patterson,William,	2	1	Aug.
Patterson,William,Jr.,			Aug.
Patteson,Charles,	1	19	Buck.
Patteson,Charles,	1	2	Lun.
Patteson,Charles,	2	15	Buck.
Patteson,David,Sr.,	1	22	Buck.
Patteson,David,Jr.,	1	10	Buck.
Patteson,Edward,	1		Buck.
Patteson,John,est.,		14	Buck.
Patteson,John,est.,		14	Buck.
Patteson,James,	1	10	Buck.
Patteson,John,	1		Buck.
Patteson,Mary,	1	13	Buck.
Patteson,Peter,	1	5	Buck.
Patteson,Richard,	1		Lun.
Patteson,Thomas,Sr.,	4	18	Buck.
Pattie,John,	1	4	Caro.
Patton,Alexander,	1		Lin.
Patton,George,	3		Cul.
Patton,George,Jr.,			Cul.
Patton,Henry,	1	1	Mont.
Patton,Jacob,	1		Aug.
Patton,Jacob,	1		Lin.
Patton,James,	1		Mont.
Patton,James,	1		Rock.
Patton,James,	2		Fay.
Patton,John,	1		Rock.
Patton,John,	1		Fay.
Patton,Roger,	1	1	Fay.
Patton,Samuel,	1	1	Berk.
Patton,Thomas,	1		Mont.
Patton,Thomas,			Cul.
Patton,Will,	1	1	Lin.
Patton,William,	1		Rock.
Pau,John,	1	1	Henry
Pau,John,Jr.,	1	1	Henry
Paul,Adley,	1		Bot.
Paul,Andrew,	1		Berk.
Paul,Daniel,	1		Pr.Wm.
Paul,Hugh,	1		Pr.Wm.
Paul,James,	1		Lou.
Paul,John ,	1		Pr.Wm.
Paul,John,Sr.,	1	1	Rock.
Paul,John,Jr.,	1		Rock.
Paul,John,	1	2	Eli.Cy
Paul,John Christian,	1		Berk.
Paul,Thomas,			Hen.
Paul,William,	1		Din.
Paulett,Jessee,	1	10	Loui.
Paulett,Capt.Richard,	1	10	Loui.
Paveley,John,	1		Cha.Cy
Pawling,Henry,	1	10	Lin.
Paxton,James,	1		Lou.
Paxton,John,Sr.,	1	5	Rock.
Paxton,John,	1	1	Rock.
Paxton,John,	1	1	Rock.
Paxton,Joseph,	1		Henry
Paxton,Samuel,	1		Rock.
Paxton,Thomas,	1		Rock.
Paxton,Thomas,	1	7	Rock.
Paxton,William,	1	9	Rock.
Paxton,William,	1	3	Rock.
Payar,Nicholas,	1		Rock.
Payne,Abraham,	1		Henry
Payne,Absalom,	1		Pr.Wm.
Payne,Ann,		10	Fau.
Payne,Archer,	1	47	Gooch.
Payne,Barnett,	1	2	Spots.
Payne,Charles,			Fau.
Payne,Flail,	1	2	Bed.
Payne,Francis,	1	5	Fau.
Payne,Francis,	2	1	Caro.
Payne,Col.George,	2	26	Gooch.
Payne,George,Sr.,	1	5	Gooch.
Payne,George,Jr.,	1	5	Gooch.
Payne,George,	1	1	Loui.
Payne,George,Sr.,	2	25	West.
Payne,George,Jr.,	1	2	West.
Payne,Henry,	1	8	Lou.
Payne,Jesse,	1	5	Gooch.
Payne,Jesse,est.,		15	Gooch.
Payne,Col.John,	1	38	Gooch.
Payne,John,Jr.,	1	19	Gooch.
Payne,John,	1	12	Bed.
Payne,John,	1	2	Bed.
Payne,John,	1		Bed.
Payne,John,	1		Bed.
Payne,John,Jr.,	1		Bed.
Payne,John,	1	1	Fau.
Payne,Maj.Joseph,	1	6	Gooch.
Payne,Joseph,	1		Bed.
Payne,Joseph,	1	11	Gooch.
Payne,Josias,	1	8	Gooch.
Payne,Mary,	1	4	Caro.
Payne,Marianne,			Pr.Wm.
Payne,Nicholas,	1	15	Spots.
Payne,Robert,	1	1	Spots.
Payne,Reuben,	1	3	Henry
Payne,Reuben,	1		Pr.Wm.
Payne,Smith,		22	Camp.
Payne,Thomas,	1		Bed.
Payne,Thomas,	1	3	Eli.Cy
Payne,Thomas,	1	2	Fau.
Payne,William,	1	25	West.
Payne,William,	1	4	Lou.
Payne,William,	1		Fau.
Payne,William,	1		Bed.
Pays,James,	1	2	Caro.
Payte,Jacob,	1		Mont.
Payte,Jeremiah,	1	3	Mont.
Payte,John,	1	2	Mont.
Payte,Thomas,	1	10	Mont.
Payton,Anthony,	1	21	West.
Payton,Benjamin,	2		Cul.
Payton,Charles,	1		Cul.
Payton,Henry,	1		Mont.
Payton,James,	1		Fay.
Payton,Lewis,	1		Lin.
Payton,Philip,	1		Lin.
Payton,Thomas,	1	4	West.
Payton,Valentine,	1	1	Lin.
Payton,Will,	1		Lin.
Payton,William,	1		Fay.
Payton,Yowroth,		5	Cul.
Paytoon,William,	1	5	Cul.
Pea,John,	1	4	Loui.
Peace,Samuel,	1		Lun.
Peach,Daniel,	1		Fau.
Peachey,Samuel,		6	K.&Q
Peacocke,B.,	1		Pr.Wm.
Peade,Philip,	1		West.
Peade,Thomas,	1		West.
Peadervill,Garret,	2		Berk.
Peak,John,	1		Henry
Peak,Jonathan,	1		Henry
Peake,Ignatius,	2		Pr.Wm.

Name			County
Peake, James,			Pr.Wm.
Peake, Mary,		6	Fau.
Peake, William,	1		Fau.
Peare, William,	1		Caro.
Pearce, John,	1	2	K.Geo
Pearce, Thomas,	11		K.&Q
Pearce, William,			Gooch.
Pearceall, Samuel,			Lou.
Pearcey, John,	1		Bed.
Pearcy, Ann,			Brun.
Pearks, Solomon,	1		Acco.
Pearks, Tabitha,	1		Acco.
Pearl, Edward,	1		Fau.
Pearle, Charity,			Fau.
Pearle, Samuel	1	6	Fau.
Pearle, William	1	15	Fau.
Pearman, John, est.		9	Cha.Cy
Pearman, James	1		Hen.
Pearman, William	1		Cha.Cy
Pearson, Benjamin	1	5	Brun.
Pearson, James	1	4	Brun.
Pearson, John	1	6	Brun.
Pearson, John, Jr.	1	2	Brun.
Pearson, Robert	1		Henry
Pearson, Shadrick	1		West.
Pearson, William	1		Pr.Wm
Pearson, William	1	1	Brun.
Pearson, William	1		Brun.
Peary, David	1		Fay.
Peary, James	2		Bot.
Peary, James	1		Bot.
Peay, Ostin		1	Caro.
Peasley, William	1	2	Buck.
Peatross, Amey	1	14	Caro.
Peatross, James	1	6	Caro.
Peatross, Matthew	1	8	Caro.
Peatross, Thomas	1	5	Caro.
Peck, Adam	1		Bot.
Peck, Daniel	2		Fay.
Peck, David	1		Henry
Peck, George	1		Mont.
Peck, Isaac	1		Hen.
Peck, Jacob	1		Bot.
Peck, Jacob	2	3	Aug.
Peck, Jeffery	1	3	Buck.
Peck, Jessee	1		Fay.
Peck, John	1		Fay.
Peck, John	2		Bot.
Peck, John	1	12	K.Geo
Peck, Philip	1	1	Buck.
Peck, Peter	1		Aug.
Peck, Peter	1		Lou.
Peck, Sarah	1	2	Acco.
Peck, Stephen	1		Aug.
Peck, William	1		K.Geo
Peck, William	1		Buck.
Pectel, Frederick	1		Bot.
Pedge, John	1	5	Fau.
Pedegoe, Robert	1		Henry
Pedegore, Edward	1		Henry
Peden, James	1		Bot.
Peden, John, Jr.	1		Bot.
Peden, John, Sr.	1		Bot.
Pedin, James	1		So'n
Pedley, Thomas	1		Hen.
Peebles, Briton	1	3	Brun.
Peebles, James			Pr.Geo
Peebles, Jehu	1	2	Brun.
Peebles, Sterling	1	17	Brun.
Peebles, Lemuel	1	4	Pr.Geo
Peebles, Mary			Pr.Geo
Peebles, Peter, Sr.	1	1	Pr.Geo
Peebles, Peter			Pr.Geo
Peed, John	1		K.Geo
Peed, Margaret		3	K.Geo
Peed, Sarah		1	K.Geo

Name			County
Peek, Henry	1	3	Buck.
Peeke, John	1		Spots.
Peel, James	1		Rock.
Peeley, Guilbert	2	12	Acco.
Peelnovrick, Jacob	1		Mont.
Peerey, James	1		Mont.
Peerey, Thomas	1		Mont.
Peerey, William	1		Mont.
Peerie, Thomas	1		Berk.
Peers, Anderson	1	25	Gooch.
Peers, Thomas	1	18	Loui.
Peery, George	1		Mont.
Peery, James	1		Aug.
Peery, John	1		Aug.
Peery, John, Jr.	1		Mont.
Peery, Robert	1		Rock.
Pees, Bernard	1	2	Pr.Geo
Pegg, William	1		Brun.
Pegram, George, Jr.	1	3	Din.
Peirce, Francis	1		Hen.
Peirce, Francis, Jr.	1	7	Hen.
Peirce, James	1		West.
Peirce, John	1	1	Berk.
Peirce, Joseph	1	6	Hen.
Peirce, Joseph	2	21	West.
Peirce, Joseph, Jr.	1	11	West.
Peirce, Lovell	1	7	West.
Peirce, Sarah		19	West.
Peirce, Thomas	1	1	Eli.Cy
Pelfrey, John	1		Henry
Pelham, Abraham	1		Lin.
Pelmar, Benjamin	1	1	Bed.
Pelter, James	1		Lou.
Pelter, John	1		Lou.
Pemberton, Abisha	1	9	K.Wm.
Pemberton, Bennett	1	3	Spots.
Pemberton, Charles	1	6	Spots.
Pemberton, George	1	1	Mont.
Pemberton, James	1		Buck.
Pemberton, John	1	4	K.&Q.
Pemberton, John	1	24	K.Wm.
Pemberton, Richard	1	5	Caro.
Pemberton, Walter	1	5	Caro.
Pemberton, William			Hen.
Pemberton, William	1	8	Spots.
Pendleton, Benjamin	1	19	K.&Q.
Pendleton, Benjamin	1	1	Buck.
Pendleton, Edmund, Jr.	3	24	Caro.
Pendleton, Edmund	5	56	Caro.
Pendleton, Henry	2	32	Cul.
Pendleton, Henry, Jr.	1		Spots
Pendleton, Henry	1	10	Spots
Pendleton, James	4	53	Cul.
Pendleton, John	1		Spots
Pendleton, John	1		Bot.
Pendleton, John	1	12	Hen.
Pendleton, John		-	Cul.
Pendleton, John	1	2	Buck.
Pendleton, Mace	1	1	Buck.
Pendleton, Micajah	1		Buck.
Pendleton, Nathaniel	1	4	Cul.
Pendleton, Philip	1	2	Berk.
Pendleton, William	3	12	Cul.
Pendrie, James	1		Mont.
Penn, Abraham	1	16	Henry
Penn, Abraham		2	Hen.
Penn, George	1		Spots
Penn, Mary		2	Spots
Penn, Thomas	1		Spots
Penn, Matthew	1		Aug.
Penn, Thomas	1	7	Brun.
Pennicks, John	1		Loui.
Pennington, Benajah	1		Mont.
Pennington, Ephraim	1		Mont.
Pennington, Joel	1	7	Din.
Pennington, Micajah	1		Mont.

Name			County
Pennington, Richard,	1		Mont.
Pennington, Sack,	1	8	Brun.
Pennington, Timothy,	1		Mont.
Pennington, William,	1	13	Brun.
Penniston, Anthony, est.		6	Din.
Penniston, Anthony, est.	1	6	Din.
Penniston, Thomas,	1	24	Pr.Geo.
Pennock, William,	4	6	Hen.
Penny, John,			Spots.
Penny, Pemuel,	1	7	York.
Pennybaker, John,	1		Berk.
Penrise, Joseph,	1		So'n
Penticost, Scarbrough		5	Brun.
Penticost, Scarbrough			Brun.
Penticost, William,	1	1	Din.
Pennyman, Robert,	1		Henry
Peoples, James,	1		Aug.
Peoples, James	1		Aug.
Peoples, John	1	1	Aug.
Peoples, John	1	2	Rock.
Peoples, Nathan	1		Rock.
Peper, Robert			Cul.
Pepher, George	1		Aug.
Pepper, Joshua	1		Brek.
Pepper, John	1		Har.
Pepper, Nathan	1	2	Din.
Pepper, Samuel	2	7	Fau.
Pepper, Samuel, Jr.	1		Fau.
Pepper, Samuel	1		Mont.
Pepper, William	1		Har.
Pepes, Philip	1		Mont.
Percy, John	1		Aug.
Percy, Thomas	1		Aug.
Perdue, Mesheck	1		Henry
Perew, Peter	1		Gooch.
Perin, Josephus	1	4	Lin.
Perkins, Anne		9	Din.
Perkins, Anthony	1		Loui.
Perkins, Baker	1	13	Ja. Cy
Perkins, Benjamin	1	4	Gooch.
Perkins, Benjamin	1	4	Din.
Perkins, Christian	1	10	Henry
Perkins, Edward	1	6	Din.
Perkins, Capt, Hardin	2	20	Buck
Perkins, Harden		5	Bed.
Perkins, James	1	8	Din.
Perkins, John	1	4	Din.
Perkins, John	1	7	Din.
Perkins, John	1		Ja. Cy
Perkins, John	1	2	Loui.
Perkins, John	1		Buck.
Perkins, John	1	8	Gooch.
Perkins, Joseph	1	14	Loui.
Perkins, Joshua	1		Din.
Perkins, Judith		6	Gooch.
Perkins, Lewis	1		Din.
Perkins, Molly		5	Gooch.
Perkins, Polly		12	Gooch.
Perkins, Stephen	1	2	Buck.
Perkins, William	1	9	Din.
Perkins, William	1	8	Din.
Perkins, William	1	1	Gooch.
Perkins, William, Sr.	1	10	Buck.
Perkins, William, Jr.	1	10	Buck.
Perkins, William	1		Fay.
Perren, John	1		Bed.
Perren, Joseph	1	1	Wash.
Perrin, John	1	32	K. Wm.
Perrin, John	1	53	K. Wm.
Perron, Charles, Jr.			Buck.
Perron, Charles	2	13	Buck.
Perron, Daniel	1	7	Buck.
Perry, Agnes		10	Din.
Perry, Benjamin	1	1	Spots.
Perry, Franklin	1	7	Lou.
Perry, James			Lou.

Name			Co.	Name			Co.	Name			Co.
Perry,John,Sr.,	1		Mont.	Petty,J..,	1	1	Pr.Wm.	Phillips,John,Jr.,	1	1	Acco.
Perry,John,	1		Eli.C	Petty,Joseph,	1	11	Pr.Wm.	Phillips,John,	1		Acco,
Perry,John,	1		Lou.	Petty,Joseph,	3		Har.	Phillips,John,	2	1	Brun.
Perry,Joseph,	1		Spots	Petty,Presly,	1		Pr.Wm.	Phillips,John,	1		Aug.
Perry,Joshua,	1		Aug.	Petty,Rawleigh,	1		Pr.Wm.	Phillips,John,	1	1	Eli.Cy
Perry,Larkin,	1		Spots	Petzer,Elizabeth,			Lou.	Phillips,John,			Din.
Perry,Littlebury,	1	4	Cha.C	Pewett,Joel,	1	8	Lun.	Phillips,John,	1		Lou.
Perry,Lovel,	1		Spots	Pewsey,Robert,	1		Henry	Phillips,John,	1		Lou.
Perry,Nathan,	1		Lou.	Peyton,Burr,	1	4	Pr.Wm.	Phillips,John,	2		Cul.
Perry,Rhodorick,	1		Loui.	Peyton,Daniel,	1		Lin.	Phillips,John,	1	16	Pr.Geo.
Perry,Richard,	2		Lin.	Peyton,Col.Francis,	2	15	Lou.	Phillips,John,		2	Pr.Geo.
Perry,Robert,			Lou.	Peyton,Henry,	1	14	Fau.	Phillips,Joseph,	1	1	So'n.
Perry,Samuel,	1		Henry	Peyton,S..,	1	10	Pr.Wm.	Phillips,Matthias,			Acco.
Perry,Thomas,	2	2	Spots	Peyton,Timothy,	1	13	Pr.Wm.	Phillips,Moses,	1	11	So'n.
Perry,Thomas,	1	2	Cha.C	Peyton,V.,	1	8	Pr.Wm.	Phillips,Rhoda,			Lou.
Perryman,Anthony,	2		K.& Q.	Peyton,William,	1	16	Lou.	Phillips,Capt.Rich'd	1	15	Loui.
Perryman,Philip,			K.& Q.	Peyton,Yelverton,	1		Lin.	Phillips,Richard,	1		Pr.Wm.
Persize,Daniel,	1		Lin.	Peytons,M.,	1	18	Pr.Wm.	Phillips,Richard,	1	2	Caro.
Person,William,		3	So'n.	Phares,John,	1		Aug.	Phillips,Robert,	1	8	Fau.
Person,George,			Acco.	Pharis,Samuel,			Fau.	Phillips,Thomas,	1	1	Lou.
Person,Turner,	1		So'n.	Phariss,James,	1		Har.	Phillips,Thomas,	1		Acco.
Persons,Thomas,	2	6	Har.	Pharos,William,	1		Wash.	Phillips,Thomas,			Acco.
Pescud,Elizabeth,		22	York	Pheabin,Paul,	1		Nor.	Phillips,Thomas,	1	1	Berk.
Peter,Tunis,			Lou.	Pheazle,Bernard,	1		Bed.	Phillips,William,Sr.	1	3	Acco.
Peter,Walter,	2	32	Pr.Geo	Pheazle,Jacob,	1		Bed.	Phillips,William,	1		Din.
Peterik,Thomas,	1		Berk.	Pheazle,Philip,Sr.,			Bed.	Phillips,William,	1	6	Loui.
Peteroe,Francis,	1		Lou.	Phelps,Cary,			Buck.	Phillips,William,	1	7	K.& Q.
Peters,Edmund,	1	4	Buck.	Phelps,John,	3	2	Buck.	Phillips,William,	1		Cha.Cy
Peters,Elizabeth,		9	Fau.	Phelps,John,Jr.,			Buck.	Phillips,William,	1	13	York
Peters,Jacob,	1		Berk.	Phelps,John,			Bed.	Phillips,William,	1		York
Peters,James,	1	3	Fau.	Phelps,John,	1	8	Bed.	Phillips,William,	1	2	Pr.Geo.
Peters,John,	1		Lou.	Phelps,William,	1	8	Buck.	Phillups,George,	1	10	Lun.
Peters,John,	1		Lin.	Phenix,Drury,	1		Brun.	Phillups,Robert,	1		Lun.
Peters,Johnathan,	1		Lin.	Phenix,John,	1		Brun.	Philpot,Samuel,			Henry
Peters,Mary,			Fau.	Phenton,Jesse,	1		Har.	Philpots,John,	1		Gooch.
Peterson,Henry,	1		Cul.	Philbert,Archibald,	1	7	Lun.	Philpots,Oakly,	1		Gooch.
Peterson,Isaac,	1		Mont.	Philbert,Horton,	1		Pr.Wm.	Phlippo,John,	1		Caro.
Peterson,Jacob,	3		Har.	Philip,Charles,	1		Lin.	Phlippo,Joseph,	1	1	Caro.
Peterson,John,	1		Berk.	Philips,Abner,	1	1	Cul.	Phlippo,Joseph,	1		Caro.
Peterson,Lucy,		17	Din.	Philips,Anthony,	1	1	Brun.	Phlippo,Sarah,		1	Caro.
Peterson,Lucy,		10	Brun.	Philips,James,	1	2	Cha.C.	Phlippo,William,	1		Caro.
Peterson,Martin,	5		Har.	Philips,John,	1		Cul.	Phinekin,Mary,			Lou.
Peterson,Michael,	1		Har.	Philips,John,	1		Mont.	Phipps,Benjamin,			Mont.
Peterson,Michael,	1		Har.	Philips,Joseph,	1		Cul.	Phipps,James,	1		Mont.
Peterson,Thomas,	1		Berk.	Philips,Hezekiah,	1		Mont.	Phipps,Joshua,	1		Bot.
Peterson,Thomas,	1	20	Pr.Geo	Philips,Mary,		7	York	Phipps,Samuel,	1		Mont.
Petholt,Zachariah,	1		Berk.	Philips,Mary,	1		Bed.	Phipps,William,	1		Mont.
Petrie,John,			Rock.	Philips,Philip,	1		Mont.	Phips,Benjamin,			Brun.
Petro,Leonard,	1		Har.	Philips,Richard,	1	13	K.& Q.	Phips,John,	2		Brun.
Petsor,Matthias,			Berk.	Philips,Samuel,	1		Bot.	Phips,John,	1		Wash.
Petters,Col.William,	1	7	Loui.	Philips,Tobias,	1	3	Mont.	Phyllips,Elizabeth,		5	Brun.
Pettey,Zachary,	1	3	Cul.	Philippe,John,	2		Mont.	Phyllips,James,	1		Brun.
Petticrew,Matthew,	2	3	Camp.	Phillips,Abner,	1	1	Fau.	Phyllips,Thomas,	1		Brun.
Pettipool,Baxter,			Lun.	Phillips,Benjamin,Sr.	2		Acco.	Pick,John,	1		Berk.
Pettipool,Colwell,	1	7	Lun.	Phillips,Benjamin,Jr.	1	1	Acco.	Pickels,John,	1	3	K.& Q.
Pettipool,Frederick,	1	1	Lun.	Phillips,Catherine,		1	Loui.	Pickens,Aaron,	1		Lin.
Pettipool,John,	1		Din.	Phillips,Christian,			Lou.	Pierce,Ann,	1	6	K.& Q.
Pettipool,Mary,	1	2	Lun.	Phillips,Christopher,	1	4	Caro.	Pierce,Daniel,	1		Mont.
Pettipool,Seth,	1	11	Din.	Phillips,David,	1		Lou.	Pierce,Jeremiah,	1	3	Lin.
Pettipool,William,	1	3	Lun.	Phillips,David,	1		Wash.	Pierce,John,	1	16	Jas.Cy
Pettipool,William,	1		Din.	Phillips,Elias,	1	4	Fau.	Pierce,John,	1		Spots.
Pettis,John,	1		Caro.	Phillips,Elizabeth,	1	11	York	Pierce,John,	1		Lou.
Pettitt,Andrew,	1		Lou.	Phillips,Ezekiel,	1		Fau.	Pierce,John,	1	5	York
Pettitt,Andrew,	1		Lou.	Phillips,Frederick,	1		Caro	Pierce,John,	1		Cul.
Pettitt,John,Sr.,	1		Nor.	Phillips,Gabriel,	1		Lou.	Pierce,John,Jr.,	1		Cul.
Pettitt,John,Jr.,	1		Nor.	Phillips.George,	1	7	Caro.	Pierce,John,	1		York
Pettitt,Leah,			Nor.	Phillips,Henry,	1		Fau.	Pierce,John,	1		Fau.
Pettitt,Nathaniel,	1		Fau.	Phillips,Isaac,	1		Lou.	Pierce,Lewis	1		Lou.
Pettitt,Obediah,	3		Fau.	Phillips,Jacob,	2		Acco.	Pierce,Matthew,			York
Pettitt,Rodam,			Lou.	Phillips,Jacob,			Acco.	Pierce,Rice Bolton,	1	10	So'n.
Pettitt,William,	1	1	Nor.	Phillips,James,	1		Pr.Wm.	Pierce,William,	1	1	Eli.Cy
Pettitt,William,	1	4	Loui.	Phillips,James,	1	1	Aug.	Pierceful,Perter,	1		Mont.
Pettus,David,	1	7	Lun.	Phillips,Jenkin,		1	Lou.	Pierceful,Samuel,	1		Mont.
Pettus,John,	1	16	Lun.	Phillips,Jenkin,	1	3	Lou.	Piercey,Martha,			Din.
Petty,Benjamin,	1	1	Cul.	Phillips,Jessee,	1	1	Pr.Geo	Piercey,Thomas,	1	3	Din.
Petty,Dudley,	1		Pr.Wm	Phillips,John,Sr.,	2		Acco.				

Name			County
Pickerell,Richard,	1		Pr.Wm.
Pickerill,Frederick,	1		Pr.Wm.
Pickings,Thomas,	1		Mont.
Pickins,John,	1		Rock.
Picket,Abram,	1		Eli.Cy
Pickett,Elizabeth,		7	Fau.
Pickett,John,	1	2	K.Geo.
Pickett,John,	1		Lou.
Pickett,Martin,	1	24	Fau.
Pickett,William,	1	19	Fau.
Pickitt,Jeconias,	2		Acco.
Pichimore,Abraham,	3		Bot.
Pickle,Christian,	1		Aug.
Picklemore,John,Sr.,	1		Bot.
Picklemore,John,			Bot.
Pigg,Francis,	1	6	K.Wm.
Pigg,George,		2	K.&Q
Pigg,James,	1		Henry
Pigg,John,	1		K.&Q
Pigg,John,	1	6	K.&Q
Pigg,Nathaniel,	2		Loui.
Pigg,Rachel,		1	K.&Q
Pigg,Rachel,		4	K.&Q
Piggott,John,	1	1	Ja.Cy
Piggott,John,	1		Ja.Cy
Piggott,Pearson,	1	9	Ja.Cy
Piggott,William,	1	1	Ja.Cy
Pigmore,John Fred'k	1		Berk.
Pigram,Baker,	2	5	Din.
Pigram,Capt.Edward,	1	21	Din.
Pigram,Edward,	1	9	Din.
Pigram,Elizabeth,	1	4	Din.
Pigram,George,	1	3	Din.
Pigram,John,	1	10	Din.
Pigram,William,est.		1	Din.
Pike,Benjamin,	1		Bot.
Pike,George,	1		Lun.
Pike,Jonathan,	3	1	Lou.
Pilcher,James,	1		Pr.Wm.
Pilchor,Stephen,	1		Pr.Wm.
Piles,John,	2	4	Lou.
Pilgrim,Amos,Sr.,	1		Henry
Pilgrim,Amos,Jr.,	1		Henry
Pilgrim,Michael,	1		Henry
Pilgrim,Thomas,	1		Henry
Pilgrim,William,	1		Henry
Pilkington,Joel,	1		Pr.Geo
Pilkington,Richard,	1	4	Brun.
Pilkington,Richard,J	1		Brun.
Pilkington,William,	1	3	Brun.
Pilkington,Willis,	1		Brun.
Pilsbury,John,	1	2	West.
Pilson,Samuel,	1		Aug.
Pilson,Richard,	1		Henry
Pilson,Robert,	1		Henry
Pilson,William,	1		Henry
Pinchback,Thomas,			Hen.
Pinckard,James,	1	1	Fau.
Pinckard,William,	1		Fau.
Pinckard,William,		1	Fau.
Pines,John,	1	6	Cul.
Pines,Lewis,Sr.,			Spots.
Pines,Lewis,	1		Spots.
Ping,John,Sr.,	1		Lin.
Piniger,Peter,	1		Cul.
Pinkerton,Robert,	1		Berk.
Pinkstone,Henry,	1		Fau.
Pinland,Alexander,	2		Fay.
Pinnex,James,	1		Lin.
Pinninger,Mathias,	1	1	Cul.
Pinninger,William,	1	1	Cul.
Pinnon,John,	1		Cul.
Pinnon,William,	2	4	Cul.
Pinter,John,	1		Bot.
Piper,Ann,		2	K.Geo.
Piper,Benjamin,	1	13	Fau.

Name			County
Piper,Josiah,	1	1	Nor.
Piper,William,	1	23	K.Geo
Pippen,George,			Buck.
Pirkey,Daniel,	1		Mont.
Pirkey,Henry,	1		Mont.
Pirkle,Henry,			Wash.
Pitillo,James,	1	13	Brun.
Pittinger,Richard,	2	1	Cul.
Pitcher,Thomas,	1		Bot.
Pitgor,Michael,	1		Berk.
Pitman,Isaac,	1	6	K.Geo
Pitman,James,	1	1	Henry
Pitman,John,	1	6	Buck.
Pitman,Samson,	3	1	So'n
Pitser,Conrod,	1		Lou.
Pitt,William,	1	1	Ja.Cy
Pittman,Hipkins,	2	3	Caro.
Pittman,James,	1	5	Caro.
Pittman,Lee,	1		West.
Pittman,Mary,		6	Caro.
Pitts,Ambrose,	1	8	Caro.
Pitts,Ann,		2	K.&Q
Pitts,David,	2	7	K.&Q
Pitts,Hezekiah,	2	10	Nor.
Pitts,James,	1	5	Caro.
Pitts,James,Jr.,	1	4	Caro.
Pitts,John,			Acco.
Pitts,Lewis,	1		Wash.
Pitts,Musco,	1	1	Caro.
Pitts,Stark,	1	1	Caro.
Pitzer,John,	1	3	Bot.
Plake,John,	1		Fay.
Plank,John,	1	1	Mont.
Plankenpiper,Zacharia	1		Mont.
Planton,William,			Brun.
Plaster,Michael,	1		Henry
Pleasants,Archibald,	1	9	Gooch
Pleasants,Isaac,	1	13	Gooch
Pleasants,Jacob,est.		5	Hen.
Pleasants,John,	1	9	Hen.
Pleasants,Joseph,			Hen.
Pleasants,Joseph,	1	8	Hen.
Pleasants,Joseph,	1	12	Gooch
Pleasants,Mary,	1	14	Hen.
Pleasants,Mary,		10	Gooch
Pleasants,Phillip,	1	4	Gooch
Pleasants,Richard,	1	4	Gooch
Pleasants,Robert,	1		Gooch
Pleasants,Robert,		18	Gooch
Pleasants,Robert,	1	7	Hen.
Pleasants,Robert,Jr.,	3		Hen.
Pleasants,Thomas,	2	23	Hen.
Pleasants,Thomas,	1	21	Gooch
Pleckinstalver,John,	1		Mont.
Pledge,Archer,	1	4	Gooch
Pledge,Francis,	1	2	Gooch
Pledge,Ursula,		3	Gooch
Pledger,John,	1		So'n
Pledgit,James,	1		So'n
Plesley,Jacob,	1		Mont.
Plotner,John,	3		Berk.
Plough,Elias,	1		Har.
Plumb,John,	1		Har.
Plumby,John,	1		Bot.
Plunkett,John,	1		Aug.
Plunkett,William,	2	4	Spots
Poage,Elijah,	1	1	Fay.
Poage,George,	1	4	Aug.
Poage,John,	3	7	Aug.
Poage,Robert,	1	2	Har.
Poage,Thomas,	1	7	Aug.
Poague,Robert,			Mont.
Poague,Robert,	2		Bot.
Poague,Thomas,	1		Mont.
Poe,Jack,	1		Ja.Cy
Polson,Andrew,	1	11	K.Wm.

Name			County
Pomfritt,John,	1	11	K.Wm.
Pomfrey,John,		1	K.Wm.
Pomroy,John,	1		West.
Pond,Daniel,	1	10	So'n.
Pond,John,	1		So'n
Pond,John,	1		Cha.Cy
Pond,John,H.,	1	12	So'n
Pond,Richard,	1	3	So'n
Pond,Richard,	1	6	So'n.
Pool,Daniel,			Lou.
Pool,George,	1		Henry
Pool,Micajah,	1	5	Henry
Pool,Thomas,	2	12	Lou.
Poole,Francis,	1	1	Eli.Cy
Poole,John,			Spots.
Poole,John,	1	1	Eli.Cy
Poole,Joseph,	1		Lou.
Poole,Micajah,	1		Spots.
Poole,Robert,	1	4	Eli.Cy
Poole,William,	1		Har.
Poolman,John,	1	5	Acco.
Poor,Abraam,	1	2	Gooch
Poor,Charles,	1		West.
Poor,Elisha,	1		Buck.
Poor,James,	1		Fay.
Poor,John,	1		Gooch.
Poor,John,	1		Fay.
Poor,Joseph,	1		Lou.
Poor,Robin,	1	11	Gooch
Poor,Thomas,	1	9	Gooch
Poore,George,Sr.,	1		Henry
Poore,George,	1		Henry
Poore,William,	1		Henry
Poorch,Bridges,		4	Brun.
Pope,Andrew,			So'n.
Pope,Ann,		3	So'n.
Pope,Britain,	1	4	So'n
Pope,George,	1		Lin.
Pope,Hardy,	1	9	So'n
Pope,Henry,	1		Lin.
Pope,Henry,	1		So'n.
Pope,Isaac,	1		So'n
Pope,Jesse,			So'n
Pope,John,	1		So'n.
Pope,John,	1	9	Pr.Wm.
Pope,Joseph,	1		So'n.
Pope,Josiah,	1	2	So'n.
Pope,Laurence,	1	7	West.
Pope,Lazarus,	1		So'n
Pope,Martha,			So'n
Pope,Mattew,	1	5	York
Pope,Melchor,	2		Berk.
Pope,Mich.,	1	1	So'n
Pope,Nathaniel,	1		So'n
Pope,Nathaniel,	1	1	West.
Pope,Nathaniel,	1	2	Mont.
Pope,Sarah,		4	So'n
Pope,Simon,	1		So'n
Pope,Thomas,	1		So'n.
Pope,Thomas,	2	5	Lin.
Pope,William,	1		Lin.
Pope,William,	1		So'n
Pope,William,	1	3	So'n
Pope,William,	1	3	So'n.
Popegay,Terrence,	1		Har.
Popham,Jonathan,	2	8	Cul.
Popham,Thomas,			Cul.
Popkins,John,	1		Lou.
Poteet,Benjamin,	1		Bed.
Poteet,James,	1		Bed.
Poteett,James,	1	2	Henry
Poteett,Thomas,	1		Henry
Poteett,William,	1		Bed.
Poracle,Moses,	1		Camp.
Porch,Thomas,	1	17	So'n
Porter,Britain,	1		So'n

Name			Loc	Name			Loc	Name			Loc
Porter,Charles,	1	1	Cul.	Potts,Samuel,	1	1	Lou.	Powter,John,	1		Brun.
Porter,Demsey,	1	5	West.	Potty,George,			Loui.	Poynter,George,	1		Lin.
Porter,Edward,			Lou.	Poudry,Ralph,	1		Berk.	Poynter,John,	1		Lin.
Porter,Edward,	1	2	West.	Poulson,Edmund,	3		Acco.	Poynter,John,Jr.,	1		Lin.
Porter,Elizabeth,		3	West.	Poulson,George,	3	4	Acco.	Poynter,Thomas,	1		Lin.
Porter,James,	1	10	So'n	Poulson,John,			Acco.	Poynthress,Joshua,	1	24	Pr.Geo.
Porter,John,	1		Henry	Poulson,William,	1	4	Acco.	Poythress,Mary,		18	Pr.Geo.
Porter,John,	2	3	So'n	Pound,William,	1		Cul.	Poythress,Mary,		10	Pr.Geo.
Porter,Joseph,			Cul.	Povall,Robin,	2	28	Hen.	Poythress,Meridith,			Brun.
Porter,Joseph,	3	2	Cul.	Powe,Marsom,	1	4	Spots.	Poythress,Thomas,	2	6	Brun.
Porter,Joseph,	1		Mont.	Powel,William,Sr.,	1	4	Pr.Wm.	Poythress,William,	1	16	Pr.Geo.
Porter,Joseph,	1		Lou.	Powel,William,Jr.,	2	6	Pr.Wm.	Poythress,William,			So'n
Porter,Mary,	1	3	Lou.	Powell,Aaron,			Bed.	Poythriss,Francis,	2	1	Din.
Porter,Margaret,		1	Mont.	Powell,Ambrose,	2	32	Cul.	Poythriss,John,			Din.
Porter,Nicholas,Sr.,	1	7	Cul.	Powell,Ambrose,	1		Fay.	Poythriss,Peter,		26	Din.
Porter,Nicholas,Jr.,	1	2	Cul.	Powell,Benjamin,	2	24	York	Poythriss,Peter,	1	17	Din.
Porter,Patrick,	3		Wash.	Powell,Benjamin,	1	1	Cul.	Poythrop,Peter,	1	87	Pr.Geo.
Porter,Philip,			Lou.	Powell,Edmund,	1	7	Lin.	Prail,John,	2	15	Fau.
Porter,Robert,	1		Mont.	Powell,Elizabeth,	1		York	Prator,Thomas,	1		Henry
Porter,Robert,	1		Har.	Powell,Ezekiel,	1	2	Cha.Cy	Pratt,Bable,	1		Acco.
Porter,Samuel,			Wash.	Powell,George,	1	6	Nor.	Pratt,Comfort,			Acco.
Porter,Samuel,	1	7	Fau.	Powell,Honorius,	1	3	Din.	Pratt,John,	1		Bed.
Porter,Thomas,	1	3	So'n	Powell,Hudson,	1	9	K.Wm.	Pratt,John,	1		Lou.
Porter,Thomas,	1	2	Cul.	Powell,Isaac,	1		Acco.	Pratt,John,	1		Mont.
Porter,Thomas,	1	2	Fau.	Powell,James,	1	6	Acco.	Pratt,Jonathan,	1		Cul.
Porter,Thomas,	3	11	Cul.	Powell,James,	1	12	K.Wm.	Pratt,Joseph,			Cul.
Porter,William,	1	7	Spots.	Powell,James,	1	8	Cul.	Pratt,Joseph,	1		Cul.
Porter,William,			Hen.	Powell,James,	1		Cul.	Pratt,Scarburgh,	1		Acco.
Porter,William,	1		Aug.	Powell,Jane,	1	16	York	Pratt,Thomas,	1	4	Cul.
Porter,William,			Cul.	Powell,Jasse,			Cul.	Pratt,William,	2		Cul.
Porter,William,	1	1	Rock.	Powell,John,	1	6	Lun.	Pratt,Zaphaniah,	1		Cul.
Porter,William,	1		Mont.	Powell,John,	1	6	Brun.	Preest,David,	1		Wash.
Porter,William,			Fau.	Powell,John,	1	10	So'n	Preest,William,	1		Wash.
Porter,William,	1	8	West.	Powell,Joseph,	1	2	So'n	Prentis,Joseph,		3	Jas.Cy -
Porter,William,	1	3	West.	Powell,Joshua,	1		Lin.	Pretlow,Thomas,	1	7	So'n
Porter,Winny,			So'n	Powell,Levin,	1	17	Lou.	Presgrove,Barnut,	1		Mont.
Porterfield,Alexander	1		Berk.	Powell,Moses,	1		Camp.	Presley,Charles,			Lou.
Porterfield,James,	1		Wash.	Powell,Nathaniel,	1	5	Nor.	Presley,James,	1	1	West.
Porterfield,John,Sr.,	1		Wash.	Powell,Richard,	1		Cul.	Presscote,Thomas,	2		Acco.
Porterfield,John,Jr.,	1		Wash.	Powell,Robert,			Berk.	Presstidge,William,	1		Cul.
Porterfield,William,	3		Berk.	Powell,Robert,	1	4	Henry	Pretlow,Thomas,	1	7	So'n
Porterfield,Wm.Jr.,	1		Berk.	Powell,Samuel,	1	5	Gooch.	Prim,Abraham,	1		K.Geo.
Portlock,Thomas,	1		Bed.	Powell,Samuel,	1		Har.	Primon,William,	2		Fau.
Portor,Elijah,	2		Fay.	Powell,Samuel,	1		Lou.	Prince,Francis,	1		K.& Q.
Posey,Benjamin,	1		Pr.Wm.	Powell,Sith,	1	12	Nor.	Prince,Joseph,	1	3	Brun.
Posey,Humphry,	1		Henry	Powell,Dr.Thomas,	1	17	Spots.	Prince,Levy,	1		Lou.
Post,Valentine,	2		Har.	Powell,Thomas,	1	2	York	Prince,Robert,	1		K.& Q.
Poston,Leonard,,	1	2	Lou.	Powell,William,	1	5	Gooch.	Prince,Sylvanus,	1	15	York.
Postwood,Thomas,	1		Wash.	Powell,William,	1	1	Cul.	Prince,Sylvanus,	1	20	Jas.Cy
Potten,Henry,	1		Lou.	Powell,William,	2		Lin.	Priner,Peter,	1		Berk.
Potten,John,	1		Lou.	Powell,William,	1	2	K.Wm.	Pringle,William,	1		Har.
Potter,Benjamin,	1		Henry	Powell,William,	1		Lou.	Prior,Silas,	1		Lou.
Potter,James,	1		Mont.	Power,David,	1	2	Caro.	Probalt,William,	1	1	Mont.
Potter,John,	1		Acco.	Power,Edward,	1	25	Jas.Cy	Procter,John,	1	6	Cul.
Potter,Labin,	1		Acco.	Power,Edward,	2	1	Caro.	Proctor,John,			Brun,
Potter,Lewis,	1		Mont.	Powers,Bernard,	1	14	K.Wm.	Proctor,Joseph,	1		Brun.
Potter,Nicholass,	2		Acco.	Powers,Bernard,	1	2	K.Wm.	Proctor,Pamely,		2	Pr.Geo.
Potter,Ralph,	1		Berk.	Powers,Charles,	1		So'n	Proctor,Thomas,Sr.,	2	1	Brun.
Potter,Rouse,	1		Mont.	Powers,Daniel,	1		Gooch.	Proctor,Thomas,			Brun.
Potter,Solomon,	1		Wash.	Powers,Daniel,	1		Gooch.	Proderah,Thomas,	1		Bot.
Potter,Thomas,	1		Mont.	Powers,David,	1		Mont.	Profitt,William,	1	1	Gooch.
Potter,Thomas,	1		Wash.	Powers,David,	1	2	K.Wm.	Proso,Matthew,	1	2	York
Potterfield,Adam,	1		Lou.	Powers,George,	1		Mont.	Prosser,John,	1	5	Pr.Wm.
Potterson,Samuel,	1	6	Henry	Powers,Henry,	1		Camp.	Prosser,Thomas,	2	55	Hen.
Potts,David,	1	1	Lou.	Powers,Isaac,	1	2	K.Wm.	Pruit,Byrd,	1	2	Mont.
Potts,David,Jr.,			Lou.	Powers,John,	1	3	K.Wm.	Pruit,Fuller,	1		Mont.
Potts,Ephraim,	1		Din.	Powers,Julius,	1	6	K.Wm.	Pruit,John,			Mont.
Potts,Ezekiel,	1		Lou.	Powers,Major,	1	4	Gooch.	Pruit,Severancy,			Mont.
Potts,Frederick,	1		Berk.	Powers,Martin,	3		Har.	Pruitt,Frances,			K.& Q.
Potts,Jeremiah,	2	1	Din.	Powers,Michael,	1		Har.	Prunier,Daniel,	1		Mont.
Potts,Jesse,	1	5	Brun.	Powers,Milley,			K.Wm.	Prunty,James,	1		Henry
Potts,John,	1	2	Berk.	Powers,Susanna,			K.Wm.	Prunty,Robert,	1	1	Henry
Potts,John,			Berk.	Powers,Thomas,			Hen.	Prunty,Thomas,	1		Henry
Potts,John,	1		Brun.	Powers,Thomas,	1	3	K.Wm.	Prus,***	1		Cul.
Potts,Nathan,	2		Lou.	Powers,Valentine,	1		Har.	Prusley,William,	1		Rock.
Potts,Nathan,	1		Brun.	Powers,William,	2	11	Gooch.	Pruther,Jerimiah,	1	4	Berk.

Name			County	Name			County	Name			County
Presley,William,	2		Rock.	Price,Pugh,	2	17	Fay.	Puckett,Jacob,	1		Buck.
Presson,Nicholas,	1	14	York	Price,Richard,	1		Wash.	Puckett,Jeremiah,	1		Bed.
Presson,Robert,	1	13	York	Price,Richard,	1	5	Cul.	Puckett,John,	2	8	Cul.
Presson,Samuel,	1	1	York	Price,Richard,	1	1	Hen.	Puckett,Peter,			K.Geo.
Presson,Thomas,	1	1	York	Price,Richard,	1		Lou.	Puckett,Richard,	1	1	Lun.
Presson,Thomas,Jr.,	1	2	York	Price,Richard,	1		Wash.	Puckett,Thomas H.	1	2	Lun.
Preston,Joshua,	1		Brun.	Price,Richard,	1	12	K.&Q	Puckett,Thomas,	1		Henry
Preston,Jacob,	1		Fau.	Price,Robert,	1	29	Hen.	Puckett,William,			Lun.
Preston,Joel,	1	1	Bed.	Price,Samuel,	1		Lin.	Pugh,Jacob,	1		Har.
Preston,John,	1		Fau.	Price,Samuel,est.,		4	Hen.	Pugh,Jesse,	1		Har.
Preston,John,	1		Henry	Price,Samuel,	2	3	Fau.	Pugh,Spencer,	1		Lou.
Preston,Joshua,	1		Fau.	Price,Thomas,		6	Loui.	Pugh,Thomas,	1		Lou.
Preston,Moses,	1		Bed.	Price,Thomas,	1		Bed.	Puire,George,	1		Bed.
Preston,Moses,	1		Bot.	Price,Thomas,	1		Wash.	Pukler,Peter,	1		Lou.
Preston,Nathan,	1		Bed.	Price,Thomas,	1		Bot.	Pukett,John,	1	34	Caro.
Preston,Robert,	1		Wash.	Price,Thomas,Jr.,	1		Wash.	Pukett,John,	1		Fay.
Preston,Sarah,			Henry	Price,William,	1	2	Spots.	Pukett,Thomas,	1	7	Caro.
Preston,Stephen,	1	2	Bed.	Price,William,	1	16	Loui.	Pukett,William,	1	1	Caro.
Preston,Thomas,	1	6	Bed.	Price,William,	1		K.Geo.	Pukett,William,	1		Caro.
Preston,Thomas,Jr.,	1		Brun.	Price,William,	1	1	So'n	Pullen,Charles,	2	1	Lou.
Preston,Thomas,	2		Brun.	Price,William,	1		Lin.	Pullen,Robert,			Lou.
Preston,Walter,	1		Wash.	Prickett,Edward,	1		Din.	Pullen,Joseph,	1		Lou.
Preston,William,	2	34	Mont.	Priest,Cornelius,	1		Lun.	Pullen,Joseph,Jr.,			Lou.
Preston,William,	1		Brun.	Priese,George,			Berk.	Pullen,Moses,	1	6	Bed.
Preston,William,Sr.,	1		Fau.	Priest,John,	2		Fau.	Pullen,Thomas,	1	2	Bed.
Preston,William,	1	1	Fau.	Priest,Thomas,	1	2	Fau.	Pullen,William,	1		Bed.
Pruett,John,	1	1	Spots.	Priest,Thomas,		3	Fau.	Puller,James,	1	2	Caro.
Prewit,David,	1		Henry	Prigman,Matthew,	1		Har.	Puller,James,	1		Berk.
Prewit,Elijah,	1		Henry	Prigmore,Dorsey,	1		Berk.	Puller,John,	1	13	Caro.
Prewit,Mrs.Elizabeth			Bed.	Prill,John,	1		Lou.	Puller,Thomas,			Loui.
Prewit,Henry,	1		Bed.	Prilliman,Jacob,	1		Henry	Pulliam,Benjamin,	1	8	Cul.
Prewit,James,	1		K.&Q	Prilliman,Jacob,Jr.,	1		Henry	Pulliam,David,	1	7	Spots.
Prewit,John,	1	5	Gooch.	Prilliman,John,	1		Henry	Pulliam,James,	1		Loui.
Prewit,Richard,	1		Henry	Prior,Joseph,	1	6	Bot.	Pulliam,Jennings,	1	1	Gooch.
Prewitt,Abigail,		2	Acco.	Prior,Joseph,	1		Bot.	Pulliam,John,	1	2	Lou.
Prewitt,James,	1		Ja.Cy	Prior,Luke,	1	14	Bot.	Pulliam,Joseph,	1	4	Spots.
Prewitt,Levin,est.,		1	Acco.	Pritchard,John,	1		Buck.	Pulliam,Nathan,	1		Loui.
Prewitt,William,	2		Acco.	Pritchard,Thomas,	1		Lou.	Pulliam,Thomas,	3	2	Cul.
Price,Abraham,	2		Lin.	Pritchett,Aaron,	2		Din.	Pulliam,Zachariah,	1		Loui.
Price,Anthony,	1	2	K.Geo.	Pritchett,Francis,		2	Din.	Pulliam,Zachariah,	1		Loui.
Price,Barret,	1	12	Hen.	Pritchett,Francis,	1		Din.	Pullin,George,	2		Fau.
Price,Bird,	1	8	Fay.	Pritchett,George,	1		Cul.	Pullin,John,	1		Aug.
Price,Bourne,	2	18	Camp.	Pritchett,James,Jr.,	1		Spots.	Pullin,John,	1		Aug.
Price,Charles,	1	17	Hen.	Pritchett,James,	1	23	Din.	Pullin,John,	1	7	Cul.
Price,Copland,		6	Caro.	Pritchett,Jeremiah,	1	4	Din.	Pullin,Loftus,	1	1	Aug.
Price,David,	1		Mont.	Pritchett,Jesse,			Din.	Pulling,William,	1		Lou.
Price,David,	1	1	K.Geo.	Pritchett,John,	1		K.Geo	Pully,William,	1		Lun.
Price,David,	1		Berk.	Pritchett,John,	1	11	Din.	Punter,Henry,			Hen.
Price,Elisha,			Hen.	Pritchett,Joshua,	1	5	Brun.	Purcell,Jonathan,	3		Har.
Price,Elizabeth,	1	2	Lin.	Pritchett,Joshua,	1	7	Din.	Purcell,William,	1		Har.
Price,Henry,	1		Mont.	Pritchett,Moses,	1		Brun.	Purdom,Benjamin,	1		Lou.
Price,Isaac,			Lin.	Pritchett,Peter,	1		Din.	Purdom,Jeremiah,	1		Lou.
Price,James,	1	16	Hen.	Pritchett,Thomas,	1	11	Spots.	Purdom,Thomas,	1		Cul.
Price,James,	1	5	Loui.	Pritchett,William,	1		Brun.	Purdue,Daniel,			Mont.
Price,Joel,	1		Brun.	Pritchett,William,	1	2	Brun.	Purdue,Isaiah,	1		Mont.
Price,John,	1		Lou.	Pride,James,	1	18	Ja.Cy	Purdue,William,	1		Mont.
Price,John,	1		Aug.	Pride,Peter,	1	3	Din.	Puree,John,	1	2	So'n
Price,John,	1		Mont.	Priddy,George,	1	6	Gooch.	Purkerson,Seth,	1		Lun.
Price,John,	1	22	Hen.	Proctor,Charles,	1	2	Spots.	Purkins,William,	1	2	Hen.
Price,John,	1	8	Hen.	Proctor,George,			Spots.	Purks,Joseph,	1	3	K.&Q
Price,John,Jr.,	1	4	West.	Proctor,George,	1		Fay.	Purel,Thomas,	1	5	Nor.
Price,John,	1	11	K.Geo.	Proctor,Hezekiah,	1	3	Fay.	Purnell,John,	1		Pr.Wm.
Price,John,	1	2	K.Geo.	Proctor,John,	2		Spots.	Pursel,Thomas,	1		Lou.
Price,John White,			Hen.	Proctor,John,	1	5	Fay.	Pursel,John,	1		So'n
Price,Jonathan,	1		Lou.	Proctor,Joseph,			Lou.	Pursell,John,	1		Henry
Price,Joseph,	1	25	Hen.	Proctor,Thomas,	1	2	Spots.	Pursley,George,	1	2	Pr.Wm.
Price,Joseph Shores,	1	7	Henry	Pryor,David,	1	1	Buck.	Pursley,John,	1	5	Pr.Wm.
Price,Mary,	1	16	Hen.	Pryor,John,	1	10	K.&Q	Purson,John,	1		Fay.
Price,Mary,		1	K.Geo.	Pryor,Lucy,		1	Buck.	Purss,Gabriel,	1		Acco.
Price,Meredith,		4	Lou.	Pryor,Nicholas,	1		Bot.	Purvess,William,	1		Cul.
Price,Michael,	2		Mont.	Pryor,Samuel,	1	19	Gooch.	Purvess,William,Jr.,	1		Cul.
Price,Michael,Jr.,	1		Mont.	Pryor,William,	1	12	Gooch.	Purvis,Francis,	1	11	Spots.
Price,Moses,	1		Lin.	Pue,William,	1		Caro.	Purvis,James,	1	6	Spots.
Price,Jacob,	1		Berk.	Puckeril,John,	1		Mont.	Puryear,Jesse,			Hen.
Price,Moses,	1		Wash.	Puckett,Drury,	1		Wash.	Puryear,Hezekiah,	1	18	Gooch.

Name			Loc.
Puryear,Susannah,	1	10	Hen.
Putlaw,Alexander,	1	10	Wash.
Putman,Edward,	1		Cul.
Putman,Daniel,	1		Cul.
Putney,Ellis,		3	Buck.
Putney,James,	1	10	Din.
Pyle,William,	1	9	Berk.
Pynes,Benjamin,	3	6	K.&Q
Pynes,Benjamin,Jr.,			K.&Q
Pynes,Clement,	1		K.&Q
Pynes,Nathaniel,	1	1	K.Wm.
Pyrtle,John,	1	4	Henry
Pysell,Adam,	1		Berk.
Pyzell,Bostian,	1		Berk.
Pysell,Peter,	1		Berk.
Quaintance,William,	3		Fau.
Qualls,David,	1		Bot.
Qualls,John,	1		Buck.
Qualy,Patrick,	1	5	Berk.
Quarles,Aaron,	1	10	K.Wm.
Quarles,Ann,	1	4	K.Wm.
Quarles,Dorothy,		7	K.Wm.
Quarles,Frances,		1	K.Wm.
Quarles,Hannah,		13	K.Wm.
Quarles,Henry,		7	K.Wm.
Quarles,Isaac,	1	23	K.Wm.
Quarles,Jack,		3	K.Wm.
Quarles,James,	1	15	K.Wm.
Quarles,James,	1	10	Brun.
Quarles,James,Jr.,	1		Brun.
Quarles,Col.John,		6	Bed.
Quarles,John,	2	16	K.Wm.
Quarles,John,	1	1	Din.
Quarles,John,	1	12	Camp.
Quarles,John,	1	7	Brun.
Quarles,John,est.,			K.Wm.
Quarles,Moses,	1	15	Brun.
Quarles,Moses,Jr.,	1	1	Brun.
Quarles,Roger,	1	31	Caro.
Quarles,Samuel,	1		Brun.
Quarles,Thomas,		5	K.Wm.
Quarles,William,	1	33	Spots.
Quarles,William,	1	4	Bed.
Quarles,William,	2	5	Caro.
Queen,John,	1		Lou.
Queen,John,Jr.,	1		Lou.
Quesenberry,James,	1		Fau.
Quesenberry,James,	1		Fau.
Quesenbury,James,	1	1	Pr.Wm
Quick,Casper,	1		Lou.
Quick,John,	1		Lou.
Quick,Tunis,	2		Brun.
Quinn,Benjamin,	1	3	Cul.
Quinn,James,	1	5	Cul.
Quinn,John,	1	2	Cul.
Quinn,Jinney,	1	4	Cul.
Quinn,Richard,Sr.,	1	6	Cul.
Quinn,Richard,Jr.,	1		Cul.
Quinsberry,James,	1	2	Fay.
Quisenbury,Elizabeth,			K.Geo
Quisenbury,James,	1	10	West.
Quisenbury,Nicholas,	1	4	West.
Quisenbury,William,	1		West.
Rabourn,Robert,	1		Lin.
Racey,Elkana,	1		Fay.
Rachell,Susanna,		10	Din.
Radcliff,Benjamin,	1	1	Har.
Radcliff,Edward,	1		Har.
Radcliff,Richard,	1		Har.
Radcliff,Stephen,	2		Har.
Radebaugh,Adam,	1		Har.
Radebaugh,Henry,	1		Har.
Radebough,John,	3		Har.
Radford,John,	2	7	Buck.
Radford,John,	2	1	Henry
Radford,William,			Lun.
Rafferty,Easter,			Wash.
Ragan,Robert,	1		Caro.
Ragland,Isaac,	2	7	Gooch.
Ragland,Jacob,	1		Bed.
Ragland,John,	1	19	Loui.
Ragland,John,			Hen.
Ragland,John,Jr.,	1	1	Hen.
Ragland,Judith,	1	8	Loui.
Ragland,Rhodes,			Loui.
Ragland,Samuel,	1	15	Loui.
Ragland,Samuel,	1	37	Loui.
Ragland,William,	1	13	Loui.
Raglin,Edward,	1	1	Fay.
Raglin,James,	1	2	Fay.
Ragon,Amos,	1		Lin.
Ragsdale,Drury,	1		Lun.
Ragsdale,Drury,		7	K.Wm.
Ragsdale,Edward,	1	5	Lun.
Ragsdale,John,	1	6	Lun.
Ragsdale,Capt.John,	1	13	Lun.
Ragsdale,John,Sr.,	1	10	Lun.
Ragsdale,John,Jr.,	1		Lun.
Ragsdale,Joseph,	1	11	Lun.
Ragsdale,Joshua,	1	6	Lun.
Ragsdale,Milly,		3	Lun.
Ragsdale,Samuel,	1		Lun.
Ragsdale,William,	1	1	Lun.
Ragsdale,William,	1	21	Pr.Geo.
Rail,Peter,	1		Berk.
Pailey,John,	1		Lin.
Railey,Thomas,	1	4	Fau.
Raine, G.	1	1	Pr.Wm.
Raine,Nathaniel,	1	9	Gooch.
Raines,Allen,	2		Cul.
Raines,Ambrose,	1	1	Bed.
Raines,Charles,	1	2	Pr.Geo
Raines,Epharim,	1	11	Pr.Geo
Raines,Hannah,			Bed.
Raines,Hartwell,	1	25	Pr.Geo.
Raines,Isaac,	1		Caro.
Ranes,James,	1		Cul.
Raines,James,			Cul.
Raines,John,	2	4	Pr.Geo
Raines,Nathaniel,	1	19	Pr.Geo
Raines,Phebea,		6	Pr.Geo
Rainey,Herbert,	1		Brun.
Rainey,William,Sr.,	1	2	Brun.
Rainey,William,Jr.,			Brun.
Rains,James,	1		Spots.
Rains,John,	1		Lou.
Rainy,Frederick,			Brun.
Rainy,Thomas,	2	4	Pr.Wm.
Rainy,William,			Pr.Wm.
Raisher,John,	1		Berk.
Reisor,George,	1		Lou.
Raizer,Abraham,	1		Mont.
Raiser,Peter,	1		Mont.
Raizer,Paul,	1		Mont.
Rakes,Henry,	2		Buck.
Rakes,William,	1		Buck.
Raley,John,	1		Hen.
Raley,Phillip,	1		Henry
Ralliff,Reuben,	1		Bot.
Railliff,Richard,	1		Bot.
Ralls,Natt,	1	1	Pr.Wm
Ralston,John,	1		Aug.
Ralston,Matthew,	1		Bot.
Ralston,Samuel,	1		Aug.
Ralston,William,	1		Aug.
Ramey,Daniel,	1	1	Fay.
Ramey,Daniel,	1	4	Henry
Ramey,James,			Lou.
Ramey,Jacob,	1		West.
Ramey,Jacob,	1	6	Lou.
Ramey,Sandford,	1	1	Henry
Ramines,Leton,	1		Bot.
Ramsay,Catherine,	1	6	So'n
Ramsay,Henry,	1	4	So'n
Ramsay,Patrick,est.		24	
Ramsbottom,James,	1		Cul.
Ramsey,Anderson,	1		Brun.
Ramsey,Andrew,	1		Aug.
Ramsey,Benjamin,	1	1	Ja.Cy
Ramsey,Charles,	1		Aug.
Ramsey,George,	1		Henry
Ramsey,James,	1	1	Rock.
Ramsey,James,	1		Henry
Ramsey,John,	1		Henry
Ramsey,John,	1	4	Aug.
Ramsey,John,	1		Aug.
Ramsey,John,	1		Aug.
Ramsey,John,Jr.,	1	5	Aug.
Ramsey,Josiah,	2		Mont.
Ramsey,Larkin,	2		Lin.
Ramsey,Patrick,	1	22	Brun.
Ramsey,Richard,	1		Bot.
Ramsey,Richard,	1	5	Brun.
Ramsey,Robert,	2		Wash.
Ramsey,Samuel,			Acco.
Ramsey,Samuel,	1		Rock.
Ramsey,Sarah,			Ja.Cy
Ramsey,William,	1	7	Rock.
Ramy,Prisley,	1		Berk.
Randal,Thomas,	2	4	West.
Randall,Abel,	2		Har.
Randall,Alexander,	1		Har.
Randall,George,	1		Berk.
Randall,Jacob,	1		Har.
Randall,John,	1		Fau.
Randall,John,			Pr.Wm.
Randall,John,	1		Henry
Randall,Jonas,	1		Lou.
Randall,Jonathan,	1		Lou.
Randall,Samuel,	1		Henry
Randall,William,	1		Fau.
Randell,John,	1	6	Fay.
Randle,Beverly,	1	5	Brun.
Randle,Isham,	1		Brun.
Randle,James,	1	13	Brun.
Randle,John,	1		Berk.
Randle,William,	1	15	Brun.
Randle,Richard,	1		Mont.
Randolp,William,	1	28	Ja.Cy
Randolph,Beverley,	1	6	Hen.
Randolph,Harrison,	1	13	Hen.
Randolph,Henry,	2	14	Din.
Randolph,Hull,	1	2	Cul.
Randolph,Isham,		1	Pr.Geo.
Randolph,John,	1	14	Din.
Randolph,Peyton,	3	103	Hen.
Randolph,Richard,	2	74	Hen.
Randolph,Richard,Jr.			Hen.
Randolph,Thomas,	1	17	Buck.
Randolph,Thomas,	1		Lou.
Randolph,Thomas,	1	35	Gooch.
Randolph,Thomas M.,	1	37	Hen.
Randolph,Thomas,M.,	4	193	Gooch.
Randolph,William,	1		Eli.Cy
Randon,John,	1		Rock.
Ranes,Giles,	1	9	Caro.
Raney,Buckner,	1	6	Din.
Raney,Daniel,	1	3	Din.
Raney,John,	1		Pr.Geo.
Raney,Robert,	1		Lou.
Range,Peter,	1		Berk.
Rankin,Benjamin,	2	14	Berk.
Rankin,David,	1		Berk.
Rankin,George,	1		Berk.
Rankin,James,	1	3	Aug.
Rankin,John,	1		Aug.
Rankin,Richard,	1	1	Aug.
Rankin,Robert,	1	3	Aug.
Rankin,Capt.Thomas,	1	3	Aug.

Name			County
Rankin,Thomas,	1		Aug.
Rankin,William,	1		Mont.
Rankin,William,			Aug.
Rankin,William,	1		Berk.
Rankin,William,	1		Fay.
Rankins,Benjamin,			Fay.
Rankins,Elizabeth,			K.Geo
Rankins,John,	1		K.Geo
Rankins,Reuben,	1	4	Fau.
Rankins,Sarah,			K.Geo
Rankins,William,	1		K.Geo
Rannels,William,	1		Mont.
Ransdell,John,	1	4	Fau.
Ransdell,Wharton,	1	3	Fau.
Ransdell,Wharton,	1	5	Fau.
Ransdell,Capt.Wharton	2	16	Fau.
Ransom, J.	1		Pr.Wm
Ransone,Flamstead,	1	10	Buck.
Ransone,Richard,	1	18	Berk.
Rascon,James,	1	3	Berk.
Rases,William,	1	8	Nor.
Rash,John,	1		Lun.
Ratcliff,John,	1	2	York.
Ratcliff,Thomas,	1	1	Rock.
Ratcliff,William,	1	2	York
Ratcliff,Zaphania,			Pr.Wm
Ratcliffe,Thomas,			Hen.
Rateliff,Edward,	1		Lou.
Rathborn,John,	1		Mont.
Rathborn,John,	1		Mont.
Rather,William,	1	3	Din.
Ratliff,James,	1		Camp.
Ratliff,James,	1		Loui.
Ratliff,John,	1		Henry
Ratliff,Robert,	1		Cul.
Ratliff,Silas,	1		Henry
Ratliff,William,	1		Cul.
Rattekin,James,	1		Lou.
Rattikin,John,	1		Camp.
Rattikin,John,	1		Camp.
Rattekin,Patrick,	1		Camp.
Rattering,Adam,	1		Mont.
Rause,Palsen,	1		Wash.
Ravenscroft,Charles,	1		K.Wm.
Rawlaneu, * * ,			Rock.
Rawleigh,John,	1	11	Ja.Cy
Rawlings,Henry,	1	4	Brun.
Rawlings,Henry,	1		K.Geo
Rawlings,John,	1	20	Brun.
Rawlings,James,Sr.,	1	2	K.Geo
Rawlings,James,Sr.,	1	12	Spots
Rawlings,John,	1	3	Brun.
Rawlings,Joseph,	1		K.Geo
Rawlings,Joseph,Sr.,	1		K.Geo
Rawlings,Joseph,Jr.,	1		K.Geo
Rawlings,Margaret,		8	Pr.Wm
Rawlings,Reace,			Brun.
Rawlings,Richard,	1	4	K.Geo
Rawlings,Richmond,			Din.
Rawlings,Robert,	1	4	Hen.
Rawlings,Samuel,	1		K.Geo
Rawlings,Sarah,	1		K.Geo
Rawlings,Susanna,		3	Pr.Wm
Rawlings,William,	1	2	Lou.
Rawlings,William,			K.Geo
Rawlings,William,Jr.	1	1	Brun.
Rawlings,William,Sr.	2	2	Brun.
Rawlins,Baron,			Brun.
Rawlins, J.	1		Pr.Wm
Rawlins,Jeremiah,	3	15	Caro.
Rawlins,John,		4	Caro.
Rawlins,Samuel,	1	8	Caro.
Rawlins,Vincent,	1		York.
Rawls,Hardy,	2	1	Lin.
Rawlsback,John,	1		Cul.
Ray,Andrew,	1	?	Henry
Ray,Ann,		11	Spots.
Ray,Daniel,	1	1	Aug.
Ray,John,	1	1	So'n
Ray,Joseph,	1		Aug.
Ray,Luke,	1		Berk.
Ray,Luke,	1	5	Bed.
Ray,Nathaniel,	1		Brun.
Ray,Robert,	1		Berk.
Ray,Samuel,	1		Berk.
Ray,Thomas,	1		Lou.
Ray,Thomas,	1		Henry
Ray,William,	1		Lin.
Rayburn,David,	1		Mont.
Rayburn,Robert,	1		Fay.
Rayburn,William,Sr.,	1		Mont.
Rayfield,Curtis,	3		Acco.
Rayfield,Jacob,	2		Acco.
Rayfield,Major,	1		Acco.
Rayfield,Peter,	1	1	Acco.
Rayfield,William,			Acco.
Raysor,George,	4		Cul.
Razor,Christian,	1		Cul.
Razor,Jacob,			Cul.
Razor,Peter,			Cul.
Rea,Benjamin,		1	Henry
Rea,James,		1	Henry
Rea,John,		1	Henry
Reaburn,George,		1	Mont.
Reaburn,Robert,		1	Mont.
Reaburn,James,Sr.,		1	Bot.
Reaburn,James,Jr.,		1	Bot.
Reaburn,John,		1	Aug.
Reaburn,John,	1	2	Bot.
Reace,Richard,			Brun.
Reach,James,	1	1	Fau.
Reach,James,		1	Cha.Cy
Read,Andrew,		1	Bed.
Read,Andrew,	1	31	West.
Read,Elizabeth,		1	Camp.
Read,Francis,	1	3	Bed.
Read,Gaspar,		1	Bot.
Read,George,		1	Bed.
Read,George,Sr.,		1	Bot.
Read,George,Jr.,		1	Bot.
Read,Griffin,			Cul.
Read,Hankenson,	2	12	Cul.
Read,Dr.J.K.,	1	2	Gooch.
Read,James,	3	7	Cul.
Read,James,			Cul.
Read,James,	1	3	Bed.
Read,John,	1	11	Brun.
Read,John,			Cul.
Read,John,			Cul.
Read,John,			Cul.
Read,John,	2	8	Acco.
Read,John,	1		So'n
Read,John,	2	14	Henry
Read,Jonathan,	1		Lou.
Read,Jones,		3	Bed.
Read,Peter,	1	1	Bot.
Read,Peter,	1	1	Bot.
Read,Richard,	1	8	Acco.
Read,Robert,	1		Bot.
Read,Robert,	1		K.&Q
Read,Samuel,	2	4	Cul.
Read,Samuel,			Cul.
Read,Samuel,	2		Bot.
Read,Tabitha,	1	1	Acco.
Read,Torobable,			Acco.
Read,William,	1	19	Bed.
Read,William,	1	3	Acco.
Read,William,			Pr.Wm.
Read,William,	1	7	Camp.
Read,William,	1	5	Brun.
Read,Zachariah,	1		Camp.
Reace,Hawkins,	1	12	York
Reade,John,	1		Pr.Wm.
Reader,Benjamin,	1		Cul.
Readin,William,	1		Cul.
Readock,Collin,	1	7	Hen.
Reah,Archibald,	1		Rock.
Reah,William,	1	1	Rock.
Ream,John,	1		Berk.
Reames,John,	1		Din.
Reames,Wood,	1	2	Din.
Reams,Edward,	2	1	Din.
Reams,Jesse,	1		Din.
Reams,Robert,			Din.
Reams,Simion,	1	1	Din.
Reamy,Daniel,	1	1	West.
Reamy,John,	1		Wash.
Reany,Matthew,	1		Henry
Reany,Stephen,	1		Henry
Rease,David,	1		Henry
Rease,John,	1		Cul.
Rease,John,	1		Mont.
Reason,Hemson Veach,	1		Har.
Reasons,William,			Cul.
Reaugh,Archibald,	1		Mont.
Reaugh,James,	1	1	Aug.
Reaugh,John,	1		Mont.
Reaves,William,	1		Brun.
Rector,Benjamin,	2	4	Fau.
Rector,Charles,	1		Fau.
Rector,Frederick,	1	2	Fau.
Rector,Harman,	1	2	Fau.
Rector,Henry,Sr.,	1		Fau.
Rector,Henry,Jr.,	1		Fau.
Rector,Jacob,Sr.,	1	4	Fau.
Rector,Jacob,Jr.,	1		Fau.
Rector,James,	1		Fau.
Rector,Jane,		1	Camp.
Rector,Jesse,	1		Fau.
Rector,John,	1		Fau.
Rector,Mary,		8	Fau.
Rector,Nathaniel,	1		Fau.
Rector,Peter,	1		Fau.
Rector,Uriah,	1		Bot.
Red.Allen,	1	3	Fau.
Red,Richard,	1		Hen.
Redcross,John,	1		York
Redd,Frances,		10	K.Wm.
Redd,James,	1	8	Caro.
Redd,James,	1	16	Spots.
Redd,John,	1	8	Gooch.
Redd,John,	1		Henry
Redd,John,	1	9	K.Wm.
Redd,Mordecai,	1	5	Spots.
Redd,Samuel,	2	16	Caro.
Redd,Thomas,	1	21	K.Wm.
Redd,William,	1	14	Caro.
Reddick,John,	1		Mont.
Reddick,Solomon,	1		Mont.
Reddick,William,Jr.,	1		Mont.
Reddiford,John,	1		Lin.
Reddiford,Joseph,	1	1	Lin.
Redding,James,	1		Aug.
Redding,John,	1	2	Pr.Geo.
Redding,Matthew,	1	1	Brun.
Redding,Rachel,		1	Pr.Geo.
Redding,William,	1		Fau.
Redford,Edward,	1	7	Gooch.
Redford,Francis,	2		Hen.
Redford,James,	1	4	Hen.
Redford,John,	1	4	Hen.
Redford,John,			Hen.
Redford,Milner,	1	13	Gooch.
Redford,Milner,	1	3	Hen.
Redford,Milner,Jr.,	1	3	Hen.
Redford,Ware,			Hen.
Redford,William C.,	2	1	Hen.
Redford,William,Jr.,			Hen.

Name			Place
Redman,Ann,		4	West.
Redman,Harmon,	1		Cul.
Redman,Henry Sissom,	1	20	West.
Redman,Jacob,	1		Cul.
Redman,John,	1		Cul.
Redman,Nathaniel,	1		Cul.
Redman,Patrick,	1		Cul.
Redman,Samuel,			Cul.
Redmond,Ignatious,	1		Henry
Redmond,John,			Lou.
Redmond,Rhodum,	1		Henry
Redmore,Stephen,	1		Bot.
Redshaw,Joseph,	1		Wash.
Redsleeve,Michael,	1		Har.
Redwood,John,	1		So'n.
Redwood,William,			Lou.
Reeble,Richard,		1	Pr.Wm.
Reece,David,	1		Lou.
Reece,Lewis,	1		Lou.
Reed,Alexander,	1	1	Aug.
Reed,Andrew,	1		Lou.
Reed,Cornelius,	1		Lou.
Reed,Edmund,	2	14	Acco.
Reed,Elizabeth,		1	Har.
Reed,George,	1	2	Har.
Reed,James,	1		Aug.
Reed,James,	1		Lou.
Reed,Jasper,	1		Berk.
Reed,John,	3		Berk.
Reed,John,	1		Lin.
Reed,John,	1	5	Lin.
Reed,John,	1	5	Lou.
Reed,John,	1		Har.
Reed,Joseph,	2		Lou.
Reed,Levern,	1	2	Acco.
Reed,Reuben,			Lou.
Reed,Robert,	1	8	Aug.
Reed,Robert,	1		Aug.
Reed,Samuel,	1		Hen.
Reed,Solomon,	1	3	Acco.
Reed,Solomon,			Berk.
Reed,Stephen,	1		Lou.
Reed,Thomas,	1	1	Bot.
Reed,William,	1	4	Lin.
Reed,William,	1	5	Lou.
Reed,William,	1		Lou.
Reeder,Jacob,			Lou.
Reeder,John,	1		Lou.
Reeder,Joseph,	1		Lou.
Reeder,Thomas,	1		Lou.
Reeder,William,	1		Lou.
Reeder,William,	1		Lou.
Reedy,Isaac,	1		Bed.
Reedy,John,	1		Berk.
Reedy,William,	1		Bed.
Reel,David,Sr.,	1		Har.
Reel,David,Jr.,			Har.,
Reel,Michael,	1		Henry
Reel,Nicholas,	1		Har.
Reeley,Andrew,	1		Berk.
Reeley,John,	3		Berk.
Reeley,Thomas,	1		Berk.
Rees,David,	2		Berk.
Rees,Amey,		7	Din.
Rees,Edward,	1	9	Din.
Rees,Francis,	1	1	Din.
Rees,Frederick,	1	2	Din.
Rees,Henry,	1	17	Din.
Rees,Hugh,	1	7	Din.
Rees,Isham,	1	9	Din.
Rees,Jacob,	2		Berk.
Rees,Jacob,	1		Berk.
Rees,James,	1	1	Din.
Rees,John,Jr.,	1		Berk.
Rees,Jordan,	1	9	Din.
Rees,Josiah,	1	3	Din.
Rees,Mary,			Lou.
Rees,Morris,	1		Berk.
Rees,Robert,	1		Din.
Rees,Thomas,	1		Loui.
Rees,Thomas,	2		Berk.
Rees,William,	1	1	Din.
Rees,William,	1	6	Din.
Rees,William,	1	1	Din.
Reese,Caleb,	1		Mont.
Reese,David,	1		Mont.
Reese,Hannah,		3	Pr.Geo.
Reese,Isham,	1		Brun.
Reese,John,	1	7	So'n.
Reese,Joseph,	1	15	So'n.
Reese,Mary,		8	So'n.
Reese,Olive,		7	So'n.
Reese,Randolph,	1		So'n.
Reese,Thomas,	1	7	Pr.Geo.
Reesler,William,	1		Lou.
Reeve,Christian,	1		Lou.
Reeves,A.,			Pr.Wm.
Reeves,George,	1	3	Mont.
Reeves,J.,	1	5	Pr.Wm.
Reeves,Jane,			Pr.Wm.
Reeves,John,	1		Bed.
Reeves,John,	1		Pr.Geo.
Reeves,Jonathan,			Pr.Wm.
Reeves,Joseph,	1	9	Pr.Geo.
Reeves,Nathaniel,	1		Berk.
Refia,George,	1		Cul.
Refia,Jacob,	2		Cul.
Refia,Jacob,Jr.,			Cul.
Regar,Anthony,	1		Har.
Regar,Burkett,	1		Berk.
Regar,Leonard,	1		Berk.
Regney,Charles,	1		Mont.
Reid,Adam,	1		Rock.
Reid,Alexander,			Hen.
Reid,Andrew,	1	1	Rock.
Reid,Daniel,	1		Rock.
Reid,Hermon,	1		Brun.
Reid,Jacob,	1		Lou.
Reid,James,	1	9	Brun.
Reid,James,	1		Camp.
Reid,Michael,	1		Rock.
Reid,Patrick,	1		Rock.
Reid,Thomas,	1		Rock.
Reid,Thomas,	1		Din.
Reid,William,	1		Rock.
Reins,Giles,	1	9	K.Wm.
Reins,John,	1	5	K.Wm.
Reins,John,			Buck.
Reins,John,			Hen.
Reives,Jeremiah,		6	Pr.Geo.
Reives,John,	1	1	Pr.Geo.
Reives,Mary,		8	Pr.Geo.
Reives,Timothy,	1	11	Pr.Geo.
Reives,Capt,Timothy,	1	6	Pr.Geo.
Reives,William,	2	21	Pr.Geo.
Remey,Sandford,	2	12	Lou.
Render,Joshua,	2	5	Cul.
Render,Lewis,	1	1	Cul.
Render,Robert,	1	1	Cul.
Reney,John,	1		Wash.
Renicks,William,	2		Lin.
Renix,James,	1		Lin.
Renix,John,	1		Har.
Renix,William,	1	3	Har.
Rennard,Richard,	1	5	Hen.
Renno,Stephen,	1		Henry
Rennoch,Samuel,	1	2	Aug.
Rennolds,Elizabeth,		7	Caro.
Rennolds,Elizabeth,		6	Caro.
Rennolds,Jacob,	1	5	Caro.
Rennolds,Rob,	1		Caro.
Rennolds,William,	1		Caro.
Renny,John,	1		Berk.
Reno,David,	1	5	Pr.Wm.
Reno,Eli,	1	1	Pr.Wm.
Reno,Enoch,	1	2	Pr.Wm.
Reno,Lewis,	1	1	Pr.Wm.
Renock,Robert,	1	2	Aug.
Renolds,Phillip,	1		Loui.
Renolds,Robert,	1	2	K.Geo.
Rentfro,John,	1	5	Henry
Rentfro,John,	1		Henry
Rentfro,Joshua,	1	5	Henry
Rentfro,Mark,	1	5	Henry
Rentfro,Moses,	1	2	Henry
Rentfro,William,	1	2	Henry
Rentfro,William,	1	3	Henry
Rentfroe,Isaac,	1	2	Bed.
Rentfroe,John,	1		Mont.
Rentfroe,Samuel,	1		Mont.
Reonald,William,	1		Loui.
Rep,John,	1		Fay.
Reresh,Nicholas,	1		Berk.
Resor,Martin,	1		Berk.
Respress,Thomas,	2	19	Lou.
Ressor,David,	1	7	Camp.
Retherford,John,	1		Bot.
Reticoe,Amava,	1		Lou.
Reudesellor,Jacob,	1		Cul.
Revel,Holliday,	1	1	So'n
Revely,John,	1	9	Buck.
Rever,Sithman,	1		Har.
Revil,Edward,	2	11	Acco.
Revil,John,	2	11	Acco.
Rew,Charles,	1		Acco.
Rexrout,George,	1		Aug.
Reyburn,George,	1		Bot.
Reyburn,Henry,			Bot.
Reyburn,James,	1		Bot.
Reyburn,John,	1	1	Bot.
Reynold,Joseph,	1	3	K.Wm.
Reynolds,Bartlett,	1		Henry
Reynolds,Benjamin,	1	3	Spots.
Reynolds,Charles,	1		Bed.
Reynolds,Cornelius,	1	1	Lou.
Reynolds,Elizabeth,	2	13	Caro.
Reynolds,George,	3		Berk.
Reynolds,George,	1		Henry
Reynolds,Isaac,	1	1	Camp.
Reynolds,James,	1	14	Caro.
Reynolds,James,	1		Bot.
Reynolds,James,	1	1	Lun.
Reynolds,James,	1		Camp.
Reynolds,James,	1		Camp.
Reynolds,Jesse,	1		Cul.
Reynolds,Jesse,	1		Bed.
Reynolds,Jessee,	1		Henry
Reynolds,John,	1		Bed.
Reynolds,John,	1		Lou.
Reynolds,John,	1		K.Wm.
Reynolds,John,	1		Bot.
Reynolds,John,	1		Camp.
Reynolds,John,	1		Camp.
Reynolds,John,	1		Camp.
Reynolds,John,	1		Berk.
Reynolds,Jones,	1	3	Bed.
Reynolds,Richard,	1		Henry
Reynolds,Susannah,			Henry
Reynolds,Thomas,	1	6	K.Wm.
Reynolds,William,			Camp.
Reynolds,William,			Camp.
Reynolds,William,	1		Bot.
Reynolds,William,	1	16	York
Reyns,Zele,	1	1	Lou.
Rhea,John,	1	1	Aug.
Rhea,William,	1	1	Aug.
Rhimore,George,	1		Aug.
Rhoads,Thomas,	1		Aug.

Name	A	B	County
Rhodes,Bazil,	1		Lou.
Rhodes,Randle,	1		Lun.
Rhodes,Robert,	1		Rock.
Rhodes,Tholemiah,	1		Berk.
Rhodes,William,	1	5	Lun.
Rhodes,William,	1	5	Lun.
Rhodes,William,	1		Lou.
Riblin,William,	1		Fay.
Rice,Benjamin,	1	2	Bed.
Rice,Charles,	1	3	Bed.
Rice,Charles,	1		Fay.
Rice,Charles,	1		Lin.
Rice,Charles,	1	6	Gooch.
Rice,Daniel,			Henry
Rice,David,	1	1	Bed.
Rice,Fisher,	2	7	Cul.
Rice,George,	1		Buck.
Rice,James,	1		Lou.
Rice,James,	1		Mont.
Rice,John,	1		Rock.
Rice,John,	1	3	Mont.
Rice,John,	1	2	West.
Rice,Nicholas,	1		Berk.
Rice,Richard,	1	1	Cul.
Rice,Sarah,		7	Cul.
Rice,Simon,	1	1	Cul.
Rice,Spencer,	1		Mont.
Rice,William,	1	2	Brun.
Rice,William,	1	9	Loui.
Rice,William,	1		Mont.
Rice,William,	2	7	West.
Rice,William,	1		Fau.
Rich,Nimrod,	1		Camp.
Rich,Samuel,	1		Lou.
Richard,Christian,	1		Bot.
Richards,Benjamin,	1		Lou.
Richards,Certia,		14	K.Wm.
Richards,Chillamon,	1	12	Aug.
Richards,Edward,	1	6	Henry
Richards,George,	1	3	K.&Q
Richards,Isaac,	1		Bot.
Richards,James,			Spots.
Richards,John,	1	3	Pr.Geo
Richards,John,		12	K.&Q
Richards,John,			K.&Q
Richards,John,	1	1	Bed.
Richards,John,	1		Gooch.
Richards,John,	1	1	Spots.
Richards,Joshua,	1		Berk.
Richards,Josiah,	2		Fay.
Richards,Mary,		10	K.&Q
Richards,Richard,	2		Bed.
Richards,Richard,	1		Lou.
Richards,Robert,	1	3	Fay.
Richards,Robert,	1	3	Wash.
Richards,Shadrick,	1	1	Henry
Richards,Stephen,	1		Wash.
Richards,Thomas,	1	1	Camp.
Richards,Coleman V.,	2	6	Pr.Geo
Richards,William,		4	Spots.
Richards,William,	1		Gooch.
Richards,William,	1		Fay.
Richards,William,	1	5	Henry
Richards,William,	1	25	K.&Q
Richards,William,	1	6	K.&Q
Richardson,Amos,	1	2	Henry
Richardson,Amos,Jr.,	1		Henry
Richardson,Benjamin,	1		Bot.
Richardson,Benjamin,			Hen.
Richardson,Charles,	1	6	Acco.
Richardson,Daniel,	1		Acco.
Richardson,Daniel,	1		Acco.
Richardson,Daniel,	1	9	Henry
Richardson,Daniel,	1		Har.
Richardson,Dudley,	2	15	Ja.Cy
Richardson,Dudley,	1	10	Loui.
Richardson,George,			Hen.

Name	A	B	County
Richardson,George,	1	35	Gooch.
Richardson,Isham,	1	13	Gooch.
Richardson,James,	1		Bot.
Richardson,James,	1		Acco.
Richardson,James,			Loui.
Richardson,Jane,			Bed.
Richardson,Jessey,	1		Lin.
Richardson,Joel,	1		Bot.
Richardson,John,			Henry
Richardson,John,	1		Henry
Richardson,John,	1		West.
Richardson,John,	2		Acco.
Richardson,John,	1		Berk.
Richardson,John,	1		Loui.
Richardson,John,	2		Mont.
Richardson,John,Jr.,	1		Camp.
Richardson,Jonathan,	1		Har.
Richardson,Joseph,	1		Bot.
Richardson,Joseph,	1		Lin.
Richardson,Joshua,	1		Mont.
Richardson,Kendal,	1		Acco.
Richardson,Landie,	1	13	Loui.
Richardson,Levi,	1		Acco.
Richardson,Matthew,			Hen.
Richardson,Richard,	1	2	Pr.Geo
Richardson,Richard,	1		Loui.
Richardson,Robert,			York.
Richardson,Samuel,	1	15	Gooch.
Richardson,Stanup,	1		Henry
Richardson,Walker,	1	16	Ja.Cy
Richardson,William,	1	1	Brun.
Richardson,William,	1	6	Brun.
Richardson,William,	3	44	Ja.Cy
Richardson,William,	1		Loui.
Richardson,William,			Har.
Richardson,William,	1		Berk.
Richardson,William,	2	4	Hen.
Richardson,William,	1		Acco.
Richardson,William,	1		Acco.
Richardson,William,	1		Acco.
Richardson,William,	2		Lin.
Richer,Peter,	1		Berk.
Richerson,Elias,	2	1	K.&Q
Richerson,George,	1	4	Caro.
Richeson,Giles,	1	6	Caro.
Richeson,Holt,	1	34	K.Wm.
Richerson,James,	1	2	K.&Q
Richerson,James,			K.&Q
Richerson,Joseph,	3	18	Caro.
Richerson,Peter,	1	12	K.Wm.
Richerson,Rachel,		3	K.&Q
Richerson,William,	1	3	K.&Q
Richeson,Elizabeth,		8	Caro.
Richeson,James,	1		Bed.
Richeson,Capt.Jona'n,	1		Bed.
Richeson,Joseph,	1		Bed.
Richeson,Thomas,	1	12	Caro.
Richeson,Thomas,	1		Bed.
Richeson,William,	1		Mont.
Richeson,William,	1	1	Caro.
Richey,Robert,	1		Mont.
Richey,Samuel,	1		Mont.
Richie,Alexander,	1		Lin.
Richie,James,		2	K.Wm.
Richie,James,	1		Lun.
Richie,James,	1	2	Bed.
Richman,Elizabeth,	1	23	Cha.Cy
Rickman,Peter,			Henry
Richmond,John,	1	3	Henry
Ricks,Ann,		16	So'n
Ricks,Mary,		10	So'n
Ricks,Richard,	1	5	So'n
Ricks,Richard,est,		16	So'n
Ricks,Robert,	1	5	So'n
Riddle,George,	1		Lou.
Riddle,Matthew,	1		Gooch.
Riddle,Moses,	1		Lin.

Name	A	B	County
Riddle,Rebecca,		8	Caro.
Riddle,Thomas,	1	9	Gooch.
Riddle,Wellinder,	1		Caro.
Riddle,William,	1	3	Caro.
Riddle,William,	1		Fau.
Riddle,Zachariah,	1		Lou.
Riddle,Zachariah,	1		Lou.
Riddlehurst,Francis,	1	7	Eli.Cy
Riddlehurst,Judith,		9	Cha.Cy
Riddlehurst,William,		4	Cha.Cy
Riden,George,		4	Spots.
Ridenbaugh,Frederick	1		Lou.
Rideout,John,	1		Brun.
Rideout,William,	1	4	Brun.
Rider,Alexander,Sr.,	1	1	Cul.
Rider,Alexander,Jr.,	1		Cul.
Rider,John,	1		Lou.
Rider,Thomas,	1		Lou.
Rider,William,	1		Aug.
Ridgecreek,John,	1		Lou.
Ridgecreek,Phillip,			Lou.
Ridgle,Mariam,			Lin.
Ridgway,John,	1	13	Berk.
Ridgway,John,Jr.,	1		Berk.
Ridgway,Phebe,		7	Buck.
Ridgway,Philip,	1	2	Berk.
Ridgway,Richard,	1		Berk.
Ridgway,Richard,	1	6	Buck.
Ridgway,Samuel,	1		Buck.
Ridgway,William,	1	1	Berk.
Riding,George,	1	8	K.Geo.
Riding,William,	1	12	K.Geo.
Ridinour,Joseph,			Aug.
Ridle,Moses,	1		Henry
Ridley,Sarah,		24	So'n
Ridley,Maj.Thomas,		25	So'n
Reid,Abraham,	1		Wash.
Reid,Elizabeth,			Rock.
Reid,John,	1		Wash.
Reid,Joseph,	1		Rock.
Rieley,Garat,	1		Berk.
Rieley,George,	3	3	Berk.
Rieley,George,	1		Berk.
Rieley,Thomas,	1		Berk.
Rieves,Bathia,		9	Pr.Geo.
Rieves,Elizabeth,		8	Pr.Geo.
Rieves,Frederick,	1	13	Henry
Rieves,George,	1		Henry
Rieves,William,	2	11	Din.
Rievly,John,	1		Cul.
Rigar,Burkett,	1		Berk.
Rigby,Alexander,	2	3	Pr.Wm.
Rigg,Thomas,	1		West.
Riggons,Moses,	1		Lun.
Right,Christopher,	1		Lin.
Right,Joseph,	1	1	Fay.
Rightmire,James,	1		Lou.
Rightsman,John,	1		Bot.
Riglesby,Christopher,	1	1	K.Geo.
Rigney,Charles,	1		Bot.
Rigsby,William,	1		Gooch.
Rihm,Tobias,	1		Bot.
Riley,Abraham,	2		Lou.
Riley,Ann,			Lou.
Riley,Barney,	1		Rock.
Riley,Bennett,			Acco.
Riley,Charles,	1		Fau.
Riley,Edward,	1		Fau.
Riley,Hugh,	1		Fau.
Riley,John,	1		West.
Riley,Robert,	1		Lou.
Rinehart,Matthias,	1		Cul.
Ringland,James,	3		Fay.
Ringland,Christopher	1		Wash.
Ringo,Cornelius,			Fay.
Ringo,H.,	1		Pr.Wm.
Ringo,P.,	1		Pr.Wm.

Name			Place	Name			Place	Name			Place
Ringoe,Cornelius,	2		Lou.	Roberson,Thomas,Jr.,	1		Henry	Robertson,Colin,			Hen.
Ringoe,Philip,	1		Lou.	Roberson,William,	1		Bed.	Robertson,David,	1	3	Din.
Ripley,Jacob,	1		Lou.	Roberson,William,	1		Fay.	Robertson,David,	1		Wash.
Ripley,Matthias,	1		Lou.	Roberts,Ann,		15	Nor.	Robertson,Donald,	1	9	K.& Q.
Ripley,Richard,	1	2	Buck.	Roberts,Arthur,	3	14	Acco.	Robertson,Field,			Hen.
Rippen,William,	1	1	Nor.	Roberts,Benjamin,	1		Aug.	Robertson,George,	1		Henry
Rippy,Matthew,	2		Berk.	Roberts,Benjamin,	1	5	Cul.	Robertson,George,	1		Pr.Wm.
Riser,Martin,	2		Berk.	Roberts,Burton,			Caro.	Robertson,Hannah,	1		Lin.
Rispass,John,	1	37	Nor.	Roberts,Charles,			Acco.	Robertson,Israel,	2	4	Cul.
Ritchey,Dr.Hugh,	1	10	Aug.	Roberts,Mrs.Christian,		3	Bed.	Robertson,James,	1	4	Bot.
Ritchey,James,	2		Rock.	Roberts,Cornelius,	1		Mont.	Robertson,James,	1		Fau.
Ritchey,John,	1		Aug.	Roberts,Daniel,	1		Berk.	Robertson,James,	1		Lou.
Ritchey,John,	2		Aug.	Roberts,David,Jr.,	1		Har.	Robertson,James,	1		Wash.
Ritchie,Adam,			Lou.	Roberts,Eleab,	1		Cul.	Robertson,James,	1	6	Camp.
Ritchie,Francis,	1		Lou.	Roberts,Eliza,		5	York.	Robertson,James,	1	1	Loui.
Ritchie,John,			Lou.	Roberts,Elizabeth,		5	York	Robertson,James,	1		Aug.
Ritchie,John,	2		Lun.	Roberts,George,	1	5	Cul.	Robertson,James,	2		Rock.
Ritchy,William,	1	3	Bot.	Roberts,Gerrard,			York	Robertson,James,			Rock.
Rivers,Joel,	1	5	Din.	Roberts,Hugh,	1	1	Cul.	Robertson,John,	1		Lou.
Rivers,John,			Lun.	Roberts,James,	1		Henry	Robertson,John,	2		Hen.
Rivers,John,	1	2	Brun.	Roberts,James,	1		Wash.	Robertson,John,	1		Fau.
Rivers,Robert,	1	5	Din.	Roberts,James,	1		Berk.	Robertson,John,	1	3	Lun.
Rivers,Thomas,	1	16	Brun.	Roberts,James,	1		York	Robertson,John,	1		Wash.
Rivers,William,	1	9	Din.	Roberts,James,	1		Bed.	Robertson,John,	1	6	Loui.
Rivers,William,	1	2	Lun.	Roberts,Jamis,	2		Bot.	Robertson,Joseph,	2	4	Fau.
Rives,Benjamin,	1	6	Brun.	Roberts,Joachim,	2	5	Acco.	Robertson,Mathew,	2		Rock.
Rives,William,	1		Pr.Wm.	Roberts,John,	2		Lou.	Robertson,Matthew,	1	6	Aug.
Rivis,John,	1		Mont.	Roberts,John,	1		Din.	Robertson,Osea,	1		Lin.
Rix,Nicholas,	1	9	Hen.	Roberts,John,			Cul.	Robertson,Samuel,			Cha.C.
Rixey,Richard,	1	9	Fau.	Roberts,John,	2	9	Cul.	Robertson,Samuel,	1		Loui,
Roach,Henry,	2		Fay.	Roberts,John,	1		Din.	Robertson,Samuel,	1		Wash.
Roach,James,	1		Lou.	Roberts,John,	1		Din.	Robertson,Thomas,	1		Rock.
Roach,James,	1	1	Pr.Wm.	Roberts,John,	1		Mont.	Robertson,William,	1	27	Din.
Roach,John,	1		Fau.	Roberts,John,	1		York	Robertson,William,	2	8	Aug.
Roach,Richard,Sr.,	1		Lou.	Roberts,John,	1		Bed.	Robertson,William,	1		Aug.
Roach,Richard,			Lou.	Roberts,John,		1	Bed.	Robertson,William,	1		Cul.
Roach,William,	1	2	Fau.	Roberts,Joseph,	2	30	Cul.	Robertson,William,	1		Fau.
Roads,Christian,	1		Lou.	Roberts,Joseph,	1	1	Cul.	Robertson,William,	1	39	Pr.Geo.
Roads,Jacob,	1		Fay.	Roberts,Joseph,Jr.,			Cul.	Robey,Benjamin,	1		Har.
Roan,Ann,	1	2	York	Roberts,Joshua,	1		Har.	Robey,Prior,	2		Har.
Roan,J.,			York	Roberts,Mark,	1		Nor.	Robins,Auther,	1	13	Nor.
Roan,John,	1		Pr.Wm.	Roberts,Mildred,		1	York	Robins,Charles,	1		Spots.
Roan,Thomas,	1	36	Caro.	Roberts,Morris,	1		Loui,	Robins,Edward,	1	9	Nor.
Roan,William,	2	1	York	Roberts,Moses,	1	2	Nor.	Robins,Elizabeth,		12	Nor.
Roane,Alexander,	1	7	Caro.	Roberts,Richard,	1	1	Cul.	Robins,Jonathan,	1		Mont.
Roane,Charles,	1	11	K.& Q.	Roberts,Richard,	1		Bed.	Robins,Jonathan,	1		Bot.
Roane,James,	1	4	Hen.	Roberts,Richard,	1		Bed.	Robins,Joshua,	1	6	Nor.
Roane,John,	1	57	K.Wm.	Roberts,Richardson,,	1		Lou.	Robins,Nelson,	1		Nor.
Roane,Major,	1	4	K.& Q.	Roberts,Samuel,	1	3	Brun.	Robins,Thomas,	1	1	Wash.
Roane,Thomas,	2	37	K.& Q.	Roberts,Samuel,	1	1	Berk.	Robins,Thomas,	1	7	Acco.
Roane,Thomas,		6	K.& Q.	Roberts,Sarah,		12	Cul.	Robins,William,	1		K.& Q.
Roane,William,	1	22	K.& Q.	Roberts,Thomas,	1		Berk.	Robinson,Absolam,	2		Fay.
Roark,Charles,	1		Mont.	Roberts,Thomas,	1	2	Brun.	Robinson,Alexander,	1		Berk.
Roark,Elijah,	1		Henry	Roberts,Thomas,	1		Henry	Robinson,Anthony,		8	York
Roark,John,	1		Henry	Roberts,Thomas,	1		Har.	Robinson,Benjamin,	1	16	Fau.
Roark,Timothy,	1		Mont.	Roberts,Thomas,	1		Din.	Robinson,Benjamin,	1	49	K.& Q.
Robards,George,	1		Gooch.	Roberts,Thomas,Jr.,	1		Din.	Robinson,Benjamin,			Bot.
Robards,James,	2	11	Gooch.	Roberts,Thomas,	2	13	York	Robinson,Benjamin,		1	Spots.
Robards,John,	1	4	Gooch.	Roberts,Thomas,Jr.,	1	1	York	Robinson,Blaze,	1		Berk.
Robards,William,	1	26	Gooch.	Roberts,William,	1		Mont.	Robinson,Brittin,	1		Rock.
Robards,William,Jr.,	1	5	Gooch.	Roberts,William,	1		York	Robinson,Caleb,	1		Wash.
Robb,John,	1		Berk.	Roberts,William,	1	1	Berk.	Robinson,Charles,	1	1	Caro.
Robbers,Jacob,	1		Bot.	Roberts,William,			Cul.	Robinson,David,			Bot.
Roberson,Benjamin,	1		Bed.	Roberts,William,	2	16	Cul.	Robinson,David,	1		Bot.
Roberson,Benjamin,	2	2	Fay.	Roberts,William,	1		Henry	Robinson,David,	1		Rock.
Roberson,George,	1	5	Bed.	Roberts,William,	1		Brun.	Robinson,Dickson,	1		Pr.Wm.
Roberson,James,	1		Bed.	Roberts,William,	1		Lou.	Robinson,Drury,	1	9	Brun.
Roberson,John,	1		Henry	Roberts,William,	1		Bot.	Robinson,Edward,	1	26	Brun.
Roberson,John,	1		Fay.	Roberts,William,Sr.,	1	3	Nor.	Robinson,F.,	1		Pr.Wm.
Roberson,Jonathan,	1		Fay.	Roberts,William,Jr.,	1		Nor.	Robinson,George,	1		Bot.
Roberson,Joseph,	1	3	Fay.	Robertson,Alexander,			Aug.	Robinson,George,	1		Caro.
Roberson,Margett,		3	Fay.	Robertson,Alexander,	1	1	Aug.	Robinson,George,	1	1	Caro.
Roberson,Richard,	1		Henry	Robertson,Arthur,	1	9	Bed.	Robinson,George,	1		Lou.
Roberson,Robert,			Fay.	Robertson,Charles,	1		Cha.C	Robinson,George,	1	8	West.
Roberson,Thomas,	1		Henry	Robertson,Christopher,	1	11	Lun.	Robinson,George,	1		Loui.
Roberson,Thomas,	1		Bed.	Robertson,Christopher,	1		Lun.	Robinson,George,	1		K.Geo.

Name			Co.
Robinson,James,	1		Bot.
Robinson,James,	1		Wash.
Robinson,James,	1	5	West.
Robinson,James,	1		Har.
Robinson,James,	1		Berk.
Robinson,Jayres,	1		Berk.
Robinson,Jessee,			Fay.
Robinson,Joel,	2	2	Har.
Robinson,John,	1		Bot.
Robinson,John,	2	10	Brun.
Robinson,John,	1	12	Eli.Cy
Robinson,John,	1		Wash.
Robinson,John,	1		Wash.
Robinson,John,	1	5	Camp.
Robinson,John,	1	4	Spots.
Robinson,John,	1		Brun.
Robinson,John,	1	2	Har.
Robinson,John,			Cul.
Robinson,John,	1		Rock.
Robinson,John,			Rock.
Robinson,John,	1	24	York
Robinson,Joseph,	1		Bot.
Robinson,Joseph,	2	36	Caro.
Robinson,Judith,		5	Loui.
Robinson,Littleberry	1	6	Brun.
Robinson,Mary,		1	Caro.
Robinson,Miss Mary,		12	Caro.
Robinson,Michael,	2	25	Spots
Robinson,Michael,Jr.	1	7	Spots
Robinson,Moses,	1		Caro.
Robinson,Nathaniel,			Fau.
Robinson,Nathaniel,	1	6	Brun.
Robinson,Patience,		3	Acco.
Robinson,Richard,	1	3	Pr.Wm
Robinson,Robert,	1		Rock.
Robinson,Starkey,	1	17	York
Robinson,Starkey,Jr.	1	10	York.
Robinson,Stephen,	1		Fau.
Robinson,Taylor,	1		West.
Robinson,Thomas,	1		West.
Robinson,Thomas,	1		Har.
Robinson,Thomas,	1	2	Cha.Cy
Robinson,Thomas,	1	34	K.Wm.
Robinson,William,	1		Bot.
Robinson,William,			Bot.
Robinson,William,	1		Bot.
Robinson,William,	1		Bot.
Robinson,William,			Lou.
Robinson,William,			Lou.
Robinson,William,	1	7	Hen.
Robinson,William,	1		Hen.
Robinson,William,	2	18	Brun.
Robinson,William,est	2	99	West.
Robinson,William,			Fay.
Robinson,William,			Fay.
Robinson,William,			Wash.
Robinson,William,	1	10	Spots
Robinson,William,	1	7	Spots
Robinson,William,	2	19	Cul.
Robinson,William,	1	2	Brun.
Robinson,William,	1	10	York.
Robinson,William,	1		Berk.
Robinson,William,	1		Berk.
Robinson,William,	1		Rock.
Robinson,William,Jr.	1	7	Cul.
Robinson,Maj.William	2	7	Spots
Robuck,Robert,	2	7	Cul.
Robuck,Robert,			Cul.
Roby,Benjamin,Sr.,	1		Har.
Roby,Thomas,	2		Har.
Roby,Vincent,	1		Har.
Roby,Widdow,			Har.
Roby,William,	1		Har.
Roby,William,	1		Pr.Wm
Rochester,John,	2	10	West.
Rod,Benjamin,	1	4	Pr.Wm

Name			Co.
Rod,Richard,	1	9	Pr.Wm
Roddy,Taylor,	2	3	Spots
Rodefer,John,	2	3	Cul.
Rodgers,Arthur,			Lou.
Rodgers,Easter,		9	Acco.
Rodgers,Enuch,	1		K.Geo
Rodgers,Hambleton,			Fay.
Rodgers,Hamilton,	4		Lou.
Rodgers,Hamilton,Jr.,			Lou.
Rodgers,Hamutal,		7	Nor.
Rodgers,Hosea,	1		K.Geo
Rodgers,James,			Lou.
Rodgers,James,	1		Acco.
Rodgers,James,	1		K.Geo
Rodgers,John,			Acco.
Rodgers,John,	1	9	Acco.
Rodgers,John,	1	9	Cha.Cy
Rodgers,John,	1		Bed.
Rodgers,John,	1		K.Geo
Rodgers,John,	1		K.Geo
Rodgers,John,	2	3	Acco.
Rodgers,Joseph,	1	2	K.Geo
Rodgers,Levie,			Acco.
Rodgers,Levin,	3	7	Acco.
Rodgers,Peter,	3	2	Acco.
Rodgers,Rodham,			Lou.
Rodham,Rodham,			Lou.
Rodgers,Robert,	1		Aug.
Rodgers,Robert,	1		Nor.
Rodgers,Robert,Jr.,	1	3	Acco.
Rodgers,Robert,Sr.,	2	1	Acco.
Rodgers,Seth,	1	3	Aug.
Rodgers,Severn,	1	1	Acco.
Rodgers,Thomas,			Lou.
Rodgers,Thomas,	1		Lou.
Rodgers,Thomas,	1	7	Acco.
Rodgers,Tinley,			Acco.
Rodgers,Torobable,Sr.	3	18	Acco.
Rodgers,Torobable,Jr.,			Acco.
Rodgers,William,			K.Geo
Rodgers,William,	2		Fay.
Rodgers,William,	1		Lou.
Rodman,John,	1	1	Pr.Wm
Rodman,Robert,	1		Berk.
Rodman,Samuel,	1	1	Aug.
Roe,Alexander,	1		Fau.
Roe,Edward,	1		Lou.
Roe,James,	1		Lou.
Roe,Jemima,	2	8	West.
Roe,John,	1		So'n
Roe,John,est.,		4	Caro.
Roe,Samuel,	1		So'n
Roe,William,	1	7	West.
Roeman,Richard,	1		Cul.
Roger,John,	2		Har.
Rogers,Alexander,	1		Mont.
Rogers,Alexander,	1		Berk.
Rogers,Anthony,	1		Lin.
Rogers,Benjamin,	1	6	West.
Rogers,Benjamin,	1		Mont.
Rogers,Bird,	1	7	K.&Q
Rogers,David,	1		Henry
Rogers,Edward,			Pr.Wm.
Rogers,George,	1	21	Caro.
Rogers,George,	1		Henry
Rogers,George,	2	7	Fau.
Rogers,Hannah,	1	7	Ja.Cy
Rogers,Henry,	2		Fau.
Rogers,Jacobs,	1		Wash.
Rogers,Jeremiah,			Fay.
Rogers,John,	1		Aug.
Rogers,John,	1	4	Cul.
Rogers,John,	1	11	Spots
Rogers,John,	1		Mont.
Rogers,John,	1		Lin.
Rogers,John,		6	Fay.

Name			Co.
Rogers,John,	1	5	Eli.Cy
Rogers,John,	1	1	Fau.
Rogers,John,	1	12	Brun.
Rogers,John,	1		Lou.
Rogers,John A.,	1	9	So'n
Rogers,John Adustan,	1	9	York
Rogers,Capt.John,	1	15	So'n
Rogers,Joseph,	1	11	Cul.
Rogers,Joseph,	1		Mont.
Rogers,Joseph,Sr.,	3	20	Fay.
Rogers,Joseph,Jr.,	1		Fay.
Rogers,Lucy,		10	Spots.
Rogers,Mary,			Gooch.
Rogers,Robert,	1		Buck.
Rogers,Rubin,			Mont.
Rogers,Stephen,	2		Fau.
Rogers,Steven,	1		Cul.
Rogers,Thomas,	1	4	Din.
Rogers,Thomas,	1	1	Mont.
Rogers,Thomas,	1	2	Aug.
Rogers,Thomas,	2	3	Cul.
Rogers,William,		2	Pr.Wm
Rogers,William,	1		Henry
Rogers,William,	1	8	Fay.
Rogers,William,	1		Mont.
Rogers,William,	1		Aug.
Rogers,William,	1	5	Ja.Cy
Rogers,W.A.,	1	9	York
Roher,Michael,			Berk.
Rokard,Thomas,	1	4	Lou.
Roland,Phobe,		4	Eli.Cy
Roler,John,	1		Lou.
Roles,Christopher,	1		Henry
Roles,William,	1		West.
Rollings,Burwell,	1		So'n
Rollings,John,		6	Spots.
Rollings,Mary,		1	So'n
Rollins,Darnall,	1		Fay.
Rollins,Nathan,	1		Fay.
Rollinson,Hughlitt,	1	1	Ja.Cy
Rollison,Joseph,	1		Lou.
Rolston,David,	2		Fay.
Rolston,James,			Fay.
Rolston,John,	2		Fay.
Romaine,James,	1		Mont.
Roman,Abraham,	1		Cul.
Roman,Abraham,	1		Fay.
Roman,Abraham,	1		Berk.
Roman,Joshua,	1		Wash.
Roman,Phillip,	1		Cul.
Roman,Thomas,	1		Berk.
Roman,William,	1		Wash.
Romaine,Abel,	1		Mont.
Romanie,John,	1		Lou.
Romaine,Layton,			Lou.
Romaine,Peter,	1		Lou.
Romaine,Peter,Jr.,	1		Lou.
Row,Thomas,	1	9	Caro.
Ronald,Andrew,	2	5	Hen.
Roney,Joseph,			Berk.
Roney,Thomas,	1	14	Din.
Ronimus,Andrew,	2		Berk.
Ronimus,Lewis,	1		Berk.
Ronle,Jonathan,			Acco.
Rook,William,	1		Cha.Cy
Rookard,William,	1	4	Pr.Wm
Roop,Barnett,	1		Bot.
Rootes,George,	1	17	Berk.
Roove,Michael,	1		Lou.
Roox,James,	2		Acco.
Rope,John,	1		Pr.Wm
Roper,Benjamin,	2	1	Cha.Cy
Roper,Charles,Sr.,	2	3	Din.
Roper,Charles,Jr.,	1		Din.
Roper,David,	1	3	Brun.
Roper,David,	1	8	Cha.Cy

Name			County
Roper,George,			Fay.
Roper,Jesse,	1	9	Hen.
Roper,John,	3	3	Hen.
Roper,Nicholas,	1		Berk.
Roper,Randolph,			Cha.C.
Roper,Samuel,	1	1	Cha.C.
Roper,Thomas,	1	4	Lou.
Roper,William,	1	2	Brun.
Ropewalk,Richmond,		20	Hen.
Rossar,William,	1	1	Camp.
Rose,Alexander,	1	25	K.Geo.
Rose,Caytom,	1		K.Geo.
Rose,Clack,			K.& Q.
Rose,Conrod,	1		Berk.
Rose,Dun,	1	14	Din.
Rose,Enuch,	1		K.Geo.
Rose,Francis,	1	2	K.Geo.
Rose,George,	2	1	Spots.
Rose,George,	1		K.& Q.
Rose,Isaac,			Lou.
Rose,J.,	1	4	Pr.Wm.
Rose,Jacob,	1	2	Nor.
Rose,Jesse,	1		Berk.
Rose,John,	1	1	Spots.
Rose,John,	1	11	Brun.
Rose,John,	1		K.Geo.
Rose,John,Sr.,	1		K.Geo.
Rose,John,Jr.,	1		K,Geo.
Rose,Jonathan,	1	1	Berk.
Rose,Silas,	1		Lou.
Rose,Thomas,	1	3	Nor.
Rose,Thomas,	3	37	K.& Q.
Rose,William,	2		Fau.
Rose,William,	1	2	Hen.
Rose,Zachariah,	1		K.Geo.
Roseberger,Erassmus,	2		Berk.
Roson,Jonathan,			Cul.
Roson,Ruebin,	2		Cul.
Ross,Alexander,	1		Camp.
Ross,Alexander,	1		Camp.
Ross,Alexander,	1		Bot.
Ross,Charles,	1	2	So'n
Ross,Coleman,	1		Caro.
Ross,Daniel,	1		Henry
Ross,Daniel,	1		Lin.
Ross,David,	1	9	Gooch.
Ross,David,		125	Camp.
Ross,David,		125	Camp.
Ross,David,	3	65	Gooch.
Ross,David,		9	Hen.
Ross,David,	1	10	Henry
Ross,David & Co.,	4	2	Din.
Ross,Edward,		2	Caro.
Ross,Francis,	1	4	Eli.Cy
Ross,Isaac,	1		Har.
Ross,Isaac,	1	3	York
Ross,Ishmael,	1	3	Nor.
Ross,J.M.,			Eli.Cy
Ross,Jacob,	1		Acco.
Ross,James,	1		Cul.
Ross,John,	1		Bot.
Ross,John,	1		Pr.Wm.
Ross,Joseph,	1	1	Acco.
Ross,Mallory,	3	4	Eli.Cy
Ross,Mallory,Jr.,	1	1	Eli.Cy
Ross,Margaret,			Berk.
Ross,Michael,	1		Fau.
Ross,Robert,	1		Aug.
Ross,Sarah,		2	York
Ross,Thomas,			Eli.Cy
Ross,Thomas,			Bot.
Ross,Thomas,	1	6	Din.
Ross,Thomas,	1		Bed.
Ross,William,	1		Bed.
Ross,William,Sr.,	1	3	Pr.Wm.
Ross,William,Jr.,	1		Pr.Wm.
Rosser,Burwell,	1	5	Pr.Geo
Rosser,David,	1	4	Pr.Geo
Rosser,John,	1	5	Brun.
Rosser,John,	2	10	Fau.
Rosser,Jonathan,	2	9	Camp.
Rosser,Martha,		3	Pr.Geo
Rosser,Michael,	1	1	Din.
Rosser,Peter,	1	4	Pr.Geo
Rosser,Richard,	1	3	Fau.
Rosser,William,	1	1	Camp.
Rosson,Jerome,	2	10	Cul.
Rosson,Joseph,	1		Cul.
Rosson,Ruebin,			Cul.
Rosson,William,	1		Cul.
Rossor,Jonathan,	2	9	Camp.
Roswell,George,	1		K.& Q.
Roswell,Peter,	1		Spots.
Roszell,Stephen,	1	6	Lou.
Rotch,James,	1		Mont.
Rotchell,John,	1	14	So'n
Rouand,Thomas,	1	32	West.
Roulet,James,			K.& Q.
Roundtree,Dudley,	1	2	Bed.
Roundtree,Samuel,	1		Bed.
Roundtree,William,	1	3	Pr.Wm.
Rounsavel,Benjamin,	2		Har.
Rountree,Erasmus,	1		Hen.
Rountree,Randol,	1	7	Gooch.
Rountree,Samuel,	1	1	Gooch.
Rourk,P.,			Hen.
Rouse,Jacob,	1		Cul.
Rouse,John,	1		Loui.
Rouse,Lewis,	1		Cul.
Rouse,Matthias,	1	6	Cul.
Rouse,Michael,	1		Cul.
Rouse,Samuel,	1		Cul.
Rouse,Samuel,	1		Din.
Roussau,William,	1	8	Fau.
Rout,George,			Fay.
Rout,James,	1	2	Fau.
Rout,John,	1		Fau.
Rout,John,	1	6	Cul.
Rout,Peter,	1	3	Fau.
Rout,Richard,	1	1	Fau,
Routen,John,	1		Bed.
Routen,Richard,	1		Bed.
Routon,James,			Buck.
Routon,Richard,	1		Eli.Cy
Routon,Richard,	3		Buck.
Row,Edmond,	1		Fay.
Row,William,	1		Har.
Rowan,James,	1		Aug.
Rowar,William,	1		Rock.
Rowe,Benjamin,	3		Cul.
Rowe,George,Sr.,	3	1	Cul.
Rowe,James,	1		Loui.
Rowe,Jane,			Loui.
Rowe,Jesse,	1		Loui.
Rowe,John,	1		Loui.
Rowe,John,est.,		4	K.& Q.
Rowe,Johnson,	1		Loui.
Rowe,Joseph,	1	23	K.& Q.
Rowe,Joseph,Jr.,	1	1	K.& Q.
Rowe,Richard,	1	8	K.& Q.
Rowe,Thomas,	1	2	K.& Q.
Rowland,Baldwin,	1	2	Henry
Rowland,George,Sr.,	1	3	Henry
Rowland,James,	2	8	Bot.
Rowland,John,	1	3	Henry
Rowland,Michael,	1	8	Henry
Rowland,Thomas,	1	4	Bot.
Rowles,John,	1	11	Acco.
Rowlet,William,	2		K.Geo.
Rowlett,Elizabeth,		4	Lun.
Rowlett,John,	1		Lun.
Rowlett,Phillip,	1		Lun.
Rowley,Ann,	1	16	K.Geo.
Rowley,Moses,			K.Geo.
Rowley,William,	1		Acco.
Rowsey,Thomas,	1		Camp.
Rowson,Charles,	1		Bed.
Rowzey,John,	1	8	Cul.
Rowzey,Richard,	1	12	Cul.
Roy,John,	1	4	Caro.
Roy,Joseph,	1		Har.
Roy,Mungo,	2	37	Caro.
Roy,Peter,	1		Buck.
Roy,Richard,	1	5	Caro.
Roy,Thomas,	1	19	Fau.
Roy,Wily,	1	13	Fau.
Royal,John,			Henry
Royal,John,	1		Lin.
Royale,William,	1	15	Cha.Cy
Royall,Isham,	1		Henry
Royall,James,	1	9	Hen.
Royalty,John,	1		Henry
Royes,James,	1		Pr.Wm.
Royes,Robert,	1		Pr.Wm.
Royster,Charles,	1		Cha.Cy
Royster,David,	1		Hen.
Royster,George,	1	8	Cha.Cy.
Royster,John,			Hen.
Royster,Littleberry,	1	1	Hen.
Royster,Peter,	1	12	Cha.Cy
Royster,William,	1	7	Cha.Cy
Royston,John,		2	Pr.Wm.
Royston,John,			Pr.Wm.
Royston,Robert,	1	12	Caro.
Royston,Thomas,	2	22	Caro.
Royston,Thomas,Jr.,	1	1	Caro.
Royston,William,	1	2	Caro.
Rozaro,Lawrence,	1		York
Rubell,Owen,	1		Henry
Rucker,Angus,		7	Cul.
Rucker,Augustine,	2	4	Cul.
Rucker,Eliott,		4	Cul.
Rucker,Ephram,	3	13	Cul.
Rucker,George,	1		Cul.
Rucker,James,	1		Aug.
Rucker,James,	1		Aug.
Rucker,John,	1	2	Cul.
Rucker,John,	1		Cul.
Rucker,Joseph,	1	5	Cul.
Rucker,Julis,	1		Cul.
Rucker,Lemuel,	1		Aug,
Rucker,Thomas,	1	1	Cul.
Rucker,Wiatt,	1		Aug.
Rucker,William,	1	1	Bed.
Rucker,William,	1		Cul.
Rucker,William,	1	5	Cul.
Rucks,William,	1	4	Lun.
Rudd,Edward,	1	8	Eli.Cy
Rudd,Thomas,	1	4	Lun.
Ruddell,Stephen,	3		Har.
Rudder,Alexander,	1	17	Lun.
Rudder,John,			Lun.
Rudder,Samuel,	2	3	Lun.
Rudder,Samuel,Jr.,			Lun.
Ruddle,Cornelius,	1	7	Aug.
Rudolph,George,	1	5	West.
Rue,Benajat,	1	2	Cul.
Ruffin,Benjamin,Sr.,	1	30	So'n
Ruffin,Benjamin,Jr.,	1	21	So'n
Ruffin,Edmund,	1	51	Pr.Geo.
Ruffin,Edmund,Jr.,	2	30	Pr.Geo.
Ruffin,Edward,		15	Brun.
Ruffin,James,	1	37	K.Wm.
Ruffin,Sterling,		21	K.Wm.
Ruffmin,Mary,		39	K.Wm.
Rugor,John,	1	1	Lou.
Ruix,Daniel,	1		West.
Rule,Henry,	1		Har.

Name			Loc.	Name			Loc.	Name			Loc.
Rnling,Lewis,	1		Mont.	Rust,Enos,			Camp.	Saerey,Isaac,	1		Caro.
Rum,Adam,	1		Lou.	Rust,Enos,			Camp.	Sagathy,Peter,	1		Berk.
Rumbaugh,William,	1		Berk.	Rust,George,	1	16	West.	Sage,Jesse,	1		Har.
Rummons,Andrew,	1		Lou.	Rust,George,	1		Camp.	Sage,William,	1		Har.
Rumsay,Edward,	1		Berk.	Rust,George,	1		Camp.	Said,William,	1		Fay.
Rundall,Henry,	1		Mont.	Rust,Jacob,	1		Har.	Sailor,Jacob,	1		Mont.
Runkle,Samuel,	1		Aug.	Rust,James,	1	7	West.	St.John,Issac,	1	1	K.&Q
Runnals,Thomas,	1		Fay.	Rust,Jeremiah,	1	5	West.	Sale,Anthony,	1	14	Caro.
Runnels,Isam,	1		Mont.	Rust,John,	1	4	Fau.	Sale,Hannah,	1	9	Caro.
Runner,Adam,	1		Mont.	Rust,John,	1	10	West.	Sale,Richard,	1	3	Caro.
Runnick,James,	1		Lou.	Rust,Matthew,			Lou.	Sale,Robert,	1		Caro.
Runnie,Thomas,	1		Mont.	Rust,Matthew,	1	3	Fau.	Sale,Samuel,	1	3	Caro.
Runyan,Isaac,	1		Mont.	Rust,Samuel,	1	5	Fau.	Sale,Samuel,	1	11	Spots.
Runyan,John,			Mont.	Rust,Samuel,	1	9	West.	Sale,Thomas,	1	8	Caro.
Runyan,John,			Mont.	Rust,Vincent,	1	5	West.	Sallard,William,	1	7	Din.
Rush,Benjamin,	1		Cul.	Rust,William,	1	7	Lou.	Salle,Isaac,	2		Buck.
Rush,Daniel,	1		Lou.	Ruth,Joseph,	1		Rock.	Salle,Jacob,	1	4	Buck.
Rush,John,	1		Cul.	Rutherford,Absalom,	1	2	Mont.	Salle,Stephen,			Bick.
Rush,John,	1		Har.	Rutherford,Dudley,			Henry	Salle,William,	1		Buck.
Rush,Leonard,	1	2	Berk.	Rutherford,George,	1		Loui.	Salle,William,	2	5	Buck.
Rush,William,	1		Cul.	Rutherford,John,Jr.,	2		Mont.	Salley,George,	1		Rock.
Rusher,Andrew,			Berk.	Rutherford,Joseph,	1		Lin.	Salmon,Benjamin,	1		Gooch.
Rusher,George,	1		Bed.	Rutherford,Julian,	1		Mont.	Salmon,Elizabeth,			Gooch.
Rusk,David,			Aug.	Rutherford,Robert,	2	17	Berk.	Salmon,Hezekiah	1		Henry
Rusk,James,	1		Berk.	Rutherford,Thomas,	1	11	Berk.	Salmon,John,	1		Gooch.
Rusk,John,	1	1	Rock.	Rutherford,William,	1	16	Gooch	Salmon,John,	1	1	Bed.
Rusk,Margaret,			Aug.	Rutherford,William,Jr	1		Mont.	Salmon,John,	1	2	Henry
Rusk,Robert,	1		Berk.	Rutherford,William,Sr	1		Mont.	Salmon,Nancy,			Gooch.
Rusk,Robert,	1	1	Aug.	Ruthrell,Samuel,	1		Henry	Salmon,Rowland,	1		Henry
Rusk,Samuel,	1		Aug.	Rutledge,Edward,	1		Aug.	Salmon,William,			Gooch.
Rusk,William,	1	1	Aug.	Rutledge,Thomas,	3	1	Aug.	Salt,Humphrey,	1		Aug.
Russ,George,			Lou.	Rutlidge,George,	1	1	Bot.	Salter,Ann,		3	Sou'n.
Russell,Andrew,	1		Aug.	Rutlidge,Thomas,	2		Bot.	Salter,Daniel,	1		Berk.
Russell,Andrew,	1		Wash.	Rutter,George,	1		Lou.	Salts,Edward,	1		Berk.
Russell,Anthony,	1		Fau.	Ryan,Darby,	1		Henry	Salts,William,	1	1	Nor.
Russell,Edward,	1	8	Cha.Cy	Ryan,George,	1		Har.	Samford,James,	1		Brun.
Russell,Enock,	1		Caro.	Ryan,James,	1		Har.	Samford,William,	1		Brun.
Russell,George,	1		Caro.	Ryan,John,	1		Har.	Samford,William,	3	1	Brun.
Russell,George,	1		Brun.	Ryan,John,Jr.,	1		Har.	Sammons,James	1	1	Lun.
Russell,James,	1		Lou.	Ryan,Whitfield,	1		Gooch	Sammons,Newit,	1		Sou'n.
Russell,James,	1	5	Camp.	Ryan,William,	1	3	Henry	Sammons,William,	1		Lun.
Russell,James,	1	5	Camp.	Ryance,Jane,			Aug.	Sample,James,	1		Lin.
Russell,Jeffrey,	1	2	Lun.	Rybott,Jacob,	1		Fay.	Sample,John,			Acco.
Russell,John,	1		Cul.	Ryburn,John,	1		Wash.	Samples,Samuel,	1		Wash.
Russell,John,	1		Lou.	Ryburn,Matthew,	1		Wash.	Sampson,Ann,		15	Nor.
Russell,John,	1	5	Caro.	Ryburn,William,	1		Wash.	Sampson,Charles,est.		4	Gooch.
Russell,John,	1		Har.	Ryland,Sarah,	1		York	Sampson,John,	1	1	Cul.
Russell,John,	1		Wash.	Ryland,Thomas,	1	2	York	Sampson,Joseph,	1		Cul.
Russell,John,	1		York	Ryley,John,	1		Fau.	Sampson,Mary,	1	7	Cul.
Russell,Joshua,	1		Aug.	Ryley,John,			Fau.	Sampson,Richard,	1	9	Gooch.
Russell,Milby,Jr.,	1		Acco.	Ryley,John,	1		Cul.	Sampson,Richard,	1		Pr.Wm.
Russell,Philemon,	1	3	Lun.	Ryley,Thomas,	1		Fau.	Sampson,Sarah,			Lin.
Russell,Richard,	1	8	Brun.	Ryne,Lazarus,	2		Har.	Sampson,Capt.Steph.	1	21	Gooch.
Russell,Robert,	1		Aug.	Ryner,Christian,	1		Cul.	Sampson,Thomas,	1	4	Cul.
Russell,Robert,	1		Lou.	Ryner,Daniel,			Cul.	Sams,John,			Spots.
Russell,Robert,	1		Lou.	Ryner,Everyhart,	1		Cul.	Sams,Joseph,	1	2	Spots.
Russell,Robert,	1	1	Camp.	Ryner,John,			Pr.Wm	Sams,William,	1		Henry
Russell,Robert,	1	1	Camp.	Ryner,John,	1		Cul.	Samson,John,	2		Cul.
Russell,Samuel,	2		Lou.	Rynolds,John,	1	4	Cul.	Samson,Thomas			Cul.
Russell,Solomon,	1		Acco.	Rynor,George,	1		Berk.	Samuel,Andrew,			K.Q
Russell,Stephen,	1		Lou.	Rynor,John,	1		Berk.	Samuel,Anthony,		15	Caro.
Russell,Thomas,	1		Lou.	Ryon,John,	1		Berk.	Samuel,Elizabeth,	1	16	Caro.
Russell,Thomas,	1		Rock.	Ryon,John Bowen,	1	2	Lou.	Samuel,Giles	2	8	Caro.
Russell,Thomas,	1		Ja.Cy	Ryon,Michael,	1		Fay.	Samuel,Grey,	1	6	Caro.
Russell,William,		2	York.	Ryon,Phillip,	1	2	Henry	Samuel,Henry,			K.&
Russell,William,	1	2	Fay.					Samuel,Henry,	2		K.Q
Russell,William,	1		Wash.	Sacry,Ann,			K.Geo	Samuel,James,	1	2	Cul.
Russell,William,	2		Fau.	Sadler,Benjamin,Jr.,	1		Gooch	Samuel,James,	1	6	Caro.
Russell,William,		2	Fau.	Sadler,Charles,	1		So'n	Samuel,John,	1	3	Caro.
Russell,William,	1		Lou.	Sadler,Featherston,			Brun.	Samuel,Mordecai,	1		K.&Q
Russell,William,			Lou.	Sadler,John,	1		K.&Q	Samuel,Samuels,	1		Augu.
Rust,Benjamin,	1	10	Fau.	Sadler,Thomas,	2		Brun.	Samuel,Thomas,	1	4	Caro.
Rust,David,	1		Camp.	Sadler,William,	1		Gooch	Samuel,William,	1	28	Caro.
Rust,David,	1		Camp.	Sadusky,Samuel,	3		Har.	Samuels,Shadriack,	1		Lou.
Rust,Elizabeth,		8	West.	Saero,James,	1		Caro.	Sandage,James,	1	4	Loui.

Name			Loc.	Name			Loc.	Name			Loc.
Sanders,Aaron,			Lou.	Sanford,William P.,	1	4	Fau.	Savage,George,	1	24	Nor.
Sanders,Benjamin,			Lou.	Sanford,Youil,	3	3	West.	Savage,Jacob,	1	1	Acco.
Sanders,Caty,		13	Spots.	Sanger,Stephen,	1		Pr.Wm	Savage,John,	1	5	Acco.
Sanders,Francis,	1		Lou.	Sangster,Alexander,	1		Fau.	Savage,John,			Acco.
Sanders,George,	1	1	West.	Sansom,Elijah,	1		Loui.	Savage,John,	1	3	Nor.
Sanders,Gunnell,	1		Lou.	Sansom,Philip,	1	1	York.	Savage,John,Sr.,	1	18	Nor.
Sanders,Henry,			Lou.	Sansum,James,	1	2	Lun.	Savage,John,Jr.,	1	20	Nor.
Sanders,James,	1		Lou.	Sansum,William,	1	1	Lun.	Savage,Kendal,	1		Acco.
Sanders,James,	1	2	Fau.	Saphell,John,	1		Berk.	Savage,Lettiston,	4		Acco.
Sanders,John,	1	1	Caro.	Sappleton,Hartley,			Acco.	Savage,Littleton,	1	99	Nor.
Sanders,John,Younger,	3	5	Caro.	Sarvar,John,	1	1	Bot.	Savage,Margaret,	1	7	Acco.
Sanders,John,Jr.,	1	9	Caro.	Sarver,Gewper,	1		Bot.	Savage,Mary,	1	3	Acco.
Sanders,John,	1		West.	Satchell,Charles,Sr.	1	4	Nor.	Savage,Mary,	1	11	Acco.
Sanders,John,	1		Lou.	Satchell,Charles,Jr.	1	1	Nor.	Savage,Peter,	2	4	Acco.
Sanders,John,			Lou.	Satchell,Christopher,			Acco.	Savage,Richard,	2	6	Acco.
Sanders,John,	1	1	Cul.	Satchell,Southy,	2	3	Acco.	Savage,Richard,	1		Nor.
Sanders,John,	1	24	Spots.	Satchell,William,	1	13	Acco.	Savage,Robert,	1		Nor.
Sanders,Judith,			Eli.C	Satchell,William,	1	45	Nor.	Savage,Robert,			Acco.
Sanders,Mary,		3	Caro.	Satchill,Southy,			Acco.	Savage,Robinson,	2	2	Acco.
Sanders,Moses,			Lou.	Satterly,Samuel,			Har.	Savage,Thomas,			Acco.
Sanders,Nathaniel,	2	2	Spots.	Satterwhite,George,	1	2	K.& Q.	Savage,William,	2		Acco.
Sanders,Nicholas,	1		Lou.	Satterwhite,James,	1	2	Caro.	Savage,William,	1		Nor.
Sanders,Peter,	1	2	Caro.	Satterwhite,John,	1	5	Caro.	Sawright,Alexander,	1		Aug.
Sanders,Philip,	1		Lou.	Satterwhite,Mann,	1	12	K.Wm.	Sawther,Jacob,	1	1	Cul.
Sanders,Philip,	1		Lou.	Satterwhite,William,	1	1	K.& Q.	Sawyers,James,	1	6	Aug.
Sanders,Reuben,	2	3	Caro.	Saulsbury,John,	3		Acco.	Sawyers,Sampson,	1	3	Aug.
Sanders,Reuben,	1	1	West.	Saulsbury,Mosses,			Acco.	Sayer,William,	1		Berk.
Sanders,Richard,	2		Nor.	Saulsbury,Nathan,	2		Acco.	Sayers,David,	1	1	Mont.
Sanders,Robert,	1	6	Fau.	Saulsbury,Thomas,			Acco.	Sayers,Robert,	1		Mont.
Sanders,Sarah,	1	8	Caro.	Saunders,Alexander,	1		So'n	Sayers,Robert,	1		Mont
Sanders,Sarah,	3	9	Lou.	Saunders,Daniel,	1	1	Lou.	Sayers,Robert,	1	5	Mont.
Sanders,Stuart,	1	1	Nor.	Saunders,David,	1		Eli.C	Sayers,John Thompson	1	11	Mont.
Sanders,Thomas,	1		Lou.	Saunders,Ebben,	1	3	Brun.	Sayne,William,	1		Gooch.
Sanders,Thomas,	1		Fau.	Saunders,Edward,	1	6	Brun.	Scale,John,	1		Cul.
Sanders,William,	1		Fau.	Saunders,Elizabeth,		1	West.	Scales,Joseph,	1	13	Henry
Sanders,William,	1	2	West.	Saunders,Henry,	1		Fay.	Scales,Richard,	1		Cul.
Sanderson,John,	1	2	Buck.	Saunders,James,			Lou.	Scanland,Robert,	1	4	Bot.
Sanderson,Joseph,est.	1	1	Caro.	Saunders,James,	1		Lou.	Scandling,Jeremiah,	1		Henry
Sandford,Daniel,	1	5	Lou.	Saunders,James,	1	10	Buck.	Scantling,James,	1		Bot.
Sandford,Edward,	1	18	West.	Saunders,Jessie,	1	17	Lun.	Scarborough,Howell,	1	1	So'n
Sandford,George,	2		Henry	Saunders,John,	1	14	Buck.	Scarborough,Isaac,	1		Bed.
Sandford,Jeremiah,			Lou.	Saunders,John,	1		Din.	Scarborough,Mary,	1		So'n
Sandford,John,	1		Henry	Saunders,John,		1	Lou.	Scarbrough,John,	1	4	Brun.
Sandford,T.,	1	4	Pr.Wm	Saunders,John,	1	1	Pr.Wm	Scarbrough,Lewis,	1	5	Brun.
Sandford,Robert,	1		Henry	Saunders,John,	1	2	Pr.Wm	Scarbrough,William,	1	2	Brun.
Sandford,W.,		6	Pr.Wm	Saunders,John,	1		Buck.	Scarbrough,William,	1		Brun.
Sandford,William,	1		Lou.	Saunders,Jonathan,	2	1	Caro.	Scarburgh,Americus,	2	11	Acco.
Sandidge,David,Sr.,	1	15	Spots.	Saunders,Juxon,	1		York	Scarburgh,Bennet,			Acco.
Sandifer,Sam,	1		So'n	Saunders,Peter,est.,	1	9	Caro.	Scarburgh,Edmund,	4	16	Acco.
Sandifer,Samuel,	1	3	Din.	Saunders,Peter,	1	4	Henry	Scarburgh,Edmund,Jr.	1	8	Acco.
Sandifur,Samuel,	1		Eli.C	Saunders,Presley,	1	1	Lou.	Scarburgh,Henry,	3	9	Acco.
Sandifur,Samuel,Jr.,	1		Eli.C	Saunders,Richard,	1	5	Caro.	Scarburgh,William,	2	8	Acco.
Sandiper,Samuel,	1		Eli.C	Saunders,Robert,	2	21	Buck.	Scherer,Samuel,	3	11	Hen.
Sandiper,William,	1	1	Eli.C	Saunders,Robert,	1	4	Fay.	Schnider,Joseph,	1		Cul.
Sandrews,John,	1		Acco.	Saunders,Samuel,	1		Buck.	Schoels,Jacob,	1		Camp.
Sands,Domined,	1	1	York	Saunders,Samuel,	1	15	Buck.	Scholefield,David,	1		Lou.
Sands,Isaac,	1		Lou.	Saunders,Stephen,	1		Din.	Scholl,Abraham,	1		Fay.
Sands,Jacob,	1		Lou.	Saunders,Stephen,		3	Bed.	Scholl,Joseph,	2		Fay.
Sandy,Uriah,	1	11	West.	Saunders,Stephen,	1	7	Buck.	Scholl,Peter,	1	1	Fay.
Sandys,Samuel,	1	3	Caro.	Saunders,Stephen,	1	6	Mont.	Scholl,William,	1		Fay.
Sanford,Augustine,	1	3	West.	Saunders,Tachariah,	1		Buck.	Schools,Gabriel,	1		K.& Q.
Sanford,Charles,	1	5	West.	Saunders,Thomas,	1	11	Buck.	Schools,George,	1		K.& Q.
Sanford,Joseph,	1	9	Cul.	Saunders,Thomas,	1	5	Caro.	Schooler,John,		3	Spots.
Sanford,James,	1	10	Nor.	Saunders,William,	2	7	Caro.	Schooler,Peter,	1		Spots.
Sanford,John,	1	4	Lun.	Saunders,William,	1	1	Gooch	Schooler,Wharton,	1	2	Spots.
Sanford,Patrick,	1	2	West.	Saunders,William,	1	4	Buck.	Schooley,Garrett,	1		Lou.
Sanford,Reuben,		2	West.	Saunders,William,	1		Din.	Schooley,John,	1		Lou.
Sanford,Richard,	1	2	West.	Saunders,William,	3	2	Lou.	Schooley,Samuel,	1		Lou.
Sanford,Richard,	1	8	West.	Sautts,Thomas,			Har.	Schooley,William,	1		Lou.
Sanford,Robert,est.,		4	West.	Savage,Abel,			Acco.	Schoonover,Benjamin,	1		Har.
Sanford,Robert,			York	Savage,Abel,	2		Acco.	Sclater,John,	1	30	York
Sanford,Robert,		2	York	Savage,Abel,	1	8	Nor.	Scoby,John,	1		Lou.
Sanford,Thomas,Sr.,	1	7	West.	Savage,Babel,	1		Acco.	Scogins,Gardner,	1	2	Brun.
Sanford,William,	1	7	West.	Savage,Francis,	1	8	Acco.	Scoggin,William,		1	Pr.Geo.
Sanford,William,	2		West.	Savage,Frederick,	1	5	Pr.Ge	Scott,Abraham,	1		York
Sanford,William,	1		West.	Savage,George,			Acco.	Scott,Abraham,			York

Name			County
Scott,Alexander,	1		Wash.
Scott,Alexander,	1	1	Fay.
Scott,Andrew,	2	1	Augu.
Scott,Anderson,	1	14	K.&Q
Scott,Andrew,	1	2	Rock.
Scott,Rev.Archbald,	1	2	Augu.
Scott,Axton,	1		Bed.
Scott,Benjamin Jr.,	1		Har.
Scott,Burrell	1		Henry
Scott,Catherine,		10	Acco.
Scott,Charles,	1		Wash.
Scott,Charles,	1	1	West.
Scott,Charles	1		Bot.
Scott,Cornelius,	1	1	Cul.
Scott,Daniel,	1	9	Nor.
Scott,David,	1		Mont.
Scott,David,est.,		3	Pr.Geo
Scott,Elizabeth,		29	Fau.
Scott,John,Epes,	1	1	Din.
Scott,Francis,	1	1	Din.
Scott,Francis,	1		Hen.
Scott,George,	1	7	Berk.
Scott,George	1		Bed.
Scott,Henry,	1		Cul.
Scott,Hugh,	1		Buck.
Scott,Jacob,	1		Lou.
Scott,James,	1		Mont.
Scott,James,	1		Bot.
Scott,James,	1	25	Lun.
Scott,James ,	1	2	Bed.
Scott,James,	1		Berk.
Scott,James,	1		Berk.
Scott,Rev.James.,	1	17	Pr.Wm.
Scott,Rev.James,	1	18	Fau.
Scott,James,	1		Wash.
Scott,James,	1	1	Cul.
Scott,Jesse	1		Cha.Cy
Scott,John,	2	1	Har.
Scott,John,	1	6	Spots
Scott,John,	1		Hen.
Scott,John,	1	12	Din.
Scott,John Jr.,	1		Nor.
Scott,John Jr.,	1	2	Nor.
Scott,John,	1	19	Caro.
Scott,John,	1	1	Fay.
Scott,John,	1		Fau.
Scott,John,	1		Mont.
Scott,Rev.John,	2	20	Fau.
Scott,John,	1		Wash.
Scott,John,	1		Cul.
Scott,John,	1		Augu.
Scott,Jonathan	1	1	Acco.
Scott,Joseph,	1		Har.
Scott,Joseph,	1		Lou.
Scott,Joseph,	1		Hen.
Scott,Joseph,		5	Sou'n.
Scott,Joseph,	1		Wash.
Scott,Joseph,	1		Buck.
Scott,Laban,	1	1	Nor.
Scott,Levern,	1	2	Acco.
Scott,Margett	1	1	Fay.
Scott,Mathew,	1		Bot.
Scott,Miley,	1		Cul.
Scott,Miriam,		15	Sou'n.
Scott,Nathan,	1		Bot.
Scott,Richard,	1	19	K.&Q
Scott,Robert,	1	1	Lou.
Scott,Robert,	2	6	Lun.
Scott,Robert,	1		Fau.
Scott,Robert,	1		Augu.
Scott,Robert,	1		Cha.Cy
Scott,Robinson,			Augo.
Scott,Sackor,	1	1	Acco.
Scott,Samuel,	1		Mont.
Scott,Samuel,			Cul.
Scott,Samuel,Jr.,	1		Wash.

Name			County
Scott,Samuel,	1		Wash.
Scott,Samuel,Sr.,	1		Wash.
Scott,Samuel,	1	1	Bot.
Scott,Samuel,	1		Lou.
Scott,Samuel,	1	16	Camp.
Scott,Samuel,		2	Brun.
Scott,Samuel,			Brun.
Scott,Stephen,	1	11	Din.
Scott,Thomas,	1	2	Lun.
Scott,Thomas,	3	17	Cul.
Scott,Thomas,	1		Wash.
Scott,Thomas,	1	18	Caro.
Scott,Thomas,			Bot.
Scott,Thomas,	1		Aug.
Scott,Thomas,Sr.,	4		Aug.
Scott,Thomas,Jr.,	1		Aug.
Scott,Thomas,Sr.,	1		Nor.
Scott,Thomas,Jr.,	1	1	Nor.
Scott,Thomas,	1	2	York
Scott,Maj.Thomas,	3	57	Din.
Scott,Thomas,Jr.,	2	11	Din.
Scott,Walter,Sr.,	3		Acco.
Scott,Walter,Jr.,	1		Acco.
Scott,William,	2	1	Aug.
Scott,William,	1		Aug.
Scott,William,	1		Acco.
Scott,William,	2	1	Acco.
Scott,William,	1		Pr.Wm.
Scott,William,	1		Pr.Wm.
Scott,William,	1		Pr.Wm
Scott,William,	1	6	Caro.
Scott,William,	1	6	Spots
Scott,William,	1	7	Lun.
Scott,William,Sr.,	1		Bed.
Scott,William,Jr.,	1		Bed.
Scott,William,			Cul.
Scott,William,	1	22	Camp.
Scott,William,(Indian	1		Hen.
Scott,William,	1		Hen.
Scott,William,	1	9	Din.
Scott,William,		6	So'n.
Scott,William,Sr.,	1	14	Nor.
Scott,William,Jr.,	1		Nor.
Scott,William,	1		Bot.
Scott,William,	1		Wash.
Scott,Zachariah,	1		Hen.
Scott,Zerubable,	1	12	Nor.
Scouts,John,	1		Lin.
Screech,Stephen,	1		Mont.
Scrghan,Mary,			Spots
Scroggin,Walter,	1	5	Pr.Wm
Scruggs,Allen,	1		Buck.
Scruggs,Britain,	1		Bed.
Scruggs,Edward,		1	Gooch
Scruggs,Edward,	1	3	Buck.
Scruggs,Gross,	1	8	Bed.
Scruggs,James,	1		Gooch
Scruggs,James,	2	4	Buck.
Scruggs,Jesse,			Buck.
Scruggs,Richard,	1		Gooch
Scruggs,Theodorick,	1	13	Buck.
Scruggs,Thomas,	1	12	Bed.
Scruggs,Valentine,	1	5	Buck.
Scruggs,William,	2	12	Buck.
Scruggs,William,	1		Mont.
Scubra,Joseph,	1		Bot.
Scuddy,Judith,	1		Spots
Sea,John,	1		Rock.
Sea,Josiah,	1	4	Gooch
Sea,Martin,	1		Rock.
Seabrook,Nicholas,	1	4	Hen.
Seaburn,George,	2	1	Berk.
Seaburn,Peter,	1		Berk.
Secee,Henry,	1		Aug.
Seager,Richard,	1	18	Caro.
Seaglor,Jacob,	1		Lou.

Name			County
Seagraves,Samuel,	1		Bot.
Seagraves,William,	1		Bot.
Seal,Anthony,	1		Caro.
Seal,David,	1	1	Caro.
Seale,Anthony,	2	8	Pr.Wm.
Seale,Anthony,Jr.,			Pr.Wm.
Seale, J.,	2	7	Pr.Wm.
Seale,J.,Jr.,			Pr.Wm.
Seale,John,			Pr.Wm.
Seale, R.,	1	1	Pr.Wm.
Sealock,Thomas,	1		Lou.
Seaman,Jacomiah,	2		Berk.
Seaman,Jonah,	1		Berk.
Seaman,Jonathan,	2		Berk.
Seaman,Jonathan,	1		Berk.
Searlf,John,	1	3	Caro.
Searcy,Robert,	1		Henry
Searjeant,William,	1		Loui.
Searng,John,	1		Henry
Sears,Albin,	1	10	Caro.
Sears,John,	2		Har.
Sears,Philip,	1	2	K.&Q
Sears,Robert,			Lou.
Sears,William,	1		Spots
Sears,William,	1		Har.
Sears,WilliamB.,	2	2	Lou.
Seaser,John,	1	3	Caro.
Seatt,David,	1		Rock.
Seaton,Augustine,	1	15	K.Wm.
Seaton,John,	1		Fau.
Seaton,William,	1	5	Fau.
Seawright,James,	1		Aug.
Seawright,Jean,		1	Aug.
Seawright,John,	1	2	Aug.
Seay,Abner,	1		Buck.
Seay,Benjamin,			K.Wm.
Sebra,James,	1		Cul.
Sedberry,George,	1	1	Brun.
See,George,	4	5	Har.
See,George,Jr.,	2		Har.
See,Michael,	2	1	Har.
Seelch,Nich,	1		Lin.
Seeright,George,	2		Fay.
Seever,Hannah,		1	Berk.
Seidmons,Thomas,	1		Wash.
Seigler,John,	1		Lou.
Seirvin,John,	1		Lou.
Seizer,Reubin,	1	1	K.Wm.
Selden,Ann,		4	Eli.Cy
Selden,Cary,	1	38	Eli.Cy
Selden,John,	1		Eli.Cy
Selden,Joseph,	1	1	Eli.Cy
Selden,Rev.Miles,	1	32	Hen.
Selden,Miles,	1	26	Hen.
Selden,Rev.William,	1	17	Eli.Cy
Selder,Elizabeth,		8	Pr.Geo.
Selder,John,	1	1	Pr.Geo.
Self,Charnock,	1	2	Lou.
Self,Charnock,	1		Fay.
Self,Elizabeth,			Lou.
Self,Jeremiah,	1		Loui.
Self,Jeremiah,	1		Loui.
Self,John,	1		K.&Q
Self,Moses,	1	1	West.
Self,Presley,	1	2	Lou.
Self,Stephen,	3	2	West.
Sellavan,Daniel,	1	3	Acco.
Selby,Clement,	1		Lou.
Belby,Thomas,	1	3	Berk.
Sellers,Frederick,	1		Har.
Sellers,John,			Har.
Sellers,Susanna,			Har.
Sellers,John,	1		Lin.
Sellers,John,	1		K.&Q
Sellers,Joseph,			Lin.
Sellers,Nathaniel,	3		Lin.

Sellers,John,	1		Cul.	Shacken,Benjamin,	1		Gooch.	Sharpe,Elizabeth,	2	4	Hen.
Sellers,Nathaniel,	1		Henry	Shackleford,Ambrose,	1		Spots.	Sharpe,Hales,	1	2	Hen.
Selling,Andrew,	1		Berk.	Shackleford,Ann,			Spots.	Sharpe,Isaac,			Hen.
Selman,Ann,			Fau.	Shackleford,Benjamin,	1	17	Fau.	Sharpe,Jacob,	1	1	Hen.
Semonis,John,	1		Lou.	Shackleford,Dicey,		2	Din.	Sharpe,James,	1	1	Cul.
Senter,Samuel,	1		Brun.	Shackleford,Edward,			Lin.	Sharpe,John,	1		Aug.
Sensibak,John,	1		Rock.	Shackleford,George,			Lin.	Sharpe,John,Sr.,	1		Aug.
Sergant,Stephen,	1		Wash.	Shackleford,James,Sr.,	1	2	Lin.	Sharpe,Julius,			Hen.
Sergant,William,	1		Wash.	Shackleford,James,Jr.,	1		Lin.	Sharpe,Peter,	1	8	Hen.
Sergeant,Richard,	2		Berk.	Shackleford,James,	1	27	Fau.	Sharpe,Richard,	2	13	Hen.
Serimsher,Walter,			West.	Shackleford,James,	2		Cul.	Sharpe,Richard,Jr.,			Hen.
Setliff,John,	1		Buck.	Shackleford,James,	2	2	Buck.	Sharpe,Thomas,	1	1	Spots.
Settle,Benjamin,	1	2	Cul.	Shackleford,Samuel,	2	4	Lin.	Sharpe,William,	1	2	Aug.
Settle,Benjamin,Jr.,	1		Cul.	Shackleford,William,	1		Mont.	Sharper,James,(F.N.)			Hen.
Settle,Edward,			Cul.	Shacklett,Edward,	1		Fau.	Sharpless,Jesse,	1		Har.
Settle,Edward,	1	16	Fau.	Shacklett,Hezekiah,	1	3	Fau;	Sharrod,Jacob,	3		Acco.
Settle,Francis,	1	3	Cul.	Shade,Jacob,	1		Lou.	Sharrod,Henry,	2		Acco.
Settle,Francis,			Fau.	Shadden,Alexander,	1		Wash.	Shatz,Henry,	1		Berk.
Settle,Gayton,	1	1	Fau.	Shadden,James,	1		Wash.	Shaver,Adam,	1		Lou.
Settle,George,	1	2	Fau.	Shaddon,Joseph,	1		Bot.	Shaver,Boston,	3	2	Bot.
Settle,Henry,	1	7	Fau.	Shaddon,Robert,	1		Bot.	Shaver,Frederick,	1		Bot.
Settle,Joel,	1	2	Fau.	Shadrer,James,	1		Camp.	Shaver,Frederick,			Bot.
Settle,John,	1		Fau.	Shadrick,Thomas,Sr.,		2	West.	Shaver,George,	1		Lou.
Settle,Newman,	1		Cul.	Shadrick,Thomas,Jr.,	1	1	West.	Shaver,Jacob,	1		Lou.
Settle,Newman,	1		Cul.	Shadrock,John,	1		Lin.	Shaw,Archibald,	1		Fau.
Settle,William,	1	2	Fau.	Shadwong,Frank,	1		Buck.	Shaw,Jervis,	1		Pr.Wm.
Settle,William,			Fau.	Shaffer,Conrod,	1		Lou.	Shaw,John,	1		Cul.
Settles,Benjamin,	2		K.Geo	Shaffer,Simon,	1	2	Lou.	Shaw,John,			Bed.
Settles,Hannah,	1	1	K.Geo	Shakleton,John,	1		Hen.	Shaw,John,	1		Rock.
Settles,Thomas,	1	2	K.Geo	Shan,Thomas,	1		Cul.	Shaw,Josiah,	1	4	Henry
Settlington,John,	1		Aug.	Shanar,George,	1		Har.	Shaw,Mary,	2		Fay.
Seundland,John,	1	3	Caro.	Shanklin,Andrew,	1		Lin.	Shaw,Philip,	1		Pr.Wm.
Seundland,John,	1	4	Caro.	Shanklin,Richard,	1		Bot.	Shaw,Robert,	1	1	Rock.
Seundland,Robert,	1	2	Caro.	Shanklin,Robert,	1		Bot.	Shaw,Thomas,	1		Lin.
Seward,Benjamin,			Brun.	Shanks,Henry,	1		Fau.	Shaw,William,	2		Mont.
Seward,Benjamin,	1	2	K.& Q	Shanks,John,	1		Fau.	Shawn,Isaac,	1		Fau.
Seward,Edwin,	1		So'n	Shanks,Thomas,	1	10	Lou.	Shay,John,	1	15	York
Seward,John,	1	15	Brun.	Shannan,Thomas,	1		Bed.	Shay,Stephen,	1		Lou.
Seward,Joseph,	2	1	Brun.	Shannon,Hugh,	1	1	Fay.	Shay,William,	1		Jas.Cy
Seward,Mary,		5	Din.	Shannon,Hugh,	1		Lin.	Shearer,Archibald,	2	1	Berk.
Seward,Robert,			Brun.	Shannon,James,	1		Mont.	Shearer,James,	1		Camp.
Seward,William,			Brun.	Shannon,John,	1		Mont.	Shearer,Leeney,			Camp.
Sewel,Thomas,	1		Bot.	Shannon,John,Sr.,	1		Mont.	Shedaker,John,	1		Lou.
Sewell,Benjamin,			Lun.	Shannon,John,jr.,	1		Mont.	Shedelkett,Christian,	1		Aug.
Sewell,David,	1		Berk.	Shannon,Robert,Sr.,	1		Mont.	Sheely,David,	1	1	Berk.
Sewell,John,	1		Berk.	Shannon,Samuel,	1		Mont.	Sheep,John,	1		Berk.
Sewell,Leonard,	2		Pr.Wm.	Shannon,Thomas,	1		Lin .	Sheerwood,Robert,	1	2	Henry
Sewell,Timothy,	1		Berk.	Shannon,Thomas,	1		Mont.	Sheets,Jacob,	2		Aug.
Seymore,Abel,	1	2	Har.	Shard,James,	1		Henry	Sheets,George,	1		Aug.
Seymore,George,	1		Har.	Sharer,James,	1		Cul.	Sheill,Ann,		1	Lin.
Seymore,Felix,	2	3	Har.	Sharlock,John,	1	5	Acco.	Shelburn,James,	1	1	Jas.Cy.
Seymore,Richard,	1	3	Har.	Sharp,Abram,	1		Bed.	Shelburn,William,	1		Jas.Cy.
Seymore,Thomas,	3		Har.	Sharp,Adam,	1		Bed.	Shelburne,Augustine,	1		Lun.
Seymore,William,	1		Har.	Sharp,Ann,			Fau.	Shelburne,James,	1	8	Lun.
Seymour,John,	1		Eli.Cy	Sharp,George,	1		Caro.	Shelburne,John,	1		Lun.
Seymour,William,	1	1	Eli.Cy	Sharp,Henry,	1		Bot.	Shelburne,Thomas,	1		Lun.
Seymure,Leah,		12	Acco.	Sharp,Isaac,			Hen.	Shelby,Isaac,	1	24	Lin.
Seyvert,Henry,	1		Aug.	Sharp,James,	1	4	Hen.	Shelby,John,	1		Wash.
Seyvert,Nicholas,	1		Aug.	Sharp,John,	2		Fay.	Shelby,Phillip,	1		Wash.
Shackelford,Daniel,	1	4	K.& Q	Sharp,John,	1		Wash.	Shell,John,	1	1	Brun.
Shackelford,Daniel,			Cul.	Sharp,John,	1		Mont.	Shell,Lemon,	2	6	Brun.
Shackelford,Drucilla,		4	K.& Q	Sharp,John,	1		Bed.	Shell,Lemon,		42	Brun.
Shackelford,Dudley,			Cul.	Sharp,John,	1		Bed.	Shell,Stephen,		1	Cha.Cy
Shackelford,Frances,		6	K.& Q	Sharp,John,	1		Bot.	Shell,Stephen,			Cha.Cy
Shackelford,Henry,	1	5	K.Wm.	Sharp,M.,	2	12	Pr.Wm.	Shell,William,			Brun,
Shackelford,James,	1	1	K.Wm.	Sharp,Martha	1	3	Hen.	Shell,William,	1	17	Brun.
Shackelford,John,	1	3	Caro.	Sharp,Moses,	1		Buck.	Shell,William,Jr.,	1		Brun.
Shackelford,John,	1	4	Cul.	Sharp,Richard,Sr.,			Buck.	Shelladay,George,Sr.	1	2	Mont.
Shackelford,John,	1	5	K.& Q	Sharp,Richard,Jr.,	1		Buck.	Shelladay,George,Jr			Mont.
Shackelford,John,	1	1	K.& Q	Sharp,Richard,	1		So'n	Shelley,Nathan,	1		Mont.
Shackelford,Leonard,	1	3	K.& Q	Sharp,Robert,	1	11	Hen.	Shelton,David,	2	28	Loui.
Shackelford,Lyne,	1	20	K.& Q	Sharp,Thomas,	2		Berk.	Shelton,Eliphaz,	1		Henry
Shackelford,Richard,	2		Cul.	Sharp,William,	1		Buck.	Shelton,George,	1		Cul.
Shackelford,William,	2	13	K.& Q	Sharp,William,	1	1	Loui.	Shelton,Henry,	1	2	Loui.
Shackelford,Zachariah,	1	2	Lin.	Sharp,William,	1		Henry	Shelton,James,	1	4	Henry
Shackelford,Zachary,	1	6	K.& Q	Sharpe,Abraham,	1	2	Hen.	Shelton,John,	1	16	Spots.

Name			County
Shelton,John,(Han.)	1	8	Gooch.
Shelton,John,	1	17	Gooch.
Shelton,Joseph,(Loui)	1	14	Gooch.
Shelton,Joseph,(Loui)	1	25	Gooch.
Shelton,Joseph,	2	40	Loui.
Shelton,Joseph,Jr.,			Loui.
Shelton,Joseph,			Loui.
Shelton,Medley,			Cul.
Shelton,Palatiah,	1	2	Henry
Shelton,Peter,	1	16	Loui.
Shelton,Ralph,Sr.,	1		Henry
Shelton,Ralph,Jr.,	1		Henry
Shelton,Roger,	1		Henry
Shelton,Samuel,	1	6	Henry
Shelton,Sil,	1	1	Brun.
Shelton,Thomas,	2	8	Loui.
Shelton,William,	1		Henry
Shelton,William,	1		Henry
Shelton,William,	3	21	Loui.
Shepard,Ann,		12	Eli.Cy
Shephard,Benjamin,			Hen.
Shepard,Hezekiah,		5	Acco.
Shepard,John,	1	5	Ja.Cy
Shepard,Solomon,			Acco.
Sheperd,John,	1		Cul.
Shepherd,***,	1		K.&Q
Shepherd,Abraham,	2	4	Berk.
Shepherd,Charles,			Lou.
Shepherd,Daniel,	1		Har.
Shepherd,George,	1		Fay.
Shepherd,James,	1		Har.
Shepherd,James,	1		Gooch.
Shepherd,John,	2		Lou.
Shepherd,John,	1		Lou.
Shepherd,John,	1	1	Berk.
Shepherd,John,	2		Har.
Shepherd,John,	1		Lin.
Shepherd,Laurence,	1		Lou.
Shepherd,Molly,		1	K.&Q
Shepherd,Solomon,	1	25	So'n
Shepherd,Thomas,			Fau.
Shepherd,Thomas,	1		Berk.
Shepherd,Thomas,	2		Berk.
Shepherd,Thomas,	1		Mont.
Shepherd,William,			Lou.
Shepherd,William,	1		Bed.
Shepherd,William,	1		Berk.
Shepherd,William,	2		Mont.
Sheppard,Benjamin,	1	16	Hen.
Sheppard,Benjamin,			Hen.
Sheppard,John,	1	1	Eli.Cy
Sheppard,Mary,		7	Hen.
Sheppard,Robert,	2	4	Hen.
Sheppard,Samuel,			Hen.
Sheppard,William,	3	7	Hen.
Sheppard,William,	2	7	Hen.
Sheppard,William,			Hen.
Shepperd,Dubartis,	3	3	Bot.
Shepperson,John,	1		Loui.
Sheredon,Phillip,	1		Henry
Sherer,Patrick,	1	1	Caro.
Sherley,***,		8	K.&Q
Sherman,Benjamin,			Cha.Cy
Sherman,Robert,			Hen.
Sherrill,William,	4		Cul.
Sherrington,Robert,	1		York
Sherwood,Robert,	1		Cul.
Shevelier,Anthony,	1		Fay.
Shewmake,Joshua,	1		Cul.
Shick,Andrew,	1		Rock.
Shield,Aser,	2	1	Acco.
Shield,Nicholas,	1		Acco.
Shield,Peter,	1		Acco.
Shield,Robert,	1	19	York
Shield,Sacker,	1	1	Acco.
Shield,Thomas,		1	So'n
Shields,David,			Aug.
Shields,Eris,	1		Caro.
Shields,James,	2	30	York
Shields,James,Jr.,			York
Shields,James,	2	40	Ja.Cy
Shields,John,	1		Berk.
Shields,John,	1		Aug.
Shields,John,	1		Berk.
Shields,Margaret,			Aug.
Shields,Moss,	1		So'n
Shields,Peter,	1		Har.
Shields,Richard,	1		Bot.
Shields,Robert,	1	3	So'n
Shields,Robert,	1		Aug.
Shields,Robert,	1		Bot.
Shields,Thomas,	1		Bot.
Shields,Thomas,	1		Aug.
Shields,William,	1		Aug.
Shields,William,Jr.,	1		Aug.
Shields,William,	1		Aug.
Shields,William,Jr.,	1		Aug.
Shields,William,	1		Berk.
Shilcott,John,	2	3	K.&Q
Shilcott,William,	1		K.Geo.
Skill,George,	1		Har.
Shilough,Daniel,	1		Bot.
Shilough,Jacob,	1		Bot.
Shim,John,	1		K.Geo.
Shin,Clement,	1		Berk.
Shin,David,	1		Berk.
Shinton,Abraham,	1		Har.
Shinton,Ramon,	1		Har.
Ship,Edmund,	1	6	Caro.
Ship,Isbel,	1	2	Cul.
Ship,Laban,	1	8	Fau.
Ship,Nanney,		2	Caro.
Ship,Richard,	1	7	Caro.
Ship,Richard Watt,	1	11	Fau.
Ship,Richard,Jr.,	1	10	Caro.
Ship,Samuel,	1	5	Caro.
Shipe,Peter,	1		Aug.
Shipler,Henry,	1		Har.
Shipler,Richard,	1		Har.
Shipman,Stephen,	1		Lou.
Shipp,Colley,	1	2	Fay.
Shipp,Laban,	1	7	Fay.
Ships,John,	1		Fau.
Ships,Joseph,	1		Fau.
Shirley,James,	1		Pr.Wm.
Shirley,John,	1	8	Spots.
Shirley,John,Jr.,	1	1	Spots.
Shirley,John,	1	1	Fau.
Shirley,Richard,	1		Pr.Wm.
Shirley,Thomas,	1	1	Pr.Wm.
Shirley,Thomas,			Spots.
Shiveley,George,	2		Lou.
Shivly,Daniel,	1		Berk.
Shively,John,	1		Berk.
Shreeves,Joseph,	1		Har.
Shrider,George,	1		Mont.
Shriegly,Joseph,	1		Lou.
Shriegly,Lawrence,	1		Lou.
Shires,John,	1		Aug.
Shires,Richard,	1		Aug.
Shirkey,James,	2	4	Bot.
Shirkey,Patrick,	1	2	Bot.
Shoat,Peter,	3		Har.
Shoats,George,	2	1	West.
Shobe,Jacob,	1		Har.
Shobe,Martin,	4		Har.
Shobe,Martin,Jr.,	1		Har.
Shobe,Rudolph,Sr.,	3		Har.
Shobe,Rudolph,Jr.,	1		Har.
Shock,Andrew,	1		Berk.
Shockley,Levy,	1		Henry
Shockley,Richard,	1		Mont.
Shockley,Thomas,	1		Mont.
Shoemake,Daniel,Jr.,	1		Lou.
Shoemaker,Daniel,	1		Lou.
Shoemaker,George,	2		Lou.
Shoemaker,George,	1		Har.
Shoemanker,Jacob,Sr.,	1		Lou.
Shoemanke,Jacob,Jr.,	1		Lou.
Shoemaker,Jeremiah,	1		Hen.
Shoemaker,John,			Lou.
Shoemaker,Leonard,			Bot.
Shoemaker,Lindsay,	1		Buck.
Shoemaker,Peter,	3		Har.
Shoemaker,Simon,	1		Lou.
Shoemaker,Solomon,	1		Lin.
Shoemaker,Thomas,	1	4	Gooch.
Shoemaker,Thomas,	1	2	Gooch.
Sholas,Jacob,	1		Camp.
Sholders,Conrod,	1		Har.
Shook,David,	1		Har.
Shook,Hammon,Sr.,	1		Har.
Shook,John,	1		Har.
Shook,Jonas,	1		Har.
Shook,Lawrence,	2		Har.
Shook,Peter,	1		Har.
Shoots,Benjamin,	1		Lou.
Shore & McConnico,	7	14	Din.
Shore,Charles,	1		Fay.
Shore,Richard,	1		Henry
Shore,Thomas,	1	9	Lou.
Shores,Edward,	1		Acco.
Shores,Richard,	1	1	Fay.
Shores,Thomas,	1	6	Fay.
Shores,William,	1	1	Lou.
Short,David,	1		Mont.
Short,Jacob,	1		Lou.
Short,James,	1		Wash.
Short,John,	1		Lou.
Short,John,	1		Henry
Short,John,	2		Lin.
Short,John,	1	5	Brun.
Short,Obediah,	1		Lin.
Short,Theodocia,		38	K.Geo.
Short,Thomas,	1	1	Brun.
Short,William,Jr.,	1	1	Brun.
Shorter,Henry,	2	2	Cul.
Shorter,James,			Cul.
Shorter,William,	1	1	Cul.
Shortridge,George,	2		Fay.
Shortridge,George,	1		Fay.
Shortridge,John,	1		Fay.
Shortridge,Samuel,	1		Fay.
Shortridge,William,	1		Fay.
Shotwell,Robert,	1	1	Cul.
Shotwell,William,	2		Cul.
Shound,Leonard,	2		Aug.
Showns,James,	1		Bot.
Shreve,Caleb,	1		Lou.
Shrewsbury,Dabney,	1	1	Bed.
Shrewsbury,Nathaniel	1	5	Bed.
Shrewsbury,Samuel,	1	6	Bed.
Shrither,Henry,	1		Bot.
Shrieve,Benjamin,	1		Lou.
Shrieve,John,	1		Lou.
Shriver,Peter,	1		Berk.
Shrives,Abraham,	3		Acco.
Shrives,Bartholomew	1		Acco.
Shrote,Peter,	3		Har.
Shroul,Alexander,	1		Aug.
Shroul,James,	1		Aug.
Shroul,William,	1	7	Aug.
Shroves,Daniel,	1		Berk.
Shryrock,Michael,	2	3	Lou.
Shuckman,Nicholas,	1		Lou.
Shuffield,Adam,			Pr.Geo.
Should,Rev.Samuel,	1	24	Caro.
Shull,Jacob,	3		Mont.
Shults,George,	1		Aug.
Shumate,Bailey,	1	4	Fau.
Shumate,Daniel,Sr.,	1	1	Fau.

Name			County
Shumate,Daniel,	1	2	Fau.
Shumate,James,	1	7	Fau.
Shumate,James,		1	Fau.
Shumate,James,	1	3	Har.
Shumate,John,Sr.,			Fau.
Shumate,John,	1	7	Fau.
Shumate,John,	1	1	Fau.
Shumate,Samuel,	1	1	Fau.
Shumate,Thomas,	1	1	Fau.
Shumate,William,	1		Fau.
Shurley,Argibill,	1		Pr.Wm.
Shurley,George,	1		Pr.Wm.
Shurley,James,	2	3	Cul.
Shurley,James,	1		Pr.Wm.
Shurley,Richard,	1		Pr.Wm.
Shurley,Valentine,	1	1	Aug.
Shurley,William,			Pr.Wm.
Shute,John,			Aug.
Shute,John,	2	4	Pr.Wm.
Shutts,John,	1		Fay.
Shuttle,John,			Camp.
Sibbey,John,	1		Har.
Sicklor,Jacob,	1		Mont.
Siddall,John,	1		Fau.
Sidebottom,Charles,	1		Lin.
Sidebottom,William,	1		Pr.Wm.
Siders,Isaac,	1		Lou.
Siglor,Jacob,	1		Lou.
Silar,Wimor,	1		Wash.
Siler,Jacob,	1		Aug.
Silkwood,Solomon,	1		Berk.
Silor,Jacob,	1		Aug.
Silor,Jacob,	1		Berk.
Silver,Aaron,	1		Aug.
Silvers,Joseph,	1		Lin.
Silvey,Abraham,		1	Fau.
Simbala,Matthias,	1		Lou,
Simmerman,Earhart,	1		Mont.
Simmerman,Henry,	1		York
Simmerman,Jacob,	1		Aug.
Simmerman,Joseph,	1		Mont.
Simmerman,Strophel,	1		Mont.
Simmonds,Thomas,	1		Lou.
Simmonds,William,	1		Lou.
Simmons,Anderson,	1	11	Pr.Geo
Simmons,Benjamin,	1	10	Pr.Wm.
Simmons,Charles,	1		Bot.
Simmons,Charles,			Camp.
Simmons,Charles,			Camp.
Simmons,Charles,	1		Bed.
Simmons,Daniel,		16	So'n
Simmons,Demsy,	1		So'n
Simmons,Edwin,			So'n
Simmons,George,	1		Bed.
Simmons,George,	1		Bed.
Simmons,George,	1		Aug.
Simmons,George,	1	3	Din.
Simmons,Harry,		1	So'n
Simmons,John,	1		Mont.
Simmons,John,	1		So'n
Simmons,John,	2	18	So'n
Simmons,John,Jr.,	1	13	So'n
Simmons,John,Sr.,	1	24	So'n
Simmons,John,	1		Henry
Simmons,John,			Lou.
Simmons,John,	1		Aug.
Simmons,John,	1		Camp.
Simmons,John,	1		Camp.
Simmons,Joseph,	1		Bed.
Simmons,Joseph,	1	4	Din.
Simmons,Joseph,	1	4	Pr.Geo
Simmons,Leonard,Sr.,	1		Aug.
Simmons,Leonard,Jr.,	1		Aug.
Simmons,Mark,	1		Aug.
Simmons,Mrs.Martha,		38	Brun.S
Simmons,Martha,		40	Brun.

Name			County
Simmons,Michael,	1		Aug.
Simmons,Nicholas,	1		Aug.
Simmons,Olive,		6	So'n
Simmons,Peter,	1		Bed.
Simmons,Randol,	1	1	Pr.Geo
Simmons,Reubin,	1	1	Camp.
Simmons,Reubin,	1	1	Camp.
Simmons,Spratley,	1	9	So'n
Simmons,Susanna,	1	26	Brun.
Simmons,Thomas,	1	13	So'n
Simmons,William,	1		Pr.Geo
Simmons,William,	1	9	Pr.Geo
Simmons,William,	1	4	Pr.Geo
Simmons,Winnifred,		4	Din.
Simmons,Zachariah,	1		Mont.
Simms,Edward,	1	1	Cul.
Simms,Ignatius,	1	7	Henry
Simms,J.,	1		Pr.Wm.
Simon,Christian,	1		Har.
Simon,George,	1		Har.
Simon,Philip,	1		Har.
Simons,Thomas,	1		Har.
Simons,Abram,	1	4	Spots.
Simons,John,	1		Berk.
Simonus,William,	1		Cul.
Simonton,Alexander,	1		Berk.
Simpkins,Coventon,	1	8	Nor.
Simpkins,James,	1		Bed.
Simpkins,John,	2	2	K.Wm.
Simpkins,William,	1		Bed.
Simpkins,William,	1	28	Nor.
Simpson,Alexander,	3	1	Har.
Simpson,Alexander,	1	1	Cul.
Simpson,Charles,	1		Spots.
Simpson,Daniel,	1		Spots.
Simpson,Edward,	1	5	Spots.
Simpson,Francis,	2	7	Spots.
Simson,Gilbert,	3	8	Fay.
Simpson,Hugh,	1		Mont.
Simpson,James,	1		Bot.
Simpson,James,Sr.,	1		Mont.
Simpson,James,Jr.,	1		Mont.
Simpson,John,	2	14	West.
Simpson,John,	1		Lin.
Simpson,John,	1		Pr.Wm.
Simpson,John,	1	3	Cul.
Simpson,John,	1		Mont.
Simpson,John,	1		Mont.
Simpson,John,	1	5	Lou.
Simpson,Jonathan,	1		Har.
Simpson,Robert,	1		Mont.
Simpson,Robert,	1		Rock.
Simpson,Samuel,			Fay.
Simpson,Solomon,	1		Bot.
Simpson,William,	1		Spots.
Simpson,William,	1		Pr.Wm.
Simpson,William,	1	12	Cul.
Sims,Asa,	1		Loui.
Sims,Bartlet,	1	1	Brun.
Sims,Benjamin,	1		Loui.
Sims,David,	1	1	Luui.
Sims,David,			Loui.
Sims,Elijah,	1	5	Cul.
Sims,Elijah,	1		Har.
Sims,Franklin,	1	2	West.
Sims,George,	1		Cul.
Sims,James,	2	7	Cul.
Sims,James,	1	1	Cul.
Sims,Jeremiah,	1		Cul.
Sims,John,	1		Loui.
Sims,John,	1	6	Brun.
Sims,John,	2	3	West.
Sims,Joseph,	1	1	K.Geo.
Sims,Matthew,	1	1	Henry
Sims,Micajah,	1		Loui.
Sims,Micajah,Jr.,	1		Loui.

Name			County
Sims,Reubin,	1		Cul.
Sims,Reubin,	1	6	Loui.
Sims,Richard,	1	2	Cul.
Sims,Sarah,		1	Henry
Sims,Thomas,	2		Cul.
Sims,William,	1	5	Brun.
Sims,William,	1		Har.
Sims,William,	1	1	Cul.
Sims,William,		4	Loui.
Sims,Zachariah,	1	2	Brun.
Sinclair,Alexander,	1	8	Aug.
Sinclair,Amos,			Lou.
Sinclair,Charles,	1		Wash.
Sinclair,George,	1		Bed.
Sinclair,Isaac,	1	7	Bed.
Sinclair,Henry,			Eli.Cy
Sinclair,James,	1		Lou.
Sinclair,James,	1		Fau.
Sinclair,John,	2	5	Lou.
Sinclair,Joseph,	1		Wash.
Sinclair,Robert,	1		Bed.
Sinclair,Weaman,	1	1	Bed.
Sinclair,William,	1	6	Fau.
Sines,John,	1		Cul.
Singer,John,	2		Fau.
Singleton,Andrew,	1	12	Aug.
Singleton,Christopher	4	2	Lin.
Singleton,Edmund,	1		Lun.
Singleton,James,			Brun.
Singleton,John,	1	4	Lou.
Singleton,John,	1		Bed.
Singleton,Joshua,	½	5	Lou.
Singleton,Robert,	1		Lin.
Singleton,Robert,	1		Lun.
Singleton,Standley,	2	10	Fau.
Singleton,Titus,	1	3	Brun.
Singleton,William,	1		Brun.
Sink,John,	1		Aug.
Sinker,John,	1	19	Fau.
Sinker,Robert,	1	4	Fau.
Sinkler,William,	2	11	Fau.
Sisham,John,	1		Henry
Sisk,Bartlett,	1		Cul.
Sisk,James,	2		Cul.
Sisk,Martin,	1	1	Cul.
Sisk,William,	2		Cul.
Sissell,James,	1		Pr.Wm.
Sissell,John,			Pr.Wm.
Sisson,Cobb,	1	5	Rock.
Sites,George,	2		Har.
Six,Richard,	1		Hen.
Skaggs,Henry,	1		Mont.
Skaggs,Moses,	1		Mont.
Skean,Henry,	1		Rock.
Skean,Jonathan,	1		Rock.
Skean,Joseph,	1		Rock.
Skean,Robert,	1		Rock.
Skeaths,Mary,		3	Spots.
Skeely,John,Jr.,	1		Berk.
Skeetz,Philip,	4	2	Berk.
Skelton,Gilliam V.,	2		Pr.Geo.
Skelton,John,	1		Berk.
Skelton,John,	1	2	Pr.Wm.
Skelton,Thomas,	1	6	K.&Q
Skelton,William,	1	5	K.&Q
Skidmore,James,	2		Bot.
Skiller,Joseph,	1		Mont.
Skillern,George,	1	17	Bot.
Skillman,Christopher,	1		Henry
Skinker,John,		7	Fau.
Skinker,Col.John,	1	56	K.Geo.
Skinker,Samuel,	1	9	K.Geo.
Skinker,Thomas,	2	3	Fau.
Skinker,William,		17	Fau.
Skinker,William,	1	23	Pr.Wm.
Skinner,Burdett,	1		K.Geo.

Name			Loc.	Name			Loc.	Name			Loc.
Skinner,Cornelius,Jr.,			Lou.	Slinker,Christopher,	1		Bed.	Smith,Charles,	1	11	Bed.
Skinner,Cornelius,Jr.,			Lou.	Sloan,David,	1		Mont.	Smith,Charles,	1		Fau.
Skinner,Ellyson,	1	6	Eli.Cy	Sloan,James,	1		Aug.	Smith,Charles,est.,		76	Loui.
Skinner,Howard,	1		Eli.Cy	Sloan,John,	1		Lin.	Smith,Charles,	1	9	Brun.
Skinner,Isaac,			Lou.	Sloan,John,	1		Lin.	Smith,Christian,	1		Har.
Skinner,John,	1	3	Eli.Cy	Sloan,Thomas,	1		Lin.	Smith,Christopher,	1	28	Loui.
Skinner,John,Jr.,	1	2	Eli.Cy	Sloan,William,	1		Lin.	Smith,Christopher,	1	2	Caro.
Skinner,Nathaniel,	2		Lou.	Sloane,James,	1	1	Bed.	Smith,Clator,			Lou.
Skinner,Phinehas,	1		Lou.	Sloane,Thomas,	1		Bed.	Smith,Clator,		4	Lou.
Skinner,Richard,	1	2	Hen.	Sloane,Thomas,Jr.,			Bed.	Smith,Clator,Jr.,	1		Lou.
Skinner,Richard,	3		Lou.	Sloane,William,	1		Bed.	Smith,Clement,	1	10	Din.
Skinner,Willis,	1		Eli.Cy	Slocum,Susanah,	1	13	Acco.	Smith,Damaras,	1	3	York
Skinner,William,	1		Berk.	Slone,Michael,	1		Cul.	Smith,Daniel,	1		Henry
Skipwith,Fulwar,			Hen.	Slone,Patrick,	1		Bed.	Smith,Daniel,	1		Henry
Skipwith,Robert,est.	1	44	Din.	Slorter,John,	1		Din.	Smith,David,	1		Mont.
Skirvin,John,	1		Fay.	Slush,Fredrick,	1		Mont.	Smith,David,			Loui.
Skyring,Henry,	1	8	K.Wm.	Slusher,Coonrod,	1		Aug.	Smith,David,	2		Har.
Slacht,Cornelius,	2		Lou.	Small,Jacob,	2		Berk.	Smith,David,	1	1	Din.
Slacht,Enoch,			Lou.	Small,James,	1		Berk.	Smith,David,	1		Mont.
Slack,Jacob,	1		Lou.	Small,John,	1		Berk.	Smith,David,	1		Mont.
Slade,Joshua,	1		So'n	Small,John,	1	1	Henry	Smith,David,	1		Bot.
Slade,Sam,Sr.,	1		So'n	Small,Lewis,	1		Cul.	Smith,Downing,	1		Cul.
Slade,Sam,Jr.,	1		So'n	Small,Mathew,	1		Henry	Smith,Edmond,	2		Wash.
Slade,William,	1		Pr.Wm	Small,William,	1		Henry	Smith,Edmund,			Wash.
Sladen,William,	1		Loui.	Smalley,David,	1		Lou.	Smith,Edward,	1		Wash.
Slagle,Jacob,	1		Har.	Smalley,William,			Lou.	Smith,Edward,			Wash.
Slamp,Frederick,	1		Mont.	Smallwood,General,	2	26	K.Geo.	Smith,Edward,	1	2	Pr.Geo.
Slater,James,	1		Berk.	Smallwood,George,	1	2	Berk.	Smith,Edward,	1	5	Gooch.
Slater,Thomas,	2		Har.	Smallwood,John,	1		Bot.	Smith,Edward,	1	8	Lou.
Slator,Jacob,	1		Lou.	Smallwood,William,	1	11	Cul.	Smith,Edward,	1		Cul.
Slatton,Tyre,	1		Lin.	Smarr,John,	1	10	Lou.	Smith,Edwin,	1		Cul.
Slatts,Henry,		1	Lou.	Smarr,Robert,			Lou.	Smith,Elijah,	1		Bot.
Slaughter,Alice,		6	K.Wm.	Smart,Elisha,	1	5	Brun.	Smith,Elisha,	1		Camp.
Slaughter,Ann,		4	K.Wm.	Smart,Flisha,Carter,			Buck.	Smith,Elisha,	1		Cul.
Slaughter,Cad,	1	7	Cul.	Smart,James,	1	1	Caro.	Smith,Elizabeth,		7	K.Geo.
Slaughter,Cadwalader,	1	25	Cul.	Smart,John,	1	7	Caro.	Smith,Elizabeth,		1	Acco.
Slaughter,Charles,	1	4	Cul.	Smedley,John,	1		Lou.	Smith,Elizabeth,		63	West.
Slaughter,Edgcomb,			Cul.	Smelser,Catherine,		1	Bed.	Smith,Elizabeth,	1	1	West.
Slaughter,Edward,	1		Lun.	Smelt,Anna,		11	Caro.	Smith,Elizabeth,		11	Loui.
Slaughter,Edward,	1		K.& Q.	Smelt,David,	1	3	Eli.Cy	Smith,Elizabeth,		6	Loui.
Slaughter,Francis,	1	13	Cul.	Smelt,James,	1	6	Lun.	Smith,Elizabeth,	1	20	Brun.
Slaughter,Francis,Jr.	1	10	Cul.	Smith,***,	1	2	K.& Q.	Smith,Elizabeth,		3	Hen.
Slaughter,George,	1	13	Cul.	Smith,Abraham,			Brun.	Smith,Elizabeth,		2	Eli.Cy
Slaughter,George,	1		Cul.	Smith,Abraham,	1		Berk.	Smith,Elizabeth,	1		Buck.
Slaughter,George,	1		K.Wm.	Smith,Absolem,	1		Bot.	Smith,Enoch,	1	5	Lou.
Slaughter,Henry,	1	16	K.Wm.	Smith,Alexander,	2	4	Buck.	Smith,Ericus,	1		Wash.
Slaughter,James,			Cul.	Smith,Alexander,	3	1	Fay.	Smith,Ezechiel,	1		Lou.
Slaughter,James,	1	9	Cul.	Smith,Alexander,	1		Berk.	Smith,Francis,		5	West.
Slaughter,James,	1	28	Cul.	Smith,Ambrose,			K.& Q.	Smith,Francis,	1	7	Pr.Geo.
Slaughter,Jemima,	1	1	Cul.	Smith,Ambrose,	1	10	Spots.	Smith,Francis,	1		Caro.
Slaughter,John,	1		Cul.	Smith,Andrew,	1		Lou.	Smith,Francis,	1	6	Din.
Slaughter,Johnsue,	1	5	Cul.	Smith,Ann,	1		Cul.	Smith,Francis,	1	8	Bot.
Slaughter,John,	2	19	Cul.	Smith,Anthony,	1	2	Henry	Smith,Frederick,	1		Bot.
Slaughter,John,			Lun.	Smith,Archibald,			Din.	Smith,Frederick,	1	2	Pr.Geo.
Slaughter,Joseph,	1		Fau.	Smith,Aron,	1		Brun.	Smith,George,	1		Wash.
Slaughter,Joseph,	1		Wash.	Smith,Arthur,			Lun.	Smith,George,	1	16	Acco.
Slaughter,Laurence,	1	33	Cul.	Smith,Augustin,	1	4	Fau.	Smith,George,	1		Acco.
Slaughter,Martin,	1	13	K.Wm.	Smith,Azwell,	1		Mont.	Smith,George,	1		Mont.
Slaughter,Martin,		7	K.Wm.	Smith,Barnett,	1	6	Loui.	Smith,George,	1	1	Loui.
Slaughter,Philip,		18	Cul.	Smith,Bartlett,	1	1	Henry	Smith,George,	1	14	Din.
Slaughter,Reuben,	1	11	Bed.	Smith,Batt,	1	9	Din.	Smith,George,	1		Lou.
Slaughter,Robert,	1	20	Cul.	Smith,Ben,	1	1	Pr.Wm.	Smith,George,			Lou.
Slaughter,Robert,	1	25	Cul.	Smith,Benjamin,	1	10	Cul.	Smith,George,			Fay.
Slaughter,Robert,	1	4	Cul.	Smith,Benjamin,	1	4	Lun.	Smith,George,	2	6	Fay.
Slaughter,Thomas,	1	8	Cul.	Smith,Benjamin,	1		Mont.	Smith,Gideon,	1		Henry
Slaughter,Thomas,	2	37	Caro.	Smith,Benjamin,	1	5	Fay.	Smith,Gideon,	1	4	Lou.
Slaughter,William,	1		Lun.	Smith,Bert,			Wash.	Smith,Giles,	1		Henry
Slaughter,William,	1	18	Berk.	Smith,Bradley,	1		Henry	Smith,Gregory,	3	30	K.& Q.
Slaughter,K.Thomas,	1	14	K.Wm.	Smith,Bridgit,		15	Din.	Smith,Guy,	1	4	K.& Q.
Slaughter,William,	1		K.Wm.	Smith,Buckner,	1	4	Brun.	Smith,Guy,	2	4	Bed.
Slaytor,James,	3		Spots	Smith,Caleb,	1	12	Nor.	Smith,Guy,est.,		15	Bed.
Sled,John,	1		Hen.	Smith,Caleb,	1		Henry	Smith,Hannah,		1	Bot.
Sledge,Charles,	1		So'n	Smith,Caleb,	1		Fay.	Smith,Henry,	1		Aug.
Sleet,John,	1	8	Lin.	Smith,Caty,		8	Pr.Geo.	Smith,Henry,			Cul.
Slevin,William,	1		Aug.	Smith,Charles,	1		Acco.	Smith,Henry,	1	30	So'n
Slimer,Christian,			Lou.	Smith,Charles,	1		K.Geo.	Smith,Henry,	1		Henry

Name			Co.	Name			Co.	Name			Co.
Smith,Henry,	1	11	K.& Q.	Smith,John,	1		Henry	Smith,Ralph,	1		Spots.
Smith,Henry,	3		Lou.	Smith,John,	1		Henry	Smith,Ralph,	1		Berk.
Smith,Henry,est.	1	5	K.Geo.	Smith,John,	1		Cul.	Smith,Randolph,	1		Henry
Smith,Henry,	1	1	Buck.	Smith,John,	1		Fau.	Smith,Reubin,	1		Fau.
Smith,Herbert,	1		Din.	Smith,John,Jr.,	1	1	Fau.	Smith,Rhodes,			Fay.
Smith,Hugh,	1		Wash.	Smith,John,	1		Fau.	Smith,Richard,	1	1	Brun.
Smith,Humphrey,	1		Bot.	Smith,John,			Fau.	Smith,Richard,	1	4	Nor.
Smith,Isaac,	1		Nor.	Smith,John,	1	8	Fau.	Smith,Richard,	1		West.
Smith,Isaac,	1	3	Henry	Smith,John,	2	6	Din.	Smith,Richard,	1	3	Din.
Smith,Isaac,	1		Berk.	Smith,John,	1	1	Din.	Smith,Richard,	1	2	Din.
Smith,Isaac,	1		Gooch.	Smith,John,	3		Berk.	Smith,Robert,	1		Cul.
Smith,Isaac,	1	1	Cul.	Smith,John,	1		Berk.	Smith,Robert,	1		Fau.
Smith,Isaac,	1		Bot.	Smith,John,	1		Mont.	Smith,Robert,	3		Har.
Smith,Isaac,	1	2	Buck.	Smith,John,	1		Mont.	Smith,Robert,	1		Mont.
Smith,Isabella,			Rock.	Smith,John,	1		Lou.	Smith,Robert,	1	4	Gooch.
Smith,Isabella,	1	9	Hen.	Smith,John,	1		Lou.	Smith,Robert,	1	9	Spots.
Smith,Isham,	1	5	Brun.	Smith,John,			Lou.	Smith,Robert,	1		K.Wm.
Smith,J.,	1		Pr.Wm.	Smith,John,	1		Cul.	Smith,Robert,	1		Wash.
Smith,Jacob,	1	2	K.Geo.	Smith,John,	2	18	Hen.	Smith,Robert,			Acco.
Smith,Jacob,	2	12	Hen.	Smith,John,Jr.,			Hen.	Smith,Robert,	1		Gooch.
Smith,Jacob,	1	3	Hen.	Smith,John,	1		Lin.	Smith,Robert,	1	2	Gooch.
Smith,Jacob,	2		Har.	Smith,John,	5		Fay.	Smith,Robert,	2	21	K.& Q.
Smith,Jacob,	1		Lou.	Smith,John,	1		Lou.	Smith,Robert,	1		K.& Q.
Smith,Jacob,	1		Bot.	Smith,John,	1		Lou.	Smith,Robert,	1		Buck.
Smith,Jacob,	1		Bot.	Smith,John,	2		K.& Q.	Smith,Robert,	1		Buck.
Smith,James,	1		Rock.	Smith,John,	1	3	Brun.	Smith,Robert,	1		Bot.
Smith,James,	2	3	Loui.	Smith,Joshua,	1	11	Din.	Smith,Robert,	1		Bot.
Smith,James,	1		Nor.	Smith,Joseph,		7	Fau.	Smith,Robert,	1		Bot.
Smith,James,	1		Spots.	Smith,Joseph,	2	14	Fau.	Smith,Rowley,	1	9	Fau.
Smith,James,	1		Caro.	Smith,Joseph,	1	8	Fau.	Smith,Ruben,	1		Lin.
Smith,James,	1		Pr.Wm.	Smith,Joseph,	1	20	Lun.	Smith,Samuel,	1	2	West.
Smith,James,	1		Mont.	Smith,Joseph,	1		Camp.	Smith,Samuel,	1		Mont.
Smith,James,	1		Cul.	Smith,Josiah,			Pr.Wm.	Smith,Samuel,	1		Mont.
Smith,James,	1		Lou.	Smith,Josiah,	1	8	Henry	Smith,Samuel,	1		Lou.
Smith,James,Jr.,	1		Lou.	Smith,Jonathan,			Mont.	Smith,Samuel,	1		Lou.
Smith,Capt.James,	2	5	Bot.	Smith,Jonas,	1		Wash.	Smith,Samuell,	2	11	Fay.
Smith,James,	1		Bot.	Smith,Larkin,		30	K.& Q.	Smith,Sarah,	1	1	West.
Smith,James,	1		K.& Q.	Smith,Larkin,	1	6	Spots.	Smith,Sarah,	1		Pr.Wm.
Smith,James,Jr.,	1	3	K.& Q.	Smith,Laurence,	1	31	York	Smith,Scarlet,	1		Lin.
Smith,James,			Brun.	Smith,Lawrence,		4	Brun.	Smith,Solomon,	3	4	Acco.
Smith,James,	1		Fay.	Smith,Leonard,			Lou.	Smith,Solomon,	1		Berk.
Smith,James,	1		Buck.	Smith,Levin,		1	Acco.	Smith,Stephen,	1	3	Henry
Smith,James,	2	4	Brun.	Smith,Lewis,		1	Aug.	Smith,Stephen,	1	5	Brun.
Smith,Jarvis	1		Mont.	Smith,Lewis,	1	2	West.	Smith,Stephen,	1		K.Wm.
Smith,Jesse,	1		Pr.Wm.	Smith,Lucy,	1	1	Caro.	Smith,Stephen,	1	2	K.Wm.
Smith,Jesse,	1		Cul.	Smith,Mahlon,	1		Lou.	Smith,Stephen,		3	Bed.
Smith,Jesse,	2	28	Hen.	Smith,Martha,		12	So'n	Smith,Temple,	1	9	Lou.
Smith,Jessee,	1	1	Caro.	Smith,Mary,			Lou.	Smith,Rev.Thomas,		41	West.
Smith,Jessee,	1		Lin.	Smith,Mary,	1	78	West.	Smith,Thomas,			Buck.
Smith,Joel,	1	1	Cul.	Smith,Mary,		10	Fau.	Smith,Thomas,	1		Aug.
Smith,John,	1	1	So'n.	Smith,Mary,		4	Cul.	Smith,Thomas,	1	1	Aug.
Smith,John,	1		Henry	Smith,Mary,	1		Cul.	Smith,Thomas,	2	4	K.Wm.
Smith,John,	1		Henry	Smith,Matthew,	1		Mont.	Smith,Thomas,	1		West.
Smith,John,	1		Spots.	Smith,Matthew,	1	1	So'n	Smith,Thomas,	1	1	Wash.
Smith,John,	1	1	Spots.	Smith,Matthew,est.,		3	Fau.	Smith,Thomas,	1		Caro.
Smith,John,	1		Har.	Smith,Merideth,	1		Mont.	Smith,Thomas,	1		Cul.
Smith,John,	1		Pr.Geo	Smith,Michael,	1		Cul.	Smith,Thomas,	2	1	Henry
Smith,John,	1	1	Pr.Wm.	Smith,Millington,	1	3	Din.	Smith,Thomas,est.		1	Lun.
Smith,John,	2	11	Acco.	Smith,Munford,	1	1	Henry	Smith,Thomas,	1	13	Nor.
Smith,John,	2	16	Acco.	Smith,Nathan,	1	12	Loui.	Smith,Thomas,	1		Mont.
Smith,John,	2	14	Acco.	Smith,Nathaniel,			Din.	Smith,Thomas,	1	5	Pr.Geo.
Smith,John,	1	6	Bed.	Smith,Nathaniel,	1	7	Lou.	Smith,Thomas,	1	25	York
Smith,John,	1	10	Bed.	Smith,Nathin,	1		Wash.	Smith,Thomas,	2	16	Loui.
Smith,John,			Loui.	Smith,Natt,	1		Pr.Wm.	Smith,Thomas,	1		Henry
Smith,John,	1	7	Loui.	Smith,Nicholas,	1		Cul.	Smith,Thomas,	1	4	Henry
Smith,John,	1	6	Loui.	Smith,Nick,	1		Cul.	Smith,Thomas,	1	1	Fau.
Smith,John,	1		Loui.	Smith,Obediah,	1	7	Hen.	Smith,Thomas,	1	4	Fau.
Smith,John,	1		Spots	Smith,Oswald,	1	7	Spots.	Smith,Thomas,	1		Mont.
Smith,John,	1	12	K.Wm.	Smith,Owen,			Cul.	Smith,Thomas,	1		Mont.
Smith,John,	1		K.Wm.	Smith,Patrick,	1		Gooch.	Smith,Thomas,	1		Lou.
Smith,John,	1	2	K.Geo	Smith,Peter,	1		Henry	Smith,Thomas,	1	3	Buck.
Smith,Col,John,		5	Wash.	Smith,Peter,	1		Mont.	Smith,Thomas,	1	2	Brun.
Smith,John,	2		Wash.	Smith,Peter,	1	6	Pr.Wm.	Smith,Thomas,			Hen.
Smith,John,	1		Aug.	Smith,Philip,	1		Berk.	Smith,Thomas,	1		Fay.
Smith,John,	1		Aug.	Smith,Phillip,	1		Bot.	Smith,Thomas,	1		Fay.
Smith,John,	1	2	Henry	Smith,Postean,	1		Har.				

Name			Place
Smith,Thomas,	1		Lin.
Smith,Thomas,	1		Lin.
Smith,Thomas,	1		Lin.
Smith,Tilman,	1		Wash.
Smith,Tilman,	1		Wash.
Smith,Valley James,	1		Wash.
Smith,William,	1		K.Wm.
Smith,William,	1	14	K.Wm.
Smith,William,	1		Acco.
Smith,William,	1		West.
Smith,William,	1		Aug.
Smith,William,	1		Wash.
Smith,William,	1		Wash.
Smith,William,	1	1	Wash.
Smith,William,			Bed.
Smith,William,	1		Loui.
Smith,William,	1	28	Loui.
Smith,William,	1	11	Loui.
Smith,William,	1	2	Loui.
Smith,William,	1	8	Loui.
Smith,William,	1	8	York
Smith,William,	1	5	Pr.Geo
Smith,William,	1		Har.
Smith,William,	1		Har.
Smith,William,	1	2	Pr.Geo
Smith,William,	1	8	Lun.
Smith,William,Sr.,	1	7	Henry
Smith,William,Jr.,	1		Henry
Smith,William,	1	4	Fau.
Smith,William,Sr.,	1		Fau.
Smith,William,Jr.,	2	11	Fau.
Smith,William,	1	14	Fau.
Smith,William,Jr.,	1		Fau.
Smith,William,	1		Fau.
Smith,William,	1	1	Fau.
Smith,William,	2	11	Fau.
Smith,William,	1		Fau.
Smith,William,	1		Fau.
Smith,William,	1		Berk.
Smith,William,	1		Berk.
Smith,William,	1		Mont.
Smith,William,	1		Mont.
Smith,William,	1		Lou.
Smith,William,	1		Cul.
Smith,William,			Cul.
Smith,William,	1		Cul.
Smith,William,	1	1	K.&Q
Smith,William,	1		Lou.
Smith,William,	1		K.&Q
Smith,William,			Brun.
Smith,William,			Brun.
Smith,William,			Brun.
Smith,William,			Hen.
Smith,William,	1		Buck.
Smith,William,	1		Bot.
Smith,William,	1		Bot.
Smith,William,	1		Fay.
Smith,William,	2	14	Fay.
Smith,William,	3		Lin.
Smith,William,	1	1	Lin.
Smith,William,	1		Spots.
Smith,William,	3	30	Spots.
Smith,Rev.W.,	1		Cul.
Smith,William F.,	1	6	Spots.
Smith,William S.,	1	10	Hen.
Smith,Withers,	1	2	Lou.
Smithe,Robert,	1		Bot.
Smither,John,	2		Pr.Wm.
Smither,John,			Pr.Wm.
Smither,William,	2	4	Spots.
Smithers,Sarah,			Rock.
Smithey,Leonard,	1	3	K.&Q
Smithy,Matthias,	1		Lou.
Smithey,Robert,	1	4	K.&Q
Smithson,Bartley,	1	2	Lun.
Smithson,Charles,	1	4	Lun.

Name			Place
Smithson,Florestina,	1		Lun.
Smithson,Francis,	1	8	Lun.
Smithson,John,	1	9	Lun.
Smithson,Menoah,	1	2	Lun.
Smithson,Micajah,	1	1	Lun.
Smithson,William,	1	2	Lun.
Smithy,Reubin,	1		Cul.
Smiley,Alexander,	1		Rock.
Samiley,Andrew,	1		Rock.
Smiley,Catherine,			Wash.
Smiley,James,			Hen.
Smiley,James,	1		Rock.
Smiley,John,	1		Rock.
Smiley,Walter,Jr.,	1		Rock.
Smock,Garnott,	1		Cul.
Smock,William,	1	1	Spots.
Smoot,Benjamin,	1		Cul.
Smoot,Edward,	1	1	Berk.
Smoot,James,			Fau.
Smoot,John,	1		Fau.
Smoot,John,	1		Fau.
Smoot,Leonard,	1		Fau.
Smoot,Thomas,	1	4	Pr.Wm.
Smouse,Adam,			Lou.
Smouse,John,	2		Lou.
Smouse,Peter,	1		Lou.
Smurr,Andrew,	1		Berk.
Smurr,Jacob,	1		Berk.
Smurr,Martin,	1		Berk.
Smute,Benjamin,	2		Hen.
Smuty,Ben,			Hen.
Smyth,Francis,	1	1	Hen.
Smyth,Widow,		7	Bot.
Smythes,William,	1		Caro.
Snow,Mary,			Pr.Wm.
Snoddy,Cary,	1	1	Buck.
Snead,Annabella,	2	1	Acco.
Snead,Charles,	3	10	Acco.
Snead,Charles,	1	3	Hen.
Sneed,Christopher,	1		Hen.
Sneed,Elizabeth,	1	8	Acco.
Sneed,George,			Acco.
Sneed,Isarel,	1	10	Caro.
Sneed,John,	1	2	Caro.
Sneed,John,	1	3	Lun.
Sneed,John,	1		Henry
Sneed,Philip,	1	1	Lun.
Bneed,Presson,	1	5	Acco.
Sneed,Richard,	1	8	Caro.
Sneed,Robert,	1	3	Hen.
Sneed,Robert,	1	4	Acco.
Sneed,Samuel,	1	4	Lun.
Sneed,Tully,	1		Acco.
Sneed,William,	3	2	Acco.
Snelson,Nathaniel,	1	2	Loui.
Snelson,Nathaniel,Jr.,	1	1	Loui.
Snevely,Peter,	2		Mont.
Snickers,Edward,	1	11	Berk.
Snido,Christian,	1		Mont.
Snido,Philip,	1		Mont.
Snider,Adam,	1		Berk.
Snider,Catherine,	2		Har.
Snider,Catherine,	1	1	Har.
Snider,Jacob,	1		Lou.
Snider,Jacob,	1		Berk.
Snider,John,	1		Berk.
Snider,Philip,	1		Cul.
Snider,William,	1		Mont.
Snidor,Nicholas,	1		Mont.
Snipes,John,	1	2	Cha.Cy
Snoddy,James,	1	1	Buck.
Snoddy,John,	1		Buck.
Snoddy,John,	1		Fay.
Snody,John,	1		Wash.
Snodgrass,Alexander,	1		Bot.
Snodgrass,David,	1		Wash.

Name			Place
Snodgrass,James,(big)	1		Bot.
Snodgrass,James,(lit)	1		Bot.
Snodgrass,James,			Wash.
Snodgrass,John,	1		Bot.
Snodgrass,John,	1		Berk.
Snodgrass,John,Sr.,	4		Berk.
Snodgrass,Joseph,	1		Wash.
Snodgrass,Joseph,(longl	1		Bot.
Snodgrass,Joseph,	1		Bot.
Snodgrass,Joseph,	3		Rock.
Snodgrass,Robert,	1		Rock.
Snodgrass,Robert,	1		Bot.
Snodgrass,William,	1		Bot.
Snodgrass,William,	1		Wash.
Snouts,Widow,			Lou.
Snowder,Jacob,	1		Bot.
Snuffer,George,	1		Bot.
Snyder,Adam,	1	4	Cul.
Snyder,Jacob,	1		Fau.
Snyder,Jacob,	1	1	Cul.
Snyder,Michael,	1	3	Cul.
Snyder,Michael,	1		Cul.
Soister,Daniel,	2		Berk.
Soister,Michael,	1		Berk.
Sollers,William,	1		Berk.
Sollis,James,	1		Mont.
Solofint,John,	1		Berk.
Solomon,Drury,	1	1	Henry
Solomon,Isham,	1		Henry
Somerson,Gowin,	1	1	Caro.
Somervell,James,	1	2	Spots.
Somervell,James,	1	14	Spots.
Sommervill,Joseph,	2	1	Berk.
Sommers,Joshua,	1		Mont.
Sork,Matthias,	1		Lou.
Sorrell,James,	1	8	West.
Sorrell,James,	1		Cul.
Sorrell,James,	3		Caro.
Sorrell,John,	1	3	Caro.
Sorrell,John,	1		Spots.
Sorrell,Rhueben,	1	4	Pr.Wm.
Sorrell,Judith,		10	West.
Sorrell,Thomas,	1	3	West.
Sorrels,Joseph,	1		Aug.
Souder,Rudolph,	1		Berk.
Sousberry,Jeremiah,	1	4	Henry
Soseberry,John,	1		Brun.
South,John,	1	9	Fay.
Southall,Furnea,	1	17	Cha.Cy
Southall,Henry,	1	24	Cha.Cy
Southall,James,	1	14	Ja.Cy
Southall,James,	1	10	Cha.Cy
Southall,John,	1	3	Cha.Cy
Southall,Philip,			Hen.
Southall,Turner,	4	23	Hen.
Southall,William,			Hen.
Southall,William,	1	26	Cha.Cy
Southard,Laurence,	1		Lou.
Southard,M.,	1	1	Pr.Wm.
Southard,William,	1	4	Lou.
Southerland,Ann,		4	K.Wm.
Southerland,Fendal,	1	52	K.Wm.
Southerland,James,	2		Bed.
Southerland,Joseph,	1	5	K.Wm.
Southerland, J.,	1		Pr.Wm.
Southerland,Samuel,	1	3	Henry
Southerland,William,	1	17	K.&Q
Southern,Henry,			Cha.Cy
Southern,James,	2		Buck.
Southern,Joseph,	1		Buck.
Southern,Samuel,	1		Buck.
Southern,Samuel,	1	2	Buck.
Southling,Gibson,	1		Bed.
Southling,John,			Bed.
Southwood,Edward,	1		Berk.
Southworth,John,			Caro.

Name			County
Southworth,John,	1		Caro.
Southworth,Thomas,	1		Caro.
Southworth,William,	1	2	Caro.
Southworth,William,	1		Caro.
Southworth,William,Jr.	2	11	Caro.
Sowasher,Henry,	1		Berk.
Sowder,Anthony,	1		Lou.
Sowell,Joseph,	1		Henry
Sowell,William,	1		Henry
Sowther,Michael,	1		Cul.
Spady,Abraham,	1		Nor.
Spady,Jacob,	1		Nor.
Spady,Thomas,	2	7	Nor.
Spaggins,William,	1	4	Bed.
Spahar,Theodorus,	1		Berk.
Spain,Abram,	1		Din.
Spain,Batt,	1	3	Din.
Spain,Daniel,Sr.,	2	4	Din.
Spain,Daniel,Jr.,	1	1	Din.
Spain,Eppes,	1	5	Din.
Spain,Henry,	1	10	Din.
Spain,John,	1	12	Din.
Spain,John,Jr.,	1	1	Din.
Spain,John P.,	1	4	Din.
Spain,Joshua,			Din.
Spain,Matthew,	1	1	Din.
Spain,Robert,	1	2	Din.
Spain,Thomas,			Din.
Spain,Thomas Sr.,	1		Din.
Spain,Thomas Jr.,	1	3	Din.
Spain,William,	1	3	Din.
Spain,William,Sr.,	1	13	Din.
Spair,William,Jr.,	1	1	Din.
Spakar,Malern,	1		Berk.
Spanglar,Henry,	1		Berk.
Spangler,Daniel,	1		Henry
Spangler,Jacob,	3		Mont.
Sparey,Peter,	1		Har.
Spark,Alexander,est.,	1	49	West.
Spark,Caty,	1		West.
Sparkes,Elizabeth,			Cul.
Sparkes,Henry,	1		Cul.
Sparkes,Humphrey,	1	1	Cul.
Sparkes,Thomas,	2	1	Cul.
Sparkes,Thomas,Jr.,	1		Cul.
Sparks,Isaac,	2		Fay.
Sparks,James,			Pr.Wm.
Sparks,John,	1	1	Cul.
Sparks,John,	1		Pr.Wm.
Sparks,John,	1		Pr.Wm.
Sparks,Thomas,	1		Lin.
Sparks,William,	1		Pr.Wm.
Spaulding,Thomas,	1	3	Bed.
Spaw,Henry,	1		Wash.
Speace,Coonrod,Jr.,	1		Camp.
Speace,Lewis,			Camp.
Speakman,John,	1		Nor.
Speakman,Thomas,	1		Nor.
Spearman,John,	1		Camp.
Spearman,John,			Bed.
Spearman,John,	2		Caro.
Spearman,Thomas,	2	8	Caro.
Spears,James,	1		Buck.
Spears,John,	1	5	Buck.
Spears,John,	1		Rock.
Spears,Robert,	2	11	Hen.
Specht,Andrew,	1	1	Lou.
Speed,Charles,	1	1	So'n
Speed,Martha,			So'n
Speers,George,	1		Lin.
Speers,Jacob,	1		Lin.
Speers,John,	1	5	Acco.
Spelman,John,	1		Har.
Spelman,Nathaniel,	1	3	Lin.
Spence,James,	1		Aug.
Spence,John,	1		Rock.
Spence,Joseph,	1	1	Mont.
Spence,Thomas,	1	7	West.
Spence,William,	1		Rock.
Spencer,Ahimaz,	1		Henry
Spencer,C.,			Camp.
Spencer,Edmund,	1		So'n
Spencer,Edward,	1	8	K.& Q.
Spencer,Elizabeth,		4	Din.
Spencer,Frances,		15	Buck.
Spencer,Francis,	1	22	Buck.
Spencer,James,Sr.,	1		Henry
Spencer,John,Jr.,	1	4	Henry
Spencer,John,	2		Lou.
Spencer,John,	1	2	Bot.
Spencer,Joseph,	1	2	Buck.
Spencer,Lewittin,	1	2	Jas.Cy
Spencer,Maneil,	1	6	Jas.Cy
Spencer,Martin,	1		Bot.
Spencer,Moses,	1		Henry
Spencer,Moses,	1		Buck.
Spencer,Nathan,	1		Lou.
Spencer,Samuel,	1	21	Buck.
Spencer,Samuel,			Lou.
Spencer,Samuel,			Lou.
Spencer,Thomas,	1		Fay.
Spencer,William,	1		Buck.
Spencer,William,	1		Mont.
Spencer,William,	1		Bed.
Spencer,William,Sr.,	1		Bed.
Spencer,William,Jr.			Bed.
Spenner,Benjamin,	1		Bed.
Spenny,James,			Fau.
Spicer,John,	1		Lou.
Spicer,William,	1	1	Fau.
Spidding,William,			Lou.
Spiers,Adam,	1	1	Pr.Geo.
Spiers,James,	2	12	Acco.
Spiers,Margaret,			Acco.
Spiller,Benjamin,C.,	1	20	K.Wm.
Spiller,Jeremiah,	1		Fau.
Spiller,Philip,	1	1	Fau.
Spiller,Waronton,	1		Wash.
Spiller,William,	1	9	K.W.
Spillman,William,	1	2	K.Geo.
Spilman,Benjamin,			Cul.
Spilman,Frances,			K.Geo.
Spilman,George,	1		Caro.
Spilman,James,	2	3	Cul.
Spilman,James,Jr.,	1		Cul.
Spilman,John,	1	1	Cul.
Spilman,John,			K.Geo.
Spilman,Robert,	1	1	Cul.
Spilman,Thomas,	1	2	K.Geo.
Spilman,Thomas,	1	3	Cul.
Spilman,William,	1		Cul.
Spindle,John,	1	2	Spots.
Spindle,William,	1	4	Spots.
Spires,William,	1		Fay.
Spiter,Conrod,	1		Lou.
Spittle,J.,	1		Pr.Wm.
Spivey,Albridgton,	1		So'n
Spivey,Benjamin,	1	12	So'n
Spivey,Elizabeth,		2	So'n
Spivey,Ephraim,	1		So'n
Spivey,William,	1		So'n
Spivey,William,	1	1	So'n
Spoar,John,	2		Har.
Spolding,John,	1		Cul.
Sponogil,George,	1		Lou.
Spooner,G.W.,	1		Spots.
Spotswood,Alexander,	1	53	Spots.
Spotts,George,	1		Aug.
Spraggins,Thomas,	1	9	Cha.Cy
Spraggins,William,	2	11	Jas.Cy
Sprags,William,			Pr.Wm.
Spratley,Mrs.,		12	Jas.Cy
Spratley,Thomas,	1		So'n
Spratlin,James,	1		Henry
Spratt,William,	1		Wash.
Spraybrough,James,	1		Brun.
Sprayberry,John,	1		Brun.
Spring,Andrew,,			Lou.
Spring,Frederick,	1		Lou.
Spring,Nicholas,	1		Aug.
Springate,William,	1		Aug.
Springer,Edward,	1		Bot.
Springer,Edward,			Bot.
Sproul,James,	1		Wash.
Sproul,Samuel,	1		Berk.
Sproul,William,	1		Rock.
Sprout,John,	1		Mont.
Spruce,David,	1		Eli.Cy
Spruce,David,	1		York
Spurling,Jeremiah,	1		West.
Spurlock,Jesse,	1		Mont.
Spurlock,John,	1	1	Hen.
Spurlock,John Sr.,	1		Mont.
Spurlock,John Jr.,	1		Mont.
Spurlock,William,	1		Bot.
Spurr,Richard,	1	11	Lou.
Squires,Ann,		1	Lou.
Squires,Elizabeth,		3	Fau.
Squires,George,	1	1	Lou.
Squires,Levie,	1		Bed.
Squires,Uriah,	1		Bed.
Stabler,Edward,	2	1	Din.
Stabler,John,	1		Lou.
Stacey,John,	1	3	York
Stacy,Benjamin,	1		Mont.
Stacy,James,	1		Lun.
Stacy,John,	1		Mont.
Stacy,Kinchin,	1		York
Stacy,Robert,	1	1	York
Stadaran,John,	1		Mont.
Stadler,Jacob,	2		Lou.
Stadler,John,	1		Lou.
Stadler,John,	1	6	Spots.
Stadler,Robert,	1		Lou.
Stafford,Absalom,	1		Mont.
Stafford,Henry,	1	6	Fay.
Stafford,Martin,			Fay.
Stafford,William,	2		Fay.
Stafford,William,	2		Fay.
Stafford,William,	1		West.
Stage,Richard,	1		Fau.
Stagg,John,	1	11	Hen.
Stagg,Mary,		1	Cha.Cy
Stagg,Thomas,	1	13	Cha.Cy
Stailey,Abraham,	1		Mont.
Stailey,Martin,	1	1	Mont.
Stainbac,Francis,			Brun.
Stainbac,William,			Brun.
Stainback,Edmund,		5	Pr.Geo.
Stainback,Francis,		6	Brun.
Stainback,Francis,	1	12	Pr.Geo.
Stainback,George,	1	9	Pr.Geo.
Stainback,George,	2	5	Brun.
Stainback,William,		3	Brun.
Stainback,Capt,Wm.,	1	10	Din.
Stains,Joseph,	1		Aug.
Stakes,Simon,	1		Nor.
Stallard,Samuel,	1	1	Wash.
Stallard,Walter,		1	Fau.
Stallard,Walter,	1	6	Cul.
Stallcup,John,	1		Lou.
Stallings,Jacob,	1	2	Henry
Stallord,Randolph,	1	2	Cul.
Stamps,John,	1		Henry
Stamps,Thomas,	1		Henry
Stamper,Isiah,	1		Mont.
Stamper,Jacob,	1		Mont.
Stamper,James,	1		Mont.

Name			County
Stamper,Joel,	1	1	Mont.
Stamper,Jonathan,Sr.,	1	1	Mont.
Stamper,Jonathan,Jr.,	1		Mont.
Stamper,Powell,	1	1	Mont.
Stanard,Larkin,	1	26	Spots.
Stanard,William,	1	29	Spots.
Standley,John,	1	1	Caro.
Standley,Pleasant,	1		Bed.
Standley,Thomas,	1		Buck.
Standly,Thomas,	1		Brun.
Standifer,Israel,	1	1	Henry
Standifer,James,Sr.,	1		Henry
Standifer,Luke,	1	3	Henry
Standifer,William,	1	1	Henry
Standiford,Isaiah,	1		Bed.
Standoff,John,	1		Rock.
Stanfield,Ephraim,	1	4	Caro.
Stanfield,Samuel,	1		Mont.
Stanhepe,William,	2	10	Lou.
Stanhope,Robert,			Fay.
Stanley,Isaac,	1		Berk.
Stanley,John,	1	1	Loui.
Stanley,John,	1		Henry
Stanley,Joseph,	1		Henry
Stanley,Nathan,	1	3	Loui.
Stanley,Richard,	1		Henry
Stanley,Thomas,	1		Cul.
Stanley,William,	1		Henry
Stanley,William,Jr.,	1		Henry
Stanley,Zachariah,	1	1	Loui.
Stanton,George,	1		Henry
Stanton,James,	1	8	So'n.
Stanton,John,	1		Henry
Stanton,Samson,	1	1	So'n
Stanton,Thomas,	1		Mont.
Stanton,Thomas,	1		Bed.
Stanton,William,	1	29	Cul.
Stanton,William,	1		Camp.
Staples,Charles,	1		K.Geo.
Staples,Christian,		2	Buck.
Staples,David,	1		Buck.
Staples,Garland,			Buck.
Staples,Isaac,	3		Buck.
Staples,Isaac,Jr.,			Buck.
Staples,Isaac,	2		Camp.
Staples,James,	1		K.Geo.
Staples,John,	1		Buck.
Staples,John,	1	8	Henry
Staples,John,	1		Hen.
Staples,Mary,			K.Geo.
Staples,Samuel,	1	10	Buck.
Staples,Samuel,Jr.,	1		Buck
Staples,Stephen,	1	2	Lun.
Staples,Thomas,	1	2	Lun.
Staples,William,	1		Hen.
Staples,William,	1		Buck.
Stapleton,Charles,	1		Bot.
Stapleton,Edward,	1		Wash.
Stapleton,Thomas,	1		Fay.
Stapleton,William,	1		Bot.
Stapleton,William,	1		Lou.
Stare,Henry,	1		Har.
Stare,John,	1		Har.
Stark,Abraham,	1		Lou.
Stark,Elizabeth,		9	Din.
Stark,James,	1	6	Fau.
Stark,Jeremiah,	1		Fau.
Starke,Bolling,	1	24	Pr.Geo.
Starke,Thomas,	1	15	Lun.
Starke,William,	1	7	K.Wm.
Starkey,John,Sr.,	1		Bed.
Starkey,John,Jr.,	1		Bed.
Starkey,Joseph,	1		Bed.
Starkey,Joshua,	1	1	Bed.
Starks,Daniel,	1	2	Spots.
Starks,Zerobabel,	1	1	So'n
Starling,Isaac,	2	2	Acco.
Starling,John,	1		Bot.
Starmer,George,	1		Lou.
Starr,John,	1		Bed.
Starrit,Robert,	1	3	Aug.
Starrit,William,	1		Aug.
Statham,Love,est.		10	Loui.
Statler,Abraham,	1		Lou.
Statler,John,	1		Berk.
Staton,James,	1		Buck.
Staton,John,	1	6	Buck.
Staton,Thomas,Sr.,	1		Rock.
Staton,Thomas,	1		Rock.
Staton,William,	1		Rock.
Staton,William,Sr.,	1	5	Buck.
Stayden,Arthur,	1	2	Gooch.
Stayden,John,	1		Gooch.
Stayley,Jacob,	3		Berk.
Steagall,Bottom,	1	2	Brun.
Steagall,George,			Brun.
Steagall,Rabun,	1		Brun.
Steagall,Samuel,	1		Brun.
Steagall,Thomas,	1	7	Brun.
Stears,Achillis,	1		Caro.
Stears,Betty,			Spots.
Stears,Mary,			Spots.
Stedman,Christ.,Jr.,	2	18	K.& Q.
Steed,John,	1	7	Brun.
Steed,John,Jr.,	1	2	Brun.
Steed,Mark,	1	4	Brun.
Steel,Alexander,	2	12	Camp.
Steel,Andrew,	1		Mont.
Steel,Andrew,	1	2	Aug.
Steel,David,	1		Rock.
Steel,George,	1		Camp.
Steel,J.,	1	9	Pr.Wm.
Steel,James,	1	6	Aug.
Steel,John,	1		Bed.
Steel,John,	1		Mont.
Steel,John,	1		Har.
Steel,Richard,	2	5	Fay.
Steel,Robert,	1	2	West.
Steel,Robert,	1	2	Rock.
Steel,Robert,	1		Bot.
Steel,Robert,	1		Mont.
Steel,Samuel,Sr.,	2		Aug.
Steel,Samuel,Sr.,	2		Aug.
Steel,Samuel,	1	6	Fau.
Steel,Samuel,	2	1	Rock.
Steel,Thomas,	1		West.
Steel,Thomas,	1		Rock.
Steel,William,	1		Fay.
Steel,William,	1		Fay.
Steel,William,	1		Berk.
Steel,William,	1		Loui.
Steele,David,	1	1	Aug.
Steele,David,	1		Aug.
Steele,James,	1		Aug.
Steele,John,	1		Aug.
Steele,Nathaniel,	1	3	Aug.
Steele,Robert,	2		Aug.
Steele,Samuel,	1		Aug.
Steele,Samuel,	2		Aug.
Steenberger,William,	1		Har.
Steerman,Valentine,	1		Bed.
Steers,Benjamin,	1		Lou.
Steers,Isaac,	1		Lou.
Steers,John,	1		Lou.
Steers,Joseph,	1		Lou.
Steet,John,	2	6	Cul.
Steevins,John,	1		Aug.
Stegar,& Co.		1	Din.
Stegar,William,	1	1	Din.
Stell,Charles,	1	4	Din.
Stell,George,	1	6	Din.
Stell,John,	1	5	Din.
Stell,Mary,		1	Din.
Stembridge,John,Sr,,	1	3	Lun.
Stembridge,John,Jr.,	1		Lun,
Stembridge,Wm.Sr.,,	1		Din.
Stembridge,Wm.Jr.,	1		Din.
Stemmons,Jacob,	1		Camp.
Stenneth,Benjamin,	2	3	Mont.
Stephen,Adam,	1	28	Berk.
Stephen,Jacob,	1		Berk.
Stephen,Robert,	1	8	Berk.
Stephen,Robert,	1		Aug.
Stephen,Samuel,(F.N.)	1		Hen.
Stephen,Thomas,	1		Berk.
Stephen,Thomas,	1		Berk.
Stephen,John,	1		Rock.
Stephens,Abraham,	1		Lin.
Stephens,Annabella,			Acco.
Stephens,Elizabeth,			Acco.
Stephens,Jacob,	1		Lin.
Stephens,Jacob,	1		Lin.
Stephens,James,			Caro.
Stephens,James,	1	1	Cha.Cy
Stephens,James,	1	3	Fay.
Stephens,Jehu,	1	1	Mont.
Stephens,John,	1		Henry
Stephens,John,	1	1	Buck.
Stephens,John,	1		Henry
Stephens,John,	1		Buck.
Stephens,John,	1		Lou.
Stephens,John,	1		Camp.
Stephens,John,	1		Mont.
Stephens,Joseph,	1		Pr.Wm.
Stephens,Joseph,	1	1	Fay.
Stephens,Joshua,	1		Mont.
Stephens,Matthews,			Acco.
Stephens,Richard,	1	2	Lou.
Stephens,Robert,	1		Lou.
Stephens,Robert,	1		Mont.
Stephens,Robert,	1		Camp.
Stephens,Solomon,	1		Acco.
Stephens,Soloman,B.			Bed.
Stephens,Thomas,	2	3	Buck.
Stephens,Thomas,	1		Acco.
Stephens,William,	1		Acco.
Stephens,William,	1	1	Lou.
Stephens,William,	1		Henry
Stephens,William,	1		Henry
Stephenson,Andrew,	1		Bot.
Stephenson,Ann,			Berk.
Stephenson,Ann,		6	Berk.
Stephenson,Edmund,	1		So'n
Stephenson,Francis,		15	Lun.
Stephenson,James,	1		Fay.
Stephenson,James,	1	2	Rock.
Stephenson,John,	1		Wash.
Stephenson,Joseph,	1		Rock.
Stephenson,Mary,			Fay.
Stephenson,Robert,	1		Wash.
Stephenson,Sarah,			So'n
Stephenson,Thomas,	1	9	So'n
Stephenson,Thomas,	1	2	Aug.
Stephenson,Wm.Sr.,,	1	2	So'n
Stephenson,Wm.Jr.,	1	4	So'n
Stepp,James,	1		Camp.
Stepp,James,	1		Camp.
Steptoe,George est.		48	West.
Sterling,Jean,		9	K.& Q.
Stern,David,	1	9	Caro.
Stern,Peyton,	2	20	Caro.
Sterret,James,	1	1	Fay.
Sterret,John,	1		Fay.
Stevens,Alice,			Lou.
Stevens,Charles,	1		Bot.
Stevens,Drury,	1		Pr.Geo.
Stevens,Edward,	3	16	Cul.
Stevens,Edward,	1		Lou.

Stevens,George,	1	1	So'n	Stewart,John,	1	1	Henry	Stockdell,Thomas,	3	10	Cul.
Stevens,George,	1	15	K.& Q.	Stewart,John,	1		Henry	Stockdell,William,			Cul.
Stevens,Jacob,	1		Bot.	Stewart,John,	1	5	Buck.	Stockhart,George,	1		Lou.
Stevens,James,	1		Bed.	Stewart,John,	1		Bed.	Stockly,William,	1	7	Acco.
Stevens,James,	1		Lou.	Stewart,John,	1		Berk.	Stockton,Robert,		8	Henry
Stevens,John,			Cul.	Stewart,John,	1		Din.	Stockton,Robert,	1	6	Henry
Stevens,John,			Cul.	Stewart,John,	1		Berk.	Stoker,Mary Jr.,			Lou.
Stevens,John,	1		Spots.	Stewart,Joseph,Sr.,	1	2	Cul.	Stokes,Allen,	2	12	Lun.
Stevens,John,	1		Spots.	Stewart,Joseph,	1	16	Cul.	Stokes,Danus,			Bot.
Stevens,John,	1	5	Caro.	Stewart,Richard,	1	8	Din.	Stokes,David,	1	18	Lun.
Stevens,John,	1		Pr.Geo	Stewart,Robert,	1		Brun.	Stokes,David,Jr.,	1		Lun.
Steven,Joseph,	2		Cul.	Stewart,Robert,	1		Berk.	Stokes,Elizabeth,		13	Lun.
Stevens,Micajah,	1		Cul.	Stewart,Samuel,	1		Bot.	Stokes,Henry,	1	20	Lun.
Stevens,Mumford,	2	5	Cul.	Stewart,Thomas,	1	17	Din.	Stokes,John,	1	1	Henry
Stevens,Peter,	2		Mont.	Stewart,Rev.William,	1	10	Fau.	Stokes,Martha,		3	Lun.
Stevens,Richard,	1	20	Caro.	Stewart,Rev.William,	1	24	Fau.	Stokes,Peter,	1		Lun.
Stevens,Sampson,	1		Henry	Stewart,Rev.William,	1	25	Fau.	Stokes,Richard,	1	4	Lun.
Stevens,Solomon,	1		Mont.	Stewart,William,	1		Lou.	Stokes,Shadrack,	1	6	Lun.
Stevens,Solomon,	1		Bot.	Stewart,William,	1		Brun.	Stokes,Thomas,	1	10	Brun.
Stevens,Thomas,	1	12	K.&Q.	Stewart,William,	2	4	Henry	Stokes,William,	1	16	Lun.
Stevens,Thomas,	1		Lou.	Stiffey,Henry,	1		Mont.	Stokes,William,	1	1	Cul.
Stevens,Thomas,			Eli.Cy	Stiffey,John,	1		Mont.	Stokes,Young,	1		Lun.
Stevens,Thomas,			Lou.	Stiffey,Michael,	1		Mont.	Stombough,Phillip,	1		Har.
Stevens,Thomas,	1	1	Brun.	Stiffey,Peter,	1		Mont.	Stone,Ashwell,		5	Jas.Cy
Stevens,William,	3		Mont.	Stigal,Robert,	1		Mont.	Stone,Bastian,	1		Aug.
Stevens,William,	1		Pr.Geo	Stigall,Jesse,			Din.	Stone,Benjamin,	1		Fau.
Stevenson,Adam,	1	1	Aug.	Stiglar,Mary		7	K.Geo.	Stone,Daniel,			K.& Q.
Stevenson,Amos,	1		So'n	Stigler,James,	2	5	Cul.	Stone,David,	1		Lou.
Stevenson,James,	2		Fau.	Stigler,Samuel,	1	9	Cul.	Stone,Eusebrus,	1	8	Henry
Stevenson,Rev.James,	1	13	Cul.	Stiles,John,	1		Lou.	Stone,Eusibius,	2	9	Caro.
Stevenson,James,			Cul.	Still,Dinnis,	1	5	Din.	Stone,Francis,	1		West.
Stevenson,John,	1		So'n	Still,Sarah,		1	Buck.	Stone,Jacob,	1		Lou.
Stevenson,Sarah,		4	Brun.	Still,Shadrack,	1	1	Din.	Stone,James,	2		Har.
Stevenson,William,	1	1	Lou.	Still,William,	1	1	Buck.	Stone,Jeremiah,	1		Mont.
Stevenson,William,Jr.,	1	4	So'n	Stinett,James,	1		Henry	Stone,Jesse,	1	1	Brun.
Stevill,Adam,	5		Har.	Stingley,George,	1		Har.	Stone,Job,			K.& Q.
Stevill,George,	1		Har.	Stingley,Jacob,	1		Har.	Stone,John,	2	1	Cul.
Stevins,Richard,	1		Bot.	Stinisyfer,Henry,	1		Cul.	Stone,John,	1	5	K.& Q.
Steward,Alexander,	1		Fay.	Stinson,Alexander,	1	10	Buck.	Stone,John,	1	1	K.& Q.
Steward,Benjamin,	2	2	Spots	Stinson,Alexander,	1	19	Buck.	Stone,John,			Lun.
Steward,Benjamin,	1	7	West.	Stinson,Cary,	1	2	Buck.	Stone,John,			Mont.
Steward,Benjamin,	1	1	So'n	Stinson,David,	1	2	Buck.	Stone,John,		3	Fau.
Steward,Charles,	1	4	Loui.	Stinson,George,	1	2	Buck.	Stone,Joseph,	1	4	Pr.Wm.
Steward,James,	1		Har.	Stinson,John,	1	12	Buck.	Stone,Josias,	1	5	Cul.
Steward,John,	1	1	Spots	Stinson,Thomas,,	2		Lin.	Stone,Lancelott,	3	4	Pr.Geo.
Steward,John J.,	1	10	Spots	Stinton,William,	1	18	Cul.	Stone,Manoah,	1	2	Fau.
Steward,Joseph,	1		Spots	Stipe,Frederick,	1		Berk.	Stone,Micajah,	1		Bed.
Steward,Joseph,	1		Har.	Stipe,John,	1		Berk.	Stone,Richard,	2	5	Lun.
Steward,Joseph,	1	21	Cul.	Stipe,Martin,	1		Berk.	Stone,Richard,Sr.,	2	17	Lun.
Steward,Richard,Sr.,	2	17	Pr.Geo	Stirgiss,John,	1	1	Nor.	Stone,Richard,Jr.,			Lun.
Steward,Walter,		2	Bot.	Stirgiss,Richard,	1		Nor.	Stone,Richard,	1		Brun.
Steward,Walter,	1		Fay.	Stirling,John,	2		Aug.	Stone,Richard,	1		Henry
Steward,William,	1		Spots	Stith,Ann,	18	34	K.Geo.	Stone,Robert,	3	1	K.& Q.
Stewart,Andrew,	1		Din.	Stith,Buckner,Sr.,	2	28	Brun.	Stone,Robert,Jr.,			K.& Q.
Stewart,Andrew,	1	9	Acco.	Stith,Buckner,Jr.,	1	14	Brun.	Stone,Sarah,	1	3	K.& Q.
Stewart,Ann,	2	5	Acco.	Stith,Buckner,Jr.,			Brun.	Stone,Spencer,	1		Lin.
Stewart,Bernet,	1		Brun.	Stith,Drury,	1	21	Brun.	Stone,Stephen,	1		Henry
Stewart,Charles,	1		Henry	Stith,Griffin,		12	Brun.	Stone,Thomas,	1		Brun.
Stewart,Daniel,	1	2	Lou.	Stith,Griffin,	2	31	Nor.	Stone,Thomas,	1	1	Fau.
Stewart,Daniel,	1		Bed.	Stith,James,	1		Bed.	Stone,Uriah,	1		Mont.
Stewart,David,	1		Henry	Stith,John,		26	Ja.Cy	Stone,Uriah,	1	5	Bed.
Stewart,Henry,	2	17	Caro.	Stith,Capt.John,		7	Brun.	Stone,William,			Cul.
Stewart,& Hopkins,	3	2	Hen.	Stith,John,	2	57	Cha.Cy	Stone,William,	1	4	Jas.Cy
Stewart,Hugh,			Lou.	Stith,Joseph,	1	6	Bed.	Stone,William,Sr.,	2	15	Lun.
Stewart,Murdock,	1		Henry	Stith,Mrs.Lucy,		29	Brun.	Stone,William,Jr.,	1	6	Lun.
Stewart,James,Sr.,			Henry	Stith,Richard,	1	24	Camp.	Stone,William,	1		Lin.
Stewart,James,Jr.,	1		Henry	Stith,Robert,	16	24	K.Geo.	Stone,William,			Din.
Stewart,James,	1		Din.	Stith,Thomas,	1	11	Brun.	Stone,William,	1		Fau.
Stewart,James,	1		Din.	Stith,Thomas,Jr.,		11	Brun.	Stone,William,	1	1	Lou.
Stewart,James,Sr.,	1		Bot.	Stith,Col.William,	2	35	Brun.	Stoneburner,Fred'k	1		Lou.
Stewart,James,Jr.,	1		Bot.	Stith,William,Jr.,			Brun.	Stoneburner,Jacob,Sr.	1		Lou.
Stewart,James,	1		Brun.	Stivers,Peter,	1		Spots.	Stoneburner,Peter,	1		Lou.
Stewart,James,	1		Brun.	Stoakley,Eyres,	1		Nor.	Stoneman,John,			Pr.Geo.
Stewart,John,	1	19	Fau.	Stoakley,William,	1	10	Nor.	Stoner,Michael,	1	2	Fay.
Stewart,John,Sr.,	1		Henry	Stobal,Ralph,	1		Mont.	Stonesever,John,	1	1	Cul.
Stewart,John,Jr.,	1		Henry	Stockdell,John,			Cul.	Stonestreet,Bazel,	1	4	Lou.

Name			County
Stonestreet,John,	2	7	Lou.
Stomum,James,	1		West.
Stoop,Robert,			Rock.
Stores,Charles,	1		Eli.Cy
Stores,Frazier,Sr.,	1	3	Eli.Cy
Stores,Frazier,Jr.,	1	1	Eli.Cy
Stores,John,	1		Eli.Cy
Stores,Savage,	1		Eli.Cy
Storke,Frances,		20	K.Geo.
Storke,John,	1	12	K.Geo.
Storke,William,	13	10	K.Geo.
Storke,William,		9	West.
Storm,Jacob,	1		Bot.
Storm,Peter,	1		Bot
Storman,Jacob,	1		Berk.
Stort,Patty,			Bed.
Story,Daniel,	1		So'n
Story,James,	1		Cul.
Story,James,	1	2	Aug.
Story,James,	2		So'n
Story,Lewis,			So'n
Story,Samuel,	1		So'n
Stotts,Andrew,	1		Mont.
Stotts,David,	1		Nor.
Stott,Elias,	1		Nor.
Stott,Jonathan,	1	6	Nor.
Stott,Laban,	1	14	Nor.
Stott,Ralph,			Nor.
Stous,T.,			Pr.Wm.
Stout,Able,	1	2	Cul.
Stout, B.,	1		Pr.Wm.
Stout,Daniel,			Aug.
Stout,Elijah,	2		Cul.
Stout,George,	1		Aug.
Stout,Hezekiah,	1		Aug.
Stout,Joseph,			Cul.
Stout,Reuben,	1		Cul.
Stoutt,Joseph,	1		Henry
Stoutt,Samuel,	1		Henry
Stovall,Bartholomew,	1	3	Camp.
Stovall,George,	1	17	Camp.
Stovall,John,	1	1	Camp.
Stoveines,Edmund,	1	1	Bot.
Stover,Jeremiah,	1		Bed.
Stover,Jeremiah,	1		Bot.
Stow,John,	1	9	Din.
Stow,John,	1		Din.
Stow,William,	1	5	Din.
Stowers,John,	1		Mont.
Stowers,Mark,	1	1	Cul.
Stowers,William,	1		Cul.
Strachan,AlexanderG.	1	17	Din.
Strachan,AlexanderG.	1	24	Din.
Strachan,Peter,			Hen.
Strader,Christopher,	1		Har.
Strahorn,Robert,	1		Rock.
Strain,James,	1		Aug.
Straine,Henry,	1		Lou.
Strange,Anne,			Lou.
Strange,Benjamin,	1		Hen.
Strange,James,	1		Henry
Strange,Jesse,	1		Buck.
Strange,John,	1		Buck.
Strange,John,			Buck.
Strange,John,	1	11	Camp.
Strange,John,	1	1	Camp.
Strange,John,	1	11	Camp.
Strange,Owen,	2	2	Brun.
Strange,Owen,Jr.,			Brun.
Strange,William,	1		Fau.
Stratton,Benjamin,	1	13	Nor.
Stratton,Henry,	1	9	Bed.
Stratton,Henry,Jr.,	1		Bed.
Strafford,Issac,	1		Bed.
Stratton,James,	1		Loui.
Stratton,John,Sr.,	1	49	Nor.
Stratton,John,Jr.,	1	15	Nor.
Stratton,Owen,	1		Henry
Stratton,Solomon,	1		Mont.
Stratton,William,	1		Nor.
Straughan,Reuben,	2	1	Spots
Straughan,Thomas,	1	21	Spots.
Straw,Leonard,	1		Mont.
Strawther,Francis,			Har.
Straya,Nicholas,	2		Berk.
Strayley,Christian,	1		Har.
Strayley,Jacob,	1		Bot.
Strechley,Thomas,	1	34	West.
Street,Anthony,	1	14	Lun.
Street,Dudley,	1	2	Buck.
Street,Henry,			Buck.
Street,Joseph,	1		Henry
Street,Samuel,	1		Henry
Streetman,Elizabeth,			Lou.
Streets,William,	1	7	Bot.
Streshly,William,	2	25	Caro.
Sreatchberry,John,	1		Lou.
Strickland,William,	1		Har.
Stricklen,Joseph,	1		Rock.
Strickling,Benjamin,	1		So'n
Strickling,Drewry,	1		So'n
Strider,Philip,	1	1	Berk.
Stringer,Benjamin,	1		Acco.
Stringer,Edmond,	1		Loui.
Stringer,Hillary,	1	24	Nor.
Stringer,Hillery,		9	Acco.
Stringer,Jacob,	2	3	Acco.
Stringer,John,	1	27	Nor.
Stringer,John,	1		Loui.
Stringer,Thomas,Sr.,	1	12	Acco.
Stringer,Thomas,Jr.,	1		Acco.
Stringer,William,	1		Lin.
Stringfellow,Henry,	2	4	Cul.
Stringfellow,Robert,	2	5	Fau.
Stripe,John,	1		Nor.
Striplin,Thomas,			Fay.
Stroat,Sabert,	1		Henry
Strode,James,	1	14	Berk.
Strode,Jeremiah,	1	8	Berk.
Strode,John,	1	5	Berk.
Strode,John,	2	31	Cul.
Strode,William,	2		Cul.
Strong,John,	1	5	Gooch.
Strong,Mary,			Gooch.
Strong,Samuel,	1	6	Lun.
Strong,Sherwood,			Buck.
Strong,William,	2	12	Buck.
Stroop,Henry,	1	3	Berk.
Stroop,Melchor,	1	1	Berk.
Stroop,William,	2	1	Berk.
Strother,Ann,	1	4	Cul.
Strother,Benjamin,	1	18	West.
Strother,French,	3	26	Cul.
Strother,James,	1	2	Fau.
Strother,John,	1	2	Cul.
Strother,John,	2	6	Cul.
Strother,Joseph,	4	7	Cul.
Strother,Margaret,		11	K.Geo
Strother,Reubin,	1	7	Fau.
Strother,Robert,	2	8	Cul.
Strother,Solomon,	1	9	Cul.
Strother,Tabitha,	2	17	K.Geo
Strother,William,	1	1	Lou.
Strother,William,	1	1	Fau.
Stroud,Adam,	1		Har.
Stroud,John,	1		York
Stroud,William,			York
Stroud,William,	1		York
Struton,Benony,	1	1	Spots
Stryder,Isaac,	1	4	Berk.
Stuart,Alexander,	1		Aug.
Stuart,Alexander,	1	1	Rock.
Stuart,Alexander,	1		Rock.
Stuart,Allen,	1	5	Fau.
Stuart,Benjamin,	1	4	Aug.
Stuart,Charles,	1		Bot.
Stuart,Edward,	1		Aug.
Stuart,Frances,Sr.,	1	52	K.Geo.
Stuart,Frances,	21	30	K.Geo.
Stuart,James,	1		Rock.
Stuart,James,	1		Aug.
Stuart,James,	1	3	Fau.
Stuart,James,	1		Mont.
Stuart,John,	1	1	K.Geo.
Stuart,John,	1		Wash.
Stuart,John,	1	3	Rock.
Stuart,John,	1	2	Nor.
Stuart,John,	2		Aug.
Stuart,John,	1		Aug.
Stuart,Jonathan,	1		Rock.
Stuart,Price,	1	7	K.Geo.
Stuart,Ralp,	1		Aug.
Stuart,Robert,	1		Aug.
Stuart,Robert,	1	5	Cul.
Stuart,Robert,	2		Aug.
Stuart,Robert Wm.,	15	14	K.Geo.
Stuart,Thomas,	2	12	Aug.
Stuart,Thomas,	1		Wash.
Stuart,Titus,	1		Lun.
Stuart,William,	1	15	K.Geo.
Stuart,William,	1	5	Fau.
Stuart,William,	1		Aug.
Stuart,William,	1		Rock.
Stuart,William,	1		Mont.
Stuart,William,G.,	1	35	K.Geo.
Stubblefield,Edward,	2	20	Cha.Cy
Stubblefield,Eliz.,		3	Cha.Cy
Stubblefield,John,est.		5	Cha.Cy
Stubblefield,John,est.		19	Cha.Cy
Stubblefield,George,	1	11	Spots.
Stubblefield,George,	1	30	Spots.
Stubblefield,Harry,	1	11	Spots.
Stubblefield,Peter,	1	19	Spots.
Stubblefield,William	1		Henry
Stubbs,Adam,	1		Henry
Stucker,David,	1		Fay.
Stucker,Jacob,	1		Fay.
Stukey,Abraham,	1		Har.
Stukey,Magdaline,			Har.
Stults,George,	1		Hen.
Stull,George,	1		Bot.
Stullivite,Charles,	3	4	Fay.
Stump,Catherine,			Har.
Stump,George,	1	4	Har.
Stump,Jacob,	1		Lin.
Stump,John,	1		Bed.
Stump,Leonard,	1	2	Har.
Stump,Michael,	2	1	Har.
Stump,Michael,	1		Mont.
Sturdivant,Ann,		13	Pr.Geo
Sturdivant,David,	1	23	Pr.Geo
Sturdivant,Mrs.Fran.		8	Din.
Sturdivant,James,	1	5	Lun.
Sturdivant,James,	1	8	Pr.Geo
Sturdivant,Joel,est.	1	31	Pr.Geo.
Sturdivant,John,	1	10	Pr.Geo
Sturdivant,John,	1	3	Din.
Sturdivant,John,	3	31	Pr.Geo
Sturdivant,John,	1	13	Brun.
Sturdivant,Robert,	1	3	Din.
Sturgeon,* * *,			Mont.
Sturgeon,Ambros,	1		Mont.
Sturgeon,Francis,	1		Mont.
Sturgeon,John,est.,		6	So'n
Sturgiss,America,	1		Acco.
Sturges,Daniel,		10	Berk.
Sturges,John,	1	2	Acco.
Sturges,Richard,	1		Acco.
Stump,Thomas,	2		Lou.
Stump,Thomas,Jr.,			Lou.

Name			Co.
Sturm,John,	1		K.&Q
Sturman,Hannah,		12	West.
Sturman,Richard,	1		Har.
Sublet,James,	2		Buck.
Sublet,William,			Buck.
Suchan,James,	1		Lou.
Suckmond,Peter,	1		Henry
Suddoth,Benjamin,	1		Fau.
Suddoth,James,	1		Fau.
Suddoth,James,	1		Cul.
Suddoth,John,	1		Fau.
Suddoth,Lawrence,	1		Fau.
Suddoth,William,	2		Fau.
Suddoth,William,	1		Lou.
Suffolk,John,	1		Har.
Suggett,Jemima,		8	Fay.
Suggett,John,	1	2	Fay.
Suills,Thomas,	1	3	West.
Suling,Gaspar,	1		Aug.
Sullinger,John,	1	10	Caro.
Sullinger,Mary,	1	5	Caro.
Sullinger,Reuben,	1	2	Caro.
Sullinger,Robert,	1	6	Caro.
Sullinger,Thomas,	1	2	Cul.
Sullivan,Burgess,	1		K.Geo
Sullivan,Sarah,		8	Fau.
Sullivan,Silvester,	1		Fau.
Sullivan,Thomas,			K.Geo
Sullivan,William,	1		K.Geo
Sullivant,John,	1		Henry
Sullivant,Samuel,	1		Henry
Sullivant,Thomas,	1		Henry
Sully,Samuel,	1		Lou.
Summerell,Boaz Gwin,	1	3	So'n
Summerell,George,	1		So'n
Summerell,Jacob,	1		So'n
Summerell,James,	1	8	So'n
Summerell,John,	1	1	So'n
Summerell,Stephen,	1	4	So'n
Summerell,Thomas,	1		So'n
Summers,Edward,			Fay.
Summers,Francis,	1	15	Lou.
Summers,George,	3	7	Lou.
Summers,John,	1		Caro.
Summers,John,	1		Aug.
Summers,John,	3		Wash.
Summers,John,Sr.,	1		Lin.
Summers,John,Jr.,	1		Lin.
Summers,John Loque'k	1		Berk.
Summers,Paul,	1		Aug.
Summers,Samuel,	1		Lou.
Summers,Thomas,	1		Lin.
Summerville,Richard	1		Bot.
Summors,John,	1		Aug.
Sumner,Hezekiah,	1		Bot.
Sumner,James,	1		Mont.
Sumner,Samuel,	1		Mont.
Sumter,Henry,	1	1	Henry
Sumvalt,Andrew,	1		Aug.
Sumvalt,George,	1		Aug.
Sumvalt,John,	1		Aug.
Sunderland,William,	2		Berk.
Sunefrank,Jacob,	1		Lou.
Surbrus,Adam,	1		Wash.
Surbrus,John,	1		Wash.
Susson,Jesse,	1		Brun.
Suster,Philip,	1		Camp.
Suter,Alexander,	1	1	Mont.
Suter,Ann,	1	7	So'n
Suter,John,	1	11	So'n
Suter,William,	2	1	Pr.Wm
Suthard,Laurence,	2		Pr.Wm
Sutherd,Robert,			Pr.Wm
Sutherlane,Enos,	1		Wash.
Sutherland,Travis,	1	1	Cul.

Name			Co.
Sutherlin,Lantin,	1		Cul.
Sutlington,Robert,	1		Aug.
Suttin,William,	1		Bot.
Suttle,Henry,			Lou.
Suttle,John,	1		Ja.Cy
Suttle,Reuben,	1	1	Lou.
Suttle,Strother,	2	9	Pr.Wm
Suttle,William,			Pr.Wm
Suttles,Amy,		1	K.Geo
Suttles,Joel,	1	1	K.Geo
Suttles,John Price,	1	3	K.Geo
Suttles,William,	1	24	Loui.
Suttles,William,	1	24	Loui.
Sutton,Benjamin,	1		Lin.
Sutton,Benjamin,	1		Berk.
Sutton,Christopher,	3	11	Cul.
Sutton,Daniel,	1		Berk.
Sutton,Elijah,	1		West.
Sutton,Elijah,	1		Berk.
Sutton,James,	2	20	Caro.
Sutton,Jesse,	1		West.
Sutton,John,	1	1	Cul.
Sutton,John,	1		Cul.
Sutton,John,			Lou.
Sutton,John,	2	28	Caro.
Sutton,John,Jr.,	1	13	Caro.
Sutton,John,	1	1	Lin.
Sutton,Joe,	1	1	West.
Sutton,Joseph,	1		Aug.
Sutton,Josiah,	1		West.
Sutton,Nathaniel,	1	9	Cul.
Sutton,Richard,			West.
Sutton,Rolin,	1		Lin.
Sutton,Rowel,			Cul.
Sutton,Thomas,	1		West.
Sutton,William,	1		West.
Sutton,William,	1	13	Caro.
Sutton,William,			Caro.
Swain,Charles,	1		Bed.
Swaine,James,	1	7	Pr.Geo
Swallow,Andrew,	1		Mont.
Swallow,Jacob,	1		Aug.
Swango,Abraham,	1		Berk.
Swango,Jacob,	1		Berk.
Swann,Jonathan,	1		Henry
Swanson,Joe,	1	1	Brun.
Swanson,Nathaniel,	1	1	Henry
Swanson,William,Sr.,	1	10	Henry
Swanson,William,Jr.,	1	1	Henry
Swart,Adrian,	3		Lou.
Swart,George,	1		Berk.
Swart,Guisber,			Lou.
Swart,Henry,			Lou.
Swart,Jacob,	1		Berk.
Swart,James,			Lou.
Swart,John,	1		Lou.
Swearingen,Hezekiah,	1	3	Berk.
Swearingen,Josiah,	1	7	Berk.
Swearingen,Sarah,		10	Berk.
Swearingen,Thomas,	1	4	Berk.
Swearingen,Van,	1	14	Berk.
Swearingen,Van,	1		Aug.
Sweat,Anthony,	1		Brun.
Sweat,William,	1		Brun.
Sweatman,John,	1	3	K.Geo.
Sweatman,William,			K.Geo.
Swift,Flower,	1		Mont.
Swift,Godwin,	1	8	Berk.
Swift,Richard,	1	17	Loui.
Swillivan,Ann,			K.Geo
Swilly,David,	1	1	Caro.
Swim,Matthew,	1		Berk.
Swim,Matthias,	1		Berk.
Swindle,George,	1		Cul.
Swindle,John,	1		Cul.

Name			Co.
Swindle,Michael,	1	1	Cul.
Swindler,Henry,	1		Lou.
Swindol,John,	1	5	Cul.
Swiney,Edmund,	1		Henry
Swiney,Moses,	3	2	Lin.
Swingle,Peter,	1		Berk.
Swink,Henry,	1		Aug.
Swink,John,	1		Lou.
Swink,Lawrence,	1		Aug.
Swinton, * * *,	1	1	Hen.
Swinton,James,	1	2	Hen.
Swipe,Robert,			Pr.Wm.
Swisher,John,	1		Har.
Swisher,Lawrence,	1		Lou.
Switzer,Henry,	2		Bot.
Switzer,William,	1		Bot.
Swope,George,	1		Lin.
Sword,Michael,	1		Wash.
Sydburn,Charles,	1		Wash.
Syner,Benjamin,	1		Cul.
Syner,James,	1		Cul.
Syner,John,	1		Cul.
Sydnor,Joseph,	1	3	Din.
Sydnor,William,	1	9	Din.
Sykes,Bernard,	2	8	Pr.Geo.
Sykes,John,	1		So'n,
Sykes,Robert,	1		Har.
Sylvester,Ward,	3	2	Har.
Syme,John,		29	Loui.
Syme,Capt.John,Jr.,	1	46	Loui.
Syme,Nicholas,	1	21	K.Wm.
Sympson,Alexander,	1		Bot.
Sypole,Casper,	2		Lou.
Sypole,Casper,Jr.,	1		Lou.
Sypole,James,	1		Lou.
Sypole,John,			Lou.
Tabb,Adam,	1		Berk.
Tabb,Bailey Seaton,			York
Tabb,Edward,	2	19	Berk.
Tabb,George,			Berk.
Tabb,John,	3	27	Eli.Cy
Tabb,John,est.,		34	Din.
Tabb,Johnson,			Eli.Cy
Tabb,Mary,	1	5	York
Tabb,Robert,	2	11	York
Tabb,Thomas,			Eli.Cy
Tabb,William,	1	10	York
Tables,George,	1	1	Berk.
Tackett,Christian,	1		Aug.
Tackett,Lewis,	1		Aug.
Tackett,William,	1		Henry
Tackett,William,	1	4	Pr.Wm.
Tackett,William,Jr.,	1	4	Pr.Wm.
Tade,James,	1		Rock.
Tait,Tenas,	1	1	Hen.
Taite,James,	1		West.
Taite,Peter,	1	6	Fau.
Taite,William,	1		West.
Talbot,Bazil,	1	2	Wash.
Talbot,David,	1	1	Camp.
Talbot,David,	1	1	Camp.
Talbot,Drucilla,		3	Camp.
Talbot,Druscilla,		3	Camp.
Talbot,Henry,	1	5	Lou.
Talbot,Isham,	1	3	Bed.
Talbot,John,		8	Bed.
Talbot,Matthew,	1	6	Bed.
Talbot,Samuel,	1	1	Lou.
Talbot,William,	1	6	Camp.
Talbot,William,	1	11	Berk.
Talbot,Williston,	1	6	Camp.
Taler,William,	1		Ja.Cy
Taliaferro,Christo.	2	36	K.Wm.
Taliaferro,Col.	1	39	Brun.

Taliaferro,Francis,est.	2	40	Caro.	Tarpley,Charles,	1		Brun.	Taylor,Daniel,	1	3	Henry
Taliaferro,Francis,	1	7	Spots	Tarpley,John Sr.,	1	10	Din.	Taylor,Daniel,	1	9	Jas.Cy
Taliaferro,Harry,	1	23	Cul.	Taroley,John,	1	2	Din.	Taylor,David,	1		Mont.
Taliaferro,John,Sr.,			K.& Q	Tarpley,William,	1	8	Brun.	Taylor,David,	1		Din.
Taliaferro,Col,John,			K.& Q	Tarr,Elizabeth,			Lou.	Taylor,Edmund,	1	4	Jas.Cy
Taliaferro,Col.John,	1	15	Spots	Tarrant,Carter,	1	9	Eli.Cy	Taylor,Edward,	1	8	Brun.
Taliaferro,John,	1	22	Spots	Tarrent,John,	1		Henry	Taylor,Edward,			So'n
Taliaferro,John,		10	Caro.	Tarrent,Rubun,	1		Henry	Taylor,Elizabeth,			Fau.
Taliaferro,Lawrence,		5	Cul.	Tarrents,Leonard,	1	4	Henry	Taylor,Elizabeth,			Fau.
Taliaferro,Nicholas,	1	11	Cul.	Tate,Agness,		4	Loui.	Taylor,Elizabeth,			Lun.
Taliaferro,Peter,	2		Cul.	Tate,Caleb,	1		Camp.	Taylor,Mrs.Elizabeth,		8	So'n
Taliaferro,Philip,	1	20	K.& Q	Tate,Charles,	1	1	Bed.	Taylor,Elizabeth,			Rock.
Taliaferro,Richard,	1	39	Ja.Cy	Tate,Edmund,	1	1	Camp.	Taylor,Etheldred,	1	13	So'n
Taliaferro,Richard,		5	K.& Q	Tate,Enos,	1	8	Loui.	Taylor,Evan,	1		Lou.
Taliaferro,Richard,	1	43	Din.	Tate,Henry,	1	6	Camp.	Taylor,Francis,	1		Fay.
Taliaferro,Richard,			Cul.	Tate,James,	1	2	Loui.	Taylor,Francis,Jr.,	1		Fay.
Taliaferro,Robert,	1	28	Caro.	Tate,James,	1	11	Loui.	Taylor,George,			Acco.
Taliaferro,Robert,	4	59	Caro.	Tate,Jesse,	1	11	Bed.	Taylor,George,	3	32	Caro.
Taliaferro,Sally,	1	65	Caro.	Tate,John,	1	1	Aug.	Taylor,George,		1	Caro.
Taliaferro,Walker est.	1	24	Spots	Tate,John,Jr.,	1	5	Aug.	Taylor,George,	1	1	Rock.
Taliaferro,William,	1	34	K.& Q	Tate,Joseph,	1		Rock.	Taylor,George,	2		Bot.
Taliaferro,William,	1	10	Caro.	Tate,Magnus,	1	8	Berk.	Taylor,George,Sr.,	1	10	Lou.
Tallent,Andrew,			K.& Q	Tate,Nathaniel,	1	4	Bed.	Taylor,George,	1		Mont.
Talley,James,	1	1	Hen.	Tate,Nathaniel,			Loui.	Taylor,George,	1		Mont.
Tallman,Benjamin,	1		Aug.	Tate,Robert,	1	1	Aug.	Taylor,George,	1		Henry
Tally,Abram,	1		Din.	Tate,Robert,	1		Wash.	Taylor,Griffin,			Fay.
Tally,Elkanat,	1		Cha.Cy	Tate,Sarah,		2	Aug.	Taylor,Harman,	1		Acco.
Tally,John,	1		Din.	Tate,Thomas,	1	2	Aug.	Taylor,Henry,	1		Fau.
Tally,Nathan,	1	6	Loui.	Tate,Uriah,	1	7	Loui.	Taylor,Henry,	1	11	So'n
Tally,Story,	1		Loui.	Tate,William,	1	3	Loui.	Taylor,Col.Henry,est.		1	So'n
Tally,Takariah,			Buck.	Tate,Capt.William,	1	2	Aug.	Taylor,Isaac,	1		Fau.
Tamplen,John,	1	1	Caro.	Tate,Zedekiah,	1	11	Loui.	Taylor,Isaac,	1		Bot.
Tan,John,	1		So'n.	Tate,Zimry,	1	7	Loui.	Taylor,Isaac,Jr.,	1		Bot.
Tandy,Achilles,	1	4	Fay.	Tatem,Samuel,	1		Cul.	Taylor,Jabez,	1		Acco.
Tandy,John,	1	1	Fay.	Tatham,James,Sr.,	2	6	Acco.	Taylor,Jacob,	3	3	Acco.
Tandy,Smyth,	1	2	Aug.	Tatham,James,Jr.,	2	2	Acco.	Taylor,Jacob,	1		Acco.
Tandy,William,	1	7	Fay.	Tatham,John,	1	1	Acco.	Taylor,James,	1		Camp.
Tandy,William,	1		Camp.	Tatham,Michal,			Acco.	Taylor,James,			K.& Q.
Tanent,Larkin,	1	2	Henry	Tatum,Benjamin,	2	3	Lun.	Taylor,James,	1	13	Nor.
Tanent,Samuel,	1	4	Henry	Tatum,Chany,	2		Brun.	Taylor,James,	1	1	Henry
Tankard,Stephen,	1	20	Hen.	Tatum,Edward,	1	1	Henry	Taylor,James,	1		Rock.
Tankersley,George,		6	K.Geo	Tatum,Eppes,	1	13	Pr.Geo	Taylor,James,	1		Rock.
Tankersley,George,		4	Caro.	Tatum,George,	1		Brun.	Taylor,James,			Hen.
Tankersley,George,	1		Henry	Tatum,James,	1		Brun.	Taylor,James,	3	53	Caro.
Tankersley,John,			K.Geo	Tatum,Jesse,	1		Brun.	Taylor,James,	1		Fau.
Tankersley,John,	1	14	Spots	Tatum,Jessee,	1		Henry	Taylor,James,	1		Bed.
Tankersley,Mary est.,		10	K.Geo	Tatum,Joseph,	1		Lun.	Taylor,James,	1	1	Henry
Tankersley,Mary,	1	6	Caro.	Tatum,Joseph,	1		Brun.	Taylor,James,G.,	1	2	Lin.
Tankersley,Richard,	2	4	Henry	Tatum,Nathaniel,			Brun.	Taylor,Jeremiah,	1	7	Jas.Cy
Tanner,Benjamin,	1		Camp.	Tatum,Paul,		11	Brun.	Taylor,Capt.John,	1	20	So'n
Tanner,Benjamin,	1		Camp.	Tatum,Rebecca,	1	12	Pr.Geo	Taylor,John,Jr.,		13	So'n
Tanner,Dorata,			Cul.	Tatum,Reuben,	1	1	Lun.	Taylor,John,	1		Bot.
Tanner,Frederick,	1		Cul.	Tatum,Richard,	1		So'n.	Taylor,John,	1		Buck.
Tanner,George,	1		Har.	Tatum,Robert,	1	3	Pr.Geo	Taylor,John,			Buck.
Tanner,George,	1		Har.	Tatum,Sarah,		3	Pr.Geo	Taylor,John,	1	9	Caro.
Tanner,Jacob,	1	2	Lou.	Tatum,William,			Lun.	Taylor,John,	1		Caro.
Tanner,James,	1		Aug.	Tavener,George,	1		Lou.	Taylor,John,	1		K.Geo.
Tanner,James,	1		Fay.	Taws,Andrew,	1	3	Berk.	Taylor,John,	1		Mont.
Tanner,John,	2		Cul.	Taylo,Col.,est.,		11	K.Geo	Taylor,John,			Hen.
Tanner,John,	1	9	Fay.	Tayloe,John,est.,	1	19	K.Geo	Taylor,John,	1	6	Mont.
Tanner,Mary,			Camp.	Taylor,Abraham,			Acco.	Taylor,John,	1	1	Brun.
Tanner,Mary,			Camp.	Taylor,Alec,		11	Acco.	Taylor,John,	1		Lun.
Tanner,Meredith,	1		So'n	Taylor,Alexander,	2	4	Pr.Geo	Taylor,John,	1	1	York
Tanner,Seth,	1		Camp.	Taylor,Alsey,		12	Caro.	Taylor,John,	1		Camp.
Tanner,Seth,	1		Camp.	Taylor,Ann,		5	Caro.	Taylor,John,	1		Cul.
Tanner,William,	1		Fay.	Taylor,Barton,	1	2	So'n	Taylor,John,	1		Bed.
Tansell,William,	1		Pr.Wm	Taylor,Benjamin,	1		Fau.	Taylor,John,	1	15	Lou.
Tapp,Lewis,	1	6	Cul.	Taylor,Benjamin,	1		Lun.	Taylor,John,			Henry
Tapp,Moses,			Cul.	Taylor,Charles,	1	5	Acco.	Taylor,John,	1	2	Berk.
Tapp,Vincent,	1	1	Cul.	Taylor,Charles,	1		Camp.	Taylor,Jonathan,	1	24	Bot.
Tapp,William,	1	1	Cul.	Taylor,Charles,	1		Camp.	Taylor,Jonathan,	2		Lin.
Tapp,William,Jr.,	1		Cul.	Taylor,Charles,	1		Fau.	Taylor,Joseph,	1	9	Fau.
Tapscott,George,	1	9	Buck.	Taylor,Charles,	2		Cul.	Taylor,Joseph,	1		Lun.
Tarbet,Nathaniel,	1	2	Aug.	Taylor,Coffie,	1		Bot.	Taylor,Joseph,	1		Aug.
Tarbit,Hugh,	1		Aug.	Taylor,Daniel,	1		Buck.	Taylor,Joseph,	1		Bot.
Tarflinger,Henry,	1		Lou.	Taylor,Daniel,	1		Lun.	Taylor,Joshua,			Lou.

Name			Loc.
Taylor,Joshua,Sr.,	3	9	Acco.
Taylor,Joshua,			Acco.
Taylor,Judith,		16	Fau.
Taylor,Manly,	1	3	Lou.
Taylor,Mary,		4	Ja.Cy
Taylor,Miles,	3	1	Hen.
Taylor,Muse,Sr.,	1		Caro.
Taylor,Muse,Jr.,	1	1	Caro.
Taylor,Nathan,	1		Mont.
Taylor,Nathaniel,	1	7	Berk.
Taylor,Nathaniel,			York
Taylor,Nimrod,			Fau.
Taylor,Oliver,	1		Har.
Taylor,Patience,	1	5	Acco.
Taylor,Paul,	1		Berk.
Taylor,Peter,		1	Fau.
Taylor,Peter,	1		Acco.
Taylor,Pinkethman,	1	5	Ja.Cy
Taylor,Rebecca,		2	Ja.Cy
Taylor,Redigal,	1	4	Acco.
Taylor,Col,Richard,		13	Bot.
Taylor,Richard,	1	5	Pr.Geo
Taylor,Richard,	1		Pr.Wm.
Taylor,Richard,	3	23	Ja.Cy
Taylor,Richard,	1	56	K.Wm.
Taylor,Richard,		6	Caro.
Taylor,Richard,		31	Caro.
Taylor,Richard,Sr.,	1	2	Buck.
Taylor,Richard,	1	4	Buck.
Taylor,Richardson,	1		York.
Taylor,Robert,	1		Berk.
Taylor,Robert,	1	1	Rock.
Taylor,Robert,		4	So'n
Taylor,Samuel,	1		K.&Q
Taylor,Samuel,Jr.,	1		K.&Q
Taylor,Samuel,	2		York
Taylor,Samuel,	1		Lou.
Taylor,Samuel,	1		Berk.
Taylor,Sarah,			Bed.
Taylor,Sinah,	2		Acco.
Taylor,Skelton,	1	1	Bed.
Taylor,Sophia,	1	3	Acco.
Taylor,Stephen,	1	1	Acco.
Taylor,Mrs,Temperence,		13	So'n
Taylor,Thomas,	1	2	Lun.
Taylor,Thomas,	1	3	Cul.
Taylor,Thomas,			Lou.
Taylor,Thomas,	1	1	Bot.
Taylor,Thomas,	1		Fay.
Taylor,Thornton,		5	Caro.
Taylor,William,	2	4	Acco.
Taylor,William,	1		K.Geo.
Taylor,William,	1	1	Caro.
Taylor,William,	1		Fau.
Taylor,William,	1		Cul.
Taylor,William,	1		Lou.
Taylor,William,Jr.,	1		Lou.
Taylor,William,	1	2	Lou.
Taylor,William,	1		Hen.
Taylor,William,	1	26	Lun.
Taylor,William,	1		Bed.
Taylor,William,	1		Bed.
Taylor,William,	1		So'n
Taylor,William,	1		Bot.
Taylor,William,	1		Bot.
Taylor,William,	1		Buck.
Taylor,William,	1		Henry
Taylor,William,	1		Aug.
Taylor,William,	1		Rock.
Taylor,William,	1		Mont.
Taylor,William,			Lin.
Taylor,Wm.Patterson,	1	1	Buck.
Taylor,Woolrick,	1		Mont.
Taylor,Zachary,	1	12	Fay.
Tayner,Britain,	1	1	So'n
Tayner,Nathan,	1		So'n
Tayner,William,	1	3	So'n
Tazewell,Henry,	1	15	Brun.
Tazewell,John,		16	Nor.
Teaford,Jacob,	1		Aug.
Teackle,Arthur,	1	13	Acco.
Teackle,John,Jr.,	1	11	Acco.
Teackle,Levin,	2	22	Acco.
Teackle,Severn,	1	9	Acco.
Teakle,Richard,	1		Fau.
Teaney,John,	1	2	Pr.Geo
Tear,Jane,			Lou.
Teas,Charles,	1	1	Aug.
Teas,Mary,		9	Aug.
Teas,Thomas,	1		Camp.
Teate,John,	1		Wash.
Teate,William,	1		Wash.
Tebbs,F.,	1	1	Pr.Wm.
Tebbs,Foushee,	1	5	Lou.
Tebbs,Foushee,	1	3	Lin.
Tebbs,M.,	1	1	Pr.Wm.
Tebbs,M.,		6	Pr.Wm.
Tebbs,Towshed,	2	15	Pr.Wm.
Tebbs,William,,	1	24	Pr.Wm.
Tebbs,William,	1	9	West.
Tedford,Alexander,	3		Rock.
Tedford,Alexander,Jr.			Rock.
Tedford,David,			Rock.
Tedford,David,	1		Rock.
Tedford,George,	1		Rock.
Tedford,James,	1		Rock.
Tedford,James,Jr.,	1		Rock.
Tedford,Capt.John,	1	1	Rock.
Tedford,John,	1		Rock.
Tedford,Robert Sr.,	1		Rock.
Tedford,Robert,Jr.,	1		Rock.
Tedford,Robert,	1		Rock.
Tedford,William,	1		Rock.
Telford,John,	1	3	Loui.
Telly,Michael,	1		Brun.
Temple,***,	1	17	K.& Q.
Temple,Augustine,	1	1	Pr.Geo
Temple,Benjamin,	1	36	K.Wm.
Temple,Burivell,	1	8	Pr.Geo
Temple,David Sr.,	1		Pr.Geo
Temple,David,	1		Pr.Geo
Temple,Eppes,	1		Pr.Geo
Temple,Francis,	1		Pr.Geo
Temple,James,	1		Pr.Geo
Temple,Joshua,	1	2	Pr.Geo
Temple,Liston,		6	K.Wm.
Temple,Mary,		6	K.Wm.
Temple,Peter,	1	2	Pr.Geo
Temple,Sam,	1	1	Pr.Geo
Temple,Samuel,	1	25	Caro.
Temple,Samuel,.	1	12	Pr.Geo
Temple,Stephen,	1	9	Pr.Geo
Temple,William,	1	2	Pr.Geo
Templeman,Samuel,	1	16	West.
Templeman,Thomas,	1	9	West.
Templeton,James,	1	3	Rock.
Templeton,John,	1	3	Rock.
Tenham,Elizabeth,	-	6	Loui.
Tenley,William,	1		Fau.
Tennent,John,	1	11	Caro.
Tennison,William,	1	2	Pr.Wm.
Tentiman,Henry,	1		Lou.
Teny,William,	1		Bot.
Terrance,Achibald,	2		Berk.
Terrant,Manlove,	1		Lou.
Terrell,Ann,		2	Loui.
Terrell,Charles,	1	10	Caro.
Terrell,Christopher,	1	4	Caro.
Terrell,Edmond,	1	8	Cul.
Terrell,Elizabeth,		8	Loui.
Terrell,George,	1	10	Caro.
Terrell,James,	1		Caro.
Terrell,Joel,			Loui.
Terrell,Richard,	1	4	Loui.
Terrell,Richard,		1	Loui.
Terrell,Richmond,	2	28	Cha.Cy
Terrell,Thomas,	2	12	Caro.
Terrell,Thomas,	1	8	Loui.
Terrell,William Sr.,	2	22	Loui.
Terrell,William,Jr.,	1	19	Loui.
Terrell,William,	1	2	Cha.Cy
Terrill,Benjamin,	1		Loui.
Terrill,Henry,	1		Cul.
Terrill,John,	2	16	Cul.
Terrill,John,Jr.,	1	4	Cul.
Terrill,Joseph,	1		Cul.
Terrill,Joseph,	1		Lin.
Terrill,Oliver,			Cul.
Terrill,Robert,		7	Cul.
Terry,Christian,			Loui.
Terry,David,	1		Loui.
Terry,Emanuel,	1		K.Wm.
Terry,George,	1		Har.
Terry,Gidion,	1		K.Wm.
Terry,James,	1	6	Henry
Terry,James,	1		K.Wm.
Terry,James,	1		K.Wm.
Terry,James,	1	10	Loui.
Terry,Jasper,			Bed.
Terry,John,	1		K.Wm.
Terry,John,	1	1	K.Wm.
Terry,John Sr.,	3		Buck.
Terry,Josiah,	1		Bot.
Terry,Martha,			Bed.
Terry,Mary,	1		K.Wm.
Terry,Obediah,	1	1	Spots.
Terry,Prudence,			Henry
Terry,Stephen,	1		K.Wm.
Terry,Stephen,	1		K.Wm.
Terry,Stephen,	1		Har.
Terry,Stephen,	1		Rock.
Terry,Tasher,	1		Bot.
Terry,Tasher,	1		Bot.
Terry,Thomas,	1		Bed.
Terry,Thomas,	1	1	Cul.
Terry,Thomas,	1	3	Spots.
Terry,Thomas,	2	22	Caro,
Terry,William,	1	3	K.Wm.
Terry,William,			Bot.
Terry,William,	1		Bot.
Terry,William.	1	3	Bed.
Tster,Samuel,	1		Lin.
Torick,Henry,	2		Lou.
Tetrick,Jacob,			Lou.
Tavault,Nicholas,	1		Har.
Teverbough,Daniel,	2	1	Har.
Tewell,Charles,	1		Fay.
Tewell,John,		13	Pr.Geo.
Tewell,Hugh,	1	3	Pr.Geo.
Thacker,John,			Loui.
Thacker,William,			Brun.
Thackfield,Thacker,	1		Caro.
Thatcher,John,	1		Lou.
Thatcher,Richard,	1		Lou.
Thatcher,Stephen,	1		Lou.
Tharp,Jesse,	1		Fau.
Tharpe,William,	1	1	Hen.
Tharpe,Zachariah,	1		Lou.
Thaxton,William,	2	1	Lun.
Thead,George,	1		Cul.
Thilman,John,	2	32	Caro.
Thilman,Paul,	1	5	Caro.
Thilley,Gordon,	1		Cul.
Thilsjarel,John,	1		Cul.
Thing,William,	1		Bot.
Thomas,***,	1		Wash.
Thomas,Aaron,	1		Fau.
Thomas,Ann,	1		Buck.

Name			County
Thomas, B.B.,	1	5	Pr.Wm
Thomas, Ben,	1		Pr.Wm
Thomas, Benjamin,	1		Wash.
Thomas, Benjamin,	1		Fau.
Thomas, Benjamin,	1		Mont.
Thomas, Charles,	1	4	Loui.
Thomas, Charles,	1		Henry
Thomas, David,	1	6	Fau.
Thomas, David,	1		Gooch
Thomas, David,	1		Bed.
Thomas, David,	1	5	Lun.
Thomas, Edward,			Cul.
Thomas, Elisha,	1		Fau.
Thomas, Elizabeth,		4	Cul.
Thomas, Emmet,	1		Lou.
Thomas, Enoch,	1		Lou.
Thomas, Enoch David,	3		Har.
Thomas, Evan,			Lou.
Thomas, George,	1	2	Lou.
Thomas, George,	1	10	Cul.
Thomas, Griffin,	1		Wash.
Thomas, Harrison,	1	2	Nor.
Thomas, Henry,	1		Buck.
Thomas, Henry,	1	4	So'n
Thomas, J.,	1	1	Pr.Wm
Thomas, Jacob,	1	1	Hen.
Thomas, James,		8	Cul.
Thomas, James,	1		West.
Thomas, James,	1		West.
Thomas, James,	1	12	Cul.
Thomas, James,	2		Gooch
Thomas, James,	1		West.
Thomas, James,			Hen.
Thomas, James,	1		Hen.
Thomas, James,	1		Buck.
Thomas, James,	1	1	Bed.
Thomas, James,	4		Har.
Thomas, Jason,	1		Cul.
Thomas, Jesse,	1	1	Buck.
Thomas, Jesse,	1	1	Cul.
Thomas, Job,	1	2	West.
Thomas, John,	1	4	Cul.
Thomas, John,	1	2	Brun.
Thomas, John,	1	5	Brun.
Thomas, John,	1		West.
Thomas, John,	1		West.
Thomas, John,			Lou.
Thomas, John, Sr.,	1	5	Cul.
Thomas, John, Jr.,	1	3	Cul.
Thomas, John,			Lou.
Thomas, John,	1	9	Nor.
Thomas, John, Sr.,	2		Buck.
Thomas, John,	1	2	Buck.
Thomas, John,	1		Bed.
Thomas, John,	1		Bed.
Thomas, John,	1		Cul.
Thomas, John,	1		Lou.
Thomas, Joseph, Sr.,	1	9	Buck.
Thomas, Joseph, Jr.,	1	2	Buck.
Thomas, Joseph,	1		Bot.
Thomas, Rev.Joseph,	1		Lou.
Thomas, Leonard,	1		Lou.
Thomas, Leonard,	1		Lou.
Thomas, Lucy,			Aug.
Thomas, Lucy,		4	K.Wm
Thomas, Mary,	1	2	Hen.
Thomas, Michael,	1		Mont.
Thomas, Morriss,	3		Har.
Thomas, Moses,	1	8	Lou.
Thomas, Nathan,	1		Wash.
Thomas, Nathan,	1		Loui.
Thomas, Olive,	1		Hen.
Thomas, Owen,	1		Lou.
Thomas, Owen,	1	1	Lou.
Thomas, Philip,	1		Henry
Thomas, Price,	1	5	West.

Name			County
Thomas, Reuben,	1		Wash.
Thomas, Reuben,	1	1	Cul.
Thomas, Robert,	1	5	Lou.
Thomas, S.,	1		Pr.Wm
Thomas, Sarah,			K.Geo.
Thomas, Sarah, est.,		4	Cul.
Thomas, Thomas,			Lou.
Thomas, Thomas,			Lou.
Thomas, Thomas,	1		Buck.
Thomas, William,	1		Bed.
Thomas, William,	1	1	Lou.
Thomas, William,	1		Lou.
Thomas, William,			Lou.
Thomas, William,	1		Pr.Wm.
Thomas, William,	1	15	So'n
Thomas, William,	3		Lou.
Thomas, William,	1		Cha.Cy
Thomas, William,	1		Mont.
Thomason, Fleming,	1		Loui.
Thomason, Gentry,			Loui.
Thomason, George, Sr.,	2	16	Loui.
Thomason, George,	1	10	Loui.
Thomason, George, Jr.,	1	1	Loui.
Thomason, John,	1		Bed.
Thomason, Nathaniel,	1	1	Loui.
Thomason, Richard,			Loui.
Thomason, Richard,			Henry
Thomason, Samuel,	1	7	Loui.
Thomason, Thomas,	1	4	Loui.
Thomason, Turner,	1.		Henry
Thomason, William,	1	1	Henry
Thomason, William,			Loui.
Thomley, Ann,		7	K.Geo.
Thomley, Aaron,	1	12	K.Geo.
Thomley, Eppa,	1		K.Geo.
Thomley, John,	1	7	K.Geo.
Thompson, Alexander,	1	1	Aug.
Thompson, Alexander,	1	1	Aug.
Thompson, Alex.,	1		Lin.
Thompson, Andrew,	1		Lou.
Thompson, Andrew,	1		K.Geo.
Thompson, Andrew,	1		Mont.
Thompson, Archibald,	1		Mont.
Thompson, Charles,			Lun.
Thompson, Daniel,	1		Pr.Wm.
Thompson, David,	1	10	Lun.
Thompson, David,	1	2	Cul.
Thompson, Edward,	1		Aug.
Thompson, Elenor,			Camp.
Thompson, George,	1		Mont.
Thompson, Henry,	1		Fay.
Thompson, Henry,	1		Mont.
Thompson, Hugh,	1		Mont.
Thompson, Isaac,			Lou.
Thompson, Isarel,	3		Lou.
Thompson, Capt.James,	1	16	Wash.
Thompson, James,	1	2	Lin.
Thompson, James,			Rock.
Thompson, James,	1		Rock.
Thompson, James,	1		Rock.
Thompson, James,	1		Lou.
Thompson, James,	1	8	Lun.
Thompson, James,	1		Gooch.
Thompson, James,	1		Henry
Thompson, Jeremiah,	1	3	Cha.Cy
Thompson, Jeremiah,	1		Lou.
Thompson, John,	1	1	Rock.
Thompson, John,	1	8	Rock.
Thompson, John,	1	6	Cha.Cy
Thompson, John,	1	6	Din.
Thompson, John,	1	1	Din.
Thompson, John,	1	7	Pr.Geo.
Thompson, John,	1	18	Cul.
Thompson, John,	1		Cul.
Thompson, John, Sr.,	1	17	Caro.
Thompson, John, Jr.,	1	3	Caro.

Name			County
Thompson, John,	1		Aug.
Thompson, John, Sr.,	1		Bot.
Thompson, John, Jr.,	1		Bot.
Thompson, John,	1		Mont.
Thompson, John,	1	12	Camp.
Thompson, John, Sr.,	1		Wash.
Thompson, John,	1		Wash.
Thompson, John,	1		Lin.
Thompson, Jonah,	1	3	Lou.
Thompson, Joseph,			Lou.
Thompson, Joseph,			Aug.
Thompson, Joseph,			Berk.
Thompson, Joseph,	1		Aug.
Thompson, Joseph,	1		Rock.
Thompson, Lawrence,	2	8	Fay.
Thompson, Mary,		3	Cha.Cy
Thompson, Mayton,	1		Lun.
Thompson, Matthew,	2		Aug.
Thompson, Perkin,	1	5	Cha.Cy
Thompson, Philip, est.		14	Cul.
Thompson, Richard,	1		Aug.
Thompson, Robert,	1	1	Aug.
Thompson, Robert,	1		Aug.
Thompson, Samuel,	1		Bed.
Thompson, Samuel,	1	3	Mont.
Thompson, Sarah,		5	Bed.
Thompson, Sarah,			Lou.
Thompson, Sherwood,	1		Henry
Thompson, Smyth,	1		Aug.
Thompson, Stephen,	1		Pr.Geo.
Thompson, Susanna,			Pr.Geo.
Thompson, Thomas,	1		Aug.
Thompson, Thomas,	1	1	Lou.
Thompson, Thomas,	1		Cul.
Thompson, Thomas,	1		Lou.
Thompson, Thomas,	1		Fay.
Thompson, William,	1	1	Wash.
Thompson, William,	2	20	Spots.
Thompson, William,	1		Rock.
Thompson, William,	1	22	Din.
Thompson, William,	1		Bot.
Thompson, William,	2	4	K.Geo.
Thompson, William,	1		Henry
Thompson, William, Jr.,	1		Henry
Thompson, William,	1	11	Mont.
Thompson, William,	1		Mont.
Thompson, William, Jr.,	1		Din.
Thompson, William,	1		Aug.
Thompson, William,	2		Aug.
Thompson, William,	1		Aug.
Thompson, Winerford,	1	3	Cul.
Thomson, Anderson,	1		Loui.
Thomson, Anne,		14	Loui.
Thomson, Anthony,	1	14	Loui.
Thomson, Charles,	1	2	Loui.
Thomson, Clifton,	1	1	Loui.
Thomson, David,	1	2	Loui.
Thomson, David,	1		Loui.
Thomson, Eli,	1	5	Fau.
Thomson, Francis, est.		14	K.Geo.
Thomson, Hugh,			Fay.
Thomson, Rev.James,	1	6	Fau.
Thomson, James,	1	6	Fau.
Thomson, Jesse,	1	2	Fau.
Thomson, Jeremiah,	1	3	Loui.
Thomson, John,	1		Fau.
Thomson, John,	1	2	Acco.
Thomson, John,	1	4	Loui.
Thomson, Joseph,	1	19	Loui.
Thomson, Matthew,	1	7	Loui.
Thomson, Nelson,	1	9	Loui.
Thomson, Peggy,		2	West.
Thomson, Richard,	1		Wash.
Thomson, Robert,	2		Fay.
Thomson, Robert,	1		Loui.
Thomson, Rodes,	1	6	Loui.

Name			County
Thomson, Thomas,	2	40	West.
Thomson, Waddy,	1	15	Loui.
Thomson, William,	2	4	West.
Thomson, William,	1		Loui.
Thomson, William,	1	4	Loui.
Thorn, Alexander,	1	12	Cul.
Thorn, Frederick,	2		Har.
Thornberry, Abraham,	1		Berk.
Thornberry, Benjamin,	1		Berk.
Thornberry, Henry,	1		Fau.
Thornberry, John,	3	5	Fau.
Thornberry, John,	1		Berk.
Thornberry, John,	1		Berk.
Thornberry, Samuel, Sr.	1	19	Fau.
Thornberry, Samuel, Jr.	1		Fau.
Thornberry, Thomas,	1		Berk.
Thornbrough, Thomas,	3		Berk.
Thornbrough, Thomas, Jr.	1		Berk.
Thornell, William,	2		Bed.
Thornhill, John,	1		Bed.
Thornhill, John,	1		Cul.
Thornhill, Reubin,			Cul.
Thornhill, Tam,	1		Cul.
Thornhill, Thomas,	1	1	Cul.
Thornhill, Thomas,	2	8	Buck.
Thornton, Anthony,	2	32	Caro.
Thornton, Elizabeth,		26	Caro.
Thornton, Elizabeth,		13	Fau.
Thornton, Elizabeth,		20	K.Geo
Thornton, Francis,	17	19	K.Geo
Thornton, Francis,	3	26	Spots
Thornton, Mrs.Frances,	1	11	Spots
Thornton, Mrs.George,	1	28	Spots
Thornton, Henry,	1		Wash.
Thornton, James,	1	1	Brun.
Thornton, James,			Brun.
Thornton, John,	1	2	Spots
Thornton, John,	2	41	Cul.
Thornton, John,	1		Henry
Thornton, Luke,	1		Henry
Thornton, Reuben,	1		Spots
Thornton, Reuben,	1		Brun.
Thornton, Samuel,	1		Lou.
Thornton, Seth,	2	19	Caro.
Thornton, Sterling,	1	22	Hen.
Thornton, Susanna,	1	28	Caro.
Thornton, Thomas,	1	11	Pr.Wm
Thornton, William,	2	27	Cul.
Thornton, William,	1		Spots
Thornton, William,	1	10	Brun.
Thorp, Andrew,	1		Har.
Thorp, David,			Cul.
Thorp, Frances,		7	Bed.
Thorp, Francis,	1	21	Camp.
Thorp, Henry,	1		So'n
Thorp, Henry,	2		Cul.
Thorp, Jeremiah,	1	4	So'n
Thorp, John,	1		So'n
Thorp, John,	1		So'n
Thorp, John,			So'n
Thorp, Joshua,	1	10	So'n
Thorp, Mrs.Martha,		15	So'n
Thorp, Martha,		9	So'n
Thorp, Moses,	1	11	So'n
Thorp, Phoebe,		5	So'n
Thorp, Samuel,			Cul.
Thorp, Susanna,		1	So'n
Thorp, Thomas,	1		Bed.
Thorp, Thomas,	1	1	Hen.
Thorp, Timothy,	1	19	So'n
Thorp, William,	1		Bed.
Thorp, William,	1		Henry
Threadgill, Randol,	1		Brun.
Threadgill, Capt.Thomas,	2	2	Brun.
Threlkeld, Elijah,		4	Fau.

Name			County
Threlkeld, Elijah,			Cul.
Threlkeld, George,	2	1	Fau.
Threlkeld, George,			Cul.
Threlkeld, James,	1	1	Cul.
Threlkeld, John,	3	3	Cul.
Threlkeld, John,	1	3	Cul.
Threlkild, Moses,	1	3	Cul.
Threlkild, Steven,	1	3	Cul.
Thrift, William,	1	3	Lou.
Thrink, Valentine,	1		Bot.
Thript, Drury,	1		Din.
Thript, William,	1	1	Din.
Throckmorton, Gabriel,	1	16	Berk.
Throckmorton, Robert,	1	57	Bed.
Throckmorton, Robert,	1	3	Berk.
Thrower, Christopher Jr.	1	9	Brun.
Thrower, Edward,			Brun.
Thrower, Hezekiah,	2	20	Brun.
Thukston, Thomas,	2		Har.
Thurman, Charles,	1		Buck.
Thurman, David,	1	1	Lin.
Thurman, J.,	1	1	Pr.Wm.
Thurman, Joseph,	1		Pr.Wm.
Thurman, Philip,	1		Lin.
Thurman, William,	1		Pr.Wm.
Thurmon, John,	2	13	Camp.
Thurston, John,	1		Gooch.
Thurston, William,	1		Gooch.
Thweatt, Alexander,	1	4	Din.
Thweatt, Burwell,	1	6	Din.
Thweatt, Charles,	1		Din.
Thweatt, David,	1	3	Din.
Thweatt, Drury,	1	5	Din.
Thweatt, George,	1	12	Din.
Thweatt, George, Jr.,	1		Din.
Thweatt, Henry,	1	5	Din.
Thweatt, Henry, Jr.,	1	11	Din.
Thweatt, James,	1	2	Din.
Thweatt, James,	1	23	Din.
Thweatt, John,	1	33	Pr.Geo
Thweatt, Joseph,	1	2	Din.
Thweat, Mary,		16	Brun.
Thweatt, Peter,	1		Din.
Thweatt, Thomas,	1	18	Pr.Geo
Thweatt, William,	1	11	Din.
Thweatt, William,	1	2	Din.
Tidds, William,	1		Har.
Tidwell, Ann Barbara,		6	West.
Tiffee, Catlett,	1		Cul.
Tiffey, Charles,	1		Cul.
Tigart, James,	1		Wash.
Tignal, Phillip,	2	1	Acco.
Tignal, William,	1	5	K.&Q
Tignor, Jemima,		2	K.Wm.
Tignor, Thomas,	1	1	K.Wm.
Tignor, Thomas,	1	2	K.Wm.
Tilford, Andrew,	1		Bot.
Tiller, Ann,	1	1	Carb.
Tiller, Daniel,	1		Caro.
Tiller, Henry,	1	6	So'n
Tiller, Thomas,	1		Caro.
Tillery, Thomas,	1	2	Cul.
Tillett, Samuel,	2	6	Lou.
Tilman, John,	1	2	Brun.
Tilman, Lucy,	1	7	Brun.
Tilman, Tobias,	1		Bot.
Timberlake, Benjamin,	1	13	Loui.
Timberlake, Charles,	1	2	Camp.
Timberlake, Epaphro's	1	4	Fau.
Timberlake, James,	1	11	Cha.Cy
Timberlake, John,	1		Loui.
Timberlake, Joseph,	1	2	Caro.
Timberlake, Joseph, Jr.	2	7	Caro.
Timberlake, Phillip, Sr.	1		Loui.
Timberlake, Phillip, Jr	1		Loui.

Name			County
Timberlake, Richard,	1	4	K.Wm.
Timberlake, Richard,	2	12	K.Wm.
Timberlake, Richard,	1		Camp.
Tisdale, Shirley,	1	2	Loui.
Timberlake, William,		1	Caro.
Timmons, Bryan,	1		Berk.
Timson, Sarah,		2	York
Tinch, Henry,	2	7	Pr.Geo.
Tindal, Benjamin,	3	30	Buck.
Tinney, James,	1	1	York
Tinney, John,	1	1	York
Tinney, William,	1		Ja.Cy
Tinsbloom, John,	1		K.&Q
Tinsley, Ann,	1	1	Caro.
Tinsley, Edward,	2	6	Cul.
Tinsley, Elizabeth,			Caro.
Tinsley, James,			Cul.
Tinsley, John,	1		Henry
Tinsley, John,	1	1	Cul.
Tinsley, Joshua,	1	2	Caro.
Tinsley, Phillip,	1		Gooch.
Tinsley, Reaves,	1	1	Gooch.
Tinsley, William,	1		Fay.
Tinsley, William,	1	1	Caro.
Tinsley, William,	1	5	Caro.
Tinsley, William,	1		Buck.
Tipton, Aequilla,	1		Berk.
Tipton, Shadrack,			Bot.
Tipton, Mordecai,	1		Bot.
Tippert, Samuel,	1		Cul.
Tirdall, William,	1		Henry
Tisdale, Daniel,	1	1	Din.
Tisdale, John,	1	1	Loui.
Tisdale, John,	1	9	Loui.
Tisdale, William,			Lun.
Title, Anthony,	1		Henry
Titmarsh, Jeremiah,	1	3	Pr.Geo.
Tittle, John,	1		Henry
Toamin, Joshua,	1		Henry
Tobet, John,			Lou.
Tobler, Jacob,	1		Mont.
Todail, Littleton,	1		Nor.
Todd, Bernard,	1	15	K.Wm.
Todd, Elizabeth,			Din.
Todd, George,	2	14	Caro.
Todd, George,	1	5	Hen.
Todd, Henry, est.,	2	33	K.&Q
Todd, Henry,			Din.
Todd, Jane,		5	Fay.
Todd, Rev.John,	2	21	Loui.
Todd, John,	1		Fay.
Todd, John,	1		Din.
Todd, Levi,	2	6	Fay.
Todd, Levi,			Bot.
Todd, Owen,			Fay.
Todd, Richard,	1	2	Spots.
Todd, Robert,	1		Lou.
Todd, Robert,	1		Lou.
Todd, Robert,	3	8	Fay.
Todd, Robert, Jr.,			Fay.
Todd, Samuel,	1	3	Spots.
Todd, Samuel,	1		Bot.
Todd, William, est.,		45	K.&Q
Todhunter, Jacob,	1		Fay.
Todhunter, John,	1	1	Lou.
Toknson, Moses,	1		Mont.
Tolberts, Thomas,	2		Har.
Toleman, William,	1		Nor.
Toler, John,	1		K.Wm.
Toler, Joshua,	1		K.Wm.
Toler, Joseph,	1	5	Bed.
Toler, Martin,	1		K.Wm.
Toler, William,	1	3	K.Wm.
Tolle, George,	1		Fau.
Tolle, Jonathan,	1		Lou.
Tolle, Sarah,	1	1	Fau.

Name			Co.	Name			Co.	Name			Co.
Tolle,Stephen,	1		Lou.	Townsend,Joseph,	1	1	Lun.	Trimble,Capt.James,	1	4	Aug.
Tollet,John,	1		Mont.	Townsend,Taylor,	1		Aug.	Trimble,James,	1		Wash.
Tolley,Christian,	1		Rock.	Townshend,Gerard,	1		Fay.	Trimble,John,	1	1	Rock.
Tolliver,* * *,	1		Mont.	Townshend,Henry,	2	6	Acco.	Trimble,Moses,	1		Wash.
Tomlin,John,	2	12	Fau.	Townshend,James,	1		Fay.	Trimble,Moses,	2	3	Rock.
Tomlin,John,Jr.,	1	1	Fau.	Townshend,James,			Lou.	Trimble,Capt.Robert,	1		Wash.
Tomlin,Walker,	1	20	K.Wm.	Townshend,William,	1	4	Acco.	Trimble,William,			Fay.
Tomlinson,Benjamin,	1	12	Lun.	Tracewell,Edward,	1		Aug.	Trimble,William,	2		Fay.
Tomlinson,Harriss,	1	1	Lun.	Tracey,William,	1		Bed.	Trimier,Obediah,	1	2	Loui.
Tomlinson,Nicholas,	1		Fay.	Tracy,George,	1		Pr.Wm.	Trimmer,William,	1		K.Wm.
Tomlinson,Richard,	1		Fay.	Trader,Arthur,	1	1	Acco.	Triplett,Daniel,	1	7	Cul.
Tomlinson,William,	1		Fay.	Trader,Henry,	3	4	Acco.	Triplett,Daniel,	1	1	Hen.
Tommerson,John,	1		Hen.	Trader,Lett,			Acco.	Triplett,Eliza.	1		Lou.
Tompkins,Ann,	1	17	Caro.	Trader,Lettiston,	1	2	Acco.	Triplett,Enoch,	1		Lou.
Tompkins,Ann,		27	Nor.	Trader,Samuel,			Acco.	Triplett,Francis,	1	2	Lou.
Tompkins,Christopher	1	33	K.Wm.	Trader,William B.,	1		Acco.	Triplett,Francis,	1	6	Fau.
Tompkins,Benjamin,	1	29	Caro.	Trahorn,James,	2		Lou.	Triplett,James,	3	7	Pr.Wm.
Tompkins,Bennet,	1	21	Nor.	Trahorn,William,			Lou.	Triplett,James,Jr.,			Pr.Wm.
Tompkins,Edward,	2		Lin.	Trainam,Obediah,	1		Spots.	Triplett,John,Sr.,	2	4	Cul.
Tompkins,Francis,	1	10	Caro.	Trammel,Sampson,Sr.,	1	7	Lou.	Triplett,John,	1	8	Cul.
Tompkins,Guinn,		3	Fay.	Trammel,Sampson,Jr.,	1	6	Lou.	Triplett,John,	1	11	Cul.
Tompkins,James,	1	13	Caro.	Trammell,Thomas,	1		Lou.	Triplett,Nat,			Pr.Wm.
Tompkins,John,	1	19	Cul.	Tranham,David,	1		Caro.	Triplett,Reuben,	1	1	Lou.
Tompkins,John,	1	29	Nor.	Tranham,Samuel,Sr.,	1	1	Caro.	Triplett,Col.Simon,	1	16	Lou.
Tompkins,Robert,	1	33	Caro.	Tranham,Samuel,Jr.,	1	1	Caro.	Triplett,Thomas,			Lou.
Tompson,George,	2	1	Cul.	Trap,Martin,	1		Lin.	Triplett,William,	1	11	West.
Tompson,William,	1	18	Cul.	Trapwell,Jacob,			Cha.Cy	Triplett,William,			Fau.
Tomson,John,	1	1	K.&Q	Travice,John,	1	4	Pr.Geo	Triplet,William,	1	4	Fay.
Toney,Harriss,	1		Bed.	Travillion,Cetivia,		1	Ja.Cy	Tripplett,Abel,	1		Lou.
Toney,John,	1	8	Buck.	Travis,Britain,			So'n	Tristrem,Thomas,	1		Bot.
Toney,Reuben,	1		Bed.	Travis,Champion,	1	24	Ja.Cy	Trivillian,Thomas,		4	Caro.
Toney,William,	1		Bed.	Travis,Edward,	1	34	Brun.	Trivillian,Thomas,Jr		3	Caro.
Toney,William,Jr.,	1		Bed.	Travis,John,	2	17	York	Trotter,David,	1	2	Aug.
ToolWilliam,	2	7	Fau.	Traylor,George,			Din.	Trotter,George,	1	9	Brun.
Toole,James,	1		Lou.	Traylor,John,	1		Din.	Trotter,Isaac,	1		Aug.
Toole,John,	1		Berk.	Traylor,Joseph,	1		Din.	Trotter,Isham,	1	7	Brun.
Toombs,Gabriel,	1	2	Caro.	Trebby,James,	1	1	Lou.	Trotter,James,	1	11	Brun.
Toombs,Mary,	1		K.Wm.	Trebby,John,Sr.,	2		Lou.	Trotter,James,	1	4	Fay.
Toomey,Michael,	1		Bot.	Trebby,John,Jr.,	1		Lou.	Trotter,James,	1	3	Din.
Toomes,John,	2	8	York	Trebby,Jonathan,			Lou.	Trotter,James,	1	3	Aug.
Topping,Garret,	1	5	Acco.	Trebell,William,	1	27	Ja.Cy	Trotter,James,Jr.,	1	7	Aug.
Topping,John,	2		Acco.	Treble,Andrew,	1	5	Fay.	Trotter,Joseph,	1	2	Aug.
Topping,Levi,			Acco.	Tremble,James,	1		Aug.	Trotter,Richard,	1		Aug.
Topping,Major,	1		Acco.	Tremble,John,Sr.,	2	4	Aug.	Trotter,Samuel,	1	1	Aug.
Topping,Robinson,	3	3	Acco.	Tremble,John,	1		Aug.	Trotter,William,	3	3	Fay.
Topping,Smith,	1		Acco.	Tremble,Robert,	1		Aug.	Trotters,William,	1	2	Aug.
Torrance,Joseph,	1		Camp.	Tremble,Walter,	1	1	Aug.	Troup,Mary,			Henry
Torrence,Joseph,	1		Camp.	Trent,Alexander,	1		Camp.	Trousdale,John,	1		Wash.
Torrann,Andrew,	1	2	Cul.	Trent,Alexander,	1		Camp.	Trout,Jacob,	1		Bot.
Tosher,Christian,	1		Har.	Trent,Elijah,	1		Camp.	Trout,Paul,	1		Lou.
Tounsin,Jabres,	1		Lin.	Trent,Elijah,	1		Camp.	Trower,John,	1		Har.
Towler,Cornelius,	1		Gooch.	Trent,Henry,	1		Henry	Trower,Robert,	1	4	Nor.
Towler,Cornelius,	1		Gooch.	Trent,Obediah H.,	1	2	Bed.	Trower,Solomon,	1		Loui.
Towler,George,	1		Gooch.	Trent,Peter F.,	1	24	Hen.	Trower,William,	2	10	Nor.
Towler,Jopheth,	1	7	Gooch.	Trent,William,			Henry	Troxell,Christian,	1		Lou.
Towler,John,			Gooch.	Tribble,George,	1	1	Caro.	Troxell,David,	1		Lou.
Towler,Mary,		4	Gooch.	Tribble,George,Jr.,	1		Caro.	Troxell,George Jacob			Lou.
Towler,Matthew,	1	3	K.Wm.	Tribble,John,	1		Camp.	Troxell,John,	1		Har.
Towler,Matthew,	1		K.Wm.	Tribble,Joseph,	1		Caro.	Truax,John,	2		Lou.
Towler,Capt.Stockley,	1	19	Gooch.	Trice,James,Sr.,	1	12	K.&Q	Trudaway,John,	2		Fay.
Towler,William,	1		K.Wm.	Trice,Jane,		6	K.&Q	True,Henry,	1	5	Spots.
Towles,Elizabeth,		19	Spots.	Trice,William,	1		K.&Q	True,James,	1		Fay.
Towles,Henry,	1		Cul.	Trice,William,	1	19	Loui.	True,Joseph,	1		Spots.
Towles,Henry,	1	6	Cul.	Trigg,Abraham,	1	5	Mont.	True,Margaret,est.,			Spots.
Towles,Joseph,	1		Cul.	Trigg,Daniel,	1	10	Mont.	True,Martin,	1		Spots.
Towles,Col.Oliver,	2	34	Spots.	Trigg,James,	1		K.&Q	True,Thomas,	1		Spots.
Towles,Stokely,	1		Cul.	Trigg,John,	1		Berk.	Truman,Susanna,		4	Hen.
Towles,Thomas,	1	19	Spots.	Trigg,John,	1	12	Bed.	Truman,Cuffey,(F.N.	1	1	
Towman,Peter,	1		Lou.	Trigg,Mary,			Spots.	Trumbo,Andrew,			Har.
Townley,Robert,	1	15	K.&Q	Trigg,William,	1	10	Spots.	Trumbo,George,	1	1	Har.
Townsend,Ezeliel,	1		Aug.	Trigg,Col.William,	1	15	Bed.	Truslow,Thomas,			K.Geo.
Townsend,James,	1		Aug.	Trigger,Francis,	2		K.Geo.	Trussell,Rhody,	1		Pr.Wm.
Towsend,John,	1	2	Lun.	Trigger,William,			K.Geo.	Trussell,Thomas,	1		Pr.Wm.
Towsend,John,			Lun.	Triman,Robert,	1		Pr.Wm.	Trussell,William,	1		Pr.Wm.
Townsend,John,	1		Har.	Trimble,David,	2		Aug.	Tuck,Bennett,	1		K.Wm.
Townsend,John,	1		Henry	Trimble,Isaac,	1		Rock.	Tuck,Cary,	1	1	K.Wm.

Name			County
Tuck,Jack,	1		K.Wm.
Tuck,Joseph,	1		K.Wm.
Tucker,Abraham,	1		Berk.
Tucker,Benjamin,			Lou.
Tucker,Benjamin,	1	1	So'n
Tucker,Benjamin,	1	12	Din.
Tucker,Berryman,	1	10	Din.
Tucker,Daniel,	1	12	Din.
Tucker,David,	1		Din.
Tucker,David,	1	22	Brun.
Tucker,George,	2	5	Lun.
Tucker,Henry,	1		So'n
Tucker,Isaac,	1	23	Din.
Tucker,Isaac,	1	7	Din.
Tucker,Isaac,	1	9	Din.
Tucker,Joel,			Lun.
Tucker,John Sr.,	1	24	Din.
Tucker,John Jr.,	1	13	Din.
Tucker,John,			Din.
Tucker,John,	1	1	Din.
Tucker,John,	1	1	Lin.
Tucker,John,	1		So'n
Tucker,Joseph,	1	1	Lun.
Tucker,Joseph,	2	9	Din.
Tucker,Capt.Joseph,	1	20	Din.
Tucker,Joseph,	1	4	Din.
Tucker,Martha,		2	Lun.
Tucker,Miles,	1	2	Pr.Geo
Tucker,Moses,	1		Cul.
Tucker,Nicholas,	1		Lou.
Tucker,Nicholas,	1		Lou.
Tucker,Robert,	1		Din.
Tucker,Robert,	1	1	Din.
Tucker,Robert,	1	10	Din.
Tucker,St.George,	1	11	Din.
Tucker,Susanna,		1	Pr.Geo
Tucker,Thomas,			Camp.
Tucker,Valentine,	2	1	Camp.
Tucker,William,	1	2	Lun.
Tucker,William,	1	3	Lun.
Tucker,Wood,	1	11	Din.
Tucker,Wright,	1	9	Brun.
Tuder,John,	1		Brun.
Tuder,Robert,	1		Brun.
Tuell,William,	1		Lou.
Tuggell,Henry,			Berk.
Tuggle,Henry,	1		Gooch.
Tuggle,Henry Jr.,	1		Gooch.
Tuggle,James,	1		Gooch.
Tuggle,William,	1		Gooch.
Tul,Samuel,	1		Lou.
Tull,Isreal,	1		Fay.
Tull,Lewis,	1	2	Cul.
Tulley,Alexander,	1		Cul.
Tullor,Rodham,	1	5	Fau.
Tully,Jonathan,	1		Bot.
Tumblestone,Nathaniel,	1		Lou.
Tumblin,Richard,	1		Lou.
Tummings,Edward,	1		Bot.
Tuner,Shadrick,	1		Henry
Tunkersby,John,	1	9	Caro.
Tunly,John,	2		Bot.
Tunnel,Mary,			So'n
Tunnel,Stephen,	1		Lou.
Tunstall,Ann,	1	12	K.& Q.
Tunstall,Benjamin,	1	1	Brun.
Tunstall,Esther,		50	K.& Q.
Tunstall,Leonard,			K.& Q.
Tunstall,Molly,		43	K.& Q.
Tunstall,Richard,	1	9	K.& Q.
Tunstall,Richard Jr.,			K.& Q.
Tunstall,Sarah,	1	25	K.& Q.
Tunstall,William,	1	40	Henry
Turberville,George,	1	17	Fau.
Turberville,George,	1	23	Lou.
Turberville,George,	1	51	West.

Name			County
Turberville,John,	1	18	Lou.
Turberville,John,	6	106	West.
Turberville,Richard,	1		Din.
Turbifell,John Sr.,	1	9	Brun.
Turbifell,John Jr.,	1	1	Brun.
Turibfell,William,	1	1	Brun.
Turboun,Elinor,			Henry
Tureman,Ignatius,	1	5	Spots.
Tureman,Margaret,		5	Spots.
Turk,Thomas Jr.,	1	1	Aug.
Turley,Charles,		2	Lou.
Turley,Charles,			Lou.
Turley,Ignatius,	1		Lou.
Turley,James,	1		Camp.
Turley,James,	1		Camp.
Turley,Jiles,			Lou.
Turley,John,	4	5	Lou.
Turley,John,			Lou.
Turley,John,	1	4	Lou.
Turley,Robert,	1		Bed.
Turley,Sampson,			Lou.
Turlington,Edmund,	1	1	Acco.
Turlington,Jacob,	1		Acco.
Turlington,James,	1		Acco.
Turlington,James,	1		Acco.
Turlington,Mary Ann,	1		Acco.
Turman,Benjamin,	1		Bot.
Turman,Benjamin,	1		Bot.
Turman,Charles,			Bot.
Turnal,George,	1		Acco.
Turnbull,Amey,		4	Din.
Turnbull,George,	1	6	Bed.
Turnbull,James,	1	6	Din.
Turnbull,Robert,	2	81	Din.
Turnbull,Robert,	1		Fau.
Turnbull,Stephen,	1	13	Eli.Cy
Turnbull,Stephen,	1	5	West.
Turner,Admiah,	1	1	Bed.
Turner,Alexander,	1		Fau.
Turner,Andrew,	1		Buck.
Turner,Andrew,	2		Acco.
Turner,Anothy,	1		Berk.
Turner,Arthur,			Brun.
Turner,Arthur,		1	Lun.
Turner,Arthur,	1		So'n
Turner,Arthur,		13	So'n
Turner,Bartholomew,	1	4	Gooch.
Turner,Ben,			Hen.
Turner,Benjamin,	1		Loui.
Turner,Benjamin,	1	6	So'n
Turner,Benjamin,	1	10	So'n
Turner,Benjamin,	1	15	So'n
Turner,Caleb,	1	16	K.Wm.
Turner,Charles,	1	2	K.Wm.
Turner,Dabney,	1	9	K.Wm.
Turner,Daniel,	8	15	Caro.
Turner,Daniel,	1		Henry
Turner,David,	1		So'n
Turner,Edward,	1		Nor.
Turner,Edward,	1	14	Fau.
Turner,Elijah,	1	2	Bed .
Turner,Ephraim,	1		So'n
Turner,Fielding,	3	13	Lou.
Turner,Francis,			Pr.Wm.
Turner,George,	2	1	Caro.
Turner,Harris,			So'n
Turner,Henry,	1	8	So'n
Turner,Henry,	1	13	So'n
Turner,Hezekiah,	1	5	Fau.
Turner,Hillery,	2		Acco.
Turner,Isaiah,	1	1	Bed.
Turner,Jacob,	1		So'n
Turner,Jacob,	1	3	So'n
Turner,Jacob,	1	9	So'n
Turner,Jacob,	2		So'n
Turner,Jacob,	1		So'n

Name			County
Turner,James,			Cul.
Turner,James,	1	2	Henry
Turner,James,Sr.,	1	10	Bed.
Turner,James,	1	7	Bed.
Turner,James,	1		Caro.
Turner,Jerimiah,	1		Cul.
Turner,Jesse,			Brun.
Turner,Jesse,	1	4	So'n
Turner,John,	1		Bed.
Turner,John,	1		Henry
Turner,John,	1		Buck.
Turner,John,	1		Cul.
Turner,John,	1		Berk.
Turner,John,	1		Camp.
Turner,John,	4		K.Geo.
Turner,John,	1		Fau.
Turner,John,	1		Fau.
Turner,John,	1	2	Caro.
Turner,John,	1	6	Caro.
Turner,John,	1		So'n
Turner,John,	1	2	Ja.Cy
Turner,John,			Acco.
Turner,John,	1	2	Lou.
Turner,John F.,	1	7	Nor.
Turner,Joseph,	1		Fay.
Turner,Joseph,			So'n
Turner,Joseph,	1	2	So'n
Turner,Joseph,		1	Din.
Turner,Joseph,	1	14	Din.
Turner,Joseph,	1	1	Berk.
Turner,Joshua,			So'n
Turner,Joshua,	1	7	Acco.
Turner,Josiah,	1		Henry
Turner,Lewis,	1		Bed.
Turner,Lewis Ellzey,	2	4	Lou.
Turner,Littleton,	1	8	So'n
Turner,Lucy,	1	12	So'n
Turner,Martha,			So'n
Turner,Mary,		6	Berk.
Turner,Mary,		1	Ja.Cy
Turner,Matthew,	1	1	Lun.
Turner,Matthew,	1		So'n
Turner,Nathan,	1	3	So'n
Turner,Patience,			So'n
Turner,Pearce,	1		Fau.
Turner,Phoebe,		1	So'n.
Turner,Pleasants,	1		Gooch.
Turner,Rachael,		24	K.Wm.
Turner,Reubin,	1	24	K.Wm.
Turner,Richard,	1	4	Caro.
Turner,Richard,	1	3	Cul.
Turner,Rodger,	3	1	Fay.
Turner,Samuel,			Fau.
Turner,Samuel,	1		So'n
Turner,Samuel,	1		So'n
Turner,Thomas,	1	22	So'n
Turner,Thomas,	1	7	Berk.
Turner,Thomas,	3	118	K.Geo.
Turner,Thomas,	1	76	West.
Turner,Thomas,	1	9	So'n
Turner,Thomas,	1		Spots.
Turner,Thomas,	1		Spots.
Turner,Thomas,			So'n
Turner,William,			Cul.
Turner,William,	1		Henry
Turner,William,	1	1	Bot.
Turner,William,	1		Acco.
Turner,William,	1		Spots.
Turner,Williams,	1		Hen.
Turnley,Francis,	1	1	Hen.
Turpin,Alexander,			Hen.
Turpin,David,			Buck.
Turpin,Henry,	1		Hen.
Turpin,John,	1	1	Hen.
Turpin,Lusby,	2	15	Henry
Turpin,Margaret,			Lun.
Turpin,Michael,	1	5	Hen.
Turpin,Michael,	2	3	Hen.
Turpin,Peter Field,	1	14	Buck.

Name			Co.
Turpin,William,			Fay.
Turpin,William,	1		Lun.
Turrence,John,	1		Fay.
Turvey,Daniel,	1		Har.
Tusady,Joseph,	1	5	Camp.
Tushemer,Jacob,	1		Lou.
Tushler,George,	1		Lou.
Tutt,Benjamin,	1	10	Cul.
Tutt,Hansford,			Cul.
Tutt,James,	2	11	Cul.
Tutt,James,	1	6	Cul.
Tutt,James,	1	16	Spots
Tutt,John,	1	13	Cul.
Tutt,Million,		16	Cul.
Tutt,Richard,	1	2	Cul.
Tuttle,James,	1	1	Mont.
Tuttle,James,			Pr.Wm
Twiford,Bartholomew,	1		Acco.
Twiford,George,	1		Acco.
Twiford,James,			Acco.
Twiford,John,			Acco.
Twiford,Robert,	3	3	Acco.
Twiford,Torobable,	3		Acco.
Twink,Andrew,	1	2	Berk.
Twyman,George,			Cul.
Twyman,Reubin,			Cul.
Twyman,William,Sr.,	3	15	Cul.
Twyman,William,Jr.,	1	2	Cul.
Twing,Henry,	1		Berk.
Twopence,James,	1		Loui.
Tye,Henry,	1		Cul.
Tye,Solomon,	1	3	Din.
Tyler,* * *,	2	8	Pr.Wm
Tyler,Charles,			Pr.Wm
Tyler,Charles,			Pr.Wm
Tyler,Charles,	1	5	Lou.
Tyler,Daniel,	1		Gooch
Tyler,Edmund,	1	6	So'n
Tyler,George,	2	20	Caro.
Tyler,Henry,	1	3	Pr.Wm
Tyler,Jeremiah,	1	1	So'n
Tyler,John,	1	4	K.Geo
Tyler,John,	1	4	K.Geo
Tyler,John,	2	18	Cha.Cy
Tyler,John,	1	10	Lou.
Tyler,John,Sr.,	3	19	Pr.Wm
Tyler,Nat,			Pr.Wm
Tyler,Nat,	1		Pr.Wm
Tyler,Richard,	1	21	Caro.
Tyler,Sarah,		1	Nor.
Tyler,Thomas,	1		Nor.
Tyler,William,			Pr.Wm
Tyler,William,	1	8	K.Geo
Tyler,William,	3	24	Caro.
Tynes,West,	1	4	So'n
Tyre,David,	1		Buck.
Tyree,William,	1	1	Ja.Cy
Tyree,William,	1	11	Cha.Cy
Tyree,William,Jr.,	1	2	Cha.Cy
Tyrie,James,	1	5	York
Tyson,Nathaniel,	1	4	Nor.
Underhill,Amas,	2	8	Acco.
Underhill,Daniel,	3	9	Acco.
Underhill,Thomas,	1	8	Acco.
Underwood,Elijah,	1		Cul.
Underwood,Elizabeth,			Brun.
Underwood,Francis,	1	10	Gooch
Underwood,George,	1	10	Gooch
Underwood,Gideon,	1		Cul.
Underwood,Joel,	1	1	Cul.
Underwood,John,	1		Bed.
Underwood,John,	1	10	So'n
Underwood,John,Jr.,	1	1	So'n
Underwood,Joseph,			Lin.
Underwood,Joseph,	1		Cul.
Underwood,Lewis,			Cul.
Underwood,Matthew,	1		So'n

Name			Co.
Underwood,Nathan,	1	12	Cul.
Underwood,Richard,	1		Cul.
Underwood,Samuel,	1		Henry
Underwood,Seth,	1		Cul.
Underwood,Thomas,	1	2	Fau.
Underwood,Thomas,	1	24	Gooch.
Unkerfere,Philip,	1		Lou.
Upchurch,George,	1		Brun.
Upchurch,Hermon,	1		Brun.
Upchurch,James,Sr.,	1	3	Brun.
Upchurch,James,Jr.,	1	3	Brun.
Upchurch,John,	1		Brun.
Upchurch,Michael,	1		Brun.
Upchurch,William,	1		Brun.
Updike,Aman,	1		Bed.
Updike,Rufus,	1		Lou.
Upshan,Leroy,	1	5	Buck.
Upshaw,James,	1	27	Caro.
Upshaw,Jeremiah,	1	21	Caro.
Upshur,Abel,	1	33	Acco.
Upshur,John,	1	29	Nor.
Upshur,Leah,	1	14	Acco.
Upshur,Littleton,	1	12	Nor.
Upshur,Thomas,	1	30	Nor.
Urquert,Walter,	1		Camp.
Urquhart,William,	2	20	So'n
Urton,John,	1		Lou.
Urton,John,	1		Lou.
Urven,Annanias,	1		Lin.
Useler,Christian,	1		Fau.
Usher,William,	1		Aug.
Ussery,John,	1	2	Lun.
Ussery,John,	2	11	Lun.
Ussery,Mary,	1	1	Lun.
Ussery,Mastin,			Lun.
Ussery,Thomas,			Lun.
Utley,Hezekiah,	1	2	Gooch.
Utley,Josiah,	1	2	Gooch.
Utley,Obediah,	1	1	Gooch.
Utley,William,	1	1	Gooch.
Utman,Joseph,	1		Lin.
Utman,Peter,	1		Lin.
Utterback,Agness,	1		Fau.
Utterback,Harman,		1	Fau.
Utterback,Henry,		1	Fau.
Utterback,Henry,	1		Cul.
Utterback,Henry,	1		Cul.
Utterback,Jacob,	1		Cul.
Utterback,John,	1	4	Fau.
Utts,Frederick,	1		Mont.
Utts,Silvester,	1		Mont.
Utz,Adam,	1	3	Cul.
Utz,George,Sr.,	1	9	Cul.
Utz,George,Jr.,	1	2	Cul.
Utz,George,Jr.,	1	1	Cul.
Utz,Michael,	1	8	Cul.
Utz,Michael,Jr.	1	1	Cul.
Vace,Patrick,	1		Berk.
Vahub,John,	1		Aug.
Vahub,Robert,	1	1	Aug.
Vaiden,Joseph,		10	Cha.Cy
Vanlandingham,George,			Fay.
Vale,William,	1		Ja.Cy
Valentine,Batchelder	1	9	K.Wm.
Valentine,Edward,	1	15	K.Wm.
Valentine,Edward,	1		Ja.Cy
Valentine,George,	1		Har.
Valentine,Lucy,			Camp.
Valentine,Luke,	1		Camp.
Valentine,Sarah,		8	York
Valentine,Teabid,	1		Har.
Vallangham,Richard,	1	1	Lou.
Vance,Abner,	1		Mont.
Vance,Rev.Hugh,	1	1	Berk.
Vance,John,	1		Rock.
Vance,Joseph,	1		Wash.
Vance,Joseph,	1		Rock.

Name			Co.
Vance,Martha,	1	1	Aug.
Vance,Patrick,	1		Rock.
Vance,Robert,	1		Berk.
Vance,Samuel,	1	2	Aug.
Vance,Samuel,	1		Wash.
Vance,Thomas,	1		Mont.
Vancel,Edmund,	1	1	Mont.
Vancenthiller,John,	2		Berk.
Vancleve,Ralph,	1	1	Fay.
Vandegrift,Ganott,			Henry
Vandegriff,Leonard,	1		Henry
Vandergriff,Leon'dJr	1		Henry
Vanderwall, * P,		6	Hen.
Vanderwall,John,	1		Hen.
Vanderwall,Jeffry,	1		Hen.
Vanderhoof,John,	3		Berk.
Vandeval,Daniel,	1		Hen.
Vandervort,Nicholas	3		Berk.
Vandevinter,Abraham	1		Henry
Vandevinder,Jacob,	1		Har.
Vandevinder,Isaac,	1	1	Lou.
Vanduren,Barnett,	1		Lou.
Vandyck,David,	1	1	Lun.
Vandyke,Garriot,	1		Cul.
Vandyck,Henry,	1	2	Lun.
Vandyke,Peter,	1		Cul.
Vandyke,Peter,	1		Cul.
Vanelif,Isaac,	1		Berk.
Vaney,Henry,	1		Berk.
Vanhook,Aaron,	1		Wash.
Vanhook,Lawrence,	1	8	Wash.
Vanhook,Samuel,	1		Wash.
Vanhorne,Barnett,	1		Lou.
Vanhorn,John,	1		Lou.
Vanlear,Jacob,	1	2	Aug.
Vanleare,John,	1	1	Bot.
Vanmeter,Abel,	1	3	Berk.
Vanmeter,Abraham,	1		Berk.
Vanmeter,Henry,	1	6	Berk.
Vanmeter,Isaac,	1	1	Berk.
Vanmeter,Isaac,	1		Lin.
Vanmeter,Jacob,	1	2	Berk.
Vanmeter,Jacob,	1		Har.
Vanmeter,John,Sr.,	1		Berk.
Vanmeter,John,	1		Berk.
Vanmeter,Joshua,	1		Lin.
Vanmeter,Nathan,	1		Berk.
Vn Meter,Abraham,	2	5	Har.
Vn Meter,Garret,	3	14	Har.
Vn Meter,Joseph,	2	9	Har.
Vannoy,Cornelius,	1		Lou.
Vanorsdale,Cornelis	3		Berk.
Vanorsdale,John,	1		Berk.
Vanover,Cornelius,	1		Lou.
Vanover,Henry,	1		Bot.
Vanpelt,Joseph,	1		Mont.
Vansandt,Elijah,	1		Bot.
Vansandt,Isiah,	1		Bot.
Vanvartor,Benjamin,	2		Berk.
Vanveckley,Evert,	1		Berk.
Vardiman,Amml,	1		Lin.
Vardiman,John,Sr.,	2		Lin.
Vardiman,John,Jr.,	1		Lin.
Varell,John,	1	23	Brun.
Varnall,Richard,	1		Henry
Varne,Jacob,	1		Lou.
Varner,John,	1		Rock.
Vass,Mary,		4	Spots.
Vass,Rice,	1	3	Spots.
Vass,Thomas,	1	3	K.&Q
Vass,Vincent,	1	1	Spots.
Vasser,Benjamin,	1	1	So'n
Vasser,Etheldred,	1		So'n
Vasser,John,	1	2	So'n
Vasser,Joseph,Sr.,	1	1	So'n
Vaugh,George,	1		Mont.
Vaughan,Ambrose,	1		Din.
Vaughan,Ambrose,	1	3	Caro.

Name			Place
Vaughan,Benjamin,	1		Lun.
Vaughan,Benjamin,	1		Lun.
Vaughan,Bland,	1	1	Caro.
Vaughan,Chaney,			Caro.
Vaughan,Caty,			Caro.
Vaughan,Cornelius,	1	2	Lou.
Vaughan,Cornelius,	2	12	Caro.
Vaughan,Craddock,	1	6	Lun.
Vaughan,David,	1	5	Din.
Vaughan,David,	1		Brun.
Vaughan,Drury,	1		Din.
Vaughan,George,	1		Brun.
Vaughan,George,			Brun.
Vaughan,Henry,	1	3	Din.
Vaughan,Henry,	1	3	So'n
Vaughan,Henry,	1	6	Cha.Cy
Vaughan,James,	1		Din.
Vaughan,James,	1	7	Gooch.
Vaughan,James,	1	2	Brun.
Vaughan,James,	1	1	Brun.
Vaughan,James,	4	9	
Vaughan,John,	1	4	Din.
Vaughan,John,	1		Caro.
Vaughan,John,	1	5	Caro.
Vaughan,Leroy,	1		Lou.
Vaughan,Littleberry,	1		Hen.
Vaughan,Mary,			Cul.
Vaughan,Matthew,	1	17	Gooch
Vaughan,Morriss,	1		Din.
Vaughan,Peter,	1	10	Din.
Vaughan,Richard,	1	2	Pr.Wm
Vaughan,Richard,	1		Brun.
Vaughan,Richard,	1		Cul.
Vaughan,Richard,	1		Din.
Vaughan,Samuel,	1	10	Din.
Vaughan,Shadrack,	1	27	Gooch
Vaughan,Thomas,	1	2	Henry
Vaughan,Thomas,	1		Mont.
Vaughan,Thomas,	1		Spots.
Vaughan,Thomas,	1	2	So'n
Vaughan,William,	2	2	Cul.
Vaughan,William,	1	5	Brun.
Vaughan,William,Jr.,	1	1	Brun.
Vaughan,William,	1	17	Brun.
Vaughan,William,	1	5	Din.
Vaughan,William,	1		Din.
Vaughan,William,	1		Hen.
Vaughan,William,	1	8	So'n
Vaughan,William,	1		Bed.
Vaughan,William,	1		Bed.
Vaughan,William,			Cha.Cy
Vaughan,William,	1	9	Cha.Cy
Vaughan,William,	1		Fau.
Vaughan,William S.,	2	4	Cha.Cy
Vaughan,Willis,	1	3	Brun.
Vaughan,Zachariah,	1		Din.
Vaught,Andrew,	1		Mont.
Vault,Chrisley,	1		Mont.
Vault,David,	1		Mont.
Vault,Gaspar,	1		Mont.
Vault,Henry,	2		Mont.
Vault,John,	1		Mont.
Vaun,James,	1		Lin.
Vaun,John,	1		Lin.
Vause,William,	2	1	Har.
Vawter,Elliott,	1		Caro.
Vawter,Margaret,			Caro.
Vawters,Thomas,	1	4	Buck.
Veal,David,	1		Berk.
Veal,Thomas,	1		Mont.
Veale,Cinar,			Lou.
Veale,John,	1	5	Lou.
Veale,William,Sr.,	2	7	Lou.
Veale,William,Jr.,			Lou.
Veatch,Silas,	1	6	Loui.
Venable,Abraham,	2	8	Fay.
Venable,Jacob,	1	6	Camp.
Venable,Jacob,	1	6	Camp.
Venermon,Garret,	2		Fay.
Venie,Thomas,	1		Lou.
Veniell,Adam,	1		Lou.
Venpelt,John,	1		Wash.
Veraity,Charles,	1		Cul.
Verdee,James,	1		Berk.
Verick,Michael,	1		Mont.
Vermilion,Jesse,			Wash.
Vernon,Abner,	1	6	Cul.
Vernon,Richard,	2	9	Cul.
Verrell,John,	1	40	Din.
Vessells,Elijah,	1		Acco.
Vest,John,	1	3	Spots.
Vest,John,	1		Buck.
Vest,Samuel,	1		Henry
Vestervell,Abraham,	1		Berk.
Vestervell,James,	1		Berk.
Vestervelt,David,	1		Berk.
Vice,Jenry,	1		Mont.
Vick,Arthur,	1	2	So'n
Vick,Council,	1	1	So'n
Vick,Elizabeth,	1	2	So'n
Vick,Elizabeth,	1	2	So'n
Vick,Howell,	1		Brun.
Vick,Jacob,	1	2	So'n
Vick,Jacob,Jr.	1	1	So'n
Vick,James,Sr.,	1	8	So'n
Vick,James,Jr.,	1		So'n
Vick,Jesse,	1		So'n
Vick,Jesse,	1		So'n
Vick,Jesse,	1		So'n
Vick,John,	1	5	Brun.
Vick,John,Jr.,	1		Brun.
Vick,Jordan,	1		So'n
Vick,Joseph,	1	1	So'n
Vick,Josiah,	1	3	So'n
Vick,Lewis,	1		So'n
Vick,Matthew,Jr.,	1		So'n
Vick,Pilgrim,	1		So'n
Vick,Robert,	1		So'n
Vick,Sam,	1	1	So'n
Vick,Shadrack,	1	1	So'n
Vick,Simon,	1	3	So'n
Vick,Thomas,	1	4	So'n
Vick,William,	1	17	So'n
Vick,William,	1	6	So'n
Vickars,James,	1		Bot.
Vicker,Rawleigh,	1		Fay.
Vickers,Robert,	1		Wash.
Victor,John,	1	9	Caro.
Vigor,Sarah,		7	West.
Vigor,William,	1	3	Spots,
Vincarver,Harmon,	1		Cul.
Vince,John,	1		Cul.
Vincent,Charles,			Bed.
Vincent,William,	1		Henry
Viney,Stephen,	1		Har.
Vineyard,Christian,	1	1	Bot.
Vineyard,John,	1		Bot.
Vineyard,John,	1		Cul.
Vinson,Henry,	1		Henry
Violett,Edward,	1	2	Berk.
Violett,John,	1		Lou.
Virlander,John,	1		K.&Q
Vivin,John,	1	1	Fay.
Vivion,Charles,	2	19	Caro.
Voden,Henry,	1		Fay.
Voden,William,	1		Fay.
Voss,Edward,	1	29	Cul.
Vottaw,Isaac,	1		Lou.
Vowls,Richard,	1	2	Fau.
Wabraven,John,	1		Mont.
Waddell,John,	2	4	Fau.
Waddill,James,	1	4	Hen.
Waddill,Mary,		1	Cha.Cy
Waddill,Richard,	1	5	Cha.Cy
Waddill,Samuel,	1	5	Cha.Cy
Waddle,Benjamin,	1		Mont.
Waddle,James,	1		Aug.
Waddle,Rev.James,	1	20	Aug.
Waddle,Joseph,	1	1	Aug.
Waddle,Joseph,	1	1	Aug.
Waddle,Noel,	1	1	Din.
Waddle,Thomas,	2	1	Aug.
Waddle,William,			Din.
Waddy,John,	1	11	Nor.
Waddy,Samuel,	1	10	Loui.
Wade,Bancks,	1		Hen.
Wade,Childrey,	1	5	Ja.Cy
Wade,Dabney,	1	9	Gooch.
Wade,Daniel,	1	7	Gooch.
Wade,David,	1		Bed.
Wade,Dawson,	1		Bot.
Wade,Dawson,	2		Fay.
Wade,Dawson,Jr.,	1		Fay.
Wade,Edward,			Hen.
Wade,Elizabeth,		3	Brun.
Wade,Hood,	1		Gooch.
Wade,Isaac,	1		Bed.
Wade,Jacob,	1		Bed.
Wade,Jeremiah,	1		Ja.Cy
Wade,Jeremiah,	1		Bed.
Wade,John,	1	4	Gooch.
Wade,John,			Fay.
Wade,John Utley,	1		Gooch.
Wade,Jose ph,	1	14	Ja.Cy
Wade,Joshua,	1		Bed.
Wade,Matthew,	1	2	Ja.Cy
Wade,Nathaniel,	1		Loui.
Wade,Pierce,	1	5	Camp.
Wade,Richard,	1	3	Gooch.
Wade,Robert,	1		Lou.
Wade,Robert,	1	4	Gooch.
Wade,Willson,	1		So'n
Wade,Zepheriah,	1		Lou.
Wadkins,David,	1		Lou.
Wadkins,Edward,	1		Lou.
Wadkins,John,	1		Lou.
Wadkinson,Cornelus,			Acco.
Wadlington,Francis,	1	2	Pr.Geo.
Wafford,Thomas,	1	4	Gooch.
Wafford,Thomas,	1	6	Gooch.
Wagar,William,	1	5	Eli.Cy
Wagener,Conrod,	2		Lou.
Wagener,Frances,	1		Berk.
Wagener,John,			Lou.
Wagener,Lewis,			Lou.
Wagginer,Thomas,			Cul.
Waggoner,Andrew,	1	2	Har.
Waggoner,* *nsby,	1	1	Cul.
Waggoner,Christian,	1		Aug.
Waggoner,Jacob,	1		Mont.
Waggoner,James,	3	7	Cul.
Waggoner,James,	1		Cul.
Waggoner,John,	1		Cul.
Waggoner,Reubin,	1	1	Cul.
Wagnon,Daniel,	1		Brun.
Wagoner,Christopher,	2		Berk.
Waid,John,	1		Aug.
Waide,James,	1	4	K.Wm
Waide,John,	2	5	K.Wm
Waide,Mary,		10	K.Wm
Wain,Adam,	1		Lin.
Wainwright,Cornelis,	1	8	Din.
Wainwright,Samuel,	1	6	Din.
Wainwright,Thomas,			So'n
Wait,John,	1		Cul.
Wait,John,Jr.,	1		Cul.
Wake,John,	1	12	Fau.

Name			Co.	Name			Co.	Name			Co.
Walden, Charles,	1		Caro.	Walker, Joseph Jr.,	1		Rock.	Wallace, Joseph,	2		Lou.
Walden, Edward,	1	2	K.&Q.	Walker, Levin,	2	11	Acco.	Wallace, Michael,	1	24	K.Geo.
Walden, George,		2	Caro.	Walker, Mary,		17	Cul.	Wallace, Peter,	1	1	Rock.
Walden, James,	1		Henry	Walker, Mathew,	1		Fay.	Wallace, Robert,	1	1	Rock.
Walden, James,	1		K.& Q.	Walker, Moses,	1		Camp.	Wallace, Robert,	1		Wash.
Walden, James,	1		K.& Q.	Walker, Peter,	1	6	Gooch.	Wallace, Robert,	1	11	Eli.Cy
Walden, James,	1		Lin.	Walker, Peter,	1	11	Gooch.	Wallace, Samuel,	1	2	Rock.
Walden, John,	1	5	K.& Q.	Walker, Prissilla,		9	Din.	Wallace, Samuel,	1	1	Lin.
Walden, John,	1	20	Caro.	Walker, Randolph,	1		Buck.	Wallace, Thomas,	1	6	Cul.
Walden, Lewis,	1	5	Caro.	Walker, Rebecca,		13	Cha.Cy	Wallace, William,	1	4	Pr.Geo.
Walden, Lewis,		4	K.Wm.	Walker, Richard,	1	3	Lun.	Wallace, William,	1		Bot.
Walden, Lewis,	1		K.& Q.	Walker, Richardson,		1	Cha.Cy	Wallace, William,	1	1	Rock.
Walden, Richard,	1	8	K.& Q.	Walker, Robert,	1	1	Spots.	Wallen, Elisha Jr.	1	3	Mont.
Walding, Isham,	1		Din.	Walker, Robert,	1	5	Eli.Cy	Wallen, James,	1		Mont.
Waldrope, Welthy,	1		K.Wm.	Walker, Robert,	1	24	Brun.	Wallen, John,	1		Mont.
Walds, William,	1		Lou.	Walker, Robert,	1	2	Fay.	Wallen, Joseph,	1		Mont.
Wales, Isaac,	1		Cul.	Walker, Robert,	1	52	Din.	Wallen, William,	1		Mont.
Walke, Thomas	1	4	Din.	Walker, Robert,	1	5	Acco.	Waller, Mrs.Ann,	1	29	Spots.
Walker, Adam,	1		Mont.	Walker, Robert,	1	4	Camp.	Waller, Arthur,	1	9	So'n
Walker, Alexander,		6	Ja.Cy	Walker, Samuel,	1		Rock.	Waller, B.,		8	York
Walker, Alexander,	1		Rock.	Walker, Samuel, Jr.,	1		Rock.	Waller, Benjamin,	1	21	Spots.
Walker, Alexander,	1		Din.	Walker, Samuel,	1		Bot.	Waller, Benjamin,	1	22	Ja.Cy
Walker, Alexander,	3	7	Cha.Cy	Walker, Samuel,	1	4	West.	Waller, Benjamin,	1	1	So'n
Walker, Alexander, Sr.,	1		Rock.	Walker, Sarah,		31	Cha.Cy	Waller, Benjamin C.,	1	13	York
Walker, Alexander, Jr.,	1	6	Rock.	Walker, Shadrack,	1	3	Gooch.	Waller, Charles,	1	5	Fau.
Walker, Anna,		27	Cha.Cy	Walker, Solomon,	1	1	K.Wm.	Waller, Edward,	1	8	K.& Q.
Walker, Asaph,	1	7	Buck.	Walker, Sylvanus,	1	6	Lun.	Waller, Edward,	2	14	Fau.
Walker, Benjamin,	1		Cul.	Walker, Thomas,	1	8	Lun.	Waller, Elizabeth,		7	K.Wm.
Walker, Benjamin,	3	7	Lun.	Walker, Thomas,	1		Din.	Waller, George,	1	18	Henry
Walker, Buckley,	1		Camp.	Walker, Thomas,		3	Brun.	Waller, Jesse,	1		Lou.
Walker, Edward,			Brun.	Walker, Thomas,		3	Brun.	Waller, John,	1	2	Spots.
Walker, Elmore,	1		Buck.	Walker, William,	1		K.& Q.	Waller, John,	1	11	Spots.
Walker, Frances,	1	11	Buck.	Walker, William,	1	23	Brun.	Waller, John,	1	3	K.& Q.
Walker, Frances,		32	K.& Q.	Walker, William,	2	14	Ja.Cy	Waller, John,	2	37	K.Wm.
Walker, Freeman, est.,		1	Din.	Walker, William,	1		K.Wm.	Waller, John,	1		Lou.
Walker, George, est.,		3	Brun.	Walker, William,	1	5	Rock.	Waller, John,	1		So'n
Walker, Henry,	1	5	Cha.Cy	Walker, William,			Rock.	Waller, John,			Acco.
Walker, Henry,	1		Mont.	Walker, William,	1	5	Gooch.	Waller, Joshua,			Acco.
Walker, Henry,	1		Cul.	Walker, William,			Bed.	Waller, Leonard,	1	5	Spots.
Walker, Henry,			Brun.	Walker, William,	1		Buck.	Waller, Pomfeet,	1	9	Spots.
Walker, Capt.Henry,	1	2	Bot.	Walker, William,	4	26	Cul.	Waller, Thomas,	1	1	Spots.
Walker, James,			Cha.Cy	Walker, William,	1	4	Cha.Cy	Waller, Thomas,	1	16	Spots.
Walker, James,	1	13	Cul.	Walker, William,			Cha.Cy	Waller, Thomas,	1	7	K.Wm.
Walker, James,	1		Buck.	Walker, William,	1		Camp.	Waller, William,	1		Berk.
Walker, James,	2	12	Buck.	Walker, William,	1		Camp.	Waller, William,	1	5	Spots.
Walker, James,	1		Bot.	Walker, William,	1		Loui.	Wallerson, Henry,	1	1	Bot.
Walker, James,	1	3	Rock.	Walker, William,	1		Bot.	Wallingsford, Benj.	1		Berk.
Walker, James,	1		Rock.	Walker, William, Jr.,	1		Bot.	Wallingsford, Benj.	1		Berk.
Walker, James,	1		Rock.	Wall, Adam,	1		Mont.	Wallingsford, James,	1		Berk.
Walker, James, N.,	1	2	Jas.Cy	Wall, Apple,			Mont.	Wallingsford, Joseph,	1		Berk.
Walker, Joel,	1	1	Henry	Wall, Benjamin,	1		Brun.	Wallis, John,	4	9	Cul.
Walker, John,		3	Cha.Cy	Wall, Coonrade,	1		Mont.	Wallis, John Jr.,			Cul.
Walker, John,			Cha.Cy	Wall, Frathias,	1		Wash.	Wallis, Michael,	1	9	Cul.
Walker, John,	2	8	Cul.	Wall, Isaac,	1	6	Din.	Wallis, Robert,	1		Aug.
Walker, John,			Cul.	Wall, John,			Cha.Cy	Wallis, Robert,			Cul.
Walker, John,	1		Bed.	Wall, John,	1		Din.	Wallis, William,		2	Lub.
Walker, John,			Bed.	Wall, John,	1-		Mont.	Wallis, William,			Cul.
Walker, John,	1	5	West.	Wall, Jonathan,	1	4	So'n	Walmack, Richard,	1		Gooch.
Walker, John,	1		Wash.	Wall, Joshua,	1	1	Din.	Walpoles, Thomas, est.	1	12	Brun.
Walker, John,	1		Wash.	Wall, Peter,	1	1	Din.	Walten, George,	1		Lou.
Walker, John,	1		Gooch.	Wall, William,	1		Cul.	Walter, John,	1		Berk.
Walker, John,	1		Fau.	Wall, Zachariah,	1	1	Cul.	Walter, Michael,	1		Mont.
Walker, John,	1	20	Ja.Cy	Wallace, Andrew,			Lou.	Walter, Richard,	1	2	Acco.
Walker, John,	1	3	Ja.Cy	Wallace, David Sr.,	2		Bot.	Walters, Absalom,	1		Mont.
Walker, John,			Lou.	Wallace, Edward,	1		Brun.	Walters, John,	1	2	Mont.
Walker, John,	1		Lou.	Wallace, James,	1		Rock.	Walters, Jonathan,	1		Rock.
Walker, John Sr.,	1	10	Acco.	Wallace, James,	1		Bot.	Walters, Richard C.,	1	5	York
Walker, John, Jr.,	2	8	Acco.	Wallace, James,	1		Aug.	Walters, Thomas,	1		Berk.
Walker, John, Sr.,	2	1	Rock.	Wallace, James Jr.,	1		K.Wm.	Walthall, Francis,	1	7	Buck.
Walker, John,	2		Rock.	Wallace, Jane,		4	Aug.	Waltham, Sarah,		3	Acco.
Walker, John,	1		Rock.	Wallace, John,	1	1	Spots.	Waltham, Susannah,		1	Nor.
Walker, John,	1		Rock.	Wallace, John,	1	1	Lou.	Waltham, William,	1	5	Nor.
Walker, John,	1		Rock.	Wallace, John,	1		Wash.	Waltman, Jacob,	1		Berk.
Walker, John,	1		Rock.	Wallace, John,	1		Rock.	Weltman, Manuel,	1		Lou.
Walker, Joseph,	1	7	Rock.	Wallace, John,	1		Aug.	Walton, George,	1	9	Lun.
Walker, Joseph Sr.,	1		Rock.	Wallace, John,	1	4	Brun.	Walton, George,	1	4	Brun.
								Walton, Henry,	1	5	Brun.

Walton,James,	1	1	K.& Q.	Ware,Malichi,	1	1	Loui.	Warthen,Elizabeth,Sr.		2	Pr.Geo.
Walton,John,	2	14	Brun.	Ware,Markham,	1		Fay.	Warthen,Elizabeth,		1	Pr.Geo.
Walton,John,	1	8	Loui.	Ware,Mary,		2	K.& Q.	Warthen,James,	1		Pr.Geo.
Walton,John,	1		Hen.	Ware,Mary,			Brun.	Warthen,Jeremiah,	1	1	Pr.Geo.
Walton,John,	1		Bed.	Ware,Nicholas,	1	2	Pr.Wm.	Warts,Conrod,	1		Lou.
Walton,John,	1	7	K.& Q.	Ware,Reuben,	1	5	Caro.	Warts,Michael,	1		Lou.
Walton,Mary,		1	K.& Q.	Ware,Robert,est.,		7	K.& Q.	Wash,Ezekiel,	1	1	Loui.
Walton,Robert,		22	Henry	Ware,Robert,	1	5	K.& Q.	Wash,John,	1	3	Loui.
Walton,Thomas,	1	2	Brun.	Ware,Robert,	3	26	Caro.	Wash,John,	1	8	Henry
Walton,William,	2		Bed.	Ware,Sarah,		3	K.& Q.	Wash,Mary,		14	Loui.
Walton,William,			Brun.	Ware,Thomas,	1	7	K.Wm.	Wash,Susanna,			Loui.
Walton,William,	2		Bed.	Warford,Abraham,	1		Lou.	Wash,Thomas,	1		Loui.
Walton,William,	1	8	Bot.	Warford,John,	1		Lou.	Wash,Thomas,			Loui.
Walwood,George,	1		Bot.	Warmsley,John,	1		Aug.	Wash,William,	1	3	Loui.
Wammock,James,	1	6	Pr.Geo.	Warmsley,William,	1		Aug.	Washboun,Thomas,	2	11	Cul.
Wampler,George,	1		Mont.	Warnell,Roby,	1	11	Lou.	Washington,Arthur,	1	15	So'n
Wampler,Michael,	1		Mont.	Warner,Jacob,	1		Buck.	Washington,Charles,	1	22	Berk.
Wann,William,	1		Henry	Warner,Leonard,	1		Lou.	Washington,George,Sr.	1	2	So'n
Wans,Susanna,		1	Din.	Warner,Peter Sr.,	2		Lou.	Washington,George,Jr.	1	2	So'n
Waples,Samuel,	1	2	Acco.	Warner,Peter,Jr.,			Lou.	Washington,H.,	1	14	Pr.Wm.
Warberton,Benjamin,	1		Cha.Cy	Warner,William,	1		Lou.	Washington,Henry,	1	16	Lou.
Warberton,John,	1	2	Cha.Cy	Warrack,John,	1		Wash.	Washington,Jesse,	1	6	So'n
Warburton,Benjamin,	1	29	Jas.Cy	Warrder,Catharine,			Lou.	Washington,John,	2	21	Caro.
Warburton,John,	1	10	Ja.Cy	Warren,Ambrose,	1		Henry	Washington,John,	1	20	Spots.
Ward,Benjamin,	1		Fay.	Warren,Bartholomew,	1		Loui.	Washington,John,	1		West.
Ward,Daniel,	1		Henry	Warren,Benjamin,	1	12	Brun.	Washington,John,	1	26	West.
Ward,Ephraim,	1		Mont.	Warren,Benjamin,	1	3	So'n	Washington,John,	24	24	K.Geo.
Ward,Henry,	1	5	Cul.	Warren,Burress,	1		Lin.	Washington,John Aug.	1	9	Lou.
Ward,Isaac,	2		Fay.	Warren,Catharine,		5	K.& Q.	Washington,John,Aug.	1	44	Berk.
Ward,Jacob,	1		Berk.	Warren,Charles,	1		Wash.	Washington,John Aug.	2	64	Berk.
Ward,James,	1		Bot.	Warren,David,	1		Lin.	Washington,Joseph,	1	15	So'n.
Ward,James,	1		Mont.	Warren,Drury,	1		Henry	Washington,Landers,	19	25	K.Geo.
Ward,John,	1	3	Brum.	Warren,Henry,	1		Nor.	Washington,Nat,	9	13	K.Geo.
Ward,John,	1		Spots.	Warren,Henry,	1		Henry	Washington,Robert,	13	15	K.Geo.
Ward,John,			Fay.	Warren,Hiliray,	1	7	Nor.	Washington,Robert,	1		So'n
Ward,John,	1		Bed.	Warren,James,	1	8	Din.	Washington,Samuel,est.		80	Berk.
Ward,John,	1		West.	Warren,James,	1		Spots.	Washington,Sarah,	2	18	Brun.
Ward,John,	1		Lun.	Warren,James,	1	1	Lin.	Washington,Susanah,		17	Berk.
Ward,John,	2		Mont.	Warren,Jesse,	1	2	Din.	Washington,Thacker,	1	76	K.Geo.
Ward,John Jr.,	1		Mont.	Warren,John,	1	15	K.Wm.	Washington,Thomas,	1		West.
Ward,Joseph,	1	11	Hen.	Warren,John,	1		Cul.	Washington,Thornton,	1	23	Berk.
Ward,Joseph,	1		Bot.	Warren,John,	1		Din.	Washington,William,	1	48	West.
Ward,Lawrence,	1		Lou.	Warren,Joseph,	1		Nor.	Washington,Wm.Aug.,	1	60	West.
Ward,Littleton,	1	6	Nor.	Warren,Obijah,	1		Aug.	Wason,John,	1		Rock.
Ward,Livy,	1		Din.	Warren,Robert,	1	4	Pr.Wm.	Wason,Robert,	1		Rock.
Ward,Marget,			Fay.	Warren,Robert,	1	4	Nor.	Waterfield,Isaac,	1		Acco.
Ward,Mrs.,		5	Spots.	Warren,Rose,		10	Nor.	Waterfield,Philip,	1		Bed.
Ward,Nancy,			Aug.	Warren,Sally,		10	Brun.	Waterfield,William,	1	8	Nor.
Ward,Nathan,	1		Mont.	Warren,Samuel,	1		Spots.	Waters,John,	1		Pr.Wm.
Ward,Richard,	1		Cul.	Warren,Thomas,	1	3	Henry	Waters,Joseph,	2		Cul.
Ward,Roland,		11	Lun.	Warren,Thomas Jr.,	1		Henry	Waters,William,	1		Cul.
Ward,Samuel,	1	3	Lun.	Warren,William,	1		Spots.	Watkins,Benjamin,	1		Camp.
Ward,Stephen,	1		Nor.	Warren,William,	1	4	Lin.	Watkins,Benjamin,	1	4	Gooch.
Ward,Thomas,	1		Henry	Warren,William,	1		Henry	Watkins,Benjamin,Jr.	1	5	Gooch.
Ward,Wells,	1		Mont.	Warren,William Davis,			West.	Watkins,Charles,			Pr.Wm.
Ward,William,			Loui.	Warrick,Jacob,	1	14	Aug.	Watkins,Dorothea,		1	Gooch.
Ward,William,	1	2	Bot.	Warrick,James,	1		Hen.	Watkins,Edward,	1	27	Cul.
Ward,William,	1		Mont.	Warrick,Robert,	1		Mont.	Watkins,Elinor,			Bot.
Ward,William,	1		Henry	Warrick,William,	1		Aug.	Watkins,Elizabeth,	1	8	K.Wm.
Ward,William,	1	1	Cul.	Warrick,William,	2	20	Brun.	Watkins,Francis,	1	15	Hen.
Ward,William,	1		Brun.	Warrin,Charles,	1		Lin.	Watkins,George,			Eli.Cy
Ward,William,	2	4	Acco.	Warrin,Zachariah,	1		Henry	Watkins,George,	1		Henry
Warden,John,	1	1	K.Wm.	Warriner,Ann,		2	Hen.	Watkins,H.,	1	1	Pr.Wm.
Warden,Robert,	1		Henry	Warriner,Benjamin,	2	3	Hen.	Watkins,Henry,	1	4	Pr.Geo.
Wardlaw,James,	1	1	Rock.	Warriner,Daniel,	1		Hen.	Watkins,Henry,			Pr.Wm.
Wardlaw,Robert,	1		Rock.	Warriner,David,			Hen.	Watkins,Humphrey,	1	5	K.& Q.
Wardlaw,William,	1	3	Rock.	Warriner,Freeman,	1		Hen.	Watkins,Isham,	1	10	Loui.
Ware,Christopher,	1	25	K.& Q.	Warriner,Hezekiah,	1	2	Hen.	Watkins,Jacob,	1		Camp
Ware,Dudley,	1		Lin.	Warriner,James,	1	3	Hen.	Watkins,James,			Lou.
Ware,Isaac,	1	9	Loui.	Warriner,John,	2	3	Hen.	Watkins,James,			Loui.
Ware,James,	1	8	Caro.	Warriner,John,			Hen.	Watkins,James,	1	6	Loui.
Ware,John,	1	18	K.& Q.	Warriner,Joseph,	1		Hen.	Watkins,Joel,	2	7	Buck.
Ware,John,	1		K.& Q.	Warriner,Lucey,		1	Hen.	Watkins,Joel,	1	2	Loui.
Ware,John,	2		Henry	Warriner,Mordecai,			Hen.	Watkins,John,	1	2	Gooch.
Ware,John,	1		K.Wm.	Warriner,Sarah,		1	Hen.				
Ware,John,	1	23	Gooch.	Warrington,John,	1		Hen.				

Name			Co.	Name			Co.	Name			Co.
Watkins,John,	1		Caro.	Watt,George,	1		Caro.	Weaver,Zachariah,		2	West.
Watkins,John,	1		Aug.	Watt,William,	1	25	Buck.	Web,James,	1		Aug.
Watkins,Joseph,	1		K.&Q	Watt,Arter,Est.,		4	K.&Q	Webb,Aaron,	1		West.
Watkins,Joseph,	1	14	Gooch.	Watts,Benjamin,	1	3	Cul.	Webb,Aaron,	1		K.Geo.
Watkins,Joseph,	1	21	Gooch.	Watts,Edward,	1	5	Bed.	Webb,Abraham,	1	1	Buck.
Watkins,Joseph,	1	5	Loui.	Watts,Francis,	1		Fau.	Webb,Armiger,	1	1	Eli.Cy
Watkins,Mary,		1	Pr.Wm.	Watts,Frederick,	1	2	Cul.	Webb,Augustine,	1		Bot.
Watkins,Moses,	1		Camp.	Watts,Haron,	1		Cul.	Webb,Charles,	1		Hen.
Watkins,Robert,	1	2	Din.	Watts,John,	1	4	Fau.	Webb,Edmund,	1	2	K.Wm.
Watkins,Robert,Jr.,	1		Camp.	Watts,John,	1	9	K.&Q	Webb,Edmund,	1	1	K.Wm.
Watkins,Silas,	1	9	Buck.	Watts,John,	1		Din.	Webb,Edmund,	1	5	Brun.
Watkins,Stephen,	1		Henry	Watts,John,	1	4	Pr.Geo	Webb,Elizabeth,		3	Henry
Watkins,Thomas,	1	10	Gooch.	Watts,John,	1	2	Cul.	Webb,Foster,	1	4	Hen.
Watkins,Thomas,	2	12	Hen.	Watts,Johnson,			Cul.	Webb,Foster,Jr.,	2	6	Hen.
Watkins,Thomas,	1		Lou.	Watts,Kauffman,	1	9	K.&Q	Webb,George,	3	36	Hen.
Watkins,Thomas,Jr.,		4	Hen.	Watts,Littleton,	1		Eli.Cy	Webb,George,	1	28	Buck.
Watkins,William,	1	1	Pr.Wm.	Watts,Richard,	1	2	Bed.	Webb,George,Jr.,			Hen.
Watkins,William,	1		York	Watts,Samuel, ½ of	2	20	Eli.Cy	Webb,Henry,	1		Mont.
Watkins,William,	1	1	Caro.	Watts,Samuel,Jr.,	1	8	Eli.Cy	Webb,Isham,	1		Henry
Watkins,William,		3	Caro.	Watts,Thomas,Jr. ½of	2	20	Eli.Cy	Webb,Jacob,	1		Buck.
Watkins,William,	1	38	Din.	Watts,Thomas,Sr.,	1	6	Eli.Cy	Webb,James,	1		K.Wm.
Watkins,William&Geo.	2	1	Eli.Cy	Watts,Thomas,Jr.,			Eli.Cy	Webb,John,	1	1	K.Wm.
Watlington,Edward,	1	17	Din.	Watts,Thomas,	1		Cul.	Webb,John,			Hen.
Watlington,John,	1		Din.	Watts,Thomas,	1	2	Bed.	Webb,John,	1		Lou.
Watmoreland,Robert,	1	8	Din.	Watts,Thomas,	1		Fau.	Webb,John,	1	8	Brun.
Watson,Americus,	1		Acco.	Watts,Thomas,	1	4	Fau.	Webb,John,	1	1	Lun.
Watson,Benjamin,	1		Mont.	Watts,William,	1		Pr.Geo	Webb,John,	1		Aug.
Watson,Charles,	1		Din.	Watts,William,	1	15	Cul.	Webb,John,	1	12	Buck.
Watson,David,	1		Henry	Watts,William,	1		Bed.	Webb,John,	1		Bot.
Watson,Caleb,	1		Acco.	Watts,William,	1	8	K.&Q	Webb,John,	1		Bot.
Watson,Custis,	2	4	Acco.	Waugh,Abner,		28	K.Geo.	Webb,John,	1	1	Buck.
Watson,Edmund,	1	2	Acco.	Waugh,Alexander,	1	2	Cul.	Webb,John,	1		Eli.Cy
Watson,Elijah,	3	17	Acco.	Waugh,John,	1	16	Cul.	Webb,Julius,	1		Bot.
Watson,Epharim,	1	4	Acco.	Waugh,Lewis,		9	K.Geo.	Webb,Julius,			Henry
Watson,Gilbert,	1		Wash.	Waugh,Richard,	1	18	Cul.	Webb,Micajah,Jr.,	1	1	Brun.
Watson,Isarel,	2		Acco.	Waugh,Mrs.Abner,rector		30	Caro.	Webb,Micajah,Sr.,	1	7	Brun.
Watson,James,	1		Wash.	Way,John,	1		Fau.	Webb,Morris,	1		Henry
Watson,Capt.James,	1	9	Loui.	Wayland,Henry,	1	1	Cul.	Webb,Moses,	1		K.Geo.
Watson,Capt.James,	1	23	Loui.	Wayland,John,	2	4	Cul.	Webb,Richard,	1		Fau.
Watson,Jesse,	1	1	Acco.	Wayland,John,Jr.,	1	2	Cul.	Webb,Samuel,	1		Bed.
Watson,Johannis,	2	4	Acco.	Wayland,Joshua,	1	1	Cul.	Webb,Simion,	1		Bot.
Watson,John,			Acco.	Wayland,Mary,		8	Cul.	Webb,Smith,	1	1	Henry
Watson,John,	1	6	Henry	Wayman,Henry,	1	1	Cul.	Webb,Theoderick,	2	19	Bed.
Watson,John,	3	1	Berk.	Wayman,Harmon,	1		Cul.	Webb,Theoderick,	1	12	Buck.
Watson,John,	1		Berk.	Wayman,Joseph,	1		Cul.	Webb,William,	1		Bot.
Watson,John,	1		Wash.	Wayt,Richard,	1	8	Cul.	Webb,William,	1		Mont.
Watson,John,	1	5	Bed.	Weagle,George,	1		Berk.	Webb,William,	1		K.Wm.
Watson,John,Jr.,	1		Berk.	Weakland,William C.,	2	4	Buck.	Webb,William,Jr.,	1	1	Buck.
Watson,Johnson,	1	12	Bed.	Weaks,William,	2		Henry	Webb,William,Sr.,	1	5	Buck.
Watson,Littleton,	1	2	Nor.	Wease,Adam,	4		Har.	Webber,John,	1	5	Spots.
Watson,Michael,			Henry	Wease,Magdaline,		4	Har.	Webber,John,	1		Camp.
Watson,Patrick,Jr.,	1		Wash.	Wease,Michael,	1		Har.	Webber,Phillip,	1	1	Gooch.
Watson,Peggy,	1	2	Acco.	Weasegar,Daniel,		6	Bed.	Webber,William,	2	10	Gooch.
Watson,Randolph,	1	7	Loui.	Weatherford,Archibald	1		Henry	Webber,William,Sr.,	1	8	Gooch.
Watson,Rebecca,	1	42	Cha.Cy	Weatherford,Daniel,	1		Lun.	Webber,William,Jr.,			Gooch.
Watson,Revil,	1	1	Acco.	Weatherford,John,	1		Henry	Webley,John,	1	4	K.&Q
Watson,Robert,	1		Henry	Weatherford,William,Srl			Lun.	Webster,David,			Gooch.
Watson,Robert,	1		Henry	Weatherford,William,Jrl		2	Lun.	Webster,George,	1		Cul.
Watson,Robert,	1		Fay.	Weatherly,William,	1	2	Hen.	Webster,John,	1		Bed.
Watson,Robert,	1		Berk.	Weathers,Isaac,	1	2	Brun.	Webster,Joseph,	1		Henry
Watson,Robert,	1		Mont.	Weathers,John,			York	Webster,Landel,	1		Cul.
Watson,Samuel,	1		Henry	Weathers,John,	2	5	Ja.Cy	Webster,Luke,	1	5	Gooch.
Watson,Samuel,	1		Henry	Weatherspoon,William,	1	1	Henry	Wenster,Reubin,	1		Mont.
Watson,Samuel,	1		Berk.	Weaver,Christopher,			Berk.	Webster,Samuel,	1	3	Buck.
Watson,Severn,	3		Acco.	Weaver,Daniel,	1		Cul.	Webster,Thomas,	1	5	Eli.Cy
Watson,Teackle,			Acco.	Weaver,Isaac,	1		Mont.	Wedderburn,Lydia,		6	K.&Q
Watson,Thomas,	1		Fau.	Weaver,Jacob,	1	8	Fau.	Weddinger,George,	1		Berk.
Watson,Thomas,	1		West.	Weaver,John,	2	2	West.	Wedze,John,Jr.,	2		Har.
Watson,Thomas,	1		York	Weaver,John,	1		Lou.	Weedon,George,	1	7	West.
Watson,Torobable,	1	6	Acco.	Weaver,John,	1		Lou.	Weedon,George,	1	9	Spots.
Watson,William,	1	1	Fau.	Weaver,John P.,			Bed.	Weedon,George,		8	K.Geo.
Watson,William,	1	1	Lun.	Weaver,Leonard,	1		Bot.	Weedon,James,	1		K.Geo.
Watson,William,	1	7	Brun.	Weaver,Matthias,	2	5	Cul.	Weedon,John,Sr.,	1	4	West.
Watson,William,	1		Lou.	Weaver,Peter,	1		Aug.	Weedon,John,Jr.,	1	2	West.
Watson,William,	1		Wash.	Weaver,Tilman,	1	5	Fau.	Weedon,Joseph,	1		K.Geo.
Watson,Zachariah,	1		Cul.	Weaver,William,	1	1	Brun.	Weedon,Nathaniel,	1	6	Lou.

Name			Co.
Weekly,John,	1		Cul.
Weeks,Abraham,	1		Nor.
Weeks,Alderson,	1	3	Fau.
Weeks,Benjamin,	1	23	West.
Weeks,Benjamin,	2		Cul.
Weeks,John,	1	5	Pr.Geo.
Weeks,Joseph,	1		Pr.Geo
Weir,Abraham,	1	1	Rock.
Weir,Hugh,	1		Rock.
Weir,Hugh,	1		Wash.
Weir,James,	1	1	Spots.
Weir,James,	1		Wash.
Weir,James,	1		Rock.
Weir,Jeane,		2	Rock.
Weir,John,	1		Rock.
Weir,Jonathan,	1		Wash.
Weir,Joseph,	1		Rock.
Weir,Samuel,	1		Wash.
Welch,Ann,			Wash.
Welch,Isaac,	1		Har.
Welch,James,	1		Buck.
Welch,James,	2		Buck.
Welch,James,			Lou.
Welch,James,	1		Rock.
Welch,John,	4		Spots.
Welch,Joseph,	1		Henry
Welch.Patrick,	1		Rock.
Welch,Richard,	1		Henry
Welch,Samuel,	1		Rock.
Welch,Silvester,	1	5	Fau.
Welch,Thomas,	1		Rock.
Welch,William,	1		Fau.
Weldon,Benjamin,	1	9	Ja.Cy
Weldon,Fanny,		1	Hen.
Weldon,George,	1		West.
Well,Laban,	1		Pr.Geo
Wellons,Charles,	2		So'n
Wellons,Henry,	1		So'n
Wellons,John,	3	11	So'n
Wells, * * *,	1	6	Pr.Wm.
Wells,Abner,	1	3	Lun.
Wells,Abraham,	1		Mont.
Wells,Carty,	1	4	Pr.Wm.
Wells,David,	1		Lou.
Wells,David,	1		Pr.Geo
Wells,George,	1		Mont.
Wells,Jerry,	1	1	Pr.Geo
Wells,John,	1		West.
Wells,John,	1		Lou.
Wells,Moses,	1		Mont.
Wells,Peter,	1		Fay.
Wells,Richard,	1	1	Din.
Wells,Thomas,	1		K.Geo.
Wells,Thomas,	1		Buck.
Wells,William,			Brun.
Wells,Zachariah,	1		Lou.
Welsh,Jacob,	1		Berk.
Welsh,Jacob,	1		Berk.
Welsh,James,	1		Berk.
Welsh,James,	1		Fay.
Welsh,John,	1		Lou.
Welsh,John,			Buck.
Welsh,John,	1		Fay.
Welsh,Michael,	1		Berk.
Welsh,Philip,	1		Berk.
Welsh,Thomas,	1		Mont.
Welsh,Thomas,	1		Cul.
Welton,David,	2	3	Har.
Welton,David,	1	2	Har.
Welton,Job,	3	9	Har.
Welton,William,	1	4	Har.
Wemmer,Jacob,	1		Bed.
Wenlock,Fielding,			Cul.
Wenlock,Marget,	1		Cul.
Wenlock,James,	1		K.Geo.
Went,Lucy,		5	K.Geo.

Name			Co.
Westcoat,Joshua,	1	8	Nor.
Westcoat,Littleton,	1	8	Nor.
Wesley,Robert,	1	2	Loui.
Wessenberger,George	1		Berk.
Wesson,Edward,		1	Brun.
Wesson,Henry,	1		Brun.
Wesson,Isaac,	1		Brun.
Wesson,James,	2	4	Brun.
Wesson,John,	1		Brun.
Wesson,Sterling,	1		Brun.
Wesson,William,	1		Brun.
West,Abel,	2	18	Acco.
West,Ann,		6	Caro.
West,Ann,	1	6	Acco.
West,Ann,	1	10	Acco.
West,Anthony,	4	14	Acco.
West,Anthony,			Acco.
West,Benjamin,	1	1	Loui.
West,Benjamin,	1	10	Bot.
West,Charles,	1	10	Caro.
West,Charles,	1		Fau.
West,Maj.Charles,	2	6	Lou.
West,Drury,	1		Hen.
West,Edmund,	1	2	Acco.
West,Edmund,	2	1	Caro.
West,Francis,	1	6	K.Wm.
West,George,			Acco.
West,Col,George,	1	13	Lou.
West,James,	1	1	K.Geo.
West,James,	1		Caro.
West,Jeremiah,	1	10	Acco.
West,John,	1		Lou.
West,John,	1		Spots.
West,John,	1		Spots.
West,John,	3	18	Acco.
West,John,			Acco.
West,John,	2	10	Acco.
West,John,			Acco.
West,John,	1	9	Acco.
West,John,			Hen.
West,John,			Lou.
West,John,	2	10	Cha.Cy
West,John,	1	9	Din.
West,John,	1		Lun.
West,John,	1	8	Camp.
West,John,Jr.,	1		Bed.
West,John,	1		Bet.
West,Joseph,	1		Lou.
West,Joseph,	2		Cul.
West,Joseph,	1	1	Nor.
West,Major,	2		Acco.
West,Mary,		16	Lou.
West,Nathaniel,	1		Lou.
West,Philip P.	1	3	Acco.
West,Resan,	1	2	Bot.
West,Revel,			Acco.
West,Richard,	1	2	Buck.
West,Robert,	1	1	Lun.
West,Robert,Sr.,	1	9	Din.
West,Selathiel,	1	4	Acco.
West,Thomas,	1		Cul.
West,Thorogood,	1	2	Acco.
West,William,	1		So'n
West,William,			Cha.Cy
West,William,	1	1	Caro.
West,William,	1	10	K.Wm.
Westbrook,Amos,	1	1	Lun.
Westbrooke,Burwell,	1	5	So'n
Westbrooke,Burwell,	1		So'n
Westbrooke,Henry,	1	32	So'n
Westbrooke,Jacob,	1	2	So'n
Westbrooke,John,	1	4	So'n
Westbrooke,Joshua,	1	1	So'n
Westbrooke,Samuel,	1	10	So'n
Westbrooke,Samuel,Jr.,	1	8	So'n
Westbrooke,Thomas,	1		So'n

Name			Co.
Westerhouse,Abraham	1	1	Nor.
Westfall,Jacob,	1		Har.
Westfall,Jacob,	1		Har.
Westfall,John,	2	3	Har.
Westly,Thomas,	1	4	K.Wm.
Westmoreland,Alex'r	1	1	Brun.
Westmoreland,Reaves,	1	6	Din.
Westmoreland,Thomas,	1	8	Din.
Westra,Will,	1	1	So'n
Westra,William,	2	1	So'n
Westwood,Wolrich,	2	14	Eli.Cy
Wetherall,John,			Cul.
Wetherall,Milly,	2	16	Cul.
Wetherley,James,	1		Fau.
Wetmiller,John,	1		Har.
Wetherspoon,Reu.,	1		Gooch
Wettle,Peter,	1		Fay.
Wever,John,	3	6	Cul.
Wever,Peter,	1	2	Cul.
Weyford,George,	1		Aug.
Whailon,Patrick,	1		Fau.
Whale,Thomas,	1		Cul.
Whaley,James,	1	5	Lou.
Whaley,James,	2	6	Lou.
Whaley,James,	2	2	Fay.
Whaley,James,Jr.,	1	1	Lou.
Whaley,Jilson,			Lou.
Whaley,John,		3	Lou.
Whaley,John,			Lou.
Whaley,William,	1	2	Lou.
Whaley,William,			Lou.
Whaley,William,Jr.,		2	Lou.
Wharton,James,	1		Wash.
Wharton,John,	1	1	Spots.
Wharton,John,	1	10	Cul.
Wharton,Joseph,	1		Spots.
Wharton,Long,	1	5	Spots.
Wharton,Samuel,	1		Spots.
Wharton,Samuel,Sr.,	2		K.Geo.
Wharton,Thomas,	2	4	York
Wharton,William,	1	1	K.&Q
Whary,John,	1		Berk.
Whayley,William,		1	Lou.
Whayne,John,			K.&Q
Whayne,William,	1		K.&Q
Whealer,John,Sr.,			Nor.
Whealor,John,Jr.,	1		Nor.
Whealy,William,	1		Berk.
Wheat,Basill,	1	4	Bed.
Wheat,Benjamin,	1		Henry
Wheat,John,	1		Bed.
Wheatley,James,	1	11	Fau.
Wheatley,John,	1	4	Fau.
Wheatley,Joseph,	1	4	Fau.
Wheatley,Thomas,	1		Lin.
Wheatley,William,	1	4	Fau.
Wheehoun,Margaret,			Din.
Wheeler,Benjamin,Sr.	1	2	Brun.
Wheeler,Benjamin,Jr.	1		Brun.
Wheeler,Charles,	2		Buck.
Wheeler,Charles,Jr.	1		Buck.
Wheeler,James,			Buck.
Wheeler,John,	1		Lou.
Wheeler,Mark,	1	3	Loui.
Wheeler,Thomas,	1		Har.
Wheeley,Josiah,	1		K.Wm.
Wheelock,James,	1	1	Lou.
Wheelon,John,	1		Spots.
Wheelor,Archelas,	1		Bed.
Wheelor,Benjamin,	1	2	Bed.
Wheelor,Clement,		10	Lou.
Wheeler,Ignatius,	1	6	Lou.
Wheelor,James,	1		Spots.
Wheelor,Leonard,	1	2	Lou.
Wheelor,Rowlan,	1		Bed.
Wheelor,Samuel,	1	1	Lou.

Name			Loc.
Wheelor,Thomas,	1		Bed.
Wheeley,John,	1	1	K.&Q
Wheeley,John,	1		K.Wm.
Wheeley,Phillip,	1		K.&Q
Whimmer,John,	1	1	Berk.
Whisenhunt,Paul,	1		Wash.
Whit,Joseph,	1	2	Cha.Cy
Whit,Littleberry,			Cha.Cy
Whitaker,Benjamin,	1		Lou.
Whitaker,Caleb,	1		Lou.
Whitaker,George,	1		Lou.
Whitaker,John,			Buck.
Whitaker,Joseph,	1		Lou.
Whitaker,Joshua,	1		Lou.
Whitaker,Richard,	1	5	York
Whitaker,Thomas,	1	1	Eli.Cy
Whitaker,Thomas,	1	1	Eli.Cy
Whitaker,William,	1		York
Whitby,John,	1	2	Brun.
White,Abbott,			Cul.
White,Archelaus,			Buck.
White,Alexander,	1	1	K.Geo
White,Alexander,	1		Bot.
White,Ambrose,	2	6	Caro.
White,Ann,		1	Fau.
White,Annamariah,		2	K.Wm.
White,Archibald,	1		Aug.
White,Armistead,	2	12	Cul.
White,Augustus,	1		Lou.
White,Basil,	1	8	Spots
White,Benjamin,			Lou.
White,Blumer,	1	1	Brun.
White,Burgess,	1		Brun.
White,Caleb,	1	6	Nor.
White,Carter,	1		Lun.
White,Catherine,	1	27	Hen.
White,Charles,	1		Har.
White,Chilion,	1	15	Caro.
White,Daniel,	1	5	Brun.
White,Daniel,	1	9	Cul.
White,Daniel,	1		Cul.
White,Daniel,	1		Lou.
White,David,est.,		7	Hen.
White,David,	1		Caro.
White,David, ½ of	2	6	Aug.
White,Ebenezer,	1		Har.
White,Elizabeth,			K.Geo
White,Elizabeth,			Bed.
White,Francis,	1	9	Caro.
White,Galin,			Acco.
White,Garrison,			Lou.
White,George,	1		Bed.
White,George,	1		Lin,
White,George,	1		Lin.
White,Hannah,	1	3	Nor.
White,Henry,	1		Henry
White,Henry,	1	4	K.&Q
White,Henry,	1		Buck.
White,Henry,	1		Bot.
White,Henry,	1	4	Hen.
White,Hezekiah,	1		Mont.
White,Isaac,	1		Wash.
White,Isaac,	1	1	Aug.
White,Jacob,	1		Bed.
White,Jacob,			Acco.
White,James,	1		Lou.
White,James,	1	8	Pr.Wm
White,James,	1	5	K.&Q
White,James, ½ of	2	6	Aug.
White,James,	1	5	Mont.
White,James,			Fay.
White,Jesse,	1		Buck.
White,Joachim,	2		Acco.
White,Joel,			Lou.
White,Joel,	1		Fay.
White,John,	1	10	Spots
White,John,	1		Spots
White,John,	1	1	Buck.
White,John,	1		Aug.
White,John,	1	4	Cul.
White,John,	1	2	Cul.
White,John,	1		Berk.
White,John,	1		Berk.
White,John,	1		Ja.Cy
White,John,	1	47	K.&Q
White,John,	1	5	Loui.
White,John,	1	3	Loui.
White,John,	1		Loui.
White,John,			Lou.
White,John,	1	27	K.Wm
White,John,			Lou.
White,John,	1	1	Caro.
White,John,	1	1	Hen.
White,John,	1		Nor.
White,John,Sr.,	1	7	Lun.
White,John,	1		Mont.
White,Joseph,	1	9	Nor.
White,Joseph,	1		Bed.
White,Joseph,			Lou.
White,Josiah,	1		Lou.
White,Levin,Sr.,	4		Acco.
White,Levin,	2	5	Acco.
White,Lovell,	2	2	K.Geo.
White,Mary,		12	K.Wm.
White,Matthew,	1		Lou.
White,Moses,	1	7	Lou.
White,Nathan,	2		Acco.
White,Obedience,	1	3	Nor.
White,Richard,	3		Lou.
White,Robert,		4	Berk.
White,Robert,	1		Lou.
White,Samuel,			Din.
White,Samuel,	1	6	K.Geo.
White,Samuel,	1		Lou.
White,Sarah,	1		Acco.
White,Solomon,			Acco.
White,Solomon,			Acco.
White,Stephen,	1		Bed.
White,Tarpley,			Hen.
White,Thomas,	1	11	Spots
White,Thomas,	1	4	Berk.
White,Thomas,	1	10	K.Wm.
White,Thomas,	2		Lou.
White,Thomas,	1		Lou.
White,Valentine,	1		Aug.
White,Westley,	1		Wash.
White,William,	1	2	Brun.
White,William,	1		Hen.
White,William,	1		Caro.
White,William,	1		Lou.
White,William,			Acco.
White,William,	1	9	K.Wm.
White,William,	1		Loui.
White,William,Jr.,	1	7	Loui.
White,William,	1	4	Loui.
White,William,	1	1	Cul.
White,William,	1		Spots.
White,William,	1	5	West.
White,William,	1		Fau.
White,William,	1	6	Fau.
White,William,			Eli.Cy
White,William,	1	9	Nor.
White,William,	1	2	Lun.
White,William,	1		Mont.
White,William,	1		Wash.
Whitecotton,Melia,	2	4	K.Geo
Whitecotton,James,	1		Har.
Whitehead,Anthony,			Pr.Wm.
Whitehead,Benjamin,	1	2	Brun.
Whitehead,James,	1		Cul.
Whitehead,Jesse,	1	20	So'n
Whitehead,John,	1	3	Cul.
Whitehead,John,	1	10	So'n
Whitehead,John,	1		Nor.
Whitehead,Joseph,	1	6	Din.
Whitehead,Mary,		6	So'n
Whitehead,William,	1	4	So'n
Whitehouse,Daniel,	1		Lou.
Whitely,William,	1	5	Lou.
Whitemore,Jocob,	1		Bed.
Whiteneck,Henry,	1		Berk.
Whitehurst,Tully,	1	2	Spots.
Whites,Mary,	1	5	K.Geo.
Whitesides,John,	1	1	Cul.
Whitesides,John,			Fay.
Whitesides,John,	1		Mont.
Whiteside,Moses,	1		Rock.
Whitesides,William,	2		Fay.
Whitfield,William,	1	1	Gooch.
Whiticur,Mark,	1		Fay.
Whiting,Beverly,		22	Berk.
Whiting,Henry,	1	32	Berk.
Whiting,Henry,est.,		3	Pr.Wm.
Whiting,John,			Pr.Wm.
Whiting,John,	2		K.Geo.
Whiting,Mary,		26	K.&Q
Whiting,Matthew,	4	73	Pr.Wm.
Whiting,Maxwell,	1		Spots.
Whiting,Peter,	1	25	Pr.Wm.
Whiting,Thomas,			Pr.Wm.
Whitledge,John,	2	3	Pr.Wm.
Whitledge,William,	1	4	Pr.Wm.
Whitler,Jacob,	2	3	Spots.
Whitley,Aquilla,	1		Lin.
Whitley,Jonathan,	1	4	Rock.
Whitley,Robert,	1		Mont.
Whitley,William,	1		Lin.
Whitlock,Ann,		14	Hen.
Whitlock,Ann,		1	Gooch.
Whitlock,Euclid,	1	2	Caro.
Whitlock,James,	1		Gooch.
Whitlock,John,	1	1	Hen.
Whitlock,John,	1	7	K.Wm.
Whitlock,Josiah,	1	6	Lun.
Whitlock,Mary,		1	Hen.
Whitlock,Sarah,	1	1	Caro.
Whitlock,Thomas,	1		Gooch.
Whitlock,Thomas,	1		Mont.
Whitlock,William,	1	2	K.Wm.
Whitlock,William,	1		Loui.
Whitlock,William,	1	2	Gooch.
Whitlow,Henry,Sr.,	1	6	Gooch.
Whitlow,Henry,Jr.,	1	1	Gooch.
Whitlow,James,	1		Hen.
Whitlow,Mary,		1	Hen.
Whitlow,Nathan,	1	1	Hen.
Whitlow,Sarah,		1	Hen.
Whitmore,Charles,			Din.
Whitmore,Eliza.,		7	Din.
Whitmore,John,	1		Pr.Geo.
Whitmore,Michael,	1		Mont.
Whitmore,Thomas,	1		Pr.Geo.
Whitmore,William,	1	2	Din.
Whitnell,Robert,	1		Berk.
Whitney,Elijah,	1		Wash.
Whitney,Francis,	1		Wash.
Whitney,Francis,	1	34	Fau.
Whitney,Giles,		3	So'n
Whitney,Jeremiah,est.		19	Buck.
Whitney,Joshua,		2	So'n
Whitsel,John,	1		Mont.
Whitsill,William,	1	6	Henry
Whitt,Richard,	1		Mont.
Whittemore,Clement,	1	1	Lun.
Whitten,William,			Henry
Whittimore,Nathan'l			Rock.
Whittington,Howell,	1	2	So'n
Whitto,Stephen,	1		Bot.
Whitto,William,	1		Bot.
Whitton,Jeremiah,	1		Mont.
Whitton,Thomas,Sr.,	1		Mont.

Name			Co.	Name			Co.	Name			Co.
Whitton,Thomas,Jr.,	1		Mont.	Wiley,John,	1		Aug,	Wilks,John,	2		Bed.
Whooly,William,	1		Bot.	Wiley,John,	3		Rock.	Wilks,Joseph,	1	12	Brun.
Whooly,William,Jr.,	1		Bot.	Wiley,Peter,	1		Rock.	Wilks,Minor,	1	5	Lun.
Whorley,Silas,	1		Buck.	Wiley,Robert,	1		Aug.	Wilks,Samuel,	1		Lou.
Whorton,James,	2	2	Acco.	Wiley,William,	1		Bed.	Willell,Nathan,	1		Berk.
Whorton,Reuben,	1		Caro.	Wilhite,Daniel,	1		Cul.	Willeroy,James,	1	8	K.Wm.
Whyley,Benjamin,	1		Din.	Wilhite,George,	1	4	Cul.	Willeroy,John,	1	5	K.Wm.
Wiatt,Conquest,		11	Pr.Wm.	Wilhite,John,	1	1	Cul.	Willet,Elizabeth,		8	Nor.
Wiatt,James,	1	2	Pr.Wm.	Wilhite,Michael,	1	1	Cul.	Willet,Jonathan,	2	2	Acco.
Wiatt,John,	1		Lou.	Wilhite,Nicholas,	1	4	Cul.	Willet,Thomas,	1		Acco.
Wiatt,John,	1	30	Pr.Wm.	Wilhoit,Gabriel,	1	1	Cul.	Willet,William,	2	3	Acco.
Wiatt,William,	1	4	Pr.Wm.	Wilhoit,Jesse,	1		Cul.	Willett,Charles,	1		Lou.
Wiatt,William Edw'd			Pr.Wm.	Wilhoit,John,	2	1	Cul.	Willett,Charles,	1		Berk.
Wickham,John,	1		Bot.	Wilhoit,Margaret,	1	5	Cul.	Willett,James,	1		Berk.
Wickliff,David,	3	4	Fau.	Wilhoit,Tobias,	1		Cul.	Willett,Nathan,	1		Berk.
Widdows,Robert,	1	1	Eli.Cy	Wilhoite,James,	1		Cul.	William,Ben,	1		K.&Q
Widgeon,Esther,		2	Nor.	Wilhoite,Joel,	1		Cul.	William,David,	1	8	Din.
Widgeon,Isaac,	1	1	Nor.	Wilhoite,Michael,	2		Cul.	William,Henry,	1		Bot.
Widgeon,John,	1	15	Nor.	Wilhoite,William,	1		Cul.	William,Henry,	1		Caro.
Widgeon,Littleton,	1		Nor.	Wilkerson,Benjamin,	1		K.Geo.	Williams,Absalom,	1	6	Brun.
Widgeon,Robert,	1		Nor.	Wilkerson,David,	1	3	Cha.Cy	Williams,Alexander,	1	6	Brun.
Widgeon,Severn,	1		Nor.	Wilkerson,Elizabeth,			Lun.	Williams,Anthony,	1	13	Pr.Geo.
Widner,Jacob,	1		Har.	Wilkerson,Frederick,	2	10	Pr.Geo	Williams,Benjamin,		15	So'n
Wickliff,Isaac,	1	3	Pr.Wm.	Wilkerson,Gerard,	1	1	K.Geo.	Williams,Benjamin,	1	1	So'n
Wickliff,Nat,	1	3	Pr.Wm.	Wilkerson,James,	1		K.Geo.	Williams,Benjamin,	1		Hen.
Wickliff,Robert,	1	2	Pr.Wm.	Wilkerson,James,			Lou.	Williams,Benony,		1	Spots.
Wickliff,William,	1	4	Pr.Wm.	Wilkerson,James,			Lou.	Williams,Brazure,	1	31	Cha.Cy
Widdows,Robert,	1	1	Eli.Cy	Wilkerson,James,Jr.,	1		K.Geo.	Williams,Charles,			Din.
Widgeon,Esther,		2	Nor.	Wilkerson,Jarrett,	1		Loui.	Williams,Charles,		10	Din.
Widgeon,Isaac,	1	1	Nor.	Wilkerson,John,	1		K.Geo.	Williams,Charles,	1	1	Brun.
Widgeon,John,	1	15	Nor.	Wilkerson,John,	1	9	Din.	Williams,Charles,	1		Spots.
Widgeon,Littleton,	1		Nor.	Wilkerson,John,	1	2	Lou.	Williams,Charles,	1	13	K.&Q
Widgeon,Robert,	1		Nor.	Wilkerson,John,	1	3	Lin.	Williams,Charles,	1		Lin.
Widgeon,Severn,	1		Nor.	Wilkerson,John,Jr.,	1		K.Geo.	Williams,Charles,	1		Fay.
Widner,Jacob,	1		Har.	Wilkerson,Joseph,	1		Lou.	Williams,Clement,			Din.
Wiekle,Philip,	1		Berk.	Wilkerson,Major,	1	1	Buck.	Williams,Col.,	1	7	Gooch.
Wiggenton,John,	1	15	Cul.	Wilkerson,Margaret,			K.Geo.	Williams,Daniel,			Lun.
Wiggenton,Richard Y.,			Cul.	Wilkerson,Suttles,	1	1	K.Geo.	Williams,Daniel,			Lun.
Wiggins,Abram,	1		So'n	Wilkerson,Taylor,Sr.,			K.Geo.	Williams,David,	1		Lun.
Wiggins,William,	1		So'n	Wilkerson,Taylor,Jr.,			K.Geo.	Williams,David,	1	2	Pr.Geo.
Wigginton,Eleanor,		5	Lou.	Wilkerson,Thomas,	2	6	K.Geo.	Williams,David,	2		Lou.
Wigginton,Henry,	1	1	Lou.	Wilkerson,Thomas,		1	K.Geo.	Williams,David,	1		Aug.
Wigginton,John,	1		Pr.Wm.	Wilkerson,Thomas,	1		K.Geo.	Williams,Dice,	1		So'n
Wigginton,Sarah,		5	Lou.	Wilkerson,Turner,	1	4	Buck.	Williams,Drury,	1	7	Pr.Geo.
Wigginton,Spencer,	1	14	Lou.	Wilkerson,William,	1	7	Buck.	Williams,Drury,	1	3	Gooch.
Wigginton,William,	1	1	Lou.	Wilkerson,William,	1	8	Cha.Cy	Williams,Edward,	1		Nor.
Wiggonton,B.,	1	5	Pr.Wm.	Wilkie,James,			Din.	Williams,Edward,	2	1	Har.
Wigglesworth,James,	1	14	Spots.	Wilkins,Benjamin,	1	14	Pr.Geo	Williams,Edward,	1		Fay.
Wigglesworth,James,Jr	1	5	Spots.	Wilkins,Benjamin,	1	4	Nor.	Williams,Edmund,	1	5	Din.
Wigglesworth,John,Jr.	1	1	Spots.	Wilkins,Catherine,	1	4	Nor.	Williams,Elias,	1	1	Gooch.
Wiglesworth,William,	1	5	Caro.	Wilkins,George,	1		Har.	Williams,Elias,	1		So'n
Wigley,Abraham,	1		Wash.	Wilkins,Henry,	1	7	Nor.	Williams,Elijah,	1		Berk.
Wigley,James,	1		West.	Wilkins,Joachain,	1	1	Nor.	Williams,Elijah,	1		Wash.
Wilborn,Lewis,	1		Gooch.	Wilkins,John,	1	27	Pr.Geo	Williams,Elisha,	1		Bed.
Wilburn,William,	1	1	Gooch.	Wilkins,John,	1	19	Nor.	Williams,Elizabeth,	1	19	Brun.
Wilcox,George,	1	7	Lin.	Wilkins,John,Jr.,	1	8	Nor.	Williams,Elizabeth,			Henry
Wilcox,Herman,	1	11	Cha.Cy	Wilkins,John,Sr.,	2	20	Nor.	Williams,Elizabeth,			So'n
Wilcox,Isaac,	1	1	Lin.	Wilkins,Major,	1	1	Nor.	Williams,Elizabeth,			Lou.
Wilcox,Major,	1	9	Cha.Cy	Wilkins,Nathaniel,	1	2	Nor.	Williams,Enock,	1		Wash.
Wilcox,Thomas,			Cha.Cy	Wilkins,William,	1	27	Pr.Geo	Williams,Epharim,	1		So'n
Wild,Thomas,			York.	Wilkins,William,	1	11	Nor.	Williams,Evan,	1	5	Pr.Wm.
Wildman,Abraham,	1		Lou.	Wilkinson,C.,	1	9	Pr.Wm.	Williams,Euan,	2	1	Mont.
Wildman,Jacob,	1		Lou.	Wilkinson,Cary,	2	26	Ja.Cy	Williams,Francis,	1	6	Gooch.
Wildman,John,			Lou.	Wilkinson,James,	1	1	Fay.	Williams,Frederick,	1	5	Din.
Wildman,John,	1		Lou.	Wilkinson,John,	2	22	So'n	Williams,George,	1		Brun.
Wildman,John,	1		Lou.	Wilkinson,John,Jr.,			So'n	Williams,George,	1	7	Brun.
Wildman,Joshua,			Lou.	Wilkinson,Joseph,	1	1	Bed.	Williams,George,			Fau.
Wildman,William,Sr.,	3		Lou.	Wilkinson,Nathaniel,	3	39	Hen.	Williams,George,	1		Fau.
Wildman,William,Jr.,	1		Lou.	Wilkinson,Peter,	1	2	Bed.	Williams,George,	2	1	Pr.Geo.
Wildridge,William,	1		Aug.	Wilkinson,Sherwood,			Buck.	Williams,George,	1		Mont.
Wile,Felty,	1		Berk.	Wilkinson,William,			Henry	Williams,Henry,	1		So'n
Wiley,Adam,	1		Bed.	Wilkinson,William,Sr	1	4	Ja.Cy	Williams,Henry,	1		Lou.
Wiley,Alexander,	1		Rock.	Wilkinson,David,	1	7	Pr.Geo	Williams,Howard,	1	6	K.&Q
Wiley,Andrew,			Rock.	Wilkinson,Jessee,	1	11	Pr.Geo	Williams,Isaac,	1	15	So'n
Wiley,James,	1		Cul.	Wilks,Burwell,	1	2	Brun.	Williams,Ishmael,	1		Wash.
Wiley,James,			Rock.	Wilks,John,	1		Henry	Williams,J.,	1		Pr.Wm.

Name			County
Williams,Jacob,	1	4	So'n
Williams,Jacob,	1		So'n
Williams,Jacob,	1		Mont.
Williams,James,	2		Pr.Wm
Williams,James,	1	6	Lun.
Williams,James,	1	1	Fau.
Williams,James,			K.Geo
Williams,James,	1		Lou.
Williams,James,	1	6	Cul.
Williams,James,	2	5	Din.
Williams,James,	1	2	Brun.
Williams,James,	1	8	Eli.Cy
Williams,James,	1		Gooch
Williams,James,	1		Mont.
Williams,Jeremiah,	1		Mont.
Williams,Jesse,	1	1	Cul.
Williams,Jesse,			Hen.
Williams,Jesse,	1	10	Hen.
Williams,Jiles,	1		Lin.
Williams,John,	1	10	Lou.
Williams,John,	1	3	Lou.
Williams,John,	1	17	Cul.
Williams,John,	2	15	Cul.
Williams,John,	1		Fau.
Williams,John,	1		Fau.
Williams,John,			Lou.
Williams,John,	1		Lou.
Williams,John,	1		Lou.
Williams,John,	1	5	Gooch
Williams,John,	1	4	Gooch
Williams,John,			Hen.
Williams,John,	1	2	Brun.
Williams,John,			So'n
Williams,John,	1	10	Nor.
Williams,John,	1		Bed.
Williams,John,	1		Bed.
Williams,John,	1		Aug.
Williams,John,	1		Aug.
Williams,John,	1		Mont.
Williams,John,	1		Berk.
Williams,John,	1		Har.
Williams,John,	1	10	Lin.
Williams,John Pope,	1	9	Fau.
Williams,Jonas,	1		Fau.
Williams,Jonathan,	1		Hen.
Williams,Jones ,	1	11	Brun.
Williams,Joseph,			Brun.
Williams,Joseph,	1	1	Fau.
Williams,Joseph,	1		Fau.
Williams,Joseph,	1		Pr.Wm
Williams,Joseph,	1	7	Pr.Geo
Williams,Joseph,	2		Fay.
Williams,Joseph,			Lou.
Williams,Joshua,	1		Din.
Williams,Joshua,	1		Lou.
Williams,Lazarus,	1	15	Lun.
Williams,Lazarus,	2	5	Brun.
Williams,Lessenbery,	1	8	Pr.Geo
Williams,Lewis,	1	1	So'n
Williams,Lucey,		23	Cul.
Williams,Lucy,			Pr.Geo
Williams,Ludwell,	1	8	Pr.Geo
Williams,Martha,		3	So'n
Williams,Mary,		1	Pr.Wm
Williams,Mary,			Brun.
Williams,Mary,		4	Brun.
Williams,Mary,		2	Gooch
Williams,Mary,	1	4	Hen.
Williams,Matthew,	1	1	So'n
Williams,Matthew,			Lun.
Williams,Miles,	1	5	Din.
Williams,Miles,	1	5	Brun.
Williams,Mordecai,	1		Berk.
Williams,Moses,	1		Aug.
Williams,Moses,	1		Wash.
Williams,Nathaniel,	1		Gooch
Williams,Neremiah,	1		Wash.
Williams,Nicholas,	1	17	So'n
Williams,Nicholas,Jr.,	1	3	So'n
Williams,Notley,	3		Lou.
Williams,Original,	1		Lou.
Williams,Paul,		2	Cul.
Williams,Paul,	1	2	Cul.
Williams,Paul,	1	18	Fau.
Williams,Peter,	1	4	Pr.Geo
Williams,Peter,	1	11	Pr.Geo
Williams,Peter,		2	Brun.
Williams,Philip,	1	10	Gooch.
Williams,Philip,	1		Mont.
Williams,Philip,	1		Fay.
Williams,Powell,	1		Gooch.
Williams,Rachel,	1	2	West.
Williams,Rachel,		1	Din.
Williams,Richard,	1		Lou.
Williams,Richard,	1	6	Pr.Geo
Williams,Richard,	1		So'n
Williams,Richard,	1		Din.
Williams,Richard,	1	1	Hen.
Williams,Richard,	1		Lun.
Williams,Richard,est.	1	12	Lun.
Williams,Robert,	1		Wash.
Williams,Robert,	2		So'n
Williams,Thomas,			Lou.
Williams,Robert,	1		So'n
Williams,Robert,			Din.
Williams,Roger,	1	1	York
Williams,Samuel,	1		Cul.
Williams,Sarah,			Brun.
Williams,Silas,			Henry
Williams,Sion,	1		So'n
Williams,Susannah,	1		Cul.
Williams,Thomas,	1	1	Brun.
Williams,Thomas,	1		Fau.
Williams,Thomas,	1		So'n
Williams,Thomas,	1		Bed.
Williams,Thomas,	1	3	Bed.
Williams,Thomas,Sr.,	1	13	Lou.
Williams,Thomas,Jr.,	1	2	Lou.
Williams,Thomas,			Lou.
Williams,Thomas,	1		Buck.
Williams,Thomas,	1		Bot.
Williams,Thomas,			Hen.
Williams,Thomas,			Hen.
Williams,Thomas,	1	1	Hen.
Williams,Thomas,	1	21	Lun.
Williams,Thomas,	1	3	Lun.
Williams,Thomas,	1		Berk.
Williams,Thomas,	1		Berk.
Williams,Thomas,	1		Mont.
Williams,Thomas,Jr.,			Mont.
Williams,Thomas,Sr.,	1	14	Lin.
Williams,Thomas,Jr.,	1	7	Lin.
Williams,Vincent,	2	1	Har.
Williams,William,	1		Lou.
Williams,William,	1		Bed.
Williams,William,	1		Bed.
Williams,William,			West.
Williams,William,	1		Pr.Geo
Williams,William,	1	1	So'n
Williams,William,	1	1	So'n
Williams,William,	1	8	So'n
Williams,William,	1	20	Gooch.
Williams,William,	1		Henry
Williams,William,	1	3	Brun.
Williams,William,	1	5	Din.
Williams,William,	1		Pr.Geo
Williams,William,Jr.	1		Pr.Geo
Williams,William,	1		Mont.
Williams,William,Jr.,	1		Mont.
Williamson,Absalom,	1	7	So'n
Williamson,Allen,	3	5	Hen.
Williamson,Aulden,	1		West.
Williamson,Aulden,	1		Wash.
Williamson,Benjamin,			Cha.Cy
Williamson,Benjamin,			Cha.Cy
Williamson,Benjamin,	1		Rock.
Williamson,Burwell,	1	28	So'n
Williamson,Charles,	1	13	Brun.
Williamson,Charles,			Din.
Williamson,Charles,	1	4	Pr.Geo.
Williamson,Daborsua,	1		Camp.
Williamson,David,	1		Fay.
Williamson,David,	1		Rock.
Williamson,Edmund,			Hen.
Williamson,George,	1	4	Hen.
Williamson,George,			Cha.Cy
Williamson,George,			Berk.
Williamson,Jacob,	1		Berk.
Williamson,James,	1		Pr.Geo.
Williamson,James,	1	1	Bed.
Williamson,James,	1	3	Mont.
Williamson,John,	1		So'n
Williamson,John,	2	14	Hen.
Williamson,John,	2	12	Hen.
Williamson,John,			Hen.
Williamson,John,	2	11	Din.
Williamson,John,			Brun.
Williamson,John,			Mont.
Williamson,John,	1		Gooch.
Williamson,John,	1	5	Pr.Geo.
Williamson,John,	1		Lou.
Williamson,Joseph,	1	5	Mont.
Williamson,Mildred,		14	K.Geo.
Williamson,Peter,	2	2	Berk.
Williamson,Peter,Jr.,	1	2	Berk.
Williamson,Richard,	1		Lun.
Williamson,Richard,	1		Rock.
Williamson,Richard,			Hen.
Williamson,Robert,	1	4	Camp.
Williamson,Samuel,,	2	30	Hen.
Williamson,Samuel,	1	16	Hen.
Williamson,Smith,	1		Rock.
Williamson,Stephen,	1	7	Din.
Williamson,Mrs.Ste'n	3	19	Hen.
Williamson,Thomas,	1	4	Hen.
Williamson,Thomas,	1		Lun.
Williamson,Thomas,	2		Buck.
Williamson,Thomas,			Rock.
Williamson,Col.Thos.	1	65	So'n
Williamson,William,			Buck.
Williamson,William,	1	4	So'n
Williamson,William,	1		Berk.
Williamson,William,	1	9	Camp.
Williamson,William,	1	9	Camp.
Williamson,William,			Hen.
Willie,Epharim,	1		Lou.
Willie,John,	1	1	Lou.
Williford,Charles C.	1		So'n
Williford,Jordan,	1		So'n
Williford,William,Sr	1	2	So'n
Williford,William,Jr	1		So'n
Willingham,Jessee,	1		Henry
Willingham,Thomas,	1		Henry
Willis,Bartlett,	1	4	Gooch.
Willis,Custis,	1		Acco.
Willis,Cuthbert,			Hen.
Willis,David,	1	5	Cha.Cy
Willis,David,	1	1	Henry
Willis,Edward,	1		Cul.
Willis,Edward,	1		Gooch.
Willis,Ellener,			Gooch.
Willis,Francis,		14	Berk.
Willis,Francis,	1	14	Pr.Wm
Willis,George,	1	2	K.Wm.
Willis,George,	1		Lou.
Willis,Henry,	5		K.Geo.
Willis,Henry,	1		Wash.
Willis,Isaac,	1		Henry

Name			Place
Willis,James,	1	5	Cul.
Willis,James,	1		Cul.
Willis,Joel,	1		Lin.
Willis,John,	1		Acco.
Willis,John,	1		Henry
Willis,John,	1	1	Lin.
Willis,Joseph,	1	1	Brun.
Willis,Joshua,	1	13	Cul.
Willis,Josiah,	1	7	Nor.
Willis,Lewis,	1	26	Spots.
Willis,Lewis,	1	21	K.Geo.
Willis,Major,	1	4	Lin.
Willis,Major J.,	1	23	Pr.Wm.
Willis,Martha,			Pr.Wm.
Willis,Peter,	1	14	Brun.
Willis,Pleasant,	1	4	Gooch.
Willis,Reubin,	1	2	Cul.
Willis,Robert,	1		Lun.
Willis,Robert Carter,	1	15	Berk.
Willis,Rich,	2	16	Berk.
Willis,Severn,	1		Acco.
Willis,William,	1	1	Nor.
Willis,William,	1		Gooch.
Willis,William,	1		Gooch.
Willis,William,	1	2	Brun.
Willis,William,			Brun.
Willis,William,	1	7	Cul.
Willis,William,Sr.,	2		Hen.
Willoughby,Andrew,,	1		Wash.
Willoughby,John,	1		Fau.
Willoughby,Joseph,	2		Spots.
Willoughby,Nathaniel,	1		Wash.
Willoughby,William,	1		Wash.
Willoughby,William,	1		Wash.
Wills,Abram,	1		Din.
Wills,Adam,	1	9	Din.
Wills,Adam Jr.,	1	2	Din.
Wills,Alexander,	1		Din.
Wills,Drury,	1		Din.
Wills,Euclid,	1		Camp.
Wills,George,	1	2	K.Wm.
Wills,Herbert,	1	1	Din.
Wills,Igntias,	1		K.Wm.
Wills,Jacob,	1		Wash.
Wills,James,	1		Fay.
Wills,John,	2	4	Henry
Wills,John,	1		Bot.
Wills,John,			Cha.Cy
Wills,Mathew,	1	2	Henry
Wills,Matthew,	1	8	So'n
Wills,Randolph,	1		Din.
Wills,Reubin,	1		Din.
Wills,Robert,	2	1	Cha.Cy
Wills,Thomas,			Fay.
Wills,William,	1		Henry
Wills,William,	3		Bot.
Wills,William,Sr.,	1	1	Din.
Wills,William,	1	5	Din.
Wills,William,	4		Fay.
Wills,William Jr.,			Fay.
Willson,Andrew,	1	1	Aug.
Willson,Andrew,	3		Bot.
Willson,David,			Lou.
Willson,David,	1		Aug.
Willson,Eliab,	1		Aug.
Willson,Elizabeth,		7	So'n
Willson,Henry,			Lou.
Willson,Isaac,	1		Fay.
Willson,Isaaih,	1	4	Cul.
Willson,Jacob,	1		Mont.
Willson,James,	1		So'n
Willson,James,	1	10	Pr.Geo
Willson,Jeremiah,	1		Mont.
Willson,John,	1		Mont.
Willson,John,	1	6	Buck.
Willson,John,	1		So'n
Willson,John,	1	1	Aug.
Willson,John,	1	1	Aug.
Willson,John,	1		Aug.
Willson,Jonathan,			So'n
Willson,Joseph,	1		Fay.
Willson,Matthew,	3		Aug.
Willson,Ralph,	1		Aug.
Willson,Robert,	1		Aug.
Willson,Robert,	1		Aug.
Willson,Robert,	2	1	Aug.
Willson,Stephen,	1		Aug.
Willson,Thomas,	1		Aug.
Willson,William,	1	4	Aug.
Willson,William,	1		Aug.
Willson,William,	1	1	Bed.
Willson,William Sr.,	1		Mont.
Willy,Alexander,	1		Aug.
Wilmith,Charles,			Hen.
Wilmore,Henry,	1		K.& Q.
Wilmore,Thomas,	1		K.& Q.
Wilmoth,Jeremiah,	1		Lun.
Wilmoth,John,	1		Lun.
Wilson,Abraham,	1	14	Caro.
Wilson,Abraham,			Rock.
Wilson,Alexander,	1		Rock.
Wilson,Alexander,	2	1	Lou.
Wilson,Allin,	1		Lin.
Wilson,Ann,		1	Eli.Cy
Wilson,Barnard,	1	1	K.& Q.
Wilson,Charles,	1		Har.
Wilson,David,	1		Har.
Wilson,David,	1		Bot.
Wilson,David,	1		Bot.
Wilson,David,	2		Rock.
Wilson,Ebenezer,	1		Lou.
Wilson,Edward,	1	2	Lun.
Wilson,Edward,			Lou.
Wilson,Edward,	1		Bed.
Wilson,Edward,	1		Berk.
Wilson,Ephraim,	1		Bot.
Wilson,Ester,		1	Fay.
Wilson,George,	1	4	Din.
Wilson,George,	1		Berk.
Wilson,George,	I		Cul.
Wilson,George,	1		Lin.
Wilson,George,	1	2	York
Wilson,George,		1	Pr.Geo
Wilson,George,	1		Rock.
Wilson,H.,	1	1	Pr.Wm.
Wilson,Harris,	2		Henry
Wilson,Henry,	1		Har.
Wilson,Hugh,	1		Rock.
Wilson,Hugh,	1		Berk.
Wilson,Isaac,	1	10	K.& Q.
Wilson,Jacob,	1		Berk.
Wilson,James,	4	3	Berk.
Wilson,James,	1		Berk.
Wilson,James,	1		Cul.
Wilson,James,	1		Lou.
Wilson,James,	1		Lou.
Wilson,James,	1		Aug.
Wilson,James,	1		Bot.
Wilson,James,	1		Bot.
Wilson,James,	1	3	Camp.
Wilson,James,	1	3	Caro.
Wilson,James,	1	15	Caro.
Wilson,James,	1		Bed.
Wilson,James,	1	2	Lin.
Wilson,James,	1		Henry
Wilson,James,	1	1	Rock.
Wilson,James,	1		Rock.
Wilson,James Jr.,	2		Rock.
Wilson,James,			Rock.
Wilson,Jane,	1		Fay.
Wilson,Jeremiah,	1	4	Spots.
Wilson,John,	1	10	Spots.
Wilson,John,	1		Berk.
Wilson,John,	1		Berk.
Wilson,John,	1		Berk.
Wilson,John,	1	5	Brun.
Wilson,John,	1	1	Eli.Cy
Wilson,John,	1		Eli.Cy
Wilson,John,	1		Bot.
Wilson,John,	1		Camp.
Wilson,John,	1	3	Cha.Cy
Wilson,John,			Lou.
Wilson,John,	1		Henry
Wilson,John,	1		Henry
Wilson,John,	1		Henry
Wilson,John,	1	2	Henry
Wilson,John,	3		Rock.
Wilson,John,	1		Rock.
Wilson,John,	1	3	Rock.
Wilson,John,	1		Rock.
Wilson,John,		1	K.Geo.
Wilson,John,	1		Rock.
Wilson,John,	1		Rock.
Wilson,Joseph,	1		Bed.
Wilson,Joshua,	1		Bot.
Wilson,Littleton,	1		Nor.
Wilson,Lodwick,	1		Din.
Wilson,Margaret,			Lou.
Wilson,Martha,		3	Henry
Wilson,Martha,		7	K.& Q.
Wilson,Mary,			Lou.
Wilson,Mary,			Fay.
Wilson,Mary,			Berk.
Wilson,Mathew,	1		Bot.
Wilson,Molly,		3	K.& Q.
Wilson,Moses,	1	1	Henry
Wilson,Moses,	1		Henry
Wilson,Nathaniel,	1		Fau.
Wilson,Nathaniel,	1		Har.
Wilson,Nathaniel,	1		Rock.
Wilson,Richard,	1		Henry
Wilson,Richard,		9	Caro.
Wilson,Richard,	1	3	Lun.
Wilson,Richard,	1		Fau.
Wilson,Robert,	1	1	K.& Q.
Wilson,Robert,	1		York
Wilson,Robert,	1		Wash.
Wilson,Robert,	1	11	Lun.
Wilson,Robert,	1	5	Din.
Wilson,Robert,	1	1	Brun.
Wilson,Sampson,	1		Aug.
Wilson,Sampson,	1	1	York
Wilson,Samuel,	1		Berk.
Wilson,Samuel,	1		Berk.
Wilson,Samuel,	1		Bot.
Wilson,Samuel,	1		Bot.
Wilson,Samuel,	1		Rock.
Wilson,Samuel,	1	1	Rock.
Wilson,Samuel,Jr.	1		Rock.
Wilson,Samuel,	1		Lou.
Wilson,Spencer,	1	3	Nor.
Wilson,Spicer,	1	4	Cul.
Wilson,Tarpley,	1	1	Cul.
Wilson,Thomas,	1		Lun.
Wilson,Thomas,	1		Camp.
Wilson,Thomas,	1	4	Rock.
Wilson,Thomas Sr.,	1		Henry
Wilson,Thomas Jr.,			Henry
Wilson,William,	1		Rock.
Wilson,William,	1		Rock.
Wilson,William,	1	5	K.Wm.
Wilson,William,	1		K.Geo.
Wilson,William,	1		Nor.
Wilson,William,	3	3	Har.
Wilson,William,	2		Berk.
Wilson,William,	1		Berk.
Wilson,William,	1		Berk.
Wilson,William,	1		Berk.
Wilson,William,	1	8	Lun.
Wilson,William,		1	Lun.

Wilson,William,	1		Eli.Cy	Winston,Anthony,	1	1	Caro.	Witt,David,	1	1	Henry
Wilson,William,Jr.,	1	1	Lun.	Winston,Anthony,	1	9	Loui.	Witt,Jessee,	1	5	Henry
Wilson,Willis,	1	9	York	Winston,Anthony,Sr.,	2	34	Buck.	Witt,John,	1		Henry
Wilson,Woodrough,	1	3	Brun.	Winston,Anthony,Jr.,	1	13	Buck.	Wittinghill,Peter,	1		Aug.
Wilson,Zachariah,	1	5	Caro.	Winston,Edmond,	2	18	Camp.	Wodd,Richard,	1		Har.
Wilton,Jonathan,	1	1	Har.	Winston,Edmund,	2	18	Camp.	Woddrop,Mary,	1	25	Cha.Cy
Wiltshire,Benjamin,			Spots.	Winston,Isaac,	1	11	Gooch.	Wodrow,Andrew,	1	5	Har.
Wilshire,Joseph,	1		K.&Q	Winston,John,	1	17	Loui.	Wolf,Adam,	1		Lou.
Wily,John,	1	2	Camp.	Winston,Nathaniel,	2	14	Caro.	Wolf,Conrod,	1		Lou.
Wily,John,	1	2	Camp.	Winston,Peter,	1	51	Hen.	Wolf,John,	1		Lou.
Wilye,John,	1		Wash.	Winston,Samuel,	1	8	Caro.	Wolf,John,	1		Har.
Winch,Peter,	3		Har.	Winston,Wm.Overton,		6	Camp.	Wolf,John,	1		Har.
Windham,Eustace,	1		So'n	Winter,James,	1		So'n	Wolfkale,John,	1		Lou.
Windham,Jesse,	1		So'n	Winters,George,			Lou.	Wolgmot,David,	1		Berk.
Windham,John,Jr.,	1		So'n	Winters,Jacob,			Lou.	Wollage,Peter,	1		Cul.
Windham,John,Sr.,			So'n	Winters,Mordecai,	1		Berk.	Wollan,James,	1		Lou.
Window,Abel,			Acco.	Winters,Martin,	3	1	Lou.	Wollard,William,	1	5	Lou.
Window,Abel,	1	1	Acco.	Winton,Mathew,	1	2	Pr.Wm	Wollis,James,	1		Acco.
Window,Henry,	1		Acco.	Wires,John,	1		Lou.	Wolston,Henry,Sr.,	1		Bot.
Window,Robert,	1		Acco.	Wirt,Conrad,	1	1	Pr.Wm	Wolston,Henry,Jr.,	1		Bot.
Wine,Richard,	1		Fau.	Wisdom,Joseph,	1		Spots	Wolston,Stephen,	1		Bot.
Winegarner,Henry,	1		Lou.	Wise,Charles,	1		Acco.	Woltz,Peter,	1		Berk.
Winegarner,Herbert,	1		Lou.	Wise,Christopher,	1		Har.	Womack,Alexander,	1		Lun.
Winfield,John,	1		Bot.	Wise,Bostain,	1		Har.	Wombwell,Calia,		2	So'n
Winfred,John,	1		Bot.	Wise,Broox,			Acco.	Wommack,Burwell,	1		Pr.Geo.
Winfrey,Jesse,			Hen.	Wise,Edmund,	3	2	Acco.	Wommack,Elizabeth,		18	Pr.Geo.
Winfrey,John,	1		Lun.	Wise,Edward,	1		Acco.	Wommack,Isham,	1	1	Pr.Geo.
Winfrey,Judith,		3	K.Wm.	Wise,George,			Acco.	Wommack,James,	1	5	So'n
Winfrey,Mary,		11	York	Wise,George,			Acco.	Wommack,John,	1	6	Pr.Geo.
Winfry,William,	2	10	Buck.	Wise,Jacob,	1		Har.	Wommack,Miles,	1	2	Pr.Geo.
Wingate,Jocob,	1		Nor.	Wise,Johannis,	1	4		Wommack,Thomas,	1	1	So'n
Wingate,William,	1		Nor.	Wise,John,	4		Cul.	Wommack,William,	1		Pr.Geo.
Wingfield,Edward,	1	4	Brun.	Wise,John,	1	1	Hen.	Wood,Alise,	1		Cul.
Wingfield,Joshua,	1	14	Brun.	Wise,John,	1	1	Acco.	Wood,Andrew,	1		Bot.
Wingfield,Robert,	1	1	Gooch.	Wise,John,Sr.,	3		Har.	Wood,Christopher,	1	17	Loui.
Wingfield,Thomas,	1	7	Buck.	Wise,John,Jr.,	1		Har.	Wood,Daniel,		1	Din.
Wingo,James,	1	2	K.Wm.	Wise,Martin,	1		Har.	Wood,David,	1		Fau.
Wingo,William,	1		K.Wm.	Wise,Peter,			Acco.	Wood,Dickinson,	1	2	Fau.
Winigar,John,	1		Rock.	Wise,Solomon,	1	5	Acco.	Wood,Drury,	1	16	Hen.
Winkey,Isarel,	1	11	Buck.	Wise,Tabitha,	1		Acco.	Wood,Ebenezer,	1		Har.
Winkey,John,	1	3	Buck.	Wise,Tulley,	1	9	Acco.	Wood,Edmund,	1		Camp.
Winkey,Reubin,	1	5	Buck.	Wise,William,	1	1	Eli.Cy	Wood,Elijah,	1		Pr.Wm.
Winkey,Samuel,	1		Buck.	Wise,William,	2	7	Acco.	Wood,Elijah,	1		Pr.Wm.
Winn,Adam,	3	12	Fay.	Wisehart,Christopher,	1		Berk.	Wood,Elijah,Jr.,	1		Pr.Wm.
Winn,Alexander,	1	4	Lun.	Wiseman,John,			Mont.	Wood,Theldred,	1	1	Din.
Winn,Benjamin,	1	9	Caro.	Wiseman,Peter,	1		Aug.	Wood,George,	1		Berk.
Winn,Daniel,	1	13	Lun.	Wiser,Henry,	2		Lou.	Wood,Hezekiah,	1		Pr.Wm.
Winn,Elisha,	1	3	Lun.	Wiser,Michael,			Lou.	Wood,Jacob,	2	3	Cul.
Winn,Erasmus,	1		Lun.	Witcher,Daniel,	1		Mont.	Wood,James,	1	1	Fau.
Winn,Galanus,	1		Lun.	Witcher,Epharim,	1	1	Mont.	Wood,James,	1		Camp.
Winn,Gloucester,	2	11	K.Wm.	Witcher,John,	1		Mont.	Wood,James,	1		Camp.
Winn,James,	2	8	Fau.	Witchliff,A.,	1	2	Pr.Wm	Wood,James,	1		K.Wm.
Winn,Jesse,	1	5	Caro.	Witchliff,M.,	1	1	Pr.Wm	Wood,James,	1		Camp.
Winn,John,	1	9	Lun.	Withers,Cain,	1	2	Fau.	Wood,Jesse,	1	1	Camp.
Winn,John,	1	5	Lun.	Withers,James,	1	7	Fau.	Wood,Jesse,	1	1	Camp.
Winn,John,Jr.,	1	5	Lun.	Withers,James,	1	12	Fau.	Wood,John,	1		Lou.
Winn,Joseph,	2	7	Lun.	Withers,James,	1	12	Fau.	Wood,John,			Cul.
Winn,Margaret,		6	Fau.	Withers,James,	1	8	Cul.	Wood,John,	1	1	Din.
Winn,Miner,	1		Lun.	Withers,James,	1		Bot.	Wood,John,	1		Lun.
Winn,Minor,			Lun.	Withers,James,Sr.,	1	15	Fau.	Wood,John,	1	3	Lun.
Winn,Minor,	2	11	Fau.	Withers,John,	1	6	Fau.	Wood,John,	1		Hen.
Winn,Owen,			Fay.	Withers,John,	1	4	Bot.	Wood,John,	1	2	Hen.
Winn,Owen,	1	9	Lou.	Withers,John,	1	1	Lin.	Wood,John,	1	9	So'n
Winn,Peter,	1	2	Lun.	Withers,Spiner,			Cul.	Wood,John,	1	2	K.&Q
Winn,Robert,	1		Lou.	Withers,Thomas,	2	19	Fau.	Wood,John,	1		Eli.Cy
Winn,Samuel,	1		Lun.	Withers,William,	2	15	Fau.	Wood,John,	1		Fau.
Winn,Tavernes,	1	9	Caro.	Withers,William,	1	3	Fau.	Wood,John,	1	6	Camp.
Winn,Thomas,	1	1	Lou.	Withers,William,	1	10	Fau.	Wood,John,	1	7	K.Wm.
Winn,Thomas,	1	2	Lun.	Withers,William,	1	17	Brun.	Wood,John,est.,		18	Cul.
Winn,Thomas,	1	4	Lun.	Withers,William,		7	Cul.	Wood,Jonathan,	1	1	Wash.
Winn,William,	1	4	Lun.	Withers,William,	2	2	Berk.	Wood,Joseph,	1		Pr.Wm.
Winning,James,	1		Berk.	Withers,William,	1	6	Lin.	Wood,Joseph,	2	15	Cul.
Winning,William,	1		Lou.	Withers,William,Sr.,	3	29	Fau.	Wood,Joshua,	2	9	So'n
Winrow,Richard,			Loui.	Witman,George,	1		Har.	Wood,Joshua,	1	1	Fau.
Winsburg,Jacob,	1		Lou.	Witt,Ann,			Bed.	Wood,Laskly,	1		Lou.
Winscot,Isaac,	1		Wash.	Witt,Charles,			Buck.	Wood,Malcom,	1	2	Cha.Cy
Winslow,Beverley,	1	13	Spots	Witt,David,			Henry	Wood,Mary,		6	Eli.Cy
								Wood,Peter,	1	2	Cul.

Name			Loc.	Name			Loc.	Name			Loc.
Wood,Peter,	1		Har.	Woods,Thomas,	1		Bed.	Wootten,Thomas,	1	4	Spots.
Wood,Richard,	1		K.& Q.	Woods,William,			Henry	Wootten,Thomas Sr.,	1	9	Eli.Cy
Wood,Samuel,	1		Fau.	Woodside,John,	5	4	Fau.	Wootton,Bartley,	1		Buck.
Wood,Samuel,	1		Gooch.	Woodson,Benjamin,		6	Gooch.	Wootton,Dudley,	1		Buck.
Wood,Samuel,	1		Camp.	Woodson,Charles,	1	18	Hen.	Wootton,John,	1		Buck.
Wood,Stephen,est.		11	Lun.	Woodson,Jacob,	1	4	Gocch.	Wootton,Simon,	1		Buck.
Wood,Thomas,	1	2	Lun.	Woodson,Jacob,	1	8	Buck.	Wootton,Turner,	1		Buck.
Wood,Thomas,	1	2	So'n	Woodson,John,	1	5	Gooch.	Wootton,William,	1	2	York
Wood,Thomas,	1	1	Loui.	Woodson,John,	1	7	Gooch.	Word,John,	1	1	Cul.
Wood,Thomas,	1		Har.	Woodson,John,	1	9	Gooch.	Word,Thomas,	1		Cul.
Wood,Thomas,	1	4	Buck.	Woodson,John,	1	4	Gooch.	Word,Thomas,	1		Spots.
Wood,Valentine,est.,		41	Gooch.	Woodson,Col.John,	2	21	Gooch.	Word,Thomas,	1	4	Buck.
Wood,Valentine,est.,		14	Loui.	Woodson,Joseph,	1	8	Gooch.	Wordon,William,	1		Har.
Wood,William,	1	4	Nor.	Woodson,Jos.Jr.,½.of	2	22	Gooch.	Workman,Isaac,	1		Lou.
Wood,William,	2	4	Spots.	Woodson,Maj.Joseph,	1	16	Gooch.	Workman,John,	1		Aug.
Wood,William,	1	6	Loui.	Woodson,Matthew,	1	35	Gooch.	Workman,Peter,	1		Lou.
Wood,Zachary,			Cul.	Woodson,Moses,			Hen.	Workman,William,	2		Aug.
Woodall,Charles,	1		Loui.	Woodson,Robert,½ of	2	22	Gooch.	Worldley,William,	1		Bed.
Woodall,David,	1		Buck.	Woodson,Samuel,	1	10	Gooch.	Worldly,Matthew,	1		Bed.
Woodall,James,	1		Buck.	Woodson,Shadrick,	1	9	Henry	Worley,Caleb,	1	9	Bot.
Woodall,John,	1	2	Henry	Woodson,W.N.,			Gooch.	Worley,David,	1		Bot.
Woodall,William,	1		Gooch.	Woodward,Benjamin,	1		Gooch.	Worley,John,	1		Buck.
Woodall,William,	1		Buck.	Woodward,Benjamin,	1	23	Din.	Worley,John,	1		Buck.
Woodard,Charles,	1		Fau.	Woodward,Chesley,	1	4	Bed.	Worley,Peter,	1		Buck.
Woodard,Elizabeth,		2	So'n	Woodward,Jesse,	1		Lou.	Wormley,Ralph,	2	83	K.Wm.
Woodard,John,	1	2	So'n	Woodward,John,	1	7	Din.	Wormley,Ralph,	1	69	Berk.
Woodard,Lewis,	1		Fau.	Woodward,Joshua,	1		Bed.	Wornald,William,	1		Lou.
Woodard,Luke,	1		Fau.	Woodward,Launce,	1		Bed.	Worner,George,	1	5	Acco.
Woodard,Samuel,	1	2	So'n	Woodward,Richard,		1	Bed.	Worrell,Benjamin,	1		So'n
Woodard,William,			Cul.	Woodward,Samuel,	1	12	Gooch.	Worrell,Benjamin,Jr.,	1		So'n
Woodcock,Mark,	2		Hen.	Woodward,Samuel,	1		Bed.	Worrell,Elijah,	1	1	So'n
Woodcock,Thomas,	1		Cha.Cy	Woodward,Thomas,	1	10	Din.	Worrell,John,	2		So'n
Woodcocke,Henry,			Hen.	Woodward,William,	1		Bed.	Worrell,Josiah,	1		So'n
Woodfin,John,	2		Hen.	Woodward,William,	1	5	Gooch.	Worrell,Richard,	1	1	So'n
Woodfin,John James,	1	22	Hen.	Woody,Henry,	1		Bed.	Worrington,James,	1	1	Acco.
Woodfin,William,			Hen.	Woody,Henry,			Buck.	Worrington,John,	1	8	Acco.
Woohford,Catesby,		12	Fau.	Woody,William,	1		Bed.	Worrington,Polley,	1		Acco.
Woodford,Henry,		9	Spots.	Woody,William,			Henry	Worrington,Stephen,	1	6	Acco.
Woodford,Mary,	1	15	Caro.	Woodyard,H.,		4	Pr.Wm.	Worsham,Thomas,	1	11	Din.
Woodford,Thomas,	1		Lou.	Woodyarde,G.,	1	3	Pr.Wm.	Worster,John,	1	1	Lou.
Woodger,John,	1	4	Loui.	Woodyarde,J.,	1		Pr.Wm.	Wortham,William,	1	5	Caro.
Woodger,Thomas,	1		Loui.	Woofter,Sebastion,	1		Lou.	Worthen,John,	1	2	Pr.Geo.
Woodleif,Ann,		2	Pr.Geo	Woolam,Baltis,	1		Berk.	Worthen,Mary,		2	Pr.Geo.
Woodleif,Betty,		1	Pr.Geo	Woolam,Matthias,	1		Berk.	Worthen,William,			Pr.Geo.
Woodleif,Edward,	1	4	Pr.Geo	Woolam,Peter,	1		Berk.	Worthington,Edward,	1	2	Lin.
Woodleif,Sarah,		6	Pr.Geo	Woolard,John,	1		Lou.	Worthington,Ephraim,	1	20	Berk.
Woodleif,Thomas,	1	33	Pr.Geo	Woolard,William,Jr.,	1		Lou.	Worthum,Charles,	1	7	Caro.
Woodlik,Thomas,		1	Din.	Wooldridge,Elizabeth,		4	Camp.	Worthum,Margaret,		7	Caro.
Woodmore,William,	1		Buck,	Wooldridge,Henry,	1	2	Buck.	Wotton,Pricilla,		3	York.
Woodroof,Fielding,	1	8	Spots.	Wooldridge,James,	1		Camp.	Wray,Benjamin,	1		Bed.
Woodroof,Richard,	1		Spots.	Wooldridge,John,	1		Camp.	Wray,Daniel,			Bed.
Woodrough,Benjamin,	1		Brun.	Wooldridge,Richard,	1		Camp.	Wray,George,	1	4	Eli.Cy
Woodrough,George,	1		Brun.	Wooldridge,Thomas,	1	2	Buck.	Wray,Jacob,	1	11	Din.
Woodrough,George,	1		Brun.	Wooldridge,Thomas,	1	6	Buck.	Wray,Jacob,	1	13	Eli.Cy
Woodrough,John,	1		Brun.	Wooldrige,John,	1		Acco.	Wray,James,	1		Bed.
Woodrough,Nathaniel,	1		Brun.	Woolery,George,	1		Berk.	Wray,John,	1		Brun,
Woodrough,Richard,	1	9	Brun.	Woolf,Joseph,	1		Fay.	Wray,Moses,	1		Bed.
Woodruf,Harden,	1		Buck.	Woolf,Michael,	1		Rock.	Wray,Moses,Jr.,			Bed.
Woodrum,William,	1		Buck.	Woolf,Peter,	1		Berk.	Wray,Reubin,	1		Brun,
Woods,Agness,			Bed.	Woolfolk,Augustine,	1	11	Loui.	Wray,Thomas,	1		Lou.
Woods,Ambrose,	1		Bed.	Woolfolk,Charles,	1	9	Caro.	Wren,Isaac,	1	4	Lou.
Woods,Hugh,	1	2	Henry	Woolfolk,Elizabeth,	1	9	Caro.	Wren,John,	1	5	K.Geo.
Woods,James,	1	1	Bot.	Woolfolk,John,	1	6	Spots.	Wren,Mary,		1	K.Geo.
Woods,Jeremiah,			Bed.	Woolfolk,Joseph,	1	5	Spots.	Wren,Richard,	1	3	So'n.
Woods,John,	1	3	Henry	Woolfolk,Richard,	1	11	Caro.	Wren,Travis,	1		Lun.
Woods,Jonathan,	1		Bed.	Woolfolk,Robert,	1	13	Caro.	Wren,William,	1		Lun.
Woods,Jonathan,	1		Bot.	Woolfolk,Samuel,	1	3	Caro.	Wrenn,James,		4	Lou.
Woods,Joshua,	1		Bot.	Woolfscalf,George,	2		Fay.	Wrenn,John,	1	7	Lou.
Woods,Martha,		5	Bot.	Woolfscalf,William,			Fay.	Wrenn,Travis,	1		Lou.
Woods,Mary,			Bot.	Woolsey,George,	1		Lin.	Wright,Alexander,	1		Aug.
Woods,Michael,	2		Lin.	Woolsey,Joel,	1	6	Brun.	Wright,Ann,			Spots.
Woods,Patrick,	1		Rock.	Woolsey,Nanny,			Brun.	Wright,Benjamin,	3	1	York
Woods,Peter,	1		Bed.	Woolsey,Randol,	1		Brun.	Wright,David,	1	2	Caro.
Woods,Samuel,	1	3	Bot.	Woolsey,Tephaniah,	1		Wash.	Wright,David,	1		So'n
Woods,Stephen,	1	3	Bed.	Wooster,Hinman,	1		Bed.	Wright,David,	1	18	Bed.
Woods,Thomas,		4	K.& Q.	Wooster,William,			York	Wright,David,	1	19	Bot.

Name			Place
Wright,Dennis,	1		Spots.
Wright,Edward,	1	8	York
Wright,Elizabeth,			Cul.
Wright,Elizabeth,		15	Caro.
Wright,Elisabeth,	1		Aug.
Wright,Francis,	1	1	Cul.
Wright,Francis,	1		Wash.
Wright,George,	1		Berk.
Wright,George,	1		Berk.
Wright,George,	1		Fau.
Wright,George,			Brun.
Wright,Jacob,	3		Acco.
Wright,Jacob,			Wash.
Wright,James,	1	1	Berk.
Wright,James,	1		Lun.
Wright,James,	1	1	So'n.
Wright,James,	1		Fay.
Wright,James,	1		Aug.
Wright,James,	1		Bed.
Wright,Capt.James,	1	7	Bed.
Wright,Jessee,	1		Lin.
Wright,Job,	1		So'n.
Wright,John,	1	2	Berk.
Wright,John,	1	9	Berk.
Wright,John,	3	13	Spots.
Wright,John,	2	5	Cul.
Wright,John,			Cul.
Wright,John,	1		Cul.
Wright,John,			Cul.
Wright,John,	1		Lun.
Wright,John,	1		Loui.
Wright,John,	1		Lun.
Wright,John,	1		So'n.
Wright,John,	1		Brun.
Wright,John,	1		Aug.
Wright,John,	1	1	Bed.
Wright,John,	1		Bed.
Wright,John,	1		Bed.
Wright,John,	1	1	Bed.
Wright,John,	1	3	York
Wright,John,	1	1	York
Wright,John,	1	1	So'n.
Wright,John,	1		Buck.
Wright,John,	1		Buck.
Wright,John,	1		K.Wm.
Wright,John,	1	14	Fau.
Wright,Joseph,	1		Caro.
Wright,Joseph,	1	1	Cul.
Wright,Joseph,	1		So'n.
Wright,Joseph,	1		Brun.
Wright,Joseph,	1		Bed.
Wright,Joseph,	1	1	Bed.
Wright,Joshua,	1		Din.
Wright,Margaret,			Cul.
Wright,Moses,	1		Buck.
Wright,Nathaniel,	1		Cul.
Wright,Parsons,			Lun.
Wright,Philipp,			K.&Q.
Wright,Pryor,		3	Camp.
Wright,Pryor,		3	Camp.
Wright,Reubin,	1	5	Brun.
Wright,Richard,	1		Mont.
Wright,Richard,			Cul.
Wright,Robert,	1	10	Brun.
Wright,Robert,	1		Camp.
Wright,Robert,	1	1	Lou.
Wright,Robert,	1	18	Caro.
Wright,Sam,	1	4	York
Wright,Samuel,	1	3	Aug.
Wright,Sarah,			Buck.
Wright,Sarah,		2	Brun.
Wright,Susanah,	1		Acco.
Wright,Thomas,	1	2	Caro.
Wright,Thomas,	2	6	Cul.
Wright,Thomas,	2		Lun.
Wright,Thomas,			Acco.

Name			Place
Wright,Thomas,	1	11	West.
Wright,Thomas,	1	9	Camp.
Wright,Thomas,	1	9	Camp.
Wright,Thomas,	1		Ja.Cy
Wright,Thomas,	1		Bed.
Wright,Thomas,	1		Buck.
Wright,William,	1		Aug.
Wright,William,	1		Lin.
Wright,William,	1	1	Fay.
Wright,William,			K.&Q.
Wright,William,	1	1	Fau.
Wright,William,			Acco.
Wright,William,	1	4	Cha.Cy
Wright,William,	1		Cul.
Wright,William,	4	14	Caro.
Wright,William,	1		Bed.
Wright,William,	1		Bed.
Wright,William,Jr.,	1		Bed.
Wright,Wm.Stanhope,	1		Brun.
Wright,Wingfield,	1		Bed.
Wrightmire,Benjamin,	1		Lou.
Writ,William,	1		Fau.
Write,William,	1	6	K.&Q.
Wroe,Grace,		4	K.Geo.
Wroe,Original,	1	1	K.Geo.
Wroe,Thomas,	1	5	K.Geo.
Wroe,Richard,	1	2	West.
Wyatt,Edward,	1	25	Din.
Wyatt,Henry,			K.&Q.
Wyatt,Ismay,			Acco.
Wyatt,John,	2	10	K.&Q.
Wyatt,Joseph,	1	1	K.&Q.
Wyatt,Joshua,	2	7	Acco.
Wyatt,Katharine,		24	Pr.Geo
Wyatt,Littleton,	1	3	Acco.
Wyatt,Overstreet,	1	1	Lun.
Wyatt,Richard,			K.&Q.
Wyatt,Richard,		1	K.&Q.
Wyatt,Richard,Sr.,	3	21	Caro.
Wyatt,Richard,Jr.,	1	10	Caro.
Wyatt,Suckey,		18	K.&Q.
Wyatt,Thomas,	1	1	K.&Q.
Wyatt,William,	1	7	K.&Q.
Wyatt,William,	1		K.&Q.
Wyatt,William,	1	2	Pr.Wm.
Wyatt,William,Jr.,	1	4	Acco.
Wyatt,William,	1	11	Lun.
Wyckoff,Isaac,			Lou.
Wyckoff,Nicholas,	2	1	Lou.
Wyckoff,William,	1	1	Lou.
Wycoff,Peter,	1		Berk.
Wycoff,Samuel,			Lou.
Wyland,Peter,	1		Berk.
Wyld,William,		10	York
Wyley,Benjamin,	1		Lin.
Wyley,John,	1		Lou.
Wylie,Alexander,	2	6	Hen.
Wylie,James,	1	1	Mont.
Wylie,Peter,	1		Mont.
Wylie,Thomas,	1		Mont.
Wymer,Frederick,	1		Fay.
Wymer,John,	1	3	Fay.
Wyne,Charles,	1	3	Din.
Wyne,John,	1		Fau.
Wyne,Thomas,	2	18	York
Wyne,Thomas,	1	6	Din.
Wynkoop,Adrian,	1	5	Berk.
Wynkoop,Cornelius,	2		Berk.
Wynn,Matthew,	1	10	Brun.
Wynn,Peter,	1	14	Brun.
Wynne,John,			York
Wynne,Jones,	1	2	Camp.
Wynne,Joshua,Sr.,	1	3	Din.
Wynne,Joshua,Jr.,	1		Din.
Wynne,Robert,	1	2	Din.
Wynne,Stith,	1	6	Brun.

Name			Place
Wynne,Susanna,		1	Din.
Wynne,William,	1	4	Mont.
Wynne,William,	1		Henry
Wyrick,Martin,	1		Mont.
Wysong,Fiat,	1		Bot.
Wythe,George,	1	26	Eli.Cy
Yacoby,John,	1		Lou.
Yager,Adam,Sr.,	1	6	Cul.
Yager,Adam,Jr.,	1	5	Cul.
Yager,Godfrey,	1	6	Cul.
Yager,John,	1	6	Cul.
Yager,John,	1		Cul.
Yager,John,Jr.,	1		Cul.
Yager,Michael,	1	7	Cul.
Yager,Samuel,	1		Cul.
Yager,Susanna,		6	Cul.
Yagy,Martin,	1		Lou.
Yance,Peter,	1		Mont.
Yancey,Ann,		6	Loui.
Yancey,Charles,	1	12	Loui.
Yancey,Jeremiah,	1	11	Hen.
Yancey,Jeremiah,	1	11	Hen.
Yancey,John,	1	4	Loui.
Yancey,John,	2	5	Cul.
Yancey,John,Jr.,	2	8	Cul.
Yancey,Lewis,	1	7	Cul.
Yancey,Ludwell,			Cul.
Yancey,Mary,		10	Loui.
Yancey,Mary,		4	Caro.
Yancey,Philemon,	1	2	Cul.
Yancey,Richard,	1	10	Cul.
Yancey,Stephen,	1	4	Loui.
Yancey,Tyree,	1	8	Loui.
Yancy,Charles,	1	14	Cul.
Yancy,Lewis Davis,	1	6	Cul.
Yancy,Nathan,	1	18	Eli.Cy
Yarbrough,Charles,	1		Brun.
Yarbrough,Henry,	1	10	Caro.
Yarbrough,Lewis,	1		Brun.
Yarbrough,Richard,	1	22	Din.
Yard,William,	1		Rock.
Yarmouth,Reuben,	1		Din.
Yates,Alice,			Lou.
Yates,Andrew,	1		Berk.
Yates,Benjamin,	1		Lou.
Yates,Benjamin,	1	1	Lou.
Yates,Charles,	3	35	Spots.
Yates,Charles,	1	5	Caro.
Yates,Elizabeth,			Lou.
Yates,Elizabeth,	9	9	K.Geo.
Yates,George,	1		Mont.
Yates,James,		4	Caro.
Yates,John,	1		Bed.
Yates,John,	1	3	Cul.
Yates,Joshua,	1	1	Lou.
Yates,Marshall,	1	4	Caro.
Yates,Michael,		2	Cul.
Yates,Michael,	2	20	Caro.
Yates,Michael,	1	7	Spots.
Yates,Richard,	1	2	Cul.
Yates,Robert,	5	5	K.Geo.
Yates,Thomas,	1		Cul.
Yates,William,	1		Berk.
Yates,William,	1		Bed.
Yates,William,	1	55	Din.
Yates,William,	1	1	Fau.
Yeager,Absolam,	1		Lin.
Yeager,Andrew,	1		Aug.
Yeago,Elisha,	1	1	Cul.
Yeargain,William,	1		Eli.Cy.
Yeargair,James,	1	5	Din.
Yeargin,John,	1		Brun.
Yearich,George,	1		Berk.
Yearley,William,	1		Lin.
Yearouse,Charles,	1		Aug.

Name			County
Yeatman,John,	1	8	West.
Yeatman,Thomas,		6	West.
Yeaton,C.,	1		Pr.Wm.
Yeazel,George,	1		Har.
Yeazel,Jacob,	1		Har.
Yell,George,	1		Lou.
Yellow,James Smith,	1		Buck.
Yerkes,Joshua,	1		Berk.
Yetton,Charles,	1		Bot.
Yoakam,John,	1		Har.
Yoakam,Powell,	4	1	Har.
Yocaby,Matthias,	1		Lou.
Yoakam,Jacob,	1	2	Har.
Yont,George,	1		Lin.
Yoakim,John,	1		Lou.
York,James,	1		Hen.
Youlle,Thomas,	1	12	Camp.
Young,Agness,			Bed.
Young,Alexander,	3	5	Hen.
Young,Daniel,	1		Bot.
Young,Daniel,	1	4	Gooch.
Young,Daniel,	1	4	Wash.
Young,Edward,	1	9	Din.
Young,Ezeliel,	1		Mont.
Young,Francis,	1	3	Din.
Young,Frederick,	1	1	Pr.Geo.
Young,Hackley,	1	3	Lou.
Young,Hackley,	2		Cul.
Young,Jacob,	1		Wash.
Young,Jacob,	1		Loui.
Young,James,			Cul.
Young,James,	1	6	Fau.
Young,James,	2	7	Din.
Young,James,Sr.,	1		Aug.
Young,James,	1		Aug.
Young,James,	1		Henry
Young,James,	1		Henry
Young,James,	1		Wash.
Young,James,	1		Fay.
Young,Jane,		3	Caro.
Young,John,	1		Cul.
Young,John,			Cul.
Young,John,	1		Caro.
Young,John,	1	18	Caro.
Young,John,	1	2	Berk.
Young,John,	1		Berk.
Young,John,	1		Aug.
Young,John,	1	1	Aug.
Young,John,	2	19	Fay.
Young,John,	1		Fay.
Young,John,	1	1	Wash.
Young,John,			Hen.
Young,John,	1		Lou.
Young,John,	1		Mont.
Young,John,	1	1	Din.
Young,John,	2	2	Lin.
Young,Joseph,			Fay.
Young,Joseph,	1		Caro.
Young,Joseph,	1		Bed.
Young,Lawrence,	1		Bot.
Young,Lawrence,	1	3	Loui.
Young,Leonard,	1	4	Spots.
Young,Leonard,	1	7	Spots.
Young,Lewis,	1	4	Loui.
Young,Margaret,			Spots.
Young,Nathaniel,			Caro.
Young,Nicholas,	1		Berk.
Young,Original,	1	10	Fau.
Young,Peter,	1		Henry
Young,Reuben,	1	6	Spots.
Young,Reuben,	1	1	Caro.
Young,Richard,	2	1	Acco.
Young,Richard,	1	6	Spots.
Young,Richard,	4	1	Caro.
Young,Robert,	1		Aug.
Young,Robert,	1	1	Pr.Geo.

Name			County
Young,Samuel,	1		Cul.
Young,Samuel,			Cul.
Young,Samuel,Jr.,	1		Aug.
Young,Thomas,	1	1	Cha.Cy
Young,Tinsley,	1	7	Din.
Young,William,	1		Aug.
Young,William,	2	4	Aug.
Young,William,	1	6	Fau.
Young,William,	1		Lun.
Young,William,	1		Aug.
Young,William,	2	12	Fay.
Young,William,	1		Fay.
Young,William,	1	20	Caro.
Younger,John,			K.&Q
Younger,Marcus,	2	1	K.&Q
Younghusband,Isaac,	2	13	Hen.
Younghusband,Isaac,	1	6	Hen.
Younghusband,Pleas't			Hen.
Yowell,David,Sr.,			Cul.
Yowell,David,	1	3	Cul.
Yowell,James,	1	2	Cul.
Yowell,James,	1	5	Cul.
Yowell,James,	1		Cul.
Yowell,John,	1		Cul.
Yowell,John,	1	4	Cul.
Yowell,Samuel,			Cul.
Yowell,William,	1		Cul.
Zachary,Benjamin,	1	1	Cul.
Zachary,John,	2	10	Cul.
Zachary,William,	1		Cul.
Zeglar,Christopher,	1		Cul.
Zeglar,Leonard,	1		Cul.
Zimely,Adam,	1		Wash.
Zimley,Jacob,	1		Wash.
Zimmerman,Christopher	1		Cul.
Zimmerman,John,			Cul.
Zimmerman,Margaret,			Cul.
Zimmerman,Mary,			Cul.
Zimmerman,Michael,	1		Cul.
Zimmerman,Rorannat,			Cul.
Zimmerman,Frederick,	1	7	Cul.
Zimmerman,John,	2	4	Cul.
Zimamon,Reuben,	1	13	Cul.

ERRATA.

Name			County
Aldridge,James,	1		Mont.
Dames,John,	1	1	Eli.Cy
Douglass, * * ,	1		Wash.
Kilpatrick,James,	1		Aug.
Kilpatrick,John,	1		Rock.
Lawler,James,	1		Berk.
Lawson,Robert,	3	51	Pr.Wm.
Lee,Samuel,	1	8	Pr.Geo.
Lee,Simmons,	1		Pr.Geo.
McColgan,Edward,	1	1	Bot.
Mastin,Richard,	2	1	Pr.Wm.
Mooseman,Henry,	1		Camp.
Mooseman,Tachariah,	1	10	Camp.
Paterson,Ezeliel,	1		Fay.
Peery,George,	1		Aug.
Prosser,Thomas,	2	55	Hen.
Small,James,	1		Fay.
Smelt,John,	1	4	Eli.Cy
Smelt,Joseph,	1		Eli.Cy
Stack,Andrew,			Cha.Cy
Stanton,Richard,	1		Bed.
Stretchberry,Jacob,	1		Lou.
Thomas,Augustine,	1	1	Henry
Thomason,Elias,	1	11	Loui.
Turner,James,			Cul.
Wakefield,Pleasant,	1		Ja.Cy
Warsham,Robert,	1	2	Mont.
Watson,Jonathan,	1		Har.
Watson,Thomas,	1		Har.
Williams,Amos,	1		Mont.